Business for Advanced GNVQ

by *Matthew Glew*
Philip Gunn
Malcolm Surridge
Michael Watts
Lis Crabtree

Collins Educational

An imprint of HarperCollins*Publishers*

Matthew Glew, Philip Gunn, Malcolm Surridge and Michael
Watts assert the moral right to be identified as the authors of
this work.

Published by
Collins Educational Ltd
An imprint of HarperCollins*Publishers*
77–85 Fulham Palace Road
Hammersmith
London W6 8JB

First published 1996
Reprinted 1997, 1998

ISBN 0003223736

Series commissioned by Richard Jackman.
Designed and edited by DSM Partnership.
Cover designed by Trevor Burrows.
Project managed by Kay Wright.
Production by Mandy Inness
Printed and bound by Scotprint Ltd, Musselburgh, Scotland

Contents

ACKNOWLEDGEMENTS

The authors and publisher wish to thank Pat McNeill for his support and enthusiasm for the original idea and its initial development.

They would also like to acknowledge the significant contribution that Melvyn Butcher, David Collinson, Murray Lauder, Steve Moulds (DSM) and Paul Stirner (DSM) have made towards its refinement and completion.

Cartoons: Nathan Betts (units 2, 3, 5 and 8)
             Daniel Betts (units 4 and 6)
             Martin Shovel (unit 1)

Photographs: Nathan Betts (pp. 176, 190, 356, 383, 396, 430, 433, 494, 511)

Interview simulation (unit 4): Lucy Gunn

The authors and publisher would like to thank the following for permission to reproduce material:

Bally Shoe Factories, Norwich, photograph (p. 224).
Bank of England *Inflation Report*, May 1994: 'Factors limiting capital expenditure' (p. 68), November 1995: 'Growth in unit wage costs' (p. 326), 'Acquisitions and mergers in the corporate sector' (p. 329).
Barclays Bank plc for the advertisements (pp. 429 and 452), 'Business plan form' (p. 518), 'Cash-flow forecast' (p. 524), extract from *Financial Planning for Your Business* (p. 444), 'Profit and loss forecast' (p. 523), 'Thinking of starting a business' (p. 546).
Bartle Bogle Hegarty Limited for the W H Smith advertisement (p. 387).
British Airways for the photograph (p. 291).
British Gas for the household gas bill (p. 380) and advertisement (p. 391).
BT 'The costs of direct calls in the UK' from *A Guide to call costs for BT Chargecard* (p. 380).
Carnaud/Metal Box plc for the photograph (p. 148).
Cartoonists & Writers Syndicate for the cartoon by Kal (p. 136).
Central Statistical Office (Crown copyright. Reproduced by the permission of the Controller of HMSO and the Central Statistical Office.) From *Annual Abstract of Statistics* 1994: 'Meat consumption' (p. 4). From *Annual Abstract of Statistics* 1995: figures from 'Consumers' expenditure at 1990 market prices' (p. 7). From Labour Force Survey: 'Trends in job-related training' (p. 323). From New Earnings Survey: 'Regional earnings, Spring 1994' (p. 312), 'Pay rates for selected occupations, Spring 1994' (p. 313). From *Regional Trends* 1995: 'The changing workforce' (p. 305). From *Social Trends* 1993: 'Age and sex structure of the population' (p. 500). From *Social Trends* 1994: 'Household expenditure 1971–1992, selected items at constant (1990) prices' (p. 160), 'Households by size, percentages and totals, Great Britain' (p. 162), 'Ethnic groups, Great Britain, 1991' (p. 164), 'Participation in the most popular sports, games and physical activities, by age, Great Britain, 1990' (p. 164), 'Savings by social class, age and sex, Great Britain, 1993 (p. 165), 'Readership of national newspapers, by sex and age, 1992 (p. 178), 'Readership of the most popular magazines, by sex and age, 1992 (p.178), 'Current and projected population statistics for selected European countries' (p. 298). From *Social Trends* 1995: 'Full and part-time employment by gender' (p. 301), 'People working at home as a percentage of those employed or self-employed, Spring 1994' (p. 303), 'Employees with flexible working patterns, Spring 1994' (p. 305), 'Percentage of the workforce receiving training' (p. 310), 'Regional unemployment in the UK' (p. 311), 'Average gross weekly earnings, Spring 1994' (p. 313), UK unemployment trends' (p. 314).
Christopher Keenan, A Line Design, for the 'Armstrong Ales' and 'The Court Hotel' logos.
Computer Weekly, Karl Schneider, 'Data transfers make the news' (p. 134).
Daewoo Cars for the photograph of sales room (p. 198).
Daily Express, Sascha Olofson, 'Virtual dream for shoppers' (p. 109).
Daily Telegraph 'Union to sue insurance firm over bullying boss' by Hugh Gurdon and Ben Fenton, 13 September 1995 (p. 213), '£30,000 damages for Irish insult' by Nigel Bunyan, 23 September 1995 (p. 218), 'Ford factories back to normal' 18 November 1995 (p. 220), 'Judges dash hope of backdated dismissal claims' by Terence Shaw, 27 January 1996 (p. 222), 'Lower prices will take time to work through' (p. 340).
Department of Trade and Industry, Application to an industrial tribunal (p. 221), Development and intermediate areas map (p. 437), 'B&B Fabrications' (p. 159).
Department for Education and Employment 'Percentage of employees receiving job related training' (p. 323).
Design to Distribution Limited for the photograph (p. 224).
Devon News, Nick Irving, 'Ambulance controller loses unfair sacking fight', 23 September 1995 (p. 216).
Dyno-Rod for their logo (p. 537).
Economist 'Elastic brands', 19 November 1994 (p. 22).
Eurostat 'Economic activity rates for selected European countries' (p. 306), 'Self-employed workforce in selected European countries' (p. 309), 'Part-time working in selected European countries' (p. 309).
Financial Times 'Employers "must take care" on job references', 8 July 1995 (p. 259).
Guardian 'Consumers' champion pulls the plug on extended cover', 17 December 1994 (p. 53), 'More trouble ferments for big brewers', 8 February 1995 (p. 54), 'Cement cartel files read like a thriller', 3 December 1995 (p. 56), 'Price cuts to

follow electricity review', 25 March 1995 (p. 60), 'ITN union staff vote to strike' by Andrew Culf, 24 January 1996 (p. 220), 'Gatt: who wins what' (p. 339).

Hertfordshire Business Link 'Support for new business start-ups' (p. 535).

High-TEC Sports UK for the case study material and photographs (p. 155–6).

Holiday Inn Worldwide for their logo (p. 537).

Independent 'Improved rights for part-time workers' (p. 301).

Independent on Sunday 'Personnel officers are a waste of time, says new study', 15 May 1994 (p. 235).

Inland Revenue for the cover from *'Self-Assessment: A Guide for the self-employed'* (p. 540).

Inskip Limited for the Pepsi-Max photograph (p. 183).

International Monetary Fund 'Growth of real GDP' (p. 318), 'The long-term fall in the value of the pound' (p. 322).

Kwik-Fit Euro Ltd. for the photograph and logo (p. 144).

Lloyds Bank plc, *Lloyds Bank Economic Bulletin* 190, October 1994, 'Economic outlook', (p. 499).

Marketing 'The Packaging Prodigies' 20 January 1994 (p. 148), 'Penguin Targets Kids', 17 February 1994 (p. 153), 'Research Propels Innovation', 27 January 1994 (p. 158), 'Live Viewing', 1 December 1994 (p. 180), 'Maximising Your Market Impact', 9 March 1995 (p. 103), Direct mail expenditure graph, 9 March 1995 (p. 185).

Marks and Spencer plc, *Annual Report and Accounts* extract (p 293).

McDonalds Restaurants Ltd. for the photograph (p. 145).

Modus Publicity and Benetton for the photograph (p. 451).

Molly Maid for their logo (p. 537).

Motorola and Macmillan Davies for the advertisement (p. 251).

National Association for Business Studies Education 'New Standing Order Mandate' (p. 371).

National Asthma Campaign for their leaflet (p. 440).

National Institute of Economic and Social Review 'Retail prices' (p. 319), 'Business investment as a proportion of GDP' (p. 319), 'Interest rates' (p.320), 'Manufacturing productivity' (p.320), 'Participation in higher education' (p. 322), 'Proportion of 16 and 17 year-olds in full-time education and training' (p. 322).

NatWest Bank plc 'Details of key staff' (p. 519), extract from business finance leaflet (p. 439).

Newsweek 'What matters to consumers?', 24 July 1995 (p. 163).

Nissan Product & Corporate Affairs for the Nissan Almera photograph (p. 352).

The Observer 'Branson puts the fizz into Iceland', 16 October 1994 (p. 503), 'Daewoo pronounces death of the salesman', 9 April 1995 (p. 198), 'DIY retailers reach for hacksaw' by Michael Tate, 29 January 1995 (p. 39), 'Virgin tastes victory in cola battle' by Roger Tredre, 16 October 1994 (p. 41).

Office of Population Censuses and Surveys 'Changes in the social class distribution of the population' (p. 9).

Organisation for Economic Co-operation and Development 'European waste paper recovery rates (percentages)' (p. 45), 'GDP totals and per capita and private fuel consumption expenditure 1990, selected countries' (p. 160), 'Government spending on research and development' (p. 324).

Pasta Information Council for the photograph (p. 355).

Pizza Express for their logo (p. 357).

PowerStock Photo Library for the photograph (p. 435).

Prontaprint for their logo (p. 357).

Reuters Business Information Unit 'Corporate information over the last decade' (p. 129), Why companies do not track the cost of computer-based information systems' (p. 135).

J Sainsbury plc for the photograph (p. 447) and the till receipt (p 373).

Science Photo Library for the photograph (p. 292).

Signs & Labels Limited, high voltage sign (p. 159).

Sony for the photograph (p. 285).

Sysdem, *Trends 17*, 'Female activity rates' (p. 308).

The Times 'A London-based design company...' (p. 138), 'Big sweetener draws Siemens to Britain' by Christine Buckley, 5 August 1995 (p. 437), 'Hutchison Telecom to raise £1bn', 13 September 1995 (p. 430), 'Preston reveals its new goal' by Jon Ashworth, 9 August 1995 (p. 435), 'Venture cash set to pour into railways' by Jonathan Prynne, 10 November 1995 (p. 436), 'Asda board moves to one-year contracts', 20 October 1995 (p. 302).

Tony Stone for the photograph (p. 288).

United Biscuits Ltd., Captain Scarlet promotion (p. 154).

Universal Press Syndicate ©, Doonesbury cartoon by Garry Trudeau (p. 135).

University of Warwick, Institute for Employment Research 'Change in employment by occupation' (p. 529), 'Labour market trends' (p. 299 and 530), 'Increasing involvement of women in the UK labour force' (p. 308).

The Voice 'Soul-d on Healthy Food!', 11 July 1995 (p. 161).

Whitbread plc, MSL Design and Woodland Animations for the advertisement (p. 251).

Every effort has been made to contact copyright holders, but if any have been inadvertently overlooked, the publishers will be pleased to make the necessary arrangements at the first opportunity.

Introduction

WHAT IS A GNVQ?

The letters GNVQ stand for **General National Vocational Qualification**. To help you to understand more about this new type of qualification, we will look at these words in turn.

First, the word 'general'. GNVQ courses provide a broad-based vocational education focused on a particular sector of the world of work, such as leisure and tourism, manufacturing or business. At present fifteen work sectors are covered. GNVQs are designed for people who are generally studying full-time at school or college. Most students are over 16, although a Part One GNVQ has been introduced for 14 to 16 year olds in schools. An increasing number of students are also taking GNVQs on a part-time basis in colleges.

Introduced in 1992, the GNVQ is a new 'national' qualification. Many GNVQs are replacing similar older qualifications including BTEC First Diplomas and BTEC National Diplomas. GNVQs are based on national standards, drawn up and published by the **National Council for Vocational Qualifications (NCVQ)**. Your school or college will be registered with one of the three organisations that award the qualification – the Business and Technology Education Council (BTEC), the City & Guilds of London Institute and the Royal Society of Arts Examinations Board – and your certificate will be awarded in the name of that organisation. However, the three bodies all work to common standards set by NCVQ.

The GNVQ is a qualification which relates to the world of work and employment, in contrast to GCSEs and A-levels, which are largely based on knowledge and the understanding of academic subjects. GNVQs should also be distinguished from **National Vocational Qualifications (NVQs)**, which are specific to a particular type of employment and are usually studied by people who are already working. GNVQs are, therefore, one of three paths open to young people wanting to continue their studies.

WHAT IS ADVANCED BUSINESS GNVQ?

Advanced Business helps you develop the skills, knowledge and understanding which prepare you for entry into employment or self-employment in business. This is achieved through practical investigations of business and markets, analysing business systems, proposing improvements to systems, proposing developments to products, producing financial forecasts and producing business plans.

As a GNVQ student you will take responsibility for your own learning, for planning your work, for carrying out your own investigations, and for keeping proper records of what you have done in connection with the course. Much of your learning will be achieved by carrying out your own enquiries and investigations, generally in connection with assignments agreed with your tutor. This may involve:

- ⊙ **carrying out research in libraries and resource centres;**

- ⊙ **visiting workplaces and talking to the people who work there;**

- ⊙ **learning about the experience of local employers and business people during their visits to school or college;**

- ⊙ **conducting surveys of people's activities, preferences and opinions;**

- ⊙ **studying company brochures and published reports in the press;**

- ⊙ **studying specific examples of people, places and firms related to your work;**

- ⊙ **arranging work experience placements with a local employer.**

Overall, you will make an active investigation of the actual world of work, presenting your findings in a variety of ways, including reports, talks and presentations both to people you know well and to others. Together, these activities develop skills which are essential in the modern world of business. You will be assessed mainly through the work that you complete during the course ('continuous assessment') rather than by a single exam. Your work will be assembled in a portfolio of evidence. In addition, there are some external tests during your GNVQ course which you must pass. These are used to confirm whether you really understand the knowledge and principles which underpin the compulsory or mandatory parts of the course.

THE STRUCTURE OF GNVQS

The structure of GNVQs is quite complicated, but it is the same for every GNVQ; once you have got the general idea, it is not difficult to understand. There are a lot of special GNVQ terms that will seem strange at first, but you will soon get used to them. We now look at some of these terms.

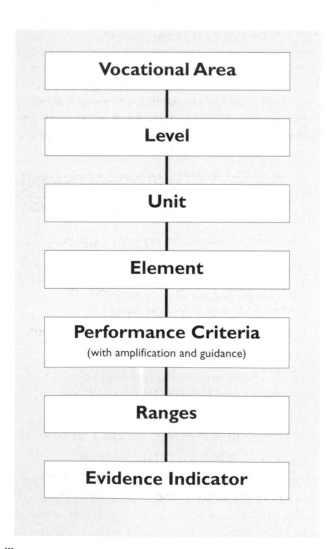

VOCATIONAL AREAS

Each GNVQ is related to a broad area of the world of work, such as business, manufacturing or health and social care. There are fifteen vocational areas currently covered by GNVQs.

LEVELS

In each of these vocational areas there are currently three levels - Foundation, Intermediate and Advanced.

- **Foundation** is broadly equivalent to four GCSEs at grades D to G, or NVQ level 1.

- **Intermediate** is broadly equivalent to four or five GCSEs at grades A to C, NVQ level 2, or BTEC First Certificate/Diploma.

- **Advanced** is broadly equivalent to two A-levels, NVQ level 3, or BTEC National Certificates/Diplomas.

UNITS

A GNVQ is made up of a number of vocational and core skills units, some of which are compulsory and some of which involve an element of choice.

The vocational units cover the knowledge, skills and understanding which you need to achieve in order to work in business or continue your studies further. There are three types of vocational unit.

- **Mandatory vocational units** cover the basic skills, knowledge and understanding needed for a wide range of jobs in business.

- **Optional vocational units** extend the scope of the mandatory units and will provide you with an opportunity to focus your studies in a particular direction, such as finance, marketing or personnel.

- **Additional vocational units** can be chosen to supplement your business studies, enhance your qualification and improve your prospects for progression into higher education.

This book contains all the mandatory vocational units needed to gain the Advanced Business qualification. HarperCollins also publish separately some of the optional vocational units, including *Behaviour at Work* and *Living and Working in Europe*.

The **core skills units** help you to develop the everyday skills and knowledge which are necessary to be effective within the workplace. There are three mandatory core skills.

- ☺ **Application of number,** which involves carrying out mathematical calculations and applying the findings in a business context.

- ☺ **Communication,** which covers the interpretation of language through listening and reading, and using it to present information and ideas through speaking and writing.

- ☺ **Information technology,** which involves using information technology in a range of business contexts.

You may also choose to study additional core skills units such as:

- ☺ **Improving own learning and performance,** which helps to develop the skills which are necessary for your own personal performance.

- ☺ **Working with others,** which helps you to enhance your ability to work effectively in one-to-one and team situations.

ELEMENTS

Each GNVQ unit consists of a number of elements. There are usually between two and five in each unit. Each element has a title which sets out what you have to do to complete that part of your course. The element lays out the skills, knowledge and understanding in detail, and indicates how you should present evidence of these. You have to complete every aspect of each element.

PERFORMANCE CRITERIA

Each element is broken down into performance criteria (PC) which describe what you have to do to complete the element. This might involve describing, identifying, explaining, discussing or giving examples of concepts, processes and procedures related to the particular subject you are studying. These various activities are usually combined in a piece of work which an assessor will judge to ensure that all the criteria are met. This means that they effectively set the standard for your work.

RANGE

The range details the areas of skills, knowledge and understanding in which you must meet the performance criteria. It can also tell you about the background knowledge (sometimes called 'underpinning' knowledge) that you must have. The external tests which are required for most of the mandatory units cover the broad scope of the range.

 ACTIVITY

Obtain a copy of the specification for Business for Advanced GNVQ. Look at the performance criteria. You will see that some words are printed in bold type. Now look at the range statements, and you will find that they relate to some of the words in bold type. This should help you to understand how performance criteria relate to range.

EVIDENCE INDICATORS

Evidence indicators describe the minimum evidence that you need to include in your portfolio in order to demonstrate that you have met all the performance criteria. They show the approximate quantity of evidence needed in order to cover the range. Providing your evidence is of the required quality and in the right quantity it may be produced in a variety of forms.

This means that the evidence 'indicated' is not the only way of meeting the requirements of the unit. For example, you might describe a business process or system diagrammatically rather than through straight narrative. However, where the required evidence refers to a specific outcome in the performance criteria such as a spreadsheet, then this must be produced.

ACTIVITY

Every unit of every GNVQ is set out in the same way. Look again at the specification for Business for Advanced GNVQ that you obtained for the activity above.

1 **Study the performance criteria, range and evidence indicators for element 1.1 and summarise the things that need to be done or produced in order to achieve the element.**

2 **By reference to the amplification and guidance statements suggest how a Saturday job in a supermarket might help you to generate some of the required evidence.**

AMPLIFICATION

Amplification notes are used to clarify key terms or words used in the element, sometimes with examples to help interpret and illustrate these terms and words. You are not required to cover all of these examples in your work.

GUIDANCE

The additional guidance is provided for your tutors and will help them in planning their teaching and learning strategies and may include advice on how evidence might be produced and how the elements link together.

WORKING TOWARDS A FULL QUALIFICATION

For an Advanced GNVQ in Business, you must study all eight mandatory vocational units included in this book, plus four optional vocational units and three core skills units – making fifteen in all. This represents the basic requirements of the qualification; however you may also take some additional units or another qualification to broaden your course.

There are five types of additional GNVQ units:

- ⊗ **additional vocational units specifically designed for business;**

- ⊗ **extra optional business vocational units;**

- ⊗ **mandatory, optional or additional vocational units selected from other GNVQ vocational areas;**

- ⊗ **additional core skills units;**

- ⊗ **language units.**

For progression purposes, it is generally agreed that six Advanced additional vocational units are broadly equivalent to the demands of one A-level. Apart from taking additional GNVQ units you might also choose to take A-levels, AS-levels, GCSEs or NVQ units.

ASSESSMENT

Your GNVQ assessment is based on your preparing a portfolio to show that you have developed the skills and acquired the knowledge required by the qualification. You will, therefore, be assessed mostly on the basis of the work you do during the course. The key point to remember is that you have to produce work that meets the requirements of the evidence indicators.

This does not mean that you have to meet the performance criteria (PC) in the same order that they are given and you can even do work which draws on elements from different units, if that suits your study programme. For example, a visit to a food processing factory, if you plan it appropriately, could provide evidence for elements in units 1, 2, 4 and 5.

The key point to remember is that in order to pass the Advanced Business GNVQ you must include evidence in your portfolio which meets all the requirements of the evidence indicators for the eight mandatory vocational units, four optional vocational units and the three mandatory core skills units. You must also pass the external tests for the mandatory vocational units.

Each unit is assessed separately to determine whether you have passed it or not.

PORTFOLIO OF EVIDENCE

You need to produce a portfolio of evidence that demonstrates what you have achieved in all your tasks and assignments. This portfolio is at the heart of your GNVQ course. Everything in it should be your own work and it must meet all the requirements of the evidence indicators and the range. It has to be carefully planned, organised and maintained, and it must have an index so that you can show how everything in it relates to the evidence indicators. A portfolio of evidence contains two types of evidence:

- ⊗ **recording documentation;**

- ⊗ **copies of assessed work.**

The **recording documentation** helps you and your tutor to keep track of your progress as you work towards your qualification. This documentation typically includes three sorts of form.

- ⊗ **Qualification tracking sheets** provide an ongoing record of which mandatory, optional and core skills units you have achieved.

- ⊗ **Unit tracking sheets** indicate your progress towards achieving vocational and core skills units element by element.

- ⊗ **Assessment front sheets** summarise the scope of the assessment activity, including coverage of vocational and core skills units and indications of grading performance.

The **copies of your assessed work** may take many forms, although obviously much of it will be written work. It may be notes on a topic, such as draft ideas for a business plan, or a brief report on the organisational

structure of a local business. A great deal of your written work will be about actual work situations, such as a detailed plan of a promotional campaign for a new product or an example of how customer service is provided in a retail organisation.

Another type of written evidence will be provided by your tutor or some other person (maybe an employer) who has witnessed you taking part in a discussion, dealing with a customer, or making a presentation, and who provides a written statement that you have reached the required standard. This is usually referred to as witness testimony or a witness statement. There may also be video or audio recordings of such events.

Your portfolio may also include letters, photographs, audio and video recordings and other certificates which demonstrate that you have done work which meets the performance criteria of your Advanced Business GNVQ; in fact, anything that shows you have met the requirements of the evidence indicators.

Each piece of assessed work should be accompanied by:

⊗ **the assessment brief** which describes the situation or scenario within which the activities/tasks are to be undertaken;

⊗ **assignment process sheets** which cover the action planning, information gathering and evaluation activities associated with the completion of the assignment and include a grade(s) for the approach you have taken towards the work;

✪ **assessment feedback sheets** which tell you how you have performed on a particular assignment and provide helpful advice about how you might improve in the future – this is very often combined with a record of the assessor's grading of the overall quality of your work.

ACTIVITIES, ASSIGNMENTS AND MULTIPLE CHOICE QUESTIONS

This book has been planned to provide you with the knowledge that you need for the eight mandatory units for your GNVQ. In addition, it also provides some special features.

ACTIVITIES

Activities are exercises that should help you understand what you have been reading and to apply it to your own experience. You can complete many of the activities at your desk, perhaps by working with one or two others, by analysing case studies, documents and figures provided in the book. However, some activities involve enquiries or investigations outside the classroom. Whatever the type of activity, you will be given clear instructions on what to do.

PORTFOLIO ASSIGNMENT

Portfolio assignments are more substantial pieces of work than activities, and are designed to match the requirements of the evidence indicators. They may take many forms. If you complete all the portfolio assignments in this book you will have all the evidence which you need to include in your portfolio for the eight mandatory units. Usually, a portfolio assignment covers the evidence requirements for a whole element and will also provide you with opportunities to meet the grading themes.

An activity will sometimes act as a starting point for a portfolio assignment and, where this occurs, you may be able to include the evidence generated from carrying out the activity in your portfolio. Again, you will be given instructions where this situation occurs.

Activities and assignments also provide you with opportunities to develop core skills and to provide evidence of your achievement. Remember, evidence for core skills must be provided in a vocational context, so check with your tutor what core skills you can claim when completing activities and portfolio assignments.

MULTIPLE CHOICE QUESTIONS

The multiple choice questions in this book are designed to help you to check that you have understood the knowledge that you will need to pass the end-of-unit tests.

These questions are not designed to be exactly like the actual unit tests (your tutor should be able to provide examples) but they do cover the main points in the unit and do represent an excellent preparation for the test. The answers are available on page 553.

WHO CARRIES OUT THE ASSESSMENT?

Your **tutor** will see you regularly to study the contents of your portfolio, discuss your progress, give you feedback on your work and help you with your planning. Your tutor will also assess your work and keep you informed about whether you are reaching the required standard.

Assessment by your tutor is supported by an **internal verifier** – another tutor who works at your college or school – whose task is to check that your assessor has been fair in assessing the evidence in your portfolio. Then, there is **external verification**. This is undertaken by the organisation that awards the qualification to ensure that the national standards set by NCVQ are being met. This helps to make sure that the standard of a GNVQ is the same across the country.

All these people have to be satisfied with your work, or with a sample from your portfolio, before your certificate is awarded. This is one reason why you must keep a careful record of all the work you do and of the contents of your portfolio. You will be provided with a record sheet or logbook for this purpose.

RECORD-KEEPING

You will appreciate by now that good record-keeping is an essential part of your GNVQ course, as it is in every area of work and employment. You must keep records of your 'action plans' (and of any changes to these plans) and of all your studies, activities and assignments, as well as of the work and evidence you produce relating to the evidence indicators. You should also keep a record or index showing how the material in your portfolio is organised.

GRADING

The basic grade in GNVQ is a **pass**. You will be awarded this if your portfolio contains the evidence required by the evidence indicators, including evidence for core skills. In addition, there are two higher grades, **merit** and **distinction**. These are based on two criteria: the **process**, that is how you have tackled your work; and the **outcome**, that is the quality of the final work.

The process involves three aspects.

☻ **Planning** – This is concerned with how well you plan your work, your ability to review your own plans of action and to recognise where and when changes need to be made. The less direction you need in doing this, especially when the plans and tasks become complex, the more chance you have of gaining a merit or distinction.

☻ **Information seeking and information handling** – This is about how well you identify what information you need for your work, where you can get it from and how to obtain it. An important part of this process involves checking the actual validity of the information that you collect. Again, the more you learn to do this without direction from a tutor, the higher your grade is likely to be.

☻ **Evaluation** – This is concerned with how well you review the work you have done and the decisions you have made, both while you are doing the work and when you have finished. You have to learn to reflect on and justify your own actions, to judge how well you are performing and, particularly, to suggest what you might do differently and better on another occasion.

The quality of the outcome is about how well you bring together your knowledge, skills and understanding in your work and how well you understand and can use the specialist language of business.

Overall, you will be graded on both the process of completing your coursework and the content and quality of the work you submit for assessment. Ask your tutor for further details and guidance on these grading themes. All portfolio assignments in this book are designed to give you opportunities to meet the criteria relating to some or all of these grading themes. Some activities can also provide opportunities for grading.

Merit and distinction are awarded only for a whole GNVQ, not for individual units. The final decision about whether you have achieved a merit or distinction is made when your portfolio is complete. If at least one third of the contents meets the criteria for each of the four themes at a particular level, you will be awarded a merit or distinction. You can expect your tutor to let you know during the course whether you work is matching up to these higher standards. Gaining a merit or distinction may be essential if you hope to progress to a higher level of study.

When you have finished the course successfully, you will be awarded a GNVQ certificate from one of the awarding bodies. It will include the NCVQ symbol, to confirm the national standard. The certificate will list all the units you have completed, including core skills units, and specify whether the award is being made at pass, merit or distinction level.

WHERE NEXT?

Once you have secured your Advanced Business GNVQ, a number of options will open up for you. You can choose between:

☻ **entering employment with the opportunity to gain an NVQ level 4, or start professional training or study part-time for an HNC;**

☻ **continue with full-time higher education leading to an HND or degree.**

Both options provide the possibility to progress even further and to study on postgraduate, professional or higher-level NVQ programmes.

GLOSSARY OF GNVQ TERMS

NCVQ — National Council for Vocational Qualifications

NVQ — National Vocational Qualification

GNVQ — General National Vocationa Qualification

AWARDING BODIES:

BTEC — Business and Technology Education Council

CGLI — City & Guilds of London Institute

RSA — Royal Society of Arts Examinations Board

GRADING:

Criteria — national standards for achieving merit or distinction in GNVQ

Unit test — compulsory test to assess your knowledge of the range of a mandatory unit

Assessor — your tutor, who will make the first assessment of your portfolio

Internal verifier — the person who will support your assessor and check the assessment

External verification — the work of the awarding bodies in supporting your tutors, assessors and internal verifier and in checking that their assessment is appropriate within a national context

GNVQ STRUCTURE:

Unit — part of a GNVQ which can be assessed and certificated

Mandatory unit — set by NCVQ, a minimum number must be achieved by all students

Optional unit — set by an awarding body and may be chosen, but a minimum number must be achieved

Additional unit — set by an awarding body and may be chosen to enhance qualification

Element — part of a unit; describes what must be done

Performance criteria — part of an element; sets the criteria standard for the tasks

Range — part of an element; describes the range of knowledge required

Evidence — anything that can be included in the portfolio to meet PCs and range

Evidence indicator — indicates the formal evidence needed in the portfolio to meet the requirements of the element.

Assessment portfolio — all the evidence of you achievement during your course, collected and organised.

Business in the Economy

OUTLINE

The aim of this unit is to help students to understand those factors which influence the level and pattern of consumer demand and the decisions taken by firms concerning the types and quantities of the goods and services which they supply to their markets. Students will also develop an appreciation of the main features of the markets where firms operate in terms of the degree of competition and how such markets are also affected by various forms of government intervention.

Analyse the forces of supply and demand on businesses

THE FACTORS THAT INFLUENCE MARKET DEMAND

People have many **wants** but unless they are backed up by spending power then they are not part of **effective demand.** The following sections identify the kinds of economic, financial and social factors which are likely to influence the demand for a particular category of a good or service. This analysis of demand concentrates on the kinds of goods and services which people pay for according to the amount which they consume and which are produced by businesses seeking to make a profit. There are other services such as health, education, justice and protection from crime but most people do not pay for these according to level of use. These services are provided by central and local government departments and funded out of taxation.

In this unit, the term **demand** is used to describe the **total market demand** for a product as a whole rather than the demand for a particular variety or brand offered by a single producer. For example, the demand for trainers deals with trainers as a kind of footwear rather than the demand for a certain style or brand of trainers. Whenever one of the factors which influence demand is being analysed it will also be assumed that all the other factors that affect demand remain unchanged. This means that any changes in demand can be related solely to changes in the factor under investigation.

THE DEMAND FOR A PRODUCT IN RELATION TO ITS PRICE

A rise in price generally produces a fall in demand. As the price of a product increases it becomes more expensive **relative** to all the other goods and services which consumers can buy and the demand for it is likely to fall.

SPECIAL OFFER

BRAND NEW CARS £20

QUEUE HERE

Similarly a fall in price increases demand as the product offers better value for money compared with other goods and services. This relationship between demand and price can be shown by the use of a **demand curve**.

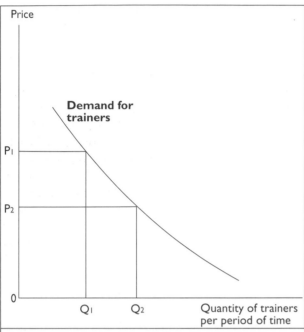

FIGURE 1.1: The relationship between the price and the demand for trainers.

The demand curve in *Fig. 1.1* shows the quantity of trainers that the total market is prepared to purchase at different price levels. If, for example, the price of trainers was P_1 then the market would be prepared to purchase the quantity of trainers as shown by Q_1. However, at the lower price of P_2 consumers would be prepared to purchase more trainers, the quantity Q_2.

Because this curve shows the **total market demand** for trainers and not the demand for a particular brand, the price axis refers to the average price of trainers. In the later sections of this unit we examine how the demand for a particular producer's brand of trainers is likely to respond to a change in price, where account is taken of the degree of competition that a single producer may face in the market where its trainers are sold.

A wide range of goods and services compete for household spending. If the producers of trainers are to increase their sales, then they must offer better **value for money**. This means that the benefit, satisfaction or enjoyment derived from buying trainers must exceed that which could be obtained by spending the same amount of money elsewhere. In order to encourage people to buy extra pairs, replace them more often or to buy for the first time, trainers must be offered at a lower price so that other goods and services offer relatively less value for money.

When showing the quantity demanded at various price levels, it is important that demand is described over of a particular **period of time** such as a month or a year. Demand is a **flow**; a time period is needed in order to assess changes in the strength of demand.

THE PRICE OF SUBSTITUTES

Although there is a wide range of goods and services competing for household spending, there are some markets where this competition is particularly strong because a specific need can be satisfied from a range of products which can be substituted for each other. In this case, the demand for one of these will be particularly affected by changes in the prices of such **substitutes**.

The demand for various types of meat, for example, is shown in *Fig. 1.2*. Changes in the pattern of consumption would have been caused partly by changes in the relative prices of meat as the different types of meat and meat products are substitutes for each other.

	1988	1989	1990	1991	1992
Beef and veal	6.35	6.03	5.25	5.35	4.98
Lamb and mutton	2.78	2.99	2.91	3.02	2.49
Pork	3.28	3.15	2.97	2.88	2.53
Beefburgers etc.	5.72	5.89	5.87	6.14	6.51
Poultry	8.09	7.76	7.95	7.63	8.16
Sausages	2.48	2.53	2.41	2.18	2.17

FIGURE 1.2: Meat consumption (ounces per person per week), 1988-92. Source: Annual Abstract of Statistics 1994, CSO.

The possible relationship between the demand for a product and the price of a substitute is shown in *Fig. 1.3*.

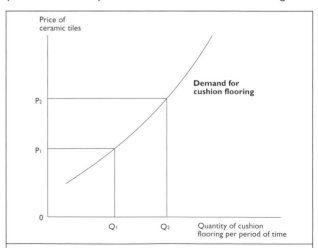

FIGURE 1.3: The relationship between the demand for cushion flooring and the price of ceramic tiles.

This deals with two kinds of flooring, ceramic tiles and cushion flooring, made from synthetic materials. When the price of tiles is P1 the demand for cushion flooring is Q1, but when the price of tiles rises to P2 the demand for cushion flooring increases to Q2.

THE PRICE OF COMPLEMENTARY PRODUCTS

The description **complementary products** is given to those products or services that must be used together to satisfy a particular need. Film and film processing, gas and gas appliances, cars and petrol, and compact discs and compact disc players are all examples of complementary products. The possible relationship between the demand for gas-fired central heating boilers and a change in the price of gas is shown in *Fig. 1.4*. When the price of gas is P1 the demand for this type of boiler is Q1, but the demand rises to Q2 when the price of gas falls to P2.

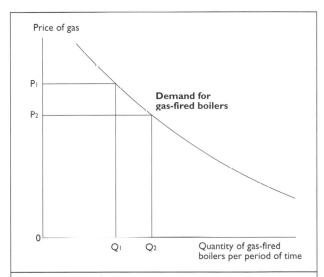

FIGURE 1.4: The relationship between the demand for gas-fired boilers and the price of gas.

THE AVERAGE LEVEL OF REAL DISPOSABLE HOUSEHOLD INCOME

In 1993, total personal (i.e. household) income in the UK was £576bn. After **taxes** and **national insurance contributions**, total personal **disposable income** was £396bn, of which £349bn was spent on consumer goods and services and the remainder went in **personal savings**. Over a period of years many households receive a rise in their disposable income but what happens to their actual **purchasing power** depends on the **cost-of-living** as measured by the rise in the **retail price index (RPI)**. The rate of increase in the RPI is referred to as the rate of inflation. Once an allowance is made for inflation, it is possible to measure the change in the level of real disposable income and thus actual purchasing power.

Between 1985 and 1993, total personal disposable income in the economy rose by nearly 60 per cent but once allowance is made for the general increase in prices over this period, real disposable income rose by only 28 per cent. It is important, therefore, that **money** disposable income is adjusted to produce **real** disposable income.

Even if total income in the economy as a whole is only rising very slowly, a **redistribution** of real disposable income may work in favour of certain groups of people. During the 1980s, for example, those on higher incomes benefited most from cuts in income tax that increased their disposable income.

A rise in income in the economy as a whole may produce a larger than expected increase in the demand for certain goods because of a redistribution of real disposable income in favour of the households which largely make up the market demand for those products.

The demand curve X in *Fig. 1.5* shows a product for which demand increases with a rise in the average level of real disposable income. As households become better off, they can afford to buy more without having to cut back in

ACTIVITY

Give examples of the existing complementary goods and services associated with the following products and services and also suggest other possible market opportunities:

1   Barbecues

2   Conservatories

3   Home computers

4   Mountain bikes

5   Natural medicine

6   Fitness gyms

7   Residential homes for the elderly

8   Child-minding services

9   Home security lighting

10   Further education courses

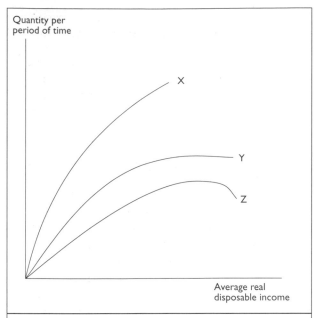

Quantity per
period of time

X

Y

Z

Average real
disposable income

FIGURE 1.5: How demand may vary with a rise in real disposable income.

ACTIVITY

After the annual budget in November, newspapers carry examples of how the chancellor's tax changes will affect the spending power of households in different income groups. Make copies of the kinds of charts used by the newspapers to illustrate this information.

Outline the reasons for any change in the purchasing power of one of the households used as an example. Suggest how different income groups may respond in terms of their demand for certain kinds of goods and services.

other areas of spending. This is generally the case with clothing, footwear, consumer durables and consumer services such as hotels, restaurants, travel and tourism.

The demand curve Y in *Fig. 1.5* shows a product for which demand at first rises with income but then remains constant despite further increases in income. This is often the case with basic food products, household cleaners and detergents, for example, where the demand is completely satisfied once certain incomes levels are reached.

There are also products, as illustrated by demand curve Z in *Fig. 1.5* where the demand may eventually fall once incomes reach a certain level. This happens when higher income allows the consumer to replace some existing purchases with what are regarded as superior substitutes. The demand for certain types of public transport, for example, has fallen over the years as more people have been able to afford private motor cars.

Fig. 1.6 shows how consumer spending on certain categories of goods and services has changed over a ten-year period. Changes in real disposable income are likely to have been a factor contributing to such changes. Just as money disposable income needs to be converted into real disposable income in order to discover what has happened to real spending power over the years, so it is also necessary to change **money expenditure** into **real expenditure** in order to assess changes in the actual quantities bought by consumers.

Over the years the actual amount of money spent on a particular product is likely to increase because of price increases. In order to discover changes in actual demand it is necessary to strip out the effects of inflation. This is done by adjusting the figures so that they are all expressed in terms of the prices which applied in a particular year.

ACTIVITY

Despite a gradual rise in the average level of spending power, the total amount of tea and coffee consumed in the UK has been falling.

Discuss the techniques that have been used by tea and coffee processors to encourage households to pay more for the tea and coffee that they continue to consume.

Give examples of other basic food products, drinks and household goods where a constant or falling demand means that the producers must develop their products in ways that mean people pay more for them.

	1983	1984	1985	1986	1987	1988	1989	1990	1991	1992	1993
										£m at 1990 prices	
Coffee, tea and cocoa	1,415	1,336	1,313	1,326	1,315	1,324	1,290	1,239	1,257	1,179	1,158
Soft drinks	2,003	2,084	2,199	2,592	2,869	2,856	3,098	3,198	3,223	3,244	3,269
Beer	11,603	11,651	11,609	11,595	11,630	11,649	11,584	11,479	11,096	10,763	10,447
Spirits	4,622	4,679	4,922	4,902	4,976	5,248	5,066	4,985	4,678	4,350	4,431
Wine, cider and perry	3,851	4,134	4,296	4,391	4,467	4,452	4,484	4,470	4,451	4,636	4,861
Cigarettes	8,400	8,113	7,923	7,700	7,648	7,690	7,716	7,703	7,533	7,252	7,085
Electricity	5,756	5,857	6,107	6,301	6,365	6,278	6,350	6,278	6,566	6,626	6,789
Gas	4,285	4,309	4,563	4,852	4,979	5,090	4,746	4,864	5,413	5,309	5,540
Coal and coke	1,050	874	1,118	966	884	835	774	660	696	538	516
Cars, motorcycles, other vehicles	14,251	13,453	14,162	15,552	16,525	19,410	21,031	19,034	15,415	14,637	16,368
Petrol and oil	7,784	8,200	8,317	8,830	9,198	9,847	10,039	10,172	9,976	9,930	9,659
Other vehicle running costs	7,985	8,577	9,570	10,635	11,561	12,194	12,573	13,137	12,910	12,992	13,965
Rail travel	1,963	2,033	2,061	2,198	2,242	2,305	2,176	2,242	2,112	2,078	2,020
Buses and coaches	2,646	2,636	2,709	2,635	2,580	2,555	2,546	2,464	2,326	2,253	2,210
Air travel	2,394	2,601	2,713	3,131	3,699	4,166	4,476	4,543	4,486	5,132	5,288

FIGURE 1.6: Consumers' expenditure at 1990 market prices.
Source: Annual Abstract of Statistics 1995, CSO.

In the case illustrated in Fig. 1.6, for example, all the data is expressed in terms of the prices that ruled in 1990. Revaluing spending at 1990 prices means, therefore, that changes in the pattern of consumer spending can be analysed without the complication of different prices.

CONSUMER CREDIT

Many people are willing to spend more than their disposable income by using various forms of **consumer credit** such as bank loans, overdrafts, credit/store cards or hire purchase agreements. In particular, hire purchase is often used to buy expensive **consumer durables** such as cars, televisions, furniture and refrigerators. The large increase in the use of credit was a major factor in fuelling the consumer boom of the late 1980s.

The willingness of households to use credit depends upon several factors. First, the **repayment period** granted by the finance company or bank. Over a longer repayment period, monthly repayments will be smaller and it will be easier for a borrower to meet the repayments. Second, the size of the **deposit** or down payment. Some credit arrangements may need a deposit and the smaller the deposit required the easier it is to buy on credit.

Third, **interest rates**. It is generally assumed that the demand for goods bought on credit is likely to be affected by changes in interest rates but this is not always the case.

ACTIVITY

Divide into groups and separate out the areas of consumer spending in Fig. 1.6 so that they are all covered. Each group should then complete the following:

1 Use a suitable computer software package to produce a series of graphs showing what happened to different kinds of spending over the ten-year period.

2 Support each graph with possible reasons for any overall trend and explain any very sudden short-term changes.

3 Each month the latest retail sales figures are reported and commented upon in the newspapers. Collect such figures and analyse the comments in the light of the factors that influence demand.

Assume, for example, that someone buys a music system for £1,000 using credit over three years at 12 per cent. A rise in interest rates to 16 per cent might be considered large but this only increases the monthly payment from £37.77 to £41.11. The level of spending financed by credit, therefore, is unlikely to be affected by such a rise in interest rates. Similarly, a cut in interest rates to 10 per cent only reduces monthly repayments to £36.11 and again this is unlikely to have much effect on sales. The demand for very expensive items such as cars, however, is likely to be more seriously affected by a rise in interest rates because of the amounts which are generally borrowed.

Fourth, the **level of business** and the state of the **labour market** affect the take up of credit. When the consumer's employer is busy people have a greater sense of **job security.** Earnings may also be boosted by regular **overtime, bonus payments** or **commissions** while a large number of **vacancies** elsewhere will suggest alternative job opportunities. This makes people confident that they can meet the monthly repayments on credit agreements. A **labour shortage** also means that employers are under pressure to grant larger pay increases. During the onset of a **recession**, however, all these factors are likely to be reversed and people are less likely to take out additional credit or enter into new agreements once any outstanding debt has been cleared.

THE HOUSING MARKET

The housing market is a major influence on the demand for the kinds of goods associated with people owning their own home or moving to another house. When, for example, a large number of houses are being bought, there is increased demand for a wide range of consumer durables and other products and services connected with home improvements.

Rising house prices will also have a **wealth effect** whereby households feel much more confident in taking on extra consumer credit. The extent to which the market value of a house exceeds any outstanding mortgage on the property also provides the **security** that may be needed to obtain a larger loan.

A downturn in the housing market exerts a depressing effect on total spending. This is particularly serious for those homeowners who face the problem of **negative equity** because the market value of their homes has actually fallen below their mortgage. At the end of 1994, some 1.3m households were affected by negative equity, and by June 1995 this figure had risen to 1.5m.

MORTGAGE INTEREST RATES

Because of the large sums of money which people borrow to buy their homes, even a small change in interest rates can have a significant effect on their monthly mortgage interest payments. A rise in the mortgage rate, for example, not only reduces the amount of money which homeowners have to spend on other goods but it also makes it more difficult for them to take on other credit agreements.

ACTIVITY

Assume that a young couple with no children and a total net monthly income of £1,200 are first-time buyers. They have an interest-only mortgage of £60,000 at 8 per cent. Calculate the increase in their monthly repayments if the rate rises to 11.5 per cent. Discuss the areas where such households are most likely to make the cuts needed to meet the extra cost of the mortgage.

CONSUMER CONFIDENCE AND THE 'FEEL-GOOD' FACTOR

This describes the net effect of some of the demand factors already described. Increased job security, rising house prices, expectations of a good pay rise and improved household finances, for example, will tend to raise the level of **consumer confidence**. In this case, people are not only likely to spend more of their income but also to

borrow more to buy the more expensive products. Consumer confidence indexes – measured by the balance between those who expect their financial prospects to improve as against those who expect their prospects to worsen – show that people have remained consistently pessimistic about the economy since the end of the consumer boom in the late 1980s.

CHANGES IN TASTES AND PREFERENCES

Tastes and preferences might be influenced by producers using **persuasive advertising** techniques to suggest that greater satisfaction or status can be achieved by purchasing a certain product. However, the increased demand for a particular product or service may originate with consumers themselves and the resulting **trend**, **fashion** or **fad** then spreads throughout the country. Market research may then identify such changes and produce advertising campaigns that seek to exploit these changes in tastes and preferences.

There are many ways of filling leisure time. A trend towards certain kinds of sporting or fitness activities, such as golf or aerobic exercise, will increase the demand for the appropriate equipment and sportswear. Similarly, the growth of DIY and garden centres is partly a result of the greater amount of leisure time being devoted to such interests. Eating habits have changed as people express a greater interest in the health and nutritional value of food, while a growing concern for the environment has also caused some consumers to shift in favour of 'green' products.

ACTIVITY

In order to try and appreciate how tastes and preferences can change within a short period of time, discuss the following:

1 Changes in fashion among young people in the last year or so in terms of clothing, footwear, cosmetics, hair styles, jewellery and other accessories.

2 The reasons why certain places of entertainment and leisure in your area have become popular among young people.

DEMOGRAPHIC CHANGES

Changes in the population with respect to **size**, **age**, **ethnic groups**, **social class** and **geographical distribution** are likely to affect the demand for various kinds of goods and services. Different age groups, for example, have particular tastes in clothing and leisure activities. More people in the age group of those setting up their own homes will have a major effect on the demand for consumer durables. The distribution of the population between inner city, urban, suburban and rural areas affects the pattern of spending in terms of car ownership, public transport and types of clothing.

		1981		1991	
Social class		Men	Women	Men	Women
I	Professional	5.7	1.0	6.9	1.9
II	Intermediate	22.5	20.6	28.0	27.6
III(N)	Skilled, non-manual	11.8	40.7	11.2	39.1
III(M)	Skilled, manual	36.6	8.5	32.8	7.2
IV	Partly skilled	17.0	22.1	15.6	16.9
V	Unskilled	6.4	7.1	5.5	7.3

FIGURE 1.7: Changes in the social class distribution of the population. (GB, percentages.)
Source: Office of Population Censuses and Surveys.

ACTIVITY

Survey a range of magazines and use the advertisements and articles to suggest which social group(s) the various publications are aimed at. Use your findings, and the information in *Fig. 1.7* to give examples of where the demand for certain goods and services would either rise or fall as people move into a higher social class.

THE PRICE ELASTICITY OF DEMAND

The **price elasticity of demand** describes the extent to which the demand for a product responds to a change in its price. *Figs. 1.8* and *1.9* show demand curves relating to two goods X and Y. In *Fig. 1.8* the percentage increase in price of good X from P_1 to P_2 is met by a smaller percentage fall in the demand from Q_1 to Q_2. Similarly, if one starts at P_2 and lowers price to P_1 then the percentage fall in price results in a much smaller

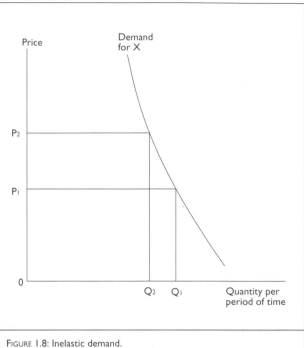

FIGURE 1.8: Inelastic demand.

percentage increase in demand from Q_2 to Q_1. In the case of good Y, however, in *Fig. 1.9*, the percentage rise or fall in price is met by a larger percentage fall or rise in demand. The demand for good X is said to be **inelastic**, while the demand for X is **elastic**.

ACTIVITY

Invite individual students who have recently bought a product that they would not usually buy to give a brief description of their purchases, covering the following:

1 The main features of the product.

2 The extent to which the decision to buy was:
  (a) taken in order to meet a need that had been carefully considered beforehand or;
  (b) simply an impulse buy.

3 In the case of (a), comment on the number of competing products considered, why they were finally rejected, the number and

kinds of shops visited and the factors that influenced the final choice.

4 In the case of (b), explain the relative importance played by an attractive display, a persuasive sales technique, a special offer, the chance to impress others or having extra money to spend.

5 Explain whether the purchase met your expectations and give reasons for being particularly satisfied or dissatisfied.

6 The group as whole should then relate all contributions to the kinds of factors which are likely to influence the level of consumer demand.

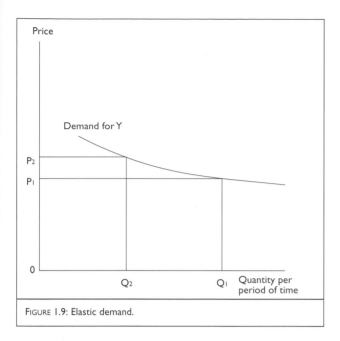

FIGURE 1.9: Elastic demand.

THE FACTORS THAT INFLUENCE THE PRICE ELASTICITY OF DEMAND

THE AVAILABILITY OF SUBSTITUTES

Where a product has many close substitutes then a price change is likely to produce relatively large changes in demand. At this point it is important to distinguish between the demand for a product in general and the demand for a particular brand or variety of a product. The market demand for petrol in general is very inelastic but the demand for the petrol supplied by a single petrol company is likely to be very sensitive to a change in the price of its particular brand only. This is because the average motorist regards the different brands of petrol as being more or less perfect substitutes for one another. Even a small change in the price of a particular brand is likely to have a large impact on sales and this would be reflected in a very elastic demand curve for that company's petrol.

The remaining points concerning the elasticity of demand concentrate upon how demand responds to a general movement in the market price of a product rather than a change in the price charged by one particular supplier.

NECESSITIES AND LUXURIES

It is often suggested that the demand for **necessities** is inelastic while the demand for **luxuries** is elastic. Putting products or services into either of these two categories depends, however, upon the kind of consumer one is dealing with. A rich person, for example, may consider a Rolls-Royce as a necessary part of their lifestyle while those on very low incomes may regard a trip to a fast food restaurant as a luxury. It was not so long ago that video recorders, dishwashers and music systems were regarded as luxuries because many people had more important demands upon their incomes. Nowadays, however, many people regard such products as essential when first setting up home. Nevertheless, necessities can be identified as products that consumers continue to purchase in significant quantities despite substantial price rises. Petrol, heating and lighting, and essential food products are examples of necessities, while luxuries are those products which are generally foregone when money gets tight.

THE PRODUCT AS PART OF TOTAL SPENDING

The price elasticity of demand will depend on the proportion of disposable income spent on the good or service over a certain period of time. Demand may prove inelastic if such spending is a small part of disposable income. A rise in the price of ballpoint pens or shoe polish, for example, will not seriously affect the demand for such items. This is because even a large percentage increase in price is unlikely to cause consumers to economise on their use, as the savings made would not be considered worthwhile.

THE FREQUENCY OF PURCHASE

Consumers are generally aware of any price changes to goods bought on a regular basis such as food products. This tends to make demand more sensitive to such changes, particularly if consumers also know the prices of substitute products. But for items which are bought only every few years, potential buyers are unlikely to know about any recent price movements. If, for example, someone is buying a music system for the first time or replacing an existing system then, unless they have monitored general price levels over a period of time, they are unlikely to be reacting specifically to a recent price change. In this case, it is again particularly important to distinguish between the price elasticity of demand for a product in general and the price elasticity of demand for individual models. If a single producer cuts the prices of its music systems then it will attract a higher proportion of both first-time buyers and those who make up the replacement demand when they visit shops to compare models and prices. This emphasises that the demand for a particular model is more elastic than the overall market demand for the product.

HABIT

The consumption of some products and services can become **a habit**. The most obvious examples include tobacco, tea, coffee and alcoholic drinks. For some people, these products almost become necessities, and demand is accordingly inelastic. But many people also show little

reaction to a change in the prices of their favourite confectionery or those goods and services connected with a particular hobby, sport or pastime to which they have become 'addicted'.

THE TIME PERIOD

In some cases demand may be more inelastic (or less elastic) in the **short run** than in the **long run**. This is because a reaction to a price change may involve complementary expenditure. A fall in the price of gas relative to electricity will not cause an immediate rise in the demand for gas, because consumers can only switch from electricity to gas when existing heating and cooking systems need replacing. Over time, a greater number of households have the opportunity to make such a choice. Moreover, as time passes new homes will be built and these are likely to have heating systems that reflect the new price differential. The relative fall in the price of gas may, however, still produce some increase in demand in the short run, as those about to install heating systems for the first time may be persuaded to change their plans and opt for gas as a fuel rather than for electricity.

THE EFFECT OF THE PRICE ELASTICITY OF DEMAND ON SALES REVENUE

The downward slope of a demand curve means that a price change will bring about a change in demand and, thus, also a change in a firm's sales revenues. The effect of a price change on sales revenue depends upon how demand reacts to this price change, i.e. the price elasticity of demand.

INELASTIC DEMAND

When demand is inelastic then a price cut will actually reduce total revenue. This is shown in *Fig. 1.8*. Here, the percentage cut in price is met by a smaller percentage rise in demand with the result that the total sales revenue falls from $P_2 \times Q_2$ to $P_1 \times Q_1$. Similarly, if the original price was P_1 and it was then raised to P_2, then sales revenue will rise from $P_1 \times Q_1$ to $P_2 \times Q_2$ because the percentage increase in price is met by a smaller percentage fall in demand.

ELASTIC DEMAND

When demand is elastic then a price cut will increase total revenue. This is shown in *Fig. 1.9*. Here, the percentage fall in price is more than compensated for by the larger percentage increase in demand with the result that total sales revenue rises from $P_2 \times Q_2$ to $P_1 \times Q_1$. Similarly if the original price was P_1 and it was then increased to P_2, then the firm's sales revenue would fall from $P_1 \times Q_1$ to $P_2 \times Q_2$ because the percentage rise in price is more than outweighed by the larger percentage fall in demand.

THE INCOME ELASTICITY OF DEMAND

The **income elasticity of demand** describes the extent to which demand responds to a change in disposable income. Over the longer period, the income elasticity of demand is a major factor in either the

expansion or contraction of the overall market for a large number of products. The income elasticity of demand depends upon the product in question and the existing level of disposable income.

INCOME INELASTIC

As disposable incomes rise from very low levels, households buy more of those products which play an important part in satisfying their most urgent needs. Thus, as households become better off the demand for basic items such as food, clothing and household goods may at first prove to be relatively elastic with respect to a change in disposable income. Eventually, however, demand will become much less sensitive and finally remain constant once a certain level of disposable income is reached. In this case demand has become totally inelastic with respect to a further rise in disposable income.

The income elasticity of demand is important because a producer's sales depend not only upon how competitive their product or service is in the market but also upon what is happening to total market demand. Those involved in products or services with a low income elasticity of demand, for example, must try to gain a larger share of a slowly growing market by persuading consumers that what they have to offer is superior to that of their competitors. Household cleaners and many foodstuffs come into this category and producers generally spend large amounts of money promoting their products to gain a competitive advantage. Food companies also respond by producing more expensive, higher value-added products.

INCOME ELASTIC

Once disposable incomes have reached a level where essential needs have been satisfied then a further rise in disposable income is likely to produce a growing demand in such areas as consumer durables and those goods and services associated with entertainment, recreational activities and travel and tourism. As disposable incomes continue to rise, some existing possessions may also be replaced with superior substitutes.

Producers of consumer durables such as cars, domestic appliances and home entertainment products also seek to attract the higher spending made possible by a rise in income by stimulating the replacement demand. A large proportion of households already have the basic consumer durables, so demand is encouraged by developing superior products based upon new technology and improved designs. Producers involved in other areas with a high income elasticity of demand, such as home improvements, furnishings, clothing and footwear and those goods and services associated with leisure, recreation and

entertainment, also seek to emphasise the style and fashion aspects of what they have to offer.

If disposable incomes fall, producers of consumer durables in particular are likely to suffer most because consumers are generally able to postpone their replacement demand.

MARKET SUPPLY AND THE IMPORTANCE OF PROFITS

Before investigating how profits are likely to be affected by changes in output, it is important to appreciate the overall importance of profits for business organisations.

THE NEED TO MAKE A MINIMUM LEVEL OF PROFIT

Capital has a wide range of uses. Apart from actually helping to produce goods and services it can also be used to buy a range of existing financial assets such as stocks, shares or unit trusts, or be placed on deposit in the banking system. Once capital has been committed to one particular use, the return which it earns will continue to be compared with what it could earn elsewhere. This assessment of the return on capital takes into account its **opportunity cost**, that is what it could currently earn in certain kinds of alternative uses, and because such opportunities have to be foregone they are likened to a **'cost'**. Thus, even if a firm is making a profit this is no guarantee that it will remain in its current line of business; shareholders will only be satisfied if this profit offers a certain **minimum return** on capital and this will be determined by what can be earned in certain kinds of alternative use.

One particular outlet for capital involves lending money by acquiring certain kinds of totally risk-free financial assets. What can be earned by lending risk free is sometimes referred to as the **pure return on capital**. There are also other areas of business where capital could be put to work to produce alternative goods and services for markets which involve the same degree of business risk. The return that could be earned from such alternative uses is known as the **risk premium**.

A firm must therefore make a return on its capital which is not only greater than risk-free alternatives but also compensates for the risks involved in operating in its particular market. If a producer is making a lower return than a line of business with the same or lower degree of risk then it will seek to move out of its existing market.

The minimum return required for a firm to maintain its capital in its current line of business is sometimes referred to as the **'normal' profit** and, because this normal profit has to be covered, it is treated as a cost. Thus, if a firm is selling its output at a price higher than its unit costs and included within its unit costs is a mark up for the normal profit, then it will be making a **super normal profit** because its return more than compensates for the risks involved.

A normal profit differs between industries because markets involve varying degrees of risk or security. Assume, for example, that a firm operates in a highly competitive market where its product is very much at risk, either in terms of being overtaken by new technology or where costs and markets can be adversely affected by factors beyond the firm's control. In order to compensate for the risks of possible severe financial setbacks, it may be looking for a minimum average annual return on its capital investment of say 22 per cent. If, however, this firm only makes profits which produce an average return on the capital invested of 14 per cent, then very soon it is likely to withdraw from the market. It may decide to use its resources in a much less risky line of business, say one which is regularly providing existing firms with a 14 per cent return. An alternative use for capital might also include buying a new issue of government stock, for example, which may be offering a guaranteed annual rate of interest of 10 per cent. Moreover, when this kind of stock matures the holders are also guaranteed to receive back their original capital investment. Thus, rather than earn just 14 per cent in a high-risk business, the firm is likely to opt for earning either the same return in a less risky venture or even settle for slightly less in a totally secure form of investment.

PROFITS AND CAPITAL INVESTMENT PROGRAMMES

Most of the funds required to finance capital investment in **plant**, **machinery**, **equipment**, **premises** and **research and development** come from **retained profits**. Spending in these areas not only protects a firm's **capacity to produce** by replacing capital items as they wear out, but can also increase its **productive capacity** so that it can meet higher levels of demand. These investment programmes must also try to use plant and machinery which uses the latest technology so that there is both an improvement in **efficiency** and in the **quality** of the end product or service. Investment spending, therefore, is vital for protecting and improving the competitive position of a producer and, along with research and development projects that yield new and improved materials, products and processes, this

investment is a major reason why the firm must seek to make the necessary level of profits.

PROFITS AND SHARE PRICES

A failure to make the best use of its assets and the resulting low **dividend payments** to shareholders may make a firm liable to a takeover. A poor return on shares depresses their price and a rival producer may believe that they do not reflect the firm's true value and earnings potential. This rival may then be able to buy up the firm relatively cheaply.

 ACTIVITY

Obtain a copy of the annual report and accounts of a major manufacturing company. Extract comments and data on the following:

1 The amount of money spent on investment projects.

2 The kinds of items of capital and premises covered by such projects.

3 How the company expects to benefit from its capital investment programme.

Use the information to produce an article for the company newspaper which is designed to explain why such investment is good for employees. Where possible include photographs of capital projects.

PROFITABILITY AS A FACTOR DETERMINING MARKET SUPPLY

The quantity which a firm is willing to supply to the market depends upon how profitable it is to do so. What happens to profits as a firm increases its supply or takes on extra business depends upon how such a move effects its **total costs** and **total revenue**. It is obviously important, therefore, that a producer has as much information as possible concerning both the likely changes in its **unit costs** as output changes and the **prices** at which products can be sold.

If, for example, a rise in demand means that a firm can sell more of its output at the existing price, and unit costs remain unchanged or even fall as output increases, then expanding production to meet the demand will obviously increase profits. If, however, a higher output leads to a rise in unit costs then profit margins will be squeezed and a producer may be willing to supply more to the market only if its customers are prepared to pay a higher price. Thus, the extent to which a firm responds to an increase in demand depends upon how the higher level of business affects both its total costs and total sales revenue and, therefore, its profits.

WHAT HAPPENS TO COSTS AS OUTPUT CHANGES

The following sections use columns of data and graphs as a means of identifying and describing the general effects on a producer's costs of a change in its output or level of business. Such an approach shows the general direction and magnitude of the changes in costs produced by an increase in a firm's output. It should not be assumed, however, that firms are able to measure and collect information relating to such changes in the same degree of detail. Nor are they able to make very precise adjustments to their supply in order to take the maximum possible advantage when there is a favourable market development. The main features of the information displayed in the data and graphs, however, are of great importance to firms and have to be taken into account when making business decisions.

THE COSTS OF PRODUCTION

The profitability of a business, and in some cases its very survival, demands that close and constant attention is paid to ways of reducing costs or at least controlling their growth. What happens to the unit costs of production as output changes will be determined partly by the costs of the inputs required (the **financial factor**) and partly by how output is affected by the increased use of such inputs (the **physical factor**). Depending upon the **time period** considered, it is possible to identify certain features concerning how a firm's unit costs are likely to change with output.

The **short run** is defined as a time period during which it is not possible to vary the use of both labour and capital. Output can be raised only by increasing the use of the input (either labour or capital) which can be varied most easily. In most cases, it is capital – in the form of plant, machinery and premises, for example – which tends to

be the most difficult to adjust; labour is generally much more adjustable. In the short run, therefore, a producer typically seeks to increase output by adding more labour in order to use the existing productive capacity more **intensively**.

THE LAW OF DIMINISHING RETURNS

Because it is not easy to adjust the use of both capital and labour, a firm will eventually be susceptible to the law of **diminishing returns**. This means, for example, that as more labour is employed to use the firm's fixed assets so, after a while, **productivity** will start to fall.

Units of labour	Total products produced	Average product of labour
1	20	20.0
2	120	60.0
3	290	96.7
4	520	130.0
5	800	160.0
6	1,120	186.7
7	1,450	207.1
8	1,770	221.2
9	2,060	228.9
10	2,300	230.0
11	2,480	225.4
12	2,560	213.3
13	2,560	196.9
14	2,460	175.7

FIGURE 1.10: Illustrative data showing changes in the productivity of labour.

The data in *Fig. 1.10* assume that a firm's premises, machinery and equipment cannot easily be expanded; output can only be increased by employing more labour. At first, the existing workers may work overtime. As the upturn in demand is large enough and expected to last for a reasonable period, then more workers are employed. The **average product (AP)** of labour is the total product (output) divided by the number of workers. As shown in *Fig. 1.10*, the average product of labour rises quite steeply at first. This rise in productivity is due to a number of factors.

1 A larger output makes it possible to take advantage of the greater **specialisation of labour**; individual workers can be employed on a much narrower range of tasks. The more frequent repetition of these tasks makes workers more skilled and this increases their productivity.

2 Increased specialisation means that new employees have to acquire the skills/knowledge relating to only a

limited range of tasks. **Training periods** are shorter and workers become productive much earlier on in their employment.

3 Because it is easier to pick up the more limited skills, the level of **wastage** during the learning period is also reduced.

4 The shorter training period also makes labour more **flexible** in terms of moving people between tasks within the organisation.

5 The greater the degree of specialisation, the less time is spent moving between operations and acquiring different tools and equipment. Savings also come from workers needing only the tools and equipment for a very limited range of tasks.

6 The more often an operation or procedure is carried out, the easier it is to identify ways to **simplify** the work. Once a complicated task is broken down into a series of simple routine operations, each of them can be more readily **automated**. This may lead to the development of more sophisticated machinery which performs several of these routine operations.

The data in *Fig. 1.10* show that, up to the employment of the tenth worker, this firm enjoys **increasing average returns**. Beyond this point the average product of labour starts to decline and the firm experiences **diminishing average returns**. This fall in productivity is likely to happen if labour shortages oblige the firm to take on workers of lesser ability. Bottlenecks produced by capacity constraints can lead to costly delays. Organisational problems may also arise as the workforce is increased in a further effort to squeeze more output from the firm's existing fixed assets. A position may even be reached where these problems become so serious that further additions to the workforce actually causes output to fall. This happens with the employment of the fourteenth worker in the illustrative data in *Fig. 1.10*.

SHORT-RUN COSTS

Because unit costs affect profitability, and thus influence the amount which a firm is willing to supply to the market, it is important to appreciate the main categories of costs and to understand how they are likely to vary in the short run with the level of output.

ACTIVITY

The marginal product of labour (MP) is the amount by which total output goes up when another unit of labour is employed. In *Fig. 1.10*, the **MP** of the first worker is 20 units, because output goes from zero to 20 units. The **MP** of the second worker is 100, because the addition of this worker causes total output to rise to 120. Similarly, the **MP** of the sixth worker is 320 units. This does not mean, however, that the sixth worker personally contributes 320 units to total output. The sixth worker does, of course, contribute to a rise in output but by joining the workforce also helps to raise the output of other workers.

1 Use the data in *Fig. 1.10* to produce a graphical representation of the marginal product (MP) and average product (AP) of labour.

2 Indicate on your graph the level of employment where:

(a) total product starts to fall;

(b) the MP of labour reaches a peak;

(c) the AP of labour reaches its peak.

3 Identify the range of employment on your graph where the MP of labour is falling but the AP of labour is still rising. Explain why this is possible.

4 Once the MP of the next unit of labour falls below the existing AP of labour, the AP of labour will immediately be pulled down. Explain the reasoning behind this statement and find the appropriate point on your graph.

FIXED COSTS

These are costs which remain the same regardless of the level of output. They include interest on capital borrowed and any repayment of the original capital sum, the depreciation on items of fixed capital, rent and local business taxes. Fixed costs are also known as **overhead** or **indirect costs** and the latter indicates that they cannot be related directly to any particular unit of output. Fixed costs must be paid even if the firm ceases production.

AVERAGE FIXED COSTS

Fig. 1.11 shows that average fixed costs (AFC) continue to fall as output is increased. This is because a fixed sum of money is being spread over a progressively larger output. The greater utilisation of capacity in the form of plant, machinery and premises can exert a very strong downward pressure on a firm's unit costs as it expands output to meet a higher level of demand. The average fixed costs are such that if an output is selected and then multiplied by its AFC, the result must always be the same. A curve with this particular characteristic is a rectangular hyperbola.

Costs (in £)

Units of output	Fixed costs	Average fixed costs	Total variable costs	Average variable costs	Total costs	Average total cost
0	200	0	0	0	200	0
1	200	200.0	280	280.0	480	480.0
2	200	100.0	380	190.0	580	290.0
3	200	66.6	440	146.7	640	213.3
4	200	50.0	480	120.0	680	170.0
5	200	40.0	510	102.0	710	142.0
6	200	33.3	534	89.0	734	122.3
7	200	28.5	554	79.1	754	107.6
8	200	25.0	572	71.5	772	96.5
9	200	22.2	592	65.8	792	88.0
10	200	20.0	614	61.4	814	81.4
11	200	18.2	644	58.5	844	76.7
12	200	16.7	682	56.8	882	73.5
13	200	15.4	742	57.1	942	72.5
14	200	14.3	822	58.7	1,022	73.0
15	200	13.3	932	62.1	1,132	75.4
16	200	12.5	1,082	67.6	1,282	80.1
17	200	11.8	1,282	75.4	1,482	87.2
18	200	11.1	1,542	85.7	1,742	96.8

FIGURE 1.11: Illustrative data showing how costs increase with output.

VARIABLE COSTS

These costs vary directly with the level of output. Because they can be related to particular units of output, they are also known as **direct costs**. They include **labour**, **raw material** and **energy costs**, as these rise and fall with changes in output.

AVERAGE VARIABLE COST

The data on average variable costs (AVC) in *Fig. 1.11* are obtained by dividing the total variable costs of producing any given level of output by that level of output. This information is also shown by the AVC curve in *Fig. 1.12*.

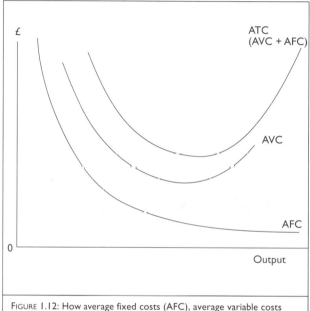

FIGURE 1.12: How average fixed costs (AFC), average variable costs (AVC) and average total costs (ATC) vary with output.

The shape and direction of the AVC curve is influenced by both the average product (AP) of labour and the costs of taking on extra workers. When the AP of labour is rising, this helps to reduce the AVC. A fall in the AP of labour tends to push up the AVC. If the firm comes up against a shortage of labour as it expands output, it may also be obliged to pay higher wages and this will exert additional pressure on AVC as output is increased.

AVERAGE TOTAL COST

The average total cost (ATC) in *Fig. 1.11* is obtained by adding together the total fixed costs and the total variable costs and dividing this total by the level of output in question. As shown in *Fig. 1.12*, the ATC curve falls at first because both the AVC and the AFC fall. Despite the continuing fall in the AFC, however, such reductions become much less pronounced and are eventually more than outweighed by the rising AVC with the result that the ATC curve starts to rise.

Units of output	Total costs
0	500
1	1,000
2	1,440
3	1,740
4	1,920
5	2,040
6	2,130
7	2,202
8	2,262
9	2,316
10	2,376
11	2,442
12	2,532
13	2,646
14	2,826
15	3,066
16	3,396
17	3,846
18	4,446

FIGURE 1.13: Illustrative data showing total costs increasing with output.

ACTIVITY

Using the data in *Fig. 1.13*, calculate the AFC, AVC and ATC. Note that the fixed costs are incurred even when there is no production; this fact allows you to calculate the fixed cost and the variable cost elements for each level of output. Use a computer software package to plot a series of graphs to illustrate this data.

LONG-RUN COSTS

The **long run** is defined as a period of time which allows a producer to vary the input of both labour and capital and generally adjust more fully to a new level of demand. Because the firm is now freed from the constraints of an important resource being fixed, it can introduce a more efficient combination of resources. These new methods of production will remove the prospect of diminishing returns. This long-run adjustment involves investment in additional **capacity**, the **training** of new labour and the further development of **management skills**. In addition, the firm will be able to take advantage of **economies of scale** as output is expanded. The net result is that, in the long run, costs rise more slowly than output.

The actual period of time which elapses before a firm embarks upon a long-run adjustment to a change in demand depends upon the industry in question. In the case of a firm producing self-assembly furniture, for example, output might be increased in the short run by changes in working practices that make a more efficient use of labour, by overtime working and by taking on more workers. If there is a very large increase in demand, a night shift can be introduced to make an even greater use of existing machinery and equipment. It may be only a few months, however, before the firm completes a long-run adjustment by extending its premises, installing extra machinery and equipment and training new workers in the appropriate skills.

In the petrochemical industry, however, while it may be possible to squeeze extra output from existing plant in the short run, it may be years before capital projects are completed and extra plant comes on stream to cope with a rise in demand. When very large amounts of capital are needed to increase productive capacity, a producer will only take such a decision if the upturn in demand is seen as being sufficiently long term to make such large-scale investment worthwhile. **Business expectations** are a vital factor in determining the extent to which a producer will commit capital funds to a long-run adjustment in the level of productive capacity.

ECONOMIES OF SCALE

As a firm expands, it can negotiate lower prices for its inputs of raw materials, components and equipment because suppliers are generally very willing to offer **discounts** to customers who buy in **bulk**. Suppliers offer discounts to attract large orders because they, in turn, benefit from the economies associated with long production runs and bulk deliveries. If a firm simply buys greater quantities of the same inputs from existing suppliers then there is also no reason why the labour costs of the **purchasing** function should increase.

When output increases, the related **sales** and **distribution** costs do not necessarily rise proportionally, especially if much of the increased business is with existing customers. Other **marketing** costs such as advertising are also spread over a higher level of sales.

As a business expands in the longer term, it may reach the stage where it has to invest in new plant, machinery and equipment. There are economies of scale in increasing plant capacity. Purchase prices, and operating and maintenance costs, do not increase in the same proportion as the productive capacity. For example, a new machine tool with double the operating capacity will not be twice as large nor involve twice the number of parts and controls. It is unlikely, therefore, that the manufacture of

a machine tool with double the capacity will involve double the production costs, and this will be reflected in the price paid for the machine. The energy used by the new machine will also rise by a much smaller proportion, while its operation will still need only one worker. Neither will it cost twice as much to maintain the larger machine.

Financial economies are available to a large and well-established firm as it can raise external capital on more favourable terms than a smaller business. It can offer greater security and point to its proven record of success. Small firms are seen as more risky ventures with less security. They may, therefore, be obliged to pay higher rates of interest to compensate for the greater risks involved, and lenders may also demand much shorter repayment periods. If a firm is raising capital from shares, then larger organisations again benefit because the costs of floating a large issue of shares do not increase in the same proportion as the size of the issue.

As output expands, firms can take even greater advantage of the specialisation of labour. More workers can be kept occupied on a very narrow area of work. For example, there might be sections within the marketing department where skilled and experienced staff can concentrate on various regions, overseas markets, market research, advertising, promotions, distribution and after-sales services.

INCREASING RETURNS AND LONG-RUN COSTS

Increasing returns in the long run, combined with other cost savings derived from economies of scale, mean that the unit costs associated with a higher level of output will

be lower in the long run than in the short run. Eventually, however, despite the application of further advances in technology, unit costs will rise in the long run. This might be because pay rises exceed the increases in productivity brought about by new technology with the result that unit labour costs rise. Efficiency may also be threatened in the longer term because of potential problems and pressures associated with managing a large-scale business operating at very high levels of output.

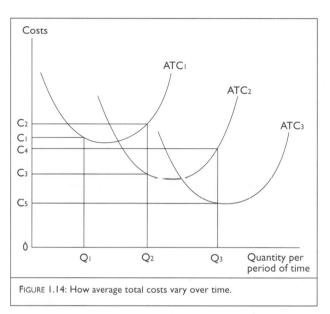

FIGURE 1.14: How average total costs vary over time.

The effects of economies of scale on long-run costs can be seen in *Fig. 1.14*. Assume that the firm in *Fig. 1.14* is currently producing Q_1 at a unit cost of C_1, and this reflects a production technique and a combination of resources geared towards that level of output. There is a

ACTIVITY

Leggo Construction receives a contract from EM Engineering to build a single-storey industrial unit which measures 40m by 30m and another one from Precision Parts Engineering to construct a similar single-storey unit but with twice the floor space.

1 Give some possible dimensions for the larger of the two units and explain why Leggo is unlikely to charge twice as much for this as it does for building the smaller unit.

2 Assuming that both the engineering companies make full use of their premises, describe some of the economies of scale associated with using and maintaining the larger premises.

3 Precision Parts' business is such that it needs a 20-tonne vehicle for distribution, while EM only needs a 10-tonne vehicle. Why will the larger vehicle be more economical?

rise in market demand and the firm wishes to increase its output. In the short run, it has to do so under the constraint of some fixed production factors. The effect on unit costs is shown by a movement along the short-run average total cost curve (ATC$_1$) and leads to a unit cost of C$_2$. In the long run, however, the producer can make a fuller adjustment by introducing a more efficient combination of resources. Because of the economies of scale and rise in productivity associated with this long-run response, the producer can now achieve the output Q$_2$ at the lower unit cost of C$_3$.

Any further rise in demand also produces a short-run response. Existing capacity is used more intensively and the resulting unit costs are shown by a movement along ATC$_2$. For example, an expansion to Q$_3$ produces a unit cost of C$_4$ in the short run. But, in the long run, a lower unit cost of C$_5$ can be achieved by further long-run adjustments.

PROFITS

The actual mark-up for profit and the price charged for goods and services depend upon factors such as the supplier's objectives and the kind of market environment in which the firm operates. This section looks at some of the strategies that firms use to set prices.

COST–PLUS PRICING

Many firms have sufficient information to produce a reliable figure for their unit costs at different levels of output. They may then add a **mark-up** to unit costs which allows them to earn the desired level of profit at different levels of output. The aim of this **cost-plus** (CP) approach is to fix a price which, when combined with the expected level of sales, provides the highest level of profit which they can reasonably expect in the light of the competition and sales forecasts derived from their market research.

The firm in *Fig. 1.15* is using a cost-plus approach. The curve labelled CP illustrates the price it will seek to charge at different levels of output in order to cover its unit costs plus mark-up. The demand curve D shows the demand for the firm's product at different prices. The information in *Fig. 1.15* can be used to identify a possible connection between the desire of the firm to make a profit and the quantity which it is willing to supply to the market.

Assume that this firm initially enters the market at the price P$_1$ expecting to sell the quantity Q. This firm's product proves to be more popular than forecast; at its price of P$_1$, it actually sells the quantity Q$_1$. Since it would have settled for a lower price at this level of sales, it is

now making a much higher level of profit than it anticipated. Quite obviously this firm's view of its potential profit proved to be rather pessimistic. As it gains market experience, it will develop a greater appreciation of the connection between the price that it charges, its sales and the level of its profits.

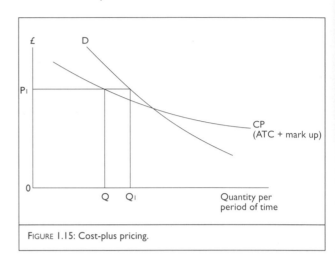

FIGURE 1.15: Cost-plus pricing.

Again, it is emphasised that the kind of graphical approach used in *Fig. 1.15* is a means of understanding the general principles which link profitability and the quantities which a firm is willing to supply to the market. In the real business world, managing directors and others taking decisions at a senior management level may not use the same cost-plus approach. However, their decisions are guided by the kind of financial information illustrated in *Fig. 1.15*. The use of diagrams in this way can also provide the basis for understanding the ways in which firms may react to changes in demand, market prices or unit costs.

THE MAXIMISATION OF PROFITS

We have already identified the importance of profits. Some firms aim to maximise profits. These firms set prices which, when combined with the resulting level of sales and measured against costs, generate profits that produce the highest possible return on the capital invested in the businesses. In this case, it has to be assumed that any departure from a price that maximises profits is a short-term strategy in response to particular market developments. It should be seen as a means of securing the firm's survival so that it can return to a profit-maximising price in the longer term.

Different pricing strategies, other than the maximisation of profits in the long run, are made possible by the **separation of ownership from control**. In a public limited company, for example, the directors and managers make decisions on objectives and strategies rather than the

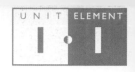

shareholders. Thus, there is the possibility that once those who control and manage a business have achieved a profit which they believe will keep shareholders happy, they may have the opportunity to seek other objectives which promote their own positions in terms of **power**, **status** and **prestige**.

THE MAXIMISATION OF SALES

Some senior managers may regard their own reputation in the business world as being enhanced if they maximise sales and achieve the largest **market share.** The price level needed to maximise the volume of sales may well produce an acceptable profit, but the resulting level of output and costs may not promote the maximisation of profits. Bonus payments for some senior managers may also be linked directly to sales rather than profits.

PRICE WITH AN INELASTIC DEMAND

When demand is inelastic (see *Fig. 1.8*), an increase in price will raise sales revenue. This occurs with a producer who has built up a high degree of **brand loyalty** among its customers – a moderate price rise will not see a significant fall in sales. In a market where brand loyalty is a dominant feature, a price reduction by the same producer will not necessarily produce a significant increase in sales, as other companies also have their loyal consumers who are not easily attracted by a fall in the price of a competing product. In times of high unemployment, however, when money is tight, price cutting by lesser brands may start to eat into the market share of leading brands.

A firm whose product or production process is protected by a **patent** may also face a relatively inelastic demand. It can raise its price without losing many customers. This also happens where the potential competitors to a dominant supplier face very high **costs of entry** – in terms of the initial capital expenditure on plant, equipment and premises – to enter the same market.

PRICE WITH AN ELASTIC DEMAND

As shown in *Fig. 1.9*, where demand is elastic a price cut will lead to a sufficiently large increase in demand so that sales revenue increases. This price cut is particularly worthwhile if the firm also enjoys economies of scale. This is because falling unit costs as output is expanded to meet the higher demand will produce even higher profits. Such a price cut, however, will not improve profits if the firm faces rising unit costs and total costs increase faster than the sales revenue. The firm must also ensure that it has sufficient spare capacity and the necessary skilled labour to meet the increase in demand.

Even if a firm is confident that consumers will notice the price reduction (perhaps because the product is bought regularly and sold alongside competing products), it must also decide if rival firms are likely to retaliate with price cuts or other measures to protect their competitive position. If the firm expects its competitors to respond with price cuts it will tend to keep its own price at the 'market' level. In this case, price will play a minor role in its marketing strategy.

ACTIVITY

Read the article over the page and then discuss the following questions:

1 How does information technology allow a large supermarket chain to respond immediately to a rival's price cuts?

2 Why might Coca-Cola have been obliged to launch a campaign aimed at 'increasing product differentiation'?

3 Select a range of supermarket products and in each case list the various brands available. Rank the top two brands for each product and explain the factors which affect the choice of the majority of consumers.

4 Give possible reasons why the demand for branded household cleaners is less elastic than the demand for bakery and dairy products.

5 What factors might encourage consumers to turn to lesser-known labels when buying certain kinds of groceries and household goods such as baked beans and kitchen towels?

6 What factors may have helped own-label products to compete with second ranked brands?

Elastic brands

It may be hard to believe, but the staid old British high street is now probably the world's toughest battleground for consumer-goods brands. For this, blame (or rather, credit) a combination of powerful supermarket chains selling sophisticated own-label products, and relatively weak trademark legislation that allows the sale of lookalikes. With point-of-sale scanning enabling competitors to match each other's price promotions instantly, costly advertising is now often the only way to keep weaker brands on supermarket shelves.

Even the mightiest brands are no longer immune to such pressures: Möet & Chandon is starting its first British advertising campaign, worth £1m ($1.5m) on 19 November. Five days earlier Coca-Cola launched a record £4m six-week campaign aimed at 'increasing product differentiation'.

Other brands look more vulnerable, as a comprehensive new study of the British market by Will Hamilton of Kingston Business School confirms.

According to the study, more than half of Britain's top 500 consumer-goods brands (including supermarket own-label products) have suffered declining sales volume over the past three years: only 184 saw sales growth. Price has increasingly become the key variable deciding a brand's fate: average prices for such grocery products as baked beans, kitchen towels and sliced bread have fallen by up to a fifth in real terms. But price cutting to gain market share can often be a loser's game with no benefit to overall profit. So what are harried marketers to do?

They might take some comfort from Mr Hamilton's study, which used AGB's data to track the price elasticity of the top 500 brands. He found that this averaged -1.85; in other words, a 10 per cent price cut should produce an 18.5 per cent increase in sales. (This excludes a small group of mainly luxury brands with a positive price elasticity whose sales increase when their price goes up.)

But the study also found wide variations across brands and categories. Thus, with an elasticity of -1.01, household cleaning products are much less price sensitive than, say, dairy and bakery products (elasticity -1.69). Unsurprisingly, across all categories, market-leading brands have lower price elasticities than their lesser brethren. However, over the past year second-ranked brands have displaced fifth-rankers as the most price-sensitive of all; they now seem to face the fiercest competition from own-label.

The study also shows that brand leaders are backed by greater advertising spending (averaging 50 per cent more than that for second rankers) and that their market share is more stable than that of minor brands; while brand leaders average a 19.2 per cent market share, second-rankers have an average 10.8 per cent. But achieving the nirvana of market leadership remains elusive. According to AGB, only three new brands have made it to the leader slot in the past three years, and all are extensions of existing products: Procter & Gamble's Pantene hair rinses; Unilever's Jif Mousse household cleaner; and Seven Seas's One-A-Day vitamins and minerals.

Mr Hamilton's study seems to prove what many marketers have long argued: that it makes more sense to support brand leaders with advertising rather than price promotions.

Economist, 19 November 1994

PRICE AND CHANGES IN DEMAND

Before responding to an increase in demand by raising prices, a producer must discover the reason for the extra sales. It could be, for example, that its rivals are also enjoying higher sales because of a rise in the total market demand. In this case, each firm may realise that the overall increase in market demand provides an opportunity to widen their profit margins by charging higher prices. The rise in total demand may also allow them to pass on cost increases that arose in an earlier period. Moreover, if the rise in demand is not expected to last very long, each firm may also decide to increase its profits by selling more at a higher price rather than being too concerned about keeping a particularly competitive price.

Extra sales may be generated because a firm has won business from its rivals as the result of having introduced a new feature that makes its product more attractive. Here, the firm may decide to keep its existing price for a period to build up the brand loyalty of the new customers. Eventually, the firm may take advantage of the increased demand to charge a price which reflects the extra value which consumers attach to the product. If, however, the rise in demand has resulted from major competitors increasing their prices, then many of the new customers are likely to return to their previous products if the firm also raises its price.

Where there is a fall in the total market demand for a product or service, a growing number of customers are likely to pay more attention to prices and shop around for the best deal. Under these circumstances, a firm will be under increasing pressure to match its competitors' price cuts. If, however, the fall in demand is because the firm is losing market share to its rivals, then it may cut prices to slow down the loss of business and use the breathing space to develop and introduce a longer-term strategy for improving its competitive position. Retaining market share will be particularly important if the firm faces very high fixed costs because a large output is needed to keep down unit costs.

PRICES AND VALUE FOR MONEY

Where goods or services are a regular part of household spending, many consumers have sufficient knowledge of competing products and their prices to form opinions on the extent to which they offer value for money. Once these opinions are firmly established, a price cut will be more successful than a price increase.

New products can be priced too low. Some consumers may be concerned that this reflects the use of inferior materials and indicates poor workmanship. They therefore may not think that the product will last very long.

If a new product is very well received, then it may be possible to charge a premium price and further exploit the consumers' view that it does represent a quality product. If there is nothing that really separates it from competing products, its price will have to be set within the range determined by the highest and lowest prices charged for these competing products.

ACTIVITY

Select a product and conduct a survey of the various brands or makes on offer in different retail outlets. Note also where they are advertised in newspapers and magazines. Identify those brands which are offering price cuts and assess them according to the following:

1　The factors which may have caused the price cut.

2　Whether the manufacturer or retailer introduced the price cut.

3　Any link with a 'money off' coupon or 'extra volume free' offer.

4　Any time limit for a 'special price'.

5　Evidence of price competition from competing brands.

Assume that you work in the marketing department of a company competing with those in your survey. You are required to use your findings as a basis for a meeting with the marketing manager. The purpose of the meeting is to discuss the pros and cons of making your own product more price competitive. Produce notes based on your findings for the meeting.

PRICE AND IMAGE

High-quality products often acquire an exclusive image. Their up-market position is then sustained by producers continuing to follow a high-price strategy. A high price will also be needed to cover the costs of producing a quality product and to compensate for the low level of sales to a small but select market. In this case, the producer must seek to ensure that the product is sold from outlets with the right image. An expensive perfume, for example, will be sold in select department stores rather than in cut-price chemists.

SKIMMING THE MARKET

If a new product is launched onto a market where it faces very little competition, there will always be some consumers who are willing to pay a relatively high price. Once, however, the demand for the product has stabilised, the price can be lowered to a level which attracts the next group of consumers. The supplier may then use a series of further price cuts to gradually cover the potential market. This short-term strategy of using progressively lower prices as a way of **skimming** or **creaming** the market ensures that a new product is not underpriced and is not sold to all consumers at a single price.

PENETRATING THE MARKET

When a supplier launches a new product onto an existing market where the demand is very elastic, a **penetration price** may be used. This involves a low price to attract consumers and to overcome any brand loyalty so that people at least try the new product. Attracting large sales as soon as possible is particularly important for a new product with very high fixed costs and where a high volume is needed to get unit costs down to competitive levels.

PREDATORY PRICING

This involves cutting prices in the short term in an all-out attempt to inflict such severe financial problems on a rival that it is forced out of business. Predatory pricing may involve the producer in much reduced profits or a loss but will be used if the competitor is reckoned to have higher unit costs and very small financial reserves. Such a strategy is also used to deter a new producer from entering a market. This is likely to be very effective where a new entrant needs to incur very high fixed costs.

LOSS LEADERS

In order to attract customers to their stores, supermarkets may offer a small number of well-known brands at below cost. Their advertising will highlight these bargain prices and, in attracting customers to the store in this way, they hope that they will buy many other items. Loss leaders may also attract customers because the emphasis on the bargain-priced products may give the impression that all other prices have also been reduced.

ACTIVITY

Use copies of *Marketing Week*, the business sections of the quality newspapers or advertisements in magazines and colour supplements to identify a product or service which is new to the market. Some products may also have special launches or promotions in retail outlets. Produce a brief written assessment of the product or service that covers the following:

1 **A picture of the product and the degree of emphasis placed on price.**

2 **Other techniques used to encourage a first purchase.**

3 **In the light of existing products or services available to consumers, describe the kinds of factors that may have helped to determine the introductory price.**

SUPPLY

In the following section, we look at the capacity and willingness of firms to alter supply in response to changes in demand, costs and other market developments.

HOW SUPPLY MAY RESPOND TO A CHANGE IN DEMAND

A change in demand affects both a producer's sales and its profits. It is important, therefore, to understand what kinds of developments will produce a change in demand and how a firm might respond in terms of altering its supply to the market.

DEVELOPMENTS THAT PRODUCE CHANGES IN DEMAND

The demand curve D in *Fig. 1.16* shows how demand is affected by a change in price. This curve is based on the assumption that all the other factors that affect the demand for this product remain unchanged. It is possible, however, to identify the effect upon this demand of changes in other demand factors.

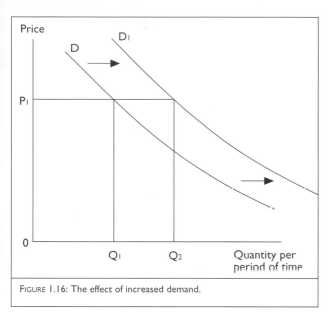

FIGURE 1.16: The effect of increased demand.

Assume, for example, that there is a rise in the average level of disposable income and the income elasticity of demand for the product is positive. This means that more of the product will be bought because people can now buy more without having to sacrifice other kinds of purchases. This means that there is now a higher demand for the product in *Fig. 1.16* at each price than previously. For example, at price P_1 consumers were willing to buy Q_1, but the rise in income means that at this same price of P_1 they are now prepared to buy Q_2. As this extra demand would be evident at all other prices, the effect of a rise in income on this demand curve D is shown by a **rightward shift** to D_1.

This shift in demand can be caused by the following kinds of development:

- ☺ **a rise in the average level of disposable income;**

- ☺ **cheaper and more plentiful consumer credit;**

- ☺ **a rise in the level of consumer confidence;**

- ☺ **a rise in the price of a competing product;**

- ☺ **a fall in the price of a complementary product or service;**

- ☺ **a change in tastes and preferences in favour of the product;**

- ☺ **a successful advertising campaign;**

- ☺ **favourable demographic trends.**

Some of these developments could produce a very sudden change in demand but it is more likely that demand will change gradually over a period of months (or even years in the case of demographic changes). Apart from hoping to benefit from the overall increase in market demand caused by these developments, each producer will follow marketing strategies designed to produce a rightward shift of the demand curve for their own particular product.

Conversely, a **leftward shift** of the demand schedule from D_1 to D in *Fig. 1.16* indicates that less is demanded at each price than previously. This fall in demand can be caused by changes which operate in the opposite direction to those above.

THE EFFECT OF AN INCREASE IN DEMAND UPON PROFITS

The effect of a rise in demand on a firm using a cost-plus approach is shown in *Fig. 1.17*. The falling CP curve indicates that the required profit margin is being achieved because unit costs are falling as output increases. Assume that this firm is currently charging the price P_1. At this price, the market is willing to buy Q_1. This means that the firm is already enjoying a much higher profit than it was looking for, as the curve CP shows it would have been willing to accept a lower price for the output Q_1.

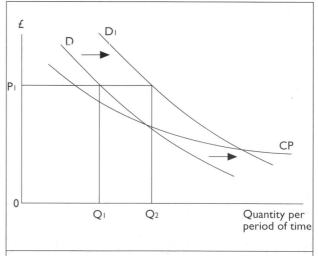

FIGURE 1.17: The effect of increased demand on a firm with falling unit costs.

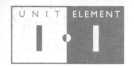
The increase in demand, as shown by the new demand curve D1, means that this firm can now sell more at the original price of P1 than previously. To take advantage of the higher demand, the firm's supply to the market increases to Q2. This higher supply produces an even healthier profit because the gap between the price P1 and the price it would have been prepared to accept for the output Q2 (as shown by the curve CP) is even greater than at Q1.

Thus, in the case of a firm with falling unit costs, it does not need to charge a higher price to make it profitable to increase its supply in response to a rise in demand. This would also be the case with a firm that experienced constant unit costs as output increased (its CP curve would be a horizontal line).

When a firm has reached a position where extra output now leads to a rise in unit costs, any further increase in output will squeeze its profit margin unless it can get a higher price for its product. It will be willing to supply more to the market in response to an increase in demand only if it can obtain the higher price needed to protect its profit margin.

The CP curve in *Fig. 1.18* shows a firm charging the price P1. According to its cost-plus approach, this is just the price it needs to supply the quantity Q1. If there is an increase in demand, the producer would need a higher price to make it worthwhile to increase its supply. Without such a price increase, its profit margin would be squeezed or it may even find itself with a price less than its unit cost. However, when the firm in *Fig. 1.18* is faced with an increase in demand as shown by the shift from D to D1 it is able to get the higher price it needs to make it profitable to increase supply to Q2. An increase in demand, therefore, which provides the opportunity for a price increase will make it profitable for some producers to increase their supply to levels that otherwise would not have been sufficiently profitable (or which would even have placed them in a position where they made a loss).

In the longer term, the vast majority of producers will experience a rise in unit costs because the improvements in productivity associated with the use of new technology are eventually outweighed by wage and salary increases. Their ability to charge a higher price to cover a rise in their unit costs is obviously important for protecting their profits and encouraging them to meet an increase in demand.

HOW SUPPLY MAY RESPOND TO CHANGES IN COSTS

A FALL IN UNIT COSTS WIDENS PROFIT MARGINS

In an effort to increase their profits, firms search for ways of reducing their costs. This could involve changes in **working practices** to make a more efficient use of labour, changes to working methods that save on energy and raw materials or the introduction of machinery and equipment which use the latest technology. Any resulting fall in unit costs means that their current price will now provide them with a wider profit margin and their existing sales will, therefore, produce higher profits.

A FALL IN UNIT COSTS ALLOWS A PRICE CUT

A fall in unit costs also provides the firm with the option of keeping its original profit margin by cutting its price and so gaining a competitive advantage over its rivals. This will be a particularly effective option if it believes that its competitors will find it difficult to match a price cut. If this price cut produces higher sales at the expense of its competitors, then the resulting increase in output may then produce further economies of scale and even lower unit costs. Thus, if a cost reduction is used to achieve a price advantage, then this may provide the firm with a self-reinforcing competitive advantage over its rivals that leads to an even greater demand for its product in the long run.

A FALL IN UNIT COSTS ALLOWS AN INCREASE IN SUPPLY

The supply curve S in *Fig. 1.19* is based upon how a firm is likely to react to a change in price given its current production methods and a cost-plus pricing strategy. The rising part of the supply curve S shows that when this firm is faced with rising unit costs, it needs a higher price to make it profitable to increase its output. Any new developments, however, which help to reduce unit costs will mean that this producer can actually supply more at each price than previously.

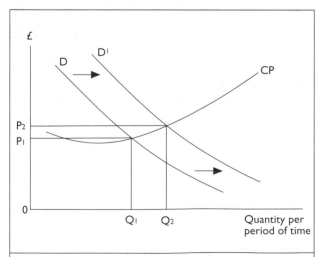

FIGURE 1.18: The effect of increased demand on a firm with rising unit costs.

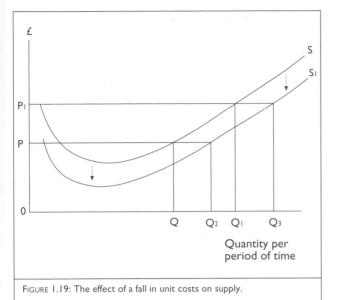

FIGURE 1.19: The effect of a fall in unit costs on supply.

THE ELASTICITY OF SUPPLY

The **elasticity of supply** describes the extent to which market supply can respond to favourable market developments. If, for example, producers can readily increase supply to the market to take full advantage of an increase in demand then supply is said to be **elastic.** If, however, producers generally find it difficult to expand output by even a relatively small amount in response to a large increase in demand then supply is said to be inelastic. The extent to which supply proves to be either elastic or inelastic will depend on the factors described below.

THE RATE AT WHICH UNIT COSTS RISE WITH OUTPUT

The extent to which firms are willing to increase output to take advantage of an increase in demand will depend upon what happens to their unit costs as output rises.

If a producer is in a position where further increases in output lead to a fall in unit costs then, as long as it receives the same price for its product as before, it will enjoy a larger profit margin on an increased volume of sales. Under these circumstances, the producer will find extra output exceptionally profitable and will have every incentive to expand output and supply more to the market. However, as the supply onto the market continues to increase, the producer will eventually have to lower prices to sell more, and profit margins will start to narrow. In this case, the producer would compare the likely reduction in the profit margin per unit and the extent to which this may be more than outweighed by the expected increase in the volume of sales. In general, falling unit costs lead to a very elastic supply.

Supply will also tend to be relatively elastic in firms with constant unit costs. Once again, the actual increase in output in response to a rise in price will depend upon

This is shown in *Fig. 1.19*. At the price P, the firm is willing to supply the quantity Q. The introduction of a cost-saving innovation, however, means that at the price P this firm would now find it profitable to supply Q2. Similarly, at the price P1 it was originally willing to supply Q1, but lower unit costs mean that it can now afford to supply Q3. In terms of *Fig. 1.19*, the lower unit costs mean that the firm's supply curve has effectively undergone a **rightward shift** from S to S1. Thus another possible effect of developments which lead to a fall in unit costs is that firms can supply more to the market without the need for a higher price to persuade them to do so. The increase in supply shown by this rightward shift of the supply curve in *Fig. 1.19* could also be caused by a fall in raw material prices, lower energy costs or the government providing the producer with a subsidy.

 ## ACTIVITY

A decrease in supply and hence a leftward shift of the supply curve would be caused by any developments which increased a producer's costs. This would mean that a firm requires a higher price than before to supply its original quantity to the market. In the paint industry, for example, manufacturers have recently been hit by large increases in the price of raw materials. Resin (which provides the gloss) has increased by 187 per cent since 1993.

Solvents have risen in price by 60 per cent since the beginning of 1995. Resin and solvents comprise 45 per cent and 10 per cent respectively of the raw material costs of a typical can of paint.

Use this information to describe the possible effects of such developments on a leading paint manufacturer. Illustrate your answer with an appropriate diagram.

how soon the extra supply onto the market puts a downward pressure upon price and slows down the rise in profits.

Constant or falling unit costs are likely to be a feature of firms where output is organised on an **assembly line** or **flow production** basis. For example, in the automobile industry extra output is unlikely to increase unit costs until overtime payments have to be paid or productivity begins to suffer because of a shortage of good quality workers.

Consider another example: there has been a large increase in demand for compact disc players in recent years. This did not produce a situation where consumers had to compete for a limited supply. Instead, the supply proved to be very elastic. As manufacturers expanded production to meet the growing demand, they experienced a fall in unit costs and, for a period of time, they were able to charge lower prices and still make higher profits.

This is also an example of a large number of producers operating in a highly competitive market. A single manufacturer of compact disc players who chose to respond to the higher demand by raising prices rather than expanding output would probably have been overwhelmed by its competitors.

Conversely, for producers who face rising unit costs, their supply will be less elastic. As these firms seek to take advantage of an increase in demand, their profit margins will be squeezed by both a rise in unit costs and the need to accept a lower price as the extra supply gets onto the market. When monitoring the results of increased supply, these firms will compare the smaller profit margin per unit sold with the expected increase in sales. Whatever the outcome, the supply of such firms will be much less elastic compared with firms still experiencing a fall in unit costs.

THE TIME PERIOD INVOLVED

The degree to which supply can be expanded also depends upon the time period considered. During the very short run, supply might prove to be very elastic if firms have a large degree of spare capacity. Output can be increased by using this existing capacity more intensively. Very soon, however, producers might suffer from both a shortage of capacity and a lack of workers with the necessary skills. In the long run, a fuller adjustment can be made to the rise in demand by firms investing in extra capacity.

This capital spending, and other economies of scale, also means that costs rise less steeply in the long run compared with the short run. Consequently, levels of output that were not profitable in the short run become profitable in the long run. Thus, the longer the time period that elapses following an increase in demand the greater the opportunity for firms to vary the input of both labour and capital. Market supply will, therefore, be more elastic.

THE ABILITY TO SWITCH CAPACITY

Where firms produce a range of products or services which essentially use the same skills and production techniques, then the supply of each of these products or services can be relatively elastic. A clothing manufacturer, for example, may have no difficulty in shifting more of its workers and equipment from denim shirts into jeans if demand for the latter is rising and offers the prospect of higher profits. Similarly, a brewer may be able to increase the output of traditional beers if demand is increasing by reducing its production of, say, lager beers (for which demand may be falling).

THE LEVEL OF STOCKS

The level of stocks held by firms will affect the extent to which supply can respond to a rise in demand. If producers are holding relatively large stocks of finished products then, even if there is an immediate problem concerning a shortage of capacity, for a while at least, extra orders can be met by drawing upon stocks. High stocks, therefore, make supply elastic in the very short run.

AGRICULTURAL PRODUCTS

In the case of an increase in the demand for agricultural products, once the existing stocks have been used up output cannot be increased until the end of the next growing period. Crops such as potatoes, wheat and green vegetables have a relatively short growing period. By comparison, it takes a long time before extra land given over to timber production produces trees which are mature enough to fell.

THE EXTRACTIVE INDUSTRIES

Firms involved in mining, quarrying or drilling operations need to obtain raw materials. They have learnt from experience that they should plan their capacity and run their operations to meet what they believe will be the average level of demand for their output over the years ahead. They will not install plant and machinery which runs the risk of being operated well below capacity for long periods of time. Instead, they invest in sufficient capacity which, when operated on a 24-hour basis, is capable of meeting their output targets. Any surplus output during a period of below average demand is put into stock and drawn upon when demand exceeds supply. However, even if demand remains high for a long time and all the stocks are used up, this will not necessarily encourage producers to generate new capacity. Not only may it be very difficult to invest in additional plant to extract more from the deposits currently being worked, but producers must be very confident that demand will remain high enough to justify the risks. There are very high costs connected with exploration and development projects

ACTIVITY

Because supply in the agricultural and extractive industries tends to be very inelastic, even a very large increase in demand will have little effect in encouraging a greater supply of these commodities. This occurs even if the resulting shortage produces a large rise in price. Similarly, these industries cannot readily reduce output during those periods when market supply exceeds demand. The resulting gluts can produce large price falls. Producers in the UK are very much affected by developments in these industries because of their impact on the prices which they pay for imported raw materials, oil and basic foodstuffs.

I   The quality newspapers regularly carry articles about movements in commodity prices in their business sections. Over a period of time collect such articles and then produce a brief report which identifies significant price movements in important commodities and the causes of such changes.

2   Identify a number of local manufacturing or processing companies where raw material prices are likely to play a significant part in their total costs. Produce a suitable communication aimed at obtaining information on the following:

(a) the most important raw materials they use and their sources;

(b) approximate percentage changes in the prices of such raw materials over the last three months;

(c) the extent to which they have been able to absorb any increases in raw material costs.

needed to obtain and refine new output. For these reasons, the supply of many raw materials tends to remain relatively inelastic once stocks have been run down.

MARKETS AND THE INTERACTION OF DEMAND AND SUPPLY

A market is formed by the existence of the forces of demand and supply. Although the items being bought and sold may be visible, the actual forces that bring about transactions between buyers and sellers are invisible. A market registers the collective strength of the total demand for a good or service and in many cases this may come from millions of potential buyers all over the country or even in different parts of the world. At the same time it registers the total amount coming from suppliers to meet demand and these too may be located large distances from each other. These forces of demand and supply interact to determine the prices which buyers have to pay and the amounts which are bought and sold.

MARKET EQUILIBRIUM

Having analysed the factors which are likely to influence demand and supply, it is now possible to bring them together and examine how their interaction in a market helps to determine a market price.

Fig. 1.20 illustrates the demand and supply curves for product X. At a price of P_2 this market would not be in a state of **equilibrium** as this is defined as a situation where the **market price** shows no tendency to change. At P_2 the current supply of X to the market is greater than the quantity which consumers are willing to buy at that price and the **surplus** will cause the price to fall. This is because consumers would recognise the opportunity to obtain a lower price while suppliers would be willing to cut prices in order to sell their surplus output. As the market price falls, however, it will gradually remove the surplus supply from the market because the lower price will both stimulate a greater demand as well as discourage some of the supply. In *Fig. 1.20* these developments are shown by a price fall which gradually closes the gap between the demand and supply curves. This fall in price continues until all the surplus supply has been removed

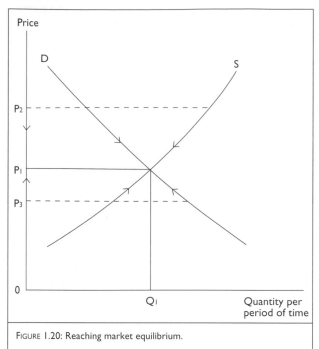

FIGURE 1.20: Reaching market equilibrium.

income. At the price P_1 demand now exceeds supply and this excess demand will cause the price to rise. The path towards the new market equilibrium can be traced by examining how the price rise will restore equilibrium by both choking off some of the excess demand as well as encouraging a greater supply to satisfy some of the increase in demand.

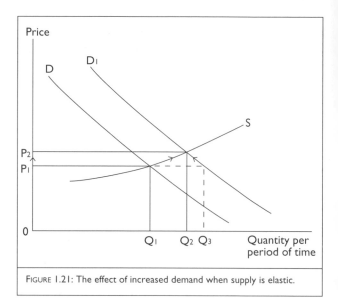

FIGURE 1.21: The effect of increased demand when supply is elastic.

from the market. This position is reached when the price has fallen to P_1. At this price, the quantity demanded is equal to the quantity being supplied and this means that a market equilibrium has been reached because neither the price nor the quantity bought and sold will show any further tendency to change.

Similarly, a price of P_3 does not represent a market equilibrium because at this price demand exceeds supply. This **excess demand** or **shortage** would cause the price to rise. This is because some consumers would be prepared to pay a higher price to obtain the product, while suppliers would recognise that the shortage gives them the opportunity to charge a higher price. The resulting rise in price will gradually remove the excess demand by both encouraging a greater supply as well choking off some of the demand. Once again a market equilibrium would be established at the price P_1 where demand is equal to supply.

CHANGES IN DEMAND AND SUPPLY

Starting from a position of market equilibrium it is possible to identify the likely effects of changes in any of the factors which effect demand and supply upon the market price and the quantity bought and sold.

AN INCREASE IN DEMAND WHEN SUPPLY IS ELASTIC

Fig. 1.21 shows the market for product A. There is market equilibrium at a price of P_1 and a quantity bought and sold of Q_1. Assume that there is an increase in demand caused, for example, by a rise in the average level of disposable

The effect of the price rise upon demand is shown in *Fig. 1.21* by the upward movement back along D_1 as demand falls back from its peak of Q_3. Similarly, the extent to which the rise in price stimulates a greater supply can be seen by the upward movement along S. Such developments come to an end when the rise in price has finally removed the excess demand from the market. This occurs at the price P_2 where demand again equals supply.

In this illustration, most of the excess demand was met by an increase in supply rather than a fall in demand. This could apply to those firms which have a large amount of spare capacity and where even a small increase in price makes a large increase in output profitable. *Fig. 1.21* shows that most of the excess demand was met by an increase in supply (Q_2-Q_1) while only a small amount (Q_3-Q_2) was choked off by a rise in price. An increase in demand, therefore, when supply is very elastic will lead to a new market equilibrium involving a relatively small price rise but a large increase in the quantity bought and sold.

The extra profits made by producers as they increase output is likely to attract other firms into the market. In the longer term, the rise in market supply may therefore be even larger than that shown in *Fig. 1.21*. Any such entry of new firms would cause a rightward shift of the market supply curve, and the resulting increase in supply and greater competition would eventually produce a lower price than P_2.

AN INCREASE IN DEMAND WHEN SUPPLY IS INELASTIC

Fig. 1.22 illustrates the effect of an increase in the demand for product B which again leads to an excess demand. In this case, however, market supply is very inelastic and not very responsive to an increase in demand. The shortage is resolved mainly by a very large price rise which has the effect of choking off much of the excess demand (Q_3-Q_2). Only a small part of the excess demand (Q_2-Q_1) is met by a rise in supply. Thus, when supply is inelastic an increase in demand will produce a new equilibrium which involves a relatively large price rise and a relatively small increase in the quantity bought and sold.

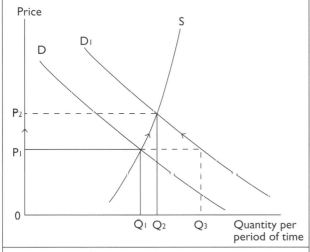

FIGURE 1.22: The effect of increased demand when supply is inelastic.

This kind of market development is often associated with what happens when there is an increase in demand for raw materials or agricultural products. Producers find it difficult to increase supply once any stocks have been exhausted.

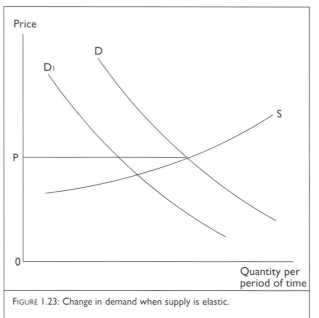

FIGURE 1.23: Change in demand when supply is elastic.

FIGURE 1.24: Change in demand when supply is inelastic.

 ACTIVITY

1 Give possible reasons for the leftward shift of the demand curve from D to D₁ in both *Fig. 1.23* and *Fig. 1.24*.

2 At the price P in each diagram label the quantity currently being supplied and the reduced amount demanded as a result of the leftward shift of demand. Label the extent of the excess supply at the price P.

3 Label the new market prices and quantities bought and sold in each diagram.

4 Explain why in the case of *Fig. 1.23* the excess supply was removed mainly by a small fall in price and a large reduction in the quantity bought and sold, while in *Fig. 1.24* the excess supply was removed mainly by a very large fall in price and a small reduction in the quantity bought and sold.

AN INCREASE IN SUPPLY WHEN DEMAND IS ELASTIC

Assume that the market for product X in *Fig. 1.25* is in equilibrium at the price P1 and a quantity bought and sold of Q1. There is then an increase in supply caused by the introduction of a cost-saving innovation.

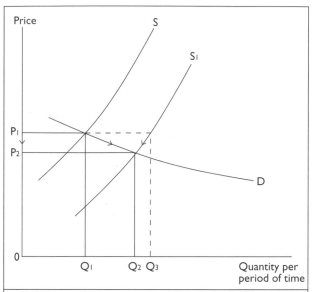

FIGURE 1.25: The effect of increased supply when demand is elastic.

The effect of this increase in supply is shown by a rightward shift of S to S1 and this means that at the original equilibrium price there is now excess supply. The market price starts to fall and this gradually removes the excess supply by encouraging a greater demand and at the same time discouraging some of the supply. The effect of the price fall on demand can be seen by a downward movement along the demand curve while the fall off in supply is shown by a downward movement along S1. In the case of product X, most of the excess demand was absorbed by an increase in demand (Q2-Q1) while the fall off in supply was only relatively small (Q3-Q2). The new equilibrium produces a relatively small reduction in price to P2 and a relatively large increase in the quantity bought and sold to Q2. This is because demand is very elastic and,

therefore, it takes only a small reduction in price to encourage the extra demand needed to absorb a large part of the excess supply.

AN INCREASE IN SUPPLY WHEN DEMAND IS INELASTIC

In the case of product Y in *Fig. 1.26* demand is very inelastic and it takes a very large price reduction to encourage even a small increase in demand. Most of the excess supply is therefore removed by a fall in price which leads to a large cut in supply (Q3-Q2) and only a small increase in demand (Q2-Q1). The new equilibrium therefore produces a relatively large price fall to P2 and only a small increase in the quantity bought and sold.

The kinds of developments shown in *Fig. 1.26* are often associated with an increase in the output of agricultural crops because of particularly favourable weather. A very good harvest of sugar beet or rapeseed oil, for example, needs a very large price fall to encourage even a relatively small increase in demand.

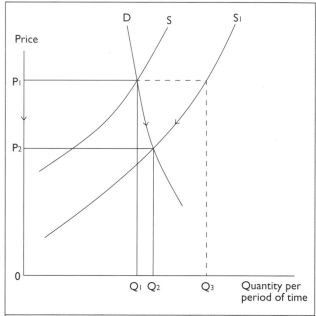

FIGURE 1.26: The effect of increased supply when demand is inelastic.

ACTIVITY

Unlike the prices of consumer durables, the prices of basic foodstuffs and beverages are subject to very sudden and unpredictable changes. This is because the demand for such products tends to be very inelastic in response to a price change, while the amount coming onto the market may be different from the planned level because of climatic factors affecting yields.

On the assumption that coffee coming from plantations around the world is bought and sold on a free market, complete the following exercise using graphs.

1 Draw a vertical price axis and a horizontal quantity axis.

2 From a point some way along the quantity axis draw a vertical line and label it S. This will show the amount of coffee supplied as a result of the latest crops coming onto the world market. Since the current supply is determined by the size of the last harvest, the same amount will be supplied regardless of price. Label this quantity Q.

3 Draw a very inelastic demand curve for coffee and label it D.

4 Use P to show the price per tonne which the market is willing to pay for coffee.

5 Particularly bad weather, however, in major producing countries means that the next coffee crop is much smaller. Show this fall in supply by the vertical line S_1 and the quantity Q_1.

6 Draw a line out from P and show that Q to Q_1 measures the extent to which the demand for coffee now exceeds the supply at the price P.

7 Label the new market price as P_1 and explain why such a large rise in price was needed to reduce demand to a point where once again demand equals supply.

8 Repeat the previous analysis to explain the effects of a very good coffee crop as shown by a new supply line S_2 being to the right of S.

PORTFOLIO ASSIGNMENT

The representatives of the catering workers in a large hotel and catering group have submitted a pay claim of 6 per cent for skilled workers, 4.5 per cent for semi-skilled workers and 3.5 per cent for unskilled workers. These claims have been made on behalf of employees in the group's 110 hotels and 120 restaurants located throughout the UK. Its hotels include both traditional and more modern establishments in city centres, urban and rural areas and range from three to five star category. The company has an ongoing programme that covers the extensive refurbishment of hotels in order to raise their star rating. It has also developed a string of country hotels with a strong sports and leisure element and a growing number of motels which provide budget-priced accommodation. All the hotels offer a range of catering services while the motels are linked to some of its fast-food establishments.

Over the previous two financial years, the company rapidly increased its level of business. Over this period, profits grew by 25 per cent. The greater demand for hotel and catering services came from both the business and leisure markets. In particular, the hotel side performed well in the market for business conferences and 'weekend breaks' where it offers a very competitive deal.

The improvement in profitability also reflects an earlier slimming down of the workforce and greater flexibility both in terms of the kinds of tasks which employees undertake and the days and hours which they work over a seven-day period. In some cases, employees have also undergone additional training to meet the needs of more flexible working.

Productivity has increased by an average of 4 per cent in the last two years.

Over the last six months, however, inflation has risen from 2.2 per cent to 3.8 per cent and the government has responded with a series of measures that have added 2.5 per cent to interest rates. A budget which has frozen tax bands and personal allowances, added 2.5 per cent to VAT and increased excise duties by 3 per cent.

As a senior manager you are required to produce an article for the next edition of the company newspaper which gives the group's views on:

1 How the factors which influence the demand for its various products and services are likely to be influenced by recent and expected changes in the economy.

2 What the company must do in order to:
   (a) minimise the effects of any adverse changes on its business; and
   (b) exploit the market opportunities provided by the more favourable changes.

3 The possible effects on the company if it were to meet the pay demand for catering staff in full and why all future pay rises should more closely reflect the performance of individual hotels and catering establishments. Your reply to the pay demand should also recognise the points which employees' representatives are likely to use to support their wage claim.

Analyse the operation of markets and their effects on businesses and communities

TYPES OF MARKET

The following analysis of market types will concentrate on the geographical size of the market, where a producer operates and the degree of competition from rival producers supplying the same market.

THE GEOGRAPHICAL EXTENT OF MARKETS FOR GOODS

An organisation involved in the extraction and refining of oil from the North Sea or a motor vehicle manufacturer in the UK operate in **world markets**. Their respective outputs are part of the world's supply of oil and cars and they hope to capture a share of their world markets by selling to customers all over the world. They must pay attention to developments in various parts of the world which are likely to affect demand. They must consider how the actions taken by producers in other parts of the world are likely to influence their own sales.

In contrast, a UK manufacturer of knitwear may believe that, although the potential market for its products extends beyond the home market, it does not go much further than most countries of the **European Union (EU)**. In this case, it will monitor developments in the EU by looking at what other producers are offering to the market and at what prices. It will also have to assess what is happening to the overall market demand for knitwear and the causes of any changes taking place.

Other organisations may operate solely in the **home market**. A brewery, for example, may sell its beers exclusively in the UK market because it does not have the right kind of products or resources to allow it to compete in overseas markets. As far as a bakery is concerned, it may be part of a **regional market**, while a poultry farmer may operate in a much more **local market** such as a city or town and its surrounding areas.

Most manufactured goods can be transported over relatively large distances without the transport costs having a significant effect on their unit costs. This means that their prices are sufficiently competitive to make them attractive to potential buyers in markets some distance from the factory where they are made. It is for this reason that even very small firms may look to sell abroad and become part of a world market.

THE GEOGRAPHICAL SIZE OF MARKETS FOR SERVICES

Markets for services also vary from the very local to those which are global. An airline or a shipping company may be part of the world market for passenger and freight transport while a bus and coach operator might operate in a very limited local market. Other services, such as banking and insurance, also cover national and international markets and these are supplied by maintaining branches and representatives at more local levels in order to reach as many potential customers as possible.

In the case of **personal** and other **consumer services**, their potential markets tend to be limited to a much smaller geographical area. The customer or client has to be in attendance to 'consume' the service. An osteopath, hairdresser, night club or snooker hall will be concerned mainly with local markets. They will not consider themselves as being particularly affected by changes in the demand and supply of similar services in other parts of the country. In the case of a personal service such as hairdressing, the owner may regard the market as being limited to the immediate neighbourhood where the salon is situated.

An important determinant of the size of a market for personal or consumer services is the extent to which a customer or client is willing to travel to use the service of one particular supplier. The more an organisation involved in the provision of a such a service can convince people that it offers exceptional value for money, then as households become more mobile, the larger will be the potential market.

The provision of services may involve suppliers that are part of very large organisations operating on a nationwide basis; examples include retail and fast-food chains. Although such organisations see themselves as operating in the national market, they are more concerned about developments in the local markets where their outlets are located. For example, sales by a branch of a DIY retail chain will be influenced by developments in the local demand for DIY products and by the strategy adopted by similar stores in the same area.

THE GROWTH IN THE GEOGRAPHICAL SIZE OF MARKETS

Several factors have helped to increase the geographical size of markets and thus the number of suppliers and customers that make up the market. Developments in **information technology** and **telecommunications systems** continue to widen the markets in which producers operate. Such developments increase the number of firms which make up the total supply to a market as well as making customers part of a larger demand. As both firms and customers become aware of new opportunities, the various regional markets for a particular kind of product within an economy merge to become a single national market. Similarly, national markets merge to become part of an international market.

International trade agreements are gradually removing barriers to international trade such as **import duties** and **quotas** which place an annual limit on the import of certain products. The elimination of these restrictions on imports allows the demand and supply of a product to be part of a much larger market.

Developments in **transport technology** in terms of speed and load capacity continue to reduce distribution costs, making an increasing number of products part of world markets.

FIRMS AS PART OF MARKET DEMAND

As consumers, we are generally unaware of markets concerned with the demand and supply of raw materials, semi-processed materials, parts and components, machinery, equipment, and industrial and commercial premises. A firm's demand for these kinds of inputs is influenced by factors such as price, quality, delivery, after-sales services, running costs and operating capacity.

Firms themselves also make up the market for various kinds of **business and commercial services** supplied by other firms. These cover areas such as banking and insurance, transport, security, legal matters, advertising,

market research and the growing number of consultancies and agencies dealing with management and information systems and the training and recruitment of employees.

COMPETITION WITHIN MARKETS

The kinds of strategies adopted by a firm to achieve its profit objective will very much depend on the level of competition that it faces in the markets where it operates. The degree of competition will be particularly important when a producer is considering a change in price or the introduction of a new or improved product or service.

COMPETITION AMONG THE MANY

The actual degree of competition between producers in markets which are generally regarded as being competitive will depend on the following kinds of factors.

THE NUMBER OF PRODUCERS

A very large number of producers generally means that customers are faced with a wide choice. No single producer can expect to raise its prices or neglect other competitive factors without suffering a loss of sales. Similarly, a price reduction or an improvement to the product or service is likely to bring about at least a short-term gain as customers are attracted from rival producers.

When there are many firms, no single firm can possibly take into account the reaction of all of its rivals when deciding upon its own prices or some other aspect of its marketing strategy. The greater the number of competing firms, therefore, the less attention any single firm is likely to pay to its competitors and the less restricted it feels when introducing a price change.

If there is a large number of producers, it is more difficult for them to come to some kind of collective agreement to avoid price competition and fix a **minimum price** and **market shares**.

In general, it tends to be the overall market demand for the product and its supply from the industry as a whole which establishes the **'market'** price for the product. Individual producers then become **price takers** as there is very little which they can do to influence that price. Each firm is such a small part of the overall market supply that even a very large increase in its own output will not depress the market price.

THE DEGREE OF PRODUCT DIFFERENTIATION

Where consumers are firmly convinced that there is no real difference between rival products or services then competitive pressures are likely to be very intense. Identical (or closely similar) products are very price elastic because consumers can select from a wide range of close substitutes. Under these conditions, individual producers have to pay particular attention to their prices.

In the case of markets for industrial materials and components, a lack of **product differentiation** is also likely to promote strong competition. This is because such products generally have to conform to very exact technical requirements. Prices are therefore an important factor in influencing choice.

The greater the degree of product differentiation that a single producer is able to achieve then the less elastic is the demand for their product with respect to a price change. Producers of consumer goods and services therefore tend to spend large sums on advertising campaigns designed to inform potential customers of the distinctive features of their products and why they represent better value for money. Consumers may see some aspects of product differentiation as being very real and obvious, such as the design and materials used for a pair of shoes or the food and surroundings in a restaurant. In other cases, it may need very persuasive advertising to convince consumers that a particular lager, toothpaste, detergent or car tyre is superior to its rivals.

The greater the extent to which a producer can convince the market that specific features of its product make it superior to others then the greater the degree of **brand loyalty** it can build up among its customers. In doing this, it hopes to reduce the impact of competitive moves by rival producers and, in the particular case of more intense price competition, the stronger brand loyalty helps to minimise the potential loss of customers.

RATE OF INNOVATION

Competition between producers acts as a spur to the development of new and improved products which

ACTIVITY

Select a type of consumer good or service which is regularly advertised in magazines or on the television, for example cars, convenience foods, shampoo/soap/ toothpaste, cosmetics, washing powders, beer/spirits, or banks/building societies.

Review the advertisements used by various suppliers in terms of how they seek to make their good or service different and therefore superior to their competitors. Where relevant, this should cover features such as price, performance, quality, customer care, design, ingredients, materials and image.

Describe how a particular supplier makes use of language, people, personalities, colours, imagery and settings to emphasise the reasons why their good or service is different to those of its rivals.

embody the latest technology. A lack of innovation and a failure to bring out new designs and styles will leave a product old fashioned and out of date. Every effort must also be made to develop and apply new technology to production methods to ensure that unit costs are low and prices are as competitive as possible. Producers must also seek innovation in training and development programmes in order to improve productivity and the quality of their output.

AN OPEN MARKET FOR NEW FIRMS

A market will remain very competitive if there are no barriers to entry so that new producers can readily enter the market. Over time, the number of producers in a market may fall because of mergers and takeovers or because some firms are forced out by competitive pressures. However, as long as other entrepreneurs are able to enter the market, then competitive pressures will be sustained.

Freedom of entry into a market will increase the pressures for existing firms to be efficient and offer competitive products so that potential new entrants deterred by both the prices and the quality they would need to offer to survive in the market.

NON-PRICE COMPETITION

In competitive markets, costs and prices may eventually settle at levels which leave very little room for further cuts. This is why resources are devoted to **non-price competition** such as advertising, packaging, tokens for mail in offers, gifts, and prizes for lucky purchases.

Indirect price competition may still take place. Companies might offer multi-packs at a discount price, money-off coupons or 12.5 per cent extra volume free. The advantage of these forms of competition is that the financial implications can be more carefully budgeted. Schemes can be introduced and then withdrawn without losing **goodwill** among customers. This is in contrast to price cuts; firms may only be able to sustain price cuts for a short period and, whereas price cuts are soon forgotten, price increases are more likely to be remembered by consumers even if the producer is simply restoring prices to previous levels.

For firms which produce plant, machinery and equipment, the non-price competition faced by a single producer includes how rival products compare in terms of **reliability**, **quality of end product**, **operating capacity**, **technology**, **running costs** and **back up services**.

Some goods differ little in technology, performance and design; examples include personal computers and other mass produced goods. In this case, a combination of price competition, customer support services and the quality of sales representatives are the main competitive factors.

COMPETITION AND POSSIBLE EFFECTS ON CONSUMERS

Producers must be efficient to survive and their need to avoid increases in costs will help to moderate price increases. As household incomes rise, competitive prices help to increase the real incomes and thus allow households to enjoy a higher **standard of living**.

A large number of firms competing to satisfy the same need will also provide consumers with a wide choice in terms of non-price features. This choice may then be widened by new producers entering the market. In their efforts to achieve a non-price advantage, producers need to improve continuously upon quality and other non-price factors.

A large number of producers will be competing for certain kinds of skills and this strengthens the bargaining power of workers when looking for better job opportunities and rates of pay.

The benefits of competition are generally described in the context of markets for consumer goods and services but consumers ultimately benefit from greater competition in the markets for materials, parts, components, plant, machinery and equipment.

ACTIVITY

Use local newspapers to list all the different techniques used by tyre and exhaust centres and garages to attract customers.

ACTIVITY

Read the article opposite on competition in DIY business. Investigate the following of the DIY business.

reference to the product range by DIY stores, explain why they are by the level of activity in the arket.

tores' use of price and/or etition in local and national aigns and in their point-of-special promotions.

3 Explain the reasons why Sainsbury was keen to expand its DIY interests and why it was confident of making a success of the Texas stores.

4 Produce an outline map of your local area and indicate the locations and names of all the DIY stores.

5 How is a location near other kinds of retailers likely to affect a DIY store's sales?

6 Give possible reasons why any small shops in your area can continue to sell DIY products.

DIY retailers reach for hacksaw

Sainsbury's £290 million swoop for the Texas Homecare chain has increased pressure on other DIY retailers, and could lead to further rationalisation.

The industry remains in turmoil. There are simply too many outlets following the rush to expand that accompanied the housing boom in the 1980s and the reluctance of anyone since to bite the bullet.

Although Sainsbury has indicated that 15 of the 241 Texas outlets will be closed because they overlap with its own stores, and up to 40 more are under review, its move is ultimately expansionist.

Among the most vulnerable is Do It All, the joint venture between WH Smith and Boots which is still running up losses and said last week it was stepping up store closures. Already more than a quarter of the 100 stores targeted have gone.

Analysts are beginning to question whether RMC, owner of the Great Mills chain, which has some 2.5 per cent of the home and garden products market, will retain its commitment to the business in the face of still more intense competition

They also believe that Focus, the business set up by Greg Stanley in the late 1980s, and which has already been forced to delay plans for a stock market flotation, may have to revise its strategy.

Management changes within Kingfisher this week could also herald changes at B&Q, market leader with a share of almost 14 per cent, even if reborn chief executive Sir Geoffrey Mulcahy's bigger problems appear to be the Woolworths and Comet chains.

B&Q is squeezing margins of around 7 per cent out of its 280 outlets, and Kingfisher has recently committed itself to investing a further £50 million in 100,000 sq. ft. warehouses. Jim Hodkinson, the highly respected and combative B&Q chief, is acutely aware that he could face a challenge this year from Home Depot, the Atlanta-based giant where he spent some months last summer, which has signalled an assault on Europe this year.

Richard Hyman, of retail specialist Verdict Research, says the Homebase deal will 'make life difficult for everyone else. I wouldn't

be at all surprised if we see more deals in this sector.'

However, he welcomed Sainsbury's move: 'It's a full price if you look at it on a short-term view, but this is a strategic move, not a tactical one. It has a compelling commercial logic.'

Sainsbury believes its Homebase management team can increase sales at Texas by 15 per cent over three years, and inflate margins currently running at a threadbare 1 per cent to around the 7.5 per cent that Homebase achieves from its 82 stores. The first looks feasible, the second much more difficult, says Paul Smiddy at Nomura.

In many ways Sainsbury's move, which propels it to second place in the DIY league table with more than 11 per cent of market share, says as much about the food retail industry as it does about the home improvement business. The supermarket chains know they will never again see the kind of returns they were used to in the 1980s. This may not be the last diversification undertaken by major supermarket groups.

The Observer,
29 January 1995

OLIGOPOLY AND COMPETITION AMONG THE FEW

Takeovers and **mergers** lead to some markets being dominated by a relatively small number of firms. This market form is known as **oligopoly** and the intensity and type of competition between the few firms in the market depends upon several factors.

The extent to which the firms in an oligopolistic market compete on prices for market share or collectively opt for a secure financial existence by avoiding damaging **price wars** is difficult to predict. Unlike a market with a large number of producers, a price cut by one producer will mean increased sales at the expense of just a few other producers. Because the loss of sales is concentrated in this way, the other producers will suffer a relatively large drop in sales and this may leave them with a large amount of expensive unused capacity. A move initiated by one producer to increase market share is likely to provoke **retaliation**. When deciding on its marketing strategy, each firm must therefore take account of the likely reaction of its rivals to any decision it takes on prices or product differentiation. Under these market conditions, firms will be aware of their **mutual interdependence**. This is in contrast to a market with a large number of firms where marketing decisions generally ignore how others may react.

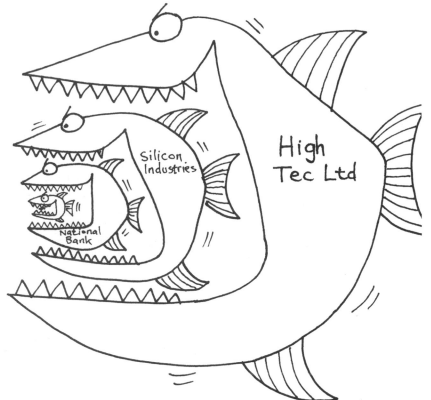

might be tempted to make the first move with a price cut to gain market share and make a fuller use of its capacity. This may trigger off a price war that eventually reduces the number of producers in the industry.

A small number of firms also makes it easier to operate a cartel arrangement on market shares. When tendering for orders, for example, firms may operate a system to ensure an agreed share of business. They might also agree to supply only certain distribution outlets.

New entrants into these markets are generally very rare. New entrants are deterred not only because existing producers may collectively agree to a price cut but also because of the **costs of entry.** A high minimum capital outlay means that a potential producer must be confident of securing a level of sales which allows it to operate at a competitive unit cost. Any new producers also face the problem of overcoming the brand loyalty to existing producers, their well-established **distribution systems** and their general **marketing expertise** with respect to the markets where they operate.

In a market with few producers and limited price competition, there will be a great deal of emphasis on non-price competition. Large amounts of money may be spent on advertising. Firms are likely to have the financial resources to establish **public relations** departments to help present the most favourable **corporate image** (while also being involved in the **sponsorship** of sports and the arts for example).

If there is no real difference between the small number of firms in a market in terms of their products, financial strength and market share, it may be difficult to predict who is likely to survive a price war. Even if the firm starting the price war survives, it may be so weakened financially that it is prey to a foreign producer looking to enter the market. Under these circumstances, firms recognise their interdependence and seek to minimise the effect of direct competition upon profits.

In this kind of market, it is easier to reach a **tacit agreement** whereby firms operate a **price cartel** and refrain from price competition. If one producer is generally accepted as being the most powerful then it may emerge as a **price leader** or **price maker**. When the total market demand is expanding, producers will recognise the benefits of a price increase. They will be keen to follow any move by the price leader. Similarly, if increased costs are squeezing their profit margins then the signal from the price leader to raise prices will be welcomed by the others. Although the emphasis will be on non-price competition, there may also be a tacit agreement to meet any new or potential competitors with a **collective price cut** in order to either deter them or to damage them when they are financially most exposed.

During a period of prolonged recession and depressed demand, producers suffer from excess capacity. This may put pressure on a price-fixing agreement. One producer

ACTIVITY

Read the article opposite about the cola battle.

1 **Design a questionnaire to find out what factors influence household choice when buying cola drinks from supermarkets.**

2 **The class as a whole should organise a blind tasting.**

3 **Produce a report on your findings.**

Virgin tastes victory in cola battle

COCA-COLA and Pepsi-Cola have slugged it out for years. But last week the two soft drinks corporations found themselves under attack from new rivals.

Woolworth's last week reported strong sales of its 29p, own-brand Genuine American Cola, launched 10 days ago, but the greater potential threat to the dominance of the American drinks giants comes from Richard Branson's Virgin Cola, to be launched next month in a joint venture with Canadian Cott Corporation of Toronto. Virgin Cola is expected to retail at 25p, undercutting Coca-Cola and Pepsi by up to 8p.

But which cola will taste the best? Even the most discerning palates may be forgiven for being confused, and regular Coca-Cola drinkers found it difficult last week to identify their favourite drink in a blind tasting conducted by *The Observer*.

All colas have much the same recipe, dominated by water and sugar, with the addition of caramel, phosphoric acid, decocainised coca leaves and caffeine. Coca-Cola's additional 'secret' ingredients – the celebrated 7X formula – are not much of a secret within the drinks industry; they are thought to comprise natural oils including orange, lemon, nutmeg, cinnamon, coriander, neroli and lime.

The first cans of Virgin Cola were dispatched to *The Observer* for the blind tasting, along with the Woolworth's cola, Marks and Spencer's Traditional Flavour Cola and Sainsbury's Classic Cola, whose can design was the subject of legal action by Coca-Cola last summer.

Virgin outscored Coca-Cola in the tasting by four regular cola drinkers. But both drinks were rated lower than Pepsi-Cola, which was considered the best of the six. Woolworth's was also ahead of Virgin and Coca-Cola. The Marks and Spencer drink, which includes 'spring water', was judged 'too watery', while Sainsbury's was given the thumbs down by all four tasters.

However, taste may not be the deciding factor in the long term. In the soft drinks industry, marketing hype and advertising spend are the most powerful persuaders of the public palate. And Richard Branson has never had any problems on the hype front.

The Observer, 16 October 1994

OLIGOPOLY AND POSSIBLE EFFECTS ON CONSUMERS

Although the possibility always exists that firms may be involved in a tacit agreement to limit price competition, many markets with few producers may see very fierce competition which benefits consumers. This will be the case, for example, where a powerful foreign producer tries to enter the market.

In a market with just a few producers, each firm may be operating at levels of output where it can benefit from economies of scale. Unit costs and, therefore, prices might be lower than in a market situation where sales are spread over a very large number of small producers. A single producer's volume of sales and profits may be such that it is able to undertake expensive investment projects involving the latest technology and which have a major impact on productivity and quality. Similarly, firms may be able to afford expensive research and development projects which lead to new and improved processes, materials and products.

Because there is less threat from new entrants, any extra profit which results from capital projects or research and development expenditure will last for a reasonable period; this can make capital investment more attractive.

It is argued that in a highly competitive market with a large number of producers, there may be very little real difference between many of the products. Consumers would not suffer if they had to choose from a narrower range of products which were much more clearly differentiated and produced on a larger scale. Where a large number of products and services are very similar, there may also be **wasteful duplication of resources** and thus higher unit costs. This would be the case, for example, with a large number of bus companies covering the same routes, building societies in the same town or steel producers supplying essentially the same products. In some industries, such as pharmaceuticals, research laboratories might also be duplicating research and development projects.

Unlike a highly competitive market where there may be a high turnover of firms, the overall situation under oligopoly is generally much less volatile. This, in turn, means **job security** for employees.

MONOPOLY

The term **monopoly** describes a market with only **one producer/supplier**. At one time such markets did exist. Before developments in transport which led to the opening up of trade either within a country or between countries, it was possible for a producer to dominate either a local or national market and to exploit the absence of competition by charging very high prices. In modern market economies, a single supplier is unlikely to dominate the market unless it is a state-owned or recently-privatised utility such as a gas, water or electricity company. Home markets are increasingly open to foreign competition while advances in technology continuously lead to new products, materials and processes which may weaken any existing monopoly power.

In the UK, the description monopoly is now given to a situation where a significant part of the market is controlled by either a single producer or a group of producers. This kind of situation is likely to arise as the result of yet more takeovers and mergers, so there are very few producers. This increases the influence which these producers have over the market price.

MONOPOLY AND POSSIBLE EFFECTS ON CONSUMERS

A producer in a strong monopoly position is able to charge a much higher price than it would charge in a more competitive market. There is less incentive to introduce cost-saving innovations and minimise costs as a monopoly can simply respond to higher costs by raising prices. The lack of competition may also mean there is no pressure to improve quality.

There is no guarantee that a monopoly will produce excessive profits. A producer may have high unit costs and be supplying a product for which the demand is falling, as was the case, for example, with British Coal. Some producers in monopoly situations cannot afford to be complacent because excessive profits and high prices may eventually persuade potential competitors that the risk and costs of entry are outweighed by the likely rewards.

If complacency leads to high unit costs and prices then this could make it viable for a potential rival to invest in a new technology that replaces existing production methods or produces a totally new substitute product.

Where the nature of the product provides very little scope for real product differentiation, consumer choice may not suffer if output is concentrated in the hands of a single producer. If, at the same time, the government is willing to prevent excessive prices, the resulting economies of scale should ensure that the monopoly producer charges lower prices compared with a market in which many firms are operating at much lower levels of output.

A **patent right** gives a producer a period during which the product, material or process cannot be used by others. Where large sums are spent on research and development as in the pharmaceutical industry, a patent provides a period during which a worthwhile return can be made on investment. Laws covering **copyright** and **intellectual property** also help to stimulate new literary works, designs and ideas.

MARKET OPERATIONS AND SOCIAL COSTS

The term **social cost** is used to describe the total cost to society of producing a particular good or service. It takes account not only of the costs incurred by the producer but also any other costs that arise elsewhere and which can be linked to the production, use or eventual disposal of the product. Social costs are therefore made up of the costs incurred by the producer, other organisations and households.

PRIVATE COSTS

In order to increase or protect their profits, firms seek to minimise their unit costs. The pressures to do this are particularly severe when a producer is faced with a rise in wage rates or an increase in the prices of raw materials, where these make up a large part of total costs. The response involves finding ways of using less of these inputs to avoid a squeeze on profit margins. This may lead to the introduction of working practices which reduces the firm's reliance upon labour. Higher raw material prices may stimulate changes in the design of the end product so that there is less reliance on high-cost raw material. In order to maximise their profits, producers will only be concerned about minimising what are known as their **private costs** of production, that is what they pay for using labour, energy, materials and capital goods, for example.

EXTERNAL COSTS

Although firms pay attention to minimising their private costs of production, there is no reason why they should seek to reduce their **external costs**. These are costs which are not met by the firm. They are associated with how a firm's production methods or the use and disposal of their end product imposes costs upon society as a whole. These costs include the harmful effects of a firm's operations on the **environment**. These might include air and water pollution, noise, traffic congestion, a deterioration in the urban, rural and coastal landscapes and any harm caused to fauna and flora. Further environmental damage may also be caused when products containing harmful materials are disposed of by the end users.

These **spillover effects** are likely to damage the health, safety and general welfare of the community. Although it may be difficult to place a precise financial value on such costs, they still represent part of the firm's overall costs of production.

THE NEED TO MEASURE EXTERNAL COSTS

In some cases it is possible to estimate some of the financial costs connected with **negative externalities**. Local or central government departments are forced to devote resources, and thus spend money, to deal with the resulting problems. (The issue still remains, however, of assessing the extent to which individual producers and certain groups of consumers are responsible for the financial aspects of dealing with these externalities.) Where these spillover effects go either partially or completely untreated, it is even more difficult to assess the true cost to society of a product or service. This is because it is difficult to put a financial cost on the various ways in which negative externalities affect the welfare of individual households.

As long as the external costs are not met by the polluters, a firm's private costs (and hence its prices) will not reflect the true social cost of its output. A firm's prices do not reflect the external costs borne by households or the extra spending incurred by central and local government as a result of harmful spillover effects.

Assume, for example, that the 'Bilko Chemical Company' has invested in technology so that it minimises its impact on the environment. As a result, its private costs produce a price of £2,100 a tonne for a certain kind of chemical. The 'Spillit Chemical Company' moves into the market. Its methods cause the release of toxic emissions. Because it is very neglectful of its effect on the environment, Spillit has lower private costs and can sell the same chemical at £2,000 a tonne. Spillit gains market share at the expense of Bilko because it is more price competitive. Spillover effects mean that Spillit's chemical is

actually produced at a much higher cost to society. Unfortunately, market forces continue to encourage the output of Spillit's product unless it is forced to introduce a much less damaging process or to meet its external costs.

SHIFTING EXTERNAL COSTS TO PRIVATE COSTS

Governments have resorted to the use of legislation supported by financial penalties to provide protection for the environment. It is argued, however, that environmental protection should be more closely linked to financial incentives. This could involve charges on producers according to the extent to which they damage the environment or oblige government to spend money dealing with their spillover effects. Many environmental costs currently borne by others would then become part of the firm's own or private costs. This is known as **'internalising'** external costs. It would put producers under far greater pressure to find ways of minimising the effects upon the environment of both their production methods and the eventual use and disposal of their products. In this way, a link is established between minimising environmental damage and minimising production costs. It might also lead to greater environmental protection compared with a system of regulations.

REGULATIONS

Government pressure on business to improve its environmental performance continues to increase. Voters demand that the government tightens and extends its regulations. UK regulations have been made stricter by the **Environmental Protection Act 1990** and by the setting up of the **National Rivers Authority** to investigate and control discharges of waste into rivers. At a local level, producers are subject to regulations administered by **Local Planning Authorities** and **Environmental Health Authorities**. They are concerned about issues such as the kind of business or building allowed in a particular area, the environmental impact of both its design and the materials used for the building, the level of noise, effect on local traffic and the disposal of waste.

EU LAWS AND ENVIRONMENTAL PROTECTION

UK producers also have to take account of EU directives concerning environmental protection. Although EU laws overrule regulations in member states, governments can still introduce environmental laws which are stricter than those of the EU. Germany, for example, actually banned the use of unleaded petrol rather than phase out its use by the year 2000. In 1991, Germany also introduced a very strict law which obliges packaging manufacturers and

ACTIVITY

Identify a local issue where people are worried about the environmental effects of a local factory or some other kind of business activity. The problem could also be connected with the siting of new business premises, a housing development or road traffic. Apart from the articles carried in the local papers, these kinds of issues generally spark off letters to the editor. Since such issues can run for quite a long time, it might be necessary to monitor events over several weeks.

Produce a brief report that covers the following:

1 The nature of the problem.

2 The pressure groups involved.

3 The responses from those who are seen as being responsible for the actual or anticipated damage to the environment.

4 The kind of solutions that are put forward by those who wish to protect the environment/welfare of the local community.

5 Any involvement on the part of local or central government.

6 The extent to which it is possible to place a financial cost on the spillover effects.

---

retailers to take back bottles, cans, cartons and general packaging in order to achieve its aim of recycling packaging waste. Some of the main EU laws and regulations are summarised below.

AIR POLLUTION

⊗ **Cars, vans and light goods vehicles** must be fitted with catalytic converters to meet strict standards on exhaust emissions.

⊗ **A 1991 directive** to cut exhaust emissions from new heavy lorries by 50 per cent.

⊗ **Air pollution controls** on new factories and a requirement to use the most up-to-date technology to limit emissions into the atmosphere.

⊗ **An agreement to reduce the emissions** from power stations and factories of pollutants such as sulphur dioxide.

⊗ **The phasing out (and banning) of products** that damage the ozone layer.

WATER POLLUTION

⊗ **Improving water quality** by setting limits on the level of harmful substances per litre. These include dangerous chemicals and nitrates from pesticides and fertilisers.

⊗ **Laws on oil pollution at sea,** the dumping of waste at sea and the movement of polluting goods by sea.

⊗ **Standards for the treatment and disposal of sewage** and the banning of treated waste being discharged into the sea or fresh water by the end of 1998.

DANGEROUS CHEMICALS

⊗ **Laws control the sale and use of dangerous chemicals** such as asbestos and PCBs. (PCBs, in particular, are extremely toxic; land contaminated by PCBs cannot be used again.)

⊗ **Factories using potentially dangerous products** must meet safety standards in their design and handling operations. Both workers and the local community must have full information on potential dangers associated with the factory.

⊗ **Regulations** demand that the EU must be informed of the import or export of some twenty-one dangerous chemicals where the trade involves a non-member state. If it is the first such trade, then the government of the non-member state must also be informed.

☻ **The introduction of 'banks'** for the collection of batteries which contain mercury, cadmium and lead. Cadmium, used in plastic products such as flooring, will be phased out.

NOISE

☻ **Regulations limit the noise from earth-moving equipment,** compressors and pneumatic drills, tractors, lorries, cars, motorcycles and aircraft.

☻ **With the exception of lawn-mowers,** the noise from other household appliances is not restricted by EU law. To be sold throughout the EU, however, they must have a label giving the noise level. This may help to make the reduction in noise a competitive factor between manufacturers of appliances.

THE NATURAL ENVIRONMENT

In order to protect the environment, the EU requires that projects which absorb large areas of land or which will affect the areas around them must be assessed in terms of their environmental impact. Individual governments are responsible for carrying out such assessments on the building of motorways, power stations and refineries. The EU, however, sets out the environmental aspects that must be covered by the assessment. If these procedures are not followed correctly – and any differences between the member state and the EU cannot be settled – the case goes before the European Court of Justice.

RECYCLING

The EU aims to prevent any further growth in packaging waste. By the year 2000 it hopes to recover 90 per cent of such waste and recycle 60 per cent of it. By 1994, no agreement had been reached on how this target would be achieved and a major reason for this was insufficient capacity for collecting and recycling the materials involved. Where waste cannot be recycled, the EU seeks to minimise the movement of waste. As much as possible, waste should be dealt with at local sites or incinerators using the latest technology.

THE RIO AGREEMENT

There are also international agreements such as that reached at the **Earth Summit** at Rio de Janeiro in 1992. Under the **Rio Agreement**, all EU governments committed themselves to stabilising the output of greenhouse gases, protecting all aspects of the natural environment such as plant and animal life and generally ensuring that economic advance is not at the expense of

(percentages)	1980	1989	1995
Australia	30	33	n.a.
Austria	33	48	50
Canada	22	28	42
Denmark	26	32	50
Finland	42	48	n.a.
France	30	34	n.a.
Germany	34	43	48
Greece	20	28	35
Italy	30	26	33
Netherlands	45	49	55
Norway	20	26	50
Portugal	32	42	50
Spain	37	39	50
Sweden	33	44	50
Switzerland	30	47	50
United Kingdom	32	30	36
United States	27	32	40

n.a.: not available.

FIGURE 1.27: European waste paper recovery rates (percentages). Source: Organisation for Economic Co-operation and Development (OECD).

the environment. The Rio Agreement also required governments to produce detailed reports on how they intend to implement such commitments. Companies need to consider the implications of such future action for environmental protection and take early steps to introduce the necessary changes.

'GREEN' CONSUMERS

Companies also have to respond to the growing number of consumers whose concern for the environment leads them to favour **'green'** products. These consumers look more favourably on companies that have a reputation for seeking to minimise their impact on the environment. The extent to which a company can demonstrate that it takes a greater account of the environment than its competitors is a growing factor in determining its competitive position and how it is viewed by public opinion.

ACTIVITY

Each student should undertake the following:

1 Collect a range of full-page colour advertisements from magazines and newspaper supplements which make some kind of reference to environmental factors as part of an effort to win customers or improve public image. This approach may be portrayed in the picture/photograph and/or included in the accompanying text.

2 Select the two advertisements which are the most interesting examples of the use of green issues in a marketing strategy. Fix these on the wall of the class and attach underneath brief comments on:

(a) where the references to green issues occur; and

(b) what particular issues and concerns they are aimed at.

3 The class as a whole should then decide which advertisements are the best three examples of the use of green issues to promote a good or service and give reasons for their selection.

ACTIVITY

1 Select a company involved in one of the following:

paints

retailing (supermarket type)

motor vehicle manufacturing

petrol retailing

food processing/manufacturing

oil refining

household cleaning agents

steel or aluminium production

batteries

road transport

fast food

construction

brewing

refrigerators/freezers

paper manufacture

plastics

2 Write to the company requesting copies of brochures, company newspapers or magazines which describe any recent (or future) changes in connection with their inputs, production methods, technology or end products that reflect its efforts to limit effects upon the environment.

3 Produce a report that describes the environmental problems that the company is concerned with, how they have responded and what their future plans are. Assume that this report is to be used as a publication suitable for future students making similar enquiries. Where possible use pictures or photographs to illustrate your report.

MARKET OPERATIONS AND SOCIAL BENEFITS

When consumers purchase goods and services the resulting satisfaction of their needs gives rise to **private benefits**. This term is used to describe the welfare derived from the satisfaction of their needs. It is possible, however, that the production or consumption of a good may also contribute to the welfare of others even though they do not buy the product. In this case, the product is associated with **positive externalities** that produce **external benefits**. Just as governments seek to regulate the activities and outputs of firms which give rise to external costs, so there is also a case for the government using financial incentives to encourage firms which yield external benefits. Below, we consider some areas where there might be a case for government assistance.

PRIVATE SECTOR INVESTMENT

The most important factor in raising productivity and generating economic growth is the level of investment in fixed assets. This involves producers using funds to acquire additional and more technologically advanced plant, equipment, machinery and premises. For the economy as a whole, this investment in fixed assets brings the following benefits:

⊗ **Increased orders** for capital goods and premises generates jobs in firms meeting such orders.

⊗ **When goods and services are produced** more efficiently, peoples' incomes go further. This greater spending power produces a higher standard of living.

⊗ **Investment** produces new and improved goods and services, both for consumers as well as producers when they purchase parts, materials, equipment and commercial services.

⊗ **Improvements in productivity** and quality make UK firms more competitive and this helps to increase exports. In turn, this increases the UK's foreign currency earnings and allows the country to pay for a higher level of imports.

⊗ **More efficient productive capacity** means that the economy as whole can respond to a higher level of demand without a rise in inflation and without a large part of the demand being met by increased imports.

TRAINING

Capital projects should be supported by investment in **training** and **management development programmes**. These allow employees at all levels to acquire new skills or improve existing ones so that full advantage can be taken of a firm's new and improved productive capacity. Unfortunately, a shortage of skilled labour has frequently been a major factor in preventing many firms in the UK from increasing output to meet an increase in demand.

Skills shortages cause problems for the UK economy. They force up wage rates, and thus prices. This can cause a surge in imports and make exports uncompetitive.

Even during an upturn, when firms begin to face skill shortages many still hesitate to invest in training and development programmes because they are not confident that the higher market demand will last long enough to make it worthwhile.

Investment in skills is also less attractive if producers expect employees with improved skills to be poached by other firms. A low level of training throughout an industry actually increases the likelihood of a producer losing any newly-trained workers to other employers. This further reduces the incentive for individual firms to invest in skills development. During a downturn in the economy, spending on training will be even lower as firms seek to cut costs. A lack of the necessary skills will then restrict the output growth when demand picks up again.

A supply of workers with the appropriate skills yields important benefits to the economy as whole. There is a very strong case for the government playing a greater role through, for example, increased funding for vocational education and Training and Enterprise Councils (TECs).

 **ACTIVITY**

Discuss the external benefits of government spending on the following:

1 Subsidies to rail freight and unprofitable passenger services.

2 More generous grants for home insulation, plus all building products associated with saving energy being exempt from **VAT**.

3 A subsidy for organic farming methods.

4 A tax on all packaging materials such as plastic, paper, cardboard and glass but no tax on packaging made from at least 75 per cent recycled materials.

🗂 🗂 🗂 PORTFOLIO ASSIGNMENT 🗂 🗂 🗂

Assume that the European Union intends to issue a directive requiring member states to take stricter steps to deal with the litter problem caused by discarded packaging, bottles and cans. It wants a greater percentage of packaging and containers to be made from recycled materials.

Among the measures which the **UK** government intends to phase in over the next three years are:

1 There is to be a compulsory deposit of 5p on all bottles and cans of a half litre size or below and a 10p deposit on all containers above a half litre.

2 The packaging used for the products served in all fast-food/take-away outlets must be made from biodegradable materials.

3 A heavy tax is to be levied on packaging and containers made from virgin materials while those made from recycled materials will be zero rated.

4 All supermarkets (above 5,000 sq. ft.) must provide facilities for the collection of glass, metal and plastic containers.

You work in the strategic planning department of **Burgerbrew plc**, a major

producer of both alcoholic and non-alcoholic drinks with extensive interests in pubs, off-licences and pizza and hamburger restaurants.

Prepare a document for the head of strategic planning which identifies the potential problems posed by the new measures for Burgerbrew's operations. List the kind of measures which you would expect departments to take in response during the transitional period.

The head of strategic planning would also like to discuss with you:

(a) your ideas on how the shift to a greener image could be supported by the company voluntarily introducing other measures that would reduce its impact upon the environment;

(b) how the general shift towards a green image might become a feature of Burgerbrew's marketing activities;

Prepare some notes on (a) and (b) above in preparation for your meeting, along with some sketches on how these ideas might also be embodied in any advertisements, packaging or containers.

Examine the effects of government policies on markets

DEALING WITH MONOPOLIES AND RESTRICTIVE PRACTICES

One of the strongest arguments in favour of a free market economy is that competition forces producers to compete on both price and quality. However, there is also the possibility that market forces can produce market forms which operate against the interest of consumers. It is for this reason that the government assumes the power to intervene directly in the activities of businesses which are against the public interest.

THE FAIR TRADING ACT 1973 AND THE COMPETITION ACT 1980

These two Acts are the current basis for government intervention in the UK. The legislation is designed to protect consumers from monopolies and anti-competitive practices and to encourage greater competition between producers.

THE MAIN FEATURES OF THE FAIR TRADING ACT 1973
The Act set up the **Office of Fair Trading (OFT)** to monitor market developments and trading practices that may be against consumers' interests. The OFT is run by the **Director-General of Fair Trading (DGFT)**. Its tasks include:

1 Collecting detailed information about consumer matters and receiving advice from the many consumer bodies.

2 Publishing advice to consumers and explaining their rights.

3 Considering complaints from individuals or consumer groups and, if necessary, referring them to a **Consumer Protection Advisory Committee.** Any resulting new regulation or law that is needed is enforced by the **trading standards departments** of local authorities.

4 Encouraging trade organisations to draw up voluntary **codes of practice** for their members.

5 Recommending changes to close any loopholes in existing laws or stop new kinds of unfair restrictive practices.

6 Taking legal action against traders who break laws designed to protect consumers.

The Act defined a monopoly as a firm or group of firms controlling 25 per cent of a local market or the national market. Mergers can be investigated where they involve a 25 per cent market share or assets of at least £30m.

Firms supplying both goods and services are required to register with the OFT certain agreements between themselves if these could lead to competition being restricted. The DGFT has the power to refer any such agreements to the **Restrictive Trade Practices Court**.

The DGFT can refer monopoly situations to the **Monopolies and Mergers Commission (MMC)**. It is the Secretary of State for Trade and Industry, however, who actually decides if the monopoly should be investigated to assess if it is against the public interest. In reaching a decision, the MMC considers the level of competition in the industry and looks for evidence in terms of cost reductions, the rate of innovation and how easy it is for new suppliers to enter the industry. It also considers the interests of consumers in terms of prices, choice and quality.

THE MAIN FEATURES OF THE COMPETITION ACT 1980

The Act recognises that anti-competitive practices can also involve single firms which are neither monopolies nor operating restrictive practices in collusion with other firms. In particular, the DGFT can investigate any pricing or distribution policy by a firm which has become a cause of **public concern**. For example, the following kinds of business strategies can be investigated:

1 A firm charges a price below cost in order to remove a major rival from the market and then returns to much higher prices.

2 A producer gives different levels of **discount** to buyers which are not related to the size of their orders. This kind of **price discrimination** can be used by producers to persuade retailers not to stock any rival brands.

3 A firm has a subsidiary which has complete control over a **raw material**. It charges its rivals a higher price for the material, increasing their costs and, therefore, weakening their competitive positions.

4 A retailer is obliged to stock the **whole range** of a supplier's products in order to obtain just one of them.

5 A retailer will be supplied with a product only on condition that it does not stock certain **rival products**.

6 A supplier agrees to supply just **one retailer** in a particular area.

The DGFT findings are reported publicly and if necessary the matter is passed on to the MMC.

This Act also meant that for the first time nationalised industries could be referred to the MMC while their prices could be investigated by the DGFT.

ACTIVITY

Read the article reproduced opposite on extended warranties. Answer the following questions:

1 **What is meant by a 'cooling-off' period and how might it help buyers of electrical goods?**

2 **Why have retailers been able to charge 'well over the odds' for extended warranties?**

3 **Why might the changes demanded by the DGFT help to make the market for extended warranties more competitive?**

4 **What kinds of information would an independent company offering extended warranties need in order to fix the premiums it charges to various customers buying different kinds of dishwashers or music systems?**

5 **As a retailer offering extended warranties, argue the case for excluding 'non-functional parts, accidental damage or misuse'.**

6 **Why might consumers feel that these exclusions are unfair ?**

Consumers' champion pulls the plug on extended cover

BRITAIN'S 15 million owners of extended warranties on electrical goods could be forgiven for feeling duped, following yesterday's criticism by the OFT that such policies were over-priced and over-sold.

Extended warranties are offered by most retailers to protect customers against the cost of ongoing repairs. However, their cost has soared over the past few years as commissions have escalated to a point where they now offer, in many cases, questionable value to the customer.

The Consumers' Association yesterday also warned buyers that they were paying heavily for peace of mind. The association called for a cooling-off period on policies. However, this was rejected by the OFT.

The OFT launched its investigation into warranties in February after receiving complaints from customers that they were pressured into paying well over the odds for cover.

Director-General of Fair Trading Sir Bryan Carsberg agreed with the complaints when he published his highly critical report yesterday.

Stores have been ordered to display details of the cost and condition of the warranties so that customers can shop around. This should lead to a sharp reduction in the cost of many policies.

Retailers have been given up to two months to erect prominent displays detailing price and terms, with leaflets for customers to take away and study, and Sir Bryan warned that the high-pressured selling techniques must stop.

He said: 'The manner in which these warranties are sold has very little transparency. There is no advertising to speak of and very little price display. They are often sold to consumers in a way which can bring undue pressure to bear upon them to make snap, ill-informed decision.

'There is no competition in extended warranties either at the point of sale or later on, with direct marketing. It is therefore not surprising that prices for extended warranties on the same produce vary considerably.'

The OFT report also takes retailers to task for substantially widening their margins through big boosts to the commissions they receive, which can lead to them pocketing around 70 per cent of the one-off premium. This was particularly the case where the retailer actually owned the insurer.

Sir Bryan said that once customers were given adequate information to shop around then their margins would fall. He said: 'Regular and comprehensive reports on repair costs and frequency of claims should be encouraged. Consumer organisations, including the Consumers' Association, have a key role to play here. Such reports should be well-publicised in order to give consumers informed guidance on value for money.'

The Sale of Goods Act provides customers with a first line of defence if a product is deemed unfit for the purpose for which it was bought. Most manufacturers also offer free parts and labour guarantees for the first 12 months, if not longer. But according to the OFT, one in four customers buying electrical goods already covered by a manufacturer guarantee also opts for extended cover. Nor does a high premium necessarily guarantee all-inclusive cover. Some warranties exclude non-functional parts, accidental damage or 'misuse', depending on interpretation. Guarantees can also be invalidated if the customer moves house, while others require repair bills to be paid up front by the customer, then claimed back.

Guardian,
17 December 1994

More trouble ferments for big brewers

The big brewers face another investigation into their treatment of tied pubs, just six years after the huge shake-up ordered by the former trade and industry secretary, Lord Young. Office of Fair Trading officials are to look into the breweries' pricing of wholesale beer.

At the heart of their latest probe is the gap – which can be as high as 40 per cent – between the price brewers charge landlords of free houses and the higher rate they charge tenants running their own pubs.

The industry, already reeling from years of recession, sliding pub attendances and a huge black market in cheaper European beer bought supposedly for 'private consumption', faces the threat of losing a further slice of revenue should the OFT order cuts in the cost of beer to tied pubs.

The industry pointed out this would be the thirty-third government or European Commission investigation into its activities since the mid-1960s. It is thought the OFT investigation will be complete within three months.

Yesterday's statement followed a suggestion by the European Commission that the UK authorities look into the wholesale beer issue.

Should the OFT find against the brewers, the industry could face another upheaval just six years after Lord Young, then trade and industry secretary, ordered a huge shake-up in 1989, which put a ceiling on the number of tenanted pubs each brewer was allowed to own.

Ironically, this vastly increased the numbers of 'free' houses, as brewers sold pubs to comply with the law. And the brewers then had to compete fiercely on wholesale beer prices in order to capture the business of these free houses.

That widened the gap that had already existed between prices charged to free and tied houses.

Bass, Whitbread, Scottish & Newcastle and Courage were quick to defend the practice. A Courage spokeswoman pointed out that, although publicans running tenanted houses paid more for their beer, they gained in ways denied to free house landlords: they tended to pay less rent, she said, and were given technical and promotional support.

Scottish & Newcastle said it was 'disappointed the OFT has decided to investigate the brewing industry once again'.

Whitbread called on the inquiry to live up to its promise 'of examining prices in the context of the whole deal between us and the lessees'.

Bass, Britain's biggest brewer, said it would co-operate with the enquiry.

There are about 25,000 free houses across the country and 27,000 tied houses, in which the publican is effectively running a franchised business. A further 13,000 pubs are 'managed houses', run by a licensee who is a full-time employee of the brewery.

Guardian,
8 February 1995

ACTIVITY

In early 1995, the OFT started an investigation into the brewing industry. Some background is given in the article above. Investigate:

1   The reasons why in 1989 the MMC placed a limit on the number of 'tied' pubs.

2   Those factors which have contributed to falling beer sales.

3   The views of tenants running their own pubs on the prices they pay to their brewery landlords.

4   The eventual ruling made by the OFT on the two-tier pricing of beer.

CONSUMER PROTECTION

Reputable retailers are always aware of their responsibilities to their customers. They seek to ensure that they are satisfied with their purchases. This not only encourages their customers to make repeat purchases but also to recommend the retailer to friends and relatives. Although many retailers are committed to 'customer care' there will always be those who seek to sell at any cost and then ignore complaints from dissatisfied customers. There will also be consumers who seek to make a complaint which unfairly seeks to place the blame on the retailer. Thus, although the following laws are concerned with consumer protection, they also provide a legal framework to protect fair and responsible retailers from consumers who make unjustified claims against them.

THE TRADE DESCRIPTIONS ACTS 1968 AND 1972

These deal with those situations where retailers give a false or misleading statement concerning the description of a good, its country of origin or any aspect of its price.

THE SALE OF GOODS ACTS 1979 AND 1994 AND THE SUPPLY OF GOODS AND SERVICES ACT 1982

The 1979 and 1994 Acts are concerned with the rights of consumers who claim that they have not been supplied with suitable goods that meet their particular needs. The 1982 Act also covers the supply of services. For example, a building repair should be carried out with reasonable care and skill and within a reasonable period of time. The Act offers the customer some protection against 'cowboy' firms.

THE CONSUMER CREDIT ACT 1974

The main feature of this Act is the obligation of lenders to ensure that consumers are made fully aware of the total cost of goods bought on credit, the annual rate of the total charge for credit (the **APR**, annual percentage rate) and any rights to cancel the agreement.

THE CONSUMER PROTECTION ACT 1987

This particular Act reflects a directive from the EU that consumers should be given certain rights to claim **damages** arising out of a defective product.

CONSUMER SAFETY ACTS

A series of Acts have been passed over the years which make it an offence to sell goods which do not meet certain **safety** requirements. Toys for young children, for example, must be made from flame-resistant materials, have no sharp edges, use lead-free paint and have no pieces that could easily be swallowed if the toy came apart. Strict safety standards also apply to items such as electrical goods, cosmetics, night clothes, carry-cot stands and cooking utensils.

THE FOOD ACT 1984 AND THE FOOD SAFETY ACT 1990

The 1984 Act makes it an offence to sell food which is unfit for human consumption or to treat food in such a way that it becomes a danger to health. It also covers the labelling of food. Manufacturers must specify contents, ingredients, and artificial colourants and preservatives. The 1984 Act is also concerned about the ways in which consumers may be misled about the quality of food and what has been put into it. The 1990 Act strengthened many aspects of the 1984 Act and, in particular, is concerned with controlling all aspects of food safety throughout the food distribution chain. It covers such matters as what is fed to animals, the premises where the food is prepared or supplied to the public and the training of employees in food hygiene.

THE UNFAIR TERMS IN CONSUMER CONTRACTS REGULATIONS

These regulations came into force in July 1995 and reflect an EU directive designed to remove the 'small print' in contracts so that consumers are not bound by unfair terms. Tour operators, for example, have included terms in their contracts which allow them to cancel or change holidays and to limit their financial obligation to refund any money paid. In future, tour operators will have no such 'get out' clause, as a consumer will be able to claim compensation for a similar holiday with another operator even if it costs more.

THE UNSOLICITED GOODS AND SERVICES ACTS 1971 AND 1975

The aim here is to protect consumers from what is known as **'inertia selling'**, that is sending people goods through the post which have not been ordered and then relying upon their ignorance and apathy to extract payment if they are not returned within a certain period.

COMPETITION POLICY AND THE EUROPEAN UNION

The removal of all kinds of trade barriers, and distortions such as tariffs and state subsidies which prevent free and fair trade between members of the EU, is obviously vital to the creation of a true single European market (SEM). It is also important that the EU plays a part in ensuring that competition within the single market is free from market distortions caused by restrictive trade practices and monopoly power.

The **European Commission** is able to intervene in cases of anti-competitive practices because of the power given to it by the **Treaty of Rome** of 1957. This set up what was then known as the **European Economic Community (EEC)**. **Articles 85** and **86** of the treaty deal with **anti-competitive behaviour** where firms acting either together or individually use their dominant position to restrict competition between firms involved in trade within the EU. In general, the EU has been successful in implementing a common policy on competition throughout the member states; its aims are, for example, reflected in UK laws dealing with anti-competitive activities.

The increased number of mergers between firms from different member states in the 1980s increased the risk of customers being exploited by monopoly power. This led to regulations allowing the European Commission to investigate mergers. The commission can investigate when the combined world turnover of the firms involved is more than 5bn ECU (£1 = 1.31 ECU, May 1995) with each firm having at least 250m ECU of turnover within the EU. Where companies have at least two thirds of their turnover in one member state, the merger must be dealt with according to the regulations of the relevant government. Firms must give the European Commission prior notice of any such merger. It then has three weeks to decide if it should investigate.

Cement cartel files read like a thriller

IT WAS A sign that the European Commission has come of age as an anti-trust authority when the competition commissioner, Karel Van Miert, said with a mixture of pride and wonder that the voluminous file on Europe's cement cartel read like a crime thriller.

Mr Van Miert was outlining the commission's decision to impose record fines on thirty-three companies and nine trade associations accused by Brussels of working together over a ten-year period to share out Europe's £5.5bn cement market.

The commissioner said the large penalties show that Brussels is determined to crack down on anti-competitive practices. 'After what happened this year, I hope that everyone has got the message,' Mr Van Miert said.

The commission's emergence as a bold competition regulator has been helped by two European Court judgements which allow dawn raids on the offices of companies suspected of running cartels or price-fixing arrangements.

The £193.5m penalty slapped on thirty-three cement makers this week is the third time this year the EC has broken its own record for the size of fine imposed. Steel producers and cardboard makers have also felt the weight of commission disapproval.

Various factors can trigger a cartel investigation: unusual price movements, complaints from customers and, occasionally, tip-offs from within the industry itself.

The commission is cagey about what prompted the cement investigation, but it appears that one factor was the decision by Greek companies to export to the rest of Europe in the mid-1980s, when the war in Lebanon robbed them of traditional Middle East markets.

The impact of Greek exports produced complaints about government subsidies, but the Greek view is that the industry was simply newer. 'As a result,' said Dimitris Paplexopoulos, executive director of Titan Cement SA, one of the main manufacturers in Greece, 'it is more modern and cost-effective, which is why we are able to export so successfully.'

To combat the fall in prices caused by Greek exports, European cement companies allegedly set up a company to buy up Greek cement and sell it outside Europe.

The sudden appearance of a new cement-exporting company, Interciment, didn't go unnoticed in Brussels.

The commission said it found evidence to back up its suspicions in raids carried out in 1989 at cement companies and industry associations. Documents allegedly included bilateral market-sharing agreements between producers in Spain and Portugal and in France and Italy.

The affair is unlikely to make a significant impact on the structure of the European cement market, according to a NatWest Securities analyst, Robert Donald. He said there might be more vulnerability to imports – especially in France, which had the highest prices in Europe – while Europe's cement producers would want to demonstrate that they were 'whiter than white', and that might give some of their bigger customers a little more leverage on price.

Guardian,
3 December 1994

ACTIVITY

Using the article opposite on the cartel in the cement industry, discuss the following:

1   The kinds of projects that use very large quantities of cement and how cement companies could operate a system to maintain high prices and share the market between them.

2   The kinds of price movements that might suggest the existence of a cartel.

3   Why would sudden raids on companies be a necessary way of identifying cartels and obtaining the kind of documentary evidence EU officials would be looking for?

4   The reasons why someone within the cement industry might decide to inform the EU of cartel arrangements.

5   Why cement imports from Greece posed a threat to the cartel and how European producers sought to protect their position.

6   Possible features of the cement, steel and cardboard box making industries that might encourage cartel arrangements on prices and market shares.

NATIONALISED INDUSTRIES

In 1979, the state-owned industries of the UK employed about 1.5m people and dominated the transport, energy, steel, communications and shipbuilding sectors of the economy. The full list of the largest previously state-owned

industries now operating in the private sector is shown in *Fig. 1.28*. Since many of these industries had been nationalised for many years and run by governments of both political parties, there must have been strong reasons for having them under **public ownership**. The case for nationalising a particular industry was generally based upon a combination of factors.

British Aerospace	1981
Cable and Wireless	1981
Amersham International	1982
National Freight Consortium	1982
Britoil	1982, 1985
Associated British Ports	1983, 1984
Enterprise Oil	1984
Jaguar	1984
British Telecom	1984, 1991, 1993
British Gas	1986
British Airways	1987
British Ordnance	1987
Rolls-Royce	1987
BAA	1987
National Bus Company	1988
British Steel	1988
Water and sewerage companies	1989
Regional electricity companies	1990
National Power	1991, 1995
PowerGen	1991, 1995
Scottish electricity companies	1991
Northern Ireland electricity generating companies	1992
British Coal	1994

FIGURE 1.28: Major privatisation sales since 1979.

In the case of rail transport, the production and distribution of gas and electricity and the provision of telecommunications services, the companies had become very large organisations. This was due to the very extensive economies of scale which could be derived from expanding the size of their operations. Further competition was then deterred by the very high initial costs of entry, requiring substantial capital investment. Even if competition had been possible, it would have led to the wasteful duplication of resources and spare capacity that would have resulted in higher prices to make them viable. Many industries, therefore, had become **'natural monopolies'**. If left in the private sector, they could have used their position to exploit consumers with excessive prices.

In some cases, the industries required very large sums of money to finance their **modernisation programmes.** Given their weak financial positions they would have faced great difficulty in raising the necessary level of finance from the capital market. The government, however, could provide funds for such capital projects from its tax revenues or by borrowing at relatively low rates of interest on their behalf.

The government could slow down the rate at which the industries introduced **rationalisation programmes** which involved shedding labour and closing down the inefficient and high-cost parts of their operations. A policy of slowing down closures was particularly important where, for example, the steel, coal or shipbuilding industry was the main source of employment, either directly or indirectly, in particular regions of the UK. The government could pay **subsidies** to these industries to avoid sudden and large-scale redundancies. The aim was to reduce the social problems that would otherwise result from the operation of market forces. In the meantime, the government sought to attract jobs to the same areas through its regional development policy.

At a time of rising unemployment in the economy as a whole, the government could boost jobs by bringing forward capital spending programmes in the nationalised industries. A new power station, for example, would protect or create jobs in a range of firms receiving orders connected with the project. The government could also influence the siting of new steel-making capacity, for example, to help areas of high unemployment.

Governments could ensure that major investment projects or other important spending by the nationalised industries produced orders for UK rather than foreign suppliers. This is still a common practice around the world. In the developed economies, it is estimated that over 70 per cent of major public sector contracts go to home producers.

Apart from trying to alleviate the problems associated with unemployment, the government could also take account of other social needs. In the case of British Rail, for example, it could subsidise loss-making routes. This was particularly important for those in rural areas who live some distance from the main employment opportunities. Had cuts in services been on an even larger scale, this would also have aggravated the harmful effects arising from more cars and lorries on the roads.

During a period of rising **inflation**, the government could slow down the rise in the cost of living by restraining increases in rail fares and gas, electricity, telephone and postal charges. These bills are a significant part of the average household's spending. If **price restraint** was extended to keeping down energy, steel and rail freight charges, then this also helped to moderate the rise in production costs in the private sector.

PRIVATISATION

The term **privatisation** refers to the conversion of nationalised industries or public sector corporations into public joint stock companies. These industries are transferred from the public sector, where they were owned by the state, to the private sector where they are owned by shareholders. The Conservative government's privatisation programme is based mainly on its strongly held belief that market forces make industries more efficient. By the end of 1993, privatisation had brought in over £51bn for the government. Over 920,000 jobs had initially been transferred to the private sector. The sell off of the coal mines owned by British Coal was a more prolonged affair, but had been completed by the end of 1994 and brought in a further £2bn. Soon after being privatised, however, these industries engaged in rationalisation programmes that resulted in large cuts in their workforce.

THE CASE FOR PRIVATISATION

If industries could no longer rely upon financial support from the government when they made losses or an insufficient surplus to finance capital projects, then they would be obliged to pay more attention to their costs. This would accelerate both the closing down of high-cost inefficient capacity and the rationalisation of their workforce. A greater emphasis upon raising productivity would also encourage more innovation and the introduction of improvements in working practices that save on labour costs.

In order to finance investment programmes, the privatised industries would have to earn sufficient profits to pay for capital projects as well as keeping their shareholders happy. The increased importance which they would have to give to profits was another reason why they were expected to be more efficient. If they needed to obtain funds from external sources, they would also need to be profitable to attract capital from private investors.

The government was keen to see **wider share ownership** and, in particular, employees owning shares in their own companies. It was hoped that if employees had a financial stake in their company, then they would see their interests as coinciding with those of their companies. This was expected to reduce conflict between management and workers. Privatisation provided the government with the opportunity to encourage employees to take a financial stake in their own industries.

Once state-run concerns were transferred to the private sector, they would have clear objectives. Their efficiency, pricing policies and investment programmes would no longer be confused by sudden and frequent changes in the financial, social and economic objectives set for them by the government.

Industrial disputes between employees and management in the nationalised industries often turned into very serious political battles. Unions saw themselves as up against the government. Privatisation would allow the government to remove itself from the kinds of decision which it often hesitated to take, on pay and redundancies for example, because of the likely political conflict. The government was confident that the resulting private sector management would not hesitate to take such decisions in the interests of efficiency and profits.

In the case of British Steel, British Airways, Jaguar and others that faced intense international competition, their need to survive without government support was expected to have a dramatic effect on their efficiency and the quality of their output. Some large privatisations, however, meant that public sector monopolies simply became private sector monopolies. Examples are British Gas, the electricity generating companies and the regional water companies. Even in the case of British Telecom, privatisation meant that, at least in the first years, it faced very limited competition in some of its markets. The government believed, however, that these industries would still be more efficient in the private sector because of the kinds of developments described above.

Nationalised industries had been prevented from diversifying into other lines of business because private sector firms in the same market could claim that they were facing unfair competition. Nationalised industries could rely upon financial support from the government if they ran into financial problems and this was in contrast to the greater risks associated with private sector firms in the same lines of business. Privatisation allows companies greater commercial freedom.

Finally, the revenue which the government obtains from privatisation can be used to cut taxes or reduce the amount which it needs to borrow when its tax revenues do not cover its spending.

REGULATING PRIVATISED MONOPOLIES

Where the newly privatised industries would enjoy a monopoly position, the government sought to open up their markets to competition. In the case of British Telecom, for example, it required that other telecommunications companies could use the British Telecom network. It hived off the ownership of the gas pipeline system and the national grid from those that supplied gas or generated electricity. It was hoped that this would encourage companies to compete to supply gas or electricity through these distribution systems.

Public concern, however, about the ability of privatised monopolies to increase their profits by simply charging higher prices, forced the government to create a series of **regulatory agencies** to monitor their prices and to act as 'watchdogs' to ensure fair trading. **OFTEL**, **OFWAT**, **OFGAS** and **OFFER** were set up to monitor the activities of British Telecom, the water companies, British Gas and the regional power companies, respectively. They can investigate consumers' complaints.

In particular, they can put a ceiling on price increases by using what has become known as the **'RPI-X'** formula. This means that companies are restricted to price increases below the rate of inflation. If the retail price index had risen by say 5 per cent and the regulator had put a value of say 3 per cent on 'X', then the industry in question can only raise prices by 2 per cent. The regulator also has the power to change the value placed on X, raising it if the level of profits does not seem to justify the price increase produced by the formula. The formula can also be abandoned completely and an industry obliged to reduce its prices or give consumers a rebate in the case of very excessive profits.

ACTIVITY

1 Obtain details of the residential call charges made by British Telecom, Mercury and one of the cable companies. Also, investigate the special discounts they offer on certain kinds of calls or selected numbers and their rental charges.

2 What kind of information would a household need in terms of its own use of the phone in order to assess what its annual bill would be with the three different companies?

3 To what extent has competition between BT and Mercury reduced their call charges?

Price cuts to follow electricity review

THE SCALE of cuts in electricity bills will have to await the outcome of three months of bruising battles between the industry regulator and the twelve regional power companies.

A three-month review of a price regime, unveiled last August, was set to take effect from April and will be conducted by the director general of electricity supply, Steven Littlechild, in what is seen as the biggest U-turn in the brief history of utility regulation in Britain.

At stake is the prices paid for power by 23m households and many small businesses, but there are already fears that the twelve firms and the watchdog could fail to agree delaying price cuts still further while the matter is referred to the Monopolies and Mergers Commission (MMC) for adjudication.

The regulator hinted there were three ways to cut prices: an immediate rebate, altering inflation-linked price controls or a mixture of the two. The growing consensus last night was that simple rebates would be unacceptable and that a mixture of tougher price curbs and repayment was most likely.

Just over two weeks ago Prof. Littlechild caused a £3.5bn collapse in electricity share prices with a surprise announcement that he was having second thoughts about the five-year price regime which was criticised for being too lenient.

He gave himself two weeks to decide whether to continue with the existing price cuts – which impose average one-off cuts of 14 per cent and a stipulation that price rises are kept at 2 per cent below inflation for the rest of the decade – or to rewrite them.

Yesterday he said existing controls would proceed for the first 12 months, but he would revise the regime for the rest of the period. There was 'sufficient justification to consider proposals for a further tightening of these controls'.

He said that he had been convinced by representations from consumer groups and MPs that there was a case for considering tighter controls.

Guardian, 25 March 1995

ACTIVITY

Read the article opposite. Divide into two groups representing the electricity consumers and the regional power companies and then discuss the case for and against a price cut/freeze.

Investigate the eventual decision by the electricity industry regulator on 6 July 1995 and assess how it affected the average household.

DEREGULATION AND CONTRACTING OUT

In addition to its privatisation policy, in the 1980s the government also sought to give market forces a greater role in those areas where central and local government services had been largely responsible for providing services. It did this by opening up these services and their related activities to the possibility that they could be supplied by private sector firms.

DEREGULATION

Some markets had been **regulated** by the government so that once certain organisations had been granted a right to supply a market they were then protected from the entry of other suppliers. One such example of a previously regulated market was bus and coach transport.

Before 1980, local bus routes and long-distance coach travel in the UK was not open to free competition. Passengers were served by bus and coach companies who had been given licences to be the sole operators on particular routes. This approach to bus services based on regulation sought to avoid wasteful competition with too many buses operating vehicles on the same routes and running them with too many empty seats. There was concern that, in a free market, companies would show little interest in loss-making off-peak schedules and would risk accidents by saving on maintenance costs when faced with intense price competition. Over the years, this regulated market for bus and long distance coach travel had become dominated by local authority and state-owned bus and coach companies. Bus operators were also receiving increasing subsidies to run unprofitable routes. The Transport Acts 1980 and 1985 opened up the industry to free competition in the belief that **deregulation** would lead to lower fares and improved services. Companies were also able to tender for routes where they would receive a subsidy. The increased use of minibuses on local routes is one of the results of deregulation.

COMPETITIVE TENDERING IN THE PUBLIC SECTOR

Competitive pressures have also been introduced into many other parts of the public sector in an effort to reduce costs. This involves the practice of **contracting out** many of the services previously undertaken by central and local government departments. This generally involves putting services out for **competitive tendering** in order to give private companies an opportunity to compete for the contract to provide the service for a specific period of time. Many sections within government departments which had previously provided such services **'in house'** have been turned into independent organisations and also allowed to bid for contracts. This process of competitive tendering or **market testing** now covers a wide range of services from catering, cleaning, maintenance and waste disposal services to architectural and pay roll services. There are also now privately run prisons and private sector companies have also been responsible for carrying out escort duties when prisoners are being transferred.

Market forces have also been introduced into the National Health Service (NHS). Hospitals supplying health care services have been converted into hospital trusts and earn income by selling their health care services to the various health authorities. Hospital trusts also sell services to those doctors' surgeries which have become fundholders. These fundholders actually purchase the kinds of health care services they need for their patients. It is hoped that this **'internal market'** will lead to a more efficient use of resources within the NHS. The fixed budgets of those that buy services on behalf of patients will cause them to 'shop around', and hospital trusts will need to offer competitive charges to get 'business' that generates income.

The budgets of schools and colleges are also more closely linked to the numbers of their students. Colleges are expected to earn more of their income by selling courses to both the business sector and to Training and Enterprise Councils (TECs). This policy is expected to produce a more business-like approach in terms of efficiency and quality as schools and colleges compete for 'customers'.

ECONOMIC POLICY

Free market economies fluctuate between periods of **boom** which lead to labour shortages and inflation, and periods of falling demand which produce a decline in output, rising unemployment and possibly a deep **recession**. These booms and slumps happen because there is no reason why all the different kinds of spending in the economy will always produce a total level of demand that is just sufficient to absorb the total output that can be produced when all those able and willing to work have jobs. Because the economic environment can change very suddenly, from one of excess demand to one of a lack of demand, producers have to operate in very uncertain markets.

Over the years, governments have used a variety of economic policies in an effort to either dampen down or stimulate total spending in the economy so that it more closely matches what the economy is capable of producing. It does this with measures designed to influence both the level and pattern of total spending in the economy. Specific measures concern consumer spending, private sector investment, spending on imports, export demand and public expenditure.

INFLATION

If the government's economic forecasts suggest that the level of total spending in the economy is likely to increase faster than the rate at which UK producers can expand output to meet such demand, then the government may be concerned about inflation. This is because an excessive level of total spending in the economy may very soon produce labour shortages that lead to large pay rises and, thus, a rise in unit labour costs and higher prices.

The UK's **balance of trade** with the rest of the world will also deteriorate because of the following factors:

- **A sudden and large spending boom** will produce a surge in imports because UK producers cannot cope with the increased orders.

- **Higher inflation** will make import prices more attractive.

- **Export prices** become less competitive in overseas markets.

- **Some UK producers will switch output** from export markets to the buoyant home market at the expense of quoting longer delivery dates to overseas customers.

- **If the higher spending reflects a boom in the take up of credit,** then imports of consumer durables will rise.

- **A rapid rise in the level of home output** will mean much higher imports of raw materials, energy, parts and components.

DEFLATIONARY MEASURES

In order to reduce the rate of inflation and improve the UK's balance of trade, the government can use a variety of economic measures to depress or **deflate** total spending in the economy.

AN INCREASE IN INTEREST RATES

A rise in interest rates raises the costs of mortgages, loans, overdrafts and other forms of credit. This depresses the market demand for goods and services for the following reasons:

- **A rise in the interest rates paid on mortgages** leaves a large number of home buyers with less money to spend on other items. Higher mortgage interest payments also make it more difficult for many households to meet the repayments on other kinds of loans and consumer credit agreements. In particular, this will reduce the demand for a wide range of expensive consumer durables which are often bought on credit.

- **Higher mortgage rates** reduce the demand for houses from both first-time buyers and those who are moving home. This fall in the housing market, in turn, reduces the demand for furnishings, consumer durables and the kinds of services and products associated with home improvements.

- **Producers react to the fall in consumer spending** by cutting back on production and the resulting redundancies will mean an even larger fall in consumer spending.

- **Reduced overtime,** bonus payments and commissions also mean a loss of earnings and hence less spending power for those still in work.

- **Because the rise in unemployment** reduces the bargaining power of trade unions, workers can no longer be confident of securing even a small pay increase to help meet the repayments on any additional credit agreements.

- **Falling house prices** may leave many households with negative equity, where their outstanding mortgage is higher than the market value of their property. When this is combined with a lack of job security, these households will hesitate to take on additional consumer credit. If they faced financial difficulties, they could no longer rely upon selling their property at a profit to clear their debts.

- **Depressed sales, lower profits and higher interest charges** on existing loans and any future borrowing oblige firms to cut their capital investment programmes. This fall in investment will depress the demand for the plant, machinery, equipment and premises provided by firms in the capital goods and construction sectors of the economy. This means a further rise in unemployment and an even lower level of total spending in the economy. It should be emphasised that because investment is vital for the future prosperity of the economy, the damage which deflationary measures inflict on investment is a very serious and unwanted side effect of an anti-inflationary policy.

- **In order to help meet the higher interest charges** on their existing borrowing, firms need to make savings and this makes it all the more important for them to avoid excessive pay increases.

AN INCREASE IN INCOME TAX RATES

If the government is concerned about excessive levels of spending and a rise in inflation, then it can raise income tax rates in order to reduce the average level of disposable income. An increase in employees' **national insurance contributions** also reduces disposable incomes.

FREEZING TAX ALLOWANCES AND TAX BANDS

An increase in income tax rates is very unpopular with voters but there is a way for the government to increase the percentage of income paid in tax without actually raising income tax rates. Everyone is entitled to a certain amount of income which is free of income tax; for many years, it was generally the case that at budget time the chancellor raised this **personal allowance** in line with the rate of inflation in order to protect the real spending power of the tax-free income. The government also usually raised the bands of income on which the higher rates of tax would be paid in line with inflation. If, however, the government decides to freeze allowances and tax bands, then as incomes rise in the future, a larger proportion of income would be paid in income tax.

For many years, households with mortgages were able to offset their annual interest payments on the first £30,000 of their mortgage against their tax liability. If, for example, this involved an annual interest payment of £2,400, on a standard rate of tax of 25 per cent, this would save £600 in tax. In 1995, relief on mortgage interest repayments was only allowed at 15 per cent, thus reducing households spending power.

AN INCREASE IN INDIRECT TAXES

The prices which producers charge for their goods and services is also affected by changes in **value added tax (VAT)**, **excise duties** and other taxes which the government collects when consumers spend money. While taxes on various forms of income are known as **direct taxes**, the different types of **expenditure taxes** are called **indirect taxes**. These taxes mean that some of the money paid by consumers is eventually passed on to the government. In effect, firms are acting as tax collectors for the government. In the case of the excise duty imposed on beer, for example, it is far easier for the government to collect revenue from the breweries according to their beer sales than trying to collect taxes from the thousands of outlets which eventually sell their beers to consumers. Although the breweries pay the tax over to the **Customs and Excise**, beer drinkers do of course end up paying the tax because it is passed on down through the distribution chain in the prices charged by pubs, off-licences and supermarkets.

INCREASING VAT

Value added tax is levied by the government according to the value added by each firm in the various production and distribution stages until the good or service is finally paid for by the consumer. A major reason for the original introduction of VAT was to create an incentive for firms to minimise their costs because the lower their value added the less the impact of the tax on their selling price.

When VAT was first introduced in 1973 it was set at 7.5 per cent. It was subsequently raised to 15 per cent in 1979 and then increased to 17.5 per cent in 1992. In the 1994 budget, the government was defeated in its attempt to impose the full rate of VAT on domestic fuel and had to settle for a rate of 8 per cent.

An increase in VAT will dampen down the level of spending in the economy because it reduces real spending power. A higher rate of VAT means that the average household's disposable income does not go so far as before.

The actual effect of a rise in VAT on many prices can be very small. In the case of an item priced at £2.35, for example, its price will rise by only 5p if VAT is increased from 17.5 per cent to 20 per cent. Even a product priced at £470 will cost only £10 more. However, it is the cumulative effect of these higher prices that reduces real spending power and hence total demand in the economy.

At budget time, the government also has the option of extending VAT to zero-rated items. The major areas of consumer expenditure still exempt from VAT are food, children's clothing and footwear, books, newspapers and magazines, and public transport.

ACTIVITY

1 Assume that the VAT rate is 17.5 per cent. Alpha and Beta are competing firms which both buy in inputs of materials and components at £100.

   (a) What are their selling prices if Alpha incurs costs of £40 and adds a mark-up of £20 while Beta incurs costs of £32 and adds a profit of £16?

   (b) By what percentage does Alpha's price exceed Beta's:
       (i) before VAT; and
       (ii) after VAT?

2 Assume a household spends £470 a month on average on goods and services which carry the standard rate of VAT.

   (a) How much does this household pay in VAT?

   (b) What is the extra VAT paid by this household if the rate rises by 2.5 per cent?

INCREASING EXCISE DUTIES

A very large proportion of the price paid for alcohol, tobacco products and petrol is accounted for by excise duties. In the case of the typical bottle of whisky, packet of cigarettes and litre of petrol, the duty is about half the price paid. The government has selected these items for very heavy taxation because the demand for them is very inelastic. When the chancellor increases the duty on these products, they continue to be bought in very large quantities. He can therefore rely upon the higher excise duties as a way of removing spending power from households and leaving them with less money to spend on other goods and services.

INTRODUCING OR INCREASING OTHER TAXES

In addition to raising existing taxes, the government may introduce new taxes. In the November 1994 budget, for example, the chancellor set a 3 per cent tax on most general insurance premiums and a new duty on air

passengers at £5 for flights within the UK and the EU and £10 elsewhere. A rise in the road fund licence can also be used to withdraw purchasing power because, as with higher petrol duty, the government is not obliged to return the extra revenue back into the economy via increased spending on roads.

REDUCING GOVERNMENT SPENDING

A very large part of total spending in the economy is accounted for either directly or indirectly by government spending. In the early 1990s, for example, it was around 42 per cent of total spending. A large number of households and firms have incomes and order books which are affected by such spending. If the government is concerned that total spending is rising too fast, leading to higher inflation and a growing trade deficit, then the chancellor may introduce a budget aimed at restricting the growth of public expenditure in order to help slow down total spending in the economy.

SPENDING IN REAL TERMS

If the government estimates that in the next financial year inflation is likely to be about 3.5 per cent, then central and local government departments need a 3.5 per cent increase in their budgets just to maintain their existing spending in real terms. If, however, the government increases public spending by 1.5 per cent, then this amounts to a cut in spending in real terms because the money will not buy as many goods and services as before. For example, the money devoted to road building rises but it actually buys fewer miles of motorway; the construction industry, and its own suppliers and sub-contractors, receive fewer orders. They, in turn, are forced to lay off workers. The resulting fall in spending power will then work its way through to other sectors of the economy.

PUBLIC SECTOR PAY RISES

Apart from making cuts in its capital spending projects, the government can also use its position to freeze or severely restrict public sector wage rises. When deciding the budgets for central government services, and the grants which it makes to local authorities, the government may only make an allowance for an average pay rise for public sector employees of, say, 1 per cent. If, however, inflation is expected to be 3 per cent in the next financial year, then the real spending power of those in the public sector will actually fall. This again helps to reduce the pressure of demand in the economy.

CAPPING COUNCIL TAX

When faced with what they see as insufficient funding from central government, some local authorities might seek extra income by increasing the charges it imposes upon the local community in the form of council tax. To prevent this, the government can use its power to restrict rises in **council tax**. This **capping** on local authorities is a way of enforcing controls on the level of local authority spending.

THE EFFECTS OF DEFLATIONARY POLICIES

If deflationary policies are severe, and operated for a long enough period, inflation will eventually fall and the trade balance will improve. This will be due to the following developments:

- **When producers are faced with a falling market demand** then they must offer competitive price to survive. In particular, this means that employers must resist large pay demands if they are to remain competitive.

- **Any need to meet higher charges on existing borrowing** forces firms to make savings elsewhere. This is another reason for them to pay more attention to their labour costs.

- **Rising unemployment also eases pressures in the labour market.** Trade unions have much less bargaining power when negotiating wage increases.

- **As inflation falls below the average rate for other manufacturing economies,** UK goods regain some of their lost competitiveness. This makes imports less attractive compared with home output as well as making exports more competitive in overseas markets.

- **The fall in total demand in the home market** also eases the demand for imports of consumer goods as well as raw materials, parts, components and capital goods.

- **The falling home market forces producers** to pay more attention to developing export markets. In time, this helps to improve the UK's balance of trade.

- **Firms will be left with spare capacity.** The slack order book means that they can offer more attractive delivery dates, so increasing their chances of winning orders at home and abroad.

POLICIES TO DEAL WITH UNEMPLOYMENT AND TO GENERATE GROWTH

On some occasions, the government may be concerned that total spending in the economy is producing a level of output which still leaves a very high level of unemployment. In this case, the government may opt for measures which help to encourage or **reflate** total spending so that producers will hire more workers. The government can select from the same kinds of measures used to deflate demand to deal with inflation but this time use them in the reverse direction.

LOWER INTEREST RATES

Cheaper consumer credit and mortgages played a central role in the consumer spending boom of the late 1980s and in the government's attempt to move the economy out of recession and deal with the high unemployment of the early 1990s. Households which gain most from a lower mortgage rate are those with large outstanding mortgages.

CUTS IN THE VARIOUS RATES OF INCOME TAX

Governments have not generally used lower income tax as a way of stimulating consumer spending because of the political unpopularity of perhaps having to reverse the change in the future. There is also the question of fairness: lower income tax rates are of no use to those on low incomes who pay little or no tax but they bring substantial benefits to those on high incomes. A large part of extra disposable income may also go on imports. Although cuts in income tax were a feature of the 1980s and early 1990s, the government saw them as a way of stimulating **'initiative and enterprise'**. It believed that high tax rates deterred the growth of an **'enterprise culture'**. It hoped that tax cuts would encourage small firms and the self-employed.

INCREASES IN TAX ALLOWANCES AND INCOME TAX BANDS

Because increasing tax allowances and income tax bands in excess of the rise in the cost of living are not so obvious measures, they have the political advantage that they can be made much less generous in the future if the need arises without the political unpopularity associated with reversing earlier tax cuts.

LOWER INDIRECT TAXES

In reality, a cut in excise duties is very unlikely as this would increase the use of products which are a threat to both health and the environment. Again a cut in VAT is soon forgotten once a government is obliged by any future inflationary pressures to restore the rate to its previous level.

AN INCREASE IN GOVERNMENT SPENDING

Any such increase would have to be financed by the government borrowing. If it was paid for by higher tax rates, this would defeat the aim of increasing total spending in the economy. Although it takes time before the effects of more spending on capital projects eventually produce more jobs, such a policy may be preferable to tax cuts. This is because the extra spending could concentrate on health, education, training and environmental protection measures, for example, which benefit everyone in the longer term. These projects are also labour intensive and have a relatively low import content.

ACTIVITY

You are employed in the marketing department in a company concerned with one of the following industries:

- **Hotels**
- **Fitted kitchens, manufacture and installation**
- **Catering**
- **Retailing electrical goods**
- **Retailing clothing**
- **Furniture manufacture**
- **Sportswear and equipment**
- **Brewing and distilling**

Produce a report of about 250 words on the likely effects upon your company's sales of a fall in interest rates from 10 per cent to 8 per cent and the general expectation that they will go even lower over the next six months. The report is to appear in the company newspaper to keep employees informed of likely developments.

ACTIVITY

Car registration plates can be used to find out the year when cars were bought. This evidence can be used to see how the demand for cars is influenced by government economic policy.

1 Using busy but safe roadside locations and car parks, carry out a survey of as large a number of cars as possible to establish the number which were registered in each of the last ten years. It can be reasonably assumed that not too many of the earlier cars would have been scrapped.

2 Use appropriate pictorial techniques to display total registrations in each year and rate of increase over the previous year.

3 Select data from *Fig. 1.32* and *Fig. 1.33* (page 73) which you regard as affecting consumer confidence and the decision to buy a new car. Use appropriate sources of economic and financial data to update such figures.

4 Describe, explain and illustrate any correlation which you can find between the information in 2 and 3.

ACTIVITY

1 Over a month, collect articles from newspapers which comment on economic and financial data such as retail sales, unemployment, the take up of credit, interest rates, the housing market and consumer confidence.

2 Assume that you are employed in a marketing department. You are required to produce a brief monthly report on how your company's sales performance is likely to be influenced by developments in the general business environment as shown by your research above. Where possible support your comments with copies of any charts and tables taken from newspapers.

3 Briefly state what action the company can take to exploit any favourable developments or minimise the effects of any potential problems. Assume that the recipient of the report does not expect more than 600 words and prefers a concise style that makes good use of headings, listings, bullet points, bold print to highlight key words, etc.

ECONOMIC POLICIES AND ECONOMIC GROWTH

The extent to which the economy can continue to push its total output of goods and services to higher levels, and thus achieve **economic growth** depends upon improvements in productivity. Because all economies have limited resources, higher output can only be achieved if resources are used more efficiently. Producers, therefore, play a vital role in promoting economic growth because in order to strengthen their competitive positions they strive for the improvements in productivity needed to minimise their unit costs.

GOVERNMENT AND PRIVATE SECTOR INVESTMENT

Because of the vital role played by investment in promoting economic growth and raising living standards, governments have always sought to encourage investment by the private sector. Unlike consumer spending, however, governments have found it far more difficult to stimulate the level of investment.

BUSINESS CONFIDENCE

One of the problems facing companies when making decisions about their future strategy and investment programmes is the very uncertain nature of the environment in which they have to operate. A major reason for this is the effect of changes in the government's economic policy upon the total level of spending in the markets where a firm sells its goods or services. Within a relatively short period of time, a shift in economic policy can cause dramatic developments in the markets where companies operate; it impacts on where they sell their goods and where they acquire their resources such as labour and capital. If, for example, a change in economic policy produces either an actual or anticipated fall in total spending in the economy, this will depress the level of business confidence and force

many firms to cut or postpone their investment and training programmes. This is because capital projects can involve many millions of pounds and firms must be confident of a relatively long period of buoyant sales once new capacity comes on stream.

It is argued that the kind of **'stop-go' cycle** in *Fig. 1.29* has been responsible for the relatively low level of investment in the UK and thus explains why its rate of economic growth is below that of many other major manufacturing economies.

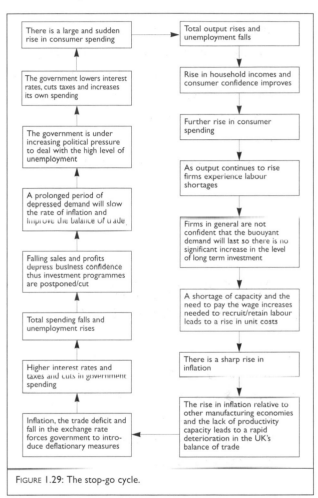

FIGURE 1.29: The stop-go cycle.

The government should therefore try to avoid the sudden changes in economic policies that contribute to an unstable business climate. It needs to follow an economic strategy that produces a steady increase in total demand so that firms can respond without suffering from a lack of productive capacity or skills shortages. If this kind of market environment can be sustained for a reasonable period of time, firms will have both the profits and the confidence to invest in additional capacity. This, in turn, means that future increases in demand can be met mainly by increases in total output rather than the inflationary pressures produced by a shortage of capacity and skilled labour.

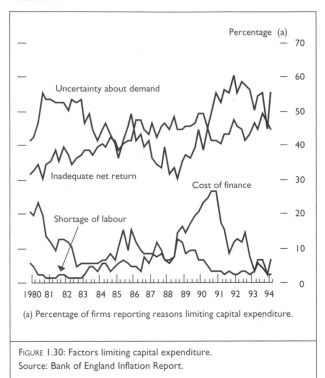

1980 81 82 83 84 85 86 87 88 89 90 91 92 93 94

(a) Percentage of firms reporting reasons limiting capital expenditure.

FIGURE 1.30: Factors limiting capital expenditure.
Source: Bank of England Inflation Report.

INTEREST RATES

Apart from the effects which higher interest rates have on sales, profits and business confidence, they also make it more expensive for firms to raise extra capital funds by borrowing. Because company borrowing often involves large sums of money, even a relatively small rise in interest rates means a large increase in interest repayments on borrowed capital. In order to meet these higher interest charges firms may need to cut back on their future capital spending programmes. The government should, therefore, seek to follow economic policies that would reduce its need to resort to an increase in interest rates.

INVESTMENT GRANTS

The use of public funds to help finance private sector investment plays a very minor role in the UK economy. Most of the grants that have been made available are linked to capital projects which protect or create jobs in areas of high unemployment or help to tackle the social, economic and environmental problems of run-down urban areas. Within the EU, the commissioner for competition seeks to ensure that member governments do not use any such financial assistance simply as a way of disguising the payment of a subsidy to an uncompetitive home producer.

COMPANY TAXATION

Investment might be encouraged by a cut in the level of **corporation tax** which firms pay on their profits. The rate of corporation tax depends upon the level of profits.

In the financial year 1995–6 it varied from 25 per cent to 40 per cent. A cut in corporation tax not only increases the net return on capital but also increases the level of internally generated funds available to finance future capital projects. The government might also find ways of increasing investment by providing firms with a more advantageous system of capital allowances. These allow spending on investment projects to be offset against tax liability in such a way that the early return on such investment is made more attractive.

ECONOMIC GROWTH AND THE SINGLE EUROPEAN MARKET

The very large **internal market** of the EU can be seen as a major factor in promoting the rate of economic growth and employment in the UK for a number of reasons. A larger **'home' market** allows producers to exploit further economies of scale and hence benefit from lower unit costs. If they maintain prices at their current levels, profit margins will increase and provide additional profits to finance future investment projects. Alternatively, they may use the opportunity provided by lower unit costs to cut prices and thus strengthen their competitive position at the expense of the higher-cost producers.

Capital intensive industries, and those which have to spend large sums on research and development, are able to undertake their capital spending programmes with a much higher degree of confidence. Investing in a new chemical processing plant or developing a new drug becomes much more worthwhile if a company sees the prospect of large sales from a potentially very large market. Advances in technology are also becoming increasingly expensive to fund, and the removal of trade restrictions and the opening up of export markets helps to generate the level of sales needed to make such projects viable.

The removal of import controls such as **tariffs** and **quotas** further increases the choice available to companies when buying raw materials, parts, components and capital goods. Having taken account of non-price factors such as quality and delivery, they are able to buy components from those suppliers which offer the most competitive prices. In the case of capital goods, it is particularly important that import restrictions do not prevent companies having access to the kind of plant and machinery which most closely meet their needs. Import controls prevent a company from selecting from the widest possible range of suppliers, and have an adverse effect upon the costs, quality and competitiveness of that company's output.

If producers are sheltered behind import barriers, they may become complacent. The lack of competition from overseas companies means that they do not have to be particularly efficient to survive in their home market. If the home economy is opened up to foreign competition, home producers have to respond to the threat of imports by paying greater attention to their costs, offering more competitive prices and generally improving other features such as quality and after sales-service. Inefficient producers will not survive in this much more competitive environment; those that do are also likely to find additional markets outside the EU.

The widespread **removal of trade barriers** and other restrictions on imports increases the purchasing power of households in the UK. The prices of many products may actually fall because of more intense competition. Producers in the UK may experience a greater demand for their output as households make use of their extra spending power. Output, jobs, incomes and further spending will thus arise out of the original rise in real purchasing power.

REGIONAL UNEMPLOYMENT

When market forces lead to the closure of a large employer or the decline of an industry as a whole, there is a large number of redundancies. If expanding firms or growth industries are located in the same area as the unemployed workers and they need the same kinds of skills, people may soon find alternative jobs. If the redundant workers do not have the right kinds of skills or are too far away from firms recruiting workers then unemployment may prove to be very long term. Unfortunately, unemployment has left its mark on the UK economy for decades because of the long-term decline in the output of the steel, shipbuilding, textile and coal mining industries. These were the main sources of employment in northern England, central Scotland, South Wales and Northern Ireland. Until more recent times, these areas have always suffered from unemployment levels well above the national average.

The problem of **regional unemployment** is made worse because of the secondary effects on local firms which supply these declining industries with equipment and commercial services. Others lose their jobs because of the general fall in consumer spending in such areas. New industries and job opportunities have tended to be concentrated in the South, the South East and the West Midlands but the **mobility of labour** in terms of the extent to which workers can move between regions or acquire new skills is generally very low.

It is also a problem that can repeat itself elsewhere if other markets are lost to overseas producers, or if technology makes a radical change to the end product. The UK motor vehicle industry, for example, suffered large-scale job losses because of increasing imports from

the mid-1970s onwards and this in turn has affected component suppliers, the manufacturers of machine tools and the engineering industry in general. Advances in technology have further reduced the demand for labour because robots have replaced workers on the assembly line, while a single computer-controlled machine tool can do the work of a whole series of traditional machine tools. These developments meant that even fewer people are employed either directly or indirectly in the motor vehicle and machine tool industries. The introduction of new technology into the workplace, however, would have had a less serious effect on unemployment if the demand for the final output had continued to rise at a healthy rate.

In more recent years, the advance in information technology has been one of the factors that has reduced job prospects in areas such as financial services. The break-up of the former Soviet Union has reduced the threat of an East-West conflict and thus reduced the number of jobs in defence-related industries.

	1990	1991	1992	1993	1994
North	8.6	10.6	11.2	11.2	11.7
Yorkshire	6.8	9.1	9.9	9.8	9.8
East Midlands	5.1	7.8	8.7	9.0	8.3
East Anglia	3.8	6.2	7.1	8.3	7.4
South East	3.9	7.4	9.4	10.3	9.6
South West	4.5	7.7	9.1	9.2	7.5
West Midlands	5.9	9.0	10.7	11.6	9.9
North West	7.5	9.9	10.1	10.9	10.2
Wales	6.6	9.2	8.9	9.5	9.4
Scotland	8.0	9.2	9.5	10.1	9.9
Northern Ireland	13.7	14.1	12.1	12.5	11.5

FIGURE 1.31: Regional unemployment rates.
Source: Employment Department.

GOVERNMENT POLICY AND REGIONAL UNEMPLOYMENT

Government intervention in recent years has been mainly concentrated on offering financial help to firms which either expand their existing operations in areas of high unemployment or which move into such areas. The policy has been one of **'taking work to the workers'** rather than providing financial incentives or affordable housing for those who wish to move to areas of labour shortages.

The areas where firms may qualify for a range of grants are known as **assisted areas** and are classified as either **development areas**, where there is a much higher than average level of unemployment, or **intermediate areas**, where serious unemployment is likely to arise in future if they do not receive such financial assistance. The whole of **Northern Ireland** has also been designated an area that qualifies for special financial assistance. The current assisted areas are still those which resulted from the last review in 1984. New areas were added in 1993, including the coal mining areas of the Midlands, parts of the South East and areas affected by the run down of the defence industry.

The level and scope of financial assistance has varied over the years and the current system is based upon either **Regional Selective Assistance (RSA)** or **Regional Enterprise Grants (REG)**. Regional Selective Assistance is discretionary and takes the form of a grant to help with the costs of capital projects and training. To qualify for a grant, the project must be viable, create or protect jobs, bring benefits to the area or the UK economy as a whole and be one which could not go ahead without money from the government.

The Regional Enterprise Grant scheme is designed to help small and medium-sized firms with the costs of capital projects and innovation. An **Enterprise Initiative Consultancy Scheme** helps firms with the costs of using outside consultancies.

URBAN AND INNER CITY PROBLEMS

Since the late 1970s increasing attention has been paid to the economic, social and environmental problems of large cities and **inner city areas**. There has been a shift of employment and population away from these older and densely populated **urban areas** into towns, smaller cities and more **rural areas**. The people who live in the traditional urban areas have had far fewer job opportunities. These areas have becomes centres of acute poverty, deprivation and social problems and have suffered a serious decline in their physical environment.

A variety of policies have been used in response to inner city problems. One current measure is the **Urban Programme** under which local authorities can obtain **City Grants**. These can be used to help finance projects involving the private sector. The overall aims of the support provided via the Urban Programme are:

✪ **the creation of jobs or training opportunities** through the building of new factories or the conversion of existing premises into industrial units that help to stimulate the local economy;

ACTIVITY

You are a member of a small team within your local authority responsible for encouraging the economic development of your area. You hear that a well-known company is thinking of moving into your region. Assume that it involves one of the following kinds of businesses:

- A large hotel
- A private hospital
- A distribution warehouse for soft drinks
- The assembly of video recorders for a Japanese company
- The manufacture of DIY furniture
- Offices for an insurance company
- A pizza manufacturer
- The manufacture of parts for the motor vehicle industry

1 Select one of the above and produce a case for the company to locate in your particular area. This should be based upon how your local area will be able to meet the needs of such an organisation in terms of labour requirements, access to markets, transport links and sites, any financial assistance from the UK government or the EU and any other factors which are likely to attract the new source of jobs.

2 You should also identify those aspects of the local area in terms of housing, the physical environment, leisure facilities and other factors which may be important for the company's key personnel moving into the area with young families.

✪ **improvements to the physical environment** through the modernisation of existing business premises and amenities such as footpaths, rivers, canals and parks;

✪ **improving the quality of life** by dealing with the problems arising out of poor housing conditions and the lack of health, leisure and recreation facilities.

Another aspect of inner city policy is the **Derelict Land Programme**. This gives grants to public and private sector organisations and individuals to improve previously derelict land so that it again contributes to the local environment and its economy.

REGIONAL UNEMPLOYMENT AND THE EUROPEAN UNION

The UK receives additional financial support for its regional policy from the EU's budget. This aspect of the EU's economic policy recognises that, as with a single economy, there is no reason why economic growth and job prospects will be evenly spread throughout the single market. The EU has therefore introduced schemes to encourage a more even economic and social development throughout the various regions and member states. The EU's assistance is aimed at:

✪ **regions whose economic development lags behind the EU average – about 80 per cent of the EU's spending on its regional policy is allocated to these areas; in 1994, the only area classified as such in the UK was Northern Ireland;**

✪ **the restructuring of areas suffering from industrial decline such as steel, shipbuilding and coal mining – the UK receives most of the funds covered by this objective as it has about 20m people living in such areas compared with 53m people in the EU as a whole;**

✪ **combating long-term unemployment;**

✪ **helping young people enter employment;**

✪ **helping agricultural sectors adapt to the reduced support from the Common Agricultural Policy and generally promoting rural development.**

Some of these aims are the concern of the **European Regional Development Fund (ERDF)** which seeks to stimulate development by helping to finance investment in **infrastructure projects** such as communications, energy, water and sewerage, and environmental improvements. Much emphasis is placed on supporting investment in capital projects (in manufacturing, for example) which help to replace jobs lost through the decline of traditional sources of employment. Most of the UK's help from the European Regional Development Fund has been to help with modernising and diversifying the industrial base in areas of high unemployment.

The **European Social Fund (ESF)** provides help for vocational training and retraining. Apart from the long term unemployed and young people it also aims to help women returning to work, migrant workers and disabled people. The UK for example has used the European Social Fund to deal with youth unemployment in inner cities and steel areas where retraining is an important factor.

The **European Agricultural Guidance and Guarantee Fund** specialises in financial help for projects which raise productivity in agriculture or improve the processing and marketing of agricultural products. This help recognises that the reduced financial support under the **Common Agricultural Policy (CAP)** requires farmers to become more efficient. Reforms to the Common Agricultural Policy will reduce jobs in agriculture. The EU aims to attract small and medium-sized firms into **Rural Development Areas (RDA)**, develop tourism and leisure activities and generally create alternative sources of employment in agricultural areas. Rural Development Areas can also qualify for financial assistance from both the European Regional Development Fund and the European Social Fund.

EU funds must be used to support a government's own regional development programme and not to replace their own spending. Any funds from the EU must therefore be matched by the government involved and produce extra regional development. If a government is found to have frozen or cut its own regional spending while receiving funds from the EU, it will have its aid withheld.

ACTIVITY

Conduct a survey of your local area and identify any new building work that either creates or renovates premises for a company moving into the area or involves the expansion of an existing local company. Investigate one of these projects and comment on:

1   The type of premises.

2   Whether the premises are designed for a particular customer or are being let by a property company looking for tenants.

3   The possible advantages associated with the site and its general location.

4   The kinds of jobs which are likely to be created by the company occupying the premises or by the kinds of companies that might be attracted to rent any office space or industrial units.

5   Any involvement which the local authority may have had in attracting jobs to the area.

PORTFOLIO ASSIGNMENT

1 Use graph paper to produce a series of charts which illustrate the movements in the economic and financial indicators shown in *Fig. 1.32* and *Fig. 1.33*. Where appropriate also produce charts which show the rate of change, for example, between 1985 and 1986 consumer spending rose by 6.8 per cent. Because both absolute and percentage changes may be relatively small and in some years negative, give careful consideration to the construction and scale used for the vertical axis. The reader should be able to clearly identify the direction and size of changes.

2 Explain the kinds of developments which may have been responsible for any trends or sudden and large changes in your charts. In doing this also try to identify any significant relationships between sets of data. Note that some may only respond after a time lag.

FIGURE 1.32: Key UK economic indicators.

	Consumer spending £m 1990 prices	Base rate %	Mortgage rate %	Export volume index	Import volume index	Retail price index	Unemployment %	Investment by manufacturing sector £m 1990 prices
1985	276,742	12.2	13.2	78.9	70.4	75.0	10.9	12,710
1986	295,622	10.9	11.8	82.2	75.6	77.6	11.2	12,097
1987	311,234	9.7	11.6	87.1	81.4	80.8	10.0	12,641
1988	334,591	10.1	10.9	89.0	92.4	84.8	8.1	13,846
1989	345,406	13.8	13.6	94.2	99.9	91.4	6.3	14,984
1990	347,527	14.8	15.1	100.0	100.0	100.0	5.9	14,227
1991	339,915	11.7	13.0	101.2	94.7	105.9	8.1	12,803
1992	339,946	9.6	10.8	103.7	100.9	109.8	9.9	11,590
1993	349,293	6.0	8.1	106.9	104.6	111.5	10.4	10,980
1994	358,370	5.5	7.8	118.4	110.6	114.3	9.3	11,239

FIGURE 1.33: Further UK economic indicators.

	Investment by rest of private sector £m 1990 prices	Savings as a percentage of disposable income	House price index	Take up of consumer credit £m	New car registrations (thousands)	Average earnings index	Production index
1985	52,147	10.7	50.1	3,820	1,842	66.3	93.0
1986	55,780	8.7	56.9	4,383	1,883	71.3	96.1
1987	65,451	7.1	66.5	6,362	2,016	76.8	98.7
1988	78,635	5.7	84.8	6,756	2,211	83.5	100.2
1989	80,761	7.2	101.2	6,530	2,304	91.1	100.1
1990	75,737	8.4	100.0	4,578	2,005	100.1	100.0
1991	68,093	10.4	98.5	2,377	1,600	116.8	100.5
1992	66,395	12.8	94.7	488	1,599	114.7	102.7
1993	67,200	11.7	92.4	2,689	1,776	118.5	105.8
1994	68,229	10.4	90.8	5,687	1,894	123.2	109.4

✓ MULTIPLE CHOICE QUESTIONS

1 The demand for a product is likely to fall if there is:

A a fall in the price of a complementary product

B a fall in the price of a substitute

C a larger rise in the price of substitutes compared to complementary products

D a rise in income relative to the rate of inflation

2 Real income differs from money income because:

A real income takes account of extra earnings from overtime or bonus payments

B money income is that part of total income upon which income tax is paid

C money income is what is left after mortgage repayments have been made

D real income takes account of the fall in the value of money

3 A rise in disposable income can be caused by:

A a reduction in the rate of VAT

B an increase in earnings

C a fall in the level of savings

D a fall in the price of essential food products

4 The price elasticity of demand measures:

A the extent to which market demand responds to a change in price

B how producers react to a rise in demand caused by a fall in price

C the effect of an increase in demand for a product on its price

D how spending power is affected by a rise in prices

5 The demand for a product will be price elastic if:

A it has very few close substitutes

B there is very little product differentiation in the market where it is sold

C there is a rise in the average level of real disposable income

D spending on the product is a very small part of the average household's total spending

6 If demand is inelastic then:

A a fall in prices leaves demand unchanged

B price does not change as demand increases

C supply cannot respond to a rise in demand

D a fall in price causes a smaller percentage change in demand

7 A firm will not need to lower its price to sell more if there is:

A a rise in the price of a complementary good or service

B a fall in the price of a substitute

C a very elastic demand for its product with respect to a price change

D a rise in purchasing power

8 If a firm in a very competitive market introduces a cost-saving innovation then the firm is best advised to:

A increase its prices to further widen its profit margin

B supply more to the market at a lower price

C cut its price because demand will be inelastic

D reduce its profit margins

9 Supply will be elastic in response to an increase in demand when:

A producers are faced with an elastic demand

B consumers have had a chance to adjust to a price cut

C further increases in output produce a fall in unit costs

D producers are operating at full capacity

10 A market is best described as existing when:

A producers respond to rising prices

B a rise in purchasing power strengthens effective demand

C there is a demand for and supply of a product or service

D an increase in demand is always met by an equal increase in supply

11 The market for a product will be increased by all of the following except:

A the lowering of import duties

B a fall in transport costs

C a reduction in import quotas

D advances in information technology

12 Markets are likely to be the more competitive:

A the higher the costs of entry

B the less the degree of product differentiation

C the lower the level of imports

D the greater their geographical size

13 Consumers benefit from intense competition because:

A choice and real incomes are maximised

B producers will spend large sums on advertising

C dominant suppliers enjoy economies of scale

D as employees they will receive higher pay

14 A monopoly situation may arise out of all of the following except:

A increasingly capital-intensive methods of production

B the removal of import restrictions

C the granting of a patent

D mergers and takeovers

15 In a market dominated by a small number of producers an agreement to change prices together is least likely when:

A they have very different cost structures

B a new producer is preparing to enter the market

C they generally hold the same view on the future level of total market demand

D their respective financial positions are very similar

16 A producer's private costs will be less than the social cost of its product if:

A costs are incurred elsewhere as a result of its impact on the environment

B local authorities pass the costs of dealing with environmental damage back to the producer

C it operates in the private sector and its prices exceed its unit costs

D the use of its product by one person brings benefits to the wider community.

17 Which of the following is a false statement:

A the harmonisation of environmental standards in the EU will help to promote fair competition

B companies in the service sector do not produce negative externalities

C taxes on toxic emissions will force firms to pay for their damage of the environment

D environmental damage means that private costs are less than social costs

18 Which of the following is least likely to protect the environment:

A an energy tax

B a tax on motor vehicles according to engine size

C recycled building products being zero rated for VAT

D extending VAT to cover rail travel

19 Which of the following will contribute to a rise in productivity:

A the purchase of lottery tickets

B spending by private sector on capital projects

C buying land in anticipation of rising prices

D buying shares in the privatised utilities

20 Which of the following is not likely to yield a positive externality:

A battery-driven cars

B road widening schemes to allow for larger and more economic freight loads

C modernising the railways

D the use of peat-free compost

21 Which of the following will not deflate consumer spending:

A a rise in excise duties

B an increase in interest rates

C an increase in the repayment period on hire purchase agreements

D the freezing of tax allowances and tax bands

22 Consumer confidence will be increased by all of the following except:

A a rise in the number of unfilled vacancies

B a rise in house prices

C expectations of a pay rise

D increased imports of consumer goods

23 If interest rates are high for a long enough period then such a policy is guaranteed to reduce inflation because:

A a combination of higher borrowing costs and falling sales will oblige firms to avoid a rise in unit labour costs

B the majority of households will decide to save much more of their income

C the resulting fall in house prices will persuade employees to accept a smaller pay rise

D the rise in the cost of credit will cut the demand for imported consumer durables

24 A firm's capital investment programme may be cut or postponed if:

A it fears that the government will respond to higher inflation by raising interest rates

B a very small proportion of its costs are accounted for by interest charges

C bank lending to households exceeds their lending to firms

D economies within the European Union achieve faster rates of economic growth

25 The UK's membership of the European Union means that:

A UK firms will face less competition from cheap labour imports from the Far East

B businesses in the manufacturing sector have the opportunity to further exploit potential economies of scale

C a major reason for mergers between UK companies and others in the EU is removed

D the existence of a single market gives all companies the same liability to tax

26 Capital intensive industries and those with high levels of research and development expenditure benefit from the dismantling of trade barriers because:

A fixed costs and risks will be lower

B interest rates on external sources of capital to fund such projects will be the same

C the larger potential market will make these projects more viable

D capital funds can flow freely between countries

27 Consumers benefit from an opening up of international trade because:

A product design will eventually conform to an internationally agreed specification

B there will be more price competition

C existing market leaders in the UK are guaranteed to strengthen their position

D brand loyalty will be rewarded

28 Which of the following will not expand consumer spending:

A a widening of tax bands

B a fall in interest rates

C a reduction in the period on hire purchase agreements

D an increase in personal tax allowances by more than the rate of inflation

29 Financial support from the EU for a member state's regional policy:

A does not cover areas where unemployment is caused by the decline of defence-related industries

B means that a government can cut back on its own spending

C is only available in areas where traditional industries have declined

D recognises that a free market will generate economic growth but that the benefits will not be evenly spread

30 Which of the following is unlikely to attract the attention of the DGFT:

A a food company only supplying a supermarket chain on condition that it does not stock a rival brand

B construction companies tendering for road building contracts in a way that shares out the work between them

C a supermarket chain selling sugar and milk below cost

D a brewer only supplying beer on condition that the outlet also buys soft drinks from its subsidiary

31 A firm may obtain a monopoly position by:

A being granted a patent

B acquiring a major supplier of components

C the removal of import restrictions

D advances in technology raising the initial capital costs

32 Which of the following is not a reason why consumers suffer when faced with a monopoly supplier:

A consumer choice is limited

B a monopoly may be supplying other firms and not consumers

C without secure sales, vital research and development will not be worthwhile

D higher costs are likely to be passed on in higher prices

33 Which of the following is not a feature of the privatised utilities:

A their shares are owned by private individuals and not financial institutions

B the government benefits from their profits

C they must raise capital at market rates of interest

D they cannot always charge the free market price

Business Organisations and Systems

CONTENTS

OUTLINE

The aim of this unit is to examine business organisations in the private (market) and public (command) sectors at both local and national levels. The unit introduces organisations in terms of the different structures, purposes, liabilities, legal constraints and obligations, and objectives. The systems that support organisations and the impact of information technology on administrative procedures are explored. The content of the unit not only develops an understanding of the functions of the business but also an appreciation of how organisations work on a day-to-day basis.

Investigate business organisations

OBJECTIVES OF BUSINESS ORGANISATIONS

The focus in this unit is on business organisations and their objectives, legal obligations, types and structures. Modern businesses operate in a global market of seemingly endless opportunities and at international level the stakes are high. Companies want appropriate legal structures which offer recognition and protection on the one hand and freedom from unreasonable constraint or intervention on the other. Government policies provide support for business. Deregulation and the changes to company law are designed to encourage not only the establishment of British businesses but to attract major foreign investors too.

THE BUSINESS CONTEXT – UK PLC

Business is the lifeblood of a nation. Although the UK economy is very much market-led, it is still regarded as a mixed economy as there remains a significant, though much reduced, public or command sector. The economy has undergone extensive restructuring since the beginning of the 1980s. A major feature has been the vast programme of **privatisation**, transferring public utilities and nationalised industries from the public sector to the private sector. The dominant economic emphasis is on **wealth creation** and the **free market**; even in the National-Health Service, education and local government, the reorganisation and refocusing of budgets has encouraged competition. Britain is often referred to as UK plc.

This country is no longer reliant on manufacturing as its main source of wealth The **service sector** has grown so fast that it now contributes more than 60 per cent of gross domestic product (GDP). Despite competition from the Singapore, Tokyo, New York and Frankfurt money markets, London is still predominant in banking, finance, and insurance. Tourism too has expanded, giving the UK a multi-billion pound business. Growth has also been seen in the leisure, distribution, hotel and catering markets.

An economy is a dynamic framework and without a healthy enterprise sector there will not be sufficient tax revenues to invest in defence, roads, schools, social services and so on. Companies operate in a climate constantly challenged by change-agents and outside forces. They need to take account of **political**, **economic**, **social** and **technological (PEST)** policies, initiatives and developments. The role of government is open to conflicting political interpretations. Many would argue that its primary objective is to create the appropriate climate and regulatory framework in which business can succeed.

ACTIVITY

Since corporate taxes have been reduced, some companies have felt they should 'put something back' into the community. For some, this may be sponsoring the planting of flower beds in roundabouts; for others it might be the equipping of a specialist room in a school.

Discuss in a small group:

1 **Whether or not you approve of this attitude.**

2 **How it benefits the community.**

3 **How it might benefit the donors.**

4 **Other examples of business sponsorship.**

BUSINESS OBJECTIVES

Although people can work for themselves, and offer a wide range of services and even products, isolated individuals are incapable of the mass production necessary to meet society's needs. Much business activity requires enormous investment and expertise. This can only be profitably managed by and through an organisation which assumes the responsibility for raising capital, co-ordinating resources, and driving projects forward to completion.

All organisations are set up with some clear purpose in mind. These objectives are essentially economic but they can also be social. The objectives of a company tend to be goal specific and can easily be measured; for example, an objective is to increase sales by five per cent. In contrast, aims are indications and intentions; for example, an aim is to become the market leader in Japan. The overriding objective for commercial companies must be **profit** or, in the case of not-for-profit organisations (such as co-operatives and charities), a surplus. However, the profit motive must be supported by other considerations like customer satisfaction. So, for example, shareholders expect British Gas to make a profit but the company is also required to ensure a safe and efficient gas supply to its consumers. Organisations in the public sector are required to break even but their objectives are, in the main, designed to meet the collective needs of society.

A company may state that its primary objective is to remain in business and to return a fair profit but the company may also want to emphasise other factors like **customer service**, **value for money**, **high quality products**; attention to these factors obviously helps to create and build up business and profits. They also reflect a business attitude which the company can encourage through its administration and communications systems, and training programmes. A profitable business will not be achievable without a committed staff, reliability, quality

assurance, and modern management and production techniques. Business leaders also argue that they require the minimum of government intervention.

The primary commercial objective then is profit, and its justification is that it rewards risk taking. Some businesses (such as oil, aerospace and pharmaceutical companies) invest very heavily in their projects and since there is a large market risk, sometimes even danger, a high profit is justified. The **net profit** – turnover less all costs and expenses – tends to be regarded as the reliable indicator of a company's performance. Net profit contributes to three charges:

⊗ **company taxation;**

⊗ **reserves;**

⊗ **dividends to shareholders.**

The reserve fund is an important source of internal capital. It is the company's savings and strong reserves which enables it to invest in plans for growth, purchase equipment, build new facilities, and avoid applying to the bank for (expensive) development capital.

A key question about profit is whether it is to be maximised or optimised. **Maximising** means winning the largest possible profit from the market, but such a strategy can open a company to the risk of diminishing returns. While turnover and profit continue to increase, unit costs instead of falling may begin to rise. Returns, measured as profit as a percentage of turnover, begin to fall. **Optimising** means getting the best possible return, by generating profit as efficiently as possible. Companies might deny some addition to turnover growth if, by doing so, they can contain unit costs so that they continue to decline.

As we have emphasised, the profit motive, though crucial, is not the sole purpose of business. Some complementary business objectives may include:

⊗ **to remain** competitive and retain market share (which requires regular monitoring of costs, advertising, market research, product development, sales drives);

⊗ **to survive** regardless of the prevailing economic climate even if it means the sale of assets;

⊗ **to respond** to and respect environmental pressures (for example, by minimising pollution);

⊗ **to achieve** customer satisfaction through reliable products or services and a high level of service;

⊗ **to offer** value for money, through price consciousness and product development.

Public limited companies

Achieve the best possible financial return on capital

Build reserves

Satisfy shareholders and the market generally

Boost or maintain share market values

Optimise profits

Improve market share

Sole trader

Earn a living and be self-supporting

Charities

Increase income from collections, bequests and trading

Support chosen causes and projects

Win public (and government) sympathy for their work

National Health Service

Improve the general health of the nation

Treat more patients in less time

Use resources efficiently

FIGURE 2.1: Summary of primary objectives of different organisations.

Other factors may demand that a company redefines its goals, introduces new products and services, or even relocates to another country. A company needs to consider the external environment, paying attention to political, economic, social and technological developments (the PEST factors).

ACTIVITY

List what you consider to be the aims and objectives of each of the following organisations:

⊗ Prudential Assurance;

⊗ British Airways;

⊗ Marks & Spencer;

⊗ General Motors.

LIMITED LIABILITY

Before looking at different types of companies, it is useful to begin with the important concept of **limited liability**. Limited liability is regarded as a privilege. It is a protection not against business loss but against unlimited personal loss. It is a major element in the legal structure of joint stock companies. Partnerships and sole traders cannot benefit from limited liability.

A working definition is that in the event of business failure, i.e. bankruptcy, a shareholder's financial liability is **limited** to the amount of capital invested or promised. If a shareholder invests £20,000 in either a public or a private limited company and then the company fails, all the shareholder can lose is that £20,000 investment. If, for example, £50,000 has been promised and only £15,000 has been contributed, the shareholder can be asked for the remaining £35,000. To illustrate the point, when British Telecom was privatised, investors paid for their shares in three tranches or instalments. The first payment secured ownership of the shares; therefore if British Telecom had soon gone under, shareholders would have been legally obliged to make the other two payments.

The essential point is that it is the company that goes bankrupt not the shareholders (although some may become bankrupt as a result). It is possible, therefore, for a joint stock company to be declared bankrupt for £200m but that does not mean the shareholders have to find that sum. The company's assets will be sold. If this sale of assets is not sufficient to meet the outstanding £200m liability, shareholders are not liable for the remaining debt. Their liability is limited to the size of their investment. In direct contrast, those business organisations which have no limited liability, such as partnerships and sole traders, must explore all ways of **meeting liabilities**. A sole trader's bankruptcy may mean the loss not just of the business but also his or her house, car and personal possessions to meet as much of the debt as possible.

Companies relying on the public subscription of shares know that limited liability is a strong selling point. It reduces the risk for individual investors and also attracts large-scale investment from financial institutions (pension funds, insurance companies, trade unions) which avoid taking excessive risks with their clients' or members' funds. Some companies may choose not to have limited liability. For example, a company limited by guarantee acquires the advantages of incorporation, but its members agree to meet certain sums in the event of failure.

TYPES OF OWNERSHIP

The economy is divided into **public** and **private** (or command and market) sectors. In the middle is the **mutuality sector** containing the not-for-profit organisations. Until recently, building societies would have appeared under this heading but, as a result of changes to the legal controls, societies are now free to compete with banks and other financial institutions on an equal footing. They are profit motivated and operate like public limited companies. Some are seeking registration as public limited companies; indeed, Abbey National is already quoted on the Stock Exchange and now ranks as one of Britain's largest banking operations.

The organisations in the mutuality sector certainly attempt to make a **trading surplus** and, in that sense, they are profit makers but with a difference – the profit supports the charitable or social aims of the organisation. In the case of mutual assurance societies (such as Norwich Union), the profits are ploughed back into the policies These societies are run without shareholders – the real owners are the **policy holders**.

PRIVATE SECTOR

THE JOINT STOCK COMPANY

A company is defined as an association of persons who contribute money (or equivalent value in goods and assets) to a common stock, employ it in some trade or business, and share the profit or loss arising out of that business. **Joint stock companies** are either public or private, and governed by and registered under the **Companies Act 1985**. A joint stock company has separate legal identity from its members and can sue or be sued in its own name. Both public and private companies require a minimum of only two members (there is no upper limit on members); each form enjoys limited liability.

THE PRIVATE COMPANY

This type of company is suitable for small and medium-sized operations. It is particularly suitable for family firms and for small enterprises involving just a handful of people. Some of its features are:

UK PLC		
Public sector	**Mutuality sector**	**Private sector**
(or command sector)		(or market sector)
Nationalised industries	Co-operatives	Public limited companies
Public corporations	Assurance societies	Private limited companies
Quangos	Friendly societies	Partnerships
Local government	Charities	Sole traders
Central government		

FIGURE 2.2: Basic structure of the British economy.

- it cannot advertise its shares for sale;
- it is not quoted on the Stock Exchange;
- it is not obliged to publish its accounts;
- the company name ends with limited;
- it may have a sole director.

THE PUBLIC COMPANY

A public company is denoted by the letters 'plc' at the end of its name. All companies which are quoted on the Stock Exchange are **public limited companies**, but not all public limited companies are listed on the stock market (e.g. Co-operative Bank plc). To become a plc, a company must have an issued **share capital** of at least £50,000 and at least 25 per cent of the nominal value of the shares (and the whole of any premium) must have been received by the company. If the shares are nominally worth 10p (that is, the face value) but are sold at 50p, a company must have received 2.5p per share plus the premium of 40p. This regulation is to stop public limited companies setting up without sufficient capital. Other requirements include:

- it is a company limited by shares;
- its memorandum of association has a separate clause stating that it is a public company;
- it is obliged to publish an annual report and balance sheet;
- its shares are freely transferable, that is, they can be bought and sold (through stockbrokers, banks and share shops).

The quoted companies can be tracked daily by reference to the Stock Exchange listings in financial pages of the broadsheet newspapers. The Stock Exchange is the **Official Listed Market (OLM)** for securities (shares). Companies which have traded for less than five years cannot join the OLM. However, if they have traded for more than three years, they may apply for admission to the **Unlisted Securities Market (USM)**.

ACTIVITY

Select five plcs which interest you and follow their share price movements over a four-week period. Imagine that you invested £1,000 in each company at the outset of the exercise. Determine your profits or losses.

REGISTRATION OF A COMPANY

The registration procedure is conducted by the **Registrar of Companies** who is an official of the Department of Trade and Industry (DTI). The Registrar must be satisfied that all statutory requirements have been fulfilled, and only then issues a **certificate of incorporation** which is conclusive evidence that a company complies with the law. It is an offence for a company to start trading or borrowing money until the certificate has been granted.

The law also requires that the company provides details of its internal rules and external relationships. It must submit two documents, the **memorandum of association** and the **articles of association**.

The memorandum of association defines the constitution and powers of the company and the scope of its activities. It includes:

- the name of the company including the word 'limited';
- the address of the registered office;
- a statement of the company's aims;
- the amount of capital the company wishes to raise;
- a statement that the shareholders' liability is limited.

The articles of association govern the internal rules of the company. The articles are a contract between the company and its shareholders in respect of their **ordinary rights** as members. The document must provide the details of:

- the nominal capital;
- when and how shareholders' meetings are to be conducted;
- the voting rights of members;
- how profits and losses will be distributed;
- the names of the directors;
- how the directors are appointed and the nature of their authority.

DIRECTORS

In law a company is regarded as 'an artificial legal person' which can only act by and through human agents. The **directors** are these agents; they are responsible to the shareholders for running the enterprise. They have the power to:

- ⊘ **sell company assets;**
- ⊘ **sue in the company's name;**
- ⊘ **declare a dividend.**

They have two statutory duties:

- ⊘ **to act as agents of the company – they are not personally liable if they act within their authority;**
- ⊘ **to exercise the duty of trust.**

Directors are required to exercise their powers and responsibilities personally and collectively but the articles and memorandum authorise them to delegate responsibilities to a managing director who is appointed to and answerable to the board. A director is a servant of the company and may delegate functions but not the exercise of discretion.

The actions of the directors are limited by the doctrine of *ultra vires* (meaning 'beyond the powers') which is a safeguard against the misuse of power and shareholders' money. The memorandum identifies the activities of the company and the directors cannot exploit any opportunities, however potentially profitable, which have been excluded. It is, however, normal practice for companies to write their objects wide enough to cover any reasonable business activity.

Directors may be executive – senior managers in the company with seats on the board – or non-executive, people outside the company but appointed to the board because they have particular expertise. If the company has borrowed from a merchant bank then the bank will often insist on one of its staff being appointed to the board to watch over the bank's interests. The shareholders may also be entitled to elect directors. A person who is an undischarged bankrupt may not be a director. There is an age limit of 70 for directors of public companies but a motion at the annual general meeting (AGM) can extend a director's service.

PARTNERSHIPS

Partnerships are governed by the **Companies Act 1985** and the **Partnership Act 1890**. Partners are bound by mutual trust and confidence. They are jointly and severally liable without limit (partners have no limited liability) for each other's actions. Thus, one partner's decision or action binds the other(s). The minimum membership is two and the maximum twenty but the Companies Act 1985 permits more for practices of accountants, solicitors and members of recognised stock exchanges. Every partner is entitled to participate in the management of the business.

According to the 1890 Act, a partnership dissolves on the death, resignation or bankruptcy of a partner, or on the agreed termination of the life and purpose of the business. In order to avoid disruption to the business, it is usual to draw up a **deed of partnership** which identifies the ways in which the partnership will be run. A deed might cover arrangements for sharing of profits, liabilities in case of debt, continuation after death or resignation of a member and so on. In the absence of a deed (or partnership articles), partnership activity will be governed by the 1890 Act.

The **Limited Partnership Act 1907** allows a partnership to claim limited liability for some of its partners, but there must be at least one general partner who is fully liable for all debts and obligations of the practice. This is not a common type of organisation – it is easier and more advantageous to set up a limited company.

You should note that it is often the case that one person in a private business refers to another as 'my

ACTIVITY

A partnership is not a particularly popular form of business organisation outside of the professions and specialised businesses. It is mainly suitable for bankers, architects, solicitors, accountants, financial advisers, stockbrokers and doctors. Bearing in mind the absence of limited liability, and the fact that many of these businesses provide professional advice, suggest reasons why the partnership is appropriate for some professional people.

partner'. However, the term only has legal significance when referring to a partnership but it is widely used to describe associates in small businesses. Partnership is rarely used in any other context. One notable exception is the famous **John Lewis Partnership**, a leading retailer. John Lewis is a private company with a nominal share value of £100. It has four shareholders (the managing director has a 40 per cent holding and three trustees each hold 20 per cent). The company has a structure that encourages staff participation and the profits are shared by the staff in the form of bonuses. The term 'partnership' here reflects the democratic nature of John Lewis.

SOLE TRADERS

By **sole trader**, we mean self-employment. This is a very common form of business in the UK. In recent years, as more people have been either made redundant or given early retirement, the number of sole traders has grown significantly. The sector continues to expand within the European Union at some at 2.5 per cent annually. Although most sole traders work on their own, this need not always be the case. Theoretically, a sole trader can employ hundreds of staff and own several factories but clearly the financial contribution and business risks would usually be too great. Typically sole traders are corner shopkeepers and market traders or have occupations such as self-employed plumbers, electricians, hairdressers and consultants.

The essential feature of this type of business is that the sole trader has full responsibility for the financial control of the business, for meeting capital requirements and running costs, and full personal liability in the case of debt. There is a minimum of legal regulation. However, if the business is to be run under a name different to the proprietor's then registration is required under the **Business Names Act 1985**. The features of the sole trader are:

- ⊗ **capital is only provided by the trader either from savings or a loan;**
- ⊗ **direct personal involvement;**
- ⊗ **unlimited liability;**
- ⊗ **independence;**
- ⊗ **easy to set up;**
- ⊗ **entitlement to all of the profits but responsible for all of the debts;**
- ⊗ **no requirement for the independent auditing of accounts.**

FRANCHISES

A **franchise** is not a form of business organisation but a way of doing business. A sole trader or a limited company can undertake franchise operations. Franchising covers a variety of arrangements under which the owner of a product or service, or sometimes just a name, **licenses** other organisations or individuals to manufacture, use, or sell it in exchange for payment (in the form of fees, royalties or commissions). Usually the licensee benefits from an exclusive territory and support from the licenser in the form of staff training, advertising and promotion. The range of franchised activity is wide. It includes car dealerships, public houses, business service centres, doorstep milk deliveries, express delivery of parcels and fast food (Wimpy is a prime example).

FINANCING THE COMPANY

A private company cannot issue a prospectus because it cannot offer its shares to the public on the open market. It raises its **capital** by selling shares by private negotiation. A public company will issue its **prospectus** explaining to would-be shareholders the nature of the business, its markets and opportunities, and proposals for the future. This gives investors the chance to assess the company and the degree of risk.

The capital of a private or public company may be divided into **ordinary** or **preference shares**. Ordinary shares (or equities) carry the most risk. They rank after the preference shares when the profits are distributed. The ordinary shareholders are the true owners of a company and have most of the voting rights at company meetings. They receive a fluctuating **annual dividend** which depends upon the distributable profit after taxation and allocation to reserves. Depending on the financial performance of the company, dividends are not necessarily paid every year.

Shares have two values – the **nominal (face or par) value** and the **market value.** The nominal value is what the share is actually worth, the market value is the price investors are willing to pay for it. So a share in a major public limited company may be bought for, say, 350p but its nominal value might only be 25p. This means that in order to become a part-owner of the company, the investor must pay fourteen times the nominal value. The market price rises or falls according to market trends and business performance but the nominal value is fixed. Dividends are paid on nominal not market value.

Preference shares take priority over the ordinary shares and have the right to a **fixed dividend**. However, like ordinary shares, there is no automatic right to the payment, a company must have a profit to distribute. Preference shares may be cumulative or non-cumulative. If the shares are cumulative preference, and in any one year there is insufficient profit to pay the dividend, then the fixed dividend is carried forward and added to the dividend for the following year. A non-cumulative share has no right to payment in full nor for any arrears for years in which dividends were not paid.

Loan capital (debentures) interest has priority and must be paid whether the company has any distributable profits or not. If there are no profits the company is obliged to pay the **debenture holders** from the sale of assets, from capital, or by raising another loan.

In addition to capital, businesses need other sources of finance. Even successful companies may require an arrangement with their bankers from time to time so that ongoing obligations such as wages, salaries and raw material costs can be met. For most firms, the real financial anxiety is **cash flow**; they need working capital to sustain the life of the business. A company may have a full order book but it can run into difficulty if its customers do not pay on time (or at all). We will now consider some other sources of finance.

TRADE CREDIT

Credit is acquired by delaying the settlement of bills. The action gives a company 'breathing space' but it can result in suppliers refusing to do further business. In resolving a cash flow situation in this way, even temporarily, a company is effectively passing the problem back to its suppliers.

LEASING

Leasing is a popular means of providing cars for the sales force and executives. It is also used to acquire other equipment, including **office furniture** and **machinery**. The main advantages of leasing are:

- ✪ **a company does not have to commit a large proportion of its cash resources to obtain equipment;**

- ✪ **the cost of servicing the agreement comes out of revenue;**

- ✪ **payments are known in advance enabling better budgeting;**

- ✪ **the opportunity arises to update equipment regularly; for example, the car fleet need never be more than two years old, computers can be updated.**

BANK LOANS

Bank loans tend to be medium to long-term arrangements to finance major developments. Resorting to such loans may be avoided if the company has healthy reserve funds.

OVERDRAFT

An **overdraft** is usually a short-term arrangement used to meet current obligations. It is not suitable for an investment programme. Banks usually set a fairly low limit on the amount that can be borrowed on overdraft.

MUTUALITY SECTOR

THE CO-OPERATIVE SOCIETY

The most significant part of the mutuality sector is the **co-operative movement** which contains a diversity of businesses (agriculture, engineering, retail and wholesale distribution, travel, funeral services, property, banking) organised in **industrial** and **provident societies**. The co-operative movement celebrated its 150th anniversary in 1994. Its essential purpose was to create a social organisation to offer protection from unfair trading practices and poverty. The ultimate aim was to establish a 'commonwealth' owning the means of production, distribution and exchange.

In recent years, there has been a renewal of interest in the co-operative society as an ideal business form for self-governing workshops such as studios of artists,

designers and printers. There is an umbrella organisation, **ICOM (Industrial Common Ownership Movement Ltd)**, which advises the co-operative development agencies and workers' co-operatives. It has a 'sister' organisation, **ICOF (Industrial Common Ownership Finance Ltd)**.

The essential features of a co-operative society are:

- ✪ **it is registered under the Industrial and Provident Societies Acts 1965-78 and the Companies Acts;**

- ✪ **it has limited liability;**

- ✪ **shares are not transferable – they can only be bought from or sold to the society;**

- ✪ **membership is available on the purchase of one share with a nominal value of £1;**

- ✪ **the maximum shareholding depends upon the rules of each society but it cannot exceed the £15,000 limit set by the law;**

- ✪ **membership is voluntary and open;**

- ✪ **society control is democratic – each member is permitted one vote regardless of shareholding;**

- ✪ **there is equitable use of any surplus or profit;**

- ✪ **a limited rate of interest is paid on capital.**

Co-operative societies use various methods to distribute profits. After taxation and reserves, there is a distribution to members. Some money is put in a patronage fund to finance social and educational activities. Traditionally retail societies paid members a dividend on purchases, but currently there are four ways of rewarding members and societies may choose to apply one of the following:

- ✪ **dividend on purchases;**

- ✪ **trading stamps;**

- ✪ **interest on the share account;**

- ✪ **special offer vouchers for members.**

ACTIVITY

Obtain the latest published trading details of the co-operative movement (the retail societies, the Co-operative Wholesale Society, the Co-operative Bank and the Co-operative Insurance Society). The information should include turnover, trading surplus, members' benefits, the number of societies, shops, brand lines and members, assets, and premium income. Present your findings in a table.

CHARITIES

Because so many people give up their time to help, charities form part of what is known as the **voluntary sector**. They are run by full-time professionals and supported by a network of volunteers. There are more than 6,000 registered charities and voluntary organisations in the UK. They are financed by collections, flag days, donations, bequests and trading activities. Company sponsorship is also important, providing support such as rent-free accommodation, a minibus or the loan of a manager. The **National Lottery** also makes awards to selected charities.

Additionally, there are charitable trusts which can be found in both the private and public health and education sectors. These organisations operate as businesses but enjoy certain tax advantages.

ACTIVITY

Make a list containing ten charities known to you, putting them in what you regard as an order of priority.

FRIENDLY SOCIETIES

Friendly societies are not quite so well known today but, until the **Welfare State** was established, they were crucial to some families who needed assistance during periods of illness or unemployment. The societies were formed for the mutual purpose of creating a fund to provide assistance to its members in time of need. In the 1930s, there were more than 3,000 societies, but today

only a few hundred exist. Among the best known are the Royal Ancient Order of Buffaloes and the Ancient Order of Foresters.

ACTIVITY

Complete the tasks below for each of the following forms of business organisations: public company, private company, partnership, co-operative society and sole trader.

1 Identify the Act(s) of Parliament which control(s) its activities.

2 Describe the nature of its liability.

3 Suggest how its profits are distributed.

Present your answers in the form of a table.

PUBLIC SECTOR

The public sector contains the remaining nationalised industries and public corporations, central government ministries and departments, local authorities and quangos. Despite the transfer of many activities from the public to the private sector, it remains a large sector of activity.

PRIVATISATION PROGRAMME

The justification for the massive programme of privatisation (which began in the early 1980s) is that companies in the private sector are more efficient than those in the public sector. It is argued that they produce a better level of service because of the pressure of **market forces** and the need to meet **profit-related targets**. The government has tried to inject **market disciplines** into the rest of the public sector by the creation of internal markets and profit centres within the remaining public bodies and organisations. Since 1979, more than thirty public enterprises have been transferred to the private sector. *Fig 2.3* demonstrates the impact of privatisation policy. It lists the major assets which each realised more than £1bn when privatised.

Under current government proposals, there are still some major public sector enterprises which will either be sold off eventually or turned into profitable businesses within the public sector. British Rail is in the process of being privatised. It has been split up into a number of companies in preparation for the transfer to the private

Asset	£bn
British Airports Authority	1.2
British Gas	6.5
British Petroleum	6.1
British Steel	2.4
British Telecom	4.8
Britoil	1.1
Cable and Wireless	1.0
Electricity distribution companies	5.2
Rolls-Royce	1.0
Water companies	5.2
Total revenue	**34.5**

FIGURE 2.3: Assets realised by major privatisation sales since 1979.

sector. There are separate companies for ownership of the track, operation of the rolling stock, and so on. Other public enterprises include London Transport, Nuclear Electric and the Post Office. It is thought that market forces will encourage cost effective organisations and lead to the better use of resources.

ACTIVITY

Discuss in a group the view that the gas, water and electricity companies, which control essential resources, should have remained in the public sector under the supervision of the government rather than have been transferred to the private sector and, thereby, been subject to market forces.

CENTRAL GOVERNMENT

Central government comprises ministries and departments which set policy for and, in many cases, administer public services. Government activity has to be funded from **taxation** and other sources. It raises revenue from personal and corporate taxation, indirect taxes (VAT, customs and excise duties), sale of public assets (privatisation), motor vehicle tax, national insurance

contributions and national savings. The government also borrows money. **Gilt-edged stock** is issued, enabling investors to loan money to the government. Some financial contributions may be made by the **European Union**, particularly to assist declining areas (where, for example, traditional coal, steel and shipbuilding industries have run down) with employment creation projects.

LOCAL GOVERNMENT

Local government is an important element in the country's democratic structure. Councils and local authorities are responsible for education, social services, police, fire, consumer protection, public transport, highways, allotments, leisure and recreation. Local government is funded by the **council tax**, **government grants**, **loans** and **charges for its services**. Business rates are levied on all commercial properties and paid to central government. This money is reallocated to local councils in accordance with a formula based on population and the level of services. District councils are the **tax raising authorities**.

Privatisation affects local government too. Its role is changing from one of providing services to one of enabling

ACTIVITY

When the council sends your household its demand for the council tax, it is accompanied by a leaflet explaining the provision and costs of local authority services. Obtain the latest version of this leaflet from your local council. Then:

1 **List the services in declining order of expenditure (for the current year).**

2 **Note (or calculate) the average charge per council taxpayer.**

3 **Identify the total cost of running your local authority.**

4 **Explain what is meant by the 'capping limit'.**

5 **Suggest who might be eligible for council tax discounts or exemptions.**

those services to be delivered. One characteristic of this change is **compulsory competitive tendering (CCT)**. This policy requires certain services to be put out to tender, that is other organisations have the right to submit a bid to carry out those services (examples include refuse collection, grass cutting and management of leisure services). Council departments are entitled to bid for the contracts, but only in their own geographical areas; they are unable, under the law, to bid for contracts elsewhere – unlike private sector contractors.

QUANGOS

Quango stands for quasi-autonomous non-governmental organisation. Their rationale is that ministers (and their departments) need some assistance in the formulation and application of their policies, so lay people with particular expertise are appointed to give advice. There are some 40,000 public appointments to quangos; approximately 10,000 people are appointed or re-appointed every year. The work can be unpaid or paid, and varies from one day a month to a full-time commitment. Examples of quangos include tribunals, public corporations (such as the BBC) and advisory bodies (on, for example, the environment, health and agriculture). Anyone can submit an application to the **Public Appointments Unit**. The unit circulates a list to the various government departments which are responsible for the appointments.

ORGANISATIONAL STRUCTURES

Management works through a framework of responsibility and authority which **co-ordinates resources**, **monitors performance**, **resolves problems** and **achieves targets**. Management is a function which exists regardless of the size of a business organisation, although a management structure usually becomes more obvious the larger the company. The sole trader (see *Fig. 2.4*) operates as sales manager, finance director, customer services manager (and more) – in reality, one person is trying to get work, to satisfy the customers and to manage the business – but these functions become highly specialised in larger organisations. The sole trader may take on an assistant to help out but the agreement about terms will most likely be verbal and even casual. Compare that to seeking a job with ICI or Ford, where the recruitment process is well defined and

organised by professional and qualified people. Although the business functions remain the same regardless of structure, size and the nature of the business, the degree of specialisation varies between different organisations.

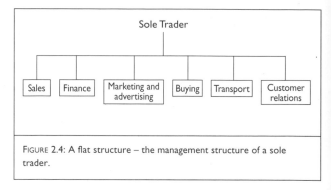

FIGURE 2.4: A flat structure – the management structure of a sole trader.

Businesses can be classified by the number of people involved:

- **micro** – **fewer than 10 staff**
- **small** – **11 to 99 staff**
- **medium** – **100 to 499 staff**
- **large** – **500 plus staff**

The size of a company largely determines the shape of the organisation. In a smaller firm, the staff have to be more flexible and multi-skilled. Participation in a micro business is a very hands-on affair. Like the sole trader model in *Fig. 2.4*, the structure is probably a straight line as the boss is closely involved in the day-to-day activities. In a small crop-spraying and air taxi business, for example, the owner is probably the sales director and the chief (and only) pilot, while the receptionist is also the bookkeeper and the secretary. Technical support is offered by a mechanic who services the plane, mows the airstrip, paints the hangar and runs errands. The ways in which an organisation's objectives are to be met must be considered in the context of the most appropriate structure.

FORMS OF ORGANISATIONAL STRUCTURE

Organisational structures can be classified under a number of headings. Before discussing the basic forms, it is worth emphasising that, in practice, hybrid forms exist – in other words, a structure may be basically one form but will assume aspects of another. It should also be acknowledged that, although a structure may be sound, people will always find ways to challenge it and promote their own agenda. Equally, in a complex system, they will find informal ways to make it work.

Received wisdom suggests that the logical division of a company's structure is by function but, in many cases, division by product might more appropriate. A multinational conglomerate might divide up according to country, broad geographical area, or by company. None of these approaches is absolutely standard – a division by product may, for example, require sub-division by function, with some other functions remaining centralised. The titles or ranks people have, the tasks they perform, their areas of responsibility and the extent of their authority, all depend upon the size, culture and organisational structure of the company for which they work.

LINE

Line structures are the simplest of all the structures and perhaps the most familiar. With a line structure, a company is usually organised by **functional departments** (personnel, marketing, production, sales, etc.) with each headed by a senior manager. The main characteristic is that there is a **line of responsibility** and authority (see *Fig. 2.5*) which decreases in power as it goes down through the structure from the managing director or chief executive officer to the unskilled manual employee. Each

level of management, supervision or operation is answerable to the one above. It is an **hierarchical structure**, simple to understand, and staff know precisely where they are in it and to whom they are responsible. It also offers an uncomplicated way of delegating tasks, monitoring performance and imposing discipline. The downside is that it may encourage strict demarcation between departments and an authoritarian management style.

FUNCTIONAL

In a functional structure, the flow of responsibility and authority is determined by function with little reference to departmental structure. Each function of the business is managed by a specialist whose authority can carry more weight than that of the line manager in whose area that function is being partially or totally carried out. This structure has the effect of reducing the authority of line management. These issues can be resolved if the functional manager liaises with the line manager so there is no confusion in line command, discipline and organisation.

Functional managers are freed from day-to-day routine management concerns and can concentrate on their areas of expertise. Because they have access to all areas of a company, they are able to contribute advice and observation on the co-ordination of the organisation's activities. This structure is flexible and specialists can respond quickly to external or internal change-agents.

LINE AND STAFF

Essentially, this is a combination of the line and functional forms but the specialists, the functional managers, have advisory rather than executive authority. In a sense, they are **trouble-shooters** who can attend to problems arising in those departments requiring their services. However, since they are appointed because of their experience and knowledge, their advice, though not binding, is usually regarded as persuasive.

A line and staff structure may encourage clashes of personality and opinion, affecting efficiency and morale. However, a specialist who is known for sound and practical advice, depth of knowledge and good personal administration will be well regarded by staff at all levels; there should be no confusion about areas of authority.

COMMITTEE

A committee structure is a familiar form in local government (see *Fig. 2.6*) where each area of the council's activity (education, public works, finance, etc.) is governed by a committee comprising elected councillors and senior council officers. The committees do not **manage**, they **determine policy**. It is left to the officers to exercise their management roles in their departments.

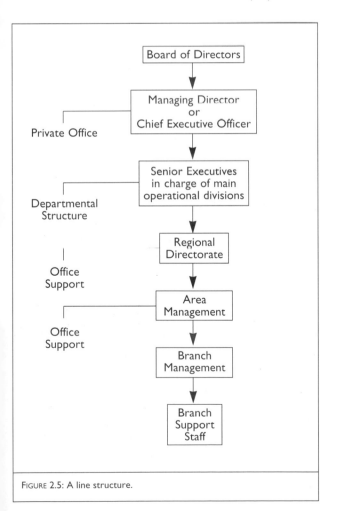

FIGURE 2.5: A line structure.

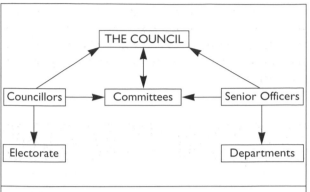

FIGURE 2.6: A committee structure – the management structure of a local authority.

The committee style has been used increasingly in business in recent years as it encourages **employee participation**. It affords the opportunity for issues to be openly debated resulting in better balanced, informed and representative decisions. Committees may be either executive or advisory. The purpose of any committee must be clearly defined before it is set up.

In many ways, the committee system is less a form of organisation than an approach within another structure. The use of committees and the value placed on their recommendations will reflect the culture of the company.

MATRIX

In a matrix structure, each function within an organisation is placed under the direction of a functional manager who leads a team of specialists. These specialists are also located in departments under the supervision of line managers. Each specialist is, therefore, subject to two sources of authority – the functional manager who is charged with technical performance and targets, and the line manager whose concern is staff management.

In a matrix, people are grouped in divisions or teams according to their areas of expertise. It is possible for a person to be responsible to several team leaders, some of whom may even be of lower status. So, in addition to

being accountable to the functional and line managements, a specialist may be a member of one or more **interdisciplinary project teams**.

The matrix ought to encourage the ready **cross-fertilisation** of experience, knowledge and opinion leading to the better use of intellectual resources.

CENTRALISATION

Centralisation is the practice of concentrating all the power – the responsibility and authority – at the top of an organisation. Typically, this places power with the managing director but also with a **senior management team (SMT)**. Centralisation occurs in complex organisations with widespread activities as there is a need to keep control of the organisation and to ensure that policies are properly carried out.

The disadvantages of centralisation can be seen as:

⊗ **removing initiative from supervisory and middle management;**

⊗ **demanding that all actions and decisions be approved by the SMT;**

⊗ **creating a bureaucracy with formal procedures;**

⊗ **encouraging reactive rather pro-active staff;**

⊗ **encouraging a lack of commitment to the overall aims of the company.**

Centralisation is administratively convenient and allows absolute control over the organisation. Although a company may have many divisions, departments or activities, certain functions will remain under firm central control to ensure uniformity, tight budget control, elimination of waste and avoidance of duplicate stock. Centralised functions may include computing, personnel, accounts, reprographics and purchasing.

ACTIVITY

Draw up the structure of an organisation familiar to you (your college or company). Comment on its features (for example, it might be basically committee with elements of functional). Indicate whether, in your opinion, it is a suitable form in which the organisation can deliver its aims and objectives and also motivate its staff.

DECENTRALISATION

In a decentralised structure, the responsibility for various functions and operations is devolved from the top and rests wherever the action is. It places decision-making and initiative directly in the hands of managers and supervisors.

Decentralisation challenges standardised procedures, even the uniform application of policy. But it can encourage the setting up of action teams with **local autonomy** and their own targets. It can offer **flexibility of operation and delivery**.

ACTIVITY

Working in a group, define the following terms (which have been used in the text) within a business context:

- **authority;**

- **responsibility;**

- **efficiency;**

- **effectiveness;**

- **management.**

PORTFOLIO ASSIGNMENT

This assignment is an investigation into business organisation. You are to compile a report which will examine and compare the structures, motives, and differences of three selected business organisations.

Choose three business organisations to investigate – one must come from the public sector and two from either the private sector or one from each of the mutuality and private sectors.

Select organisations which readily offer the required information and which are interesting. Plcs are required to make their report and balance sheets available to any enquirer (who may be a prospective shareholder) but it may be difficult to access information about a private company (unless you go to **Companies House** and ask to see the articles and memorandum).

Your report needs to be divided into three areas of investigation.

1 For each selected organisation, offer a general explanation of its broad financial objectives. Emphasis should be given to the earning and distributing of profit and/or surplus.

2 The overall objectives of each organisation must be defined. This definition should be supported by an explanation of how the financial, legal and controlling (management and structural) differences between organisations influence the achievement and outcome of those objectives.

3 Construct organisational charts illustrating the different structures of the companies. Support the charts with clear explanations of the differences and highlight recent, planned or likely changes to either structures, locations or functions.

Investigate administration systems

The word **'administration'** has several meanings. In the context of this unit, it means all the various **formal information systems** that a business uses to support the organisation and its functions and ensure that it achieves its objectives. For example, the finance department of a supplier formally informs a customer how much money she or he has to pay for goods by sending an invoice; by getting money in from the customer on time, the finance department makes an important contribution to the business achieving its objectives.

A business organisation survives by generating more income from sales than it costs to provide a product or service. It has to operate efficiently to achieve that objective. A key task of management is to design an **effective organisational structure** which brings together all the necessary functions and resources, and sets realistic objectives so that all employees are clear about their contribution to the success of the organisation.

Equally important to the efficiency of a business is the design of systems that provide specific and accurate information to all parts of the organisation and to customers and to suppliers. These are described as **'administration systems'** or sometimes **'paperwork systems'**.

ADMINISTRATION SYSTEMS

Administration is the process of:

- **gathering information (input);**

- **processing information;**

- **storing information;**

- **distributing information (output).**

Note that the terms **input** and **output** are more readily associated with computer-based systems, but they are equally applicable here. They are considered in more detail later in this unit.

FIGURE 2.7: The administrative process.

Information is the raw material of decision making. Managers make critical decisions based on the information provided by administration systems. It is therefore important that information is:

- **accurate;**

- **on time;**

- **sufficient;**

- **cost effective.**

Systems that produce information that is specifically designed to aid managers in decision making are often called **management information systems (MIS)**.

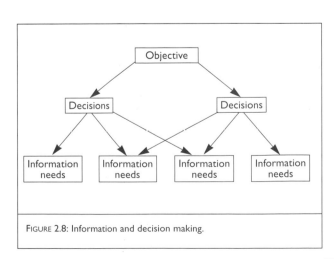

FIGURE 2.8: Information and decision making.

Managers of small businesses depend less on formal systems than managers of large companies. This is because there are relatively few transactions in a small business, the manager is familiar with all aspects of the business and, therefore, 'knows what is going on'.

In contrast, large businesses might generate millions of transactions, have a wide range of products or services and operate on many sites. Their senior managers need well-designed administration and information processing systems that supply them with accurate, timely information upon which they can make high-level decisions.

As businesses grow, the demand for better and faster information grows too. Ensuring that administration systems can grow with the organisation is important if the company is to continue to satisfy its customers.

It is worth noting that all administration creates an **overhead cost** – it does not add value to the product or service that the organisation provides to its customers. Administration systems should be adequate but not excessive – that is, they should be cost effective and provide value for money.

However, companies are required to maintain some administration systems by law; for example Pay As You Earn (PAYE) records must be maintained and returns made on Inland Revenue forms. VAT records are mandatory. Accidents must be recorded and serious incidents must be reported to the Health and Safety Executive. But these systems, too, should be **economic** and **efficient**.

PROCESSING INFORMATION

All business organisations, large and small, must process data. They will do so manually, with computers, or using calculators. There is a wide variety of tailor-made business machines for particular applications such as accounting, manufacturing and so on. The output information can be distributed on paper, electronically to visual display units (VDUs), by fax, by phone and by computer disk.

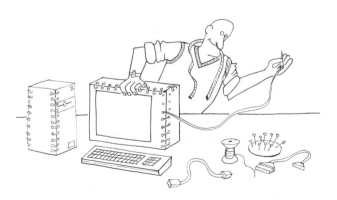

ACTIVITY

Design a simple questionnaire to get evidence from your head of department (or equivalent) of the ways data is processed within your department at school or college. Give it a reference number (for example, Item 1) and write an index to keep track of your evidence. If you can gather any forms or flow diagrams of the actual systems, give them reference numbers and file them in the same way.

Put the completed questionnaire (and other documents) in a folder of evidence which may be useful in the assignment at the end of this element.

INDEX		
Item No	Description of item	Type of evidence
1	Methods of data processing used in department	Questionnaire completed by head of department

The speed and extent of **electronic communication** is a great asset to multinational businesses and is beginning to permit trans-European administration. So, several companies in Europe that belong to the same group or parent company might set out to share the same services and systems. At present, the business areas that lend themselves to this approach, mainly because of European laws and regulations, are:

- ⊗ **human resources;**
- ⊗ **environment;**
- ⊗ **health and safety;**
- ⊗ **information technology;**
- ⊗ **business services;**
- ⊗ **public and government affairs;**
- ⊗ **tax;**
- ⊗ **purchasing.**

You can see where this is leading. If these administration systems are common across country boundaries, the parent company only needs one administration centre (or head office) in Europe to run all their businesses. Companies within the group will only need terminals linked to the centre, and they will not need any administration staff or senior management, just operational managers. Think of the costs that could be saved in this way.

ACTIVITY

The organisation in which you study – your school or college – will have administration systems to support its work. It will have systems to register students and ensure they are on the correct course; it will have systems to record all financial transactions and record income and expenditure; it will have systems to keep personnel records for all lecturers and other staff; and it may have systems to keep track of customers (students) and keep them informed about the college's services.

Bearing in mind that college administration staff are busy and have a demanding job to do, try to arrange for someone from the administration department to outline the systems that are used in the organisation. At this stage, try to get a big picture of all the systems and how they carry accurate, specific information from one department to another for the purpose of managing the affairs of the school or college effectively.

Fig. 2.9 looks at some administration activities that might result from a student applying to study Advanced Business GNVQ at a college.

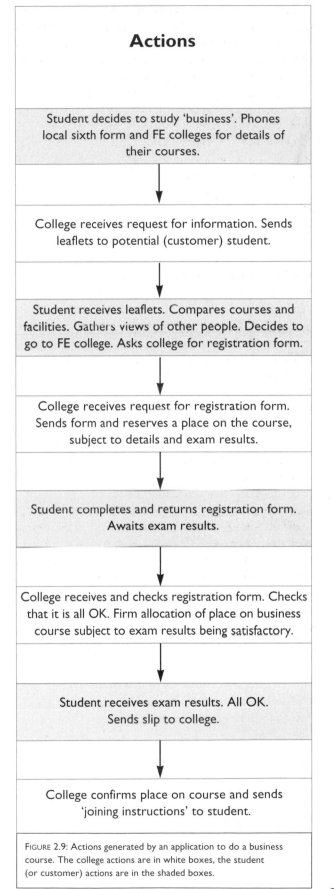

Actions

Student decides to study 'business'. Phones local sixth form and FE colleges for details of their courses.

College receives request for information. Sends leaflets to potential (customer) student.

Student receives leaflets. Compares courses and facilities. Gathers views of other people. Decides to go to FE college. Asks college for registration form.

College receives request for registration form. Sends form and reserves a place on the course, subject to details and exam results.

Student completes and returns registration form. Awaits exam results.

College receives and checks registration form. Checks that it is all OK. Firm allocation of place on business course subject to exam results being satisfactory.

Student receives exam results. All OK. Sends slip to college.

College confirms place on course and sends 'joining instructions' to student.

FIGURE 2.9: Actions generated by an application to do a business course. The college actions are in white boxes, the student (or customer) actions are in the shaded boxes.

In this example, action will not be confined to the college administration department. In processing the application, the administration department will:

- **advise the head of business that a place is allocated;**

- **request funding from the County Education Department;**

- **provide the senior management team with details of enrolments;**

- **set up central records for each student with all personal and course details.**

As a result of this information, other people in the organisation and in associated organisations take some action.

The head of the business department must:

- **allocate staff to teach the course;**

- **allocate a classroom for the course;**

- **allocate materials and books;**

- **prepare the course register;**

- **prepare the student record.**

The County Education Department will:

- **gather data about all students going to the college;**

- **make an appropriate award of funds to the college;**

- **advise central government about student numbers and use of funds.**

The college's senior management team:

- **receives information about total numbers of students in each department;**

- **reviews resources and budgets with each head of department;**

- **reallocates resources according to student numbers.**

In addition, as students accept places, the college's administration department needs to:

- **put all students' details on records;**

- **put all courses' details on records;**

- **make allocation of lockers, etc.;**

- **issue travel vouchers as appropriate.**

ACTIVITY

What might have been the scene on the first day of the new term had the administration system failed to correctly record the number of students joining the business course?

Equally, what would it be like if the head of department had received the information too late to complete the necessary planning?

Consider the following questions.

1 **How would the students (customers) have felt?**

2 **What opinion would the students (customers) have of the organisation?**

3 **How would the inaccuracies affect the head of department?**

4 **How would the inaccuracies affect the County Education Department?**

5 **How would the inaccuracies affect the decisions made by the senior management team?**

6 **Draw conclusions about the relationships between administration systems and the efficiency of an organisation.**

ACTIVITY

Gather all the forms that are used in your school's or college's enrolment system. Paste them on a large sheet of paper in the order in which they are completed. (You might find it helpful to use flip chart – A1 size – paper.) Draw lines that show the flow of data and information, just like a flow chart.

1 Can you identify the input data and the output information?

2 How are the data processed?

3 Write a short step-by-step description of the system so that a new member of staff would be able to follow it without too much help. Test it out on a friend or relative. Did she or he understand it?

4 Now give your chart and description a reference and file them with the rest of your evidence.

FUNCTIONAL ADMINISTRATION SYSTEMS

Most businesses involve four key functions: **production**, **finance**, **marketing** and **personnel**. *Fig. 2.10* shows the administration systems that might be found in each of these four main functions.

Fig. 2.10 shows the great variety of administration systems needed to support a business organisation. Each of these systems could be run in a 'stand alone' fashion with its own paperwork and procedures. However, there are often data which are common to several systems and, where that occurs, it should be possible to find links between two or more systems. Modern information technology allows systems that have common information needs to share the same database. By linking them, businesses can reduce some duplication of effort. For example:

⊗ the production section needs some raw materials, so a material requisition is raised and given to the storekeeper;

⊗ stores issues the items and updates the stock records;

⊗ if the stock records show that the item is running low, stores will raise a purchase requisition to tell the purchasing section that the item needs replacing;

⊗ purchasing will raise a purchase order to replenish the item concerned.

FUNCTION	ADMINISTRATION SYSTEMS
Production	Production control system; drawings control system; purchase order system; stock control system; quality control system; planned maintenance system; machine utilisation system.
Finance	Credit control; sales invoicing; sales ledger; purchase ledger; petty cash; wages and salaries; PAYE records; statutory payment records; budgetary control; final accounts.
Marketing	Sales budgeting; sales recording; customer analysis; product analysis; territory analysis; promotion scheduling and purchasing; marketing budget control; customer communication systems; sales and marketing analysis and reporting system.
Personnel	Recruitment and selection systems; employee records; performance review systems; accident records; attendance records; training records; training budgeting; salary and wages control systems; staff turnover system.

FIGURE 2.10: Functional administration systems.

In this example the same information – the name and reference number of the item on the documents mentioned – has been reproduced four times for different purposes. By designing all four systems together as an integrated system, it is possible to reduce or eliminate duplication.

ACTIVITY

Examine the lists of functional administrative systems in *Fig 2.10* and note down which systems might be found in each of the following organisations:

- ⊗ **a sole trader selling and fitting kitchen furniture;**

- ⊗ **a small limited company employing thirty-seven people providing packaged holidays in Europe;**

- ⊗ **a plc manufacturing washing machines, refrigerators and spin dryers;**

- ⊗ **a co-operative retail company selling a wide range of food and household goods;**

- ⊗ **the planning and maintenance department of a local council;**

- ⊗ **Save the Children Fund.**

Consider the relationship between type and size of organisation, and the need for administrative systems.

PROCESS AND PROCEDURES

The term **'administrative process'** relates to the way things are done. It might be:

- ⊗ **a manual process or an automated process;**

- ⊗ **a paper-based process or an electronic process;**

- ⊗ **an independent process or an integrated process.**

Most administration systems are now **automated** and **electronic**, even in the smallest organisations, although many still produce paper outputs and are not yet fully integrated.

Administration systems are formal communications carrying specific information around the organisation. There is a need for accuracy and timeliness. It follows that people cannot just do what they like. There must be a strict procedure which ensures all the actions that need to be taken are taken in the right order. Every administration system has a procedure which contributes to its effectiveness.

Administration systems gather, process (sometimes store) and distribute information. These are distinct stages in the process but, in addition, many systems cross boundaries between departments, sections, and often between organisations. *Fig. 2.11* shows how a sales order invoicing system might operate.

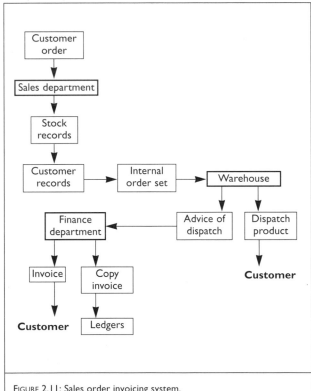

FIGURE 2.11: Sales order invoicing system.

You should notice that processing a customer's order has several stages:

1 **Check stock levels. If the item is available, the process can continue; if not, some further supplies would have to be manufactured.**

2 Check customer record. If the customer's credit **OK**, continue; if not, pass back to sales department to deal with.

3 Raise paperwork. Tell the warehouse to pack and dispatch the goods.

4 The warehouse dispatches the goods and advises finance that they have been sent out.

5 Finance raises an invoice for the goods.

6 The invoice is posted to the customer. A copy is sent to the ledgers.

ACTIVITY

Think about the differences between a process and a procedure.

1 Give three examples of processes that you find in your studies. An example is the assessment process.

2 Give three examples of procedures that you may come across in your school or college. One example is the enrolment procedure.

3 How are processes and procedures different?

4 Give three reasons for having processes and three reasons for having procedures.

SUITABILITY

In this section, we look at the suitability of administrative systems. In looking at suitability, we consider **fitness for purpose**, **value for money**, **security** and **health and safety**.

FITNESS FOR PURPOSE

Some systems are best carried out using a pen and a printed form. For example, many doctors write out a prescription for the patient to take it to a chemist to be made up. However, in some larger practices doctors have computer terminals on their desks which hold each patient's records. Simply by typing in the patient's surname and initials, the doctor can access a record of all the drugs at present being prescribed for a patient, and simply produce a new or repeat prescription. The system then 'looks up' the costs of the drugs prescribed on a database, and updates the doctors drugs budget.

Other systems are very sophisticated and rely on massive remote databases. For example, when you book an airline ticket, the travel clerk takes your requirements and accesses a database from a desktop terminal. The database holds details of every flight – the seating capacity of each flight, the number of seats that have already been booked and who has made the booking. The clerk finds a flight that meets your needs, and if it is suitable for you, books a seat on the flight and issues your ticket . The ticket is a small form containing about four copies of the booking. The database is immediately updated to prevent that seat being sold twice. Another clerk hundreds of miles away can access the database at the same time but cannot double book your seat. (Some of you may have had a different experience and found that your seat on an aircraft had been double booked. This is probably not a computer error but a policy that some companies have to overbook by a certain percentage to take account of the people who do not turn up. This policy is designed to prevent aircraft flying with unnecessarily empty seats, which costs airlines revenue.)

In setting up a new administration system, there are many questions a designer needs to ask:

- ☺ **what does the user want/need?**

- ☺ **what is the purpose/objective of the system?**

- ☺ **what is the input to the system?**

- ☺ **who will input data and how?**

- ☺ **is it a one-input system or a multi-input system?**

- ☺ **how will the data be processed?**

- ☺ **how will the data be stored?**

- ☺ **what outputs from the system are required?**

- ☺ **how will the output be presented?**

Factors that influence the system design and the way that data are processed are:

- **the size of organisation;**
- **the nature of its business;**
- **the time available for the transaction to be completed;**
- **the nature of the transaction being administered.**

A trader dealing in commodities might simply write a note in a notebook; the deal is instant and traders rely on the creed of 'my word is my bond'. In a fish market, simply sticking a printed number on a crate of fish might be enough to ensure it reaches the correct destination. There is no time or facility for anything else.

Buying something from a shop using a credit card simply requires your signature on a slip of paper for security reasons. All the other procedures are usually done electronically at high speed:

- **your credit balance is checked;**
- **the card is checked to ensure it has not been lost or stolen and is not out of date;**
- **the transaction is recorded;**
- **your account is debited.**

It is relatively straightforward to test whether an administrative system is 'fit for the purpose'. The test is 'does it do what it was intended to do' or 'does it achieve its objectives'.

For example, in credit card transactions a system would be deemed 'fit for its purpose' if it enabled customers to

VALUE FOR MONEY

pay for purchased goods quickly, accurately and securely. It is much more difficult to determine whether a system is **'value for money'**. In the past, when paperwork systems were manually processed, it was possible to draw a flow diagram and work out the cost of each stage in terms of clerical labour, the materials used, postage, etc. It was possible to say with some confidence how much it cost, for example, to raise and process a purchase order for an item of raw material stock, and to store the item until it was needed.

It is, however, much more difficult with computerised systems. There are some complex issues that would most probably require the expert input of an accountant:

- **is the computer hired, leased or bought?**
- **how is the cost to be depreciated?**
- **what is the cost of the software?**
- **what is the cost of hardware maintenance?**
- **what is the cost of the software maintenance?**
- **what is the cost of training both the administrators and the managers?**
- **what is the cost of installation?**
- **what is the cost of security?**
- **what is the cost of consumables?**
- **how are the total costs to be apportioned to each system?**

ACTIVITY

You are probably involved with administration systems every day. For example, if you travel to college by bus or train there is an administration system for collecting fares and giving you a ticket. Similarly, if you buy something in a shop, you will pay for it and receive a receipt. Taking a book from the library is another example.

1 List six different examples of activities you have been involved with in the last week

that had their own administration systems.

2 For each one, draw a simple diagram showing what happened. For example:
   (a) Got on bus near home
   (b) Paid driver 50p
   (c) Driver gave me a ticket for 35p
   (d) Stayed on the bus as far as college
   (e) Got off bus.

3 Comment on the 'fitness for purpose' of each system.

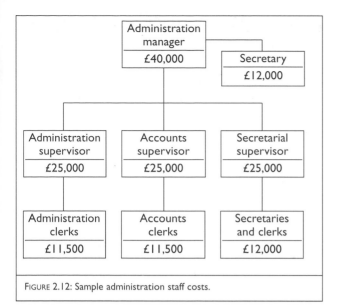

FIGURE 2.12: Sample administration staff costs.

ACTIVITY

Form a discussion group of three or four colleagues.

1 Using the evidence already filed in your folder from previous activities, discuss all the information you would need to do a thorough costing of a system. Start with how you might obtain information about the costs of the equipment being used to process the data.

2 Decide how you might calculate the costs of installation.

3 Think how you might calculate the ongoing running costs. *Fig. 2.12* shows some typical salary costs for administration work.

4 When your group has discussed the topic, write a memo for a manager highlighting the costs of the administration system.

SECURITY

There are three aspects to security in administration systems:

- ⊗ security of information;
- ⊗ security of electronic data files;
- ⊗ security of finance.

SECURITY OF INFORMATION

In most organisations there is some information that is open; anyone can know it. For example, **open information** would include the prices of a company's products; the contents of food products, etc. Some information has to be disclosed by law. But there is some **sensitive information** that a company would not like its competitors to know. For example, firms would not wish to disclose the costs of producing its products or the secret recipe that makes its food taste better or different from others in the same market.

And there is information that is classified, which only certain people may know about. For example, **classified information** would include a patient's records in a doctor's surgery or hospital, a plan to take over another company, or to develop a revolutionary new product.

Where this information could be gleaned from an administration system, there will be restrictions placed on the distribution of that information – only certain, specified people may have access to it. Documents will be marked clearly if they are confidential, restricted or secret. The government enforces secrecy of some of its data by means of the **Official Secrets Act**.

SECURITY OF ELECTRONIC DATA FILES

There are two types of security needed for files. First, security against loss of data caused by physical, electrical or electronic failure. This security is usually achieved by keeping copies of all critical files in a fireproof safe, and by holding 'father' and 'grandfather' files which could be updated to get back lost data.

Second, an organisation needs security against corruption of files by virus programs. This can be achieved by passing all new files through a virus check before they are loaded.

These issues are explained more fully in element 4 later in this unit.

ACTIVITY

Prepare a short talk of about five minutes (to be presented to your class colleagues) that sets out the moral arguments about either:

(a) the rights of people to security for their personal data held in computers; or

(b) the practice of 'hacking' into other people's computer files.

SECURITY OF FINANCE

It is said that money makes rogues of us all. That may not be true, but certainly companies have to guard against **theft** and **financial malpractice**. All administration systems that relate to receiving or spending the company's money must be designed to avoid theft or fraud. The accounting professional bodies lay down strict guidelines to be followed in this regard. All systems must be auditable; that is, all money due to a company, and all money spent by a company must be traceable by means of an audit trail.

ACTIVITY

Prepare a short questionnaire that can be given to your school or college accountant.
Ask two or three questions that enquire about the ways – internal and external – that money is kept secure.
Give the completed questionnaire a reference number and file it in your folder.

HEALTH AND SAFETY AT WORK

There are certain things in the administration environment (as opposed to the production environment) that should be considered when planning, designing and implementing administration systems. Although the **Health and Safety at Work Act 1974** is the main statute employers must comply with, **The Offices, Shops and Railway Premises Act 1963** also relates to safety in offices. The main provisions of these Acts relating to offices are:

- ✪ **each person sitting at a desk should have 40 sq. ft of floor space or 400 cubic feet of space;**
- ✪ **the temperature should be at least 16°C or 60°F within the first hour of work;**
- ✪ **there should be sufficient toilets and washing facilities;**
- ✪ **lighting should be adequate;**
- ✪ **seating should be appropriate to the job;**
- ✪ **ventilation should be adequate particularly where machinery (for example, some photocopiers) gives off fumes;**
- ✪ **fire exits should be clearly marked and access to them free from obstruction.**

The **Health and Safety Executive (HSE)** provides advice about the use of visual display units (VDUs). The key points are:

- ✪ **jobs should be designed to allow short, frequent breaks;**
- ✪ **screens should be adjustable to suit individuals needs;**
- ✪ **bright lights should not reflect in the screen;**
- ✪ **screens should not have a window or bright light behind them;**
- ✪ **the characters should not flicker.**

Failure to comply with the Health and Safety at Work Act is a criminal offence. The HSE consider that managers who control the resources are responsible for safety. Employees are required to co-operate with employers on health and safety matters.

ACTIVITY

Walk around your school or college and note all the things that are in place to keep people safe and healthy. For example, there will be fire extinguishers and fire exits.
If you can arrange it, ask the head of the science department to show you the safety equipment and procedures in the chemistry laboratory. Ask the head of science about office equipment that might give off harmful fumes, or present other types of hazards.

INFORMATION TECHNOLOGY AND ADMINISTRATION SYSTEMS

Since the mid-1980s, **information technology (IT)** has developed at such a rate that it has been called a 'revolution'. The **information revolution** has brought great changes to administration systems as well as all other areas of business, for example, computer-aided design (CAD) and computer-aided manufacture (CAM).

IT is rapidly becoming subsumed into the majority of occupations. It is no longer simply a remote data processing

tool or a piece of secretarial equipment. IT skills are no longer optional, they are essential to the successful completion of many jobs, including management. In most businesses, both large and small, there is a **personal computer (PC)** on almost every desk, from the chief executive down through all levels of administration and operations. IT is as important as a pen or a tool box. However, it is not a substitute for the skills of the artisan and the imagination and creativity of managers.

PRESENT SITUATION

Almost every area of business is affected by IT: research, design, production, training, communication, and so on. In this element, our focus is on the use of IT in administration systems.

IT equipment in regular use in administration includes:

- ✪ **mainframe computers;**

- ✪ **personal computers (PCs);**

- ✪ **laptop computers;**

- ✪ **PC workstations;**

- ✪ **laser printers;**

- ✪ **fax and telex machines;**

- ✪ **client servers.**

PCs are the most rapidly growing type of computer system. They are powerful, versatile machines which can be used by a person possessing little or no technical computer knowledge. They can support a number of input/output devices, including:

- ✪ **keyboard;**

- ✪ **mouse and joystick;**

- ✪ **colour or black and white monitor screens;**

- ✪ **floppy disk drive;**

- ✪ **hard disk drive;**

- ✪ **CD-ROM;**

- ✪ **various types of colour or black and white printers, including high quality laser printers;**

- ✪ **sound output devices.**

PCs are relatively cheap and can be purchased from a variety of sources, including high-street shops, mail order outlets and office equipment suppliers. Shopping around can produce a wide range of prices. Software, on the other hand is relatively expensive particularly if it is tailor made for an organisation (see *Fig. 2.13*). However, software packages are available for most applications.

The most popular packages are:

- **spreadsheets;**

- **word processing;**

- **database management systems;**

- **desk top publishing;**

- **graphics;**

- **integrated packages for production, accounting, payroll, marketing and personnel;**

- **special purpose software for doctors, dentists, accountants, solicitors, and so on;**

- **software for use in the home covering personal finances, inventory, home banking.**

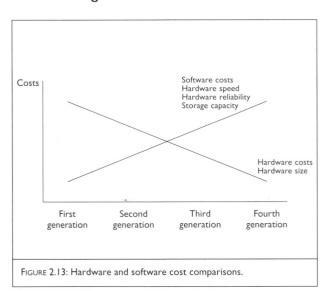

FIGURE 2.13: Hardware and software cost comparisons.

PCs can communicate over **local area networks (LANs)** or **wide area networks (WANs)**. This is a powerful facility that has resulted from the development of fibre optic digital networks over the telephone system. Through these networks all the electronic administration equipment can be interlinked. They can be connected by a single 'server' locally or, by multiple servers, to anywhere in the world.

For example, from the PC that this author is using to write this element, he is in daily contact with offices in England, Scotland, USA, Holland and Norway. All users of this network can call on a bank of twenty software systems and use them simultaneously without interfering with another user's data. These systems can be used by any number of individuals at the same time, or several users can collaborate and share data.

For example, three or four people, far apart, can be speaking through the telephone conferencing system as each of them is looking at the same data on a VDU screen on her or his desk. A one-hour telephone conference like this can save the group considerable time and expense in travelling to face-to-face meetings. Stress and fatigue are also reduced using these facilities.

ACTIVITY

1 **Find out what computer-based administration systems are used in your school or college.**

2 **What software is used on them? Is the software a package or was it designed and tailored especially for the organisation?**

3 **If you can arrange it, ask one of the senior management team to explain what information is derived from the administration systems to assist with management decisions.**

THE FUTURE

IT is developing very fast. It seems there is no end to its current progress. Whatever developments take place, IT is going to alter the way businesses are structured and the way they are administered. Tomorrow's environment will look nothing like today's.

The article opposite predicts how retailing will change in the future. Although it refers to retailing and banking, all businesses could be affected. For example, some businesses have done away with the practice of everyone having her or his own desk. Instead, each person has a personal 'environment' in the corporate computer network. When they arrive at work in the morning, they have to find a vacant place, so long as there is a PC on the desk they can work as normal. This practice is known as **'hot desking'**.

Virtual reality is in its infancy, but its potential for business is very exciting. Christopher Barnatt, author of *Cyber-Business* predicts that there will be little need to assemble people for work, only for social interaction. Meetings will be held between people thousands of miles

Virtual dream for shoppers

Can you imagine shopping without the crowds, queues and over-heated fitting rooms? Well the shopaholic's dream is soon to become a reality for millions. The time is close when we will be able to buy the perfect outfit over the Internet, and anything from holidays to books through interactive television.

Electronic shopping is still in the early stages. But US analysts Killen and Associates predict that money transactions via the Internet will expand to more than £30bn by the year 2005.

There are around 30 million Internet users world-wide, one million of them in the UK, and usage is expected to grow at 10 per cent a month. So it is not surprising major retailers are eager to bring us all virtual shopping.

Last month, Barclays Bank opened its first electronic shopping centre with secure credit card facilities called BarclaySquare. Within just 24 hours of opening, 14,000 people had visited the centre.

There are only eight major retailers to choose from, but there are plans to expand in September.

'There is no space limit to how many retailers can join the centre,' says Christine Tucker, public relations officer for Barclays. 'But we want to keep it manageable. Shoppers will get lost if there are too many options on offer. BarclaySquare is there to supplement the shopping experience, not replace it. You can buy books from Blackwells, wines from Sainsbury's, gadgets from Innovations, and even book yourself a ticket to France via the Channel Tunnel.'

Double click on the Car Shop, and motor fans are provided with a range of information on new and used cars.

Click on the shop you wish to visit, browse, click next to the item you wish to purchase and take it to the checkout. At the virtual checkout you are given a total cost for the goods selected and you are required to key in your card number to ensure it is delivered to your home.

One question many users will ask is, can someone else hack in and use my credit card number? Barclays assures customers that credit cards are safe. Interactive Telephony Ltd joined forces with Barclays Merchant Services and Netscape to develop a method of making on-line transactions hacker proof. When a BarclaySquare shopper places an order by sending their credit card number down the line, that number is individually coded and can be deciphered only at the other end.

A more sophisticated system will need to be designed for direct money transfers but, so far, simple credit card transactions over the Internet are entirely secure.

CompuServe, the on-line information service, is the main competition for BarclaySquare, with its own electronic mall. It is not as far reaching as the Internet, but does have 100,000 UK subscribers, mainly young professionals on high salaries who are the perfect target for retailers.

At on-line W. H. Smith, you can buy books from a list of 250 bestsellers, at Virgin you can by CDs and videos and you can stop off at Dixons for a selection of electrical goods. On one day, shoppers clicked in at the rate of more than one per minute. CompuServe also hopes to persuade 15 retailers to join by the end of the year.

Daily Express, 9 June 1995

apart who, wearing their low-power laser scanners, can look around the 'room' and see everyone in their places, and interact as if it were a normal gathering. Nobody will go into 'the office'. The office will be wherever there is a PC linked to the corporate computer network.

The **Internet** can offer access to millions of people worldwide. A page on the World Wide Web can already reach ten million people. The Irish Tourist Board is already using it to sell holidays to a world-wide audience. A Scottish company is selling Scottish smoked salmon and Highland holidays through the Internet. The Bank of Scotland is on-line with its own page on the Web trying to attract new customers. It believes that there is a potential market to be gathered from among young computer literates. Visa is working on techniques which will make the transfer of money through the Web safe.

Once this can be guaranteed, there is no reason why every type of business arrangement cannot be made via the Web.

The use of **'smart cards'** as a substitute for cash is also becoming a reality. A smart card is like a credit card with a chip in it. The card is put into a hole-in-the-wall bank terminal, where, after security protocols, a certain amount of money is 'down-loaded' from your bank account onto the card. You can then go shopping with the card and spend the money in any outlet with the right terminals. When all the 'money' on the card is spent, you can go back and replenish it – if, of course, there is money in your account. This system was piloted in Swindon during the second half of 1995.

All new technology takes time to bed in and become accepted. It takes time for the average operations manager to appreciate the different ways in which IT can be exploited to improve business performance. New skills have to be learned by staff from the top to the bottom of every organisation. Old attitudes about how work should be done have to give way to new attitudes – and that can cause stress and worry.

But one thing is certain, IT is not going to go away; so it is best we become knowledgeable and skilful in its use.

ACTIVITY

Read the business section of any good newspaper. Cut out any reference to the ways new technology is affecting business organisations. Make a scrapbook which you can show to your colleagues.

IMPROVEMENTS IN SYSTEMS

Organisations are changing all the time. They are like evergreen plants; they sprout, grow, flower and, unless they are tended carefully, they will wither and die. If they are well looked after they will give pleasure year after year.

Administration systems are changing too. They serve specific purposes in support of an organisation, and they must be flexible enough to change as the organisation changes. If they do not respond to their changing environment they will not serve the organisation and the organisation will certainly cease to exist in its present form.

Improvements in an administration system can be achieved by:

⊗ **constantly monitoring its performance against its objectives;**

⊗ **ensuring that the technology and equipment used to process the data are well maintained and up to date;**

⊗ **ensuring that the staff using the system are efficient and well trained;**

⊗ **ensuring that the managers using the information output from the system know what the output means and are trained in decision making;**

⊗ **taking care to see that procedures are efficient and modifying them to eliminate duplication;**

⊗ **introducing new procedures where appropriate.**

People who are not technical specialists in IT have to be trained in new skills. Unfortunately, we are not clear about what future training needs will be. Basic skills like using a keyboard efficiently, and knowing how to use applications, are unlikely to change. But where new concepts and methods are being developed, organisations will not get the full benefit unless people are trained to exploit them. That takes time. The consequence might be that opportunities to add value to performance are missed. The magnitude of time wasted by inefficient use of the technology is estimated to be 60 per cent of all real IT costs. This results in:

⊗ **increased staff costs;**

⊗ **a long timespan for the development and introduction of new applications;**

⊗ **slow implementation of change;**

⊗ **computer specialists spending up to 75 per cent of their time maintaining old applications rather than developing new ones;**

⊗ **heavy work load for computer specialists because of the need to maintain and develop systems, resulting in stress, fatigue, errors and constant staff turnover in this area of work.**

Hardware costs are reducing which encourages more companies to use more technology but the number of experts is not increasing at the same fast rate. Experience and training will correct all that, but both of these solutions take time. All new technology has shortcomings, but IT will continue its revolutionary progress in making business administration faster, more accurate, less costly and more relevant to the precise needs of the users.

PORTFOLIO ASSIGNMENT

For this assignment, you need to arrange a meeting with a businessperson who is responsible for, or uses, a business administration system. She or he might be a person in your school or college, a relative or friend, a manager in a local firm that supports work experience, or someone in a firm that you contact at your own initiative. Before the meeting, prepare a list of questions you wish to ask about one administration system. The answers to your questions should give you information about:

⊗ the purpose and objectives of the system;

⊗ a description of the stages of the system;

⊗ the forms used in the system;

⊗ the input of data to the system;

⊗ the output from the system for

   (a) suppliers, customers, clients, etc.

   (b) management decision making;

⊗ the method used to process the data;

⊗ the volume of data processed (for example, 5,000 invoices per year).

Prepare a business report which includes:

(a) some brief details of the business which operates the system, the way you contacted the business and how you gathered the information;

(b) a statement of the purpose of the system, a full description of the system accompanied by either a diagram or the actual forms used and an illustration of the data input to and the information output from the system;

(c) an analysis of the effectiveness of the system and its fitness for purpose, and an outline of the costs of the system.

Also explain, either verbally or by a presentation to your tutor, ways in which you might be able to improve the effectiveness of the system, and give your reasons for your findings.

Analyse communication in a business organisation

This element addresses some of the ways in which organisations communicate both internally and with the business world at large. Many businesses now operate in highly competitive global markets where the rapid, even immediate, response to changing trading opportunities and political situations can make the difference between profit and loss, survival and failure. It is essential that a business invests in, maintains, and regularly updates a reliable and effective communications system which makes use of efficient electronic processing and recognises the value of the human contribution.

THE NATURE OF COMMUNICATIONS

To communicate means to impart or convey information, meanings, instructions, requests and comment from one person to another using the media of speech, written text, sound, sign language, images, and even body language.

The act of communicating is arguably what human activity is all about. Nothing is achieved without communication, whether it is doing the shopping or building an aircraft. But the art of communicating is less straightforward; many problems, mistakes and disputes arise because the parties to a communication are confused by unclear instructions and misleading statements, or there is misinterpretation or a lack of understanding. In business, emphasis must be given to getting communication right.

Because we are now in the midst of an accelerating technological revolution, it is so easy to overlook the fact that even computer-generated documentation originates from people. The focus today is on the technology to the point that the computer is often blamed for errors when the true culprit is the operator who keys in the wrong information.

ESSENTIALS OF COMMUNICATIONS

Effective communication means, in simple terms, the sending of information in an appropriate form which the recipient is able to interpret exactly as the originator intends. Successful communication is reliant upon:

- ✪ **timing;**
- ✪ **clear thinking and expression;**
- ✪ **attentive and careful reading, listening and interpreting.**

During the working day, individuals and companies are dealing with many different situations and personalities. There is the need to stick to company procedures and routines but it must be recognised that at times circumstances demand flexibility and initiative. Despite a dependence on technology, a business survives on its skills in handling people. Staff need to know when to be formal, persuasive, sympathetic, firm, and to appreciate when an informal, and more personal, approach will unlock a problem.

It is good advice to reflect on the purpose of any communication and the reasons behind it. Here is an example of a code of practice or set of basic rules:

- ✪ **take the time to marshal thoughts about content, structure and objectives;**
- ✪ **present ideas, requests, suggestions and instructions logically;**
- ✪ **employ simple concise sentences;**
- ✪ **use correct grammar;**
- ✪ **avoid technical or legal jargon (except for specialists), outdated language, slang, and terms which some might find offensive;**
- ✪ **adopt tone and style appropriate to the audience or recipient;**
- ✪ **be courteous and exercise tact and sensitivity;**
- ✪ **be impersonal;**
- ✪ **use the most appropriate and effective medium;**
- ✪ **encourage feedback.**

Some communications need to be complex and involved such as a technical description of switching gear. However, where it is practicable to do so, the code should be followed. When giving instructions, in either written or verbal form, it is advisable to adopt the 'kiss' approach – keep it simple, stupid!

ACTIVITY

Bring in an example of any form of communication which you find particularly difficult to understand. It might be a letter, instructions on how to complete a tax form or assemble a piece of furniture, a circular from the church or scouts, or a refund claim form issued by a store.

Form a small group with the other members of the class. Together, rewrite the offending items using the code of practice set out above. Present the new versions to the rest of the class or training session, indicating why the changes are thought necessary and how they improve the document.

METHODS OF COMMUNICATIONS

In analysing business communications, the first step is to consider the usual methods employed by an organisation. The following lists are extensive but they are not offered as complete or definitive. They indicate the variety of methods used by business and the range of options available.

Oral or verbal methods include:

- ⊗ telephone;
- ⊗ audio-conferences;
- ⊗ conferences;
- ⊗ interviews;
- ⊗ committee meetings;
- ⊗ discussions;
- ⊗ instructions;
- ⊗ lectures;
- ⊗ role-play/business games;
- ⊗ team briefings;
- ⊗ management/staff consultative meetings.

Written or textual forms include:

- ⊗ letters;
- ⊗ memoranda;
- ⊗ reports;
- ⊗ balance sheets;
- ⊗ minutes;
- ⊗ summaries;
- ⊗ abstracts;

- ⊗ circulars;
- ⊗ notices;
- ⊗ in-house journals;
- ⊗ manuals;
- ⊗ charts and graphs;
- ⊗ statistical tables;
- ⊗ training documentation;

- job descriptions;
- application forms;
- mission statements;
- policy statements;
- press releases;
- advertisements;
- packaging;
- catalogues;
- directories;
- computer print-outs.

Other methods include:

- video-conferences;
- radio/television;
- trade fairs;
- careers conventions;
- public meetings.

Material and information can be disseminated by using a variety of support equipment and services. These include:

- fax;
- electronic networks (E-mail);
- appropriate computer interface;
- telephone;
- radio pager;
- telex;
- telemessages (USA and UK only);
- postal/parcel services;
- courier services;
- the media.

In deciding on the method and means of communication, a business needs to consider the following factors:

- type of information;
- complexity and detail;
- accuracy;
- confidentiality/security;
- convenience;
- urgency;
- need for feedback and response;
- need to keep a record;
- cost;
- distance;
- number and location of people requiring the information;
- degree of formality/informality.

 ACTIVITY

Work in a small group and define or explain what is meant by these terms:

- audio-conferences;
- memoranda;
- in-house journals;
- job descriptions;
- mission statements.

🔅 ACTIVITY

Assemble a portfolio of at least ten examples of different kinds of genuine business communications. They need not all be good examples; attach to each item a note stating how effective or important you think it is.

🔅 ACTIVITY

Consider your institution or employer. Identify and explain at least five methods of communication in regular use which you think help inform and motivate you, i.e. those communications which make you feel part of the organisation.

OBJECTIVES OF COMMUNICATION

The lists of communication methods may seem overwhelming but they demonstrate the **variety**, **complexity** and **demands** of communications. Organisations expend much time and effort on the process of communicating. The primary objective is to pass on information so that business runs smoothly. However, communications can also play a significant part in motivating people, especially if management sees it as a process to involve rather than impose upon staff.

We now consider the differences between **internal** and **external communications**. Each activity may select from the same menu of methods and media, although their objectives are quite different. Internal communications relate to the transfer of information within an organisation; external communications deal with customers, suppliers, shareholders, etc.

The objectives of internal communications are to:

- ☻ **initiate action;**

- ☻ **encourage the flow of information and ideas;**

- ☻ **give commands;**

- ☻ **delegate;**

- ☻ **report;**

- ☻ **organise people;**

- ☻ **encourage teamwork;**

- ☻ **motivate;**

- ☻ **influence attitudes;**

- ☻ **encourage the work ethic;**

- ☻ **encourage effective and efficient performance;**

- ☻ **communicate results, goals and strategies.**

Internal and external communications operations may be separate because they focus on different objectives but they are in a sense related. If internal communications systems are weak, insecure and unprofessional then external communications are unlikely to be exemplary. One reflects the other. Companies with inefficient internal systems, which may demotivate staff, will find it difficult to create positive and effective external communications and build satisfactory relations with suppliers, clients and the general public.

The objectives of external communications are to:

- ☻ **present the best image of the organisation to the world at large;**

- ☻ **inspire confidence in the organisation;**

- ☻ **encourage business.**

In supporting these main aims, a company may wish to communicate:

- ☻ **the nature of its business or activities;**

- ☻ **its record on industrial relations, equal opportunities, health and safety and the environment;**

- ☻ **geographical areas of activity;**

- ☻ **the response to and handling of complaints about products and services;**

- ☻ **the quality and content of the company's products and services.**

The following groups will be among those targeted by external communications:

- ⊗ **pressure groups such as animal rights activists;**
- ⊗ **local, national and European politicians;**
- ⊗ **government at local, national and European levels;**
- ⊗ **customers or clients;**
- ⊗ **suppliers and other supporting companies;**
- ⊗ **shareholders;**
- ⊗ **the stock market;**
- ⊗ **general public;**
- ⊗ **the media.**

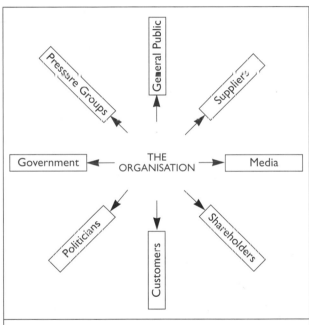

FIGURE 2.14: The organisation and the external audience.

ACTIVITY

Obtain two annual reports and balance sheets (from, for example, plcs, retail co-operatives and NHS Trusts) and examine how successful you think each is as a means of projecting the image and progress of the organisation to the world at large.

ACTIVITY

Your company wants to build a high-tech plant on a greenfield site. It is in an area of outstanding beauty and home to a variety of wildlife. The planning authority has no specific objections at this stage but public opinion is growing against your outline proposals. People believe that the area will be environmentally damaged. Your managing director thinks people should find something better to do, they should be grateful for the business coming into their area. If you are the public relations manager, explain how you would best communicate your company's plans and intentions to inform and reassure the general public.

COMMUNICATION FLOWS

The flow of information is dictated by the needs of management and by the structure of the organisation. Communications need to be co-ordinated and integrated so that the organisation can meet its corporate objectives. There are two official (or structural) and two unofficial (though often very productive) channels of communication. We shall consider each in turn.

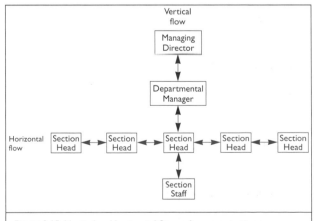

FIGURE 2.15: Vertical and horizontal flows of communication.

VERTICAL

The **vertical channel** reflects both the upward and downward flows of information. It is the route through which authority and responsibility are expressed. The downward flow is from superordinate to subordinate. It is used to:

- ⊗ **instruct;**
- ⊗ **delegate;**
- ⊗ **set targets;**
- ⊗ **inform;**
- ⊗ **persuade;**
- ⊗ **motivate.**

The downward flow, therefore, is the means to carry out the policies of the organisation. The upward flow is used to:

- ⊗ **convey feedback and response;**
- ⊗ **request approval for actions;**
- ⊗ **notify problems;**
- ⊗ **request solutions to problems;**
- ⊗ **report on target achievement;**
- ⊗ **report on human relations matters such as appraisals.**

Horizontal or lateral

Departments are organised to create areas of specialist activity such as personnel, sales, and research and development. But it must be understood that these departments or sections are part of, and must contribute to, the organisation as a whole. An activity initiated in one department may well have repercussions for several other departments and they will need to be appropriately informed so that they can respond accordingly. The **horizontal flow of information** occurs between departments (or other units of discrete or specialist activity) nominally at the level of supervision or management.

In an organisation which has a long chain of command and an authoritarian structure, the horizontal flow is often initiated by a vertical flow within a department. For example, a routine request for data by a junior clerk may be passed up through the structure to the departmental head who passes it to the head of another department who will then funnel the request down to the appropriate desk. Such a cumbersome structure is likely to encourage the informal flow.

Informal

In order to operate effectively, an organisation is obliged to introduce procedures and practices covering the management of its internal structure. Despite clear procedures and well-defined vertical and horizontal information flows, it has to be recognised that some tasks would not get completed on time without people ignoring the **'chain of command'** and departmental demarcations. All organisations comprise people who have differing and sometimes conflicting personalities. Even in the best run organisations, the flow of information is likely to meet problems and mostly they are resolved by relying on **personal relationships**. So, for example, squash partners, even of unequal status, will co-operate 'unofficially' to achieve a result.

Grapevine

A **grapevine** exists in every organisation and in terms of speed of information circulation it cannot be beaten. Its main feature, and disadvantage, is that it so often feeds

ACTIVITY

The senior management team are discussing the current position of the company over lunch in the boardroom. One manager says that the company would benefit from a 10 per cent reduction in staff and bonuses cut by half; business would grow by 5 per cent. After lunch, the personnel director is approached by a group of staff wondering if it is true that senior management has agreed to a large number of redundancies and pay cuts. Analyse this situation in a small group

1 Identify possible sources of the rumour.

2 Discuss the methods the company might use to reassure staff.

3 Suggest ways that disinformation might be discouraged in the future.

upon rumour. Even if the substance is true (prospective redundancies for 5 per cent of sales staff), by the time the information has gone around the entire organisation, probably more than once, it will have become exaggerated and distorted (25 per cent of staff and closure of the southern area warehouse). But it is also true that the grapevine can pass on reliable information well in advance of any announcements. The usual sources are the 'invisible' employees, those who move about the organisation, in and out of offices and meetings largely unnoticed – tea ladies, cleaners and messengers. The grapevine can also be used quite deliberately by management to test the reaction of staff to suggested policies and proposals.

MANAGEMENT INFORMATION SYSTEMS (MIS)

Administration and communications systems are the processes through which a business generates, distributes, co-ordinates, monitors and completes its work. When all this activity is computerised, it is known collectively as the **management information system** (or MIS for short). It is not the name of any particular software package but rather a description of the overall function or purpose of the control systems within the organisation. A management information system is the collation of information and activities which assists or supports management. It may be used as a tool to support:

- **decision-making;**
- **directing the business;**
- **forecasting;**
- **monitoring performance;**
- **progress chasing;**
- **establishing goals and targets;**
- **producing the balance sheet;**
- **identifying loss making and/or slow moving lines;**
- **calculating profitability;**
- **VAT accounting;**
- **order processing;**
- **job costing.**

Information must be processed to meet both the overall needs of the organisation and the specific needs of the different levels of responsibility and authority within the organisational structure. Those doing unskilled routines may require a minimal information input, but those charged with formulating and/or advising on company policy will require access to all information sources.

As business becomes more complex, with the need to process the increasing amount of information in numerical, textual, sound and image forms, MIS will be regarded as an organisation's main strategic communications instrument.

THE EFFECTIVENESS OF COMMUNICATIONS

Communications tend to be taken for granted. Yet, so often, seemingly minor misinterpretations of data can create **problems** and **bottlenecks**. Stress is rightly placed on the effectiveness of communications. Without regular appraisal of, and improvement in, the methods and systems there is the threat of ineffective communications. Poor systems encourage:

- **information hoarding;**
- **lack of co-operation;**
- **conflict and division;**
- **feelings of demotivation, exclusion, insecurity, and even hostility;**
- **internal pressure groups;**
- **demarcation.**

Insufficient attention to, and investment in, communications can divert a lot of energy away from meeting the organisation's stated mission objectives. Groups or individuals may develop their own agendas – a process which disrupts both the administration and working relationships. The importance of periodically reviewing the communications policy cannot be overstated.

Simplicity has already been suggested as a feature of communicating, but as business and human activity gets complicated so too will communications. Even highly intelligent people are capable of mishearing or misapplying information. This can, for example, cause a problem with far-reaching legal consequences. So, effective communications play a vital role in determining business success.

It is therefore worth reiterating the characteristics of effective communications. Any communication needs to be:

- ☺ **easily accessible;**

- ☺ **comprehensive;**

- ☺ **clear;**

- ☺ **informative;**

- ☺ **relevant to recipient's needs and circumstances;**

- ☺ **demand oriented;**

- ☺ **coherent;**

- ☺ **efficient;**

- ☺ **fast;**

- ☺ **flexible;**

- ☺ **delivered to the right addresses at the right time;**

- ☺ **unambiguous.**

In addition, you need to pay attention to the following points:

- ☺ **recipients must have confidence in the sender or originator;**

- ☺ **successful communications rely on the two-way process or exchange of information;**

- ☺ **all communications must reflect quality;**

- ☺ **the appropriate means of delivery must be employed.**

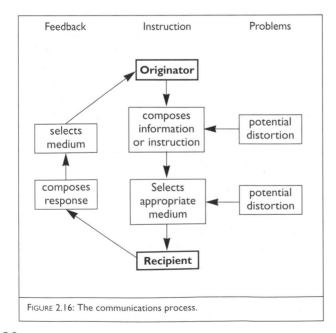

FIGURE 2.16: The communications process.

QUALITY

There is a saying 'garbage in, garbage out'. This means that careful attention must be paid to the processing of information. Computer systems do not, as a rule, make mistakes as the programs react logically to the given commands. Poor quality output reflects both poor quality input and poor information housekeeping. With global markets operating 24 hours a day, poor, ineffective or insecure communications may have formidable implications for an organisation. But, note, quality is just as imperative in verbal, handwritten and printed communications as it is in electronic forms. Limited vocabulary and a poor standard of English are as much barriers to effective communication as poor information.

MEETINGS

Many people claim to dislike meetings. Common complaints are that they go on too long, they do not focus on the issues, or they are badly run. But meetings can be highly dynamic events with important opportunities for making contacts. Notionally, they are expensive in terms of time and a budget-conscious manager may regard meetings as a lost opportunity, that is the participants could have achieved more by being at their desks. Equally, in the age of telecommunications one could ask why bother to assemble in one location when there are audio/visual conferencing or electronic messaging facilities?

However one of the disadvantages of electronic and remote media is the **lack of personal contact**. People are social animals and meetings create very different reactions to those experienced in remote conferencing. Meetings can identify the leaders and followers, the initiators and imitators, the proactive and the reactive. They can contribute to **team building** and provide **effective feedback**. For the people involved, attending a meeting means being 'in the know'. Ambitious staff use meetings to promote their own causes much more effectively than via memoranda, reports or teleconferencing.

Meetings should always be called for specific purposes. They should be positive and dynamic. Otherwise, they become affected by the 'sewing circle syndrome', with meetings being held on a regular basis almost solely for companionship.

ACTIVITY

List five advantages and five disadvantages to the individual of attending meetings.

CULTURE

Culture in this context means the attitudes and values of an organisation. Some companies have strict top-down organisational structures which may inhibit personal initiative and enterprise, and maintain long channels of communication. Others encourage a more open and democratic working climate supported by a recognition of individual contribution within a relatively flat structure. In these organisations, there is a short channel of communication between the boss and the functional teams and/or specialists. The culture of an organisation affects the working climate and it is likely to be reflected in the communications structure.

Information technology has brought considerable cultural change. As we have emphasised, organisations can now operate in a global business environment which demands they have fast, even immediate, and flexible responses. There is not the time to refer every single transaction or opportunity 'up the line'. Nor would it make business sense. IT-based companies, particularly those in international markets, encourage self-directing teams. These challenge any real (or supposed) hierarchy by imposing a flatter organisational structure.

The increasing use of IT has created more opportunity for employees to be directly involved in dealing with customers, suppliers, budgets and so on. In this sense, IT has empowered those people at the base of the organisational pyramid, who are now more frequently using and interpreting information and taking decisions.

DECENTRALISATION

In decentralised structures, the organisational pyramid is 'flattened' Long channels of communication are cut into short ones. Not only is the risk of distortion (through the rumour mill) reduced, but this process encourages employee involvement and participation. However, good intentions are not enough. If greater participation is to be achieved, companies need to introduce supporting policies.

One problem is to convince both 'them and us' (management and staff) that the organisation can work as a **people-centred operation**. It requires **open communication** and **feedback**. Organisations need to ensure that open consultation sessions are neither contrived nor starved of essential information.

There needs to be a culture of **information sharing**. The availability of data at all times to all employees confirms the staff as partners and problem-solvers. Obviously, some access has to be restricted owing to the nature of the information (such as medical records, personnel files and patent applications).

New mechanisms may be needed for **problem solving**. Some organisations have set up **corrective action teams (CATs)**. A CAT is multi-functional. It assembles in order to tackle a particular problem and then disbands. This offers the opportunity for employees to participate in 'trouble-shooting'.

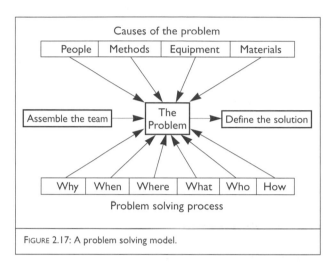

FIGURE 2.17: A problem solving model.

RESPONSES TO CHANGES IN COMMUNICATIONS

As organisations change, both management and staff can react positively or negatively to new developments. Some are regarded as **threats**, some as **opportunities**. Here, we look in turn at the negative and positive responses to changes in communications.

NEGATIVE RESPONSES

It is only to be expected that the prospect of change is accompanied by some feelings of concern. Where new electronic systems are being introduced, these preoccupations will centre on the following issues:

- ⊗ **the compatibility of the equipment with external databases;**

- ⊗ **security from eavesdropping and malicious damage;**

- ⊗ **capability of the proposed configuration to be expanded;**

- ⊗ **costs of installation, maintenance and operation;**

- ⊗ **cost and extent of training.**

These may seem reasonable questions as no investment should be made without searching enquiry, but they become negative issues if people are subject to the 'FUD' factor (fear, uncertainty and doubt). If the technology appears to be 'too clever' then the major reaction, certainly among the senior and/or non-technical staff, is likely to be apprehension. If the power of the computerised system is stressed too strongly, staff (who may already feel insecure) will convince themselves that they cannot compete with the equipment – that somehow they are incapable. They may even try to resist the introduction of IT by creating obstacles, by proving the worth of a manual system or even by absenteeism. They may see computerisation as a threat to their employment.

Most jobs these days now demand keyboard skills. A senior manager dependent upon a secretary/PA and unused to a word processor, needs convincing of its value as a personal tool. If keyboard training is to be done by a relatively low-ranking employee, an exposure of ignorance may be feared. Other fears may be territorial: an electronic communications system may threaten a department's gatekeeper status. Some staff will not be comfortable with the notion of wider access to information.

POSITIVE RESPONSES

People at all levels in an organisation will be won over to the electronic revolution in their workplace once advantages have not only been demonstrated but experienced. Innovations like user-friendly software, immediate access to data and labour-saving procedures help win staff over. With the backing of employees, an organisation will be 'switched on' and technologically responsive. It should enjoy clear advantages, including:

- **improved speed of communication;**
- **improved access to communications;**
- **better working conditions;**
- **liberation of abilities;**
- **release from repetitive routines;**
- **opportunity for more responsibility;**
- **better control over job input;**
- **enjoyment of, and involvement in, problem solving;**
- **access to a much wider market and more business opportunities;**
- **connection to global telecommunications;**
- **opportunities for business creativity through electronic partnerships.**

IMPROVING COMMUNICATIONS

Having diagnosed a communications problem the next step is to suggest a remedy. In this section we consider several factors which, though insufficient in themselves, can when put together bring about a marked change in an organisation's culture. This can result in an improvement in **adaptability**, **loyalty**, **performance** and **communications**.

TRAINING

Training, itself, is not the remedy to organisational and communications problems. However, it is the means by which people can be encouraged to be more receptive to change, to the needs of others and to the aims of the organisation. Some procedures can be taught directly, for example learning a new software package. But the process of developing team or participative work practices can only be developed effectively by using the trainees' own life skills and experiences – learning takes place through interaction with others.

The aims of training are to:

- **reduce the perceived threat of technology;**
- **learn to use the technology (and not be used by it);**
- **adapt to the changing working environment;**
- **encourage open communication and sharing of information;**
- **remove the fear of staff participation;**
- **remove the mystique of (but not the respect for) superordinate and specialist functions;**
- **understand the organisation – its structure and mission;**
- **encourage open mindedness and remove pre-packaged reactions;**
- **stimulate team building;**
- **develop social skills.**

ACTIVITY

Your company is experiencing problems with younger staff who cost a lot to train then often leave after less than a year. The personnel department is advising that recruitment should concentrate on the middle aged, particularly women who are returning to paid work after having children, because they will be more reliable. Your company is committed to IT and the new employees have no experience at all of computerised systems. Many even doubt their own competence to cope with computers.

Work in a small group. Assemble an induction training programme designed to introduce new staff to information technology stressing its user-friendly nature and the ways in which office work is now organised. Design a one-day course and bear in mind it is an introduction to IT. Consider what is required from your own experience with IT.

TELECOMMUNICATIONS

The prefix **'tele'** comes from the Greek meaning far and it is in daily use in words such as telephone and television. It could be argued that all communication which is not face to face must be remote which therefore makes it telecommunication. However, the term tends to be used to denote state-of-the-art electronic means of handling data (like sending high speed encoded messages from UK to Australia via satellite). The fax machine, which has become indispensable to business, is clearly an example of telecommunications, and so is a terminal which accesses information from a datafile stored just 20 metres away.

The merger of computers and telecommunications has produced the multi-purpose workstation. This allows a wide range of activities to be undertaken without the employee/user moving from the desk. A workstation offers:

⊗ word processing;

⊗ numerical calculations;

⊗ transmission of messages;

⊗ storage and retrieval of information.

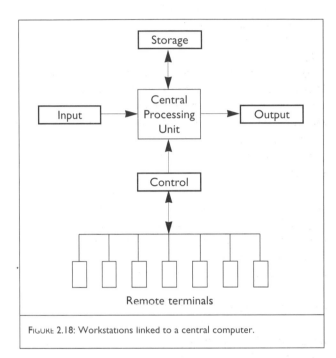

FIGURE 2.18: Workstations linked to a central computer.

A significant development in administrative work is that staff can have better control over their tasks and can enjoy more responsibility. Instead of completing just one function in a process, IT permits the integration of several functions allowing an individual to complete an entire task. The release from repetitive routines ought to be a motivating factor: staff should get more job satisfaction because they are making better use of their abilities.

ACTIVITY

Obtain the sales and publicity literature from at least two producers or retailers of hardware and software. Make notes on the range and prices of equipment and software available. If you were to set up a small business, explain what electronic equipment you would buy and how you would expect to use it.

THE PAPERLESS ORGANISATION

Information technology has encouraged the idea of the **paperless organisation** in which all information and data is treated electronically. This should remove the need to maintain physical files full of letters, memoranda, reports, price lists and so on. All storage will be on disk and the transfer (i.e. the communication) of material will be entirely by computers 'talking' to each other.

This is not a futuristic notion. It is now possible to undertake a range of activities without being dependent on paper. However, paperless offices will not become commonplace until organisations are connected to the appropriate networks through compatible equipment. Current research, known as **OSI** or **open systems interconnection**, is looking at ways to allow any computer and network to combine with any other. Difficulties persist as there are so many different systems. The problem is one of **incompatibility**: without appropriate technology one system cannot directly talk to or communicate with another.

Curiously, the use of computerised systems has increased paper consumption and there has been a rapid growth in world-wide paper production. Even in 'high-tech' organisations, manual systems of administration still exist alongside the electronic.

COMMUNICATIONS BY COMPUTER

Communications by and between computers will be increasingly important in business. Already, there are a range of applications. These include:

- ✪ **accessing electronic message networks using E-mail, for example;**

- ✪ **accessing information which may be stored remotely from the head and subsidiary offices – for example, bank branches consulting customers' accounts held on a mainframe possibly hundreds of miles away;**

- ✪ **accessing databanks of economic and trade information;**

- ✪ **an employee remotely updating company files when away from base;**

- ✪ **teleworking – for example, a journalist can send in copy to a newspaper from a portable computer; many other specialists can work from home.**

ACTIVITY

A Glasgow-based company employs a specialist who lives in Truro and works at home. List at least two advantages and two disadvantages of teleworking both for the individual and the company.

THE INTERNET

The **Internet** (short for international network of computers) originated in the USA in the 1970s when electronic links were formed between computers in the military and university sectors. Anyone with a computer, a modem, a telephone line and the appropriate software can access the Internet and communicate in **cyberspace**. By 1990, there were about two million users. The forecast is that there will be 200 million users by the end of this century. Internet really acts as a library – information can be put on-line on what are called 'sites' and users can access the datafiles.

ELECTRONIC DATA INTERCHANGE (EDI)

As speed and accuracy are essential to businesses, it is sensible to allow information (such as stock records, prices, finance proposals and manpower schedules) to be exchanged between organisations electronically. This reduces the scope for transmission errors. Information is exchanged by computers which can be linked using telephone lines. In order to make electronic data exchange work, **value-added data network services (VADS)** need to be added to the telecommunications network. These provide:

- ✪ **a means to enable terminals with differing speed of transmission rates (bits per second) to communicate;**

- ✪ **a method of conversion (effectively a computer 'handshake') enabling connection and communication between incompatible terminals;**

- ✪ **facilities for connection and message-routeing;**

- ✪ **facilities to enable messages to be stored for forwarding later;**

- ✪ **gateways to other databases and services.**

Many companies are dispersed not just within the UK but throughout Europe and the world. There is a need to maintain instantaneous communication. A telephone call is not sufficient to obtain the mass of information needed to make decisions. Electronic information exchange is the answer.

There is also a continuing need for efficiency. EDI allows the transfer of standard forms to be passed between computers of different organisations. This process bypasses postal services and fax, saves paper handling costs and makes better use of expensive time. EDI offers the prospect of a totally integrated business system when all organisations are linked via the **information superhighway**. Business can then be run with the minimum of personal contact.

EDI supports two new approaches to business administration: just-in-time methods and total customer responsiveness.

JUST IN TIME

Just in time (JIT) is a method of stock control in which little or no warehoused stock is kept within the company. Supplies are delivered 'just in time' for use. The advantages of just-in-time methods are:

- **fewer out of stock situations;**

- **lower inventory costs;**

- **reduction in staffing costs;**

- **reduction in lead order times;**

- **improved information about prices and product availability;**

- **greater accuracy in ordering procedures.**

TOTAL CUSTOMER RESPONSIVENESS

Electronic data interchange can stimulate the establishment of profitable partnerships between organisations in both vertical and horizontal directions. It offers firms the opportunity to develop more creative and effective ways of running business, generating new production and distribution systems for everything from handling raw materials to distributing finished goods and supplying commercial services. Some see this as the ultimate in organisational communications.

ELECTRONIC MESSAGING

The growth of electronic messaging systems has been encouraged by the rapid ownership of microcomputers for both personal and business use. There is, as a consequence, an ever increasing flow of information distributed in electronic form through a growing number of networks. There are many on-line systems that can be accessed over the telephone line. Some databases store financial and economic information, others will offer an up-to-the-minute news service.

A popular system is the **bulletin board**. This is the electronic equivalent of a noticeboard. It provides a convenient way of informing people about events, health and safety regulations, items for sale, etc. Many newspapers, especially the local free ones, have adopted the bulletin board approach; readers can send in their 'small ads' to dispose of a freezer or to offer gardening services. Electronic bulletin boards work on the same principle. They can contain advertisements and messages, and may stimulate the informal exchange of information.

YOU FORGOT THIS !

The advantages of these messaging or E-mail systems are:

⊗ **messages can be read and dealt with when convenient to the recipient;**

⊗ **the sender knows that contact is assured as, unlike with telephones, there are no unavailable or engaged lines;**

⊗ **they are cheaper than telephone calls;**

⊗ **messages or letters can be sent to a number of subscribers at the same time;**

⊗ **messages of any length and complexity can be sent;**

⊗ **a printed record is available to both sender and recipient;**

⊗ **a system can be protected by a password so that messages and other information can only be accessed by those subscribing to it.**

ACTIVITY

Directorate General XXIII of the European Commission is responsible for enterprise policy. It has recently introduced two initiatives:

⊗ **an information network called Euro-Info Centres;**
⊗ **the Business Co-operation Network (BC-NET).**

Obtain details of these networks. Explain how they operate and list the benefits for subscribers.

MOBILE COMMUNICATIONS

It is estimated that by the year 2000 there will be forty million users of mobile communications in the European Union. This figure will double by 2010 and, by then, 50 per cent of business people will have mobile telephones. Including cellular telephones, paging and private mobile radio, the current market is less than twenty million.

SPECIAL NEEDS

Business information systems need to take into account the needs of the disabled. Among the disabled are employees at all levels, and clients. If the disabled are to be involved in the process of communication then some arrangements must be made to accommodate their various difficulties.

VISUALLY HANDICAPPED

If a person's sight is very limited or even non-existent, he or she has to rely upon other senses, particularly touch. Obviously, the hands are used extensively and the degree of sensitivity increases from the palm to the fingertips, which are very touch sensitive. Louis Braille, himself blind at three, invented a system of writing based on six raised dots in various groupings or configurations. These are felt by the fingertips, enabling a blind person to read. Expert braille readers can read at the rate of 150-200 words per minute. Braille documentation can be very expensive to produce but advances in technology have opened up access to information sources for blind people.

SPEECH SYNTHESISERS

For people who have lost the power to speak naturally, technology has provided a valuable aid in the electronic voice or speech synthesiser. Perhaps the most famous person to use this equipment is Professor Stephen Hawking of Cambridge University (author of *A Brief History of Time*) who suffers from a wasting disease and is confined to a wheelchair. The synthesiser enables him to continue his research and teaching. He has a computer attached to his wheelchair and by pressing a switch in his hand he can select words from a series of menus on the screen. His 'voice' is produced by the synthesiser, albeit in an American accent. The programme can store his dialogue and can also be controlled by a switch operated by head or eye movement.

THE INFORMATION SOCIETY

The information society refers to the way in which our daily business and personal lives are being transformed by the continuing IT revolution. As we have discussed, the business world is well served with electronic networks and, as more advances are made in computerisation, it will be possible to install a global telecommunications facility bringing computing services and within the reach of the general public.

The medium will be the **information superhighway**. This will carry simultaneous transmission of data, sound and images at very high speed and the user or recipient will be able to choose whether to read, watch or listen to it.

Many applications are being considered. Below are just three of the potential benefits:

- ☼ **The creation of a world-wide electronic library will give every individual access to distance learning. This means that a UK student could gain a qualification by taking different modules selected from the world's universities.**

- ☼ **Business organisations will have access to expanded networks. These will, among other activities, encourage the exchange of commercial information, open up new market opportunities and enhance the efficiency of transnational payments.**

- ☼ **As the idea of the nine-to-five job becomes redundant, it is anticipated that there will be a growth in teleworking; more people will work from home or satellite offices and these locations can be anywhere in the world.**

PORTFOLIO ASSIGNMENT

You are to compile a report which investigates and analyses the internal and external communication in a business organisation.

First, select the organisation. This assignment demands much information and it is essential to choose a company or institution which is prepared to offer ready access to its communications systems. The approach must be flexible as it may be necessary to consult more than one organisation in order to collect all the evidence. If that is the case, make it clear in your report. You are advised to start with a familiar organisation such as your employer, school, college or local authority. Before you begin, consult the appropriate sections in the text and draw up your strategy.

The report needs to be divided into six sections which are identified by the specific tasks below.

1 Investigate three examples of internal and three external communication.

2 Analyse one example of internal and one external electronic communication. The examples should be considered in terms of their effectiveness in permitting access to information and encouraging interaction between people.

3 You should make two proposals for changes (or improvements) to the organisation's communications which should be justified in terms of their beneficial effects on the organisation.

4 Consider your proposals; explain two positive and two negative effects that the changes may bring about.

5 Define and explain the aims and objectives of your selected organisation.

6 Explain how this organisation uses communications to achieve its objectives.

Analyse information processing in a business organisation

INFORMATION PROCESSING

As we have discussed earlier in this unit, business is now approaching the **information age**. Organisations are investing large sums to produce systems capable of storing, retrieving, processing and communicating information. Information is now a very valuable commodity. Corporate information may be based on products, people or competitors. The effective use of information allows companies to understand their markets better and to become more efficient in supplying the products and services required. Information gives a firm a competitive edge over its rivals. Being able to predict future trends or accurately target potential customers will heavily influence the profitability of a company. The information sector is growing faster than the agricultural or manufacturing sectors, and is becoming ever more important in organisations.

In this section, we look at different types of information processing systems, analyse the effectiveness of information processing and explain the effects of the Data Protection Act on organisations and individuals.

THE PURPOSE OF INFORMATION PROCESSING

Information plays a key role in **decision making**. Companies need to respond rapidly to internal and external influences. Reports expressing changes in consumer preferences need feeding quickly through to the product design team. Changes in raw material costs must be evaluated by the finance department and acted upon. Before important company decisions are made, information will be gathered and processed to make sure that the correct actions are being taken.

It is important to **record historical information in an easily accessible form**. Companies store a range of historical information to assist in queries. This will include information for consumers, financial and personnel managers and shareholders. Information on customer purchasing may be required to generate mailing lists, last year's sales figures may be needed to evaluate advertising campaigns, or personnel records may be needed to calculate sick pay. This information needs to be stored in a form which can be quickly retrieved, and presented in the manner required.

Systems that improve information processing allow employees to **work more efficiently**. A well-organised filing cabinet allows a clerk to reduce the time spent looking for records. Similarly (low cost) cash-point machines allow (relatively expensive) bank staff to concentrate on dealing with customer queries.

Word processor, desk top publishing and spreadsheet packages allow companies to improve their presentation of written materials. This provides **more effective communication** to customers, managers and employees. Increasingly, more sophisticated applications are being used to convey large amounts of information. As we have seen, organisations are now making use of E-mail, video conferencing and multimedia information centres, all as an aid to improving communication.

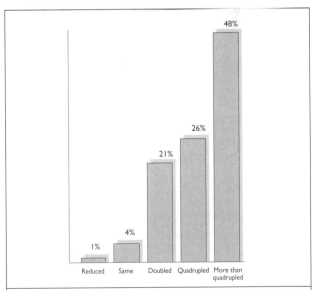

FIGURE 2.19: Growth of corporate information — executives report the extent to which information has grown over over the last decade. Source: Industrial Research Bureau for Reuters.

ACTIVITY

In groups of three or four, select one of the following areas of business activity:

- ⊗ hotel reception;
- ⊗ travel agent;
- ⊗ supermarket;
- ⊗ record store;
- ⊗ market research;
- ⊗ a large biscuit manufacturer's distribution centre;
- ⊗ a brewing process;
- ⊗ motor vehicle assembly line;
- ⊗ newspaper publisher;
- ⊗ fast-food store.

Identify and discuss those aspects of the activity where information technology is likely to have had a significant impact over the last five years in processing information.

THE PROCESS OF TRANSFERRING DATA INTO INFORMATION

Pages of unanalysed questionnaires are of little use to a company. They contain important data, but these data are not accessible. In their unprocessed form, it is difficult to extract useful and valuable information. The data – the small raw facts from which information comes – are themselves of little or no value. To give them shape, the data must be transferred into information. Whether using manual or computer-based systems, this is the purpose of **information processing**. This process can be broken down into four main components:

- ⊗ input;
- ⊗ process;
- ⊗ storage;
- ⊗ output.

INPUT

The first stage is to input the data into a manual or computer-based system. In manual systems, this may be achieved by filling out a record card in ink. A computer system may mean using an optical character reader to enter data such as multiple choice answers on exam papers. There are many methods of inputting data into a computer. Input methods include keyboard, mouse and touch screen entry, as well as the more sophisticated methods such as **optical character recognition (OCR)** and **optical mark recognition (OMR)**. These last two methods are put to good effect in the Post Office to speed up the process of reading addresses on letters.

PROCESS

To transform data into information, they must be processed. This may involve collating all the pieces of data about one person, or making calculations on the figures entered. Processing involves changing the data so that they are ordered and related. The amount of processing depends upon the type of data being input and the required output. A printed train timetable contains information on arrival and departure times. Data have been inputted and processed so that passengers can quickly look up train times.

STORAGE

Though not strictly a part of processing, storing the information allows there to be a time difference between data being entered and information being supplied. A filing cabinet acts as a manual storage device. Similarly a hard disk drive fulfils the same function within a computer system. By using a storage system, the data can be processed and then output many times at later dates.

OUTPUT

The purpose of processing information is to provide some form of output. This may be a summary table printed on a piece of paper, a figure displayed on a computer screen or a movement in a gauge. It is important that this output is in the form required by the user so that he or she can act upon it. With any system, there must always be some form of feedback to ensure that the information being produced is that which is required.

Once we have the information, we can analyse it and make informed decisions based upon it. After reading a train timetable, for example, the analysis may be that the train has already left, and the decision may be to go home.

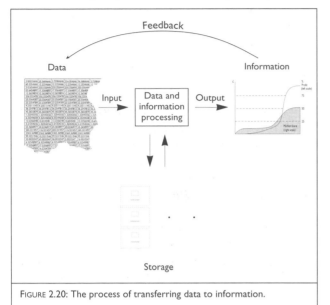

FIGURE 2.20: The process of transferring data to information.

WHO REQUIRES INFORMATION?

All departments, and all employees within departments, require information. This information may be anything from the price of an item in stock to the frequency of sales in summer compared to winter. However, although all departments may be accessing the same information, they are likely to be analysing it in different ways. The finance department will be more interested in costs and prices, whereas the marketing department may require product information on colours and sizes. It is important for all departments to have available the information they require in order to make important decisions.

At an **operational level**, organisations need to respond rapidly to daily issues. Shop assistants need to be able to give basic product information, determine which items are in stock and give prices for products. Secretaries may need to update customer details, produce well-presented letters and log incoming calls. All companies process information at an operational level each day. Without this information, many organisations would become inefficient in daily tasks.

In order to make longer-term decisions at a **strategic level**, managers and directors need to have important **performance indicators**. These may include current staff to capital ratios, sales forecasts or average sales by region. By analysing this information, senior managers and directors can make informed decisions on whether to build a new production plant, raise prices or increase capital expenditure. Without appropriate information,

they will be far less certain that decisions taken are in the best interest of the organisation.

ACTIVITY

1 Obtain the annual reports and accounts of at least three large public limited companies. You may be able to use material collected for activities you undertook earlier in this unit.

2 Cut out figures and tables containing information. Paste these onto a sheet of paper and beneath each one describe:

  (a) what the information refers to;
  (b) how it was collected and might have been processed;
  (c) the significance of the information;
  (d) why it is important and who in particular would have been interested in it.

THE REQUIREMENTS OF INFORMATION

Information is incredibly valuable to all companies. Without information, organisations will not be able to function to their full ability. Though information required may vary by department and by level of the operator within the department, there are several common requirements of all information.

Information must be **up to date**. A 1991 train timetable is worthless. The more up to date the information is, the more value it has. How recent the information needs to be depends on its use. Airline booking systems work in real-time, so their information must be accurate to the second. Here the information rapidly goes out of date. By comparison, a telephone directory system may only be updated yearly. Its value declines at a slower rate. In either case, the information must be current for its purpose.

Information must be **accurate**. Inaccurate information is worse than no information. For example, most people would prefer you told them that you do not know the time of the next train, rather than be given an incorrect time.

Information needs to be **relevant** to the task in hand. The same data may be required by different departments which each need to extract the information relevant to them. Irrelevant information requires more processing. It may be better to hold just important billing details on customers rather than to keep huge files containing information about past purchases, payment methods and other unrelated details. This way the information you require is much easier to access, and the cost of processing it will be reduced.

Only authorised personnel should have access to information. Valuable information should be **secure**. If a company has spent a considerable amount of money obtaining data, it would not wish them to be accidentally changed by an employee, nor would it wish its competitors to receive this information for free. Information should also be secure from fire, theft and (accidental and deliberate) damage.

Information is only of use if you can retrieve it when and where you require it. It needs to be **readily available**. It is important that train timetables are available at the station, and that the ticket operators can look up train connections while you wait.

THE TYPES OF INFORMATION SYSTEMS

Information systems come in various forms. At the basic level, you are processing information when you enter a new name in your address book or look up the telephone number of a relative. At the other end of the spectrum, there are systems which constantly monitor their environment and adapt under different circumstances. Submarine control systems take in direction headings and water pressure as inputs and feedback appropriate information to their operators. This ranges from position data through to engine tolerance levels. The submarine operators then make decisions using this information.

In any large organisation you will find text, number and graphic-based processing systems. There are a range of systems even in the most unlikely organisations. When you spend an evening in a disco or club, there are many information processing systems involved. Your leaflet will have been produced on a word processor or a graphics package. The takings at the bar will be processed by a spreadsheet, and there will even be a system to send output to the lights based on the music input received.

ACTIVITY

Choose a large bank or building society and assume that you have an account with it along with a cash-point card.

1 List the banks and building societies which accept your card.

2 Identify the number of different cash-point machines, within your town or shopping centre, that accept your card.

3 Apart from being able to withdraw money, what other facilities are available from the machines?

4 Why do some cash machines have the facility to operate in several foreign languages?

5 Draw a flow diagram showing what happens to the information once money is withdrawn from a cash-point machine.

6 Give one reason why cash machines should give bank details which are:

⊗ up to date;

⊗ accurate;

⊗ relevant;

⊗ secure;

⊗ readily available.

MANUAL SYSTEMS

Manual systems are operated by hand without the aid of a computer. For example, a filing clerk receives information, sorts it and places it in the correct file in a cabinet. Similarly, the clerk retrieves appropriate information from the cabinet. Though manual, this is still information processing. In any organisation there are considerable number of these types of systems. Manual systems tend to have the advantage of judgement and flexibility, however they are more prone to errors. We have all lost a friend's telephone number because we have not placed it correctly in our address book. A personal secretary to a managing director keeps the appointments diary; here, it is vital that an important client can fit into a tight schedule. A good personal assistant may be able to 'squeeze in' a brief meeting or delay a 'less important' appointment. A computer in a similar situation is unlikely to be able to make such allowances.

SINGLE-PURPOSE SYSTEMS

Single-purpose systems are introduced with the aim of targeting one function within an organisation. A computer is used to complete that function more efficiently. The single-purpose system only stores information relevant to that function or task. Examples of single-purpose systems are word processors, cash-point machines and loan repayment devices. In each of these examples, the system carries out one function only – to process words, to process account requests and to detail loan repayments to customers, respectively.

MULTI-PURPOSE SYSTEMS

Multi-purpose systems carry out a variety of functions. They may take data from many sources and process information for many different requirements. The system itself has more than one purpose. Unlike a cash-point machine which has the single purpose of processing individual account requests, the computer terminal inside the bank is able to process many different information requests. It is able to retrieve personal details about customers, list all accounts overdrawn and produce summaries showing the cash flow or transactions for that day. Different people within the organisation access the system, but for different purposes. The cashier uses it to verify your identity, while the manager uses it to analyse your banking record and make loan decisions based on this information. Multi-purpose systems are more expensive and require a greater amount of security than single-purpose systems.

MULTI-TASKING SYSTEMS

Multi-tasking systems carry out more than one task at the same time. If you can hold a conversation while you make a cup of tea, you are **multi-tasking**. You are carrying out two functions at the same time. If a computer must stop what it is doing to carry out a second task it will be multi-purpose. If, however, it can carry out a second request and continue with the first it is multi-tasking. An aircraft's navigation system must be multi-tasking. It must not stop monitoring the plane's altitude whenever the air temperature is required. It will carry out the two requests together. Many computer systems are now multi-tasking. Windows 95 and OS/2 Warp can both carry out more than one task at the same time. Using these systems, you can carry out a spell check while a spreadsheet is being recalculated in the background. Multi-tasking systems enable users to become much more efficient. Instead of waiting for a task to be completed they can carry on with another job. Their time is used much more efficiently.

ACTIVITY

Bainbridge & Anderson is a busy doctor's practice with over 6,000 patients. Currently every patient has their own record card and associated file. Each of these is stored in one of five filing cabinets. At the surgery there is one full-time and one part-time receptionist. Each doctor has an appointment book as well as a list of clients requiring home visits.

1   What would be the advantages of computerising the information systems within the surgery to:

   (a) the doctor;

   (b) the patients;

   (c) the receptionist;

   (d) the overall operation of the surgery.

2   How would a multi-purpose system enable the doctors and receptionist to work more efficiently?

THE EFFECTIVENESS OF INFORMATION PROCESSING

The process of transferring data into information is a costly one. It may involve questionnaires, manual data entry into a computer system and expensive data processing before it is of value to a company. It is important that the **benefits** of the information outweigh the **costs** involved in acquiring and processing it. There are many ways of processing the same information. Organisations must choose the most effective system, in terms of **speed**, **value for money**, **reliability** and **security**. Some video rental stores take your details and manually enter them onto a record card. Your record is updated by hand each time you rent a video. Other stores enter your details into a computer database that effectively mimics the manual process. The newer, and more sophisticated, information systems link up to other services. With these stores, your post code is sufficient to provide your address for the system. If you return a video late, the system automatically bills you. The system also monitors the frequency of your visits and possibly the types of videos you rent. All of these different systems achieve the same goal of supporting a video rental business. Some methods are more appropriate than others at processing the same information. Organisations need to consider carefully several factors before choosing the most effective method for processing data.

FITNESS FOR PURPOSE

The first factor is whether the method can deliver the required information within given **specifications**. A new travel agency would set certain targets such as accuracy of information, time limits for enquiries and levels of detail required. A manual system is very unlikely to meet these specifications.

The second factor is whether the information output from the system is in a **usable form**. A system analysing questionnaires must produce information which directly helps decision making. A company conducting market research on beauty products needs the output in a form which provides objective information such as the price consumers are willing to pay or the number of hair products purchased in one month.

Systems which provide information which can be interpreted in several ways are of far less value. If a system is processing results from a fruit survey, you might draw from this that a hair care product should have the same smell as the most popular fruit. This would be one subjective interpretation. Another might be that sweet, sickly smells are more popular to eat, but sharp, clean smells are preferable for a shampoo. To be fit for the purpose required, systems are usually expected to give **objective information**: if information remains open to subjective interpretations, a company is left with a series of unanswered questions requiring further data processing or more research.

EFFICIENCY

Typically, a computer can work many times faster than a human being. Computers like repetitive tasks, require no breaks and are totally accurate. Provided you can feed the information into a computer as fast as it can process it, a computer can be very efficient. After being 'taught' how to sort a list, or group data, it is able to repeat this task indefinitely. The efficiency of a system may be measured by the quantity of facts and figures retrieved in a time period or by the time it takes to retrieve a piece of information. With either measure, the efficiency must also take into account the cost of such processing as well as how quickly a new user can operate such a system.

Doonesbury

BY GARRY TRUDEAU

INFORMATION RETENTION

Where a human may forget a piece of information, a computer will not. It is able to store innumerable pieces of information and still be able to access the relevant data. However, a computer may become corrupt or lose data because of a **computer virus**. A filing cabinet has no such drawback. Organisations must take into account the quantity of data and the length of time that it will be stored.

SECURITY

Just as an office can be broken in to, so can a computer system. Many personal computers are not adequately protected from thieves or from intruders wishing to gain information. It is important that, whatever system is used, the information held is evaluated and appropriate security measures are taken to ensure that it is kept safe. With manual systems, fireproof safes should be used and locks placed on doors. With computerised systems, virus and password protection should be in place.

COST

A manual system is inexpensive to set up. It has fairly constant running costs. The cost of setting up a manual telephone directory system is likely to be approximately one day's training and the hourly rate for the operator from that point on. Being a manual system, the member of staff is only able to deal with a limited number of enquiries. If the volume of enquiries increases, then another operator will need to be placed on call, generating similar costs. For small volumes of processing, manual systems offer a flexible, cheap solution.

For larger quantities of processing, a computer may be more cost effective. There is a cost involved in starting up computer systems, of which staff training can be a high proportion. For this reason, increased quantities of data

must be processed before a computer system becomes economical. A computer system, however, is likely to be equally happy handling ten requests as it is handling a hundred. Within most organisations, there is a point at which a computer becomes more cost effective than a human at the same task. Depending on the requirements, single-purpose, multi-purpose or multi-tasking systems may be used, but the cost implications associated with each should be taken into account.

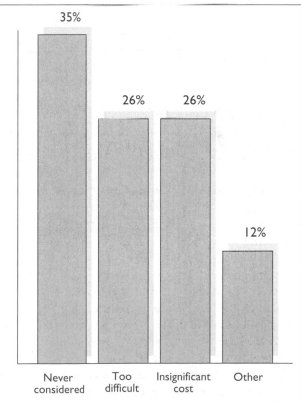

FIGURE 2.21: Why companies do not track the costs of computer-based information systems.
Source: Industrial Research Bureau for Reuters.

THE EFFECTS ON INDIVIDUALS AND BUSINESSES

The rapid progress in information processing has affected businesses and individuals alike. There has been a change in the structure of many countries' economies and output. Historically, the dependence on agriculture was followed by the dominance of industrial output. Increasingly, it is the service and information sector which is growing. Whole businesses have sprung up based on the sale of accurate, relevant information.

ORGANISATIONS

The information revolution has given organisations access to information which is more detailed, reliable and accurate than previously available. Complex management information systems allow well-informed decisions to be made, based on comprehensive and up-to-date information. Systems are available which allow tasks to be performed in a fraction of the time that it previously took, with total accuracy and near perfect reliability. Organisations are adopting a variety of these systems at all levels to improve efficiency and maintain a competitive advantage.

As well as allowing organisations to use this information for their own purposes, companies can manipulate information, and sell it on to other companies. If you enter a competition for a hi-fi system, you might later receive a string of other 'offers' ranging from compact discs to holidays. Once an organisation has information on a target group of customers, it becomes valuable to other companies with a similar market. The speed of computers and the ease with which information can be manipulated has led to a growth in **information sale and exchange**.

In order to take advantage of these improvements, organisations have had to invest in sophisticated equipment and communication lines. In many cases, the structure of the organisation has changed to reflect the increased importance of information. Where supermarkets previously had a high percentage of staff pricing and ordering stock, information systems now automatically take care of this. This equipment, and the training which must accompany it, needs to be regularly updated to ensure that the competitive edge remains.

As companies invest in new technology, they must also meet the associated costs. Old and new systems may be incompatible. Data must be converted across, printers re-configured, and new communications cables laid. Staff will require training to use the new system effectively and

security measures must be put in place to prevent the loss or theft of data. Often newer, more sophisticated, systems are introduced into competing companies only one year after the installation of the previous system. Organisations must then decide whether to follow suit or wait for the next generation of information developments.

INDIVIDUALS

The skills required by employers have changed over time because of the changing structure of the economy. Previously, workers may have based an entire career on a single skill or trade. They are now expected to have a **broad range of skills and experiences**. The increased use of computers has led to many repetitive jobs being undertaken by machines, while employees now deal more with the data entering and leaving these systems. As a result, working conditions have improved and employment opportunities for disabled or part-time workers have risen. Many jobs are office based, requiring less physical effort. As systems continue to develop, so employees will be required to adapt quickly. This has large training implications. The opportunities for computer operators, and those with associated skills, have increased, and this is likely to continue as the value of information increases. The main negative effect of these developments is the increase in computer-associated health problems. **Repetitive strain injury (RSI)** from keyboards, headache and eye strain from monitors, as well as a general rise in stress levels from equipment malfunctions, have all affected employees' health.

ACTIVITY

Read the article on data transfers opposite. Then answer the following questions.

1 Before the new system was introduced, what information might newspaper retailers send to Associated Newspapers?

2 How might the introduction of the system have 'paid for itself twice over since last July'?

3 What are some of the hidden costs in installing such a system?

4 How could the system develop in the next five years?

Data transfers make the news

ASSOCIATED Newspapers has just completed one of the UK's most ambitious electronic data transfer networks, processing newspaper sales and returns information from more than 55,000 retailers across the country.

The company claims that the system, which was completed last month, has already paid for itself twice over since last July, when the first information started flowing across it.

Associated is the first company to make full use of the national retail information network set up by Newpet, an electronic trade committee made up of newspaper and magazine publishers and their wholesalers. Under the system each wholesaler uploads information to each publisher detailing the number of papers sold and the number returned from each retailer it supplies.

Associated is processing this information and feeding its regional sales reps data on the retailers in their areas.

'The aim is to reduce returns and increase the availability of papers,' said Michael Jones, Associated's IT director. 'We have already achieved a 200 per cent payback in one year.'

The information is stored at Associated Newspapers in a database running on Digital Alpha servers. The largest wholesalers send information direct to the company, while smaller ones use value added networks or simply dial in over the public phone system. Sales reps can dial into the database from their laptops to download the latest figures.

Jones said the system, which has allocated a unique identifying number to every newsagent in the country, could be expanded beyond newspapers. 'Other groups are already applying to use the numbers,' he said, 'including confectionery firms.'

Computer Weekly, 8 June 1995

THE DATA PROTECTION ACT 1984

Systems which process data have become increasingly sophisticated over time. Analysing and transferring data has become much more cost effective. The **Data Protection Act** was introduced with the aim of preventing people abusing personal data held on computers. Any organisation, whether in the public or private sector, must register details of data held on individuals with the **Data Protection Registrar (DPR)** and adhere to the eight principles of the Act. Some information is excluded under the legislation, including data held by sports clubs and data held by individuals for personal use. These few exceptions aside, all organisations holding personal data on computer must pay the £75 registration fee and obey the principles. Organisations failing to comply face a maximum fine of £5,000.

THE EIGHT PRINCIPLES OF THE DATA PROTECTION ACT

THE DATA SHOULD BE OBTAINED AND PROCESSED FAIRLY AND LAWFULLY

It is important that a person should know that the information they are giving is being held on computer. There should be no deception involved and they should be made aware of the reason for the data being held. It would be unfair (and unlawful) to obtain personal information from an unregistered source.

THE DATA SHOULD BE HELD ONLY FOR SPECIFIED PURPOSES

Data can only be held for purposes which are registered with the Registrar. If for example, the doctors' practice Bainbridge & Anderson wishes to hold data relating to its employees for accounting and personnel reasons, it must register this use.

THE DATA SHOULD NOT BE USED OR GIVEN FOR OTHER PURPOSES

This principle focuses on not using the data outside of the purpose for which it has been registered. This includes giving the data to third parties. Bainbridge & Anderson would not legally be allowed to pass employees' details to an insurance firm as this purpose was not registered.

THE DATA HELD MUST BE RELEVANT AND NOT EXCESSIVE

It is important that a company holding computerised information does not record more information than is strictly required for its intended purpose. Similarly, they should not hold irrelevant information. It would be legal for a garage to hold customer information regarding recent repairs and the make and model of the car. They would have no reason to include the age of customers or their credit card number in customer files. This would be illegal as the information is both irrelevant and excessive for the purpose of keeping customer purchase records.

THE DATA SHOULD BE ACCURATE AND (WHERE NECESSARY) UP TO DATE

Inaccurate information is irrelevant. More important to the individual is that it may be harmful. An individual's ability to borrow money for a car or holiday is likely to be based on his or her credit rating. If this information is not correct, then credit requests will be refused, or inappropriate limits will be set.

SECURITY MEASURES MUST BE TAKEN TO PREVENT UNAUTHORISED ACCESS TO THE INFORMATION

Organisations must take precautions to prevent unauthorised access to personal information. This will involve physical barriers as well as digital methods. Information, and the computers on which they are stored, should be in a locked room. Any back-ups, disks or printouts of the data should also be locked away. If the information is available on a network of machines, adequate password protection should be in place, so that only authorised personnel may gain access to the information.

'A London-based design company, worried about the dangers of fire, stored all of its valuable information archives in a fireproof safe. The fire never came but thieves did and the only item they stole was the safe.'
The Times, 3 March 1995

THE DATA SHOULD NOT BE KEPT LONGER THAN IS NECESSARY

If there is no need to keep data after a certain period, the organisation should destroy that information. It would not be necessary to keep personal information on employees after they have left the organisation. These records should be destroyed soon after employees leave.

INDIVIDUALS ARE ALLOWED TO ACCESS AND (WHERE APPROPRIATE) CORRECT DATA HELD ON THEM

The Data Protection Act gives provision for any member of the public to find out what information is held on computer about them. An organisation is required to give this information within forty days, though may charge a small administration fee (of up to £10). The individual is then provided with a printout of all the information. If information is inaccurate, the individual can request that the data be changed, or where appropriate deleted.

ACTIVITY

In groups of three or four, discuss why computers have made it necessary to have a Data Protection Act. During the discussion, consider the following issues:

- ⊗ speed of processing;
- ⊗ cross-referencing;
- ⊗ analysis tools;
- ⊗ cost of replicating data.

Discuss why some organisations may still not have registered under the Act, despite it being on the statute books for more than ten years.

THE IMPLICATIONS OF THE DATA PROTECTION ACT

FOR THE INDIVIDUAL

The Data Protection Act has given individuals the ability to find out what information is being stored on them by any organisation. It gives them the ability to correct inaccurate information and to remove their details from computer systems where the information is no longer required or where the company does not have the right to hold such information. Under the Data Protection Act, an individual's information is secure from being used for purposes not registered with the Data Protection Registrar.

FOR ORGANISATIONS

The Data Protection Act has forced organisations to look much more closely at the information they are storing on computers. Previously, there was no structure or procedure; now, companies can no longer keep unnecessary computer files about individuals. They must manage this information responsibly. Records must be kept up to date, must be accurate and security devices must be in place to prevent unauthorised access. Although this has ensured that the information a company holds is more valuable, it has placed a large financial burden upon business. It is not uncommon for an organisation to have a data protection officer to monitor compliance with the Act and to deal with requests from individuals. If an organisation fails to register data, or does not comply with any of the eight principles, it can be fined a maximum of £5,000.

LATEST DEVELOPMENTS IN DATA PROCESSING

The methods used to process data are constantly developing. More sophisticated analytical tools, along with increased computing power are providing organisations with information which allows them to focus their activities more effectively.

DATA WAREHOUSING AND DATA MINING

Many organisations now hold data from a wide variety of sources. By creating **data warehouses** of information, they can react far more easily to new patterns and can use analytical tools to provide more information than just past sales. For example, while existing records may only be able to provide details of sales of ice cream in the previous year, the data warehousing approach would be able to put this information together with weather forecasts, consumer preferences and any other information available to the organisation. This warehouse of information can then be analysed to provide predictions. These analytical tools can sift through the data effectively. They are more complicated and, therefore, expensive but the results can be quite astounding. For example, using **data mining techniques** to find patterns might show a company that sales of fast food are linked to sales of video rentals. This may lead to joint marketing campaigns targeting this group of people.

GROUPWARE

Packages are being developed to allow employees to share information more easily within their work group. This includes documents, figures, diaries and databases. The team may be spread throughout a building, or across several countries. The software allows these individuals to work together on the same project, as if they are sharing the same machine. All of the group are able to work on their individual areas, but can then easily tie in their work with that of their colleagues. This flow of information between users provides each with a clearer view of how their input fits in with the whole team.

THE INTERNET AND DATA PROCESSING

One of the fastest growing areas of information is the **Internet**. This interconnection of thousands of computers unleashes quantities of data which are almost limitless. The data on the network covers everything from products and services through to educational establishments and even transcripts of court hearings. It is now possible to call up the weather in any country, receive copies of today's newspaper articles as well as search for specific information.

The data on this network, though freely available, is often in a very raw state. Data about drinking habits may be scattered across continents, and within these continents may be found on hundreds of different computers. In this state, the data may be of no use to Coca-Cola or Cadbury Schweppes. For organisations to fully utilise the available data, very powerful information processing and data retrieval engines need to be created. These will collect, process, and report on relevant data from around the world. Once this information source is tapped, organisations will be even better placed to make global decisions.

PORTFOLIO ASSIGNMENT

1 Arrange to visit a local organisation with a view to investigating the information processing taking place within one particular aspect of the organisation such as finance, marketing or production.

2 Find out what systems there are for numbers, text and graphics within this area and look at the efficiency of these systems.

3 Produce a brief report which explains the information processing taking place. Ensure your report includes the following:
(a) how the information is received;
(b) how it is entered into the system;
(c) what format the information is in;
(d) what information is retrieved from the system;
(e) who the information is given to;
(f) what actions are taken after this person receives the information.

4 How could any of the systems be improved upon?

5 Outline how the organisation has responded to the Data Protection Act.

6 Explain the relevance of the Act to the area you have investigated.

Marketing

CONTENTS

OUTLINE

This unit introduces the major principles which underpin marketing, namely the anticipation of market needs and opportunities; the satisfaction of consumer expectations; the maximisation of benefits to the organization, including income generation and/or profits; managing the effects of change and competition; the coordination of activities to achieve marketing aims; making use of technological developments; and enhancing the perception of the organization, product or service by consumers. Implementing these principles involves marketing research, effective communications, and sales and customer service. Each of these is the subject of an element in the unit.

Principles and functions of marketing

Marketing is the management process of identifying, anticipating and satisfying consumer requirements in such a way as to yield a profit, while also encouraging consumers to make further purchases and to recommend the products and services of the organisation.

This means that those responsible for marketing within an organisation need to be able to identify the needs of their potential customers. It is also necessary to be able to anticipate those future trends and developments which could influence customers' requirements; for example, a furniture warehouse would need to increase its stock in anticipation of an upturn in the housing market.

Marketing also involves constantly reviewing all aspects of a product or service in order to ensure that it continues to satisfy the potential customer's requirements. This means having the right product or service, at the right price, and it being on sale at the right time and place. Only when all these factors have been satisfied is it likely that a private sector organisation will be able to make a profit or a public sector organisation or charity be effective in meeting its objectives. Ultimately, an organisation can claim that its marketing is successful when consumers make repeat purchases or are prepared to make recommendations about the organisation's products or services.

OBJECTIVES

The primary aim of marketing is to ensure that consumers buy products or services. However, the ways in which marketing is carried out vary enormously between organisations according to their size and the nature of their products or services. In a small business, the marketing role may be carried out by a single person. Many sole traders have to make marketing decisions, along with other business decisions, in areas such as purchasing, production and finance. In the case of a one-person mobile hot dog stall, the owner has to purchase supplies and equipment, cook the product and control the financing of the operation, as well as make all the marketing decisions. These will include deciding on the most important features of the product for target consumers in terms of type and size of roll, sausage and sauces; how much should be charged; where the mobile unit should be located; and how the business should be promoted through, say, signs by the roadside or advertising.

In a much larger organisation there may be specialists responsible for each part of the marketing operation. *Fig. 3.1* shows how marketing could be organised in a business which has markets at home and abroad.

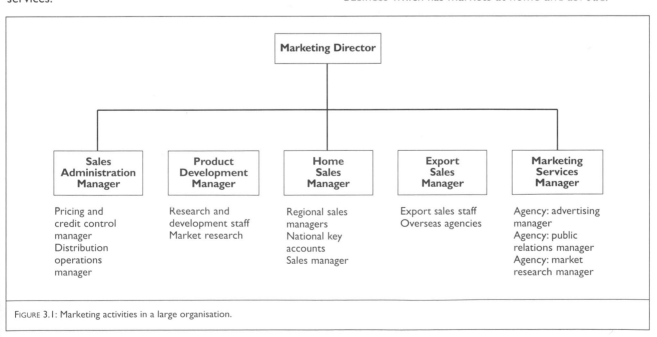

FIGURE 3.1: Marketing activities in a large organisation.

The most important domestic customers would be handled by a special key account manager. Some of the work connected with market research, public relations and advertising could be handled by outside agencies.

Hovever the marketing operation is organised, it must be well co-ordinated and have well-defined lines of communication with other departments. If this is not the case, there is always a danger that problems will arise in terms of production, purchasing and finance. Costly errors may be made about levels of production and the purchasing of raw materials and components, upsetting financial planning.

The way in which marketing activities are carried out within an organisation varies according to whether it is **product-oriented** or **customer-oriented**. In a product-oriented organisation, there may be an assumption by those working in the organisation that the existing range of products or services is the best on the market and that sales will follow automatically, so there is no need for product change or modification. Such a complacent view can lead to the downfall of an organisation if it is operating in a rapidly changing business environment. For example, some companies producing towelling nappies were badly caught out by the introduction of the paper-based disposable nappy. A customer-oriented organisation, on the other hand, is in a constant state of change, assessing, monitoring and responding to changes in the market. It will have a highly developed marketing strategy, which acknowledges and is sensitive to its customers' changing needs and wants. It will strive to find out what customers want, what causes them to buy products, and what the product or service really means to them as consumers. From the top down, the organisation and all its decision makers will be market led, recognising that tomorrow's profitability depends upon meeting today's needs.

This means taking a 'whole company' approach towards marketing, as is demonstrated in the Kwik-Fit article, opposite.

FIGURE 3.2: Marketing objectives.

(Marketing objectives diagram:)
- Achieve a target level of sales
- Expand sales revenue to a specified level
- Increase market share
- Enter new markets
- Achieve an overall specified level of profit

KWIK-FIT

From the very beginning, Kwik-Fit aimed to give its customers the benefits they really wanted – fast service, quality products and competitive prices.

Chairman Tom Farmer says that success is due to getting results in five key areas, called 'The Kwik-Fit System'. The system highlights several aspects of good marketing practice: identifying and responding to current and future motoring needs; developing specialist repair and replacement outfits; well-trained and highly-motivated staff; sophisticated computer systems and management support; and a distinctive a high-profile brand image.

Kwik-Fit's ability to identify and expl trends in its markets is illustrated by its Ch Safety Scheme, encouraging the fitting child safety seats in cars and, more recent the supply of child cycle helmets.

Staff training receives considerab investment – £2.5m last year. All servi centre staff are trained in customer service well as technical skills. The bold claim, 'Yc can't get better than a Kwik-Fit fitter', deliberately made to give staff something live up to. It's not just a TV advertising sloga it's emblazoned on the overalls of staff. 'T the public, "You can't get better than a Kwik Fit fitter" is an advertising slogan,' says Tor Farmer. 'To us, it's a philosophy.'

The customer, however, remains at th centre of the company's focus. To quote Tor Farmer: 'We aren't interested in satisfie customers. We want delighted customers.'

Marketing: the way forward
Department of Trade and Industry, 1992

Within the customer-oriented organisation, marketing features prominently in overall planning. Any market plan will be based on the strategic plan of the organisation and will be run and controlled by the systems operating within the organisation. Consequently, the objectives behind marketing activities are determined by the overall objectives of the business organisation of which there may be several (see *Fig. 3.2*).

Unfortunately, both marketing and strategic objectives may conflict with the needs of customers, who generally want:

- **high-quality goods and services;**
- **low prices;**
- **an adequate choice;**
- **an efficient and convenient system of distribution;**
- **imaginatively presented and detailed information about the products and services; and**
- **a rapid response to any changes in technology.**

Many of these factors are quite expensive to provide in terms of changes in an organisation's production methods and standards of service and this may have an adverse effect on the organisation's ability to maintain its productivity and, ultimately, its profitability.

In order to achieve its overall objectives, a non-profit making organisation, such as a charity or voluntary body, also has to pay attention to marketing and the achievement of high standards of customer (or member) care. For example, in 1994, the Royal Society for the Protection of Birds (RSPB) had a total income of over £30m and membership of around one million. The major objective of the RSPB is the conservation of wild birds and the preservation of the environment on which they depend. This involves the organisation in six major activities: research, education, advice, campaigning, the management of nature reserves and specific measures to protect birds. The RSPB's success in these areas depends on its ability

ACTIVITY

McFacts

- McDonald's has over 16,000 restaurants in at least 83 countries, serving more than 28m people each day.

- There are more than 600 McDonald's restaurants in the United Kingdom, serving 1.5m customers each day. The number of restaurants is expected to double by the end of the year 2000.

- McDonald's UK sales in 1994 were £720m. Globally, McDonald's sales reached over US $25bn. The average UK customer spends £2.99 per visit to McDonald's.

- In 1994, McDonald's UK customers consumed 42,000 tonnes of French fries, 5.5m gallons of milk and 335m hamburger buns.

- The world's busiest McDonald's is on Red Square in Moscow, serving as many as 50,000 people each day.

- Since 1955, when McDonald's first restaurant opened in suburban Chicago, McDonald's has sold over 100bn hamburgers.

- By the end of 1994, more than 60,000 people had received training at McDonald's Hamburger University in East Finchley, London, or at one of two regional training centres.

- McDonald's 'Golden Arches' is the second most recognised brand in the world. McDonald's proudly serves the best known brand in the world, Coca-Cola!

Study the McFacts above. Discuss whether you think that McDonald's success has been due to a product-oriented or customer-oriented approach towards marketing. Also, identify what you consider to be its major marketing objectives.

to market itself in order to attract income from membership subscriptions, legacies, fundraising, business support, charitable trusts, films, consultancy, grants and rents. This can only be achieved by the organisation being member-oriented, constantly monitoring and reflecting members' needs in terms of the facilities available on nature reserves, the types of publications and films produced, and by setting the membership fee at a level sufficient both to provide the required income and to sustain membership numbers.

PRODUCT, PRICE, PLACE AND PROMOTION

The ingredients of marketing are known as the **'Four Ps'**. They involve matching the product to consumer needs, determining the price, deciding where and how the product or service should be placed (distributed) in the market and promoting it through publicity, advertising and sales techniques. The marketing department will develop an appropriate marketing strategy which involves identifying the most important components of the marketing operation, so as to determine the best **marketing mix** of the 'Four Ps' for its target market.

The market has to be targeted because it is unlikely that an organisation can, or wants to, provide a range of products or services with sufficient variation to satisfy all customers. In **targeting**, the organisation should conduct detailed market research into the characteristics of its potential customers including their socio-economic class, age, household type, gender, personal values and geographical location. This information will allow the organisation to divide the market into groups or **segments**. The organisation should target the segment of the market that offers the best prospects for it to achieve its objectives. By targeting in this way, it is possible for the organisation to develop a marketing mix which satisfies the needs of a clearly defined set of customers.

PRODUCT

When designing a strategy for a product, it is important to identify precisely what is being purchased in terms of benefits and how these help to satisfy a particular need. This means that it is essential to be clear as to exactly what the product provides. For example, Theodore Levitt, a leading figure in marketing in the USA in the 1960s, identified the fact that nobody buys drills: they buy the ability to make holes, which means that if a more efficient and cost-effective way of making holes became available

people would turn to it. In fact, a product or service may provide satisfaction at three levels (see *Fig. 3.3*).

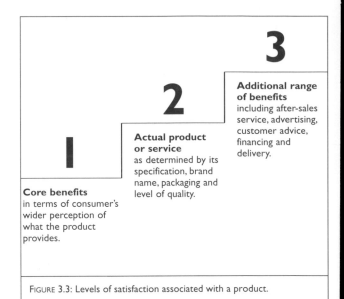

FIGURE 3.3: Levels of satisfaction associated with a product.

These levels may be applied to products sold by, for example, the Body Shop. In this case, the **core benefits** might be viewed in terms of buying natural products which make the consumer feel 'at one' with nature as they are made from ingredients which do not damage the environment or infringe animal 'rights'. The actual products are created through extensive laboratory research. They are of high quality, are associated with an internationally known brand name and are sold in a range of sizes with the minimum of packaging. The additional benefits associated with the Body Shop's products are in terms of the advice sheets which are available in the shops, the product knowledge of the staff, the recycling of containers, and the fact that, through purchasing a product, consumers feel that they are supporting a human or animal 'rights' project or action which is beneficial to the environment.

When developing a product, a marketing department must identify the three levels of satisfaction and then design a strategy that allows them to be achieved. This includes consideration of issues concerning branding, packaging, labelling and the development of a range of products to cover all the stages of a product life cycle.

Branding helps to identify a product and differentiate it from those of competitors. It is used to establish consumer loyalty and, in so doing, makes demand more price inelastic. It also can convey a feeling of quality and reliability. For example, the name of Heinz is known by most consumers. They associate it with high-quality food products, for which they are probably prepared to pay slightly more.

In certain cases, manufacturers may sell into different segments of the market under a variety of brand names.

Unilever sells washing detergents under the names of Persil, Surf, Radion, Wisk, Lux and Stergene. The ultimate success in branding is when the brand name becomes associated with the brand category, as with Levi's jeans and Kleenex tissues.

Packaging can combine with branding to differentiate the product. It also helps to attract attention, describe the product and, ultimately, make the sale. A more affluent consumer is prepared to pay for the convenience, appearance, dependability and prestige that are communicated through better packaging. This is especially true in the case of expensive cosmetics and confectionery.

Labelling contributes to the perceived quality of the packaging and, ultimately, the product. This is because it helps to identify the product type and the brand clearly. It might also grade the product, describe its features and provide promotion through suitable graphics; and it can add further value to the product by providing information on its usage.

The packaging prodigies

THERE'S a revolution brewing in the tinned food market and it's going to change the lives, we are told, of the millions of consumers who regularly battle with a can-opener and a tin.

The UK's biggest can producers believe the easy-open-end (EOE) tin is about to win widespread acceptance in food markets here – a feat it has already achieved on the Continent. After more than two decades of development, the latest EOE tins are as sturdy as traditional cans, but sport lids that can be ripped off with a ring-pull.

A changeover will not happen overnight, however. 'It's all about timing,' says Francisco Serrano, marketing manager of the food consumer group of CarnaudMetalbox (CMB), the UK's biggest producer of EOE cans. 'Both manufacturers and retailers are now ready to jump.'

According to Gerry Tipple, business and marketing director of Nacanco subsidiary Pechiney, another major supplier of EOE cans, 'the first sectors to adapt with be premium products.'

This is a trend experienced in other countries where EOE cans are now well established. CMB's figures show that EOE penetration in canned food has reached 48 per cent in Italy, 35 per cent in Spain and Portugal and 30 per cent in France.

But some UK manufacturers are already opting for EOE cans as a way of making their brands stand out from the field, even if the advantage is only temporary. 'The use of an EOE can is not something you can withdraw and you certainly can't stop competitors from following suit,' says Tipple.

It's a development that will have far reaching effects on pack design as well as the food inside. The switch to EOE is so fudamental that it is normally part of a relaunch or new product introduction, to make sure that none of its impact is lost.

An EOE can costs more, too – 'perhaps 1p per can extra', according to Tipple – and, in a product relaunch, that expense may have to be written off by the manufacturer. Yet Serrano is convinced that people are willing to pay for more convenient packs: 'Its like buying a mini – you'd pay more for one with doors, and you wouldn't need a can-opener to get into it.'

And the EOE can is not purely functional. Canners hope the easy-open factor will at last drag tins out of a commodity rut, making the packaging an advantage rather than a problem to be coped with.

Campbell's Grocery Products launched the Cianto range of pasta sauces in October 1992 in CMB's Quantum can, a trademarked design aimed at adding value to the EOE tin's existing convenience benefit. Its vertical flutes take print directly on the can's surface. This year, RHM Foods' J A Sharwood followed suit by repositioning its cook-in sauces with the help of Quantum packs.

'Our research showed that people thought the can looked original, and 72 per cent said it was an improvement on ordinary cans,' says Campbell's marketing manager Andrew Lamb. 'It's obviously easier to use and it adds quality to the product's image.'

Sharwood's is tapping into the growth of premium sauces in what is a fast-growing and highly competitive market. 'We knew the packaging would have to reflect a premium product,' says senior product manager Fergus Rose. 'The usual route is to opt for jars. 'But why,' he asks, 'should consumers pay up to 40 per cent more for something packed in glass?'

HP Foods' approach is different. It sought a longer-term competitive advantage in the children's pasta market, where its brand is dogged by Heinz, and where sales are won or lost according to which character featured on-pack is currently in vogue.

The range was re-launched in August 1993. 'The new EOE can didn't need specific advertising as its benefits are clearly on show at point-of-sale.' says HP Foods' marketing manager Paul Nevett. 'At the re-launch, the rate of sale improved 25 per cent.'

If the can producers' dreams of a ubiquitous EOE tin are realised, then there is a relatively short time available for the big brands to scoop the value-added benefit of rip-top packs. In petfoods, Mars's Pedigree brand was closely followed into EOE cans by arch-rival Spillers and own-label products.

'It gives us a head start,' sums up Sharwood's Rose. 'But in the end, the can only supports what's inside.'

Marketing, 20 January 1994.

☼ ACTIVITY

Read the article on page 147, then answer the following questions.

CarnaudMetalbox Foodcan

☻ **How might the adoption of an EOE can help food producers to differentiate their products?**

☻ **How might an EOE can add value to the product?**

☻ **Why is an EOE can more acceptable in an affluent society?**

☻ **Which level of satisfaction does the EOE relate to?**

☻ **Why is it likely that, in time, the views of the senior product manager of Sharwood's will prove to be true?**

The life cycle of products must be carefully monitored to allow the organisation to maximise its sales and profits as well as produce the optimum amount of the product. Generally, the **product life cycle** takes the form shown in *Fig. 3.4*.

An organisation's marketing strategy should reflect the product life cycle and the stage which a particular product has reached. Typically, the following actions will be necessary.

☻ **Development requires** heavy expenditure on market research and product development.

☻ **When a product is introduced,** producers should accept that it will take time to become established and, in consequence, promotional expenses will be high.

☻ **To sustain growth** the organisation may increase the quality of the product and add new features or models. Promotional activities will be focused on building consumer commitment and loyalty.

☻ **Most products are at the stage of maturity** which, in some cases, may be extended by moving into other market segments or repositioning in a larger or faster growing segment. In other cases, the quality, features or style of the product may be modified, or the marketing mix adjusted in terms of price, promotion or place.

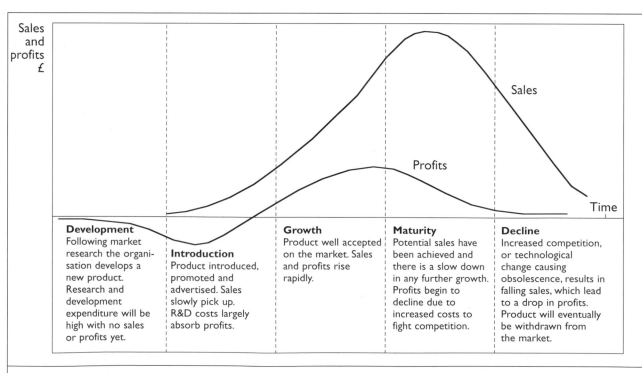

FIGURE 3.4: Product life cycle.

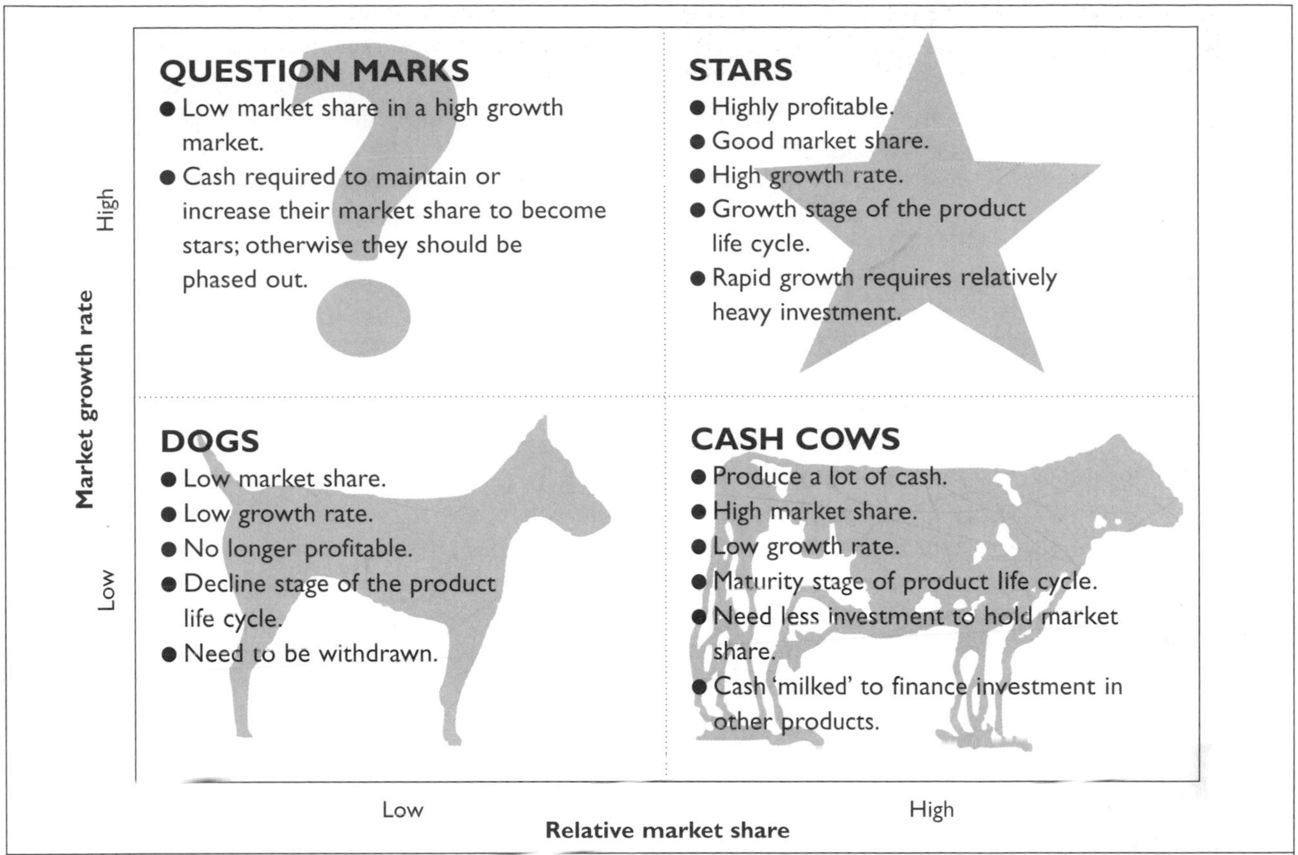

FIGURE 3.5: The Boston Consulting Group matrix.

Within the figure:

QUESTION MARKS
- Low market share in a high growth market.
- Cash required to maintain or increase their market share to become stars; otherwise they should be phased out.

STARS
- Highly profitable.
- Good market share.
- High growth rate.
- Growth stage of the product life cycle.
- Rapid growth requires relatively heavy investment.

DOGS
- Low market share.
- Low growth rate.
- No longer profitable.
- Decline stage of the product life cycle.
- Need to be withdrawn.

CASH COWS
- Produce a lot of cash.
- High market share.
- Low growth rate.
- Maturity stage of product life cycle.
- Need less investment to hold market share.
- Cash 'milked' to finance investment in other products.

Market growth rate — High / Low

Relative market share — Low / High

● **The organisation** should accept when the product has gone into decline and be prepared to drop it, attempt to reposition it, or wait for the competition to 'go under', and then pick up the rest of the market.

The Boston Consulting Group developed a growth share matrix, which can be combined with the product life cycle to enable an organisation to represent its range of products in terms of market share and growth (see Fig. 3.5).

Ultimately, an organisation should try to establish a balanced portfolio of products at different stages of development and different positions within the Boston matrix. This should allow for the revenue from one product to help with the development of another, thus ensuring the future survival of the business.

PRICE

Pricing is the only aspect of the marketing mix that directly produces revenue; the other aspects all involve costs. Therefore, it is extremely important to get the pricing strategy right as this will determine the financial success of a particular product and will contribute to the long-term viability of the organisation. The marketing department should set the price in the context of the total marketing mix. If price is not a particularly significant factor for consumers in the target market, strategies relating to quality, promotion and distribution will strongly influence price. If, within the target market, consumers are very price-sensitive, price will strongly influence the other factors making up the marketing mix.

In developing a pricing policy an organisation will have to make plans at several stages.

1 It has to decide its **pricing objectives**, which will reflect the organisation's overall objectives. If its overall objective is to maximise current profits, it will estimate the potential demand and costs and select a price which maximises current profits. But, if it is more interested in achieving security, it may do this by trying to achieve a larger market share, thus setting a lower price. Again, if it is concerned ultimately with status and prestige, it may attempt to create a product of the highest possible quality and set the price at a higher level in order to cover the necessary research and development costs.

2   Through market research, the organisation needs to establish the level of demand for the product at different prices. From this it may be possible to derive a demand schedule and determine the degree of **price elasticity**. The more inelastic the demand for the product, the higher the company can set its price.

3   The organisation needs to identify and state clearly the **costs** associated with the project. Ultimately, the price that is set must, in the long term, recover the costs of producing, distributing and selling the product, plus a profit. The total costs associated with a particular product or service are made up of fixed and variable elements. **Fixed costs** are what has to be paid regardless of output, for example plant, machinery, rent and rates. **Variable costs** vary directly with the level of output; for example, if output increases, the variable costs associated with inputs such as labour, raw materials and energy will also increase. In formulating a pricing policy, it is necessary to study the behaviour of such costs in the short, long and very long run.

4   Pricing should be competitive, therefore it is important to **analyse competitors' prices** and offers. Information can be gathered directly, by sending out researchers to compare prices and offers in the shops, or by studying the price lists of competitors.

5   The organisation can now select a **pricing method.** It must produce a price which reflects the organisation's objectives, the price elasticity of demand for the product, the organisation's costs, and competitors' prices. There are four main approaches to pricing.

Cost-plus pricing is a crude method of pricing. It involves establishing the total costs of producing a particular product, adding a standard margin or **'mark-up'** and pricing the product accordingly. For example, if it costs a manufacturer of electrical goods £12 to produce an electric kettle, it could simply add 33.3 per cent as a 'mark-up' and sell the kettle to a retailer for £16. This is a method widely used by many construction companies. In some areas a standard mark-up exists, as in the case of books sold by retailers, which normally have a 33.3 per cent mark-up. The major weakness of this system is that it fails to reflect market forces. If the price has been set too high, the level of sales will suffer; whereas, if it has been set too low, profits may be sacrificed. The system works reasonably well if all the firms within a particular industry broadly use the same methods, so that prices move together.

Target profit pricing involves using breakeven analysis (see *Fig. 3.6*), which illustrates total costs and total revenues at different volumes of sales. The price must be set at a level at which the firm at least covers its variable costs, otherwise there is no point in continuing production. Profits will occur only at a volume of sales above the breakeven level, because only then have fixed and variable costs been covered.

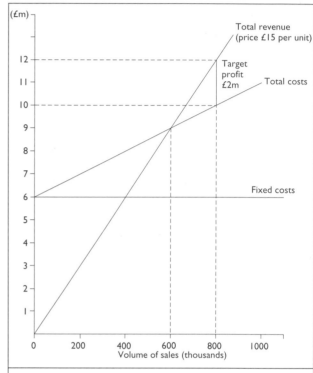

FIGURE 3.6: Target profit pricing and breakeven analysis.

In the case of the example in *Fig. 3.6*, at a price of £15 per unit and with the given cost structure, the firm will break even at a volume of 600,000 sales. If the firm's objective is to achieve a target profit of £2m, it would have to achieve a level of sales of 800,000 at a price of £15 per unit. It is possible that by charging a higher price the firm may achieve its objective of £2m profit with a lower volume of sales. This is because the slope of the total revenue curve would be steeper, so the firm would break even at a lower volume of sales. Ultimately, the price and volume of sales at which the firm will achieve this target level of profit will depend on its demand schedule and the price elasticity of demand. Therefore, this breakeven analysis is of value only if it is viewed in the context of the demand situation facing the firm.

Perceived value pricing relates to the non-price variables in the marketing mix, which help to raise consumers' perception of the product and, in so doing, their willingness to pay a higher price. Take, as an example, a simple product like fish and chips. If it was served in newspaper at a fish bar a consumer might be prepared to pay £1.75 for it. On the other hand, if the consumer ate it as a meal in a cafe a price of £3.50 might be considered acceptable. In the atmosphere of a restaurant the same meal might appear on the menu at £6.50, and in a hotel restaurant a resident might pay £8 for the same dish. The higher price can be charged due to the difference in the surroundings and atmosphere in which the fish and chips are eaten.

This method of pricing relies upon accurate research into how people view a particular product and give value to the non-price variables in the marketing mix. The consumer's perception of the value of a product may, in fact, be lowered if the organisation reduces its price. This is because the consumer may consider a lower price to indicate low quality. Such an attitude is often taken towards electrical goods where the consumer may feel that if the product is priced below the expected range, there must be something wrong with it technically, or there must be a poor after-sales service. This view is further supported by the fact that while some products such as Heinz baked beans, are more expensive than other brands, consumers are prepared to pay a higher price because they think the product is of a higher quality.

Market rate pricing is often used by smaller organisations which lack the sophisticated research techniques to determine their own prices. Under these circumstances, the solution is simply to charge what is considered to be the going market rate among the organisation's competitors. The price then at least reflects the collective wisdom of the industry.

PLACE

The marketing department has to 'deliver' the product to the consumer as and when it is required. The extent to which this is achieved depends upon decisions regarding the **location** of the production or service organisation, the availability of the product or service and the method by which it is distributed.

Location decisions should take account of the convenience of access for customers. The development of shopping precincts and out-of-town shopping centres and hypermarkets means that many consumers expect to be able to buy a range of products from one point. This is time-saving for the consumers, who can obtain all their needs 'in one go'.

The logical development of this is that certain types of businesses, which provide complementary products or services, will seek to be located close to each other. For example, estate agents, building societies and solicitors may prefer to be in close proximity to provide a comprehensive service in the buying and selling of houses.

Similarly, fast-food outlets, pubs, clubs and cinemas may combine to create an area for entertainment, or a component supplier may decide to locate its operations near a manufacturing organisation on a business park.

There are circumstances where customer convenience may have to take second place to other locational factors. Typically, this is when cost factors have a more significant effect than price in the marketing mix. These costs could include transport of the finished product, or relate to the need for special site facilities, such as storage space or a means of disposing of waste matter, or the availability of a suitable supply of skilled labour (and, thus, the wages that have to be paid). To take an example, the locational decision of a single-site chemical plant is likely to be largely determined by requirements for a particular type of site and the availability of suitable employees.

Organisations seek to make decisions regarding place which ensure the **availability** of products or services when customers need them and in the quantity they require. This means that the organisation of production, storage and distribution must contribute towards the realisation of the consumer's expectations. For example, consumers who buy a particular make of car need to be confident that, if they visit the spares department of the main dealer, the component or part they require is available immediately or can be easily obtained. This is only possible if there has been an attempt to balance the production, distribution and stocking of spares in relation to the number of complete finished vehicles which have been sold.

The channels and system of distribution determine the way in which products reach the market. The marketing department seeks to establish the most efficient system so that the product is available at the right time and in the right place. A successful system depends upon the efficiency and speed of transportation, the quality of packaging, the efficiency of the stock control and storage system and the sophistication of the ordering system.

The effectiveness of the **distribution** system also depends upon the channels the product may go through. Traditionally, manufacturers have sold products to wholesalers in large quantities which are then sold to retailers in smaller, more manageable quantities. The benefits of this system have been that it allows the wholesaler to handle large shipments from the manufacturer and provide the storage for, and transportation of, the product to the retailer. In recent years, a number of manufacturers have decided to by-pass the wholesaler and deal directly with retailers or consumers. This enables savings to be made and provides a quicker response to market trends. Boots and Laura Ashley have taken this a stage further by having a vertically integrated operation, from manufacture to retailing. Vertical integration is discussed in unit 5 (see page 329).

PROMOTION

The purpose of promotion is to communicate directly with potential or existing customers, to encourage them to purchase the product or service and recommend it to others. The main promotional tools are sales promotions, public relations and advertising. Essentially, any promotional activity concentrates on the distinctive features of a product, which are known as its **unique selling points**.

In designing a promotional activity the marketing department has to take several steps.

⊗ **Identifying and targeting the required market segment.**

⊗ **Establishing the purpose of the promotion in the context of the buying process;** that is, recognition of need, consideration and evaluation of how to satisfy that need, making a choice, and evaluating the choice which may result in a repeat purchase. This will determine whether the promotion seeks to increase potential or existing customers' awareness or knowledge of the product, or to strengthen their preference for it or their determination to purchase it.

⊗ **Taking decisions on a suitable promotional message for the target audience.** In some cases it may be appropriate to appeal to consumers' emotions, in others to their reason.

⊗ **Selecting a suitable form of media for the target audience.**

⊗ **Evaluating the promotional activity by measuring feedback** in terms of who becomes aware of the product, uses it, and expresses satisfaction with it.

The choice of promotional activity will ultimately be determined by what the organisation can afford to spend, the type of product and market, and the stage reached in the product's life cycle.

Sales promotions may be directed at the consumer or the trade. Consumer promotions are used to encourage potential consumers to try a product and, hopefully, to purchase it again. Promotions may take the form of free samples, gifts, vouchers and cash refunds. Trade promotions are aimed at encouraging distributors to stock a particular product. This may be attempted through such methods as cash incentives and the payment of bonuses.

Public relations (PR) is an area used to promote a positive image of a company's achievements. It involves gaining favourable publicity and developing a perception that the company is socially responsible. It also helps to build awareness of the organisation and develop a preference for its products. It may be aimed not only at potential and existing consumers but also the organisation's suppliers and distributors and, where appropriate, any government departments or pressure groups which might be interested in its activities. Major retailers, like Marks and Spencer, Sainsbury and Tesco, spend a great deal on public relations, to promote a responsible, caring and high-quality image. The major public relations tools involve the use of publicity, publications such as newsletters and brochures, corporate image and sponsorship.

Advertising involves the use of the media by an organisation to inform, persuade and remind potential and existing consumers about its products and activities. It may also be used to encourage customers to go into a particular retail outlet. In deciding on an appropriate method of, or medium for, advertising an organisation will take several steps:

✪ **deciding on the purpose of the advertisement:** whether it is concerned essentially with imparting information, persuading new consumers or reminding existing ones;

✪ **fixing the budget for the advertising campaign** in the context of sales and the amount spent by competitors;

✪ **identifying, designing and evaluating the required message** (often carried out by an advertising agency);

✪ **deciding on the medium or media,** including newspapers, magazines, television, cinema, radio, hoardings, catalogues, circulars and leaflets (also often carried out by an agency); and

✪ **evaluating the effectiveness of the advertisement** in terms of communications and sales.

It is possible to measure the probable value of advertising expenditure by calculating the **elasticity of advertising (EA)**. This is done by dividing the proportionate change in sales volume by the proportionate change in advertising expenditure. If EA is greater than one, increasing advertising expenditure is probably worthwhile, as it will create a more than proportionate increase in sales volume.

Penguin targets kids

McVITIE'S is turning to character licensing for the first time on its Penguin brand in a bid to strengthen its dominance of the children's countline market.

It is jumping on the Captain Scarlet bandwagon and testing out a new size multi-pack – 12 Penguin biscuits priced at 99p – from the end of this month. The pack will feature details of a Captain Scarlet promotion, offering a torch in return for proofs of purchase.

Penguin marketing manager Chris Pass admitted the decision to license an outside character instead of relying solely on Penguin's own figurehead – which itself has been licensed out to third parties in the past – is a 'potentially dangerous' move.

'It is something we have been very cognisant of in preparing the TV advertising,' he said, referring to creative work from Publicis that breaks on February 26. It continues the recent theme of using footage of live penguins, but this time in the form of a Captain Scarlett spoof.

The 1960s character was chosen, according to Pass, because 'the character is popular and topical and we are attempting to build playground credibility'.

Penguin, which McVitie's describes as the biggest selling children's countline brand with £43m sales, has an opportunity to build sales, claimed Pass. While confectionery brands are increasingly frowned upon by more health-conscious parents and school teachers, Penguin 'has a biscuit heritage and is considered much more acceptable. We've experienced a big plus.'

The new-size pack compares with the 63p seven-pack and the £1.25 14-pack. The promotion will be monitored 'very carefully' and may result in a permanent 99p pack of 12.

Marketing, 17 February 1994.

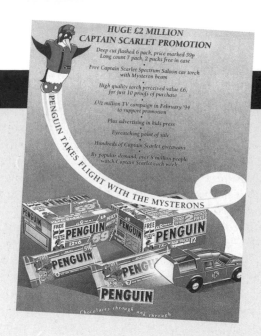

HUGE £2 MILLION CAPTAIN SCARLET PROMOTION

Deep cut flashed 6 pack, price marked 59p
Long count 7 pack, 2 packs free in case

Free Captain Scarlet Spectrum Saloon car torch with Mysteron beam

High quality torch perceived value £6, for just 10 proofs of purchase

£2½ million TV campaign in February '94 to support promotion

Plus advertising in kids press

Eyecatching point of sale

Hundreds of Captain Scarlet giveaways

By popular demand, over 8 million people watch Captain Scarlet each week

PENGUIN TAKES FLIGHT WITH THE MYSTERONS

⚡ ACTIVITY

Read the article on page 153, then answer the following questions.

1 What stage do you think that the Penguin chocolate biscuit has reached in its product life cycle?

2 Where would 'the Penguin' be positioned in terms of the Boston Matrix?

3 Does the creation of the new 12-pack for 99p suggest that McVitie's considers the demand for Penguins to be price elastic?

4 Analyse the reasons for the sustained success of the Penguin brand.

5 Identify the market segment that McVitie's is targeting with its Captain Scarlet promotion, and the major objective behind the promotion.

📖 PORTFOLIO ASSIGNMENT

INVITING SPEAKERS
As a school or college group, contact a marketing or public relations representative from a local company and a voluntary organisation or charity. In each case ask the organisation to send copies of its annual report and accounts as well as any in-house literature relating to its marketing strategy.

Invite the representatives to your school (or college) to make a short presentation on how their organisation reconciles the need to be oriented towards customers or members with its overall strategic business and financial objectives. Ask them to supply examples of how their organisation has developed through:

✪ the development of existing or new markets;

✪ the maintenance and increase of market share;

✪ innovation and the development of new products;

✪ the modification and relaunching of old products or the achievement of technological breakthroughs.

On the basis of the information supplied by the organisations prepare questions regarding the possible conflict between customer orientation, productivity and profitability; the use of market research; and the composition of the marketing mix.

Make notes individually during the presentations and prepare questions on the major points and issues covered.

Adopting the role of a business journalist, use your notes as the basis for an article entitled 'Putting the Consumer First in both the Business and Voluntary Sectors'.

PORTFOLIO ASSIGNMENT

HI-TEC MARKETING

Read the following **HI-TEC** case study.

TASK
You are employed as a marketing assistant for the family firm of Marshall's, which is a specialist producer of top of the range walking and golf shoes.

Jane Marshall, the oldest child of the founder of the business has recently taken over as managing director. She wishes to bring the company into the modern world by repositioning it in the market and diversifying into a wider range of sports goods. In preparation for designing a strategy to achieve this objective she asks you to examine the marketing activities of **HI-TEC**.

Using the information in the panel (below), produce a report which analyses **HI-TEC**'s marketing strategy and the reasons for its success. Consider whether such an approach to marketing could be adopted by Marshall's. No futher information or assistance in carrying out this assignment should be sought (or is needed) from **HI-TEC** Sports.

The development of a brand

HI-TEC Sports plc was founded in 1974 in the appropriately named village of Shoeburyness, Essex. The company's original success came as a result of the design and development of HI-TEC's first ever shoe, specifically designed for the then fast-growing game of squash – the HI-TEC Squash, of which over ten million pairs have been sold worldwide.

The HI-TEC name and logo were created and launched in 1982. The brand reflects the following:

⊗ **a stated commitment to offer all consumers advanced sports footwear which provides performance, top quality and guaranteed comfort;**

⊗ **technologically advanced research;**

⊗ **detailed design carried out with the help of computer technology; and**

⊗ **development of increasingly complex manufacturing.**

When reproduced in print, the HI-TEC brand name is always accompanied underneath by the HI-TEC 'harpoon' or 'sideflash', as it is sometimes known. The 'harpoon' is key to HI-TEC's global brand strategy since it is the single most important means of hallmarking and identifying a HI-TEC shoe, textile garment or accessory, whether appearing alone on the outer side of a show, for example, or accompanied in an embroidered format by the HI-TEC name.

The corporate colours of the HI-TEC name and logo are the same worldwide – blue and red. These colours were chosen specifically for their association with both the British and American flags: HI-TEC's two most important markets are the UK and the USA.

THE UK OPERATION
In the United Kingdom, the commercial strategy has always been to concentrate on the mid-price ranges with a wide customer base including both sports and shoe shops. This policy has meant that HI-TEC has, for the last three years, been among the top three brands in the UK market. It supplies over 4,500 retail accounts, approximately 45 per cent of which are sports retailers. Major accounts include Olympus (part of Sears), Champion (part of the Burton Group), Intersport and the British Shoe Corporation.

Sports retailers are a vital link between HI-TEC and the end consumer. They have the responsibility of helping consumers to choose the right shoe, balanced with their own need to build a profitable business.

INTERNATIONAL EXPANSION

HI-TEC is taking a planned approach to international expansion. HI-TEC believes that the sporting goods industry is increasingly global in nature with the needs of consumers increasingly homogenous. It is for this reason that competition is no longer limited to the domestic market, and the company is therefore building a worldwide brand.

HI-TEC shoe, textile and accessory collections are currently marketed in over seventy countries worldwide. Strategic markets outside the UK have been identified and subsidiary companies established. The USA and Canada, Europe (in particular Ireland) and South Africa all play a key role in HI-TEC's international expansion plans. Its American organisation is the fastest growing of all group companies, now among the 'top twenty' footwear brands in the USA, with its market leading range of lightweight rugged outdoor footwear. Elsewhere, in continental Europe HI-TEC has adapted its operations to the creation of a single European market with distributor companies in the Benelux countries, Germany, France and Spain. With the free movement of goods now permitted, all European Union countries are serviced with stocks held in a central European warehouse, in the Netherlands.

All international operations are subject to central control over product collections and quality as well as commercial policy and customer service operations. A basic central marketing directive exists but HI-TEC recognises that strong cultural and language differences still prevail, so country-specific activities are carefully monitored to local conditions and needs.

THE MARKETING OF HI-TEC'S PRODUCT COLLECTIONS

This starts with the continual feedback from HI-TEC's worldwide subsidiaries and distributors of ever-changing market information and trends, changing consumer attitudes and evolving design ideas and new sports. This data is interpreted into a twice-yearly design brief which forms the basis of the new collection.

The new collection is then presented to the sports and shoe trade by means of bulk sampling of the entire HI-TEC sales organisation, both in the UK and worldwide. During HI-TEC's selling period, it also exhibits at a number of international trade venues to assist in determining demand.

Orders are then placed with factories located all over the world, most notably in Indonesia, Korea, The Philippines, China and Vietnam. The company recognises the importance of top quality and delivery reliability which is why the production process (factory orders, quality control, scheduling and shipping) is managed by its own Far Eastern offices in Hong Kong, Korea, Taiwan, Indonesia and The Philippines. The finished product is then shipped by sea in containers to one of HI-TEC's warehouses and then sold to its customers worldwide.

Each country then operates a marketing campaign to support the products that have been developed. A typical campaign will normally concentrate on the following broad mix, adapted to local market conditions. Other elements may, of course, be added where relevant.

1   A product range constructed to meet key price points and cosmetic criteria; for example, Mediterranean countries traditionally require more brightly coloured products.

2   A distribution network capitalising on traditional sports and shoe retail outlets as well as opportunities to supply sports clubs.

3   A trade promotion campaign in which HI-TEC Sports UK invites key sports and shoe trade buyers to exhibitions and stockroom events; co-ordinates quarterly mailshots to all accounts, with brochures and informing them of company news, personnel updates, new collections, pricing issues and special offers; advertises in trade magazines and ensures 'mentions' in articles on general new product collections; and ensures the salesforce regularly presents an exciting product and explains the benefits to be gained from working with HI-TEC.

4   A consumer promotion campaign in which HI-TEC Sports UK engages the following: Ian Woosnam (golf), Henri Leconte (tennis), Roy Keane Paul Merson, Denis Wise and over fifty other Premier League players (soccer) and Jansher Khan, the world's number one squash player, and four of the world's 'top ten' lady squash players. Also, event sponsorship, including the British Open Squash Tournament, stands at all major golf events in the UK, and stands at walking and hiking events; official associations, including as official supplier to the Wimbledon Championships and the International Squash Players' Association; and a print campaign in specialist magazines.

Marketing research and product development

THE VALUE OF RESEARCH

Marketing research provides information that helps organisations to recognise and respond to market opportunities and to develop suitable products to meet market needs. It enables organisations to find out which goods and services people want, the price they are prepared to pay, where they prefer to buy the product, and how products should be promoted.

Ultimately, by carrying out marketing research, the organisation can identify key factors which relate to customer satisfaction at three levels. These are: the **essential (or 'core') benefits** associated with a product, i.e. what the customer seeks to obtain by buying it; the **product specification**, including branding, packaging and quality; and the **additional benefits** associated with after-sales service, advertising, customer advice, financing and delivery.

All these factors add value to the product, thus increasing its competitiveness and potential returns. For example, obtaining suitable information regarding the entertainment needs of young people contributed to the dominance of Sega and Nintendo in the computer games market. Similarly, it helped Horn Abbot achieve international success with Trivial Pursuit.

AREAS OF RESEARCH

Marketing research information is either **quantitative** or **qualitative**. The former is essentially numerical (how many people buy a product, how often do they buy it), whereas qualitative data relate to consumer attitudes.

In order to make sound marketing decisions, organisations need to collect and analyse research information in six main areas. We now look at each of these in turn.

PRODUCT RESEARCH

This includes both the development of new products and the improvement of existing ones. Before any changes

 ACTIVITY

Make a list of five products which have been particularly successful in meeting a market need, and suggest how marketing research may have helped to identify that need.

are made, products will be put through a series of tests to investigate features such as design, materials or ingredients, colour durability, ease of handling, fitness for purpose, and operating capacity.

One of the problems in developing a new product is that customers are obviously unfamiliar with it, so their reaction, when shown a prototype or told about it, may be misleading. This is likely to be especially true where the product breaks entirely new ground, for example in terms of technology. Initially, customers may resist the unfamiliar, but when the benefits are recognised the innovation may be quickly adopted. When the 'hole in the wall' cash dispenser was introduced, customers were wary of dealing with a machine. They felt it lacked the reassurance of a human transaction. However, the

Think of four products that consumers might think of as being of particularly high status, and explain why this should be the case.

RESEARCH INTO DISTRIBUTION

This helps to determine how consumers would prefer new or existing products to be made available.

Marketing research information may be gathered to measure the effectiveness of the sales force in terms of the cost of calls and the number and size of orders. Also, different methods of distribution, such as mail order, using a wholesaler, or direct selling can be investigated, as may the performance of individual distribution outlets. This information will help to ensure that strong distribution areas can be built upon, while unprofitable products and sales in unrewarding areas can be discontinued. Contact with those purchasing on behalf of distributive outlets or trades will provide useful opinions on the organisation's marketing techniques, when compared with those of competitors.

Sales staff will generally operate under some form of incentive scheme. New schemes may result in increased effort on the part of those seeking orders from customers

24-hour access provided by automatic tellers was soon seen as such a significant benefit that their use grew rapidly.

The importance of psychology is widely recognised in product research. This is because consumers can be motivated in their purchases by the status or prestige which they believe, and maybe know from their friends, that ownership of a particular product confers. Brand labelling can play an important part in image making.

Market tests are carried out to reach decisions as to how products should be packaged, both in terms of the type of container used (where applicable) and the overall appearance. Important factors include the materials used, the design, labelling, robustness, weight and ease of storage. Tests for comparative purposes may be carried out on competitors' products to help pinpoint advantages or deficiencies in the new or improved product.

Testing of the product and its packaging may indicate features which are superfluous and might be 'dropped', facilitating greater standardisation in production. The organisation may also be concerned to ensure that it has a sufficient range of output to allow it to compete in all areas of the market that may prove profitable. After-sales service records may indicate areas for improvement or means of raising the quality of the service provided.

In the 1990s, market research has increasingly been applied in new product development, as the article excerpt opposite shows.

Research propels innovation

INNOVATE or die. This is the daunting challenge facing companies and it's easier said than done, given the high failure of new products introduced into the marketplace.

Market research is increasingly being used to reduce those failures and save money. Answers are needed at a number of steps in the new product development cycle and research can provide the necessary guidance.

But market research has not always been regarded as a guiding light. According to Julian Bond, NPD [new product development] managing director at Research International: 'Market research used to be a very minor part of decision-making in the '80s and was used to back up decisions that were already made.' Bond says most manufacturers' historic use of market researchers was like a drunk's need of a lamp post. 'It was used more for support than illumination,' he says.

Those days are long gone. Manufacturers are now looking to research to point out how to fine-tune new products as well as predict new buyer volumes. They are listening ever more closely to their customers.

The first question a manufacturer must ask is whether or not it is reading the marketplace correctly. In other words, are new product ideas on the right track with consumers? Market research can shed light on what consumers like and don't like about a product innovation idea. This feedback can then be incorporated into the new product design to ensure it is what consumers want.

Such early testing can also be useful for helping a manufacturer choose between several alternative NPD ideas. The idea which has the most likely chance of succeeding with consumers can become a prototype.

Marketing, January 27 1994

or distributors. Research can be carried out to determine the most effective incentive scheme.

RESEARCH INTO PROMOTION

This helps to determine how effective various promotional and advertising activities are in persuading consumers to buy a particular product. The impact of advertisements, brochures, exhibitions, sales demonstrations and media publicity can be assessed; for example, in terms of the number of resulting enquiries and sales.

SOCIAL AND OTHER TRENDS

The way businesses operate is obviously influenced by the wider political, economic, social and technological environment. These are referred to by an acronym as **PEST factors**. By analysing trends and developments, organisations can spot new market opportunities and threats.

POLITICAL FACTORS

The actions of government have a major effect on business and markets, including creating (or dampening) demand for particular products or for consumer items in general. This is achieved by setting public spending levels, allocating funds for special programmes (such as to buy computers for schools), changes in taxation and interest rates for borrowers, and the introduction of new (or the abolition of existing) laws, regulations and licence arrangements.

Increasingly, in a global economy, such decisions are reached internationally, through the European Union, the biannual 'economic summit' of the heads of the seven largest economies and the work of organisations such as GATT (the General Agreement on Tariffs and Trade). For example, changes in the European Common Agricultural Policy have directly influenced opportunities for milk production by dairy farmers.

The article below shows how one organisation has gained a market advantage from both UK and European changes.

ECONOMIC FACTORS

The United Kingdom's economic performance determines its level of **national income**. How this is distributed, together with the distribution of wealth, ultimately determines the standard of living enjoyed by individual members of society. This, in turn, influences consumer spending and, thereby, market opportunities.

A standard measure of a country's economic performance is **gross domestic product (GDP)**. This is the total value of goods and services produced, usually expressed annually and per capita, i.e. the total divided by the population of the country. GDP is a useful broad indicator both of the size of a national market and of comparative living standards in different countries. However, while adjustment is made for the varying price levels in different countries in calculating GDP, the figures do not show the extent to which spending power is widely spread or concentrated in relatively few hands. Nor do they take into account levels of taxation, which can substantially reduce consumer spending power.

The trend in the UK has been for GDP to increase steadily decade by decade. Total wealth created in the early 1990s was about double that of the early 1960s. However, compared to our major economic competitors (in Europe, North America and the Pacific Rim), economic growth has been modest, and the UK has been slipping down the international league table. Nevertheless, while the UK was ranked eighteenth among the twenty-four leading industrial nations in terms of GDP per capita in 1990, once Britain's relatively low taxation was taken into account, we were ranked sixth in terms of consumer spending.

The size of various national economies, their productiveness (the amount of wealth created divided by the number of people living in the country), and how much is left on average for personal spending after

Signs and labels

DANGER
High voltage

The success of Signs and Labels Ltd shows that new laws can mean business. Formed in 1970, the company's successful identification and exploitation of market opportunities arising from Government regulations resulted in two decades of steady growth. Throughout that time, Government-introduced regulations required companies to be more thorough in labelling and signing dangers. The Safety Signs regulations of 1980 sparked huge growth in the UK market, which was recently further stimulated by Control of Substances Hazardous to Health rules. A member of the British Standards Institution (BSI), the company monitors safety developments through BSI publications and safety journals. Since safety signs are based on common [European Union] standards, Signs and Labels sees growth opportunities in the European market and has opened an office in Germany.

Marketing: the way forward, Department of Trade and Industry, 1992

	GDP totals (US $ bn.)	GDP per capita	Consumption per capita (US $)
Australia	272.5	15,951	9,458
Belgium	163.5	16,405	10,153
Canada	509.0	19,120	11,289
Denmark	86.2	16,765	8,773
France	983.5	17,431	10,516
Germany	1,156.6	18,291	9,883
Greece	74.5	7,349	5,317
Ireland	37.3	10,659	5,904
Italy	923.6	16,021	9,907
Japan	2,178.5	17,634	10,073
Netherlands	235.7	15,766	9,276
Spain	459.4	11,792	7,360
Sweden	144.4	16,867	8,733
Switzerland	142.7	20,997	11,982
United Kingdom	902.5	15,720	9,948
USA	5,392.2	21,449	14,465

FIGURE 3.7: GDP totals and per capita and private final consumption expenditure 1990, selected countries, in US dollars
Note: Private final consumption expenditure is the total spent by households and non-profit organisations on new goods and services less net sales of second-hand goods.
Source: *National Accounts Vol.1 Main Aggregates 1960-1990*, Organisation for Economic Co-operation and Development, Paris, 1992.

taxation are shown in *Fig. 3.7*. For example, Greece's economy is twice as big as Ireland's, but the Irish economy is 45 per cent more productive and, after taxation, the average Greek or Irish person has roughly the same amount to spend. Note the very high levels of taxation in some countries, such as Sweden and Denmark, and the

	GDP total (US $ bn.)	GDP per capita (US $)
Algeria	45	1,698
Brazil	358	2,300
Ghana	6	400
Iran	90	1,500
Israel	55	12,000
Jamaica	4	1,400
Nigeria	30	250
Singapore	38	13,900
South Africa	104	2,600
South Korea	270	6,253

FIGURE 3.8: GDP totals and per capita for selected less developed countries 1992, in US dollars.

huge size of the American market. *Fig. 3.8* gives the GDP totals and per capita figures for some less developed countries.

As has already been remarked, the national picture does not tell us about the distribution of spending power among various groups. If you break down the UK population into five groups in terms of its disposable household income, in 1991 the 'top fifth' accounted for slightly more than 40 per cent of overall spending, whereas the 'bottom fifth' accounted for about only six per cent. The disparity between rich and poor becomes even more marked when wealth (income and assets) is considered. In 1991, just one per cent of the population accounted for 18 per cent of 'marketable wealth' in the UK and the richest 10 per cent accounted for half. Moreover, if you remove the value of housing (by far and away the biggest asset for most people), the disparities become even greater, with the richest five per cent owning half of the wealth.

Differences in **wealth distribution** obviously have implications for marketing, with greater opportunities amongst the top 20 per cent of households for the sale of luxury items such as large houses, lavish furnishings, fast cars, expensive boats and exotic holidays. On the other hand, amongst the poorest 20 per cent a market opportunity exists for basic items including food, clothing and household goods. This may be reflected in the number of discount shops and street traders in poorer areas.

Changes in the composition of the assets included as personal wealth may result in market opportunities as individuals switch between property, shares and financial assets. Such changes may be brought about through inheritance.

Ultimately, changes in income and wealth normally affect overall expenditure. *Fig. 3.9* gives a detailed

	1971	1981	1986	1990	1992
Food	87	91	95	100	101
Alcohol	72	91	96	100	95
Tobacco	138	122	102	100	93
Clothing/Footwear	52	67	92	100	99
Fuel/Power	86	94	102	100	106
Household durables	53	69	86	100	100
Buying vehicles	51	59	81	100	77
Running vehicles	47	65	84	100	97
TV/Video	19	46	77	100	101
Books/Newspapers	101	97	92	100	96
Meals/Catering	55	58	72	100	92

FIGURE 3.9: Household expenditure 1971–1992, selected items, at constant (1990) prices.
Note: Household durables cover items such as washing machines, refrigerators and microwave ovens.
Source: *Social Trends 1994*, CSO.

breakdown of **household expenditure** at constant (1990) prices, which removes the inflation element and makes comparisons possible. Total household expenditure increased by 66 per cent in real terms between 1971 and 1992, which was in line with the overall increase in national income during the period.

there has been a growing 'grey market'. A good example is the success of Saga Holidays, which caters specifically for the retired. Meanwhile, the 'baby boomers' have become middle-aged, creating a lucrative market for restauranteurs, travel companies and those selling financial services, such as insurance and pension plans.

 ACTIVITY

Using data in *Fig 3.9* draw a graph plotting the changes in household spending for various consumer items in the period 1971 to 1992.

Calculate percentage changes in spending for different items between 1971 and 1992, and suggest reasons for these changes in spending.

Compare the results and draw up a league table ranking the rates of change.

Draw conclusions about the extent to which the rankings have been influenced by changes in the distribution of income and wealth and consider the implications for market opportunities.

 ACTIVITY

Make a list of products for which demand is likely to increase due to the move, in the next two decades, of the baby boom generation into retirement. Clues can be found by looking at the growing current 'grey market'.

SOCIAL FACTORS

These largely involve **demographic changes** which cover age, ethnicity and other characteristics. They are important for marketing because they reveals trends which influence demand for particular types of products. Take age, for example. The UK has an ageing population. This is because people are living longer and, compared to the 'boom' years from the late 1940s into the early 1960s, couples are having fewer babies. By the year 2021, nearly one in five of the population will be aged over 65, compared to only one in ten in 1951. One in 27 people (and one in 20 women) are now aged 80 or older. Conversely, under-16s today comprise only one in five of the population compared to one in four in the 1960s. It is not surprising, therefore, that while the late 1950s and 1960s saw the rapid growth of 'youth culture', with new entertainment and clothing products, in recent times

Soul-d on healthy food!

Black people spend more money on nutritious food and eat better quality diets than White people, according to a recently published survey by the Joseph Rowntree Foundation.

Its report says: 'Black households had more varied and healthier diets and to some extent better mineral and vitamin intakes. Evidence supports the study's findings that Black parents always cooked their food from raw, fresh ingredients, and provided a highly varied diet for their families.'

Ironically, Black families spent slightly less – an average of £40 a week, compared to £42 for a counterpart White family.

Liz Dowler of the Joseph Rowntree Foundation said their survey revealed that Black families put more emphasis on eating well-seasoned, quality food. 'It is a traditional thing that has nothing to do with income. Many Black people still cook the traditional way. Good food is a priority.'

The Voice, 11 July 1995

However, overall population trends can disguise what is happening with particular groups. For example, some ethnic minority groups have very young populations. Over four in ten of those from the Pakistani and Bangladeshi communities are aged under 16. Among the Afro-Caribbean population there is a disproportionate number of 16 to 29 year-olds (30 per cent of the total compared to only 21 per cent among whites). This reflects the wave of immigration from the Caribbean in the 1950s, with couples starting families in the 1960s and 1970s. Market evidence of the purchasing power of young black people can be seen in sales of sportswear and leisure products, but also in mobile phones and demand for college places and educational products (a higher proportion of black young people go to college than do whites). About one-tenth of the UK population now comprises 'people of colour', and this has influenced demand generally, for example in young people's fashions. It has also created important new product areas, such as black hair and beauty products.

Movement of the population geographically also has significance for marketing. The counties with the fastest population growth in the 1980s were Cambridgeshire, Buckinghamshire and Cornwall, with Belfast and the Scottish Isles experiencing the biggest decreases. Such changes may create opportunities or pose threats for construction companies, makers of furniture and durable household goods, and service and entertainment providers.

Another indicator is **household size**. This has fallen in the last three decades, with a considerable increase in the proportion of people who live alone (see *Fig. 3.10*). The biggest group comprises women aged 60 or older, although in the period 1971 to 2001 the proportion of this group within the population as a whole is not expected to increase greatly. The big increase concerns men of working age (under 65). By the year 2001, one in ten households is expected to come into this category, compared to fewer than one in 25 at the beginning of the 1970s.

From a marketing point of view, the decline in household size and the associated growth of one-person households has led to a number of market opportunities. For example, construction companies have been able to build more flats, maisonettes and sheltered accommodation; furniture retailers have faced an increased demand for smaller items to go into reduced living areas; demand has risen for home security systems, particularly by elderly people living alone; and food producers and retailers have experienced a growing demand for items packaged in smaller units and as individual meals.

Another significant social trend is the decline in the predominance of the traditional family. Between 1961 and 1991, the proportion of all households comprising a married couple with dependent children fell from just over half (52 per cent) to two-fifths. Nevertheless, it still should be recognised that more people live in this type of family unit than in any other. However, the rise in lone-parent families has implications for the way products are promoted. Advertisers need to be careful not to give the impression that only traditional families buy their products.

TECHNOLOGY FACTORS

Developments in technology give rise to new products and market opportunities. For example, the application of technology in the home led to the development of the **'white goods'** industry, which makes washing machines, refrigerators, dishwashers, etc. This, in turn, led to the creation of materials and services associated with these goods, such as special types of paints, new materials and plastics, and appropriate detergents for use in the machines.

Many companies have research departments specifically to carry out scientific and technical work leading to new products. For example, pharmaceutical companies spend considerable sums on the development of new drugs and medicines.

Equally, social and market factors may spark the widespread adoption of a particular technology or create a demand for technologically innovative products. Facsimile technology was invented in the middle of the last century, but it was not until the 1980s that business uses emerged that made it attractive.

Ecological problems can arise from the use of new technologies, for example the pollution of the environment and the disturbance of the balance of the natural forces of

	1961	1971	1981	1991
1 person	14	18	22	27
2 people	30	32	32	34
3 people	23	19	17	16
4 people	18	17	18	16
5 people	9	8	7	5
6 or more people	7	6	4	2
Number of house-holds (millions)	16.2	18.2	19.5	21.9

FIGURE 3.10: Households, by size percentages and totals (Great Britain).
Source: *Social Trends 1994*, CSO.

ACTIVITY

Select a group of ten household items bought weekly. Visit a supermarket and identify which of the items have been packaged, presented and promoted to meet the needs of both the one-person household and the traditional family.

From a variety of newspapers and magazines find examples of advertisements for the items included in your shopping basket. Identify those that are not household specific in their presentation.

During the period of a week, video tape any advertisements appearing on television which relate to your ten items. Classify them according to the type of household to which they are targeted.

Prepare a ten minute presentation on 'Targeting the household of the 1990s' based on your findings. Illustrate the presentation with advertising examples.

---

regeneration. Causes include the over-felling of trees, the intensive use of chemicals in farming and the uncontrolled emission of toxic waste products. Recognition of these threats to the environment has created a marketing opportunity for products which can claim to be 'green' and are sold to customers who are concerned about the environment.

CONSUMER BEHAVIOUR

Business organisations can only successfully divide the market into different groups (or 'segments') and 'position' their product in terms of giving it a distinctive appeal to particular buyers if they understand the wants of actual and potential customers. They, therefore, need to conduct research into consumer behaviour. There are several aspects of this which can be investigated.

CULTURE

Culture refers to the set of beliefs and behaviour patterns to which different groups and individuals adhere. The main influences are family, friends, teachers, politicians, religion and the media, including advertising. For example, the typical young person in Britain in the 1990s expects to own a computer and the games that go with it. This is because today's youngsters have been brought up in an age where they have developed the capacity to read and understand computer instructions, and they are surrounded at school by others who are also using computers.

Cultural shifts take place all the time. In recent years, a greater emphasis has been placed by society on health and fitness. Consequently, market opportunities have opened up for health centres and gyms, sports shops are booming and supermarkets are stocking more low-caloric and natural foods.

Any nation or group is made up of several subcultures, holding beliefs which, in some measure, make them distinctive. Determining this distinctiveness and applying it to marketing is a task of research; but there are dangers.

One is that the characteristic identified as distinctive may not be relevant. Do Catholics eat more sausages than Protestants? Probably not. Another is that the classification is too crude: it fails to recognise important sub-characteristics within the larger group. An obvious example is the grouping that sometimes happens of ethnic minorities, when, in fact, the differences between, say,

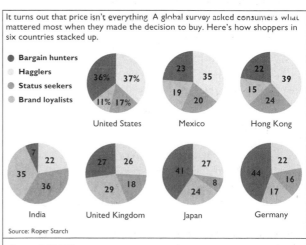

It turns out that price isn't everything A global survey asked consumers what mattered most when they made the decision to buy. Here's how shoppers in six countries stacked up.

● Bargain hunters
○ Hagglers
● Status seekers
● Brand loyalists

United States: 36% 37% 11% 17%
Mexico: 23 35 19 20
Hong Kong: 22 39 15 24
India: 7 22 35 36
United Kingdom: 27 26 29 18
Japan: 27 41 24 8
Germany: 22 44 16 17

Source: Roper Starch

FIGURE 3.11: What matters to consumers?
Source: *Newsweek*, 24 July 1995.

those of Chinese, Caribbean and Indian descent are much more significant than the fact that they are not white. There is also the risk of stereotyping, which means transferring the perceived characteristics of a group to the individuals who comprise it. Not all Yorkshire people like brass bands, no more than all Scots eat haggis! Nevertheless, some cultural differences are deeply rooted, for example Muslims do not eat pork; and generalisations can be valid. Cultural factors may also underlie shopping habits (see *Fig. 3.11*).

	Black	Indian Pakistani Bangladeshi	White	Others	Minorities *percentage*
		thousands			
ENGLAND					
North	5	21	2,988	39	1.3
Yorkshire/Humberside	37	144	4,623	33	4.4
East Midlands	39	120	3,765	29	4.8
East Anglia	14	14	1,984	15	2.1
Greater London	535	521	5,334	290	20.2
Rest of South East	74	170	10,179	104	3.3
South West	22	17	4,547	24	1.4
West Midlands	102	277	4,726	45	8.2
North West	47	147	5,999	50	3.9
WALES	9	16	2,794	16	1.5
SCOTLAND	6	32	4,936	24	1.3
GREAT BRITAIN	891	1,480	51,874	645	5.5

FIGURE 3.12: Ethnic groups, Great Britain, 1991.
Source: *Social Trends 24*.

Subcultural groups could also be based on **age**. For example, in 1961 just under 12 per cent of the population were aged 65 or over; by 1991 nearly 16 per cent were in this age group; and this number is projected to rise to just over 22 per cent by 2031. This retired group has its own needs and patterns of consumption. It might be targeted for healthcare products and medical plans, retirement homes, financial packages, particular types of holidays and restaurants, and home security systems.

CLASS

In marketing, the notion of **social class** is used to differentiate groups according to income and occupational status. The Institute of Practitioners in Advertising has identified the following classes, which are very widely applied: higher and intermediate management,

ACTIVITY

Study *Fig 3.13* and comment on how different age groups participate in particular sports, games and physical activities. Suggest how a marketing manager might use this information when seeking to introduce a sports or games product in the market.

Percentage in each group participating in each activity in the 12 months before interview

	16-19	20-24	25-29	30-44	45-59	60-69	70 and over	All aged 16 and over	Median age of partici- pants
Walking	72	70	73	73	69	61	37	65	41
Swimming	70	65	63	58	35	20	6	42	34
Snooker, pool, billiards	56	46	37	25	13	7	3	22	29
Keep fit, yoga	31	35	31	23	14	9	5	19	33
Cycling	41	23	22	22	13	8	4	17	35
Darts	29	26	21	15	10	4	2	13	31
Golf	21	19	18	15	11	7	2	12	35
Tenpin bowls, skittles	26	26	19	15	7	2	1	11	30
Running, jogging	30	20	18	13	3	1	-	9	28
Soccer	33	23	18	9	2	-	-	9	25
Weightlifting, training	27	24	20	10	3	-	-	9	27
Badminton	32	18	13	10	4	1	-	9	27
Tennis	29	16	11	9	3	1	-	7	27
Squash	15	15	15	8	2	-	-	6	27
Fishing	11	7	8	8	6	3	1	6	36

FIGURE 3.13: Participation in the most popular sports, games and physical activities, by age, Great Britian, 1990.
Source: *Social Trends 24*.

| | Social class | | | | Age | | | | | All |
	AB	CI	C2	DE	16-34	34-64	65 and over	Males	Females	adults
Percentage of adults holding:										
Building society accounts	78	70	68	49	62	68	62	63	65	65
Bank accounts	94	87	83	66	77	85	77	83	79	81
Premium bonds	45	34	25	15	16	35	34	28	28	28
Unit trusts or investment trusts	19	13	6	2	4	13	7	11	7	9
Shares	27	14	8	4	8	16	9	14	9	12
Government privatisation shares	23	13	7	3	5	14	12	13	8	10
National Savings Bank Investment/										
Ordinary account	11	13	10	7	10	10	10	10	10	10
National Savings certificates/bonds	14	12	3	4	5	7	13	8	7	7

FIGURE 3.14: Savings, by social class, age and sex, Great Britain, 1993.
Source: *Social Trends 24.*

administrative or professional (AB); supervisory or clerical, and junior management, administrative or professional (C1); skilled manual workers (C2); and semi-skilled and unskilled manual workers, those dependent on state pensions, widows without earnings, casual or low-grade workers (DE).

The value to organisations of having research information which places people in social classes is that it allows them to make generalisations about the buying behaviour of particular groups, according to their social background. For example, people from different classes show distinct preferences in such areas as newspaper reading, clothing, home furnishing, leisure activities, cars and savings schemes. In the case of savings, this is clearly demonstrated in *Fig. 3.14*, which shows that nearly all those in class AB have a bank account compared with only two-thirds in class DE. The difference is even more marked for unit and investment trusts: people in class AB are nearly ten times more likely to hold such investments as those in class DE.

PERSONAL CHARACTERISTICS

To secure a wide picture of purchasing behaviour it is important to gather information on personal factors such as the potential consumer's type of job, economic circumstances, lifestyle and self image. The pattern of demand for, say, clothing is significantly influenced by the type of job that people do. An office worker will buy a formal suit and shirt, a manual worker jeans or overalls.

Consumers' economic circumstances are determined by their level of disposable income and personal wealth, and this has a significant effect on the pattern of demand for a wide range of household goods. Households with less than £100 of disposable income per week spend nearly a quarter

of this on food and a further quarter on housing, fuel, light and power. By contrast, those with over £400 of weekly disposable income spend 15 per cent of the total on food and only a further 20 per cent on housing, fuel, light and power. Clearly, the latter group has much more available to spend on luxuries and optional leisure items.

Consumer behaviour is also influenced by **lifestyle**, which reflects consumers' patterns of living as expressed in their activities, interests and opinions. Research into these areas is important for an organisation when dividing the market into segments and identifying target groups. For example, through research, Lucozade, which was traditionally sold as a drink to aid recovery from illness, has in recent years extended into another market by being promoted as a sports drink. This has been achieved by suggesting through a range of advertisements that it is an integral part of the lifestyle of such sporting stars as Linford Christie and Daley Thompson.

Research into consumers' self images is important in determining purchasing behaviour. Those who see themselves as being active, sociable and outward going, and are looking for a new car, are likely to be attracted to a make and model advertised by, or associated with, someone sympathetic to that image.

ACTIVITY

Select four advertisements currently being shown on television and identify the type of consumer self image they are associated with.

PSYCHOLOGICAL FACTORS

Organisations need to be sure that their products match the wants of customers and that they are perceived by potential buyers as doing so. Therefore, organisations should understand the psychology of needs and perception.

In *Motivation and Personality*, Abraham Maslow explains why people are motivated by needs which are fundamental to existence and, on the other hand, by those which are associated with mental characteristics or attitudes. Maslow says these needs can be ordered in a hierarchy (see *Fig. 3.15*), with people trying progressively to satisfy them.

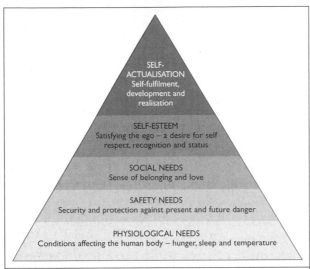

FIGURE 3.15: Maslow's heirarchy of needs.
Source: *Motivation and Personality*, Abraham Maslow.

Obviously, any marketing strategy must attempt to link the product or service to the satisfaction of a particular need. For example, in a poor country people may concentrate on the satisfaction of basic physiological needs, such as food, clothing, shelter and warmth. By contrast, in a wealthy economy, many will have moved up the heirarchy to aspire to the ownership of status goods such as fast cars, large houses and swimming pools. They may even be buying camcorders to achieve 'self-actualisation', by expressing their creativity in the making of home videos.

To place a product successfully, it is essential for an organisation to gather market information which accurately identifies the stage at which the majority of potential consumers are in Maslow's heirarchy. It is also important to try to take account of the potential customer's probable perception of the product or service. This is extremely difficult to achieve as it depends on the reaction to information, situations and messages associated with the product or service, some of which will be retained, distorted or rejected. For example, someone actively looking for a new car is more likely to notice advertisements for cars and to retain information about them. However, if someone has already decided which

type of car to buy, to reinforce the decision, the person may distort or reject other information.

ASSESSING DEMAND

Knowledge of consumer behaviour and the wider social and commercial environment makes it possible to identify, measure and monitor the factors that influence the demand for products. In addition, there is considerable value to a business organisation in being able to measure and **forecast demand**, as it provides the basis for deciding what markets to enter and which segments to concentrate on. Such measurements and forecasts may be short term, medium term or long term; cover from local to world sales; and involve individual products or an entire product range.

The aim is to inform planning. For example, short-term forecasts of demand help in making decisions concerning the optimum purchase of raw materials and components, and the scheduling and financing of production. If the extent of the market is either under-estimated or over-estimated, extra costs may be incurred and profits lost.

MEASUREMENT

Market planning requires the measurement of the total sales of the industry as a whole, the share of sales going to the particular organisation ('market share'), total demand in the market, and the level of demand in particular areas within it.

In the case of **total sales**, information is often available through the industry's trade association or from private market research firms. By expressing its own sales as a percentage of the figure obtained from these sources, it is possible for the organisation to calculate its share of the market.

The **total demand** in the market should be viewed as the total volume that would be purchased at a particular point in time, by a specified consumer group, in a defined geographical area, under particular economic conditions and a defined level of marketing in the industry. One of the most common ways of estimating this level of demand is by taking the number of buyers in the specific market, multiplying this by the quantity purchased by an average buyer in a year, and multiplying the sum by the average price per unit of the product. For example, if the manufacturer of a new type of cola estimates that, within its target market, there are 800,000 potential buyers purchasing on average 75 cans of cola a year at an average price of 50p a can, the total market demand may be valued at £30m.

The cola manufacturer may initially decide to concentrate its marketing efforts on a particular geographical area. In reaching this decision, it would need to estimate the level of market demand in the area. This is often done by identifying the most important factors influencing the size of the market, such as the percentage of disposable income, total retail sales and population. The relative importance of the factors is then assessed and weighted by use of a multiplier (if factor X is regarded as twice as significant as factor Y, the former will be multiplied by a value double that for factor Y). A calculation can then be made to project the buying power of the locality.

To take an example: if a food chain was expanding to operate nationally, it would study the relative buying power of different geographical areas before deciding where to locate new outlets. One of the areas might be Westshire. This has 0.05 per cent of the nation's disposable income, 0.08 per cent of retail sales and 0.055 per cent of the population. If income were weighted as the most important factor at 0.5, retail sales next at 0.3 and population at 0.2, the following sum could be compiled to determine the size of the Westshire market: $(0.5 \times 0.05) + (0.3 \times 0.08) + (0.2 \times 0.055) = 0.06$ per cent of national buying power. If the organisation estimated that total national sales could reach £1bn, those in Westshire could be expected to be valued at £600,000. Figures for areas could be compared in reaching a decision about the locations for expansion. However, the accuracy and value of this kind of calculation depend upon the weights selected and the quality of statistics used.

FORECASTING

Forecasting involves predictions about how buyers may behave in future in a specified set of circumstances. A general approach that can be taken to **sales forecasting** involves three stages. First, a company makes an economic forecast as to the future levels of gross domestic product; second, it applies this and a number of other indicators in estimating future sales in the industry; and third, it bases the forecast for its own sales on the assumption that it will achieve a certain proportion of the industry's total.

There are a number of other approaches that can be taken to sales forecasting. First, it is possible to carry out a survey of potential buyers' future intentions and determine the probability of a particular group of people buying a product in the future. Second, it is possible to carry out a survey of expert opinion within the industry. This could involve contacting sales representatives, suppliers, distributors and trade associations to build up a picture of what they think might happen in the future. Such an approach is often taken by car producers, who survey their dealers in order to forecast short-term

demand. Third, a statistical method known as time series analysis enables long-term movements to be charted, offering a relatively sound basis for making projections.

ACTIVITY

A chain of sports shops has estimated that total UK sales could reach £2bn. The company is considering the possibility of expanding its operation into either Middleshire or Wilburyshire.

Research has provided the following figures: Middleshire: percentage of national disposable income 0.07 per cent, of retail sales 0.08 per cent, and of population 0.085 per cent; and for Wilburyshire 0.12 per cent, 0.06 per cent and 0.075 per cent, respectively.

In terms of national buying power the relative importance of these factors is weighted thus: income 0.3, population 0.45 and retail sales 0.25. Calculate the sales potential of the two areas.

RESEARCH METHODS

There are essentially two research methods, desk research and field research.

DESK RESEARCH

This involves using existing research information, which may be **internal** or **external** to the organisation. In the case of the former, it may include information about accounts, invoices, stock control levels and sales. For example, the organisation's own records of past sales may provide valuable data by which to establish a connection between the company's performance and outside influences.

There are many external sources of information, including volumes of annual statistics published by the Central Statistical Office (CSO), of which the *Annual Abstract of Statistics*, the *Family Expenditure Survey, Regional Trends* and *Social Trends* are among the most useful. They provide data on broad aggregates in the economy such as national income and expenditure, industrial production, investment, international trade, prices and information on demographic and social trends. In addition to the CSO, the Office of Population Censuses and Surveys (OPCS) provides demographic and other census-related data. In all, the government publishes 400 series of statistics. A guide to sources of government statistics is published annually (*Government Statistics: a brief guide to sources*, available free on request from: Central Statistical Office, Press, Publications and Publicity, Great George Street, London SWIP 3AQ).

Other sources are trade publications, directories and magazines, which specialise in collecting market data in a particular business sector. These contain data, information and articles on subjects and developments of relevance to the industry, as well as expert opinion on the effects of political, economic and social trends. Two trade sources especially worth noting are the Joint Industry Committee for Television Audience Research, which produces weekly figures on commercial television audience levels, and the Audit Bureau of Circulation, which provides audited information on newspaper and magazine sales. Also useful are the journals of professional associations and institutions. If these are read in conjunction with news media such as the *Economist, Management Today, Marketing Week, Marketing* and the *Financial Times*, a good overview can be obtained of developments in the business world.

INFORMATION TECHNOLOGY

The rapid growth of information technology has made research data much more accessible and easier to analyse. This is due to the ever-increasing processing power of computers and developments, such as broadband technology, which enable large amounts of information to be moved rapidly around the world. For the first time, it is becoming possible – and commercially viable in terms of cost – to access and analyse data which previously was either too remote or could only be obtained in a predigested and simplified form. Information technology also enables data to be made available more quickly; no longer do users have to wait for printed volumes to appear. As a result, by being more up to date, information provides a more reliable basis on which to make decisions and gives an earlier indication of developments which may have commercial significance, enabling an organisation to react more quickly.

Among new developments, the use of the **Internet** to access data sources worldwide and the use of census data for 'community profiling' are worth particular note. Since 1991, census data are available by enumeration district as well as by local government ward and county. As an enumeration district comprises no more than 200 households, use of these data provides the opportunity to construct detailed profiles of local communities. 'Community profiling' can also be achieved by analysing data by postcode.

Another significant development is the computerised model of the economy developed for the Treasury. This enables fairly accurate forecasts of what is likely to happen in terms of the major economic indicators, such as income, expenditure, output, employment, growth, inflation and the balance of payments. It allows many larger companies to monitor movements in their own markets by putting market research information through the computer to analyse present and possible future trends.

BENEFITS OF DESK RESEARCH

Desk research is economical and comparatively speedy, and it has the advantage that it can be conducted with complete confidentiality, i.e. without competitors finding out! On the other hand, because the information was not generated for the particular purposes of the organisation, it may not be sufficiently relevant. Field research may be required to supplement it.

FIELD RESEARCH

When existing sources of information have been tapped, it may be necessary to supplement them by fresh enquiries, such as through the use of surveys or focus discussion groups. This enables organisations to make direct contact with potential or actual customers, and to ask them questions specific to the organisation's needs. Original research yields primary data (secondary data are found in existing sources).

Surveys may be based on a questionnaire which is conducted as part of an interview, or through a discussion group, or by post or over the telephone. Generally it is too expensive and time consuming to contact every potential customer, so only a sample of customers is included in the survey. This sample has to be very carefully selected.

SAMPLING

The vast majority of people do not intentionally distort their answers in responding to a questionnaire, but the conclusions drawn from research will not be reliable if the consumer sample used is not representative of the market being investigated.

Reliability relates to probability and the concept derives from the fact that surveys are usually carried out using only a small number (or 'sample') of the population to which the findings will be applied. When political pollsters want to find out the popularity of the government, they choose just one or two thousand people to ask, but they use the answers to make general statements about the electorate as a whole. Whether their conclusions are sound or not depends, among other things, on the extent to which error has been contained so that users can confidently rely on the accuracy of the findings. The reliability of data depends on the size of the sample group – is it big enough to enable valid conclusions to be drawn based on its opinions? – and the extent to which its composition is representative of the wider population to which the findings will be applied.

To ensure that a survey sample is **representative**, researchers first determine the wider population (or **'universe'**, as they call it). They then work out the size of the sample. If it is too small, reliability may suffer; if it is too large, unnecessary cost will be incurred. Ideally, the sample should be a small mirror image of the 'universe', in terms of its relevant characteristics, which may include gender, ethnicity, age, marital status, location, class, and so on.

The larger the number of sub-groups within the 'universe' that a researcher wishes to find out about, the larger the sample that is required. For example, if the 'universe' is estimated at one million people and the consumer sample consists of 3,000, a sub-group of the 'universe' which is only two per cent of the 'universe' will comprise 60 people in the sample. This may be too few to give an accurate indication of opinions held by the wider group which they are supposed to represent. For example, in a survey of 2,000 people, representative of the population as a whole, just over half of these will be women, but fewer than 150 will be women in their twenties and maybe no more than a dozen will be women in their twenties who live in Scotland. Two ways of tackling this problem are to create an overall bigger sample or to increase the number in the particular sub-group (although this must be taken into account when analysing the results as a whole).

Having decided upon the size of the sample, the researcher chooses a method for selecting those who will comprise it. There are four approaches.

The **probability** system involves obtaining a list of the 'universe' to be researched. Names and addresses may be available from trade and telephone directories, the electoral register, magazine subscription lists and membership lists of professional and voluntary organisations, among others. The researcher may take one name in 30 from the lists and allocate them to interviewers. They, in turn, will need to ensure that, as they conduct interviews, a representative cross-section is achieved. Inevitably, this means some of the people who have been interviewed will have to be rejected, otherwise bias may develop within the sample.

The **random selection** system involves contacting households on an speculative basis. The interviewer selects contacts by requesting the cooperation of passers-by, perhaps asking every tenth person until someone consents to be interviewed. Random selection is more acceptable than the interviewer being allowed to decide, as it prevents personal preferences coming into play. The composition of the survey group may, to some extent, be predetermined by basing the random selection upon homes which can be placed into sub-groups. For example, areas may be placed into categories in terms of regions, rural or urban location, and types of dwelling. This may be especially useful when the sample is to contain sub-groups based upon such characteristics.

The **quota** system is a very popular method of consumer research because it can be clearly defined. Once the size of the sample is decided, the sub-groups are defined and interviewers are allocated a quota of individuals which they must contact according to certain characteristics of the sub-groups. For example, an interviewer may be required to trace and interview a certain number of households which are owner occupiers, include two children of school age, where both parents work, and which are urban.

The **consumer panel** involves establishing a panel of households which acts as a representative sample of the market. Panel members are asked to provide regular details of their spending, identifying products, prices and sizes, the place and time of purchase or similar information. Such panels are expensive to establish and require continuing attention if they are to be maintained sufficiently long to make the results worthwhile. The longer a household remains on the panel, the more accustomed it becomes to making returns. It may then become less self-conscious when making purchases, ceasing to consider the implications they will have on its consumer report. It may then act more naturally in accordance with its personal tastes and preferences, and thus the information submitted to the researcher will be more valuable.

ACTIVITY

Consider the most appropriate method of sampling to employ when conducting surveys of political voting intentions and of household expenditure.

QUESTIONNAIRE DESIGN

The success of a sample survey depends to a large extent upon the quality of the questionnaire used. Questions should be designed so that the answers allow respondents to be classified into the required sub-groups of the 'universe'.

Initial questions usually seek personal facts about the respondent, such as marital status, age group and occupation. Some of these questions may be designed to stimulate the interviewee's interest in the survey and create an impression that the person's contribution is important for the research. Questions of a more deeply personal nature, required to identify sub-groups in terms of income and spending habits, can follow later when the respondent has become more relaxed.

Although the majority of people will have no reason for giving false information, many may hesitate to divulge information which could show them in an unfavourable light. Where such questions are necessary, the responses given can be checked against those to similar questions, placed elsewhere in the questionnaire. This enables the researcher to test the **validity** of the interviewee's response.

A questionnaire comprising highly structured questions, possible answers to which have been classified into predetermined categories, is quick to administer and the resulting data easy to process. By contrast, a questionnaire comprising open-ended questions creates problems of interpretation and analysis, as well as in recording data.

When writing questions, several points should be taken into account.

QUESTIONNAIRES SHOULD...

1   **Use simple language**

2   **Have clear meaning**

3   **Be administered neutrally**

4   **Avoid leading questions**

5   **Keep questions brief**

6   **Avoid embarrassing questions**

7   **Avoid two-part questions**

8   **Be expressed in positive language**

 ## ACTIVITY

What's wrong with the following questions?

'Have you travelled to France by ferry or through the rail tunnel?'

'Do you clean your car regularly?'

'Which type of car, like Ford or Vauxhall, do you feel is the most reliable?'

SURVEY METHODS

The **personal interview** is generally regarded as the most effective method of conducting a survey as it produces the best response. A personable and experienced interviewer acquires a technique which encourages participation and results in more complete and more accurate answers. The interviewer can put the person being interviewed at ease; the value of participation can be explained; and any difficulties in understanding can be overcome by rephasing questions. Where the quota system is used, the interviewer will gain experience of certain types of household and be more readily able to identify areas where they can be located. The interviewer may also become accomplished in identifying general characteristics of individuals or households, so that questionnaire responses may be supplemented by additional information.

Personal interviews are an expensive method of conducting surveys, given the time and expenses involved. This is particularly the case where the probability and random selection systems are used, which involve revisits to respondents not initially at home. Similarly, in the quota system, a sub-group may have characteristics which makes it time-consuming and difficult to trace individuals within a particular area, and this, too, adds to costs. If questionnaires are completed face to face, there is the danger that interviewees may try to give the answers expected of them, or those they believe will create the best impression.

Postal surveys are less expensive but the response rate is poor, which means large numbers of questionnaires have to be mailed to obtain a sufficient number of replies. Because there is no interviewer on hand to assist those filling them in, mail questionnaires must be especially well laid out and questions and instructions clearly expressed and in plain language. The method of answering the questions should reduce the effort involved to a minimum, for example by using ticks and crosses or circling items. Higher response rates to mail questionnaires may be achieved if a covering letter makes an appeal for participation and, perhaps, explains the purpose of the research and its use. Also, people are more likely to respond when they feel an affiliation with the purpose; for example, it is a subject they feel strongly about. However, this can introduce fresh problems in terms of the representativeness of the responses received.

Over 85 per cent of UK households have a telephone, and conducting **interviews by phone** is less expensive than personal interviewing and more likely to elicit a response than use of a mail questionnaire. However, there is a danger that bias may enter the responses if it is found that only a certain type of person is willing to provide personal information to an unknown and unseen caller.

Discussion groups bring together a representative group of people to express their tastes and preferences in relation to certain products or to give their views in general on household consumer items. The person conducting the meeting will be an experienced researcher able to create an atmosphere in which the participants feel free to express their opinions. The researcher will introduce topics and guide the conversation. The whole exercise may be filmed or recorded for subsequent analysis, including of tone and strength of expression and body language. In some cases, a group of researchers is hidden behind a glass wall, so that they can follow the proceedings without being seen. They can then relay information to the researcher with the group, including conversational leads that should be followed up. Usually, respondents selected to take part in focus discussion groups are paid to attend. There is the danger that, in a small group, one or two people will try to dominate, but an effective researcher knows how to handle this, and to 'bring out' the less forthcoming members.

TEST MARKETING

When a large capital investment is involved in the development of a new or improved product, some form of test marketing will generally be an important pre-condition for a national sales effort. Test marketing applies not only to the product but also to all the marketing activities supporting it, namely the sales organisation, the distribution system and advertising and promotional aspects. It allows the company to experience the realities of competitive pressures in a market, to discover any deficiencies and to modify the product and the arrangements. Test marketing has an impressive record:

about 90 per cent of products subsequently launched nationally are successful.

When conducting market testing it is important to ensure that several conditions apply. One is that the test area must be sufficiently large and have the required characteristics to make it representative of the marketing 'universe', so that results can be a reliable guide in selling the product to a wider public. Another is that, if the effect of advertising is being assessed, the product test area should, as nearly as possible, coincide with the readership areas of the local media.

Test marketing should not attempt to assess too many factors at the same time in the same area, as it will be difficult to disentangle the various effects. For example, if the effectiveness of promotional activities is being assessed, altering other aspects, such as packaging and price, will tend only to confuse the issue. The response of competitors should be monitored, to judge whether any competition is local in nature or could be repeated and sustained nationally.

The length of the test period should be long enough to provide evidence of seasonal fluctuations in demand as well as to enable confirmation of initial findings. The test area should be kept under scrutiny even after the product has been launched to a wider public. This may provide early warning of problems which may arise only after the product has been available for a while.

	Personal interview	Postal survey	Phone survey	Discussion group
Interviewer bias				
Depth of questioning				
Cost				
Speed in obtaining response				
Flexibility				
Control over data collected				

ACTIVITY

Rank the different survey methods with a score of one (low) to four (high) in terms of their advantages and disadvantages.

PORTFOLIO ASSIGNMENT

TEENAGE MAGAZINE

Eastern Press publishes a number of successful women's magazines and a weekly publication listing television programmes. Now, the company wants to extend its range of publications by moving into the older teenage market. In particular, it wants to assess whether there is sufficient demand for a new title among 16 to 19-year olds of both sexes and with an ABC social background.

The company's inclination is that the magazine should be weekly and cover areas such as music, sport, fashion and beauty, television and cinema, careers and higher education, social and political issues, and fiction. It should also include competitions and carry a pull-out poster. However, the editorial development team has few ideas about price, format, design, promotion and distribution of the magazine.

You work for a market research agency specialising in the magazine industry, and have been asked to investigate the feasibility of Eastern Press's idea.

Design a suitable questionnaire and conduct a survey which will allow you to confirm or reject Eastern Press' ideas. The survey should be based on a sample of 50 students at your school or college.

Eastern Press also wants to be reassured that this is the right time to be moving into such a new venture. Find out more by using secondary data.

Combine your findings in a report which also explains the methods used. Prepare a verbal presentation of your conclusions and recommendations. This is to be made to the directors of Eastern Press (your tutors/teachers).

PORTFOLIO ASSIGNMENT

SCHOOL OR COLLEGE SHOP SURVEY

The governors of your school or college are looking at a number of ways of raising funds. One involves buying a mobile building for use as a student shop. Your business studies group has been asked to conduct the initial market research, to test the feasibility of the idea.

Design a questionnaire to determine whether there is a need for a shop; who would use it and how much they would be likely to spend in it; what items the shop should stock; its opening times and location.

Compare your questionnaire with those designed by other students, then, working as a team, create a final version and conduct a survey throughout your school or college.

Write a report to the governors, presenting the findings, drawing conclusions and making recommendations. Your report should also describe the survey methods used and assess the accuracy of the findings.

Marketing communications and target audiences

THE BASIS FOR MARKETING COMMUNICATIONS

Effective communication involves the exchange of information to achieve mutual understanding and, perhaps, to promote action. In marketing, it centres on the use of advertising, public relations, sales promotions and direct marketing activities. The aim is to influence purchasing decisions, in particular as made by specific consumer groups (or 'target audiences'). A secondary aim is to obtain beneficial publicity for the organisation so as to enhance its public image.

For marketing communications to be effective, the **target audience** should comprise a group of consumers who are sufficiently alike to suggest that its members will respond in a similar way to a particular advertisement or other promotional 'message'.

ACTIVITY

The new Ford Probe is described as a 2 + 2 coupé with a choice of two engines, a sports 2.0 litre, 16-valve, double-overhead camshaft, four cylinder engine with an output of 115 PS or a refined 2.5 litre, 24-valve, four-cam V6 engine with an output of 165 PS. Both are mounted transversely and drive the front wheels through a manual five-speed close ratio transmission.

Consider the market segment that Ford would want to inform about the availability of this product.

STAGES AND TYPES OF COMMUNICATIONS

The targeted consumer requires three types of information before making a purchasing decision. The potential buyer needs to know:

- ⊗ **that the product exists and where it can be bought;**
- ⊗ **descriptive details about it; and**
- ⊗ **information useful in evaluating the product in relation to the prospective customer's needs.**

All these types of information have to pass through a number of **stages of communication**, namely origination, choice of format, choice of channel and receipt by members of the intended audience.

One of the practical problems associated with this sequence is that it is essentially one way and offers little opportunity for feedback. This makes it difficult to measure the effectiveness of marketing communications other than by the use of such broad indicators as a comparison of sales before and after an advertising campaign.

Another problem arises from the need for organisations to take account of other communications which they do not control. For example, some consumers may act as opinion leaders, influencing the views of others by making recommendations and giving advice. Such people are generally recognised by their peers because they are considered to have expert knowledge on a particular product or service. For a marketing communication to be effective, it must be received and accepted by these opinion formers. Organisations also have to pay attention to the various sources of impartial consumer advice which come from consumer group reports, newspaper articles and material issued by government agencies. These may support or damage the marketing communication put out by the organisation.

There are two types of communication that are controlled by the organisation. One is **impersonal** in that it is aimed at providing information to a large number

of people, for example an advertising campaign in the mass media. This may be appropriate for a high volume consumer product such as a new washing powder or soft drink, where the primary aim is to provide information about the existence of the product to as many people as possible. The other is **personal**, involving the supply of information directly to individuals by personal, postal or phone contact. This approach is often regarded as appropriate where the targeted consumer is taking a relatively large purchasing decision, as when buying a house or car.

In certain cases, it is appropriate to use both types of communication. For example, an organisation which is responsible for designing and building new conservatories may initially run an advertising campaign in appropriate magazines or newspapers and follow up any enquiries with a visit by a consultant or sales person.

ADVERTISING

Advertising is an impersonal form of communication. It involves the use of communications media to inform, persuade, publicise and remind potential and existing consumers about an organisation's products and activities. Essentially, it is a means of increasing sales. It may also be used to encourage consumers to purchase products or services from a particular retail outlet. The following panel gives a list of reasons for advertising.

Advertising objectives

- ⊗ **Promote and establish an image for the organisation and its products.**

- ⊗ **Tell potential buyers about a new product and to encourage them to buy it.**

- ⊗ **Increase sales by reminding potential and existing consumers about its products and activities.**

- ⊗ **Undermine the potential buyer's loyalty towards competing products.**

- ⊗ **Provide technical and general information about the product or service.**

- ⊗ **Focus on the unique selling points of a product.**

- ⊗ **Provide details of special offers, samples, brochures or promotions.**

- ⊗ **Generate initial enquiries that the salesforce may follow up.**

- ⊗ **Encourage retailers or wholesalers to stock the product.**

ACTIVITY

Identify the major types of music purchased by the members of your class or group.

List the impersonal and personal ways in which the music industry communicates its market message. Does this vary with the type of music? How effective is it?

Identify the 'opinion leaders' in your class or group. Why are they viewed as such? How do they keep themselves up to date with what is happening in the music industry?

Identify the sources of impartial advice available to consumers of music products.

THE ADVERTISING CAMPAIGN

Advertising is an important part of an organisation's promotional activities. An advertising campaign must be carefully planned, with a clear view as to whether the retailer or the consumer is to be targeted and whether it is the product or the organisation which is to be promoted.

The effectiveness of advertising is often increased if the product or organisation already has a strong brand identity. This means that it has a readily recognised name, sign, logo or design. Examples are many, including Levi's jeans, Hoover vacuum cleaners and BMW cars. High levels of recognition mean that the organisation can promote its products and publicise its activities to good effect by using these devices on sales literature, delivery vehicles, stationery or point of sale displays

Many medium-sized and large organisations seek the specialist services of an advertising agency. Agencies provide expert advice and carry out or manage a number of tasks, including copywriting; design and layout, including use of type, style and visual matter; film production for television or cinema use; space buying in media and other outlets, such as billboards; and evaluation.

The most successful agencies are those able clearly to identify the needs of an organisation and to translate them into effective advertisements. In selecting an agency, it may be helpful to follow the advice of the Advertising Association or the Institute of Practitioners in Advertising.

Any advertising campaign has to adhere to a usually strict budget, the size of which will be determined, at least ideally, by several factors. These include the objectives of the campaign (what the organisation intends to achieve by it); the amount of money competitors are spending in promoting their products; and the stage the product has reached in its life cycle. Spending on the advertising of a product is generally high when it is launched, relatively

ACTIVITY

Select an advertisement from a weekly consumer magazine and answer the following questions:

⊗ What are the main objectives of the advertiser?

⊗ What is the target audience?

⊗ How does the advertisement use images, design, colour and text to achieve its purposes?

steady during its maturity, and ceases in its period of decline.

One of the major decisions associated with an advertising campaign concerns **choice of media**. Channels of communication include newspapers, magazines, television and radio, cinema, and outdoor displays. To ensure that the marketplace is adequately covered, it is often appropriate to use a mix of media. Details about sources of advertising media, classified by area, price and potential audience, can be found in the BRAD (British Rate and Data) directory.

NEWSPAPERS

Britain has a large coverage of national tabloid and broadsheet newspapers, with a daily readership of more than 27 million, rising to 31 million on Sundays, in 1992 (see *Fig. 3.16*). The most popular daily is *The Sun,* which is read by one in four men and one in five women. On Sundays, 12 million read the *News of the World.*

Age is a significant indicator of readership, for example 25 per cent of those aged 15 to 24 read *The Sun* compared to 15 per cent of those over 65. Since 1971, new titles have come onto the market. Some like *Today* have not survived, others like *The Independent* have been more succesful. Sales of *The Independent* show a noted gender bias, with five per cent of men but only one per cent of women reading it.

This sort of information helps to determine where an advertisement should be placed so as to have the most impact on its target audience. Advertising agencies can give advice by providing **readership profiles** for newspapers which identify typical buyers in terms of social class and income. Also, newspapers themselves give advice on the best days to place advertisements. For example, it is generally thought that mail order items should be advertised at the weekend because this is when people have the leisure to browse advertisements.

Regional and local free newspapers also provide extensive coverage. They often group advertisements in classified sections. This means advertisers can be confident that their advertisement will be read by those who are most interested.

MAGAZINES

Britain has a wide range of magazines aimed at the mass market, including many that target women. Again, considerable variations exist in the age and gender of readerships (see *Fig. 3.17*). Incidentally, the large number of television listings magazines have come into being since the end of the BBC's monopoly, in 1991, on the publication of its own listings.

As for newspapers, advertising agencies can give advice on readership profiles and supply details of other types

	Percentage of adults reading each paper in 1992			Percentage of adults reading each paper in 1992				Readership (millions)		Readers per copy (numbers)
	Males	Females	All adults	15-24	25-44	45-64	65 and over	1971	1992	1992
Daily newspapers										
The Sun	24	19	21	28	23	20	15	8.5	9.7	2.7
Daily Mirror	19	15	17	18	16	18	17	13.8	7.8	2.8
Daily Mail	10	10	10	8	9	11	11	4.8	4.5	2.6
Daily Express	9	8	8	7	6	10	11	9.7	3.8	2.5
The Daily Telegraph	6	5	6	4	4	7	7	3.6	2.5	2.4
Daily Star	7	4	5	8	6	5	2	.	2.4	3.0
Today	4	3	3	4	4	3	2	.	1.5	2.9
The Guardian	3	2	3	3	4	3	1	1.1	1.3	3.1
The Independent	3	2	2	2	3	2	1	.	1.1	2.9
The Times	3	2	2	2	2	3	1	1.1	1.0	2.7
Financial Times	2	1	1	1	2	1	.	0.7	0.6	3.6
Any national daily newspaper	65	56	60	59	57	64	62	.	27.3	.
Sunday newspapers										
News of the World	29	26	28	35	31	26	19	15.8	12.5	2.7
Sunday Mirror	20	18	19	22	20	20	16	13.5	8.8	3.2
The People	14	13	13	13	12	15	14	14.4	6.1	2.9
The Mail on Sunday	13	13	13	14	14	14	9	.	5.8	2.9
Sunday Express	11	11	11	10	8	13	14	10.4	4.9	2.8
The Sunday Times	9	7	8	9	9	8	4	3.7	3.5	3.0
Sunday Telegraph	4	4	4	3	4	5	5	2.1	1.8	3.2
The Observer	4	3	4	4	4	4	2	2.4	1.7	3.1
Sunday Sport	5	1	3	7	3	1	.	.	1.3	4.1
Independent on Sunday	3	2	3	4	4	2	1	.	1.3	3.2
Any Sunday newspaper	71	67	69	71	68	72	66	.	31.3	.

FIGURE 3.16: Readership of national newspapers, by sex and age, Great Britain, 1992.

Note: Readership is defined as the average issue readership and represents the number of people who claim to have read or looked at one or more copies of a given publication during the period equal to the interval at which the publication appears.

Source: *Social Trends 24*.

of magazines, such as those produced by professional associations, those aimed at particular retail and trade groups and those covering specialist hobby and leisure interests. One of the major advantages of placing an advertisement in a magazine, rather than a newspaper, is that the publication is likely to have a longer 'life': it may be re-read over many months and seen by many more people among the target audience.

	Percentage of adults reading each magazine in 1992			Percentage of each age group reading each magazine in 1992				Readership (millions)		Readers per copy (numbers)
	Males	Females	All adults	15-24	25-44	45-64	65 and over	1971	1992	1992
General magazines:										
Reader's Digest	14	12	13	9	12	17	14	9.2	5.9	3.9
Radio Times	13	12	12	14	12	13	12	9.5	5.7	3.6
TV Times	11	11	11	15	10	11	9	9.9	5.0	4.5
Viz	14	5	10	29	11	2	.	.	4.3	1.0
TV Quick	5	8	6	9	8	5	3	.	2.9	.
What's on TV	6	7	6	9	7	4	5	.	2.8	1.9
Women's magazines										
Bella	3	14	9	10	11	8	7	.	3.3	.
Women's Own	3	14	9	10	10	8	7	7.2	3.4	4.9
Take a Break	4	13	8	12	10	8	4	.	3.0	.
Woman	2	11	6	6	7	6	5	8.0	2.6	3.8
Woman's Weekly	2	10	6	3	4	7	11	4.7	2.4	3.2
Best	2	10	6	7	7	6	3	.	2.3	3.9

FIGURE 3.17: Readership of the most popular magazines, by sex and age, 1992

Source: *Social Trends 1994*, CSO

ACTIVITY

Collect a range of daily, Sunday and local newspapers, together with examples of general and specialist magazines. Study the publications and the types of advertisements they contain.

Discuss the probable target audience for each publication and complete the readership profile below.

Use the readership profile to decide where best to place advertisements for these products:

⊗ a new record by East 17;

⊗ an all-timber conservatory;

⊗ a coach tour to Scotland;

⊗ bottom of the range kitchen units;

⊗ a hedge trimmer;

⊗ a second-hand car;

⊗ expensive jewellery;

⊗ oven-ready chips;

⊗ vintage port;

⊗ a pension plan;

⊗ holiday flats in Spain.

TITLE OF PUBLICATION	CHARACTERISTICS			
	Age	Gender	Class	Significant other

TELEVISION

The vast majority of households have a television, making it an important advertising medium. It is particularly attractive to advertisers as it allows a combination of music, speech and pictures, as well as the use of jingles, well-known personalities and mini-dramas as aids to the creation of brand interest and identity.

The effectiveness of television advertising depends on a large number of the target group of consumers watching the advertisement at the same time. Therefore, its placement in an appropriate programme slot is vital. 'Prime time' programmes, especially soap operas, provide some of the most 'penetrative' opportunities for advertising to a mass market. The link between popular programmes and advertising markets was demonstrated, in 1994, by the decision of ITV to advertise certain programmes in particular trade magazines, for example *Cracker* in *The Grocer* and *The Bill* in *Publican and Off-Licence News*.

The growth in the number of television channels has tended to spread the viewing audience across a wider range of programmes. This makes it more difficult to target a particular market segment. The situation has been complicated still further by the widespread ownership of video cassette recorders, which enable people both to 'self-schedule' television and 'fast forward' through advertisements (see panel).

The effectiveness of newspaper and television advertisements is monitored weekly in the Adwatch survey and reported in *Marketing*. A sample of 500 or more adults is asked to rank advertisements according to the frequency it remembers having seen or heard them in a given period.

Live viewing

Using the video to self-schedule TV programmes remains largely the province of young ABC1s, according to research by TGI (see Fig 3.18).

Asked whether they agreed with the statement that TV programmes are preferable 'live' rather than on video, it was the young and upwardly mobile who were more likely to reach for their remote controls.

The highest agreement index in favour of 'live' TV was among the 65-plus age band, probably because they spend more time in the house and in front of the box.

Similarly, women generally, and housewives specifically, had a higher index of agreement with the statement because they are more likely to be in the house to watch it at the time it is screened.

The highest index is among the E demograph, partly attributable to a higher proportion of unemployment and lower income levels causing them to spend more time in the home.

The lowest index of agreement is at the other end of the spectrum, with ABs having more cash, more leisure time outside the home, and more of a need to use the video.

From a buyer's point of view this excerbates the difficulty of reaching ABC1 males who, if they are recording, are probably zipping through the ads.

But it is children under 14 who agree most strongly with the statement that video scheduling is best, largely because they don't watch with their parents over their shoulders.

Marketing,
1 December 1994

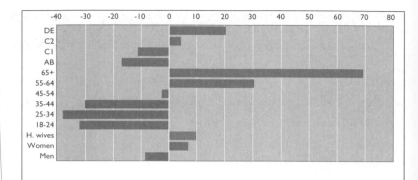

FIGURE 3.18: Who watches 'live' television?

☀ ACTIVITY

Design a suitable questionnaire and conduct a survey to find out the best remembered advertisements among the students in your school or college.

Compare the results with those appearing in the current edition of *Marketing*. Account for, and comment on, any significant differences.

RADIO

Radio provides a local and, increasingly, a national medium for placing advertisements, particularly those aimed at 16 to 24-year olds. In 1994, commercial radio accounted for four per cent of radio audiences and generated a revenue of £219m. Three stations – Virgin, Classic FM and Atlantic 252 – accounted for 22 per cent of total commercial radio hours.

Radio is a rapidly growing advertising medium and has the advantage over television of having much lower production costs. Local radio can help to develop a strong community feeling which small local businesses may benefit from in buying advertising.

CINEMA

The introduction of multi-screen cinemas and the consequent revival in cinema attendance has benefited advertising in the 1990s. Cinemas provide advertisers with a captive audience which can be reached relatively cheaply. As a medium, it is of particular value to local retailers, businesses, hotels and restaurants.

OUTDOOR DISPLAYS

Use may be made of parking meters, sandwich boards, taxis, buses and tube trains, telephone kiosks, hoardings and flashing signs.

GUIDELINES AND CONTROLS

The **Advertising Standards Authority (ASA)** is the body which regulates the UK advertising industry. The advertising profession has adopted a code of practice which the ASA administers for all non-broadcast media. The code aims to ensure that advertisements provide a fair, honest and unambiguous representation of the products they promote, including through the use of words and impressions.

The ASA gives guidance to advertisers on whether a proposed advertisement would be regarded as acceptable and deals with complaints from the general public about cases of allegedly untruthful, misleading or offensive advertisements.

The ASA is not an enforcement agency and operates on a voluntary basis. Any breaches of the law are generally referred to the Office of Fair Trading. Following an investigation the ASA can request an advertiser to amend or withdraw an unsuitable advertisement. On the rare occasion an advertiser refuses, the ASA may seek to put pressure on the offending advertiser through the Committee of Advertising Practice (CAP), which is made up of organisations representing all areas of the media, including advertisers and advertising agency associations. The ASA can issue a warning to CAP members and, as they are not supposed to accept advertisements which breach the code, this would make it difficult for the offending advertiser to continue to buy space. However, if the advertisement is still being run, the ASA can fall back on the Control of Misleading Advertisements Regulations 1988, referring the advertisement to the Office of Fair Trading.

In the case of television advertising, there are four groups that act as watchdogs over standards.

⊗ **The Broadcast Complaints Commission** is a statutory body which deals with any complaints of unjust or unfair treatment. It has no disciplinary powers.

⊗ **The Broadcasting Standards Council** is a statutory body dealing with issues of sex, violence, taste or decency. It also has no disciplinary powers.

⊗ **The Independent Television Commission** is also a statutory body, set up to regulate commercial television, which monitors the use of advertisements and can enforce action, where necessary.

⊗ **The Broadcasting Advertising Clearance Centre** is run by the ITV Centre and vets all advertising copy before it is screened.

PUBLIC RELATIONS

Public relations is a means of publicising and promoting an organisation's image with a view to influencing customers to buy products, investors to buy shares and government and others to act in ways helpful to the organisation. Essentially, it involves impersonal types of communication. In many cases it consists in the placement of information about the organisation in a suitable publication or obtaining a favourable presentation of its activities on radio, television or elsewhere without this having to be paid for. The following panel lists reasons for carrying out public relations.

Public relations objectives

⊗ **Promote confidence in, and create a favourable image of, a product or organisation in the eyes of the general public, bankers, customers and suppliers.**

⊗ **Increase understanding of an organisation, its scope and products.**

⊗ **Bring the organisation and its products to the attention of those it wishes to reach, and to do so beneficially.**

⊗ **Generate more business and profits.**

THE PUBLIC RELATIONS CAMPAIGN

Strengths

Weaknesses

Opportunities

Threats

In designing a public relations campaign it is useful to conduct a **SWOT** analysis to put the organisation and its products into perspective. This will help to highlight the main internal strengths and weaknesses of the organisation, together with any external opportunities and threats. It may be that an organisation has strengths in research development and the use of new technologies, but it suffers from weaknesses in management and labour turnover. Opportunities may be opening up in European markets; on the other hand, there may be threats from American competition. Under these circumstances, it is important to publicise the organisation's strengths and to play down any perceived weaknesses.

In addition, the findings from a SWOT analysis allow the organisation to identify the people and groups which may influence the attitudes and views of others, such as academic and commercial research organisations; management groups; existing, past and future customers; newspapers, radio and television; major suppliers; and European, national or local government officials. The public relations team should be in regular contact with these groups in order to influence their views as, ultimately, they affect the opinions of others.

Organisations, or the agencies they hire, may decide to use one or more of a number of activities in a public relations campaign.

1 **Press releases** may be issued to draw attention to the successes of the organisation. These might include an announcement concerning the creation of a new product, success in securing a new order, or some other development or achievement. An advantage of a press release is that it offers the organisation's version of a particular event (and, of course, it is free).

2 **Briefing** may be provided for those who will speak on the organisation's behalf, whether an employee or someone from outside the organisation, to ensure that the organisation's case is presented effectively on television and radio and at events. Similarly, public appearances or speeches can be used to provide opportunities to promote the name and activities of an organisation. This may involve television and radio appearances as well as local activities such as giving a speech at a chamber of commerce lunch.

3 **Sponsorship** may be offered to have the name of an organisation linked to a particular event. Examples include the Coca-Cola Cup, the Lombard RAC Rally and the Benson & Hedges Cup. Small local businesses can gain from sponsoring charity fundraising events, local sports clubs (with kit) or cultural events, such as helping to finance a theatre production. In each case, it is a matter of having the name of the organisation publicised and placed in a favourable light.

ACTIVITY

List all the sporting, cultural or general entertainment events that you can think of which are sponsored. In each case, identify what is the probable benefit to the organisation concerned.

SALES PROMOTION

A sales promotion is an attempt to communicate directly with potential consumers or distributors in order to encourage them to purchase or stock the product or service as well as to recommend it to others. It may involve both impersonal and, in some cases, personal channels of communication.

Consumer promotions are used to encourage potential consumers to try a product and, hopefully, to purchase it again. They may make use of a number of devices.

- **Free trial samples of a product**
- **Discount coupons or vouchers**
- **Cash refund of purchase**
- **Bargain packs**
- **Free gifts with the product**
- **Rewards for loyalty 'such as air miles'**
- **Point-of-sale displays or demonstrations**
- **Competitions**
- **Special deals such as zero per cent finance arrangements**
- **Loss-leaders (prices cut on particular products to encourage customers into a shop)**
- **Prizes, bonuses and other inducements to sales forces**

Trade promotions are aimed at distributors to encourage them to stock a particular product. They may involve the use of cash incentives to display and advertise a particular product, special prizes or bonuses paid to organisations prepared to stock the product or service, and exhibitions or product conventions aimed at potential distributors. The panel on page 184 gives a list of reasons for sales promotion.

THE SALES PROMOTION CAMPAIGN

For a sales promotion to achieve its objectives it is important to ensure that it keeps within budget and clearly targets the potential group of consumers or distributors. The article opposite describes how the Pepsi Max 1994 sales promotion achieved its required degree of targeting.

The 1990s have seen an increase in the number of organisations which have supported sales promotion with

Maximising your market impact

Today's 16-to-24 year-olds are notoriously difficult to reach. Their typical 'seen that, done that' attitude means they tend to be fairly indifferent to both marketing and promotional messages.

On the face of it, trying to persuade this cynical, discerning and street-wise group to participate in something as corny and old-fashioned as product sampling would appear to be a daunting task. Yet, last summer, the UK distributor for PepsiCo, Britvic Soft Drinks, targeted this very age group with a sampling campaign for its new, sugar-free cola, Pepsi Max – and managed to convince 470,000 consumers to try the product.

Britvic Soft Drinks managed to spark this level of interest among the 16-to-24 year-old age group by giving them, as it were, a taste of their own medicine. Instead of the traditionally polite 'would-you-like-one-of-these?' approach to sampling, it mounted an intrusive, but good humoured, tasting campaign which tried to mirror the irreverent behaviour and 'street-cred' image of the young characters seen in Pepsi Max's popular television commercials.

The characters represent the age group of under-25s that US marketers have dubbed 'Generation X' – a term coined five years ago by the American writer Douglas Coupland. Some observers believe it is the most important development in youth culture since the rise of the teenager in the '50s. This group might be cynical about life, but they are aware of their value and power as consumers – and they are advertising literate.

By the age of 18, most UK teenagers will have seen more than 140,000 TV ads – and their resistance to advertising and promotional campaigns is high. They know the meaning of 'branding' and 'marketing' and are sceptical about the guile of advertisers. At the same time, however, they recognise that advertising is a form of entertainment and they will respond favourably to ads which are fun – although they still won't buy products they don't want. Britvic Soft Drinks has already scored well here – with its wacky, irreverent Tango campaign – as has Golden Wonder, with its Pot Noodles brand.

So Pepsi Max aimed its high-energy ads under the banner 'Live Life to the Max' – at this target group. They were designed to overcome the negative images associated with sugar-free diet drinks by highlighting the fast-paced, exciting lifestyles that appeal to young consumers – showing 'hip' young characters taking part in various, high-risk adventure activities. According to PepsiCo, the ads 'overhauled the perception of no-sugar drinks' and gave Pepsi Max an 'unparalleled image' in the youth market.

'We needed to prove that Pepsi Max was not purely an image-based product,' says Tim Davie, marketing manager for Pepsi UK. 'We wanted to create an understanding that, with its full-bodied cola taste in a no-sugar product, it was a genuine product innovation.'

Davie says they decided to use product sampling to 'underpin' the success of the above-the-line advertising. 'Our research showed that, when people tried it, the level of repeat purchase was excellent,' he says. 'We wanted to convert a great image into repeat purchase by working the theme of the ad into the experience of receiving a free sample.'

Last summer, Pepsi Max's sales promotion agency HH&S mounted a 'Max Attack' sampling campaign which visited all the major conurbations in a two-month period.

HH&S explained that they designed the national roadshow to 'bring the brand to life on the street'. To do this, they used sampling teams of young actors who looked like, and emulated, the outrageous characters from the Pepsi Max commercials.

These 'Max Boys' toured the country in distinctive, Pepsi Max-branded white Jeeps and irreverently handed out product samples in shopping malls, stores, nightclubs and during special events. In one typical town-centre incident, a Max Boy tried to persuade a passing policewoman that a can of Pepsi Max would 'look great' on the dashboard of her police car – he was not successful.

'It was "in your face" sampling to reflect the style of the advertising,' says Paul Vines, joint managing director of HH&S. 'It was intrusive and impactful and, as it was highly-targeted, it did not suffer from any of the negative connotations of traditional sampling,' he says.

'The lookalike characters appealed to the target audience because of their 'leading edge' behaviour and image. They also enjoyed a kind of cult following at special events, with people even asking for autographs.'

According to HH&S, the roadshow was seen by 30,000 to 40,000 consumers a day. They even tied the sampling activity to on-air competitions on local radio stations.

Britvic Soft Drinks claims the sampling initiative played a 'critical part' in boosting Pepsi Max's UK sales by 300 per cent in 1994. It now has five per cent of the UK cola market – not bad, considering it was only launched in late 1993. It is a success that marketers should learn from, even if some of us are a little too old for hang-gliding off the nearest mountain.

Marketing, 9 March 1995.

television or radio advertising. In 1994, there was an increase of 160 per cent in the number of promotions supported by advertising. They included such household names as Weetabix, Coca-Cola, Esso, Shell and McDonald's. These organisations recognised that advertising helps to attract customers into retail outlets and encourages them to make purchases, while the sales promotional activity has a role in making people feel happy about a brand, thus making the sale promotion a success.

Another growth area in sales promotions has been the use of balloons. Increasingly, they are being used to launch new products, support in-store promotions, provide promotional give-aways and generate publicity. In August 1994, Walt Disney launched one and a half million balloons to support its release of *Aladdin* on video.

Sales promotion

✪ **To introduce a new product**

✪ **To encourage consumers to buy larger quantities of existing lines**

✪ **To encourage consumers to buy products at off-peak times**

✪ **To secure repeat business**

✪ **To challenge competitors**

✪ **To increase sales**

✪ **To regain former customers**

DIRECT MARKETING

Direct marketing includes direct selling, direct mail, telemarketing, use of the Internet, leafleting, roadshows, exhibitions and the sponsorship of events. In all cases, it operates through personal channels of communication where the target market is, in effect. a single customer. By approaching customers individually, an active response is required to the sales pitch.

The 1990s have seen an expansion in direct marketing activities, with the volume of sales achieved equivalent to three per cent of gross domestic product.

DIRECT SELLING

This involves selling things face to face. Typically, it takes place when the buyer visits a shop, although it may occur on the doorstep or through 'party plan' selling (home-based selling events). The advantage of direct selling is that the seller is able to respond to questions, identify customers' specific needs, select particular benefits to demonstrate, and can secure an order immediately.

Door-to-door selling is used both for domestic and industrial consumers. In the majority of cases, the sales representative will either deliver the product immediately, from stocks carried in a car or van, or take an order. The sales person may give advice on re-order quantities and display materials, and provide notice of future advertising campaigns. Where a sales representative is dealing with stockists of consumer durables, such as electrical goods, the person may also spend time attending to technical matters and complaints.

For large retail chains many sales representatives sell directly to the head office, which means much of the advice they give concerns issues of quality, packaging, discounts and special promotions. In order to sell to industrial consumers, it is often necessary to have specialist technical knowledge of plant, machinery and computer systems. These types of sales representatives are referred to as technical representatives.

Party plan selling is aimed at groups of domestic buyers who are brought together by a common contact or friend, who is recruited by the seller. The host receives financial or other benefits to organise the party, with sales being carried out by the organisation's personnel.

DIRECT MAIL

Direct mail involves posting information about an organisation's goods and services to actual or potential customers. It provides a highly targeted approach, with the names of customers, identified in terms of various socio-economic and other criteria, compiled in a list which becomes the basis for a **mail shot**. Ultimately, the success of this approach depends on the quality of the mailing list, and in many cases these are obtained from specialist agencies.

The most effective direct mail campaigns tend to be through a letter or promotional communication which is simple and to the point. It has both to stimulate interest and provide a means of response, such as a coupon or postage paid envelope. The response rate may be increased through the use of an inducement such as a prize draw.

The use of direct mail is growing rapidly. It is used by charities, book clubs, travel and leisure companies, financial services companies and political parties. In 1994, over £16m was spent on direct mail, a 12 per cent increase on the previous year's figure. This represents 2.7 billion items delivered (see *Fig. 3.19*).

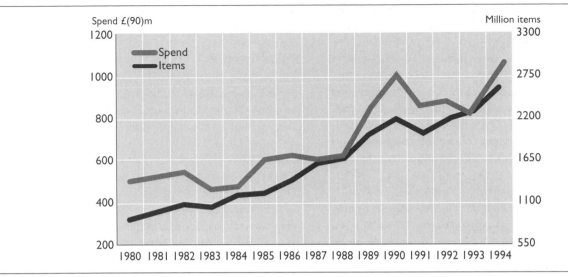

FIGURE 3.19: Direct mail expenditure and number of items delivered 1980–1994.
Source: *Marketing*, 6 April 1995.

☀ ACTIVITY

Over a period of four weeks, make a collection of the advertising and promotional literature that is posted to your home. Analyse each communication and record the following:

⊗ **organisation;**

⊗ **product, service or charity appeal;**

⊗ **ease of understanding;**

⊗ **impact;**

⊗ **form of response;**

⊗ **appropriateness of any incentives.**

On the basis of your findings, rank the communications in order of effectiveness. Write a brief report justifying your views.

TELEMARKETING

This involves the seller of a product or service communicating with customers directly by telephone. Interested customers may then be visited by a sales representative with a view to completing a sale. This method is used widely in the sale of double glazing, replacement windows, driveways, insurance and financial services. Companies like First Direct and Direct Line Insurance have managed to build very successful businesses using this sales method.

The success of telemarketing depends on the ability of the telephone sales staff. A team needs to be properly trained and staff have to be very methodical and well organised (usually, they work to a prepared script).

The use of telemarketing has been encouraged by technological advances such as the development of call centres. These provide a centralised service for receiving and also, increasingly, making telephone calls; a central computer carries out the dialling. The system works through the use of a **target database** of names and numbers. Once the call has been answered, it is routed to a salesperson. If the number dialled is engaged or an answering machine is reached, the call is routed to the back of the queue. The computer can link up with other databases to provide relevant information about the customer, such as the person's address and socio-economic group, enabling the sales person to adapt the sales pitch accordingly.

A similar approach can be taken in receiving calls, for example Abbey National Direct uses software that can recognise the telephone number of a mortgage customer and route the caller to the home loans adviser who dealt with the enquirer previously, thus providing continuity of service.

OTHER DIRECT MARKETING TOOLS

THE INTERNET

The Internet global computer network, or information superhighway, offers new opportunities for advertising and direct selling. In March 1995 there were about 30 million users of the network worldwide with over 500,000 in the United Kingdom. The development of broadband communications is expected to promote interactive use of computers, for example in 'digital shopping'.

LEAFLETING

The door-to-door distribution of leaflets can provide an effective way of targeting a particular area. It is often used by organisations offering domestic services, such as plumbers, electricians, builders, gardeners and painters and decorators. Many voluntary organisations deliver leaflets before making a collection.

ROADSHOWS

As described in the Pepsi Max campaign (see page 183), a roadshow enables a message to be communicated in a series of different locations, where representatives from the organisation can meet potential buyers.

EXHIBITIONS

These may be staffed or unattended. The purpose is to inform potential customers about products or services. One of the most effective is the **trade fair** where a manufacturer may invite a targeted group of distributors and retailers to visit the organisation's stand. Hospitality is sometimes offered.

  # PORTFOLIO ASSIGNMENT

COMMUNICATION CHALLENGE

The class should divide into small groups. Each should select two business organisations currently involved in major campaigns to advertise, publicise and promote their activities. The selection could be from such organisations as a book club, record company, manufacturer of a canned drink, a hotel chain, a credit card company, a chain of fast-food outlets, a brewery, or the manufacturer of a chocolate bar.

During a two-week period, the members of the group should monitor and record the advertising, publicity, public relations and promotional activities of the organisations, as the results of this appear in newspapers and magazines, on television and radio and at cinemas and sports, charity and entertainment events. Create a form to record your data.

The group should also find evidence of any direct marketing activities undertaken by the organisations. This may be in the form of a letter which has been sent to a member of the group, their family or a friend. (If this is not available, a request could be made to the organisation for an example.)

Each member of the group should have a set of the record sheets and write a report which compares and contrasts the campaigns and methods of communication used by the organisations.

The report should cover:

⊗ the major business activities of the organisations;

⊗ their target markets;

⊗ the main examples of the use of communications to reach the target markets;

⊗ an evaluation of the effectiveness of each communication in terms of awareness raising, securing greater brand loyalty, increasing sales and lengthening the life of the product; and

⊗ any efforts to meet the requirements of the Advertising Standards Authority. Also, suggest how a less ethical organisation might have been tempted to abuse the ASA's standards.

Customer satisfaction through sales methods and service

CUSTOMER SATISFACTION AND CUSTOMER SERVICE

The ultimate marketing objective is to make the sale, but in doing so it is important to achieve the highest possible level of customer satisfaction as this will lead to repeat sales, recommendations to other potential customers and still further sales.

Achieving customer satisfaction requires an organisation to have a **culture** which emphasises customer service. This means that all employees must have the same values, beliefs and ways of communicating which reflect the needs of the customer. Employees must be trained to have an appropriate open-mindedness and readiness to act in response to customers' needs. They must strive to achieve quality in their own work and be willing to go out of their way to deliver that same level of quality to customers. This culture, of putting the customer first, must be handed down from the top of the organisation.

Organisations, such as Marks and Spencer, have built their reputation on providing a very high standard of customer service. The staff are trained to accept the principle that the customer is always right and that their wishes can be gauged by looking at purchases on the shop floor. Similarly, when Mercury Communications was created in 1982, it provided a guide to its services which stated that: 'Mercury was created to provide the most competitive service possible at lower costs, placing the needs of the customer first.'

Organisations involved in developing a culture of customer service have to do this at both a **strategic** and **operational** level. Strategically, it is necessary to evaluate customers' wants and then to design a package of services which meets their expectations. For example, customers will have certain expectations when they enter a dry cleaners. These must be realised in terms of the standards of the counter staff, the availability of advice, the quality of the cleaning, the treatment of the items of clothing in terms of hangers and covers, the accuracy of the bill, the methods of payment, the atmosphere of the shop and the competitiveness of the price.

Operationally, any service must be well delivered with consistent standards in terms of each customer visit, different geographical locations and individual employees. For example, an organisation like McDonald's strives to maintain the same high standards of cleanliness, speed and quality of service and food whether the outlet is in London, Paris or Moscow.

Increasingly, those organisations which are committed to achieving the highest possible levels of customer satisfaction recognise that this is only possible if everyone in the organisation seeks to do their job as well as they can for the people they serve. This wider view of what is meant by a 'customer' goes beyond the **external customer**, who actually buys or uses the product or receives the service, to one which includes anyone for whom an employee within the organisation provides a service, or who has need of what is supplied. This allows for the idea of the **internal customer** – those who work in the same organisation, who have the same external customers and share the same organisational goals, and whose work is in some way dependent on that done by the employee or by others in the organisation.

ACTIVITY

List four organisations which you consider to have a culture of customer service.

In each case, identify the means by which the organisation attempts to increase consumer satisfaction and how the employees contribute towards this.

Suggest how the organisations benefit commercially by operating in this way.

Consequently, the service that an employee provides internally to fellow employees has a direct impact on the quality of the service delivered to the external customer.

In order to achieve a high level of quality employees have to think in a particular way: they have to recognise that what to them may be a routine duty may be of crucial significance for the effective performance of the internal customers that they serve. Under these circumstances, all employees need to know not only what they have to do and how to do it, but also why they are doing it and what the result will be for their colleagues if something is not done correctly and to the appropriate standard.

The commercial advantages of achieving high standards of customer service have become increasingly recognised by organisations in the 1990s. In many cases, customer service has been adopted by major business organisations as a strategic objective. These organisations have recognised that it brings the following benefits.

- ✪ **Organisations that differentiate their goods and services** on the basis of service can ask higher prices for comparative products or services and achieve higher profit margins.

- ✪ **Good customer service** is often associated with greater customer loyalty, which makes an organisation less open to attack by 'clone' competitors and ensures that it will not be as adversely affected by an economic downturn as others may be.

- ✪ **Due to the premium placed on customer service,** organisations are likely to experience more of the benefits associated with a period of economic boom.

- ✪ **Having a reputation for high-quality customer service** often means that the business does not need to spend as much on advertising.

- ✪ **A business which develops a culture of customer service** and recognises the existence of internal customers is likely to have a more contented workforce, with lower absenteeism and higher employee retention rates.

DIRECT AND INDIRECT SALES METHODS

In deciding upon the suitability of different sales methods, it is important to consider the strategic objectives of the organisation and the required culture of customer service and satisfaction. Basically, a decision has to be made as to whether an organisation should directly sell its own products or services or use an indirect selling method, working through an appropriate intermediary within the channel of distribution.

DIRECT SALES METHODS

These involve direct contact taking place only between the producer and the customer. Such methods are part of a direct marketing strategy as described previously. They include the following:

- ✪ **television and radio advertising** featuring ordering information and, often, exclusive access to the product (music compilations on compact disc);

- ✪ **door-to-door selling,** both to domestic and industrial consumers (cleaning products);

- ✪ **selling through a mail order catalogue** (holidays);

- ✪ **telephone selling,** involving an initial contact followed up with a visit from a sales representative (double glazing);

⊗ **selling directly from factory premises** (pine bookcases, bedroom furniture);

⊗ **pyramid selling,** which is a form of multi-level marketing involving a 'pyramid' of salespersons, with a few initial members recruiting others who, in turn, recruit still more, creating an expanding chain of sales people (cosmetics).

ACTIVITY

Mail order advertisements can often be seen in newspapers and magazines. Where the company selling the goods has been able to bypass both the wholesaler and the retailer, it may be able to offer the goods at attractive prices.

1 Cut out a large mail order advertisement from a magazine.

2 Explain why the company may have decided to use this direct form of selling.

3 How are both the company and the consumer likely to benefit?

4 Explain why the product is advertised in this particular magazine.

5 Do you feel that the content and style of the advert would be likely to sell the product?

6 How else might the product have been sold?

All of these methods have the advantage for manufacturers of allowing them greater control over the marketing and selling of their products. However, the 'downside' can be that they involve the manufacturer in an expensive storage and distribution operation.

INDIRECT SALES METHODS

These involve manufacturers working through a third party or intermediary in order to sell their products. These intermediaries are part of the distribution channel, which traditionally has three stages of operation:

⊗ **Manufacturing – making the product;**

⊗ **Wholesaling – the holding of large stocks and breaking bulk into retail packs; and**

⊗ **Retailing – the sale of the product to the final buyer, or consumer.**

The decision by a manufacturer to hand over the **wholesaling** and retailing activity to an intermediary is based on organisational, operational and financial considerations.

The wholesaler provides a number of benefits to the manufacturer.

1 Wholesalers buy products in relatively large quantities from the manufacturer, which they stock and then break down the bulk, selling on in smaller quantities to retailers. This allows the manufacturer to benefit from fewer but larger orders, with resulting economies of scale for longer production runs and the avoidance of what may be a high minimum outlay for storage, sales and transport facilities.

2 The manufacturer avoids having to cover the delivery costs associated with small consignments to a large number of widely dispersed retail outlets.

3 Independent wholesalers may operate a single warehouse or a chain of warehouses giving wider regional coverage and, in many cases, national distribution.

4 Specialist wholesalers may concentrate on such things as beer, wines and spirits, fruit and vegetables, meat, fish, footwear, clothing, sports equipment, carpets, china and glassware, hardware, electrical goods, books, and furniture. These specialist wholesalers are very important for goods where the demand is very high at certain times of the year. The wholesaler that deals in swimsuits, for example, will place orders for them during the winter and build up stocks in the warehouse

well before the summer months. The manufacturer of swimsuits can therefore keep the factory going at a steady rate during the whole of the year. This will help the manufacturer to run the business more efficiently. The wholesaler will also have enough swimsuits in stock to meet the very large increase in demand during the summer months. Without the wholesaler, manufacturers of swimsuits would find it very difficult to meet demand, and there would be a shortage.

5 The wholesaler may undertake specialist activities involving blending, processing or packaging, which when conducted on behalf of many producers can be carried out on a more economic scale. These specialist skills are of particular value when dealing with commodities such as tea, coffee and wool.

6 In the case of perishable products such as fruit and vegetables, the specialist wholesaler should be able to distribute the products more rapidly to a scattered market. Consider, for example, the role of the great London markets including Covent Garden (flowers, fruit and vegetables), Billingsgate (fish) and Smithfield (meat).

7 A new manufacturer with very limited trading experience and financial resources may initially use a wholesaler who will have a greater knowledge of local customers in terms of credit-worthiness and the size and frequency of orders. They can also pass on advice to the retailer regarding shelf, counter and window displays.

8 Wholesale merchants act as a link between manufacturers and the firms that need raw materials, parts, equipment and machinery. This is known as selling to the trade and could involve builders, plumbers, decorators and timber merchants. Merchants are also willing to build up their stocks in warehouses or yards with those items which are in seasonal demand. This is the case, for example, with building materials, as less building and decorating work goes on in the winter months as compared to other times of the year.

It may be concluded that selling through a wholesaler confers benefits on both the manufacturer and retailer. However, some criticisms are levelled at the wholesale function on the grounds that the wholesaler simply takes a cut and contributes to higher prices. This can mean that if either the manufacturer or retailer believes that it can perform the wholesaler's services, it will seek to do so in the interests both of profit and competitive sales. In fact, the development of large supermarket and DIY chains has meant that, in many cases, the wholesaling function of stocking and breaking bulk has become increasingly integrated with the retail function, with retailers taking advantage of price discounts associated with bulk buying.

Some products by their very nature are distributed directly by manufacturers to **retailers**. These include relatively expensive products where distribution costs can be borne by the manufacturer without a severe impact upon the competitive position or profit margins. It is not necessary for retailers to deal in large and varied stocks of consumer durables; they are not expected to buy television sets or washing-machines in bulk. Manufacturers may perhaps conduct their own wholesaling function in such products where after-sales service is required, and where close contact with retail units providing such services will be necessary.

The increased mobility of consumers has increased the popularity for manufacturers of dealing directly with retailers. This has increased the turnover of fewer but larger retail units. Where congestion in city centres has created problems, retail units have responded by taking sites in out-of-town shopping centres and by establishing hypermarkets. This also assists in deliveries and increases warehousing facilities. Manufacturers have benefited from the creation of new motorways and the development of larger commercial vehicles, which have reduced costs and improved the efficiency of their distribution system.

Some wholesalers have responded positively to these developments by offering cash and carry warehouse facilities, where retailers can choose from large displays of goods. Retailers pay for the goods before leaving and use their own vehicles to take them away. This allows the wholesaler to offer lower prices, as they save some of the costs associated with paperwork, sales representatives and delivery service. Cash and carry services may be used by people who hold a special card that allows them to buy at wholesale prices. These cards may also be issued to other businesses, such as hotels, restaurants and sports and social clubs.

The retailer operates a business which stocks a particular type of product, such as a clothes shop, or an extensive range of products, such as a department store, for making sales to consumers. In so doing, retailers have traditionally provided a convenient point of sale, at the end of the distribution channel, for manufacturers' products.

However, the relationship between retailers and manufacturers is changing. The development of supermarket and DIY chains has meant that many retailers have become much more demanding in their dealings with manufacturers. Retailers have been able to use their bulk buying power to obtain substantial price discounts from manufacturers and, in the case of larger retail groups, retailers have established an extensive own-label brand business in direct competition with manufacturers' brands. By providing retailers with the increased opportunity to use price as a competitive weapon within the marketing mix, consumers have benefited.

Agents and distributors sometimes feature within the distribution channel as another type of intermediary. The major purpose of using an agent is to generate new business contracts. In many cases, a manufacturer will employ an agent to obtain new wholesale customers, or a wholesaler will use an agent when seeking to establish new retail accounts.

Distributors are more independent than agents. They usually buy from the manufacturer at a discount and resell with a 'mark up'. In many cases a distributor will demand an exclusive sales arrangement, whereby it alone may sell the manufacturer's product in a certain area. The advantage to the manufacturer of going through a distributor is that it can offer access to additional sales outlets in new areas.

Agents and distributors are of particular value to companies wishing to establish a presence in foreign markets. The company could either sell through an export agency in the UK or appoint an agent or distributor in the country abroad. In the case of the latter, a suitable appointment could mean not only that the business sells its product abroad, but it also receives useful information in relation to factors such as developments in the market, suitable promotions and the need for product modification and updating. In many cases, the agent or distributor may also supply the after-sales service on which customers will judge the reliability of the business.

THE ROLE AND RESPONSIBILITY OF THE SALESPERSON

Selling is the part of the marketing process concerned with maintaining or increasing demand by overcoming consumer resistance or inertia. The salesperson attempts to do this by presenting the product or communicating persuasive messages to the potential client. This may be carried out at each stage of the channel of distribution, from the manufacturer to the wholesaler, the wholesaler to the retailer, and the retailer to the consumer.

Selling is unlike other aspects of marketing in that it depends entirely upon human relationships, i.e. contact between the salesperson and the customer. Consequently, the skills associated with successful selling are essentially people-oriented, including good communication, interpersonal skills and negotiating abilities.

Jobs in selling may involve working as part of a sales force, making personal or telephone contact with industrial and commercial buyers in factories, shops, local authorities, utilities, service industries and charities, or selling directly to individuals and members of households in shops and retail outlets.

STAGES IN THE SELLING PROCESS

MAKING CONTACT WITH CUSTOMERS

Sales staff provide the major link between the organisation and the customer. They must be capable of knowing how and where to make contact with existing or potential customers. For example, selling engineering components will involve building up a relationship with the purchasing departments of various engineering companies. This may be achieved by keeping the customer up to date with changes in technical specifications or design features through visits and telephone calls. In any personal dealings with existing customers, and in particular new customers, the salesperson must generate confidence by appearing honest, knowledgeable, business-like and professional, but should also be approachable, sociable and friendly.

In the case of a salesperson in a retail outlet, there is less time to establish a relationship with the customer, so first impressions are important. Sales staff should be neat and tidy, have a personality which helps them to strike up a good relationship with customers and to be able to engage their interest in a product. Customers should also be made to feel at ease and believe that the salesperson is taking a genuine interest in them and is acting in their best interest.

IDENTIFYING CUSTOMERS' NEEDS

By careful questioning and observation, the salesperson should be able to develop a knowledge of customers' circumstances and establish their real needs. This should then be taken into account when presenting a product or service to the customer.

PRESENTING AND DEMONSTRATING THE PRODUCT OR SERVICE

The salesperson should target those products or services which particularly meet the needs of the customer. Every effort should be made to stress the benefits of the product or service in terms of what the salesperson's organisation can offer and how this compares with the competition. In doing this, the salesperson must be able to draw on extensive **product knowledge** and reference should be made to satisfied customers who could vouch for the reliability of the product. The main features of the product or service should be demonstrated, and, ideally, the potential buyer should be allowed to try out the product.

If any queries are raised during the demonstration these should be viewed in a positive way, as they mean that the potential customer is expressing an interest. The salesperson should always listen very carefully to the customer's reservations and, if necessary, put forward in a calm manner an alternative point of view. Wherever possible, the salesperson should take the opportunity to reiterate the benefits, reliability and features of the product or service.

NEGOTIATING THE PRICE AND CONDITIONS OF SALE

Negotiation involves the salesperson and potential customer conferring in order to find a compromise on price or reach agreement on some aspect of the conditions of sale. Sales staff can only be effective in doing this if they have been properly briefed and have clear objectives to meet. This will allow them to make concessions and, where necessary, to move away from their original position.

Any negotiation involves both parties in making a series of theoretical proposals which are then adjusted in order to arrive at a compromise solution which should as near as possible satisfy both parties. The art of negotiation is to be firm but fair and not to become too aggressive.

Obviously, the extent to which it is appropriate to negotiate will depend upon the type of product or service, its relative price and the complexity of the conditions of sale. For example, there is very little scope to negotiate when conducting the sale of a chocolate bar, but far more when selling a car or a computerised production control system.

CLOSING THE SALE

Once all negotiations have been concluded, and an agreement has been reached, the salesperson should judge the moment to close the sale and secure a firm commitment for an order. There are a number of devices which may be used to bring this about. The salesperson may summarise the position and ask for the order, or offer a final concession to clinch the immediate sale, or assume the buyer wants the product and finalise the conditions of the sale.

ACTIVITY

TASKS

The case study about Paul Green, opposite, highlights many of the qualities that help to make a successful salesperson in a department store.

The class should divide into groups of four and one member of each group should volunteer to be assessed by the others as to the qualities in the form. Each of the assessors should have a copy of the list and give marks. The results should then be averaged to give an overall mark out of 54 (the maximum possible).

The roles may be changed, until all members of the class have been assessed by a panel of three. The top three salespeople in the class should be identified.

	MARK
Dress and general appearance	
Personal grooming - hair and nails	
Posture and general bearing	
Oral skills and method of speech	
Politeness and manners	
Friendliness towards other people	
Cheerfulness	
Ability to adapt to other people	
Ability and willingness to investigate and learn about things	
TOTAL	

MARKING SYSTEM	
Excellent	6
Very good	5
Good	4
Average	3
Acceptable	2
Below average	1
Poor	0

AFTER-SALES SERVICE

This covers all the back-up services and facilities provided by the supplier to the customer. It may include free maintenance and repairs, a telephone service to deal with customers' queries and an express parts delivery service. The provision of these services helps to enhance customer loyalty and provides valuable feedback about goods and services.

THE SALESPERSON AND THE LAW

There are several laws which seek to protect customers in their dealings with salespeople. Those involved in selling must make sure that they are aware of the implications of this legislation for their work.

Paul Green

Paul Green works as a sales assistant for Holmes and Sutcliffe, a department store belonging to the House of Lothian retail group. He joined the store after completing a GNVQ in Business and has just completed a 18-month training course. This involved working in a variety of store departments, as well as other areas such as the warehouse and display.

After the training period his first appointment has been as a sales assistant in the china and glassware department. Although he is not involved in selling highly technical items, he has quickly learned that a high degree of product knowledge is required. He needs to know what determines the quality of glass and china, the various uses of the different kinds of glasses and other items, how they should be handled and displayed; and he must be able to recognise the various traditional designs and be able to talk about their various manufacturers. In order to build up and extend his product knowledge, he spends a great deal of time studying the suppliers' catalogues and brochures.

Paul has always got on well with all kinds of people and he has a friendly personality which puts customers at their ease and makes them feel that they can trust his advice and judgement. He has a good sense of humour and is always cheerful, but manages to strike the all-important balance between being friendly to customers and giving them the respect they require.

During his training the need to be polite and well-mannered was always stressed, and his experience on the sales floor has made him realise that such an approach pays dividends. Customers usually respond to a friendly approach, and even some of the awkward customers become more reasonable when they are treated courteously and with tact and patience. This helps to create a pleasant atmosphere on the sales floor and improves Paul's job satisfaction, as well as his sales commission!

Paul is learning how to spot different types of customers and to alter his approach when necessary. For example, when a smartly dressed gentleman insisted on buying what he claimed were sherry glasses, which were in fact liqueur glasses, Paul had the delicate job of explaining that the customer was mistaken. Other 'problem' customers are parents who allow their children to run riot in the store, picking up valuable items on display and knocking into the display stands. Here, the problem is one of knowing how to complete a sale with the customer, while tactfully pointing out that the children are becoming a nuisance. Paul can also recognise the type of customer who wants to be served quickly, efficiently and with the minimum of conversation.

When he first joined the store, Paul was immediately impressed by the style and image of the assistant manager in the furniture department. In particular, he noticed that his method of speech was always clear and concise and that the way he expressed himself enabled him to 'get through' to the customer. He didn't have a 'posh' voice but was well-spoken. Paul realised that he had some faults in his own speech; he tended to be a bit hesitant and his choice of words was rather limited. As a result, he has worked hard to improve his speech and to widen his vocabulary by reading brochures and leaflets.

The store manager still feels that there are a couple of areas to which Paul should pay more attention. Although he tries to be neat and tidy, half way through the day his clothes tend to be rather crumpled and creased. This is exacerbated by his tendency to slouch a little and lean against the counter. His personal hygiene is fine, but there have been times when his hair has been a bit too 'fashionable' for the image of the store.

TRADE DESCRIPTIONS ACTS 1968 AND 1972

The 1968 Act makes it illegal to give a false description of a good. This covers descriptions in writing, in advertisements or in anything which the seller says when discussing the good with a customer. The Act also covers the way in which goods are priced. The seller cannot charge a higher price than the one marked on the good. It is also illegal to claim that the price of a good has been reduced unless the same good was previously offered at the higher price for a period of at least 28 days in the last six months.

The 1972 Act makes it illegal to sell goods that have been manufactured abroad by trying to give the customer the impression that the goods were made in the UK.

UNSOLICITED GOODS AND SERVICES ACTS 1971 AND 1975

These were designed to control what is known as 'inertia selling', i.e. sending unsuspecting people goods through the post which they hadn't ordered and relying on their ignorance or apathy to extract payment. Fines can be imposed on those businesses making demands for payment for goods and services which are unsolicited.

The Acts provide that any unsolicited goods may be kept by the recipient without payment after a period of 30 days provided that the recipient gives notice to the sender asking that the goods be collected. Alternatively, the recipient can do nothing, that is give no notice to the seller, and the goods become the recipient's as an unconditional gift after six months.

PRICES ACT 1974

This covers the ways in which a shop must show its prices. All food and drink must carry a price. In the case of pre-packed food, such as meat and cheese, the pack must also indicate the price per kg (weight). Food such as fruit and vegetables sold over a counter or on a self-selection basis in a supermarket must also have their prices clearly displayed.

CONSUMER CREDIT ACT 1974

This regulates the way in which a business may offer credit facilities to its consumers (or debtors). The main points that would have to be allowed for in a business proposal are as follows:

- **Every credit agency** must obtain a licence from the director-general of the Office of Fair Trading.

- **There is control over advertisements for credit** which may be misinterpreted, i.e. they are misleading.

- **The credit agreement must be properly drawn up** and contain terms laid down in regulations by the government, for example in relation to the debtor's principal rights and duties.

- **The credit arrangement** must show the annual percentage rate at which interest will be charged.

- **The debtor is entitled to a copy of the agreement** at the time of the contract, and a second copy within seven days if the agreement is accepted at a later date.

SALE OF GOODS ACT 1979, AS EXTENDED BY SUPPLY OF GOODS AND SERVICES ACT 1982

This indicates clearly the responsibility of any business in selling goods and services. A legal contract exists between the buyer and seller of a good or service. Once the offer to buy a good has been accepted then the seller and not the manufacturer has to deal with any complaint. The 1982 Act lays down three basic conditions regarding the quality of goods and services that a business may sell.

- **Goods must be of merchantable quality:** they must be reasonably fit for their normal purpose. A new item must not be broken or damaged and must work correctly. If a good is very cheap, however, then the customer must generally expect less quality than a more expensive version of the same good.

- **Goods must be as described.** This covers the wording on the package, display signs and oral statements by the trader.

- **Goods must be fit for any particular intended purpose.** Apart from being fit for their normal purpose, a trader may assure the customer that the good is also suitable for another use. For example, a customer may ask if a paint can also be used on plastic guttering. If the trader says that it would be suitable, the buyer can claim recompense if it proves otherwise.

A business cannot attempt to remove any of these rights by getting customers to sign a guarantee which offers less protection than is already available under the law.

FOOD ACT 1984

This lays down regulations governing the production, distribution and sale of food, which are enforced by local authority environmental health officers. Criminal prosecution may occur where, for example, food or drink is being sold which is felt to be unfit for human consumption, or the contents of any food have been wrongly described, or claims have been made about the nutritional value of food which are misleading.

WEIGHTS AND MEASURES ACT 1985

This provides detailed rules regarding the weighing and measurement of goods. For example, in the case of prepacked meat or cheese the weight must be accurately marked on the packet. Breaches of the rules can result in prosecution.

CONSUMER PROTECTION ACT 1987

This makes it a criminal offence to supply any consumer goods which do not meet with general safety requirements. Businesses have a general duty to trade safely and to meet certain standards regarding furniture and fire hazards and such products as electrical appliances, toys and babies' dummies.

OFFICE OF FAIR TRADING

A BUYER'S GUIDE

Your legal rights

How to complain

Where to get help

MANAGEMENT AND ADMINISTRATION OF THE SALES FUNCTION

The contribution of the sales function in marketing is to help to generate the volume of sales required to yield the planned profit. In certain cases, however, this may be defined as maximising sales of particular items, increasing sales abroad or providing market research information. To achieve this, those involved in sales must pay special attention to ensuring the effective operation of the salesforce and the efficient administration of the sales office. Retail selling has similar objectives, with the same need to achieve high standards of management and administration.

ORGANISING THE SALESFORCE

The sales manager has to take responsibility for organising the direct salesforce which works exclusively for the organisation. This may be divided into the internal salespeople who conduct business from the organisation's premises, either personally or on the telephone, together with the field sales force which travels to visit customers.

ACTIVITY

Select a product which you can easily bring into school or college. Efforts should be made to choose the kind of product where a customer is likely to want the help and advice of a salesperson if he or she is thinking of buying it. Examples of products that can be used for this task are:

pair of shoes	anorak
crash helmet	calculator
sports bag	hair dryer
radio	pullover
attache case	road atlas
jeans	kettle
iron	an item of sportswear
fountain pen	shaver

Determine how much the product would cost if bought today and identify all those features of the product which might be brought to the attention of a potential customer by a salesperson in the kind of shop where it is sold.

Assume the role of a salesperson and present your product to the group. At the end of each presentation the rest of the group should give their opinion on the performance and, in particular, highlight anything that might tend to mislead a customer or could potentially be in breach of the law.

In certain cases, the sales manager will also take responsibility for the sales agents, dealers or brokers who are employed on a contractual basis and paid entirely on commission.

The **direct salesforce** may be organised into territories according geographical area, product or market segment. The allocation of territories may entail sales targets.

The performance of the salesperson may be measured in a number of ways, including in terms of the following:

- ⊗ **orders secured per visit;**

- ⊗ **sales revenue generated against the number of calls;**

- ⊗ **the ratio of profit to calls;**

- ⊗ **the ratio of orders per call; and**

- ⊗ **the average value of an order.**

Obviously, if such criteria are to be applied, the allocation of territories should take account of travel time and expense, equality of sales opportunity and, hence, potential earnings.

MOTIVATING THE SALESFORCE

In order to meet the required level of sales, management must ensure that suitable people have been recruited into the salesforce and that they have received adequate training and induction into the principles of selling and customer service, as well as the organisation's product or services and its administrative procedures.

The salesforce may then be motivated to meet or exceed sales targets by:

- ⊗ **setting personal, monthly and yearly sales targets** based on the projected sales forecasts;

- ⊗ **paying the salesforce a basic salary,** together with an incentive or commission payment, based on sales achieved;

- ⊗ **raising the status of the salesforce** by giving its members appropriate job titles, expense allowances and cars;

- ⊗ **generating competition between sales personnel** through bonuses and rewards for meeting or exceeding sales targets; and

- ⊗ **improving communications by sending out sales bulletins,** newsletters or memoranda to keep the salesforce up to date with what is happening in the organisation, its successes, new product developments and the actions of its competitors.

Field selling can be a relatively lonely job, therefore it is important for the sales manager to develop a team approach by being in regular contact with members of the salesforce. This can be done more formally through holding weekly or monthly sales meetings and conferences in order to:

- ⊗ **keep the salesforce informed about the latest company developments;**

- ⊗ **introduce the salesforce to new products or modifications to existing ones;**

- ⊗ **develop strategies to deal with competitors;**

- ⊗ **introduce new credit control systems or pricing strategies; and**

- ⊗ **motivate the salesforce.**

Sales conferences are often held on an annual basis and tend to be more formal than sales meetings. In many cases, the owners of the organisation or the directors may attend. Conferences are normally held in order to:

- ☺ achieve a wider understanding of the organisation and its products or services (to this end, design, research and development, and production staff may be invited to attend);

- ☺ carry out training concerning new products;

- ☺ review the existing product range and decide whether any modifications are necessary;

- ☺ review competitors' products and decide on a policy to counteract developments in the market;

- ☺ focus on successful sales methods; and

- ☺ bring the internal sales staff into contact with the field salespeople.

ADMINISTERING THE SALES FUNCTION

The smooth and efficient operation of the sales office is vital if sales targets are to be met and a high standard of customer service achieved. The **sales office** provides several vital services.

1 It acts as a liaison between the customers and the business, which includes dealing with all incoming enquiries, making appointments and handling complaints.

2 It processes orders, which involves receiving the incoming order and checking the accuracy of price, detail and delivery; entering the order onto the manual or computerised system, passing the order to production or purchasing; and passing the completed order to the warehouse for despatch.

3 It maintains records relating to the performance of each salesperson covering: areas worked in, sales achieved, salary, bonuses received and expenses paid.

4 It receives reports from the salesforce regarding the number of calls made, the time taken, stages of negotiations, particular problems, prospecting activities for new customers and the actions of competitors.

5 It maintains records relating to existing, former and new customers. These include a list of major contracts, orders taken, discounts given, special requirements and credit rating.

6 It runs a credit control and rating system, which involves establishing a credit rating for each new customer based on the salesperson's report, trade references, and special enquiries from trade protection societies.

RUNNING A SALES CAMPAIGN

The success of any sales campaign depends upon the efficient operation of the management and administration of the sales function. The campaign has to be developed as part of the overall marketing plan which, in turn, must be tied into the organisation's overall strategic plan. Obviously, a sales campaign will only be successful if it is an integral part of the marketing mix and is coordinated with the activities of purchasing, personnel, production, finance and distribution.

The sales campaign will be targeted in accordance with the findings of market research and supported by various promotional activities, to stimulate interest in the product or service and, ultimately, to achieve higher levels of sales.

The campaign may be promoted to the salesforce, wholesaler and retailer. Letters, memoranda and bulletins may be sent out stating where the effort should be made, how it should be coordinated with the promotion, the features of the product that need to be stressed and the benefits it provides. In many cases the campaign may be accompanied by special incentives for those who manage to achieve a certain (target) level of sales. The launch of the campaign would normally be supported by either a full sales conference or a sales meeting. This would provide the opportunity to help the salesforce to develop the necessary product knowledge, appreciate the unique selling points of the product, and to understand the selling methods and promotional activities that are to be used to support the campaign.

ACTIVITY

1 Read the newspaper article over the page relating to Daewoo .

2 Discuss in small groups whether such an approach really represents the 'death of the salesman'.

3 Decide whether customers are likely to welcome such an approach.

4 Identify any potential legal problems that might be associated with selling in this way.

- a duty to act with good faith towards the employer;

- a duty of care, each party for the other;

- a duty to maintain confidence and trust between the employer and the employee;

- a duty of the employer to provide work, and a duty of the employee to carry it out conscientiously;

- a duty of the employer to give reasonable support to all employees so that they can carry out their work;

- similarly, the employer has a duty to support its managers in their managerial duties.

Have you noticed that where people have **rights**, they also have **duties** or **obligations**? It is impossible to separate them.

- **If you have a *right* to an education, you have a *duty* to attend and to learn within your ability.**

- **If your teacher has a *right* to your attention, she or he has a *duty* to make the material relevant and interesting to you.**

ACTIVITY

In a group of three or four colleagues, consider other situations in which rights have duties attached to them. Look at situations relating to education, employment, sports, social life, the environment, civil liberties, equal opportunities, and anything else you wish.

1 List the rights and associated duties.

2 What conclusions can you draw from your list about 'the nature of justice?

There are some contracts into which particular implied terms are read. For example, a skilled craftsperson would be expected to know his or her craft and to practise it to an acceptable standard of quality and safety. This not only applies to crafts but to professional people as well. For example, teachers would be expected to know their subjects and how to communicate them to students in an acceptable fashion.

Some firms also negotiate agreements with trade unions. These **collective agreements** usually relate to wages and conditions of work. For example, a teacher's salary might be agreed between the employer and the National Union of Teachers during the annual pay negotiations. These agreements are not legally binding between an employer and the union but, once they are incorporated into an employee's contract of employment, they are binding upon both the employer and the employee.

Finally, there may be occasions when **'custom and practice'** is considered to be an implied term in the contract. Custom and practice is the term given to unofficial working practices operated by the workforce which are not covered by a specific rule or procedure. They are condoned by management but have never been 'agreed' by management.

Custom and practice is hard to establish and courts tend not to be sympathetic to arguments that it constitutes an implied term of contract. However, if a custom or a practice is *reasonable*, if it is *certain* and if it is *well known*, then it may be deemed part of the contract.

Once again, in cases like this, we must look to the courts for guidance. The case *Devonald v Rosser 1906* gives us a precedent: 'a custom so universal that no workman could be supposed to have entered into this service without looking to it as part of the contract'. Although ninety years old, this judgement is still used to help decide whether something is custom and practice or not.

STATUTORY RIGHTS

In order to clarify matters, and to ensure that employee rights are protected from abuse by powerful employers, Parliament has passed numerous employment laws in the past thirty years. It is not possible to waive these rights, so they are read into (or implied in) the contract of employment of all employees in the land.

The main Acts of Parliament that relate to employment are:

- ⊗ **Equal Pay Act 1970;**
- ⊗ **Fair Employment (NI) Act;**
- ⊗ **Health and Safety at Work Act 1974;**
- ⊗ **Sex Discrimination Act 1975;**
- ⊗ **Race Relations Act 1976;**
- ⊗ **Employment Protection (Consolidation) Act 1978;**
- ⊗ **Employment Act(s) 1980 to 1990.**

These Acts provide rights to employees. Some rights are dependent on length of service; for example, you may have to be an employee for two years before some rights apply. The main rights conferred by these Acts are:

- ⊗ **not to be discriminated against on grounds of race, sex or marriage;**
- ⊗ **to receive equal pay for work of equal worth;**
- ⊗ **to receive a written statement of the main terms of the contract;**
- ⊗ **to be a member of a union or not, as the individual wishes;**
- ⊗ **to receive notice of termination of employment;**
- ⊗ **to be paid redundancy payments depending upon age and length of service;**
- ⊗ **to work in safe and healthy conditions;**
- ⊗ **to receive sick pay;**
- ⊗ **not to be unfairly dismissed;**
- ⊗ **to be given a written reason for dismissal.**

ACTIVITY

Look through the list of employee rights enshrined in law. If these are respected honestly by all employers, would we have a fair and just system of employment?

What other rights do you think should be included, if any?

If your 'other rights' are made statutory requirements, what effect might they have on the prosperity of the business?

Note that UK employment law is being amended or supplemented to meet European Union (EU) regulations and directives. Business managers must now take into account European laws and directives.

To summarise, a contract of employment is made up of many parts:

- ⊗ **the offer and acceptance of the job;**
- ⊗ **the written statement of the terms and conditions;**
- ⊗ **any other written and agreed documents;**
- ⊗ **common law duties and rights;**
- ⊗ **other implied terms;**
- ⊗ **collective agreements;**
- ⊗ **custom and practice;**
- ⊗ **UK and EU statutory rights.**

Collectively, this has an impact on business in that the contract of employment gives both employers and employees rights and confers duties, one to the other. The notion of 'British justice' applies as much in the workplace as in any other walk of life.

The average manager and employee does not usually have a detailed knowledge of law. So, they need some sort of structure to work within – and some set of procedures to guide them.

DISCIPLINE AND GRIEVANCE PROCEDURES

Every employee in companies employing more than twenty people is entitled to receive (or have available) a copy of the company's disciplinary and grievance procedure within eight weeks of joining the company. The fact that the law is so specific indicates the importance of a system of justice for both employer and employees within every place of work.

It is the legal responsibility of the employer to prepare the disciplinary and grievance procedures. If trade unions are recognised, they will doubtless want a say in the structure and content of the procedures.

ACTIVITY

1 Using a good dictionary, look up the meanings of discipline and grievance. Write these definitions in your notes, and study them so that you could explain them to any of your colleagues without reference to your notes.

2 Now get copies of your school or college's disciplinary and grievance procedures for students. Study the procedures and understand how they work. Discuss them with your teacher if you wish.

3 Prepare a short presentation (to last five minutes) in which you explain the system of justice in your school or college. Comment on the advantages of having such a process compared with not having one.

PROCEDURE FOR DISCIPLINE

Discipline can be defined as 'a system of rules for behaviour'. Disciplinary action, then, is taken against people who do not follow those rules.

The Advisory, Conciliation and Arbitration Service (ACAS) has produced a code of practice – *Disciplinary Practice and Procedures in Employment* – to act as a guide to those preparing procedures. It is not a legal requirement to follow the code, but employers would be expected to conform to the spirit of the code.

The essence of this procedure is 'fairness':

- ⊗ **fair and equal treatment of all individuals;**

- ⊗ **fair methods of dealing with people;**

- ⊗ **fair standards of work that apply to all jobs;**

- ⊗ **fair expectations – people know what is expected of them;**

- ⊗ **fair decisions – all people are treated similarly and decisions are based only on the facts;**

- ⊗ **fair outcomes – the right of appeal is given to people who have sensible grounds for disagreeing with the decision.**

Managers should be concerned with discipline all the time, not just when someone breaks the rules. They should be monitoring the behaviour of employees in three areas – **attendance**, **performance** and **co-operation** – and taking minor corrective action all the time. This action may, for example, take the form of additional training or counselling; its purpose is to ensure that people are giving of their best. If one or two people are allowed to get away with things that result in other people having to do their work or cover for them, morale is likely to suffer. Good, fair, consistent discipline is important in building high morale.

If minor corrective action fails to change an employee's unacceptable behaviour or performance, a manager might decide to invoke the disciplinary procedure. If the evidence justifies it, the manager may decide to begin disciplinary action against the offender. Always, however, the actions must be in accordance with the company's stated procedure. This usually includes:

- **one verbal warning;**

- **a first written warning;**

- **a final written warning;**

- **if these fail to correct the unacceptable behaviour or performance, then the person may be dismissed.**

Because employees being disciplined may feel under pressure, and consequently might be unable to give a good account of themselves, they are entitled to bring a trade union official or a colleague along. Disciplinary action can last weeks or months. Throughout its duration, employers must provide the support and training needed to correct the behaviour.

If an employee commits an act of **gross misconduct**, he or she may be dismissed without warning or notice – this is termed **'summary dismissal'** in consequence of gross misconduct. Matters that may be considered gross misconduct should be specified in the procedure. Examples of gross misconduct might include failure to obey an instruction, fighting, dangerous practices, drunkenness, drugs abuse, theft or other dishonesty.

The following article gives an example of the use of disciplinary and grievance procedures.

Union to sue insurance firm over bullying boss

A trade union is planning legal action against a leading insurance company over alleged corporate bullying. The case could force hostile managers to pay compensation to their staff.

The Manufacturing, Science and Finance Union said yesterday that its lawyers were preparing a case against the Co-operative Insurance Society and one of its managers on behalf of an employee who has been on sick leave for five months with a stress-related illness.

The case is believed to be one of the first of its kind, although lawyers have been saying for months that legislation introduced to conform with European law would lead to a flood of claims. The CIS case centres on the actions of one manager in a claims office in the Midlands. He is alleged to have verbally abused and mistreated all his staff for more than two years.

Bill Hamilton, a spokesman for the union, said: 'It's not just a question of employers providing machinery that is in good safe working order. They should also provide rational bosses who can treat their staff with reason rather than ranting and raving throughout the working week.'

But the company said that the manager concerned had already been subject to 'strong disciplinary action' under the normal grievance procedure, although he still worked in the same office as a manager.

A spokesman said: 'The staff concerned have been given an assurance that any repeat of the manager's unacceptable behaviour will not be tolerated.'

Daily Telegraph,
13 September 1995

- **policies and procedures** exist for promotion and transfer of employees between departments;

- **a pay policy** which sets out clearly the scales of pay that apply to each job class, and any additions to basic pay, such as overtime and holiday pay, together with a declared policy of equal pay for work of equal value;

- **sick pay** arrangements and pension schemes;

- **a health and safety policy** which ensures that the necessary organisation and arrangements are in place;

- **discipline and grievance procedures** which are fair to both employees and the employer.

Where trade unions are recognised by the employer, arrangements should be in place for negotiations to take place relating to pay, conditions, grievances, discipline and other employee relations issues within the scope of their recognition.

EMPLOYEE RESPONSIBILITIES

As with the employer, employees also have responsibilities. The main responsibilities are:

- to attend work, to be punctual and to abide by company rules;

- to work efficiently and to produce goods (or services) to the quality required;

- to comply with rules relating to equality and discrimination;

- to work safely, to comply with safety rules, and not to endanger self or others;

- to be loyal to the employer and to preserve the employer's trade secrets.

The article below illustrates the damage that can occur if employees do not take their responsibilities seriously.

ACTIVITY

Read the article about the lecturer receiving damages for being insulted. This is a case of employees not complying with the rules relating to equality and discrimination.

Please do not laugh at it. Instead, list all the people and institutions that were or will be adversely affected by it. It could run into a large number, so think widely. For example, consider the effects if a member of staff faces disciplinary action. If that person was sacked, it could affect his or her students' education; it could affect his or her family, etc.

£30,000 damages for Irish insult

The award of nearly £30,000 damages to a college lecturer called an 'Irish prat' by a colleague was criticised by a Tory councillor as 'stupidly high'.

Alan Bryans, 43, a special needs tutor at a Northumberland College of Arts and Technology, was said by an industrial tribunal to have been victim of 'particularly appalling' racial discrimination.

Besides the 'prat' remark, he was nicknamed 'Gerry Adams' by fellow staff wanting him to move his car. On another occasion a woman lecturer embarrassed him by asking him to serenade her with an Irish song.

Mr Bryans became so distressed that he lost two stone in weight. He is still receiving stress counselling.

Bill Purdoe, a Conservative councillor, described the amount of damages as 'stupidly high for what appears to have been a relatively minor incident. This is an enormous amount of money for a small college to pay – £29,000 could cover a lecturer's salary for a year.'

Mr Bryans' case was supported by the Commission for Racial Equality. His solicitor said: 'People may say this was only a bit of mickey-taking, but those people should beware – racist jokes can have expensive punchlines.'

Daily Telegraph, 23 September 1995

TRADE UNIONS AND STAFF ASSOCIATIONS

An independent trade union is defined as 'an organisation that consists mainly of work people whose principal purpose is the regulation of relations between those people and their employers'. A full definition is given in the **Trade Union and Labour Relations Act 1974**.

Since the **Employment Act 1980**, there is no obligation on employers to recognise trade unions. An employer is free to refuse to recognise a trade union even where that union has a significant number of members among the company's employees. An employer can also decide to derecognise, without negotiation, a union which has members among the company's employees.

Trade union membership has declined from 13.3 million in 1979 to under 10 million at the present time. As well as the decline in numbers, legislation has reduced trade union powers and passed the 'right to manage' back to managers. Whether this is a good thing depends on your political outlook. Despite these major changes, unions play an important role in representing their members in the employee relations field.

An employer may decide to recognise a union for certain matters. The boundaries are set out in an agreement which includes a union's right to represent its members in all or any of the following:

- **pay and conditions of work;**

- **the physical conditions in which its members have to work;**

- **the fairness of the recruitment, selection and promotion processes;**

- **the ways people are dismissed or suspended;**

- **the ways work is allocated to people or teams;**

- **the ways the discipline and grievance procedures are used;**

- **membership or non-membership of a trade union;**

- **facilities for trade union officials;**

- **procedures for conducting negotiations between employer and union.**

An individual employee is relatively powerless in a dispute with an employer. So people join unions to give them a little more security – collectively they can expect to have more influence in bargaining with an employer. In this way, they hope that the power balance between employer and employee is fairer. Unions can also exert pressure on behalf of their members at a political level.

ACTIVITY

1 **Working with a colleague, prepare an argument supporting one of the following positions:**

- **for union representation of employees in settling a dispute with an employer;**

- **against union representation of employees in settling a dispute with an employer.**

2 **When you have a sound argument, arrange to put it to a pair of colleagues who have prepared the opposite argument. It is important that you use reasoned argument and hear the other side out. Don't heckle or interrupt.**

3 **When you have completed the exercise, look again at your argument and see if you still hold the same view, or have you amended it?**

The main tool of the union is **collective bargaining**. This is a technique for controlling the basic power relationships which underlie the conflict of interest in the employee relations system. Employers have a powerful advantage when negotiating with individual employees. Trade unions try to counter this advantage by negotiating on behalf of groups of employees, by presenting collective demands.

Employees and trade unions try to establish mutually-accepted rules and procedures that provide a relatively stable framework in which to negotiate. In essence, negotiations are about distributing scarce resources –

money, status and power. Negotiators can choose collaboration or conflict. But, by whichever route, agreement has to be reached eventually. Failure to agree by collaboration can result in **industrial action**.

ITN union staff vote to strike

Journalists and technicians at ITN voted yesterday to hold a two-hour strike which could disrupt news bulletins.

Union officials warned that the strike would be the first of a series – possibly escalating into 24 hour walkouts – unless talks resumed.

ITN's management says its programmes, including News At Ten and Channel 4 News, will be screened as normal.

Members of the National Union of Journalists and the Broadcasting, Entertainment, Cinematograph and Theatre Union are protesting at ITN's decision to abandon collective pay bargaining, which they claim amounts to union derecognition.

Of 333 NUJ and Bectu members balloted, 183 voted for industrial action. ITN's work force is 674. John Fray, the NUJ's national broadcasting organiser, said: "This is an overwhelming vote of no confidence in management's intentions, which will have to be modified to avoid the risk of serious disruption."

ITN said only a small proportion of staff had voted to strike. "We are confident there will be no disruption of transmission of programmes," said a spokeswoman.

Stewart Purvis, its chief executive, is to meet staff today for a briefing. He insists that management should be allowed to pay performance-related salaries.

The historically high salaries of Bectu staff "pose a consistent problem in negotiations for new television news business contracts in a fiercely competitive market", he said.

Guardian, 24 January 1996

INDUSTRIAL ACTION

Industrial action occurs when an employer and a union are in dispute and have failed to reach an agreement. The union's members use their collective power to 'put pressure' on the employer by:

- ✪ **non-co-operation – refusing to undertake work outside job descriptions;**

- ✪ **working to rule – doing only those tasks described in the job's 'rule book';**

- ✪ **withdrawal of labour – strike action.**

This is intended to bring the employer closer to the union's demands. Sometimes it works and sometimes it does not. One thing is certain, if it damages the business, no one wins.

Ford factories back to normal

FORD'S DAGENHAM and Southampton factories returned to normal yesterday after Thursday's wildcat strikes, which cost £10 million in lost production.

Union leaders will meet on Wednesday to discuss their next move after rejecting a 9.25 per cent wage increase over two years.

Daily Telegraph, 18 November 1995

ROLE OF STAFF ASSOCIATIONS

Some employers who do not wish to recognise a trade union will encourage and finance the founding of a staff association. Staff associations invariably have little power. They pursue issues of common interest such as the provision of social events and recreational facilities. They rarely have any influence over the rights of employees, and have no negotiating rights over wages or conditions of employment. As they have no 'independence', staff associations cannot be compared with independent trade unions. They are often just a management concession to employees who wish to be consulted and have some say in the running of the business.

SETTLING INDUSTRIAL DISPUTES

If employers, trade unions and/or individual employees cannot resolve conflict, there are three bodies set up to arbitrate and adjudicate on industrial disputes. Below, we look in turn at the work of the Advisory, Conciliation and Arbitration Service, industrial tribunals and employment appeals tribunals.

ADVISORY, CONCILIATION AND ARBITRATION SERVICE

The Advisory, Conciliation and Arbitration Service (ACAS) is an independent body set up in 1976 to improve employee relations by offering an impartial service to both parties in an industrial dispute. It provides:

- **advice** to employers, employees and unions in matters of employee relations;

- **help to both sides** in resolving industrial disputes; this help might be in the form of advice or conciliation – if neither is effective, ACAS arbitrates between the sides in dispute, but it will do so only if both the union and the employer agree to be bound by ACAS's decision;

- **a code of practice and guidance** for disciplinary and grievance procedures.

ACAS has survived so long because it has maintained its impartiality, and is seen to be even handed in its dealing with both sides in a dispute. In Northern Ireland, the **Labour Relations Agency** provides a similar service.

ACTIVITY

ACAS produces excellent booklets on a wide range of employee relations issues. Write to them and ask for a list of its publications. Some are free and some are not. The address is:

Advisory, Conciliation and Arbitration Service
27 Wilton Street
London SW1X 7AZ
Telephone: 0171 210 3000

INDUSTRIAL TRIBUNALS

Any breach of contract that cannot be settled by other means may end up in a special court called an industrial tribunal.

Industrial tribunals are full members of the UK legal system. They are unique in having people on them who are chosen because they understand the work environment in matters relating to employment law. Each tribunal has a chairperson who is a barrister or solicitor with at least seven year's experience, plus two lay people, one drawn from panel of employer members, the other drawn from a panel of employee members. In some cases, a tribunal may sit without the lay members.

Industrial tribunals are more accessible to ordinary people than other courts. A complaint to an industrial tribunal by an employee or former employee is written on a very simple form – an IT1 – and sent to the tribunal office. There is no need to engage a solicitor or be represented at any hearing, although there is nothing to stop a person doing so if he or she wishes; about 50 per cent of applicants are legally represented. There are no court fees, and only in very exceptional circumstances are costs awarded against a person who loses a case. So it is easy and cheap to take a case to an industrial tribunal.

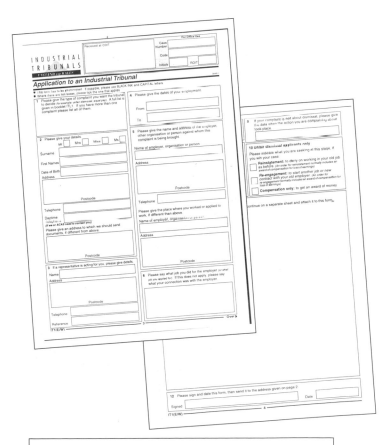

Figure 4.2: Application to an industrial tribunal.

Industrial tribunals are probably best known for their powers to hear complaints of unfair dismissal. It is easy for an ex-employee to bring a complaint against the former employer. But to avoid wasting the tribunal's time, every complaint is vetted by ACAS which conciliates between the parties and tries to reach a settlement without the need to go before the tribunal.

In 1994, 46,000 complaints of unfair dismissal were lodged. The number of complaints has more than doubled since 1989. ACAS was able to settle over 19,000 out of tribunal. More than 11,000 complaints were dropped, and only 13,200 went on to be heard at tribunal.

Altogether, only about 44 per cent of complaints for unfair dismissal are upheld by tribunals. However, it is no victory for employers to win. They should be asking themselves: 'what went wrong to cause a complaint to be made to a tribunal?' If the answer shows that their procedures are being operated by the managers in the intended fashion, and that the procedures themselves are sufficient to meet their business objectives and legal requirements, then the case may be put down to a difficult employee. But in most cases, there will be evidence of a need to reappraise the way the organisation handles these difficult matters.

The stress imposed on managers who have to justify their actions to a tribunal is considerable. It is a costly business, taking up management time that could be spent on more productive matters. The cost to the company in time and expense, is considerable.

If an industrial tribunal finds that the complainant was unfairly dismissed, the former employee has a right to compensation, reinstatement or re-engagement.

Compensation is made up of several parts. There is a basic award of over £6,000. The tribunal can award additional compensation for loss of earnings, pension and so on, of £11,000. In addition, if the employer refuses to reinstate or re-engage, the former employee may be awarded further compensation. There is also a special award payable to those dismissed because of membership or non-membership of a trade union.

As well as facing the cost of meeting these substantial compensation awards, companies that dismiss employees unfairly also often receive considerable bad publicity in the press. The effect of bad publicity is impossible to measure.

EMPLOYMENT APPEAL TRIBUNAL

An appeal may be made on a point of law against a decision by a tribunal to an employment appeal tribunal. In 1994, 940 appeals were registered with the appeal tribunal. The majority were lodged by employees. The appeal tribunal is made up of a High Court judge and two lay people. They can uphold or overrule the findings of the industrial tribunal. In rare cases, appeals to the Court of Appeal, and then to the House of Lords can be allowed.

Judges dash hopes of backdated dismissal claims

Thousands of part-time workers attempting to bring compensation claims for unfair dismissal or redundancy that occurred more than two years ago had their hopes dashed by the Court of Appeal yesterday.

Three judges ruled that a House of Lords judgement in March 1994 giving part-timers working less than 16 hours a week the right to claim compensation did not apply retrospectively.

This means that part-timers who became eligible to bring claims after the Lords' judgement will succeed only if their claims were lodged within three months of their dismissal.

The ruling was given in a case brought by Mary Biggs, 56, who alleged she was unfairly dismissed in August 1976 after working for 17 months as a part-time science teacher in Shepton Mallet, Somerset.

At the time, she was unable to bring an unfair dismissal claim because she was working for only 14 hours a week and the qualifying period was then 21 hours. The Lords ruled that the then 16-hour qualifying period was in breach of European law because it discriminated against women. Within three months Mrs Biggs lodged an industrial tribunal claim in Exeter.

But the tribunal's decision that her claim was out of time and should have been lodged within three months of her dismissal in 1976 was upheld by the Employment Appeal Tribunal.

In the Court of Appeal, it was argued that it had not been practicable for Mrs Biggs to have brought her claim within three months of dismissal and the tribunal was bound by Community law to disregard the limits.

It was also argued that she could rely on directly-enforceable rights under Article 119 of the Treaty of Rome on which the Lords' judgement was based. But, in dismissing her appeal, the court ruled that it would have been possible for her to have made her claim within the time limit.

Daily Telegraph, 27 January 1996

METHODS OF GAINING EMPLOYEE CO-OPERATION

Managing people is the most complex activity that a manager has to master. Some never master it. People are complex beings with both physical and mental needs. Although people's general characteristics can be categorised, each person is unique and is constantly changing and developing.

Physical needs include wages, sick pay, pensions, good conditions of work, safety, trade union recognition, contract of employment and business success.

Mental needs include good working relationships, a sense of belonging, knowing what is going on, self-esteem, respect, recognition for achievements, opportunity for personal improvement, a say in things that affect them, responsibility and autonomy.

To gain an employee's co-operation, all their needs should be satisfied to some extent at work. Many techniques have been developed to assist managers; each has some degree of success but they are only as good as the manager applying them. The case studies on page 224 illustrate some of the approaches that can be adopted.

ACTIVITY

Refer back to the list of items that must appear on the statement of terms and conditions of employment on page 209. Take each item from the list (do not bother about the first two – names and dates) and see where it fits into the 'model of human needs' illustrated in *Fig. 4.3*. For example, 'job title' fits into 'status'. Complete the picture of the relationship between the contract and the model of human needs.

Do you find that the contract meets mainly physical, rather than mental needs? If that is the case, we need to find other ways of satisfying mental needs at work.

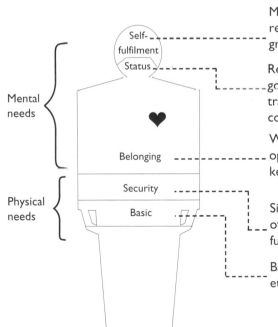

Self-fulfilment — Meaningful jobs, use of talents, participation, responsibility, autonomy, opportunity for personal growth

Status — Respect for all employees, opportunity to achieve goals, recognition for achievements, discipline, training, promotion, titles, status symbols, consultation

Belonging — Work groups, good work relationships, opportunities to socialise, sense of belonging, keeping employees informed, caring culture, loyalty

Security
Basic — Sick pay, pensions, health and safety policy, contract of employment, trade union recognition, holidays, full order book

Basic pay, working conditions (ventilation, warmth, etc.), canteen, breaks, hours of work

Mental needs

Physical needs

FIGURE 4.3: A model of human needs.

Bally Shoe Factories

In 1990, Bally Shoe Factories in Norwich was losing £1.5m on a turnover of £9m. Something had to be done. The company's operations director believed that there had to be revolutionary change. But what?

He visited twelve UK companies, including Nissan, and began to realise that Bally's own operations were out of balance. Seeing the success of other companies gave him and his colleagues courage to make some revolutionary changes.

There were two main thrusts. First, they decided to change Bally's market position to high price, high quality. Second, they sought to build much more trust and commitment with the employees.

To achieve the latter objective, they abandoned some traditional practices. They removed piecework, removed clock cards, stopped providing company cars to senior staff, and removed barriers between the managers and their staff. They developed effective ways of involving their employees in decision taking, making them aware of the value they added to the organisation.

All the changes – and the advice they sought from other companies – has been worth it. 'We were looking to break into profit in 1995,' said the operations director, 'but we actually achieved it in 1994.'

Bally's successful revolution has been based on rethinking its whole approach to its business. It moved from producing lower-priced shoes, and refocused its marketing effort to the higher end of the market. But the most impressive change has been to revise its culture from 'employees are different from managers' to 'employees are the same as managers'. The **single-status environment**!

It is often the case that people doing a job know more about its detail than the manager responsible for direct supervision. It is good sense, therefore, to develop groups (like quality circles) through which employees can give their expert advice and views to their manager. Consultation makes people feel valued, particularly when they can see that their advice is used to improve performance.

Design to Distribution

Design to Distribution, (D2D) supplies high-volume, printed circuit boards and products to a range of blue chip companies, including Dell, Hewlett Packard and Pace Micro Technology.

D2D is an example of world-class manufacturing leadership. It has achieved this enviable status by ensuring a pursuit of excellence and continuous improvement in every part of its business. To achieve this, every employee is considered a business driver. 'An operator working on a line knows the customer, the volume target, the board costs, the profit margins and, therefore, the number that we need to make in order to break even,' said D2D's quality and business planning manager.

In order to become world class other changes have been made. Operators now make decisions and deal with deviations in quality before they become problems; supervisors are more actively involved; and people from the plant have close contact with the customers. Operators are involved in the quality process rather than quality analysts – it's the only way to handle things quickly, as the customer wants. Operators are trained to carry out statistical process control. 'We don't measure as many things as we used to, but we certainly measure them more intelligently' said D2D's general manager.   ▶ ▶ ▶

> Training is not undertaken in isolation without the commitment of every employee. Days are spent explaining the importance of the quality ethos; operators get to meet the customers and publicly sign their commitment to the goal of zero defects.
>
> These are all part of ongoing improvements that are needed to keep D2D world class.

Once again, employees – the human resource – play a key part in the company's strategy. As well as the investment in advanced technology, Design to Distribution treats all staff as vital partners in creating success. It creates teams that include customers, and gives operators control over their own work area. Training, and developing good attitudes, is seen to be at the heart of the move towards world-class status.

There is an emphasis on **team working**. Most people need to work with others to achieve their job objectives. You might know the positive feeling that comes from being a member of a successful team. By creating work teams and giving them authority to use available resources, employers can make teams responsible for achieving targets, and reward them for success. Knowledge about creating balanced teams has increased over the last fifteen years. As a result, expert managers can use this knowledge to form very effective teams which prove to be more productive than keeping people working as individuals. Most people enjoy being a part of a successful team and achieving good results for which they get recognition.

Operators and shop-floor workers are given more responsibility for quality. **Quality circles** are based on the belief that several heads are better than one. Allowing people to pool their experience and expertise to examine problems and offer solutions is both good business sense and good motivation. A strategy of seeking **continuous improvement** has proved to be a great motivator and creates a feeling of worth.

A common theme in these two case studies is the pursuit of success through people. One thing that results from being a contributor to success is a feeling of personal worth. There is a virtuous circle: the more people feel valued, the greater their self-esteem, then the greater their contribution. Together, these case studies give an idea of the methods that are being employed in the best British companies to gain employee co-operation and, through that, success.

Not every company meets these high standards and ideals. In 1996, many employees in the UK are suffering from a 'lack of security', even though the UK is supposed to be pulling out of the recession of the early 1990s faster than any other country in Europe. Feeling secure in your job generates the so-called 'feel-good factor'. It is good sense for successful employers to give as much assurance as possible about job security. Insecurity causes low morale; if company morale is low, the effectiveness of schemes to gain employee co-operation will be lessened.

The best ways to secure co-operation are to:

- **treat people as adults;**

- **show them respect and value their expertise;**

- **involve them and consult them about plans;**

- **be open and honest and communicate clearly;**

- **give people lots of positive feedback on their performance;**

- **never forget to recognise good performance;**

- **always examine poor performance and find ways of preventing it happening again;**

- **let people learn – encourage personal development.**

PORTFOLIO ASSIGNMENT

This assignment is an investigation into the human resource and personnel policies of organisations. You are to research the policies of two organisations and to prepare a business report.

This assignment requires you to do a considerable amount of research. The research should provide the information you will need to write the report. Try to avoid the temptation to leave this piece of work until the last moment – you must allow time for busy business people to answer your requests for information and for their replies to arrive.

Your report should describe the human resource and personnel policies of two organisations. It should focus on:

- ❁ their health and safety policies and how these policies are carried out by managers and staff;

- ❁ their equal opportunities policies and how they are carried out and monitored by each company's managers;

- ❁ the actions that can be taken in each of your two organisations by employees if employers do not carry out their health and safety and equal opportunities obligations;

- ❁ the actions that can be taken by the employer if an employee does not co-operate with the organisation's health and safety and equal opportunities policies;

- ❁ the role that trade unions and staff associations play in negotiating pay and conditions of work and in providing information, advice and legal representation for their members.

In addition, for one of the two organisations, you should also report on how it:

- ❁ negotiates pay and conditions;

- ❁ handles disciplinary procedures;

- ❁ handles grievances;

- ❁ gains the co-operation of its employees.

Before beginning the research, ask your teacher if you are to work alone or if you can work in small groups to collect and share the data needed. If you work in small groups, you must write the report yourself, and show clearly your individual contribution to the research.

TASK 1

The first task is to prepare a research brief. You need to work out how to gather the data you need to write your report. Think of the different ways you can gather data to enable you to write an accurate report for this assignment.

Because of the complexity of this assignment, it might be best to design a questionnaire that covers all the topics specified in the assignment. In writing questions ask yourself whether they will produce the answers that give the information needed to write an informative, practical report.

You are going to have to get information from busy, professional people. So, it is important that your questionnaire is as clear and as short as possible. You should test out the questionnaire. Get a friend or colleague to read through it to see if they understand the questions. Let your teacher see the questionnaire and comment on it before you start your research.

TASK 2

Your next task is to select two organisations for your research. Choose any two organisations you like. Here are a few suggestions:

- your school or college;
- a manufacturing business;
- a hospital;
- a commercial business, say a bank or building society;
- a branch of a trade union;
- a department store;
- a farming or agricultural business;
- a mine or quarry;
- a sports centre;
- a government department, say the education department of the metropolitan or county council.

Ideally, you want to approach organisations that are local. The best source might be organisations you know through your part-time work, through work experience placements, through friends or relatives, through your school or college work experience co-ordinator, or through your own initiative.

If these are not acceptable to you, you can find a lot more ideas in the Yellow Pages, Thompson's Directory, or the Chamber of Commerce Directory. Librarians will be able to show you what directories are available.

TASK 3

To conduct the research, you need to approach the organisations that you have chosen. You need to find out which person can best answer your questions. In many cases, the best source of information is likely to be the organisation's human resources or personnel manager.

So you might write to the human resources manager. You could design your own letter-headed paper using a computer which depicts the fact that you are a GNVQ student at your school or college. Make it look professional and mature. Your letter is to explain that you need some information about human resourcing to help you complete this assignment; you might enclose a copy of the assignment if you think it would help to gain the manager's co-operation. Enclose a copy of your questionnaire.

If you do not wish to write, you may plan a telephone call that will serve the same purpose as the letter. You will need to follow this up by sending your questionnaire or arranging an interview with the appropriate managers.

TASK 4

When you have received responses to your questionnaire and any other information that you need, you need to make sense of it. You need to think about the structure of your report. Note down the headings you intend to use, and transfer all the key information under the relevant headings.

Review the information you have gathered against what you have learnt about the contract of employment. Consider whether the organisations meet the requirements of the law. Are the rights and duties of each party to the contract respected? In preparing and writing your report, you should include a summary of the main legal obligations under each of your headings.

TASK 5

The report is designed to show that you understand how human resource policies operate in local organisations and how these relate to the legal obligations imposed on employers and employees.

The report should have a structure that makes it easy for readers to understand and follow your findings. It should adopt the conventions and formats used in business reports. Agree a suitable format with your teacher before you write the final report.

Make sure that it is well presented. It should be word processed and spell checked. If appropriate, use tables and charts in the text to support your explanations.

Investigate job roles and changing working conditions

The structure of business organisations and their ownership is examined in unit 2. In this element, we examine some of the key management roles in business organisations, concentrating on the responsibility which managers have for employees – the human resource. We also consider the reasons why there have to be changes in the ways businesses are run.

Economists describe three resources of business – land, labour and capital. The business manager would break these down further.

- ☺ **Land – buildings; plant; machinery; materials; transport.**

- ☺ **People – knowledge; expertise; skills; experience; time; and energy.**

- ☺ **Capital – fixed capital; working capital; cash flow.**

Every business organisation, whether it is a charity, a school or a profit-making enterprise, needs resources to achieve its goals. The process of manipulating these resources effectively is called **'managing'**.

THE JOB OF MANAGING

There are many definitions of managing. The *Collins Dictionary* definition is 'having administrative control or authority'. Consider, now, the features of the manager's role.

- ☺ **Managers are responsible for achieving objectives.**

- ☺ **Managers work within a structured organisation and with prescribed roles.**

- ☺ **Managers use the formal authority that goes with their role to oversee the activities and performance of their staff.**

- ☺ **Managers use administrative systems and procedures to help meet stated objectives.**

- ☺ **Each manager is accountable to a more senior manager for the outcomes of the work undertaken under their authority.**

So, we could come up with a fuller definition and say that a manager has **authority** to manipulate the organisation's resources to achieve its objectives. The manager is **responsible** for using the resources only for the purpose intended, and is **accountable** to the owners of the resources for the achievement of the objectives.

ACTIVITIES OF MANAGERS

There are six main activities that managers carry out:

- ☺ **planning;**

- ☺ **organising;**

- ☺ **motivating;**

- ☺ **reviewing;**

- ☺ **communicating;**

- ☺ **co-ordinating.**

PLANNING
A plan is a design for achieving something. Planning takes place at all levels within an organisation. Plans can relate to short or long-term intentions.

Short-term plans are often called **tactical plans** and usually contain precise, detailed, measurable objectives. Short-term planning is carried out at lower levels in an organisation, at middle manager and supervisor levels.

Long-term plans are often called **strategic plans**. Long-term plans are not as detailed or measurable as short-term plans – the further they look into the future, the less certain managers can be about outcomes. They are usually made at higher levels of management.

ORGANISING

A plan on its own is a sterile thing. Nothing happens until it is turned into actions. A manager takes the resources (including people) which are allocated to a job and deploys them in such a way as to achieve the objectives.

MOTIVATING

Motivating refers to any activity carried out by a manager to obtain the co-operation of everyone who can affect the outcome of a job. Getting the optimum return from each person is in the interest of the whole organisation. Just think of the people who can affect outcomes: customers, suppliers, the manager's own staff, the boss, people in other departments, and so on. All of these must be 'motivated' to co-operate by the manager.

REVIEWING

Having made a plan and put it into action, a manager constantly reviews progress to ensure that the plan is working properly – that is, if the current activities are continued, the desired outcome will be achieved. If not, the manager modifies the activities to correct the situation. Usually there are management information systems (MIS) and procedures to ensure that relevant feedback about progress is available to the manager at all times.

COMMUNICATING

In all aspects of managing, and in all functions in an organisation, the degree of success is directly related to the quality of communication. It is the 'nervous system' of managing. (A more detailed treatment of this topic is contained in unit 2.) Managers should ensure that everyone knows and understands the importance of their own contribution to business success. Staff should receive regular feedback from their managers about how they are performing against standards.

CO-ORDINATING

Managers deploy the available resources to the different tasks that need to be done to achieve objectives. Provided that all the tasks are completed successfully (that is, each

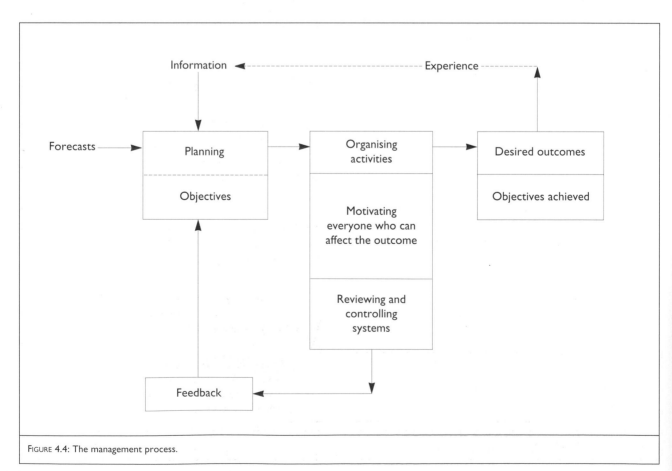

FIGURE 4.4: The management process.

meets its targets for quality, quantity, time and costs), their combined results will achieve the overall objective. Management information systems and operating procedures are designed to give the information to ensure that everyone is pulling in the same direction. Co-ordination is a unifying and harmonising activity.

Managing takes place at different levels in an organisation. The higher the level, the more general and strategic the work. The lower the level, the more tactical and specific the work. Although six levels are shown in *Fig. 4.5*, many of these levels are combined in medium and small enterprises. However, these smaller organisations still distinguish between strategic and tactical objectives.

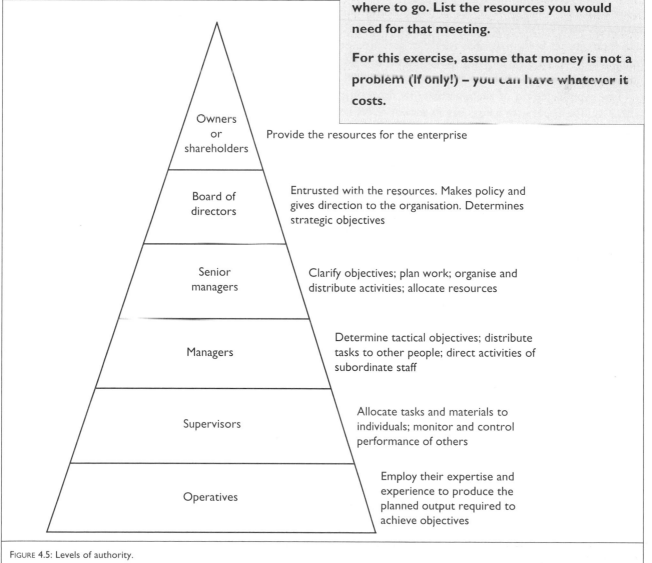

FIGURE 4.5: Levels of authority.

- Owners or shareholders — Provide the resources for the enterprise
- Board of directors — Entrusted with the resources. Makes policy and gives direction to the organisation. Determines strategic objectives
- Senior managers — Clarify objectives; plan work; organise and distribute activities; allocate resources
- Managers — Determine tactical objectives; distribute tasks to other people; direct activities of subordinate staff
- Supervisors — Allocate tasks and materials to individuals; monitor and control performance of others
- Operatives — Employ their expertise and experience to produce the planned output required to achieve objectives

DELEGATION

In order to get all the work done within an organisation, it is necessary to pass authority to lower levels of management. *Fig. 4.6* shows how authority is passed down an organisation.

By delegating authority, managers at lower levels within an organisation get the right to use the organisation's resources to produce products or services. Without authority, no manager at any level has the right to use resources – it could be fraud or theft to do so. If authority is delegated to a supervisor by his or her boss, the supervisor can use staff time by giving them work to do, spend money within budget, use raw materials, and so on.

The supervisor is now responsible for ensuring that the staff work efficiently on the job, use the materials for the products or services intended, and spend the budget only on things relating to the job. As the job proceeds, the supervisor has to account to his or her boss for the resources used, by showing the output created by their use. If targets are being met, all is well. If targets are not being met, the supervisor will be expected to take corrective action to get back on target.

You cannot get rid of accountability by delegating authority. The supervisor's boss has to answer to his or her boss in the same way. So you can see that it is not valid management behaviour to 'blame' subordinates for poor performance. They, the higher-level managers, are accountable for the performance of all their resources.

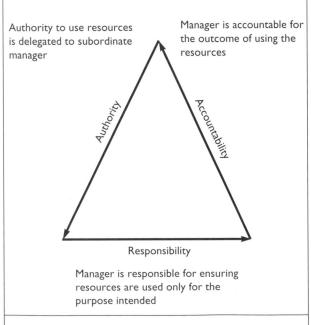

Authority to use resources is delegated to subordinate manager

Manager is accountable for the outcome of using the resources

Authority

Accountability

Responsibility

Manager is responsible for ensuring resources are used only for the purpose intended

FIGURE 4.6: The delegation model.

 # ACTIVITY

Read the section on delegation carefully, focusing on all the people involved, upwards, downwards, and sideways. Write a short essay which examines the place of 'trust' in the delegation process.

DIRECTORS

Directors are the most senior managers in a public or private limited company. In other types of organisation, such as a county council, there will be similar roles but possibly bearing different titles, like chief executive, for example.

Directors are nominated by the board of directors and appointed by the shareholders. The shareholders delegate authority to the board to manage their resources for the success of the business on a day-to-day basis. The directors are **responsible** for seeing that the resources are used only for the purpose intended and they are **accountable** to the shareholders for the outcomes of their management. If the shareholders are not satisfied with the performance of the directors, they may try to remove them from the management of the company's affairs. This is a complex process and is seldom attempted.

Directors have their duties described in legal documents called the **memorandum and articles of association**. They may take any actions needed to run the business on a day-to-day basis, provided they are not unlawful under the Companies Acts 1985. Directors have duties in common law. You will recall from our discussion about the contract of employment that duties of care and skill arise in common law. Directors must not act negligently in managing the company's affairs.

Before looking at the duties of directors in a little more detail, it is worth quoting again from case law. In the case *Re v City Equitable Fire Insurance Co (1925)*, the judge commented: 'It is indeed impossible to describe the duties of directors in general terms ... The position of a director of a company carrying on a small retail business is very different from that of a director of a railway company.'

ROLES OF DIRECTORS

The **managing director** is the most senior director on the board. Although there is no legal requirement to have a managing director, it is unusual to find a board without one.

If a managing director is appointed by a decision of the board, he or she acts in two capacities. First, as a director, all the powers, rights and duties associated with directorships apply to the managing director. Second, the board can delegate to the managing director the authority to make decisions that would normally be made by the whole board.

A **chairperson to the board** can also be appointed to preside at every board meeting and facilitate good practice. Often the chairperson is non-executive, that is, he or she does not work within the company and simply brings special expertise to the board meetings.

Non-executive directors do not work full-time in the business. As with non-executive chairpersons, the non-executive directors bring special skills or experience to the board to enhance the decisions taken. A non-executive director can be charged with negligence in the same way as an ordinary director.

THE ATTRIBUTES OF DIRECTORS

Directors need knowledge, skills and experience at two levels.

First, they should have functional expertise. For example, one director might be an engineer with responsibility for advising the board on production matters. Similarly, one would advise on financial matters, another on marketing matters, and another on human resource matters.

Second, each director should be a skilled manager. They should each be capable of:

- **planning at a strategic level;**
- **obtaining and organising resources;**
- **using social and human skills to maintain morale;**
- **offering leadership;**
- **communicating clearly;**
- **gathering and interpreting information;**
- **solving problems;**
- **taking high-level decisions.**

Directors should also be able to visualise what the business should look like in five or ten years time and start building for that now.

ACTIVITY

For this activity you will need access to a broadsheet newspaper, such as *The Times* or the *Daily Telegraph*. Turn to the business section. Many articles refer to the activities of directors and senior managers. For example, the front page of the *Sunday Times* business section on 3 December 1995 contained six stories, five of which had quotations from named senior managers.

1 Try to work out from these articles the sorts of activities that directors and senior managers undertake.

2 Make a list of all the activities you can identify and describe the skills needed to carry them out.

DIRECTORS' RESPONSIBILITIES FOR HUMAN RESOURCES

The board of directors is responsible for formulating a human resource policy. This policy would be passed down to managers who would ensure that it is followed by everyone in the organisation.

In practice, a human resources policy might be divided into a number of policies covering different aspects of personnel management. These might include:

- **equal opportunities policy;**
- **equal pay policy;**
- **non-discrimination policy;**
- **health, safety and welfare policy;**
- **pension arrangements;**
- **sick pay policy;**
- **management policies for morale and motivation;**
- **management policies relating to changes needed for future success.**

Although directors do not usually get involved in the day-to-day implementation of these policies, it is good practice for reports about their effectiveness to be presented to the board by the accountable manager on a regular basis – say, twice or four times a year.

MANAGERS

There is usually a manager in charge of each function in an organisation. Like directors, they need to be experienced and skilled in both their specialist function and in the skills of managing a department and its people.

Managers take the policies passed down from the board and turn them into activities. These activities are designed to achieve the corporate goals; a manager has no authority to use resources for any other purpose.

For example, the human resources director will hand down the human resources policy to the human resources managers. They will design procedures and processes to ensure that the policy is implemented throughout the organisation and that its goals are achieved. The human resources managers will need to consult with operational managers, and then plan and organise procedures for:

- **planning the numbers and types of staff** the organisation needs in the future;

- **attracting sufficient candidates** with the right qualities so that the organisation can select the best people for jobs;

- **training and developing staff** so that they perform to the highest level possible;

- **designing jobs** that are stimulating and interesting so that the organisation gets the best out of people;

- **ensuring that organisational structures and procedures** allow employees to have their views, ideas, worries and disputes heard;

- **designing ways of introducing and managing change** that minimise any negative impact on individuals and groups;

- **providing fair and legal procedures** for discipline and grievances, and ensuring they are applied uniformly throughout the organisation;

- **keeping within the law** on issues such as health and safety, equal opportunities, sex and race discrimination, and termination of employment;

- **dealing with trade unions,** staff associations, disputes, industrial tribunals and other legal actions.

ACTIVITY

Consider these questions about training policy. Write a short report (two pages) with your views, supported by reasoned argument.

1 **Who should be responsible for identifying the training needs of operatives in:**

    (a)   **a manufacturing business;**

    (b)   **an insurance company?**

2 **Who should carry out the training?**

3 **Who should record the training (and qualifications) held by employees?**

4 **Who should authorise the finance for the training?**

A human resources manager has objectives relating to:

- **the size and make-up of the organisation's workforce;**

- **salary negotiations and salary budget;**

- **training plans and training budget;**

- **staff turnover and morale;**

- **handling of disputes with individuals and unions.**

ACTIVITY

If you have a human resources manager (sometimes called a personnel manager) in your school or college, ask your tutor to invite him or her to give you a talk about human resources objectives.

SUPERVISORS

Supervisors are usually the first level of management in an organisation. They tend to be very skilled in the work of their department and are often promoted from within the department. They have daily face-to-face contact with their staff and deal with matters that require immediate attention. Sometimes supervisors are considered as the 'meat in the sandwich' because they are not considered a part of management, nor are they considered a part of the operational staff.

However, supervisors have management responsibilities. Departmental supervisors would be expected to manage their staff so that the department's objectives are achieved. They must operate within the contract of employment, within the law and within any procedures set out by the human resources manager. They are expected to manage staff effectively, to ensure their competence, and to ensure that high morale is maintained. Supervisors are perhaps best placed to decide upon performance standards for their staff, to monitor their actual work, to either coach them to achieve better performance or to organise their training, and to deal with day-to-day issues that might arise, such as discipline or grievance.

If a supervisor has insufficient knowledge about specialist human resource issues, he or she can call upon the human resources manager. In general, the human resources manager's role would be to advise supervisors on the handling of specialist matters only – those that might have a legal implication or such like.

⚡ ACTIVITY

Read the article opposite. Now consider a situation where a business decides to disband its human resources department and devolve 'power' to departmental managers. The department had been running for ten years with five personnel specialists.

You are one of these departmental managers. Prepare a short presentation to the managing director explaining all the steps that would have to be taken to ensure that this change could be implemented with minimum disruption.

Personnel officers are a waste of time, says new study

A team of academics led by Professor David Metcalf at the London School of Economics (LSE) has analysed job performance in 2,000 workplaces. They found that personnel directors on the board or specialist personnel officers in the workplace detracted from a company's performance.

The climate of management-employee relations was worse, productivity poorer and staff turnover rates higher when personnel managers were in place. Although human resource techniques – employee involvement, merit pay rises and blurring distinctions between managers and workers – did work, their success had nothing to do with the presence of personnel officers.

The LSE researchers' biggest problem is to explain why the work of personnel officers is not merely irrelevant but positively malign. Sue Fernie, one of the academic team, said: 'Workers see a personnel department as an external agency which distances them from their company and knows little about their work.'

Many companies are coming to the same conclusion. Only 30 per cent of British companies had a personnel officer on the board in 1993 against 70 per cent in the early 1980s. Tesco, British Gas and the RAC are all joining the list of large companies cutting or reorganising personnel departments.

It was in the 1960s that personnel work became a growth industry. Now industry has coined new buzzwords such as 'delayering' and 'flattening out the pyramid'. In practice, it means firms are devolving power to departmental managers from remote personnel officials.

But paradoxically, just as businesses are giving fewer jobs to specialist personnel officers, the government is stuffing them into quangos in the cause of making the public sector more business-like.

'NHS Trusts and further education colleges are all getting them,' said Ms Fernie. 'The anecdotal evidence we are getting is that they are helping to make relations between management and staff absolutely dire.'

Independent on Sunday,
15 May 1994

MANAGING CHANGE

Nobody can be unaware of the enormous changes that are taking place in businesses throughout the world. There is a range of forces that are acting on businesses which make change inevitable. If businesses do not respond positively and imaginatively to these forces they will almost certainly cease to exist in their present form. The greatest forces on businesses to change are:

- new technology;
- world markets;
- changing work patterns;
- workforce demands;
- environmental pressure groups.

NEW TECHNOLOGY

The rate of technological change is accelerating. It permeates every aspect of business activity: design, production planning, production control, automated production, warehousing, despatch, transportation, administration systems, management information systems, and so on. Robotics, automation and information technology are in their early stages of development. As progress continues the nature of industry and commerce will change even more dramatically. This topic is covered more fully in unit 2.

WORLD MARKETS

International companies are able to exploit world markets, enjoying considerable economies of scale as transport and communication unit costs decline. World-wide production facilities, automation, and 'instant information' anywhere in the world, have changed the nature of competition. Companies which do not deliver quality goods on time are being bypassed. Consumers demand more choice and new products. Product life cycles are shortening and product development timescales have had to speed up. Technological 'designer' products are replacing traditional versions. Premium brands are being overtaken by supermarkets' own brands – the power has shifted from the 'ability to advertise heavily' to the organisations that own the shelf space.

CHANGING WORK PATTERNS

The changes in technology and world markets are beginning to have an impact on the composition of the workforce. So, too, has the growth of service industries and the decline of manufacturing industries. There is less demand for unskilled and semi-skilled people, and growing demand for technocrats. There are greater numbers of people going to university. There is an explosion of technical and scientific journals which carry up-to-date knowledge to businesses. There are more imaginative working patterns – part-time working, job sharing, 'hot desking', working from home, and so on.

WORKFORCE DEMANDS

As employees become more expert and more aware, they are demanding better working conditions and a better quality of working life. They want to be consulted about matters that affect them at work. They have higher expectations about work than previous generations; people are not likely to become committed to employers who do not consider their needs and expectations. They want job satisfaction and know how to get it.

ENVIRONMENTAL PRESSURE GROUPS

Businesses are concerned to maintain a good relationship with their suppliers and customers. Highly intelligent people in pressure groups now monitor the workings of businesses and bring to public notice any environmentally unfriendly practices they find. This can damage a company's reputation and give its competitors an advantage. There have been examples of pressure groups staging high-profile demonstrations against a particular company and organising boycotts of its products. This makes businesses consider their practices very carefully to avoid 'upsetting' these groups.

WHY BUSINESSES MUST CHANGE

In response to these forces, businesses are having to adapt to new ways and to adopt new methods. There are good business reasons why they accept the need to change. They may embrace change:

- to improve efficiency and effectiveness;
- to improve profits;
- to respond to, or get ahead of competition;
- to adopt new technology;
- to comply with government or European Union regulations;
- to introduce new products or services;
- to take account of public pressure;
- to grow and become more influential.

You can see that the benefits of implementing changes for the business are quite attractive – increased profitability, faster growth than competitors, 'better' products than competitors, good public relations and more power in the marketplace.

IMPLEMENTING CHANGE

In order to implement changes, management must first understand why most people fear or resist change. Only if they take these reasons into account, will they be able to implement changes as quickly and successfully as Japanese industry.

REASONS FOR RESISTANCE TO CHANGE

People resist change for very good reasons; it is a normal human response which competent managers understand and deal with professionally. Change generates all sorts of fears. People fear the unknown and they are likely to feel insecure if they do not understand how change will affect them. Employees – including many managers – fear that:

- they might lose their job and hence their livelihood;

- they might not be able to handle new responsibilities;

- they might lose status, particularly if they are very good at their current job;

- they might have to change their work group and, perhaps, their social life, maybe even having to move home;

- they might be unable to do work they like, devaluing their skills;

- change is being introduced for change's sake – we have always done it this way, so why change?

- change will not work – it has been tried before and failed, so it will not work this time;

- their skills might become obsolete;

- they might have even more work and be under even greater pressure.

So, businesses must change, and there is nothing wrong with that; and people resist or fear change, and that is a very normal human reaction. How can these conflicting positions be reconciled?

ACTIVITY

1 Look at the two lists above, the reasons why businesses embrace change and the reasons why people fear and resist change. Classify each reason as either having to do with technology, the achievement of organisational goals, or outside influences (mark these reasons 'T'), or primarily concerned with social relationships, personal fears or motivations, or how hard an individual might have to work (mark these reasons 'S').

2 Now count the number of Ts and Ss you have put against each list. Calculate the percentage of reasons that you classified T and S respectively. Write your answers in a matrix like this:

	Reasons for change %	Reasons for resistance %
Technical		
Social		

When business managers complete a similar activity, their results show on average that 80 per cent of the 'reasons for change' are T reasons and only 20 per cent are S reasons. Conversely, only 20 per cent of 'the reasons for resistance' are T reasons and 80 per cent are S reasons.

This analysis highlights a real difficulty. Reasons for change are likely to be communicated in technical terms, while people want to know answers to the social question: 'how does change affect me?' Until this 'great change question' is answered, the fears – and consequently the resistance – will not decline.

If a business needs to change to keep competitive, and that change is resisted by employees, and managers have not answered the 'great change question', it will have detrimental effects on the business. These include:

⊗ **the changes are more costly to implement;**

⊗ **the changes take longer to implement, wasting time;**

⊗ **the business receives the benefits of the change later and loses potential income;**

⊗ **the morale of the employees suffers, affecting performance;**

⊗ **there may be industrial unrest, creating poor publicity;**

⊗ **the business may lose customers and make competitors stronger.**

You can see that it is a key management skill to plan changes so as to minimise resistance and to get the implementation completed as smoothly as possible. The Japanese spend time planning a change and explaining it until people are clear and understand it; then they implement it quickly with little or no resistance. The UK model is the other way around. Changes are planned quickly and very little is communicated until the time for implementation comes. Then the implementation tends to take longer with much disruption while people resist and try to stick to the old ways.

DEVELOPING AN APPROACH

There are two elements to planning a change. First, there is the problem of really understanding the dynamics of the change and 'getting a handle' on the situation. And second, there is the need to develop an implementation plan which enables the change to be made quickly and with minimum resistance.

FORCE FIELD ANALYSIS

If you imagine a blown-up balloon, it will stay that size so long as the pressure (force) inside is the same as the pressure (force) outside. If you alter either pressure, the balloon changes size. If the pressure inside is reduced compared with the pressure outside, it will change to a smaller size. If the pressure inside increases compared with the pressure outside, it will change to a larger size.

In this case, the change is brought about by changing one of the forces. This concept can be applied to any change to help us understand the dynamics of the situation.

In any stable situation, there are restraining forces pushing it one way and driving forces pushing it the other way. If both these forces are balanced, the situation will remain stable. If you want to change the situation, all you have to do is identify the nature of the restraining and driving forces, and then alter one or more of the forces to drive it in the direction you want. Just like letting some air out of the balloon.

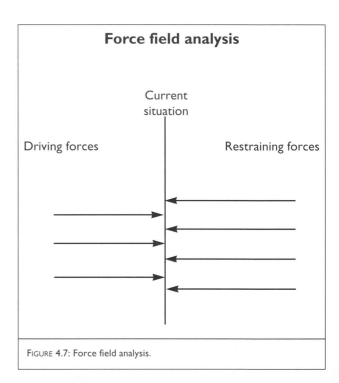

FIGURE 4.7: Force field analysis.

In *Fig. 4.7* you can take one of three actions to alter the situation:

⊗ **increase the strength of a driving force, or add another new driving force;**

⊗ **reduce the strength of a restraining force or remove it completely;**

⊗ **change the direction of a force – make a restraining force into a driving force.**

For an organisational change, the forces originate from:

⊗ **technological sources;**

⊗ **organisational sources;**

⊗ **external sources;**

⊗ **individual sources.**

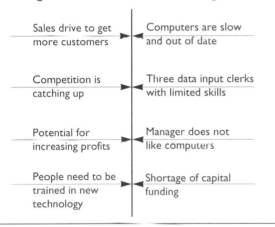

Present situation: producing 1000 documents per day
Desired situation: produce 2000 documents per day

Driving forces	Restraining forces
Sales drive to get more customers	Computers are slow and out of date
Competition is catching up	Three data input clerks with limited skills
Potential for increasing profits	Manager does not like computers
People need to be trained in new technology	Shortage of capital funding

FIGURE 4.8: Completed force field analysis.

💡 ACTIVITY

1 **In the example in *Fig. 4.8*, which of the forces do you think is the strongest?**

2 **What might be the effect of changing each force? For example, the sales drive might alter the balance by producing more customers.**

3 **Consider each force and decide upon the minimum change that might solve the problem.**

You may notice that work needs to be done on one or more force – that is called 'unfreezing'. While it is unfrozen, you can 'move' it, and then 'refreeze' it.

DEVELOPING AN IMPLEMENTATION STRATEGY

In order to ensure that changes are implemented with minimum social impact, the change plan should clearly set out to reduce resistance. To do this:

⊗ **make information available on how the change will affect people from the beginning – a person who understands social impacts should be on the change design team;**

⊗ **in communicating the change, encourage people to ask questions about its likely impact on them personally;**

⊗ **where guarantees can honestly be given, communicate information about job security, job transfer, retraining, work groups, etc;**

⊗ **obtain people's participation at the planning stage if possible, but social information must be made available as well as technical information;**

⊗ **communicate in language that is clear to the recipients – avoid jargon that excludes some people;**

⊗ **do not make people feel guilty by justifying the change 'because of their inefficiency' – to accept the change, people must admit they were wrong – and they will resist that;**

⊗ **promote the change as continuing improvements on a good base – make people feel good about themselves.**

Time spent planning changes in this way is a good investment. All these strategies are available to every manager. The skill is to pick the ones that best suit the situation. The manager's objective should be to make all changes quickly with least waste of time and money.

 **ACTIVITY**

Working in groups of three, use a force field analysis to consider a change relating to your school or college. For example, you might consider changing to a four-term year.

1 Use a large sheet of paper to record the current situation, the driving forces and the restraining forces. You may wish to interview some members of staff or students to understand the dynamics. Consider technological, organisational, external and individual sources.

2 When you have completed this, consider which forces can most easily be changed to allow the change to happen.

3 Now prepare an outline implementation plan that sets out to minimise resistance. Use the bullet point list above to guide your plan.

4 Present your findings to the whole class and be prepared to answer their questions. There will be some resistance!

PORTFOLIO ASSIGNMENT

This assignment is in two parts. The first part seeks information about job roles and the second part relates to managing change. It is based on the case study about Prodon Electronics Limited. It requires you to analyse the company and to write a business report.

Before starting the assignment, read the case study carefully. Make notes about the main issues it raises, and discuss it in depth with your colleagues so that you have a complete understanding of the situation it describes.

Prodon Electronics Limited

Jane Tomlinson is the chairperson of Prodon Electronics Limited. In her annual report, she said that 1995 had been an exceptionally good year all round. Profits had risen by 19 per cent and a dividend of 13p had been paid. She praised her colleagues on the board of directors for their strategic skills and foresight in seeing the company through the recession without harm. She singled out the new managing director in particular for praise.

The market for Prodon's products is buoyant. As interest rates have fallen, people have had more money to spend. The company is planning to expand its UK market share in the next three years from 9 per cent to 12 per cent. At the same time, it will take its first steps in establishing a foothold in mainland Europe by setting up distribution agreements with firms in Germany, Italy and Spain. From these three bases, it is intended to reach markets in all the countries of the European Union. Jane Tomlinson complimented the marketing manager and his sales team for their imaginative approach at a time when Prodon's competitors were running for cover.

Four new products are being developed, two to be introduced each year over the next two years. This will maintain Prodon's reputation of being the most innovative and forward-looking company in its sector of the industry.

This growth strategy – for increased sales and new products – will be achieved by replacing the present labour-intensive production machinery with state-of-the-art technology. Plans are being developed to increase production capacity by 25 per cent and reduce unit costs by 18 per cent through economies of scale. This will require changes throughout the organisation.

The chairperson reassured all staff that this transition will be achieved without causing hardship to those who might be affected. She complimented the production manager, his supervisors and particularly the operators who had worked with old and unreliable machines for many years without letting quality suffer. She and her board colleagues would always hold them in the highest regard.

The investment in new production technology and new product development will be financed from reserves. Steps are underway to offer shares to all staff at discounted rates to allow them to enjoy the prosperity generated by their hard work. She expressed her thanks to the finance manager and the personnel manager for working closely together to produce a very attractive scheme in which all staff, from directors to operators, have the same opportunity to benefit. The finance and personnel managers – and their staff – had played a key part in maintaining efficiency and keeping overheads under control.

Jane Tomlinson concluded her chairperson's report by announcing a major reassessment of employment policy together with an extensive retraining programme. This will give staff the opportunity to upgrade their skills and enjoy greater job satisfaction in the new high-technology environment. She thanked all the staff for their dedicated service and said she looked forward to continuing prosperity for Prodon Electronics, with all staff sharing its fruits.

The report's content is specified in task 2 and 4. It should follow a standard business report format. It should be word processed and spell-checked. Try to make it a professional piece of work.

TASK 1

This task sets out the work you have to do to analyse job roles and responsibilities.

(a) When you have a clear understanding of the case study, draw a diagram which shows the likely organisation structure of Prodon Electronics. It should identify all the job roles referred to in the case study.

(b) Draw a grid on a big piece of paper, with six columns and five rows. The amount of space available for each box should be enough to write 30-50 words. Leave the box in the top left-hand corner blank. Then, in the first column, down the left hand side of your grid, write the job roles you have identified from the case study. In the first row, at the top of your grid, write the following duties:

- identifying and meeting targets;
- working with others;
- training;
- discipline;
- implementing change.

(c) Write brief notes in the appropriate boxes about the responsibilities each role-holder in Prodon has for each of the duties listed at the top of the grid. For example, briefly note what are a director's responsibilities for 'identifying and meeting targets'. Then do the same for each of the other roles,

highlighting the differences between the roles. These notes are the raw material for your business report.

TASK 2

Now you should write part one of your business report. Using the notes you made in task 1, write a report on the job roles and responsibilities at Prodon Electronics.

(a) Explain the different job roles you have identified in Prodon Electronics.

(b) Set out in an orderly and easily understandable fashion, the responsibilities of each role for each of the five duties listed in task 1.

TASK 3

Now you should consider the management of change. The case study contains direct reference to some important changes that are being planned at Prodon. There are also some implied changes; for example, at one point it notes that 'this will require changes throughout the organisation'.

(a) Identify and list all the changes, express and implied, referred to in the case study. Where several changes are closely related, you may wish to classify them under common headings. See, for example, the classification on page 236. You may use other classifications if you prefer.

(b) Make notes that briefly explain why Prodon must make each of these changes. In addition, select one of the changes that relates to working conditions and make detailed notes that explain in depth the reasons for that change.

(c) Prodon's chairperson shows a great understanding of the reasons that people fear and resist change. Make notes of the things she said that are intended to lessen resistance.

(d) Develop a force field analysis to help you understand the dynamics of any one of the changes you identified above. Use your overall knowledge of business studies to identify 'forces'. Be imaginative and do not be constrained by tradition or convention.

(e) Develop an implementation plan based on the force field analysis, and on the need to minimise resistance. Identify the job roles which would be involved at each stage of the implementation, and state their responsibilities during the implementation.

TASK 4

Drawing on the work you undertook in Task 3, write the second part of your report.

(a) Explain briefly why a range of changes are necessary in business.

(b) Give a detailed explanation of one reason why working conditions change.

(c) Illustrate and explain a strategy for implementing a change to working conditions.

(d) Explain the responsibilities of different levels of job roles at different stages of the implementation.

Evaluate recruitment procedures, job applications and interviews

Getting the right people in the right jobs is fundamental to the success of an organisation.

If an unsuitable person is employed, the organisation will either become less efficient or managers will have to go through the whole selection process again. That would be an expensive waste of valuable management time.

In this element, we examine the process of finding the right person for the job by a series of short activities based on the following scenario.

The personnel manager

Imagine you are the personnel manager of a company making and distributing pharmaceuticals.

Working quietly in your office, you are interrupted by the sales office manager. She is flustered and irate: 'I'm fed up with the quality of sales staff we get nowadays. Can't the personnel department do something about it? Our newer recruits want to be spoon-fed, they want to have no work to do and to be paid a fortune for not doing it!'

Concerned at her frustration, you suggest that she sits down and has a cup of coffee while you discuss the problem. Once she has calmed down, you try to consider the problem rationally.

'What we've got to do,' you say, 'is to examine our recruitment and selection process, so that it helps us to choose people who can do the job we want, to the standard we want, and to fit in with our existing team.'

The sales office manager agrees, but adds doubtfully, 'if there is such a process.'

THE RECRUITMENT PROCESS

Sadly, there is no foolproof way of guaranteeing success. However, *Fig. 4.9* (on page 246) illustrates a well tried-and-tested process that reduces the risk of selecting the wrong person for a job.

Copy *Fig. 4.9* into your notes. It is quite like a 'map' that shows a logical route to a destination. (It is, in fact, called a **process map**.) The destination in this case is 'employing competent people'. The logical approach is important – it ensures that information is gathered in the right order, that it is relevant for its purpose, and that the conclusion is based on sound reasons.

Now we will look at each step in turn so that we have a full understanding of how it works.

JOB ANALYSIS

Creating a new post, or replacing someone who has left, gives a manager an opportunity to analyse the job that has to be done. Rather than just 'replace' the person who has left the post, it is often a chance to consider other (and perhaps better) ways of getting the work done.

- ☉ **The job may have changed** gradually over the years and no longer warrants a full-time appointment.

- ☉ **The departing person** may have 'bent' the job slightly to suit his or her own strengths. This might have resulted in important parts of the job not being done properly.

- ☉ **The manager** should consider whether the work could be reorganised – perhaps shared among existing staff; or even moved to another department.

- ☉ **There may be alternatives to a full-time position,** such as employing a part-timer, using temporary 'agency' staff or through more overtime by existing staff.

- ☉ **The use of more up-to-date technology** should be considered.

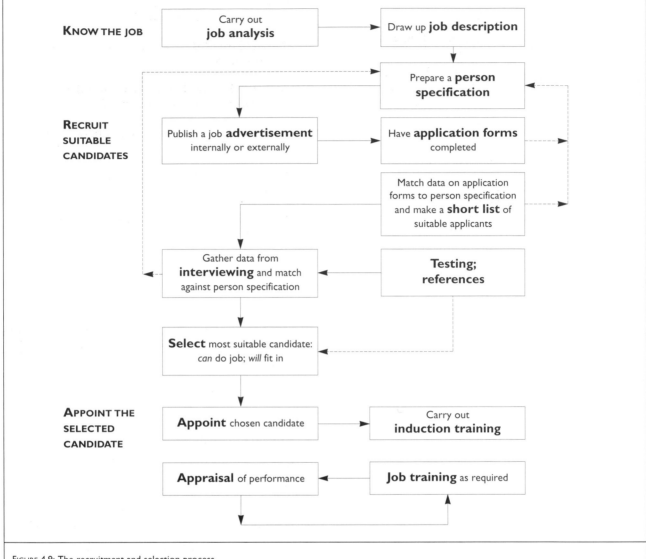

KNOW THE JOB

Carry out **job analysis** → Draw up **job description**

Prepare a **person specification**

RECRUIT SUITABLE CANDIDATES

Publish a job **advertisement** internally or externally

Have **application forms** completed

Match data on application forms to person specification and make a **short list** of suitable applicants

Gather data from **interviewing** and match against person specification

Testing; references

Select most suitable candidate: *can* do job; *will* fit in

APPOINT THE SELECTED CANDIDATE

Appoint chosen candidate → Carry out **induction training**

Appraisal of performance ← **Job training** as required

FIGURE 4.9: The recruitment and selection process.

☀ ACTIVITY

1 Read through the list of considerations about filling a vacant post given on page 245. Try to add other ways of getting work done that do not involve full-time staff. Be imaginative and innovative. For example, consider the options that are opened up by sub-contracting particular work to another business to carry out for you; or the wider use of information technology that, for example, allows people to work from home.

2 Prepare some notes on how technology might change the types of jobs that will be available in the future.

3 Form a small discussion group of up to (say) five colleagues. Use the notes you have made to contribute constructively to a discussion on 'job opportunities in the next century' with your class colleagues. After the discussion, list all the ways you have thought of to get work done.

- is there technology involved that requires special skills?

- what mental processes are required to do the job?

- is the job holder required to take decisions and use initiative?

- if so, what are the limits of his or her authority?

- is the output from the job a part or a whole?

- does the job holder have to work with others, or control the work of others?

- what are the required performance standards and how are they measured?

The simplest and most common methods of analysing jobs are:

- questioning the job holder;

- observing the job holder at work.

The information gathered is carefully recorded and analysed. Usually the job holder's manager is able to give additional information, although it tends to be rather general and would not normally be sufficient on its own. There are several other ways in which jobs can be analysed, but they are beyond the scope of this book.

In our scenario (see page 245), it might be a good idea for the sales office manager to consider exactly what the job of 'sales staff' entails. She needs to be absolutely clear about the tasks that the job holder will have to perform and the standard of work required.

She should describe the responsibilities of the job by answering the following questions:

- what tasks have to be completed by the job holder?

- how often is each task done and how important is it?

ACTIVITY

Some of your colleagues work in shops and supermarkets in the evenings and at weekends. Form a group of three or four, and make sure that at least one of the group works in a shop.

Use the nine questions above to establish the responsibilities of that person's job. Keep your notes.

JOB DESCRIPTIONS

When all this information has been gathered by the job analyst, it should be written down in a summary report setting out what the job entails. This summary report is normally called a **job description**. It contains two types of information: it describes the **tasks** of the job and it describes the **behaviour** necessary to actually do the tasks satisfactorily.

When the sales office manager in our scenario has completed the analysis, she should write a job description. This information is most valuable in trying to decide what sort of person might be able to do the job satisfactorily. *Fig 4.10* (on page 248) shows how a job description for her salesperson might look.

Job Description

Name of post:	Salesperson
Responsible to:	Sales office manager
Responsible for:	No direct staff
Relationships with:	Sales clerks; warehouse personnel; customers.
Job summary:	To call upon existing and potential customers according to the prescribed call schedule. To collect repeat orders, introduce new lines, open new accounts, arrange deliveries and returns, and collect overdue accounts. Keep customer records.
Job responsibilities:	The salesperson is responsible for selling the company's range of pharmaceuticals. He or she must know and keep up to date with the complete range of goods so as to inform and advise chemists of latest developments. He or she must behave in a professional manner and exercise care and security with samples and products. He or she must deal sensitively with complaints and errors. He or she must follow schedules and report daily on shortfalls.
Working conditions:	The salesperson will drive a company van, keep it clean and roadworthy, and ensure that any accidents or faults are reported immediately to the sales office manager.
Standards:	All calls must be made to schedule. Complaints and errors must be dealt with within 24 hours. Orders must be processed on the day they are taken. Records must be completed immediately after call. Sales targets must be met.

FIGURE 4.10: Job description for a salesperson.

ACTIVITY

Study the job description for a salesperson. Try to visualise a salesperson visiting a customer and carrying out the duties described.

Pick out and list the key tasks that a salesperson would be expected to do. Against each key task write two questions you could ask a job applicant. Your questions should be designed so that the applicant's answers will indicate whether he or she is competent to do that task to the required standard.

This is a difficult exercise, but one that interviewers have to do. So test out your questions on a colleague who has also studied the job description. Do they produce answers that show competence?

PERSON SPECIFICATION

A **person specification** (sometimes called a **personnel profile**) describes the characteristics and attributes which a person would need to be able to do the job to the required standards.

There are several ways of setting out this information. The one we will use is called the **seven point plan**. It simply describes the person you are looking for under seven broad headings. These headings are:

- ☉ **physical make-up** – what should the person look and sound like?

- ☉ **attainments** – what education, qualifications and experience should the person have?

- ☉ **general intelligence** – what intellectual capacity should the person have?

- ☉ **special aptitudes** – what special skills and talents are needed by the person?

- ☉ **interests** – what sort of pastimes or hobbies would the ideal person follow?

- ☉ **disposition** – what motivation and temperament and attitude should the person have?

- ☉ **circumstances** – what personal and domestic arrangements and location might the ideal person have?

Using this seven point plan, *Fig. 4.11* illustrates the person specification for a salesperson.

Physical make-up

Well groomed; smartly dressed.
Clear grammatical speech.

Attainments

Four GCSEs grade C, including chemistry
or a science. Formal sales training preferred.
Clean driving licence.

General intelligence

Above average. Quick on the uptake. Agile mind.

Special aptitudes

Ability to listen. High in social skills. Accuracy
and clear handwriting.

Interests

Any team sport or social responsibility.

Disposition

Pleasant and happy. Ability to cope with
customers who are upset.

Circumstances

Preferred stable, settled home life. Able to work
occasional Saturdays. Lives on territory.

FIGURE 4.11: Person specification for a salesperson.

⚡ ACTIVITY

1 **Do you agree that the characteristics listed
in *Fig. 4.11* are appropriate for a
salesperson? Justify your evaluation.**

2 **How might these characteristics differ if,
instead, you want to recruit a computer
programmer or an accounts clerk?**

There is a certain similarity between a person specification and a photofit picture used by the police in hunting suspects. The police gather information, analyse it and come up with an idea of what the offender might look like. The difference is that we are hunting for an ideal employee who will help to make our business prosper, and not someone who will 'rob' us by failing to do the job to the required standard.

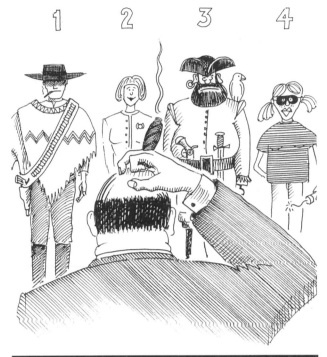

FINDING SUITABLE CANDIDATES

The next stage of the recruitment process is to attract people who fit the company's person specification, and no others. The first task is to identify, accurately, where the ideal people can be found. They may be found within the company itself, but doing a different job; they may be found through the families and friends of present staff. However, it might be necessary to advertise the position more widely. In which case, it is important to think about the type of people that the company is trying to attract and the publications they read:

⊗ **they may be readers of the *Daily
Telegraph* or the *Daily Mirror*;**

⊗ **if the post is a very technical one, or is
highly specialised, there are specialist
journals which are read by the people
suitable for these posts;**

⊗ **if someone straight from school or
college, or on a youth training
programme, would be ideal, the
company may want to contact the
careers service;**

⊗ **for specialist and management jobs,
the most popular medium for
advertising is the relevant professional
and trade press.**

The sales office manager in our scenario has the task now of deciding how to communicate her job needs in such a way as to attract suitable candidates. Let us not forget, the problem which she is trying to solve is that her 'newer recruits' are unsuitable. This is her chance to use carefully worded advertisements or notices to attract really suitable candidates.

Research suggests that there are four things that most applicants look for in a job advertisement. They are:

- **details about the organisation – who would I be working for?**

- **a clear description of the job – what would I be doing?**

- **the location – where would I be doing it?**

- **the salary scale – what financial reward would I get?**

The advertisement should also make it quite clear how any interested person should apply. Our sales office manager may decide to ask for a curriculum vitae (CV). Or she may simply ask them to write or phone for an application form.

JOB ADVERTISEMENTS

Advertising can be expensive. A national daily can charge over £80 per single column centimetre each time an advertisement is run.

In drafting advertisements, employers must respect the laws that relate to employment and recruitment.

- **The Disabled Persons (Employment) Act 1944 and 1958** provides that an employer of more than twenty people has a duty to employ a quota of disabled people.

- **The Equal Pay Act 1970** requires that equal pay is given for work of equal value.

- **The Sex Discrimination Acts 1975 and 1986** make it unlawful to discriminate against persons, directly or indirectly, on the grounds of race, gender or marital status.

- **The Race Relations Act 1976** requires that equal access to jobs and promotion is provided to people of equal ability irrespective of race, colour or creed.

- **The Employment Act 1990** makes it unlawful to discriminate against union members in a job advertisement.

The penalty for a breach of these laws can be severe. Courts can impose heavy fines and companies have to meet the legal costs involved. In addition, it costs management time in answering any charges, there is stress imposed upon those managers who must give evidence in the courts, and court cases can attract a lot of adverse publicity.

ACTIVITY

Calculate the price of an advertisement two columns wide and 15cm long in a newspaper that charges £70 per single column centimetre. How much would it cost if you published it three times?

If you publish four times, you will get a discount of 20 per cent off all four advertisements. Which option would you choose, and why?

ACTIVITY

Using the two advertisements shown in *Fig. 4.12* as a guide, design an advertisement for the job of salesperson. Make sure that your advertisement incorporates the four main points above that people look for in an advertisement, and that it stays within the law. If there is information you need for the advertisement that has not been given to you, just use your imagination and invent it.

A business wants a good return on its investment on advertising, so it makes good business sense to write a clear, precise advertisement that will attract the right sort of people. It seems sensible for a company to provide the four pieces of essential information in its job advertisements.

This clown could seriously boost your business

CHARLIE CHALK HAS A LOT OF FANS. NOT JUST THE CHILDREN HE AND HIS FUN FACTORY ATTRACT TO OUR BREWERS FAYRE PUB RESTAURANTS. BUT ALSO THEIR PARENTS. THEY CAN RELAX AND ENJOY A SELECTION OF HIGH QUALITY DISHES FROM OUR VARIED MENU, KNOWING THEIR CHILDREN CAN HAVE FUN INSIDE A SUPERB, SELF-CONTAINED AREA EQUIPPED WITH TOYS, GAMES AND ADVENTURE EQUIPMENT.

Charlie is just one example of our determination to meet the needs of the family. A determination that has made us the UK's most successful pub restaurant operation. Part of Whitbread Inns, Brewers Fayre now has over 200 thriving outlets up and down the country. Outlets where everyone - from the tiniest baby to the most senior citizen - is welcome. By capitalising on unique resources like Charlie, you'll build a business with an annual turnover of, perhaps, more than £1 million. Naturally we'll also help you excel with a comprehensive

training programme to suit your individual needs; and we'll provide you with all the necessary support and back-up to run a Brewers Fayre to the exacting standards both we and our customers expect.

MANAGEMENT

To join us on your own or as a couple you'll need impressive retail or catering management experience. An excellent organiser, you'll have the energy, imagination and team building skills to bring out the best in both your pub restaurant and your staff. Above all, you'll enjoy meeting people and you'll relish the challenge of

bringing them back time after time. We'll reward your abilities with a highly competitive salary, incentive bonus scheme and all the other benefits you would expect from the UK's leading pub retailer. You'll also have the opportunity to progress within the Whitbread Group as a whole.

If you'd like to run a business with the help of a few unusual characters, please 'phone for an application form on 071 935 6600 quoting ref: N1087/CH. Lines are open between 9am and 6pm Monday to Friday.

Working towards equal opportunities for everyone.
Four times winner of the National Training Award.
Part of Whitbread PLC, the Food, Drinks and Leisure Group.

BREWERS FAYRE

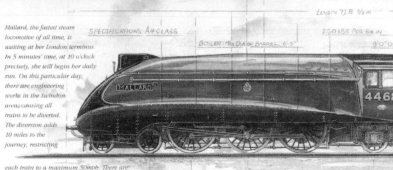

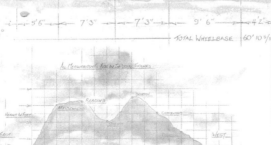

Mallard, the fastest steam locomotive of all time, is waiting at her London terminus. In 5 minutes' time, at 10 o'clock precisely, she will begin her daily run. On this particular day, there are engineering works in the Swindon area causing all trains to be diverted. The diversion adds 10 miles to the journey, restricting each train to a maximum 50mph. There are also speed restrictions between Paddington and Maidenhead (98mph) and Didcot and Swindon (100mph). For your convenience a gradient map and a cross-section of the line between London and Bristol is illustrated.

Given that Mallard, with her 8-coach train, increases her speed on level ground by 20mph every 11 miles, would she break her own world speed record of 126mph before she gets to Bristol?

MOTOROLA

Answer: No, because Mallard was an LNER locomotive and would be en route to Scotland on her daily run, having travelled northwards from Kings Cross.

AN UNUSUAL
TRAIN OF
THOUGHT FOR
PROBLEM SOLVERS

At Motorola's European Cellular Infrastructure Division in Swindon, we guarantee to set you real problems requiring real solutions. How can we make our products even smaller and more efficient? How should we reduce our cycle times and improve quality still further? How will we apply our core expertise to emerging markets?

All nice problems to have if you're a graduate-calibre engineer with a flexible mind, the vision to contribute throughout project life cycles, the ambition to learn new skills — and the desire to make the most of your hands-on design experience in:

SOFTWARE 'C', X-Windows/Unix, structured design, test and program verification tools.

FIRMWARE Electronic design and real-time embedded control experience — Firmware design, digital comms DSP, CCITT protocols, Unix and 68000 micros.

DIGITAL Sophisticated high speed, high end DSP/MCU board design, EPLD/FPGA/PAL, E1/T1/ISDN communications, and simulation tools.

ASIC Encompassing top down design tools, VHDL, logic synthesis, ATPG and DFT.

MECHANICAL Specialists in thermal analysis using simulation tools; selection of materials and new product development. Mechanical design engineers with expertise in electronic systems packaging, preferably using SDRC — Ideas for component design (moulding, casting and sheet metal).

Your remuneration and training package, of course, will not present a problem if you have the right blend of technical ability (not necessarily gained in telecoms) and interpersonal skills.

THE SOLUTION Write with a full CV to our Recruitment Consultants, Macmillan Davies, at the Colston Centre, Colston Street, Bristol, BS1 4UX, or fax it to: 0272 254903.

FIGURE 4.12: Award winning job advertisements.

INTERVIEW ROOM

CHOOSING THE BEST PERSON

The stages of the recruitment process that we have been studying so far have been designed to achieve two things: to determine precisely the sort of person needed to do the job to the required standard and then to attract such people to apply for the job.

The next stage is to gather information about each applicant. The information should allow the business to choose the best person for the job. We consider five ways of doing this:

- ✪ **application forms or CVs;**
- ✪ **interviews;**
- ✪ **testing;**
- ✪ **taking references;**
- ✪ **assessment centres.**

APPLICATION FORMS

The purpose of an application form is to gather information about the candidate that will give definite clues about personal attributes, qualifications, experience and so on.

By matching the information given on the application form (or in a curriculum vitae) with the person specification, it should be possible to decide on a shortlist of the most suitable applicants. These should be invited to attend an interview.

The remaining applicants should each receive a letter thanking them for their application, but explaining that they are not successful on this occasion. Managers and other executives are busy people. Interviewing unsuitable people both unnecessarily raises their expectations and wastes valuable management time.

The completed application form of the selected candidate will form part of the contract of employment. Any deliberate misinformation could render the contract void, resulting in dismissal.

CURRICULUM VITAE

A **curriculum vitae (CV)** is a document usually initiated and prepared by a job seeker. It serves a similar purpose to an application form. It supplies a prospective employer with the job seeker's details. It should include information on:

- ✪ **personal details;**
- ✪ **education;**
- ✪ **qualifications;**
- ✪ **work experience;**
- ✪ **interests;**
- ✪ **ambitions.**

Standard Application Form (SAF)

Please complete this form in BLACK ink or typescript. AGCAS/AGR approved form
Check employer literature or vacancy information for correct application procedure.

Name of Employer

Current/most recent University/College

Vacancies or training schemes for which you wish to apply
Job function(s)   Location(s)

First name (BLOCK LETTERS)	Surname (Dr, Mr, Mrs, Miss, Ms) (BLOCK LETTERS)
Out of term address (BLOCK LETTERS): give dates at this address	Term address (BLOCK LETTERS) give dates of address
Postcode Telephone	Postcode Telephone

Date of birth	Age	Country of birth	Nationality/Citizenship	Do you need a work permit to take up employment in the UK?

Secondary/Further Education Name of School(s)/College(s)	From	To	Subjects /courses studied and level (eg GCSE, O, A, AS,H, IB, BTEC, GNVQ) Give examination results with grades and dates		

First degree/diploma University/College	From	To	Degree/diploma (BA, HND, etc.)	Class expected/ obtained	Title of degree/ diploma course

Main subjects with examination results or course grades to date, if known

Postgraduate qualifications University/College	From	To	PhD/MA/ Diploma etc.	Title of research topic or course
				Supervisor

FIGURE 4.13: A standard application form.

CURRICULUM VITAE

Carole Iris Shiley
213 Blackbird Road
Bodwell
Great Frimouth
Suffolk
SU22 9BB

Telephone & Fax   01454 909090

Date of birth   10 06 1972   Single

Education

1985 to 1989   Alburgh High School, Brookfield Street, Nicetown, Great Frimouth.

1989 to 1991   Great Frimouth College of Further Education.

Examinations taken and results

Date	Subject	Level	Grade
6/89	Art	GCSE	A
"	Biology	"	C
"	Chemistry	"	C
"	English Language	"	A
"	English Literature	"	A
"	French	"	C
"	History	"	C
"	Maths	"	C
6/91	Art	A level	B
"	English	"	C
"	Psychology	"	C

Other school activities and hobbies:
- Choir– competed in 2 International Eisteddfods
- Swimming– represented School in County events
- Horse riding– represented North Blodborough
   Pony Club in Dressage
   my own Club in Show-jumping and Cross Country.
   Member of British Horse Society.

1991 to 1994   University of Blodborough
   BSc (Hons) Business Psychology
   Projected Grade– Upper Second

Work experience whilst at school, college and university:
   Crossgrass Riding Centre, Bowstown.
   1st Assistant to Professional Riding Instructor, including:
      Yard supervision
      Group lesson leader
      Assistance with novices in lessons
      Supervision of horse exercise and hacking.

   Gainmore Superstore, Bodwell
   Cashier & stock-taker

   Pear Blossom Holiday Park, Bodwell West.
   All job roles in small supermarket

   Bodwell Hotel, Great Frimouth
   Chambermaid

   Waverley Hotel, Great Frimouth.
   Chambermaid; barmaid; waitress; and receptionist.

Hobbies and past-time:
   Horse riding
   Travelling and walking
   Reading

Career aspirations:
My main interests are people-based rather than production-based. I am interested in applying psychology in a number of areas which include:

1. (i)   the selection process;
    (ii)   performance measurement;
    (iii)   training and development;
    (iv)   communication and motivation.

2. (i)   customer behaviour;
    (ii)   marketing research;
    (iii)   product design and innovation.

I appreciate that my degree is only a starting point and I am both willing and anxious to pursue further studies in my chosen speciality.

Referees:
Character Reference:
Mr Alan Blobby, (retired head teacher)
23 Dog Kennel Lane,
Great Frimouth SU31 6PT

Academic Reference:
Dr Anne Duckworth
The University of Blodborough
School of Behaviour
Blackhulme Street
Blodborough PQ1 1TH

Figure 4.14: A curriculum vitae.

In addition, the CV should include any other information that would be likely to persuade a prospective employer to consider granting an interview. It should also offer at least two referees who will corroborate what has been claimed – one should be a character reference and the other a work reference.

A CV should provide a pen picture of the values and skills a job seeker can bring to any prospective employer. The job seeker hopes that it will result in an interview at which he or she can further illustrate how valuable he or she could be to the business.

SELECTION INTERVIEWS

An interview can be described as a planned discussion with a specific purpose. Interviews are used in many different circumstances for many different purposes. Although we are only concerned with selection here, it is worth noting that interviews are used in appraisal, counselling, grievance and disciplinary procedures.

A selection interview is a mutual exchange of information. As well as allowing a company to find out about the applicants, it is an opportunity to give applicants as much information about the job as possible, so that they can decide whether or not they want to take the job if it is offered. Nearly 40 per cent of candidates who are made job offers do not take them up.

A company wants people who accept jobs to be motivated to work for the business. Treating them with respect at an interview is an opportunity to start nurturing this motivation. It is important that all applicants are treated in a way that is seen to be legal, fair and just.

RELIABILITY OF INTERVIEWS

There is a great deal of research evidence to show that interviewing is a very inexact process. Many researchers have shown that, given exactly the same information, different interviewers form very different opinions of the same candidate.

Some research conducted in 1964 by E C Webster of McGill University, Canada, provides some interesting conclusions that are as valid today as then.

- ☺ **Interviewers'** first impressions arise from the application form and from their first sight of the interviewee. Evidence shows that they seldom change their opinion of the candidate based on these first impressions.

- ☺ **Interviewers** make their decision about a candidate in the first few minutes of the interview, then spend the rest of the interview gathering evidence to support this initial decision.

- ☺ **Most interviewers** tend to look for reasons why candidates are *not* suitable rather than look for evidence that they *are* suitable

- ☺ **If an interviewer** has made an early decision, this is communicated to the candidate by the interviewer's body language, and the interviewee will respond accordingly.

Despite these serious weaknesses, which are reasonably well established, interviewing is still the most common selection technique used by businesses today.

PREPARING THE INTERVIEW QUESTIONS

The interviewer's questions should be designed to get the candidates to talk about their work experiences and their lives in general. These are called 'open questions'. Answers to open questions can reveal clues as to whether interviewees can do the job, whether they are motivated, and give some indication of how they cope in a variety of situations – including those where they are likely to be under pressure and stress.

The novelist and poet, Rudyard Kipling, showed how to ask open questions when he wrote:

> *I keep six honest serving-men*
> *(They taught me all I knew);*
> *Their names are What and Why and When*
> *And How and Where and Who.*

Words like what, why, when and how help to keep questions open. A question like 'how did you do your stocktaking' invites a very different answer from 'did you do stocktaking'. Phrases such as 'tell me about ...' or 'can you explain ...' should produce answers that give a great deal of useful information. Questions should not imply the answer. They should not invite a 'yes' or 'no' answer. For example, 'I expect you were very busy in your job' will almost certainly get the answer 'oh yes, I was'. It is of little or no use.

Where an applicant's answer leaves doubt, or raises an interesting issue, it should be probed further. A response like 'I was responsible for the stock' may mean that the candidate kept the records up to date, or it could mean that full budget responsibility rested on that person's shoulders.

Two important interviewing skills are **probing for clues** and **active listening**. If interviewees are to reveal their ability, experience, and motivation, they, not the interviewer, must do most of the talking. The interviewer should aim to let the interviewee speak for at least 60 per cent of the interview. That is quite difficult for the interviewer to achieve without careful preparation.

It is important to avoid asking any questions that may discriminate against a person or group of people. It is illegal to ask 'do you intend to start a family'.

THE INTERVIEW

Besides giving careful consideration to the questions that they will have to ask in order to assess interviewees' suitability for the job, the interviewer has to do other preparation.

If an interviewee is to relax and be open with the interviewer, there should be a conducive atmosphere. Comfortable chairs should be arranged to avoid barriers between the interviewer and interviewee, to allow eye contact and to allow the interviewer to use body language to remove threats from a tense situation.

It is also good manners to arrange a warm welcome for the interviewees, to take coats and hang them up, and to offer them somewhere to freshen up before the interview starts. It is also respectful to arrange that there should be no interruptions during the interview.

Before the start of the interview, all documents about the interviewees should be gathered and read again so that their details are fresh in the interviewer's mind.

Interviews should follow a structure. There are many ways of structuring an interview. Here is one suggestion:

- **tell the interviewee** how the interview will be structured;

- **then, tell the interviewee** about the job so that he or she can apply their answers to the actual job;

- **answer any questions** the interviewee has about the job;

- **ask planned questions,** taking care to avoid illegal questions;

- **listen to the answers** (remember the 60 per cent/40 per cent rule) and take notes discreetly;

- **through follow-up questions,** probe and develop issues that arise during the answers to planned questions;

- **maintain** a brisk, businesslike tempo;

- **conclude the interview** with a clear summary, and a statement of what will happen next and when.

The whole process is a commentary on the organisation's culture – interviewees will take away an impression of the business and its values. This will influence whether they want to take the job if selected.

TYPES OF INTERVIEW

There are a number of ways of organising selection interviews. The most common are:

- **one-to-one interviews;**

- **successive interviews;**

- **tandem interviews;**

- **panel interviews.**

In **one-to-one interviews**, one trained interviewer conducts all the interviews and selects the most appropriate applicant. The one-to-one interview is popular because it demands less management time, and is preferred by most interviewees. They seem to cope more easily when they need only relate to one person, and where the questions follow a logical pattern.

This process can be extended so that the candidate has successive interviews with different managers. It has been found that candidates tend to become bored with **successive interviews** and, sometimes, they become better at answering questions as the interviews proceed. It also takes a lot of their time.

In **tandem interviews**, a firm uses a line manager in tandem with a personnel specialist in the hope that each brings special knowledge and skill to the situation. This can be economical, acceptable and an efficient use of time.

Panel interviews are often used in the public sector. Up to five people sit on a panel and the candidate is interviewed once only, but by the whole panel. For most people, this is a daunting experience. It is more like a tribunal sitting in judgement than an interview.

ACTIVITY

In view of the past experiences of the sales office manager in selecting unsuitable people, which type of interview would you recommend?

Which person (or persons) should conduct the interviews? If more than one person is involved, what role should each interviewer play?

Explain why you think your choice might be more successful in getting the right sort of people.

EVALUATING INTERVIEWS

A simple way to monitor a person's interviewing skills is to use a check list (see *Fig. 4.15*). The difficulty with having a person evaluating during an actual interview is that it might add pressure and cause the interviewees not to give of their best.

Interview check list

Grade each of the following points 1 to 10 as follows:

```
0  1  2  3  4  5  6  7  8  9  10
```

Needs a lot of improvement

Acceptable standard (average)

Excellent could not be improved upon

Name of interviewer

A	B	C

Items	A	B	C
Preparation:			
1. Room layout/ arrangement			
2. All documents to hand			
3. Clear knowledge of:			
job description			
personnel profile			
application form			
4. Appropriate questions prepared for points to be investigated			

Items	A	B	C
Interview			
5. Was applicant put at ease?			
6. Was 'purpose' clearly explained?			
7. Was 'structure' clear?			
8. Talk ratio? Applicant? %			
9. Did interview follow a pattern?			
10. Use of open questions?			
11. Were issues 'followed'?			
12. Were 'gaps' in history investigated?			
13. Any long digressions?			
14. Brisk tempo? (Business like?)			
15. Clear summary?			
16. Notes taken unobtrusively?			

FIGURE 4.15: Interview check list.

TESTING

Besides being an inexact process, interviewing may not give enough information about various aspects of an applicant's ability, experience and personality. Additional data can be gathered by different types of test.

Some people consider testing an invasion of privacy, others simply doubt its value. However, if tests are to be used, there is a strong moral obligation on the user to ensure that the tests chosen are valid and reliable for the purpose for which they are used. They should be conducted by a person who is competent, trained and qualified (some require that the user holds a licence) in their use and the interpretation of the data collected.

Tests must be valid – that is, they must test what they are intended to test. Otherwise the test cannot be described as a valid predictor of successful job performance. Tests must be reliable – that is, they must be consistent in measuring what they are supposed to measure whenever they are repeated.

TYPES OF TEST

Aptitude tests are tests which are designed to show that an applicant has the basic mental and physical qualities required for success in a particular job. They are often used to help a business select people who have no previous experience of a particular job (such as new apprentices). A business that invests in training apprentices is taking less of a selection risk if it uses an appropriate aptitude test, than if it does not use any.

Achievement and **attainment tests** are used to measure skills already learned. For example, people applying for a secretarial post may be asked to do a typing test. All applicants that achieve the required standard in the test are considered further; those that do not are rejected.

Intelligence tests measure a person's intelligence quotient (IQ). People whose scores fall below a known minimum IQ for the job being filled would not be interviewed. It is important that intelligence tests are used precisely as directed, and they should always be given under the control of a psychologist.

Personality tests assess a person's emotional make-up. They attempt to predict an individual's behaviour under different circumstances. Personality is described by plotting an individual's score on a series of factors.

One of the most popular is the **Cattell Sixteen Personality Factor Test** (16PF). *Fig. 4.16* shows a completed chart for six of Cattell's factors.

Serious	☐☐☐☐☐☐☐☒☐	Outgoing
Affected by feelings	☐☒☐☐☐☐☐☐☐	Emotionally unstable
Submissive	☐☐☐☐☐☐☐☒☐	Dominant
Group dependent	☐☐☐☐☒☐☐☐☐	Self-sufficient
Conservative	☒☐☐☐☐☐☐☐☐	Experimenting
Trusting	☐☐☐☐☐☐☒☐☐	Suspicious

FIGURE 4.16: Sample of a result of Cattell Sixteen Personality Factor Test.

To take the test, a candidate completes a questionnaire which, when analysed by the expert, shows where he or she falls on each of the scales. For example, the individual shown on the scale in *Fig 4.16* is very outgoing, emotional, very dominant, quite self-sufficient, very conservative and quite suspicious.

ACTIVITY

1 **Would any of the tests we have discussed add useful information to help our sales office manager improve selection? If so, what type of test do you think would be helpful?**

2 **Let us assume that you decide to use a personality test. You have asked some consultants to carry it out for you and they have quoted a fee of £3,500. They do not guarantee that the test will assure success in selection, but they assure you that they will identify anyone who is unlikely to be successful. Write a memo to the financial director justifying the expenditure. Your memo should outline the financial advantages of 'making the right choice first time'.**

REFERENCES

A reference is an opinion, usually in writing, of a person's character, ability, honesty and reliability in support of a job application.

The problem with references is that it is usually impossible to obtain a detailed and accurate report from their current employers on how candidates are performing in their present jobs.

- **It would be unethical** to contact a present employer who may not be aware that an employee had applied for another job.

- **Some employers do give references** to current employees, for example, teachers and local government staff can get references from their current employers, but it is hard to know if these are accurate and unbiased.

- **Personal relationships** can influence some referees more than job performance, even to the extent of writing a glowing reference to get rid of someone they do not like!

Past employers are often cautious when writing references. There is no legal obligation to provide references on request, but most employers do. References must be accurate. Any fake information, or any omissions

Employers 'must take care' on job references

The legal scales tipped in favour of job hunters yesterday when the House of Lords ruled that employers have a duty to take reasonable care when writing references about former staff members.

The case opens the possibility of court actions against companies on the grounds that they have been negligent in assessing the conduct and behaviour of their employees, so damaging these people's chances of gaining work with other organisations.

The case seems certain to lead to managers thinking more deeply about the implications of the thousands of references written every day. One effect, however, could be to encourage the practice of giving confidential references given over the telephone, making it virtually impossible for disgruntled employees to bring legal cases.

Mr Morgan, director of the Industrial Society, a body promoting good employment practice, said: 'A reference can affect the rest of somebody's life, so integrity is vital. This ruling will focus employers on good practice, which is to provide references which are fair and authentic, not opinionated and anecdotal.'

Financial Times, 8 July 1995

that might cause a candidate to fail to be offered a job which he or she would have been offered had the correct information been given, may make a case for damages against the writer of the reference.

ACTIVITY

Refer back to the material on the contract of employment in element 1 and look again at the implied terms that are read into all contracts by the courts. Can you see where this House of Lords ruling fits in?

ASSESSMENT CENTRES

Many of you seeking a career in a large or medium-sized organisation may find that the selection process is carried out by means of an **assessment centre**. Some firms, like W H Smith and English China Clay, have developed their own very successful assessment centres.

The name is a little deceiving – it is not a place. It is a series of events and activities in which all candidates for a job take part. The events are designed to provide evidence against predetermined standards of competence in specific attributes and skills. The design of assessment centres is normally carried out by occupational psychologists.

Evidence is often sought relating to skills and competence in:

- ✪ **oral and written communication;**
- ✪ **openness in dealings with others;**
- ✪ **sensitivity to other people;**
- ✪ **leadership and persuasiveness;**
- ✪ **decision-making;**
- ✪ **assertiveness.**

Note is also taken of the use of initiative, common sense, energy, ability to 'come back after a fall' and, particularly, the degree of achievement and motivation exhibited by each candidate.

Assessment is usually along a scale (say from one to eight) for each of the above criteria. One is dreadful and eight is amazing. Assessors are carefully trained in observation skills, and are drawn from human resources specialists, line managers and senior managers. There is usually one assessor for every two candidates.

The focus of the assessment centre is on peoples' strengths, in the belief that there is immediate return from exploiting a person's strengths. Weaknesses that are identified are fed back to the candidate for attention, but not in a critical way. We all have weaknesses that need to be addressed.

There is an equal opportunities issue here that must be addressed by the assessors. A solitary woman or a single individual from an ethnic minority might feel inhibited. It is for the assessors to take this into account when evaluating the participants. In fact, in most situations where this inhibition might occur, it is common for at least one of the assessors to represent the minority group or groups.

Despite its expense and use of time, firms that use assessment centres claim that it reduces the incidence of selection errors markedly. If results are that good, then it is a wonderful investment.

IS ALL THIS REALLY NECESSARY TO FIND MY REPLACEMENT?

ACTIVITY

Consider the ethical issues associated with selection in general, and with assessment centres in particular.

Write a short report for the human resources manager pointing out the steps you have taken to ensure that all recruitment and selection procedures are fair and offer equal opportunity to all applicants.

The report should highlight legal requirements and how they are being met.

MAKING APPPOINTMENTS

In the entire recruitment and selection process, it is illegal to set any standards, or ask for qualifications, experience or personal qualities that would discriminate unfairly against minority racial groups, the disabled or one sex. It may be important to keep a record of reasons for appointing or rejecting candidates to show that these legal obligations are being met.

The selected candidate will be offered the job and, presumably, will accept it. At this stage, the other candidates should be informed and thanked for their time and interest.

If the sales office manager in our scenario follows this process, do you think she would stand a good chance of resolving her staffing problem? If you answer 'yes' to this, would you also agree that people are worth looking after once they have joined a company?

ACTIVITY

Many people reject job offers. Assume that you are a personnel specialist who has just made an offer to the applicant who is best suited for the job requirements, but she has declined. None of the other candidates is suitable. Your managing director has just phoned to say that the vacancy must be filled quickly and you are to offer that job to one of the other applicants.

Prepare a case to put to the managing director that sets out the disadvantages of taking the route she has ordered. You should include the financial as well as the other implications. It should also include a short-term solution to the problem while you pursue a more permanent one.

ETHICAL OBLIGATIONS

As with other professions, the personnel and development profession has a ruling body – the Institute of Personnel and Development (IPD) – which sets out codes of practice which should be followed by all practitioners, whether members of the institute or not.

The institute published a code of professional conduct in 1995. This included individual codes on:

⊗ **recruitment;**

⊗ **psychological testing;**

- ⊘ secondment;

- ⊘ employee data;

- ⊘ redundancy;

- ⊘ career and outplacement consultants;

- ⊘ employee involvement and participation;

- ⊘ equal opportunities.

IPD MEMBERS MUST RESPECT THE FOLLOWING STANDARDS

Accuracy

They must maintain high standards of accuracy in the information and advice they provide to employers and employees.

Confidentiality

They must respect their employer's legitimate needs for confidentiality and ensure that all personnel information remains private.

Counselling

They must be prepared to act as counsellors to individual employees, pensioners and dependants or to refer them, where appropriate, to other professions or helping agencies.

Developing others

They must encourage self-development and seek to achieve the fullest possible development of employees in the service of present and future organisation needs.

Equal opportunities

They must promote fair, non-discriminatory employment practices.

Fair dealing

They must maintain fair and reasonable standards in their treatment of individuals.

Self-development

They must seek continuously to improve their performance and update their skills and knowledge.

Source: The Institute of Personnel and Development Code of Professional Conduct– codes of practice.

These IPD standards and ethics are demanding on the integrity of organisations and individuals, but there is no excuse in the normal course of events for failing to observe them.

The success of a business depends very much on getting the right person in each job. It is important that expertise and experience should be deployed to achieve it. Any one of the methods or techniques we have examined for this purpose is not guaranteed to produce successful appointments. Therefore, the wise firm will gather information by a variety of means, from application forms to testing, and weigh the evidence very carefully against the person specification before arriving at its decision to appoint. Better still, it will move towards a full assessment centre process.

PORTFOLIO ASSIGNMENT

INTERVIEW SKILLS SIMULATION

In this activity, you will experience the whole process of selecting the most suitable candidate for a job. It is a group exercise which involves simulating a job interview. Some of you will play the interviewers, some the candidates.

At the end of the session you will:

(a) be able to examine and understand role-play briefs;

(b) from the briefs, understand the value of job descriptions, and person specifications;

(c) from the profile and application forms, plan the questions and conduct a selection interview;

(d) from the interviews, gather all the information you need to decide which candidate is most likely to do the job to standard and fit in with the work group;

(e) select the most suitable candidate and justify the decision;

(f) develop skills in listening;

(g) develop skills in role-playing.

THE SCENARIO

Gainmore Superstore is recruiting a purchasing supervisor. It is your task to fill this vacancy with a suitable candidate from a short list of three.

ORGANISING THE EXERCISE

Get your teacher to photocopy pages 263–76. These contain instruction sheets and handouts to enable you to complete the exercise. There are separate instruction sheets for interviewers, candidates and teachers. The handouts provide the background information and forms needed for you to play your various roles.

⊗ Handout 1: Gainmore Superstore company description and structure.

⊗ Handout 2: Job description and person profile.

⊗ Handout 3: Interview check list.

⊗ Handout 4: Profile of candidate A.

⊗ Handout 5: Profile of candidate B.

⊗ Handout 6: Profile of candidate C.

⊗ Handout 7: Application form.

Simulation designed by Lucy Gunn © 1995

INTERVIEW SIMULATION

Instruction sheet for interviewers

Interviewers work in groups of three.

1   **Read handout 1** about Gainmore's company description and structure. Know the company.

2   **Exercise:** You are a personnel officer at Gainmore Superstore. Make a list of your roles and responsibilities within the company.

3   **Read handout 2** giving the job description of the post your are trying to fill. Know the job.

4   **Exercise:** What characteristics do you think the ideal candidate for this position should display? Complete the person profile on handout 2. This profile is in the form of a seven point plan (see page 248).

5   **Exercise:** Prepare one or two questions for each of the seven points. These should be designed to reveal whether the candidates have these ideal characteristics.

6   **The students** role playing the job candidates should have completed their application forms. Read these application forms. This is your short list of candidates. Know the candidates.

7   **Exercise:** Identify any gaps between the information given on each application and the person profile that you need to make your decision. Prepare the questions that would gain this information.

8   **Exercise:** Determine which questions **must** be asked and which *should* be asked if there is time. Have a sheet of paper with these questions set out in the order in which you intend to ask them.

9   **During the interview:** Each person in your group of three will conduct an interview with one candidate, while the other two observe and complete an evaluation form using handout 3, the interview check list.

10 **After the interview:** As a group, make notes after each interview on how you think the interview went – are there any other questions you should have asked?

11 **Discuss the information** you have gained. From this make a single choice of the candidate you (as a group) wish to appoint. Ensure you can justify your decision.

INTERVIEW SIMULATION

Instruction sheet for candidates

There are three candidates for the post, so three people are required to act the different people. You will play the role assigned to you. Please read and internalise your role as an actor would a character in a play.

1   Read your individual role details (on handouts 4, 5 or 6). Know your character.

2   **Exercise:** Using this information complete the person profile on handout 2 in terms of the seven point plan to match your character.

3   Read the job description on handout 2. Know the job for which your character is being interviewed.

4   **Exercise:** Having mastered your role and understood the job, complete the application form (handout 7) extracting the relevant information from your role description.

5   **Exercise:** Write a cover letter to support the application form adding any information that you feel is not covered in the application form. Give one copy of the application form and the cover letter to each of the interview groups.

6   **Exercise:** From the information you have, prepare questions which you think you **must** be asked and questions which you *should* be asked during the interview.

7   **Exercise:** Make some notes about questions you would like to ask to help you decide if you would like to work for Gainmore Superstore.

8   **During the interview:** Only give the interviewer information for which you are asked. Do not mislead the interviewer. You may give part answers to awkward questions. If a question is asked that is not covered in the role play, answer how you feel your character would.

9   **After the interview:** Make notes about the way the interview was conducted and how it made you feel. Complete the interview check list on handout 3. Think of three good points and three points which could be improved upon.

10 Use these notes at the end of the simulation to give feedback about each interview.

INTERVIEW SIMULATION

Instruction sheet for teachers

Familiarise yourself with each of the handouts and the instructions for the interviewers and candidates. Photocopy the handouts so that you have the required number for all those participating in the exercise.

All characters can be female or male. Names and circumstances can be changed to suit the person playing the character. Nothing is rigid except the core experience and skills given in the brief. You should note that the roles are designed so that one candidate should appear under-qualified, one ideal and one over-qualified.

1   Divide the class into groups of three. Depending on the size of the class, one or two groups will be the candidates (one group for a class of twelve, two groups for a bigger class). Brief these students on role-playing technique. The remaining groups will be interviewers. They will prepare the interviews, but each group will only interview one character, while the other two groups are observers. While one interview is being conducted, the two groups of observers should complete handout 7 (interview check list).

2   After all three interviews have been completed, (recommended time for each is 15-20 minutes) each group should make a decision on a suitable candidate. Each group should present its choice of candidate with a full justification for the decision.

3   After all groups have made their presentations, the role players should provide feedback to each group about 'how they felt' during the interview, mentioning any information they were not asked for, and three positive points and three points which should be improved upon. Ensure the positive feedback comes first. You may have to brief them on feedback skills.

4   If you have the facilities, you may wish to video the interviews. It is the author's view that 'public' evaluation of the video can cause unnecessary pressure. An effective alternative is to provide a copy of the video for students to view privately.

5   Finally, it is useful reinforcement if the students put together a portfolio which contains all the documentation and the process, with a dialogue of the learning that the simulation achieved.

Suggested developments:

Here are three suggestions for extending the exercise:

● Before beginning the simulation, the whole class could design an advertisement for the position to be put in the local press. This could be based upon handout 1 (for interviewers only) and handout 2. It can then be used to aid the role-players' completion of the application form and the cover letter.

INTERVIEW SIMULATION

- On completion of the feedback session, a discussion or debate could be held on the selection process. This could focus on 'what went well and what went badly during the simulation'.

- After the simulation, each individual should write a report on the process of selecting the right person for the job. The report should cover the evidence indicators as outlined in the standards and reflect what the individual has learned from the simulation.

Handouts	Interviewers: give each individual a copy	Candidates
Handout 1: Company description	✔	✗
Handout 2: Job description and person profile	✔	✔
Handout 3: Interview check list	✔	✔
Handout 4: Role play A	✗	Candidate A
Handout 5: Role play B	✗	Candidate B
Handout 6: Role play C	✗	Candidate C
Handout 7: Application forms	Once completed by candidates	To be completed by candidates and then given to each interview group

INTERVIEW SIMULATION

Handout 1

Gainmore Superstore – company description

The company
Gainmore is a well-known superstore group retailing mainly food, with strong and growing clothing, household and leisurewear sections.

Location
Gainmore has over 200 superstores in the main cities and towns throughout the UK. One of the latest stores is in Great Filburgh, Suffolk.

The market
Gainmore traded successfully during the 1980s but suffered in the recession from 1988 to 1992. After complete restructuring the group is now successful and profits are in the top quartile for this segment of the market. Our recovery is mainly due to our policy of recruiting and training high-quality staff. We encourage self-development and support any training initiatives that will improve performance. Gainmore's turnover in 1994 was £5bn.

Operations
Sales are dependent upon the quality and price of our merchandise. Our buyers are highly skilled and qualified. They constantly seek new products to enhance our range and negotiate 'partnering agreements' with suppliers. It is in our customers' best interests that we look after our suppliers, providing continuity and the best value in the high street. We encourage suppliers to improve their products and their administration continuously.

Staffing
Gainmore employs more than 30,000 people, including part-timers. Since reorganisation, we have cut head office staff by 35 per cent and reduced levels of management. Our focus is on supervisory and middle management in our stores. Each store is a profit centre and has a high degree of autonomy. Most employee promotions are from within, and career change opportunities are considered sympathetically.

Working conditions
Gainmore values its staff. Salaries are above average for the industry, there is a contributory pension scheme, a sick pay scheme, and help with relocation if you are promoted to another store. Our equal opportunities policy is among the most robust in the country and managers are required to adhere to it in all matters relating to staff and customers. All our premises are designed to be safe for staff and customers. They are light and airy, with subsidised staff canteen and rest facilities. Holidays with pay start at 20 days, plus one day for each year's service, up to 30 days per year.

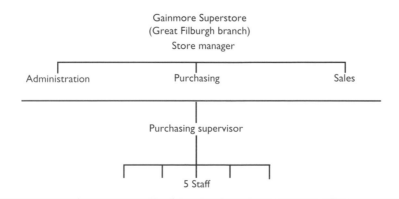

Handout 2

Job description

Job title: Purchasing supervisor
Location: Great Filburgh store
Department: Purchasing section
Answerable to: Section head

Main roles:

● to lead the work of a section dealing with the ordering, receiving and display of all fresh-food goods from local suppliers;

● to progress orders and deal with queries and matters arising from late or non-deliveries;

● to negotiate contracts with suppliers and develop partnering arrangements where appropriate;

● to liaise with customer research groups regarding range and prices of fresh fruit and vegetables;

● to maintain current records for suppliers and potential suppliers;

● to prepare monthly progress reports against milestones and report to senior management meetings on all performance and achievements;

● to constantly seek opportunities to improve performance and reduce costs.

Person profile

Job title: Purchasing supervisor

Attributes	Essential	Desirable	Disposition
Physical make-up			
Attainments			
General intelligence			
Special aptitudes			
Interests			
Disposition			
Circumstances			

INTERVIEW SIMULATION

Handout 3

Interview check list

Grade each of the following points 1 to 10 as follows:

0 1 2 3 4 5 6 7 8 9 10

Needs a   Acceptable   Excellent
lot of   standard   could not be
improvement   (average)   improved upon

Name of interviewer

X	Y	Z

Items	X	Y	Z
Preparation:			
1. Room layout/arrangement			
2. All documents to hand			
3. Clear knowledge of:			
job description			
personnel profile			
application form			
4. Appropriate questions prepared for points to be investigated			

Items	X	Y	Z
Interview			
5. Was applicant put at ease?			
6. Was 'purpose' clearly explained?			
7. Was 'structure' clear?			
8. Talk ratio? Applicant? %			
9. Did interview follow a pattern?			
10. Use of open questions?			
11. Were issues 'followed up'?			
12. Were 'gaps' in history investigated?			
13. Any long digressions?			
14. Brisk tempo? (Business like?)			
15. Clear summary?			
16. Notes taken unobtrusively?			

INTERVIEW SIMULATION

Handout 4

Candidate A

Background
Born 23 March 1966 at Acle, Norfolk. Only child. Father (now dead) was a farm labourer. Mother still lives in Acle and works for local auctioneer at Acle market.

Education
Acle Junior School then Acle High. Left in April 1982 without any qualifications, due to poor health.

Health
You were found to have a spot on your lung as a result of a TB screening at school in April 1982 just as you were preparing for four O-levels and four CSEs. You spent two months in hospital and another six months receiving treatment before being pronounced fit to start work in January 1983. Doctors say you are 100 per cent fit and you feel great.

Career
You did not return to school but were lucky to get a trainee post at a new general store in the village. Because it was a small company you gained experience at just about everything, including ordering stock and dealing with suppliers and customers. You enjoyed the selling, but you much preferred the administration.

In 1987, because of the competition from big national supermarkets, you were made redundant. You saw this disappointment as an opportunity and applied for the position of purchasing officer for a wholesale fruit and vegetable merchant in nearby Filburgh.

Keen to improve yourself, you started evening classes at the College of Further Education in accounting in September 1987 and since then you have continued to do a subject a year. This year's subject is microcomputers; you are enjoying it very much and you are good at it.

You like your current work – processing orders, liaising with suppliers, contractors and your own staff. However, new technology has made it possible to organise central purchasing from the Covent Garden office, and the Filburgh office is being phased out. You have been offered a bigger job in London, but for family reasons you decline.

Domestic
You married in 1989. Your son, Brian, was born 13 months ago. You'd like a daughter in about 12 months time. Your three-bedroom semi in Blobton is to your liking. It cost £39,500 in 1990 and you have a 95 per cent mortgage. All you need now is a little car and that is high on your list of priorities.

Interests
You make brass rubbings in local churches, travelling by bus and bike to towns and villages within a twenty-mile radius. You have given many away to friends and relatives for birthdays and Christmas presents. You are also secretary of the local sport and fitness club, and play for them regularly.

Disposition
You are a calm, persistent person, not brilliant, but hard-working, probably a late developer. You know what you want to do and you have a clear idea of how you are going to do it.

Present salary
£15,000. You have to give four weeks notice.

INTERVIEW SIMULATION

Handout 5

Candidate B

Background

Born 12 November 1969 at Thetford. You have one older sister (married to a bus driver with two children) and a younger brother (at Sussex University reading business sciences). Your parents are divorced. Your father, an area sales manager for a national firm of stationers, left home when you were nearly 15 and has never re-married. You see little of him. Your mother has a good job as manager of a ladies fashion shop in Filburgh. You now live with her in a nice house at Ellford, ten miles west of Filburgh.

Education

You left school in 1986 with three O-level passes out of six subjects taken. You believe you could have done better but the break-up of your parents' marriage undoubtedly had a disturbing effect on you.

Health

No problems of any sort since birth.

Career

Your O-levels got you into Barclays Bank as a junior and, subsequently, as a junior cashier. You studied at Great Filburgh College of Further Education for your Institute of Bankers, Part 1 (BTEC national certificate), but you failed one of the first year's subjects. You intended to retake it at the end of the second year but by June 1988, you were becoming disillusioned with banking as a career. Progress seemed too slow and the money was poor until you reached some of the higher grades.

So you decided to make the break. You watched the local papers for some sort of administration job with good prospects and you applied for the post of purchasing and supplies assistant in the direct works department of Great Filburgh Borough Council. You were successful and started on 1 June 1988. The direct works department is the central purchasing agency and your work has been concerned with issuing tender forms and processing of tenders for supplies and services for education, welfare, parks and gardens and corporation departments. You are in regular contact with all departments in writing and over the telephone.

You answer directly to the purchasing officer and have become very knowledgeable about the standards of service and the reliability of different suppliers. Success in this job requires thorough knowledge and understanding of procedures and familiarity with the organisation of a local government department. Both your boss and you feel you have these qualities.

You get through more work than most of your colleagues, some of whom seem to do no more than they have to. You get pretty angry about this and you don't mind showing it. The boss recognises your competence, he has delegated responsibility for handling some of his correspondence to you. You enjoy drafting letters and you take a pride in expressing yourself clearly and in good English.

INTERVIEW SIMULATION

You have enjoyed working for the council but, now that you've mastered the job, it seems not to have sufficient scope for initiative. You would now like some supervisory responsibility and the opportunity for advancement. The advertisement by Gainmore in the local paper could be the very place for you.

Domestic

You are very happy living at home with your mother. You get on well together and you live well. You have many friends, but you have no thoughts of marriage at this stage. Your seven-year-old Mini gives you plenty of freedom.

Interests

You are keen on pop music and have taught yourself to play the keyboards tolerably well. You really enjoy musical evenings at home and in your friends' houses. You have recently joined the Young Liberals, more because two of your friends are keen members than through any deep-felt political conviction. However, you have enjoyed the meetings so much that you intend to develop a more active role and become more involved with the party.

Present salary

£14,100. You must give one week's notice.

INTERVIEW SIMULATION

Handout 6

Candidate C

Background

Born 17 June 1953 in London where your father owned a small glazing company at Clapham. Your three older brothers are still directly or indirectly involved with the family business but you chose not to follow in their paths. Your parents recently retired and enjoy life in a quiet village in Cambridgeshire.

Education

Left school in 1969 with 8 O-levels. You could have stayed on for A-levels but you did not want an academic career – you much prefer a more business-oriented approach so you went to technical college and studied for a diploma (OND) in business studies which you passed with credits in 1971.

Career

Jobs were easy to find and you were well qualified; so you chose an appointment as a management trainee with Freeman's Mail Order near Stockwell. After two years serving in different departments following a planned programme of training and development, you were appointed supervisor – credit sanction section. You were responsible for the work of ten employees who scrutinised record cards, determined the state of the customers' accounts and decided whether they could be permitted to purchase more items on credit. It was as a result of your feasibility study that this procedure was later computerised.

In 1974, you were promoted to a 'plum' job – manager, customer relations department. You managed two supervisors each looking after eight highly-trained keyboard operators. They handled all complaints and queries from customers, using a series of standard letters which you had devised. You monitored all complaints and enquiries and produced statistics which were used in deciding which products should stay in the catalogue, which should be deleted and which should be added. The quality of your work, plus the in-depth knowledge you had gained from this job, resulted in your being promoted to assist the director of purchasing in 1981. This put you into the senior management bracket, with a company car, expense account and a 'comfortable' salary.

Sadly, within six years, your partner's health began to fail. The diagnosis was multiple sclerosis (MS) you felt you needed to spend more time together. Your partner had expressed a wish to live by the sea, and you decided to abandon your career and move out of London. Through a job agency, you applied for and got a job as office manager in a small food-processing factory (Lewguys) at Gorton, near Filburgh, Suffolk. Your partner was delighted and in June 1986 you moved to a bungalow overlooking the sea very near to the Lewguys factory.

You did not find the job very exciting. It was not a very efficient business and the equipment it made was very specialised. Still you set about establishing a good administration systems and took charge of all expenditure. You set up a proper purchasing system and insisted that quality controls were established so that materials were delivered according to specification and on time.

INTERVIEW SIMULATION

However, all your good work was to no avail. The company went bankrupt, and in February 1995, it closed down leaving you without a job.

Domestic
Your health is excellent but your partner's illness is taking its slow, natural course. Though confined to a wheelchair, your partner is still able to do most of the household chores including cooking. Your three children, Doris (11), Tim (9) and Alice (7) go to nearby Cliff Top School and are great kids. They help in the house and take a lot of the strain off you.

Interests
When you were busy building a career you had little time for outside interests. Now you're mainly occupied with your home and family. You enjoy keeping the garden beautiful – and your partner enjoys that too. You would like to play golf but that must wait. The most important thing right now is that you get this job at Gainmore.

Present salary
Unemployment benefit, but before that you earned £10,000 at Lewguys and £17,800 at Freemans. You can start immediately.

Gainmore Superstore
Please complete this form in black ink or typescript

Vacancies for which you wish to apply.
Job function(s)   Location(s)

First names (BLOCK LETTERS)

Surname (Dr, Mr, Mrs, Miss, Ms) (BLOCK LETTERS)

Address (BLOCK LETTERS)

Date of Birth

Age

Postcode   Telephone

Country of Birth

Nationality

Secondary/Further Education   From   To
Name(s) of School(s)/College(s)

Subject/courses studied and level (GCSE, GNVQ, O, A, AS, BTEC). Give examination results with grades and dates.

Any other qualifications of relevance to the position being applied for?

Work Experience:
Name of Employer   From   To   Type of Work and Main Responsibilities

Which parts of your work experience were most beneficial to you and why?

Activities and interests.
Give details of your main activities outside work and interests to date. What have you contributed and what have you got out of them? Mention any posts of responsibility.

Explain what attracts you about the type of work for which you are applying and offer evidence of your suitability.

References.
Give the names and addresses of two referees, one academic and one from your previous employment.

1.   2.

✔ MULTIPLE CHOICE QUESTIONS

1 **Which of the following statements about the contract of employment are true:**

A it must be in writing and handed to the employee when joining the company

B it is made up of express and implied terms

C it includes common law rights

D it must be recognised with trade unions

2 **Assuming that all the employees have been employed by the employer for longer than two years, dismissal may be considered 'fair' in which of the following cases:**

A the employee is not capable of doing the job he or she was employed to do

B the employee became pregnant despite being told that she might lose her job because of it

C the employees were caught sleeping whilst on duty in the security gatehouse

D the employee was found to be a member of a militant socialist group

3 **Which of the following statements are false:**

A trade unions are made up of manual workers who want to protect their rights

B an employer can refuse to recognise any trade union

C an employer can insist that all employees belong to the same trade union

D when a disagreement with an employer arises, a trade union must approach ACAS to negotiate with employers on its behalf

4 **Which of the following management actions might gain employee co-operation:**

A improving the 'payment by results' system so that those producing most earn most

B giving supervisors more authority to 'get the job done'

C making jobs as simple as possible so that people can do them without thinking

D using better lighting and background music to make the environment pleasant to work in

5 **Which of the following statements describe management activities:**

A an engineer designing the engine for a unique new motor car

B an accountant arranging training for her staff in the use of a new budgetary control system

C a supervisor examining the monthly lateness and absentee records for his department

D a secretary booking flights and accommodation for his director

6 **Which of the following are reasons why businesses must make changes:**

A to meet environmental standards

B to keep full employment

C to ensure low inflation

D to improve return on capital invested

7 **Which of the following are reasons that people fear and/or resist change at work:**

A because they need their wages

B because they do not like shareholders taking more money out of the business

C because their trade union recommends action against it

D because they do not want to lose the use of their current skills, and have to learn new ones

8 **Which of the following actions helps to reduce resistance to change:**

A be careful to keep everything 'confidential' until the plans are completed and then make the announcement

B choose the best people to implement the change, brief them well, and let others take redundancy

C be open about the change, and, where possible, invite participation in decision making

D be careful to prepare answers to the question 'how will it affect me?'

9 **Which of the following outcomes are likely results of having employees who lack competence in their jobs:**

A customers may complain about poor quality

B scrap costs may be higher

C morale may be low

D it may be difficult to recruit good staff

10 **Which of the following purposes are uses for job descriptions:**

A designing training programmes

B calculating wage rates

C writing job advertisements

D implementing disciplinary actions

11 **Which of the following approaches might be illegal when selecting a candidate for a job as a computer programmer:**

A using only male interviewers

B insisting that 'Oxford' English is spoken

C requiring specified qualifications and experience in computer programming

D requiring an ability to work on one's own

12 **Which of the following Acts of Parliament should be taken into account when writing job advertisements:**

A Employment Protection (Consolidation) Act 1978

B Health and Safety at Work Act 1974

C Race Relations Act 1976

D Sex Discrimination Act 1975

13 Which of the following distinguishes between a job application form and a curriculum vitae (CV):

A a CV contains the personal details of the applicant

B a job application form contains details of education and experience

C a CV is initiated and prepared by the applicant

D a job application form is part of the contract of employment of the successful candidate

14 Which of the following statements about interviewing skills are true:

A interviewers seldom change their first impressions of a candidate

B to get respect, interviewers must show that they are in charge

C interviewers should look thoroughly for reasons why a candidate is not suitable for the job

D interviewers should plan to let the candidate do most of the talking

15 Which of the following statements are false:

A using tests is the safest way for managers to be certain that potential new employees will be able to do the job

B tests give additional information that can help the interviewer arrive at a decision

C personality tests will show whether a candidate is telling the truth during the subsequent interview

D tests have to be valid and reliable before they are useful predictors

16 Which of the following statements are true:

A assessment centres reduce the likelihood of selection errors

B references should be used as an opportunity to warn a future employer of a candidate's weaknesses

C ethics are a matter for personal judgement

D a business will be only as successful as the quality of its staff allows

Production and Employment in the Economy

CONTENTS

OUTLINE

This unit allows students to explore the 'production' of goods and services. Production has been interpreted in a wide sense to include primary production (oil, gas and agricultural products) and services as well as manufacturing production.

Element 2 focuses upon employment and particularly upon the changes in the UK's labour market over recent years. In particular, students will learn of the rise in part-time and temporary employment alongside the decline in traditional male employment. The element also considers the implications of these changes on the type and nature of employment.

The final element takes a broad view of the UK economy and considers the competitiveness of UK businesses in world markets. It attempts to measure such competitiveness and considers actions taken by business to improve competitiveness. The element concludes with some discussion of how the government can enhance the competitiveness of UK industry.

The unit is illustrated by regular reference to current business events and up-to-date statistics are included. Students are encouraged to undertake individual and collective research.

This unit will be of help to students who are preparing a personal plan as part of unit 8 in this series.

Analyse production in businesses

Production is a broad term used to cover all the processes of adding value by businesses in the provision of goods and services to consumers and customers. Production takes place within the primary, secondary and tertiary sectors and in both the public and private sectors. The primary sector of the economy includes industries such as agriculture, forestry and fishing, the secondary sector is broadly manufacturing industry, while the tertiary sector relates to the provision of services.

ACTIVITY

Look at the adverts in a magazine or newspaper and identify two examples of production in each of the primary, secondary and tertiary sectors.

ADDED VALUE IN PRODUCTION

All businesses aim to add value to their goods or services. We can define **value added** as the difference between the cost of materials and components and the final price customers are prepared to pay for the finished product or service. Through creating added value, businesses achieve surpluses necessary to pay overheads, labour costs and dividends. If a product or service has a high value added, then it is probably in great demand. High value-added products usually have excellent reputations and/or brand images. Value can be added in a number of ways. These include:

- ☉ **buying raw materials and manufacturing an entire product;**
- ☉ **buying raw materials and manufacturing components;**
- ☉ **buying components and assembling entire products;**
- ☉ **buying components and producing part-assembled products;**
- ☉ **buying entire products and distributing them;**
- ☉ **supplying a service.**

For example, Mars purchases raw materials such as milk and cocoa and converts them into a variety of confectionery products. In this example the value added is clear. Other companies add value by buying and distributing finished products; this would be true of any retail business such as the John Lewis Partnership.

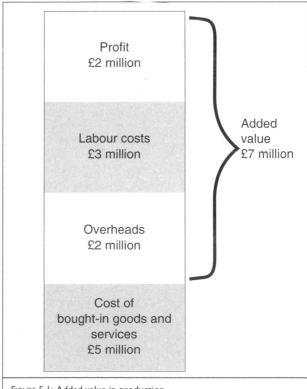

FIGURE 5.1: Added value in production.

Fig. 5.1 illustrates the relationship between value added, various types of costs, and profit. This is a fundamental relationship. Value added can be calculated using the formula:

value added = sales revenue − cost of bought-in goods and services

If a business has a total sales revenue over a year of £12m and purchases £8m of components, fuel and raw materials, then £4m value is added. We can calculate the value added to each unit of production by dividing this figure by the number of units of production produced over the year. You do this as part of the next activity.

ACTIVITY

Assume that the business produces 6 million units of production. In addition to purchasing £8m of components, fuel and raw materials, it has £2m labour costs. Calculate:

(a) the labour cost of a single unit of production;

(b) the value added by a single unit of production.

In unit 6, we consider the financial aspects of value added. In this unit, we look at some of the ways in which businesses can improve their value added and, hopefully, generate greater profits. For example, firms may be able to charge higher prices or they may be able to cut costs while maintaining price levels; in either case, value added should be increased. Other strategies include improving **quality** and increasing **productivity**.

QUALITY ASSURANCE

Since the late 1980s, quality has become an increasingly important factor in the business world. A major impetus has been the success of Japanese manufacturing companies. They have led the way in implementing quality systems within their businesses. These systems have not been implemented overnight: Japanese companies have taken between 25 and 30 years to fully develop and implement new quality systems.

The aim of quality assurance is to ensure that the customer is satisfied; by doing so, companies hope to generate greater sales, to increase value added and to make higher profits. A number of aspects of production must be taken into account when implementing quality assurance systems. These include:

- ✪ **product design;**
- ✪ **materials and components;**
- ✪ **delivery schedules;**
- ✪ **after-sales service;**
- ✪ **quality control procedures.**

The support of the workforce is critical in implementing quality systems. Quality cannot be achieved unless employees support the policy and understand and comply with the necessary procedures.

There are two main quality assurance systems in operation:

- ✪ **total quality management;**
- ✪ **quality assurance through the British Standards Institution (BSI).**

Total quality management (TQM) is a business philosophy that seeks to instil in *all* employees of a firm an *individual* as well as a *collective* responsibility for maintaining high quality standards. It is based on the notion of prevention rather than detection. Firms introduce total quality management to try and establish a competitive advantage through acquiring a reputation for quality products or services. TQM also seeks to minimise the amount of money spent detecting or correcting quality problems. Firms recognise that if faulty products have to be sent back for repair, this incurs additional costs as well as damaging the company's reputation.

The **British Standards Institution (BSI)** and the **International Standards Organisation (ISO)** jointly operate a **quality assurance standard, BS EN ISO 9000.** To obtain certification that this standard is being met, companies have to meet a number of requirements. They have to establish, document and maintain an effective and economical quality system that ensures and demonstrates that materials, products or services conform to the specified requirements. Critics have suggested that this certification shows that firms comply with systems and processes rather than guaranteeing the quality of the product. However, more than 20,000 UK firms had achieved the certification by the end of 1995.

Total quality management

Total quality management (TQM) originated in Japan. In the 1950s and 1960s, Japanese products were regarded as relatively cheap but inferior versions of products manufactured in western economies. For example, the first Japanese cars exported to the USA in the 1960s lacked sufficient acceleration to join the traffic on the freeways safely. In response, Japanese companies began to develop the philosophies and systems necessary to acquire a reputation for quality products.

Edward Deming, an American management consultant, was employed by the Japanese government to help with the reconstruction of industry in the period immediately after the Second World War. Deming gave quality a very high priority and this is why it gained credence in Japan earlier than in the USA and Europe. TQM describes the philosophy and techniques which the Japanese used to improve the quality of their products.

TQM has both an internal and an external dimension. The success of a firm depends upon its ability to satisfy the demands of its external customers. Product quality is one way in which a company can achieve a competitive advantage. TQM emphasises that the firm's ability to generate and sustain these quality advantages stems from the way in which it operates internally. The firm is comprised of a network of interrelated departments and, under TQM, each department is viewed as a customer and/or a supplier. Departments have to meet high standards in this 'internal' trading, in which raw materials, components and finished goods flow through to the dispatch department. TQM seeks to establish a unity of interest and commitment to the maintenance of the highest possible quality standards in each of these internal transactions.

TQM seeks to minimise the amount of time and money spent on quality control through the prevention of quality problems. Individual commitment to quality can be reinforced by the operation of quality circles and other employee participation schemes.

A tribute to the success of the Japanese in establishing a reputation for quality products is that it is not unknown for UK retailers of electrical goods to give their own brands a Japanese sounding name in an attempt to increase sales.

Some companies, like Jaguar for example, have a reputation for quality. A reputation for producing a high-quality product brings a number of advantages:

- **companies can charge higher prices generating greater value added and profits;**

- **sales will tend to be higher as a reputation for quality confers a competitive advantage;**

- **related products may acquire this quality image.**

ACTIVITY

Identify firms in the following product or service areas that have a reputation for supplying high-quality goods or services:

- **food and consumer durable retailing;**

- **car production;**

- **clothing;**

- **hotel accommodation;**

- **audio equipment.**

Companies have traditionally used an inspection system to identify any output that does not reach what it regards as an acceptable standard of quality. This approach to quality, however, encourages employees to take it for granted that some of their work is bound to be defective. Because work is inspected, less attention is likely to be paid to preventing errors and defects in the first place as these will be picked up later.

Apart from the need to develop quality as a competitive factor, the financial cost associated with defective output is also a powerful reason for adopting TQM. Companies can save money by improving quality. They pay a price for producing defective work.

- **By accepting that some products are bound to be defective,** companies must devote labour and other resources to various stages of an inspection system.

- **They have to rework or repair defective products,** make repairs that have to be carried out under guarantees and lose money on any output that cannot be salvaged and has to be scrapped.

- **Companies may incur financial penalties** if quality, delivery or completion dates agreed with customers are not achieved. They have to handle extra paperwork resulting from customers' complaints.

- **Reworking of defective items** can disrupt the flow of production and the organisation of the factory suffers if stocks of defective items or scrap are taking up valuable space.

- **Companies can experience delays** and lost output because plant, machinery and equipment can be damaged when they process or handle defective output.

- **Having to rework items** or deal with customers who have received a poor quality product, level of service or late delivery impacts upon staff morale, and it can reduce job satisfaction, motivation and hence productivity.

- **Companies may have to pay legal costs** and compensation if a defect leads to a customer taking legal action.

Firms are also customers themselves. They suffer if their suppliers produce defective goods. They have to devote resources to the inspection or testing of items received from suppliers and the handling of any complaints made against them.

PRODUCTIVITY

Productivity describes the efficiency with which a business turns production inputs (labour services, raw materials, for example) into output. Firms seek to improve their productivity by ensuring the best relationship between the cost of inputs and the value of the final product.

Productivity can be measured in several ways. A common method is to measure **labour output** – usually per hour. For example, if twelve fruit pickers can pick 240 boxes of cherries in a ten-hour day then their productivity per labour hour is two boxes of cherries. This is calculated by dividing output for the day (240 boxes) by the number of hours in the day (ten). The result is the output per hour, in this case 24 boxes per hour. This is then divided by the number of workers to calculate the level of output per labour hour. The following formula summarises the process:

$$\text{labour productivity} = \frac{\text{output per hour}}{\text{number of employees}}$$

An improvement in productivity will show up as an increase in output per worker hour and benefits the firm in that the labour cost in each unit of production falls. This reduction in costs will allow the company – if it so wishes – to cut prices and become more competitive. For example, over recent years labour productivity in the UK car industry has risen significantly. This has enabled the industry to compete more effectively in international markets.

Increases in productivity do not simply result from employees working harder. It could be that employees are given better equipment. Motor vehicle manufacturers have invested large amounts of money in automating their production lines. This has allowed them to reduce the number of workers, producing huge increases in labour productivity. Other factors such as training for employees and employee profit-sharing schemes may have helped improve productivity.

Businesses are increasingly using technology within their production processes. To some extent, this invalidates the use of output per worker hour as a measurement of productivity. An alternative is to measure **capital productivity**. This can be calculated using the following formula:

$$\text{capital productivity} = \frac{\text{output}}{\text{capital employed}}$$

If a furniture-making company has ten lathes which produce 320 chairs in a working day of eight hours, then the productivity of capital would be 32 chairs per lathe per day or four chairs per lathe per hour.

Both capital and labour productivity measures do not fully assess the efficiency of an enterprise since each considers only a **single input** in relation to final output. A fuller assessment would require that all inputs are considered in relation to final output.

ACTIVITY

Working in groups, investigate a range of UK industries and find out:

(a) measures of productivity in relation to capital and labour;

(b) the volume of investment (or capital formation) undertaken by these industries;

(c) the relationships (if any) between these two factors.

You should seek to include a number of manufacturing industries and a number of service industries. You should set out your work neatly and support your comments with statistical data as appropriate.

Productivity improvements can help turn around the fortunes of a business. By gaining greater output from a given amount of input, a company can reduce its costs. This gives the company the freedom to reduce its prices, to increase its competitiveness or to hold its prices and to take a greater profit margin.

ACTIVITY

Wesley Mowers Ltd produces a small range of lawn mowers for domestic use. The mowers are all based on a standard design, with minor modifications in each model in the range. The company works a 50-hour week. Profitability has been relatively low and the managers of the company have sought ways to cut costs and increase profitability.

Year	Average weekly output	Number of employees
1992	350	10
1993	360	9
1994	400	8
1995	420	7

1 Using the production data given in the table, calculate labour productivity for Wesley Mowers Ltd on a weekly and an hourly basis.

2 Suggest some reasons for any change in productivity.

3 What might be the effect on the firm of the change in productivity you have identified?

4 What reservations might you have about labour productivity as a measure of the efficiency of Wesley Mowers Ltd?

JUST-IN-TIME PRODUCTION

Holding stocks is very costly. In markets that are increasingly competitive, firms have sought to reduce their costs by holding lower quantities of all types of stocks. One of the best known methods of reducing stock levels is the **just-in-time (JIT)** system. This system originated in Japan with the Toyota Motor Company. In its broadest sense, JIT is a production management system in which materials and components are delivered to the next stage of production at the exact time they are needed. The same approach is often taken with regard to supplies to customers, delivering them 'just in time'.

Traditional mass production systems are **'push' systems**; each stage in the production process passes its output on to the next stage, regardless of the latter's actual requirements. In contrast, the JIT system is a **'pull' system**; each stage in the production process demands items from the previous production stage. This means that the items used at an assembly plant will determine the production flow at the factories of supplying firms. Nothing is produced or transported that is not required at a later stage of production.

As a result, the firm does not hold any stocks of components, raw materials or finished goods. This is why the system has been termed a **'zero inventory'** system.

JIT is ideally suited to manufacturing production where the volume of output is relatively high and sudden surges and slumps in demand are unlikely to occur. The successful operation of JIT requires good internal and external communications.

- ☉ **An internal system** is needed to ensure the smooth movement of materials and components to the appropriate part of the business at the correct time. Toyota uses a *kanban* (or card) system. Typically, such a system operates through the use of two component bins. Once one bin is emptied it is returned to the supply area and the card on it prompts further production of the component. This supply becomes available just as the second bin is emptied.

- ☉ **Excellent communications** are needed to ensure a high level of co-operation and collaboration with suppliers. It is important not to have too many suppliers or the system can become very complex to operate. Purchasers may also look to use local suppliers to avoid the problems of delays in delivery due to transport difficulties. Suppliers must be able to deliver on demand in a JIT system. Information technology has assisted businesses in their operation of the JIT system. Firms can monitor their stock levels more easily and can use automatic stock ordering systems to trigger production at the correct time.

JIT is attractive to many UK businesses. It allows retailers to hold minimal stocks, yet be sure that supplies of goods will arrive in time to fulfil customer demand. Equally, manufacturers can use the system to minimise their holdings of raw materials, components, work in progress and finished goods.

USING HUMAN RESOURCES EFFECTIVELY

By the effective use of human resources businesses can increase the value added in production. There are a number of factors that have to be considered in deploying the human resource within a business to its best effect. These include **training**, **motivation** and **flexibility**.

Training is important. It increases the skill levels of employees and enables them to carry out their work more efficiently. Training can help reduce wastage within a business as well as assist in motivating employees. It can allow delegation to take place, freeing senior employees to concentrate on strategic and long-term management issues.

FIGURE 5.2: Companies can use training to become more competitive.

Employees need to be motivated if they are to give of their best. Firms seek to involve their employees in the operation of the business as fully as possible in order to make them feel valued. Techniques such as **quality circles** provide employees with a sense of achievement and make a positive contribution to the well-being of the organisation. Shop-floor employees often have a deep understanding of the issues involved in their work and can come up with solutions to a range of problems. Employers can also rotate the jobs carried out by employees to maintain interest and motivation.

Businesses have attempted to make more effective use of employees through the adoption of **flexible contracts**. Later in this unit we will discuss the increasing use of part-time and temporary labour. Additionally, firms have increasingly employed workers on non-standard contracts. For example, some firms employ staff on an annual hours basis so that they are available to work longer hours during busy periods of the year and receive a commensurate reduction in their weekly working hours at other times. The majority of these changes in the nature and terms of employment are designed to allow businesses to match their labour supply to the level of demand for their goods or services.

WHY BUSINESSES AIM TO ADD VALUE

There are several reasons why firms seek to add value in producing a product or service. Below, we consider four main reasons.

TO MEET INTERNATIONAL COMPETITION

The UK economy is an integral part of the European and international economy and UK businesses cannot operate in isolation from their international competitors. The UK's membership of the European Union and the creation of the single market in 1993 has intensified international competition. UK consumers now face a bewildering array of goods from overseas producers; electrical goods from Taiwan, cars from Germany and wine from Australia and South Africa are just a few examples. Similarly, UK firms buy raw materials and components from all parts of the world.

ACTIVITY

Look at adverts in a national newspaper or magazine. How many of them are placed by foreign producers? Is there any pattern to the types of goods and services supplied by overseas firms?

The UK's industrial base is changing from manufacturing industry to service industry. It is important that UK firms adapt their products and their production methods to ensure that they can compete internationally.

In May 1994, the government published a white paper on international competitiveness that clearly set out the challenge facing UK businesses. The UK is falling behind its major competitors. In 1993, the UK was sixteenth in the international league table based on level of income per head of population. The US and Japan both recorded income per head figures over 20 per cent higher than the UK's. The UK is also facing increasingly fierce competition from many newly-industrialised countries, particularly from the so-called **'tiger' economies** of the Pacific rim such as Taiwan and South Korea.

TO MEET CUSTOMER REQUIREMENTS

It is true to say that successful businesses are those which produce goods and services that meet the demands of their customers. Modern businesses are increasingly **market-oriented**. This means that they first establish the requirements of their customers and then set about designing goods and services that will satisfy those needs and demands.

Collecting the information on customer requirements is usually done through **market research**. This is considered in detail in unit 3. Besides establishing the exact nature of the goods and services that customers require, market research can help identify the price that consumers are willing to pay as well as the target market. This may enable firms to sell larger quantities at a higher price and thus increase the value added in their production.

Some organisations have taken the marketing concept further. The Body Shop has a unique approach to marketing. In her autobiography, *Body and Soul*, Anita Roddick summarises the Body Shop's approach:

> *What we have tried to do is to establish credibility by educating our customers, giving them intelligent information about where ingredients come from, how they are tested and what they can be used for. It humanises the company, making customers feel that they are buying from people whose business practices they know and trust.*

This honest approach takes market orientation a stage further: it helps to shape public opinion and the nature of the demand for cosmetics. This approach, backed by public relations activity, has helped to convince the public that the Body Shop trades ethically and sells quality products. This, in turn, allows it to charge higher prices and to obtain greater added value .

TO IMPROVE PROFIT

There are many definitions of profit as we shall see in units 6 and 7. However, at this point, we shall simply define profit as the difference between the cost of producing a good or service and the income received from selling it. A business can increase the value added by lowering its costs of production as well as by increasing its income from sales.

We have discussed a number of ways in which costs might be reduced, for example by increasing productivity or by the use of just-in-time production methods. Increased sales, and higher selling prices, might be achieved by offering a better service or by the use of improved marketing or quality assurance systems. Many dry cleaners offer a 'gold star' or similar high-quality service in addition to their normal service. Inevitably, they charge a higher price for the 'gold star' service. However, dry cleaners make sure that the increase in costs associated with this 'special' quality service is less than the additional sales income received. In this way, they have increased value added and enhanced their profits.

TO SURVIVE AND GROW

Added value allows businesses to generate sufficient profits to stay in operation. The owners of small businesses need to earn an acceptable return otherwise they may decide to close the business. Larger firms need to add value to provide them with funds for investment. They have to invest to develop their business or to purchase other companies to grow through acquisition. In 1995, the Whitbread Group grew substantially by spending £1bn to purchase the Happy Eater and Little Chef restaurant chains from Forte. As a result of this purchase, the Whitbread Group, which already owns Pizza Hut and the Beefeater chain, has become the largest restaurant operator in the UK – larger even than McDonald's.

CHANGES AND IMPROVEMENTS IN PRODUCTION

The pace of industrial change is ever increasing. The last twenty years or so have proved no exception, with massive technological changes and also legislative changes and the growing influence of Japanese production and management techniques.

TECHNOLOGICAL CHANGES

Changes in technology have affected all aspects of our lives as well as many business activities. The changes in technology in businesses can be classified into a number of areas:

- ☻ **information technology;**
- ☻ **robotics and automation;**
- ☻ **computer-aided design and computer-aided manufacture.**

INFORMATION TECHNOLOGY

Information technology (IT) includes the use of microelectronic and computer systems. It is used within businesses to gather, store, analyse and distribute information. It provides the infrastructure for management information systems. It is frequently used directly when dealing with customers. For example, when booking a holiday your travel agent will interrogate a database to determine prices and availability. The same system can then be used to reserve your holiday.

⌐☼ ACTIVITY

Working in pairs, write down ten uses of information technology within a business. You should try to make these as varied and as up to date as possible.

The use of information technology within an organisation might well reflect its management philosophy. An organisation with an autocratic management style is likely to emphasise the gathering and storing functions of information technology. In this case, the communication flow will be upward. In a more democratically led organisation, the flow of information is more likely to be away from the centre and information technology will be used to disseminate information. This would be the case in an organisation in which decisions are taken at a lower level in the hierarchical structure.

In most organisations, managers require information to enable decisions to be taken. For example, data on sales would be necessary to allow decisions to be made on future production, marketing campaigns and borrowing requirements. Management information systems are designed to provide these data. Information held on these systems could include:

- ☻ **wage, raw material, component and fuel costs;**
- ☻ **sales figures, most probably based on regions or types of customer;**
- ☻ **orders and stocks held;**
- ☻ **data relating to employees.**

British Airways and information management

British Airways in one of the UK's largest businesses. In 1993, it carried 28 million passengers and half a million tonnes of freight. Many of its employees deal directly with the public as a normal part of their working life and it is important that they have the information necessary to provide the public with a high-quality service.

Because of the scale and nature of its business, British Airways has a separate department to look after its management information system. In 1992, the company invested over £49m in hardware, including computer terminals, radios and computer mainframes and over £312m in software. The department at British Airways which operates the company's management information system has:

● nearly 2,000 staff world-wide;

● two main data centres at Heathrow airport;

● over 160 mid-range processors;

● over 14,000 personal computers;

● 44,000 computer devices in over 750 locations world-wide;

● 200,000 connected terminals world-wide.

Source: *Working in Real Organizations*, Watts and Glew.

The increase in the amount of information available to managers can result in better quality decision-making. Some critics argue that management information systems can provide too much information to decision-takers, to the extent that the key data can be obscured.

ROBOTICS AND AUTOMATION

Japanese companies have been the leaders in the use of robotics in manufacturing. They have developed machines to carry out many of the manual tasks formerly undertaken by skilled and semi-skilled workers. The impact has been enormous in the limited number of industries that produce on a large scale and have sufficient funds to invest in the technology. The machines are reliable and they can work non-stop. However, their introduction has proved controversial, causing widespread redundancies and de-skilling the existing workforce.

The use of robotics in the car industry has attracted a great deal of attention. European and US motor companies have been quick to follow the lead and install their own systems. The use of robotics elsewhere has been limited mainly because of the large initial investment that is required.

Manufacturers have installed other automated systems. **Computer-integrated manufacturing (CIM)** is designed to integrate all aspects of production planning and control, including product design, factory layout planning, production scheduling and stock control. It can manage a just-in-time production system.

COMPUTER-AIDED DESIGN AND COMPUTER-AIDED MANUFACTURING

Computer-aided design (CAD) uses, as its name suggests, computers in the design of new products and components. CAD drawings can be shown on a visual display unit and then redrawn to allow for modifications and/or different specifications. When used in conjunction with the appropriate software, CAD has the facility to test new designs for robustness, longevity and performance. In this way, CAD speeds up the process of designing a new product by eliminating the need for costly prototypes and making it easier to redesign products for different markets.

When used in conjunction with computer-aided process planning, CAD can show the best method of production.

Similarly, **computer-aided manufacturing (CAM)** employs computers to send instructions to control machinery such as robots as part of the production process. When CAD and CAM systems are used together then the whole design and production process can be automated and carried through quickly and efficiently.

B&B Fabrications

It is not many small metal-working companies that can afford the type of CADCAM system now installed at B&B Fabrications at Hebburn in Tyneside.

Company owner, Bill Wilson, established the company with a partner in 1989 and bought the business outright in April 1994. A sheet-metal worker with much experience in computerised manufacturing, Mr Wilson explained: 'When I first started the company I realised that there was a growing market in metal fabrication. Larger companies were increasingly closing down their own metal fabrication operations and were buying in more compo-nents from smaller, well-run companies. But they would expect such subcontractors to have CADCAM facilities to ensure quality, speed of turn-around and low cost.'

B&B Fabrications' CAD-CAM system cost £18,000 and was purchased with the help of a grant from the South Tyneside Development Fund. The new CADCAM system was a success from the start. Operated by a full-time pro-grammer, with more staff being trained, the system has speeded up the production process by 70 per cent. As a result both capacity and sales have increased and, given its new competitive advantage, B&B is looking to increase its workforce.

The Tyneside Business Link aims to encourage busi-nesses to train their employ-ees in order to promote competitiveness and local prosperity. Unsurprisingly, it is now encouraging Bill Wilson to put more trust in his twelve-strong workforce while he concentrates on overall business strategy.

Source: *Business Link Magazine.*

Read the case study about B&B Fabrications.

1 **Research the activities which are carried out by your local Business Link.**

2 **What is meant by the term 'competitive advantage' and why did the purchase of the CADCAM equipment give this advantage to B&B Fabrications?**

3 **Suggest some disadvantages of introducing new technology into a business.**

OTHER FACTORS CONTRIBUTING TO CHANGE IN PRODUCTION

Besides technology, a number of other factors have contributed to changes in production techniques. Many of them have been initiated by Conservative governments since 1979.

CONTRACTING OUT

Firms seek to produce at minimum cost. In recent years, many businesses have placed orders with independent suppliers for goods and services which used to be provided in-house. Contracting out is based upon the belief that specialist suppliers may be more efficient, perhaps benefiting from economies of scale, and that some of these benefits can be passed on to the purchaser in the form of lower prices. In other words, it is often cheaper to buy in services rather than provide them in-house. Many private sector organisations buy in services such as cleaning and the provision of meals.

Some of the impetus for contracting out has come from the government's privatisation programme. Many services previously provided by central government and local authorities are now supplied by private sector firms. For example, the National Health Service employs private sector businesses to supply laundry, cleaning and catering services.

ACTIVITY

We have described contracting out in a very positive manner. As with all business decisions, the case is not clear cut. List and explain as many arguments as you can against contracting out.

PRICE OF TECHNOLOGY

Businesses will employ production techniques that provide the cheapest method of producing output of a given quality. Over time, rising wage levels and increases in other employment costs have encouraged employers to substitute capital equipment for labour. This trend has been accelerated by steady falls in the price of technology. So, for example, the real cost of computers has fallen in recent years; you can get machines with better technical specifications at lower prices.

ACTIVITY

Give five examples of jobs or tasks where some form of technology has replaced workers. Can you see any similarity in the types of jobs that have disappeared?

SINGLE SOURCING

Relying upon outside suppliers is always risky. Components and materials might arrive late, or not arrive at all. The quality might be too low or the price too high. Relying upon many different suppliers increases the risk, and it also makes it more difficult to operate a just-in-time production system. To reduce the risk, firms have sought to cut down on the number of businesses supplying them with components, materials and services. Taken to its extreme, some businesses adopt a single supplier policy. They reach agreements with companies to supply exclusively based upon trust and mutual understanding.

LABOUR FLEXIBILITY

In the next element of this unit, we discuss in some detail the changes in working practices that have taken place in the UK. The driving force for a more flexible supply of labour has been the need for UK industry to remain competitive with the rest of the world. Employers have

sought to increase the quality of their workforce at the same time as reducing its cost. This has been achieved in a number of ways:

- **extensive training to allow workers to acquire new skills;**

- **the increased employment of part-time and temporary workers to reduce employment costs;**

- **the use of short-term and rolling contracts to maintain motivation;**

- **the use of new technology;**

- **giving workers more responsibility within the organisation.**

The following extract from Marks and Spencer's annual report highlights the importance the high street retailer attaches to a flexible, skilled and well-motivated workforce.

Our policy remains to uphold our position as the premier employer in the retail market, attracting and retaining people of the highest calibre.

Both management and staff continue to respond well to the introduction of new systems and operating methods with a major focus on customer service. Many of our smaller stores are now run from our regional centres. That has resulted in improved standards, better utilisation of resources and lower costs. This arrangement provides more responsible and fulfilling jobs for our best managers and, in a number of cases, it has allowed younger managers a better opportunity to develop their skills and talents at an earlier stage in their careers.

Source: Adapted from Marks and Spencer plc, *Annual Report and Accounts*, 1993.

LEGISLATION

UK businesses operate in an environment that is strictly controlled by laws; nearly all aspects of their behaviour are governed by legislation.

ACTIVITY

Working with a friend, write down ten actions taken by a business that are subject to control by the law.

Firms must respect both UK legislation and European Union regulations. We shall consider two pieces of legislation and consider the impact upon businesses.

The **Health and Safety at Work Act 1974** requires that:

- ⊗ **employers have to provide a safe and secure working environment;**

- ⊗ **firms must have a written safety policy;**

- ⊗ **firms must provide safety equipment and clothing free of charge;**

- ⊗ **unions have the right to appoint safety representatives.**

The **Health and Safety Executive** was set up to enforce the provisions of the Act.

Acts like the Health and Safety at Work Act are **'enabling acts'**. These simply set out the framework of the law. Authority is delegated to some other body to draw up detailed regulations. This authority may be delegated to government departments or government ministers. In this way, governments can produce **statutory instruments** which establish rules and regulations with which individuals and businesses must comply. An example of a statutory instrument is section two of the Health and Safety at Work Act. This concerns the appointment of employee safety representatives and their role in consultations with employers. The regulations relating to section two were drafted by a government department and became law on the order of a minister.

The **Environmental Protection Act 1990** is the centrepiece of UK legislation designed to protect the environment. This Act introduced the notion of integrated pollution control which recognises that to control just one aspect of pollution is pointless. The environment is an integrated system – damage to one part is damage to the whole. This Act therefore requires businesses to minimise pollution as a whole rather then simply concentrating on one aspect such as airborne pollution.

Legal controls on businesses can force up costs as firms are obliged to take on additional, non-productive employees such as health and safety personnel. Additionally, production may become more complex and may involve more processes to ensure, for example, that pollution emissions are within legal guidelines. Some small firms can find these controls financially onerous. Being environmentally aware can work to firms' advantage. Some firms may acquire reputations for being good employers who provide a safe working environment. Firms like the Body Shop that pay a great deal of attention to the protection of the environment may benefit from increased sales to environmentally-conscious consumers.

COMPETITION

UK businesses operate in an intensely competitive world. The competitive pressures have increased with the creation of the **single European market** in 1993. This allows European firms more access to UK markets although, equally, UK firms have freer access to European markets. A number of UK manufacturing industries have declined because of their inability to compete internationally. Examples include the textile industry, the coal industry and motorbike production.

In this element, we have discussed changes in production methods and techniques. Many of these changes have been caused by the need for UK industry to remain competitive to survive.

PORTFOLIO ASSIGNMENT

Identify two local businesses on which to base your research for this assignment. You should try to choose businesses that are different in size and which produce different products. You may wish to choose one business which supplies a service.

Because you will have to visit each business and to talk with some employees, it is important to get the consent and co-operation of the businesses before you begin the assignment. It might be helpful to choose firms in which you undertook your work experience or where you have a part-time job.

1   Investigate the businesses' production methods to determine the ways in which they add value. It may be useful to read through the section on added value in production before attempting this task.

2   Identify what internal or external pressures are the force behind the businesses' efforts to add value.

3   For each industry, identify and explain at least two factors that have altered and improved their production techniques. For each of these factors, explain:

   (a) the possible causes of the changes;
   (b) the consequences for customers, for employees and for the business generally.

4   Once you have completed your research, you should write the results of your investigations in the form of a report.

Investigate and evaluate employment

In this element, we shall investigate employment within the United Kingdom and consider the changes which have taken place in the type of work which people do, the ways in which they work, the industries in which they work, the amount they are paid for their labour and the regions in which they are employed. Because the UK is a member of the European Union and because businesses are influenced by European Union employment policies, we shall look at employment trends within a European context.

SOURCES OF DATA ON EMPLOYMENT TRENDS

There are numerous sources of employment data. The major organisations which produce data (in one form or another) on employment trends are:

- ✪ **Department of Trade and Industry;**

- ✪ **Bank of England;**

- ✪ **Department for Education and Employment;**

- ✪ **Central Statistical Office;**

- ✪ **Jobcentres;**

- ✪ **Training and Enterprise Councils (TECs);**

- ✪ **Local Enterprise Companies (LECs);**

- ✪ **local authorities.**

As part of your research for this element you might need to get in touch with one or more of these organisations. There are also a number of important sources of data for you to use in your research. These may be available in the school or college library or in your local public library. Key publications include:

- ✪ **Labour Market Quarterly Report.** This provides a great deal of up-to-date data on all aspects of employment within Great Britain.

- ✪ **Labour Force Survey.** This is published four times a year by the Central Statistical Office and contains detailed information on the workforce.

- ✪ **Employment Gazette.** A monthly publication from the Department for Education and Employment setting out trends in the labour market.

- ✪ **Social Trends.** A widely used and very readable account of changes within UK society including changes in employment patterns.

- ✪ **Annual Abstract of Statistics.** This is a detailed account of the UK economy in statistical form published by the Central Statistical Office.

A useful source of data on employment in Europe is SYSDEM (the European System of Documentation on Employment). It produces a quarterly bulletin called *Trends*. It can be contacted at:

13b avenue de Tervuren
1040 Brussels
Belgium

It is important to exercise care when reading and drawing conclusions from economic data. Some data are based on figures collected for other purposes, for example some employment data relates to national insurance figures and excludes those on low incomes and those who are working in the **'black economy'**. Data may also be unreliable because certain statistics change regularly at particular times of the year. For example, unemployment figures usually fall during the spring as seasonal work in agriculture and the leisure industry becomes available. It is important to recognise these regular trends in employment data.

The government and opposition parties frequently disagree over the accuracy of economic statistics. There is, for instance, a long-running dispute about unemployment statistics. The opposition parties argue that the figures have been handled in a way which minimises the unemployment totals and which presents the government in a more favourable light. This charge is vigorously denied by the government.

	Population (millions)		Growth rate (%)
	1992	2025	1990–5
Europe	512	541.8	0.3
Austria	7.8	8.3	0.4
Belgium	10.0	9.9	0.1
Denmark	5.2	5.1	0.2
Finland	5.0	5.2	0.3
France	57.2	60.8	0.4
Ireland	3.5	3.6	-0.2
Germany	80.3	83.9	0.4
Greece	10.2	10.1	0.3
Italy	57.8	56.2	0.1
Netherlands	15.2	17.7	0.7
Portugal	9.9	10.1	0.0
Spain	39.1	40.6	0.2
Sweden	8.7	9.5	0.5
United Kingdom	57.7	60.3	0.2

FIGURE 5.3: Current and projected population statistics for selected European countries.
Source: *Social Trends 24*.

ACTIVITY

Find out the address of your local Training and Enterprise Council (TEC). Write and ask for copies of its publications that give information on the labour market in your area. From these data, try to identify two industries or towns which have experienced either a significant rise or fall in employment in recent months or years.

THE POPULATION OF THE UK AND THE EUROPEAN UNION

Before we focus on changes in employment in the UK, it is important to appreciate that employment patterns can change for two reasons. First, an industry may call for different types of employment. It may require more part-time workers or non-contract workers who are only offered employment at times when the firms concerned are busy.

Second, the structure of the labour force may change. The populations (and hence the labour forces) of most member states of the European Union are ageing. *Fig 5.3* highlights the low growth rates of the populations. In these circumstances, businesses may be forced to change their pattern of employment by, perhaps, replacing some of an ageing workforce with technology.

The low projected growth rates are caused by two underlying trends. People are **living longer** and there is a relatively **low birth rate**. This means that the workforce is gradually getting older. What are the implications for an employer whose workforce is steadily ageing? What actions can he or she take in these circumstances?

The number of retired people throughout western Europe will increase as people finish working earlier and live longer. This means that extra demands will be placed on those who are still at work to support this ever-increasing retirement group. Recognising this fact, the UK government has encouraged people to make provision for their own pensions. It wants to reduce the burden on public sector spending in the next century. Moves to raise the retirement age for women will also reduce the burden state pensions put on the government's finances.

TYPES OF EMPLOYMENT

Over recent years, there have been significant changes in the UK labour market and in patterns of employment. The tradition of getting and maintaining a full-time job is now less common. To remain competitive, employers have begun to use a variety of different contracts for hiring their workers. The most recent Labour Force Survey highlights three trends:

⊗ **full-time employment for men is still below the equivalent figure of ten years earlier;**

⊗ **part-time employment for men and women has risen steadily;**

⊗ **self-employment, though fluctuating, exhibits a rising trend.**

In this section, we shall consider the non-standard contracts which have become increasingly common as well as briefly looking at other forms of employment.

FULL-TIME EMPLOYMENT

In full-time employment, an individual is employed for the whole of the working week by a single employer. This is still the most usual type of employment. In most European countries, full-time employment means working between 35-40 hours per week. In 1994, the average working week for the European Union countries was 39 hours. This type of employment is common in most areas of the economy, but particularly common in the public sector, for example, in education and health.

One interesting feature of contemporary full-time employment is that no less than 1,280,000 people in the UK (1995 figures) have supplemented their full-time jobs with part-time or self-employed work. We could term these people as being in **multiple-employment**.

Most people work full-time because this form of employment provides a relatively high income (as well as possibly a range of perks such as company cars) and the best possible standard of living. It is also true that full-time employment offers a better chance of promotion; it is the basis for a **career**. In the past, many people would have argued that they work full-time because of the security it provides. Today, this argument rings hollow for many people. A series of surveys have shown that many people in full-time employment doubt the security of their jobs. This is one of the reasons why consumer

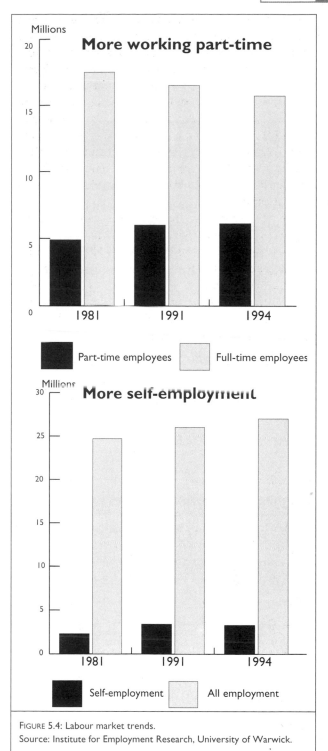

FIGURE 5.4: Labour market trends.
Source: Institute for Employment Research, University of Warwick.

spending has remained stagnant throughout much of the 1990s.

From the point of view of business, full-time employees can be highly motivated because they are often seeking to establish a career. They can be self-motivated workers who are productive and concerned to provide a high-quality service to customers. However, full-time employees can be expensive because employers have to pay **pension** and **national insurance contributions**. This can have implications for the profitability of the business if labour costs rise significantly. It can also be argued that full-time workers on secure contracts may become complacent; they may allow their standards to slip causing the business to perform less effectively.

⚡ ACTIVITY

Imagine that you are the manager of a small manufacturing business. You need to take on a new salesperson. You are considering whether to make a full-time appointment for one person or whether, perhaps, to create two part-time (and possibly temporary) posts.

1 **Make a list of the advantages and disadvantages of each course of action.**

2 **Decide on the form of employment that you would offer in these circumstances. Give your reasons.**

SELF-EMPLOYED WORKERS

Self-employed people operate as their own boss. They might either operate on a **freelance basis**, seeking work with a succession of companies or individuals, or **run their own businesses** on a permanent basis. Those who work freelance often have very specialist skills, either technical, perhaps in the area of computing, or managerial, in which case they are often called management consultants.

It is common for tradespeople, such as electricians, decorators or bricklayers, to be self-employed. In 1994, 13 per cent of the labour force – some 3.3 million people – was self-employed. It is anticipated that the numbers of self-employed in the UK will rise steadily into the next century.

Self-employment has been encouraged by a succession of Conservative governments since the early 1980s. These governments have viewed the self-employed favourably: they are seen as hard-working and entrepreneurial, prepared to adopt new ideas and enter new markets. These attributes, it is argued, are of great benefit to the economy and are likely to promote economic growth and prosperity. Self-employed people work very hard and manage businesses which, although small, can be very competitive.

The benefits of self-employment for the self-employed are less clear cut. If their businesses succeed, there can be very positive financial benefits and many people enjoy the experience of being their own boss. Self-employment has various tax advantages; self-employed workers can claim numerous business expenses that can be offset against income tax.

For many, the self-employed experience is more about working very long hours, with few holidays, for relatively poor returns. There is the responsibility of managing a business and many of the self-employed lack the necessary skills to manage their affairs to best effect.

PART-TIME EMPLOYMENT

A feature of employment in the UK has been the steady rise in the number of part-time employees (see *Fig. 5.5*). Much of this rise has been at the expense of full-time jobs. Those who work for sixteen hours or less are categorised as being in part-time employment. The growth in part-time employment reflects the trend in the UK (and the rest of the European Union) towards service industries. Service industries such as retailing have generated a great demand for part-time employees. Firms in the tertiary or service sector often require employees for only a few hours per week, and often not during the main working day. Examples include school cooks, cleaners, shelf-fillers in supermarkets and restaurant and bar staff.

Part-time employment offers benefits to those who choose to work in this way. First, the hours of work can usually be fitted in with other commitments. So, for example, part-time work suits many women who are trying to earn some money and look after their children. It allows people to pursue other interests or even other forms of employment. Following a recent government decision, part-time workers now enjoy many – but not all – of the employment rights available to full-time employees.

Improved rights for part-time workers

The Government yesterday granted improved rights to 750,000 part-time workers. This was as a result of an appeal to the House of Lords by the Equal Opportunities Commission on the grounds that 87 per cent of part-time workers are female.

The Secretary of State for Employment warned that jobs would be threatened by allowing part-time workers access to industrial tribunals and redundancy pay after two years – the same as for full-timers – instead of having to wait five years as was formerly the case.

From January 1995, those working 16 hours or less will have the same unfair dismissal and redundancy rights as full-timers. About 750,000 people who have been in part-time employment for between two and five years are expected to benefit. Yesterday's decision on part-timers still leaves them without parental leave, sick pay and pension rights.

Adapted from *The Independent*,
21 December 1994

United Kingdom				Thousands
	Males		Females	
	Full-time	Part-time	Full-time	Part-time
1984	13,240	570	5,422	4,343
1985	13,336	575	5,503	4,457
1986	13,430	647	5,662	4,566
1987	13,472	750	5,795	4,696
1988	13,881	801	6,069	4,808
1989	14,071	734	6,336	4,907
1990	14,109	789	6,479	4,928
1991	13,686	799	6,350	4,933
1992	13,141	885	6,244	5,081
1993	12,769	886	6,165	5,045
1994	12,875	998	6,131	5,257

FIGURE 5.5: Full and part-time employment by gender.
Source: *Social Trends 25*.

It can be argued that the benefits of part-time work are outweighed by the disadvantages of this form of employment. Part-timers often have a lower status than full-time employees and may be given more menial tasks to perform. Those working anti-social hours as part-timers rarely get overtime rates of pay, so from an employer's point of view they are a very economical form of labour. The national insurance system provides an additional incentive to keep pay low. If annual pay is less than a specified threshold, employers do not have to pay national insurance contributions.

ACTIVITY

Talk to your fellow students. Find out if they have a part-time job. What sort of companies do they work for? Are their jobs concentrated within a few business areas? If so, can you think of any reasons why this might be the case?

Part-time employees offer considerable benefits to employers. This type of employee provides flexibility in the sense that they can be employed only during the busy parts of the day, week or month. This means that employers can avoid having employees standing round during slack business periods with little or no work to do. In spite of the recent ruling on employment rights, part-time employees have fewer rights and are cheaper to employ. They have no rights to sick pay, nor do they have any entitlement to parental leave (time off when a child is born). Employers do not have to make pension contributions. Many fast-food chains make extensive use of cheap, part-time labour offering work during evenings and at weekends when the outlet is usually busy.

PERMANENT EMPLOYMENT

Permanent employment occurs when an employer offers an employee a contract which is not for a fixed or limited period; that is, it does not have a finite life. Such contracts suggest that people can have a job for life. In certain occupations such as university lecturing this might once have been true, but it is less and less the case in contemporary Britain. Permanent employment has benefits for the employee but, in reality, it is an illusion. If the demand for any employee's services disappears, then the employee is likely to be made redundant. An employee can also lose his or her job on other grounds – for example, through gross incompetence.

The trend today is to offer **fixed-term contracts**. Permanent contracts can be demotivating because employees can become complacent and confident in the continuity of their employment. Many firms are moving towards temporary, renewable contracts as they seek a workforce which is accountable and flexible.

Asda board moves to one-year contracts

Archie Norman, chief executive at Asda, has moved from a three-year to a one-year rolling service contract at the supermarket group. This means that his contract comes up for renewal each year and is only renewed for a one-year period.

Mr Norman revealed yesterday that all the company's directors had moved to one-year contracts. Mr Norman said: 'My attitude is that directors' notice periods should be no longer than 12 months. We have a history of longer contracts that has cost the company dear.'

The Times, 20 October 1995

ACTIVITY

Read the article about Asda's move to one-year contracts for directors.

1 **What benefits do you think that the company might gain from appointing all its directors on one-year rolling contracts?**

2 **Can you think of any disadvantages to Asda arising from its course of action?**

TEMPORARY WORKERS

In some senses, temporary workers are similar to part-time workers. They are most common in industries such as agriculture and tourism, where employers only need labour during particular months of the year. In certain parts of the UK, a high proportion of workers are on temporary contracts. In Norfolk, for example, many workers are employed in tourism, agriculture, fishing and the oil industry. These are industries which employ people for relatively short periods of time and have seasonal patterns of employment.

ACTIVITY

Obtain a recent issue of your local newspaper. Turn to the section where jobs are advertised. Count up those which are full-time and those which are part-time and, using a bar chart, illustrate the data that you have gained. Now look at the types of jobs that are being advertised as full-time and part-time positions – is there a pattern? Is it what you expected?

Employers may also use this type of employment to cover such things as the absence of full-time employees on sickness or maternity leave, an unusually busy work load or a sudden and limited need for specialist skills. They might, for example, hire computer specialists for a short-term period to oversee the implementation of a new system. Employers usually issue a temporary or fixed-term contract to the employee. This offers employers the benefits of a more flexible workforce without having to meet the costs and long-term commitments involved in hiring full-time permanent staff.

HOMEWORKING

Homeworkers are people who earn an income from working at home. In the past, homeworkers typically carried out laborious tasks for very low rates of pay. For example, a traditional homeworking industry is knitting; knitters are paid very small amounts for each garment they have completed. This is the traditional view of homeworkers – low skilled, low paid and with few benefits or rights. Homeworkers are not usually members of trade unions and are not protected by employment legislation. In 1994, there were some 650,000 homeworkers, about one person in forty of all those employed or self-employed in the UK.

Modern technology has changed the nature of homeworking. Many professional people now work from home using communication links such as faxes and

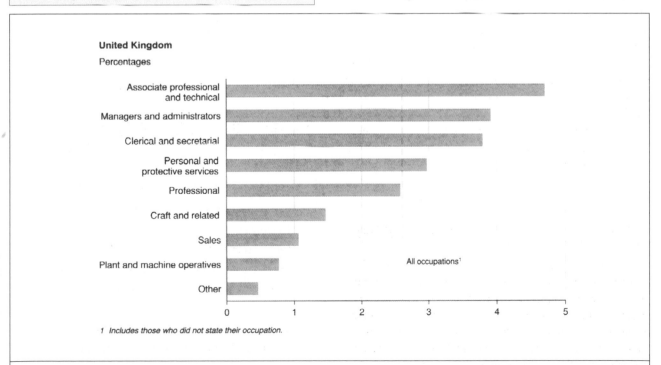

FIGURE 5.6: People working at home as a percentage of those employed or self-employed, Spring 1994.
Source: *Social Trends 25*.

electronic mail. Sometimes this is referred to as teleworking. Many books, such as this one, are written in the authors' homes and then sent on computer disk to the publisher.

Homeworking is a feature of employment that is clearly associated with rural districts in the UK. The Isles of Scilly, the Orkneys and rural parts of Wales and Scotland have the highest percentages of their workforces employed at home. This may not be surprising given that few major employers operate in these remote locations.

A major industrial example of home or teleworking is provided by the Rank Xerox 'networkers'. A number of employees left the company and set up their own small businesses which provide managerial and other services to Rank Xerox itself as well as to other organisations.

CONTRACT AND NON-CONTRACT EMPLOYMENT

As we saw in element 1, the use of contract labour is becoming increasingly common in the UK. Private firms, local authorities and nationalised industries have, in many circumstances, invited tenders from external agencies to provide services on their behalf. Since 1989, local authorities have been obliged to practise a system of **compulsory contract tendering (CCT)**. Under this system authorities are compelled to invite tenders from other firms to provide services like street cleaning and refuse collection which the local authority has traditionally offered. If an outside firm can provide the service more cheaply to an agreed standard, then the local authority has to use that firm. The firm engaged to provide the service (known as the **contractor**) is likely to use contract labour. In this way, the local authority's work is being undertaken by labour employed by someone else – **contract labour**.

Similar systems occur in the National Health Service where outside firms now provide cleaning services and may also provide hospital meals. Private firms are also contracting out services such as transport and maintenance. This means that services which were previously provided in-house are placed with independent suppliers.

Contracting out can be viewed as the opposite to vertical integration. The motive for firms to contract out their services is that costs are likely to be reduced. Contract workers usually receive low rates of pay, less favourable working conditions and reduced job security. There are benefits for employers in terms of lower labour costs, reduced administration costs and higher profit levels.

There is disagreement about whether contracting out provides the same quality of service. It is debatable whether their customers feel that the quality of the service they receive has been enhanced. This highlights a dilemma faced by business: whether to provide a service of genuine quality or one at a low price.

SKILLED AND UNSKILLED WORKERS

Workers have traditionally been categorised as **skilled**, **semi-skilled** and **unskilled**. Skilled workers are not easy to define but they include those who have undertaken long periods of training to attain professional status (such as doctors, lawyers and lecturers). An alternative type of skilled worker is those who have mastered crafts, usually as the result of a period of apprenticeship. Such skilled groups include electricians and carpenters. The unskilled worker, in contrast, is expected to perform a job for which relatively little training is required. The rewards earned for such work are relatively low as there is no shortage of people willing to perform unskilled duties.

These groupings are now changing with the advent of technology. Traditional apprenticeships are disappearing as machines do the work previously undertaken by skilled craft workers. Training is now more straightforward even for craft industries. Entry to the professions remains relatively unchanged, as such jobs are not easy to replace by technology.

The main demand for employees in the future is expected to be for those who are highly educated, perhaps to degree level. This demand will be met by the increased numbers following courses in higher education. In particular, it is anticipated that the demand for those with education and skills in computer technology will grow.

JOB SHARING AND FLEXIBLE WORKING ARRANGEMENTS

More flexible working patterns are increasingly common in the UK. These can take a number of forms of which **job sharing** is perhaps the best known, if not the most common. Job sharing occurs when employees agree to divide the working week, or the tasks which make up a job, into two parts. Usually the employer issues two contracts of employment, one to each person, and the employees decide upon the division of duties.

This is of particular benefit to those who have family commitments looking after aged relatives or young children. Employers often view job sharing favourably because frequently two people contribute more to an organisation than a single person, especially in terms of generating ideas.

In 1994, flexible working hours (commonly known as **flexitime**) were worked by roughly 10 per cent of men and 15 per cent of women. Usually employees on flexitime have to attend work during core hours – say, between

United Kingdom			Percentages
	Male	Female	All persons
Full-time			
Flexible working hours	9.7	15.4	11.7
Annualised working hours	5.6	6.4	5.8
Term-time working	1.1	4.7	2.4
Job sharing	–	0.2	0.1
Nine day fortnight	0.7	0.4	0.6
Four and a half day week	3.2	3.1	3.1
All full-time employees (=100%) (thousands)	10,573	5,681	16,254
Part-time			
Flexible working hours	7.3	9.1	8.8
Annualised working hours	3.1	5.3	5.0
Term-time working	4.9	10.3	9.6
Job sharing	1.8	2.5	2.4
Nine day fortnight	–	–	–
Four and half day week	–	0.3	0.3
All part-time employees (=100%) (thousands)	745	4,760	5,506

FIGURE 5.7: Employees with flexible working patterns, Spring 1994.
Source: *Social Trends 25*.

10 a.m. and 12 p.m. and between 2 p.m. and 4 p.m. The remainder of their weekly working hours can be made up at a time to suit the individual employee. This arrangement is most appropriate in occupations where people work mainly as individuals and not as part of a team on a regular basis. About 18 per cent of people who work in the banking industry work flexitime.

Annualised hours is also a fairly common working arrangement. This occurs when an employer sets out a number of hours which employees must complete by the end of the year. Employees can then vary their weekly working hours to suit their individual circumstances.

CHANGING TRENDS IN EMPLOYMENT

Changes are taking place in the structure of the workforce in all European countries. At the same time, the industrial structures of those countries are changing. The workforce is, on average, older, employment contracts and patterns are changing, and new industries are developing while traditional industries decline. There have been significant changes in a generation.

THE CHANGING WORKFORCE

	(thousands)	
	1976	1994
Civilian workforce	25,895	27,736
Males	16,040	15,549
Females	9,856	12,187
Employees in employment	22,557	21,562
Males	13,401	10,911
Females	9,156	10,651
Self-employed	2,073	3,290
Claimant unemployed (males & females)	1,266	2,586
Government training schemes	–	298

FIGURE 5.8: The changing workforce.
Source: *Regional Trends, 1995*.

Using the data in *Fig. 5.8*, write down the major changes that you can identify in the structure of the UK's labour force in the years between 1976 and 1994.

The UK workforce hit a low in the early 1980s of just below 24 million people. By 1994, it had risen to 27.75 million. A noticeable feature of the current labour force is that many people of working age do not work. Some are unavailable for work or choose not to work. Some people take early retirement (before the age of 65) or choose not to work for a variety of reasons, relying on a partner's income or other sources of income. A further, and very common, reason for people of working age not being in a job is that they are unemployed. In 1995, there were 2.56 million people unemployed in the UK. This is approximately 9.5 per cent of the workforce. Other European countries are experiencing similar trends.

Overall, the labour force is declining as a percentage of the total population. One reason for this is that, because people are on average living longer, there are increasing numbers of pensioners. *Fig. 5.9* shows the economic activity rates in several European countries. These economic activity rates show the percentage of the entire population who are in the labour force, whether they are employed or unemployed. However, although the numbers available for work are only expected to increase slowly, most forecasters predict that the UK economy (along with most European economies) will find it difficult to create sufficient jobs to prevent further rises in the level of unemployment.

Although the overall size of the European workforce is not expected to change significantly, there are significant changes taking place in the composition of the workforce. We saw earlier that the UK has an ageing population; unsurprisingly, its workforce is also ageing. In the mid 1980s about 25 per cent of the labour force was aged under 25. By the year 2000, the equivalent figure will be approximately 15 per cent. The proportion of people aged 45 or over in the workforce will rise from 31 per cent to 35 per cent early in the next century. Other European countries face similar demographic trends. Each member of the European Union, with the exception of the Irish Republic, predicts falling numbers of school-leavers.

	Males	Females	All
Denmark	74.8	62.0	68.3
United Kingdom	75.0	53.0	63.6
Portugal	73.7	50.5	61.3
Germany	72.8	48.6	60.1
Netherlands	71.7	45.1	58.2
France	65.9	47.6	56.2
Irish Republic	72.6	37.0	54.6
Luxembourg	69.5	36.3	52.4
Italy	67.8	36.5	51.5
Belgium	62.4	38.5	50.0
Spain	66.9	33.3	49.3
Greece	65.8	33.7	49.1

FIGURE 5.9: Economic activity rates (the labour force as a percentage of the entire population) for selected European countries, 1991. Source: Eurostat.

In the mid 1960s, the number of births in the UK rose significantly for a few years. In a group, discuss the impact this would have had on the working population in the early to mid-1980s. How do you think this might affect businesses which predominantly employ young labour?

THE CHANGING INDUSTRIAL STRUCTURE

One way of classifying businesses in the economy is to divide them into three sectors:

⊗ **primary;**

⊗ **secondary;**

⊗ **tertiary.**

Primary involves agriculture, mining and the extractive industries, secondary is essentially manufacturing industry and tertiary covers service industries.

As an economy develops, so the balance of employment between the three sectors changes. During industrialisation, workers transfer from the primary sector of the economy to the secondary sector; many agricultural workers move into manufacturing. During the later stages of industrialisation, the manufacturing sector sheds labour and these workers find employment in service industries.

A major feature of the UK economy over the last 25 years has been the change in employment provided by different industries. Today, the service sector is the largest employer of labour and makes the greatest contribution to national income. This is very different from the late nineteenth century when Britain relied heavily on manufacturing for employment and was described as 'the workshop of the world'.

ACTIVITY

Using *Fig. 5.10* as source data, illustrate the changes in employment over the period 1971 to the year 2000. Your method of illustration should make it clear which industries have employed more people and which have shed labour. Why do you think these changes have taken place?

Working in a group, investigate whether the output of these industries has risen or fallen over the same period. Why do you think that some industries have managed to reduce their labour force yet simultaneously have increased their output?

ACTIVITY

Talk to your parents or other relatives and find out the occupations in which they are now employed and those in which they have been previously employed. Do the same for your grandparents and, if possible, great-grandparents. If you can go back and find out details of further generations, do so. Now categorise the occupations of your relatives into primary, secondary and tertiary classifications.

Does your family reflect the national trend in terms of the shift of employment from primary to secondary and then to the tertiary sector? Are there any special factors at work in your locality which might affect the employment pattern?

Industrial sector	Employment in thousands			
	1971	1980	1990	2000
Agriculture, forestry and fishing	770	670	600	490
Energy and water	800	720	450	370
Manufacturing	8,190	7,070	5,460	4,430
Construction	1,550	1,620	1,810	1,830
Distribution, hotels and repairs	4,430	4,990	5,660	5,720
Transport and communications	1,630	1,600	1,570	1,420
Banking, finance and insurance	1,490	1,860	3,140	3,220
Public administration and defence	1,810	1,900	1,800	1,980
Education and health	2,370	2,980	3,290	3,950
Other services	1,390	1,820	2,580	3,330
All industries	24,430	25,230	26,360	26,740

FIGURE 5.10: UK employment trends by industrial sector.
Source: *The UK Economy*, Prest and Coppock.

This change in the industrial base centres upon the decline in the importance of manufacturing to the UK economy. Manufacturing now employs a smaller proportion of the workforce and contributes a lower proportion of output than it did 25 years ago. This process is called **deindustrialisation**.

Although the decline of the manufacturing sector has happened throughout the European Union, it has been most pronounced in the UK. Almost 3 million manufacturing jobs have been lost since the 1970s. The 1980s were characterised by rapid growth in the service sector and a consequent rise in employment in this area of the economy.

Manufacturing is very important to any economy as it is relatively easy to sell manufactured goods overseas, whereas it is difficult to export tertiary services other than perhaps financial services and tourism.

The causes of deindustrialisation are complicated, but a contributory factor was undoubtedly a lack of competitiveness of UK goods during the 1980s. In some cases, this was due to poor quality, late delivery and poor after-sales service. Another contributory factor was high prices, frequently as a result of a high exchange rate. We consider the effects of a high exchange rate later in this unit. To some extent deindustrialisation is inevitable; consumers in advanced economies choose to spend more of their rising incomes upon services. There is considerable evidence to show that as consumers become richer they increasingly purchase services such as leisure, banking and insurance. In these circumstances it is not surprising that the supplies of services increase and greater numbers of people are employed in the service industries.

The picture in the rest of Europe has been very similar. The European industrial sector shed 7.5 million jobs in the ten years to 1985, while the service sector gained 10.2 million jobs over the same period. The underlying causes, however, vary to some extent from country to country.

THE RISE IN FEMALE EMPLOYMENT

One of the most significant changes in the UK workforce has been the rise in the number of women in employment. All of the rise in the workforce in the period 1976 to 1994 was due to the increase in the number of women working.

More than 50 per cent of women aged 16 or over are now economically active (that is, at work). Of those aged between 35 and 44, three-quarters are economically active. It is likely that the trend of increasing female employment will continue into the next century.

Across the European Union as a whole about 65 per cent of women between the ages of 20 and 59 work and the numbers are expected to increase. *Fig. 5.12* shows

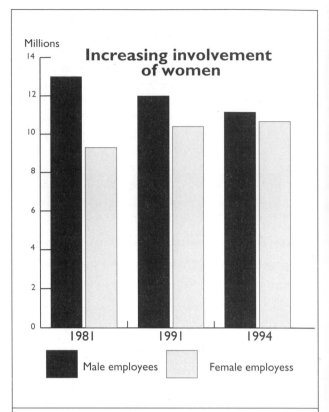

FIGURE 5.11: Increasing involvement of women in the UK labour force. Source: Institute of Employment Research, University of Warwick.

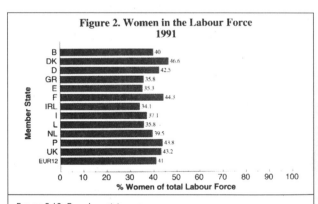

FIGURE 5.12: Female activity rates. Source: Trends 17, SYSDEM.

the female activity rates for the individual European countries. Note that these activity rates are higher than the rates in *Fig. 5.9* (see page 306) because they show the percentage of women of working age who are economically active rather than the percentage of all women (including children and pensioners) who are in the labour force.

Female economic activity rates tend to be lower in the Mediterranean countries where it is less socially acceptable in many areas for women, and particularly married women, to be in employment. In the next few years, the largest increases in female employment are expected to occur in France, Holland and Italy.

More women are working because of the increased availability of part-time jobs and because of social changes which mean that it is more acceptable for married women to be in employment. The age at which women have their first child has risen, and increasing numbers are choosing to return to work rather than stay at home with their children. The trend towards smaller families throughout Europe has also boosted female employment as it has meant that even those women who choose to remain at home while their children are young do so for a shorter period of time. The rise in the number of one-parent families has meant that many women have had to work to ensure a decent standard of living. The provision of more nursery facilities has made the return to work easier for mothers.

A further reason for the rise in female employment is due to the shift in the balance of UK industry towards tertiary or service industries. Service industries, such as banks, insurance companies and retailers, typically employ more women. The old declining manufacturing industries required male labour for what were often heavy manual jobs.

In spite of legislation to ensure that women receive equivalent rates of pay (for the same type of work) women still tend on average to receive lower rates of pay. This is partly because women are more likely to hold part-time posts which frequently attract lower rates of pay. Women tend to find employment in lower-paid sectors such as catering, nursing and retailing. By having career breaks to have children, women can also limit their career advancement and so limit their earning potential. There is some evidence that employers are less willing to offer high salaries and prestigious posts to women.

PART-TIME WORK

Another significant change in the make up of the UK workforce is the move towards part-time employment. It is anticipated that by the end of the 1990s approximately 25 per cent of the UK workforce will be part-time workers. This pattern is not common throughout Europe, however. In Germany, Italy and the Republic of Ireland there has been a decline in part-time employment.

Interestingly, the growth in part-time employment in the UK falls into two distinct groups: highly skilled work in fields such as systems analysis and less skilled work as, for example, shop assistants and gardeners.

The rise in part-time employment is partly due to lower employment costs. Part-time workers tend to be paid a lower hourly rate than full-time employees and other employment costs, such as pension contributions,

Denmark	24.3
Netherlands	22.7
UK	21.2
Germany	12.8
France	10.9
Belgium	8.6
Luxembourg	7.2
Republic of Ireland	6.5
Greece	5.3
Italy	5.3

FIGURE 5.13: Part-time working as a percentage of total employment in selected European countries.
Source: *Europe in Figures*.

are also reduced. However, the cost of employing highly-skilled part-time employees, often on a consultancy basis, can be considerable.

A further reason for the growth in part-time employment is the desire of employers to have a more flexible workforce. Part-timers are flexible: employers can use part-timers to extend their trading hours without having to pay overtime rates (shops, for example, can stay open longer) and they also enable employers to cope with fluctuations in demand. This allows business to be more competitive and market-oriented.

SELF EMPLOYMENT

The proportion of the self-employed in the workforce varies considerably between countries in Europe. In those countries with a large agricultural sector such as Spain, Italy and Ireland, there is a relatively high proportion of self-employed.

Germany	8.0
France	12.1
Italy	23.2
Belgium	15.6
UK	11.3
Ireland	21.7
Spain	20.9

FIGURE 5.14: Percentage of workforce self-employed in selected European countries.
Source: Eurostat.

In Europe, the numbers of self-employed workers have risen steadily over recent years. There has been a trend, particularly in the northern European nations, towards more owner-run businesses and a greater spirit of enterprise and self-reliance.

In the UK, self-employment is much more common as a form of employment amongst some ethnic minorities, particularly those from the Indian sub-continent. People from Pakistani or Bangladeshi ethnic groups are three to four times more likely to be self-employed than those from Afro-Caribbean ethnic groups.

ACTIVITY

Working in groups of two or three, make a chart composed of two elements. In one element you should compile a list setting out the advantages of being self-employed and in the other element of the chart you should record the disadvantages of self-employment.

TOWARDS A SKILLED WORKFORCE

There have been significant changes in the skills held by the UK workforce over recent years. A number of factors are operating here. There has been the impact of technology upon the labour force. In many industries, technology has replaced skilled workers. A notable example is the newspaper industry; many print workers were replaced by computer-based technology during a very stormy period of industrial relations culminating in the 'siege of Wapping'.

As a result of the introduction of technology, employers are able to reduce their labour costs by using cheaper semi-skilled labour in place of skilled workers. This policy, however, usually involves a substantial capital investment in technology.

Yet as many occupations have been deskilled, the government has signalled its commitment to improving the skills base of the UK workforce. This commitment is matched in other influential organisations. In 1991, the Confederation of British Industry (CBI) announced **'world class targets'**, setting out eight skills targets to improve the skills base in the UK economy.

A key target is that, by the end of 1997, 80 per cent of young people should be qualified to at least NVQ level 2, or the academic equivalent of four GCSEs at grade C or above. By supporting such targets, the government is making clear its belief that if the UK economy is to be competitive, the skills of its workforce must be improved.

As the industrial base changes, the skills that the workforce require are also changing. As production processes and commercial techniques become more complex and technologically based, it is vital that the workforce acquires the necessary skills to work effectively in these new industries.

	1984	1986	1988	1989	1990	1991	1992	1993	1994
Males	9.7	11.5	13.4	14.4	15.3	14.8	14.4	14.3	14.9
Females	8.5	9.9	13.1	14.5	15.6	15.0	14.7	15.0	16.2

Percentages

FIGURE 5.15: Percentage of the workforce receiving training. Source: *Social Trends 25*.

ACTIVITY

Fig. 5.15 shows the percentage of the workforce receiving training.

1 Why do you think that the number of women receiving training has risen so rapidly since the late 1980s?

2 Why have the overall numbers receiving training risen over the period covered by this table?

The creation of the **single European market** has placed a greater premium on managers having the skills to adapt quickly to local circumstances, to work in multi-location projects and to operate as part of a joint venture. Having the ability to speak a second European language will increasingly become an important skill. Large European firms will have either to provide training to allow their managers to acquire these skills or to recruit employees who already have such skills.

REGIONAL TRENDS IN EMPLOYMENT

There has been considerable variation in the regional pattern of employment in the UK as illustrated in *Fig. 5.16*. Traditionally, the most prosperous parts of the UK have been in the south and east. This prosperity was enhanced during the 1970s and 1980s by the proximity of these areas to the inceasingly important European export markets. The south and east remain the most prosperous parts of the UK – indeed, East Anglia enjoyed very rapid rates of economic growth in the early 1990s.

ACTIVITY

Find out which countries are currently the UK's ten major trading partners. You may need to visit a library to obtain this information. Which of these major trading partners are members of the European Union? Try to find equivalent figures for 1970. Which countries were then the UK's major trading partners? Can you explain the changes?

During the recession of the early 1990s, the south and east suffered increasing unemployment. As *Fig. 5.16* shows, the rate of unemployment in the south east has more than doubled; by comparison, in Scotland the recession had less impact and unemployment rose from 8 per cent to 10 per cent of the working population. One factor contributing to this rising unemployment was that, for the first time, service industries such as banking and finance shed substantial numbers of employees in an attempt to maintain competitiveness during the recession. This has led to a lessening of the disparity in levels of unemployment between the regions.

It remains to be seen whether the regional disparities in unemployment will return if the UK economy recovers during the late 1990s. If there is a period of sustained economic growth and prosperity, the regions in the south and east may recover the jobs that have been lost; however, employers may be atracted to other parts of the country where wages and rents are lower.

As we have discussed earlier, the last twenty years have seen the growth of service industries; this growth has been concentrated in the south and east of the country. Regions with high income and spending levels are attractive to service businesses such as financial institutions and leisure centres.

We have already seen that the UK has suffered from deindustrialisation resulting in a substantial loss of

					Percentages
	1990	**1991**	**1992**	**1993**	**1994**
North	8.6	10.6	11.2	11.2	11.7
Yorkshire and Humberside	6.8	9.1	9.9	9.8	9.8
East Midlands	5.1	7.8	8.7	9.0	8.3
East Anglia	3.8	6.2	7.1	8.3	7.4
South East	3.9	7.4	9.4	10.3	9.6
South West	4.5	7.7	9.1	9.2	7.5
West Midlands	5.9	9.0	10.7	11.6	9.9
North West	7.5	9.9	10.1	10.9	10.2
Wales	6.6	9.2	8.9	9.5	9.4
Scotland	8.0	9.2	9.5	10.1	9.9
Northern Ireland	13.7	14.1	12.1	12.5	11.5

FIGURE 5.16: Regional unemployment in the UK.
Source: *Social Trends 25*.

manufacturing firms. This has particularly hit regions in the north and west and also Scotland and Wales. Many firms in the traditional so-called **'staple industries'** have been hit hardest by job losses. Examples of the industries which have declined include coal-mining, the steel industry and textiles.

The government, however, has sought to attract firms to the less prosperous regions with some high-profile successes. Amidst much publicity, the government offered Nissan a package of financial incentives in the mid-1980s which persuaded the company to build a car factory near Sunderland. More recently, South Korean manufacturers have been attracted to the UK. Samsung, the electrical manufacturer, is opening a major factory in Billingham, in the north east, and Daewoo, the car producer is looking at the north of England as a possible site for a £350m factory capable of producing 10,000 cars a year and several thousand jobs.

PAY DIFFERENTIALS

We saw in the previous section that there are variations in employment and prosperity between the regions of the United Kingdom. Differences also exist in pay levels (see *Fig. 5.17*). Predictably, workers in London and the south east enjoy the highest incomes, while the people of Northern Ireland receive the lowest rates of pay.

ACTIVITY

Imagine that you are considering where to locate a small manufacturing business. You are looking at either west London or the north of England. Write out the advantages and disadvantages of each of the locations. Make a decision on where to site the factory.

Variations in pay rates also exist between men and women. In 1995, average annual full-time female earnings were £12,800, the equivalent figure for men was £17,500. Among top earners, there were differences but by a smaller amount: £21,000 for women against £24,340 for men. These differentials remain despite the **Equal Pay Act 1970**. This outlawed the practice of paying men and women different pay rates for the same work. We discussed the reasons why women receive on average lower pay than men earlier (see pages 308–9).

Full-time employees on adult rates	Total average gross weekly wage (£)		Increase in average total weekly pay (%) (Apr 93–Apr 94)	
	Male	Females	Males	Females
South East	419.4	301.1	1.9	3.5
East Anglia	334.8	241.6	2.6	6.5
South West	343.9	245.4	3.2	3.8
East Midlands	325.0	230.5	2.4	4.1
Yorkshire and Humberside	329.5	238.4	3.6	3.9
North West	343.9	243.6	2.8	2.8
North	327.8	237.0	1.9	5.3

FIGURE 5.17: Regional earnings, Spring 1994.
Source: New Earnings Survey.

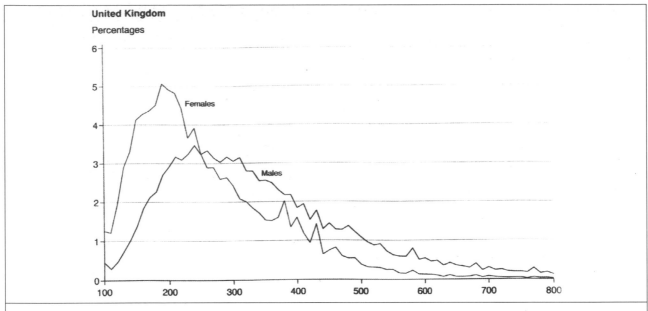

FIGURE 5.18: Average gross weekly earnings, Spring 1994.
Source: *Social Trends 25*.

Pay rates also vary significantly between the occupations. Traditionally, the professions – for example, doctors, lawyers, accountants – have received the highest rates of pay and unskilled manual workers the lowest levels of remuneration.

Private sector pay (male rates)	Total average gross weekly wage (£)	Increase in average total weekly pay(%) (Apr 93 – Apr94)
British Gas staff and senior officers (not higher management)	440.9	10.1
Gas workers	389.9	3.8
Chemical and allied-other workers	340.6	6.4
Metal trades manufacture	300.4	4.9
Vehicle building (England and Wales)	396.3	11.0
Banking (England and Wales)	290.8	-2.0
General printing (England and Wales)	379.3	12.6
Building and allied trades	243.8	12.8
BT managerial and professional	702.0	22.6
BT clerical and allied grades	320.8	2.9
Public sector pay (male rates)		
Royal Mail manuals	246.1	1.6
Nurses and midwifery staff	305.4	6.2
Prison officers	358.1	3.8
Civil Service clerical	223.1	1.9
Local authority manuals	241.0	1.8
Fire service below station officer	344.6	1.1
Primary and secondary teaching	454.7	3.4
Further educational teaching	453.6	1.5

FIGURE 5.19: Pay rates for selected occupations, Spring 1994.
Source: New Earnings Survey.

Pay varies between occupations because of the demand for, and supply of, various types of labour. Pay rates for unskilled workers are low because little or no training is required, so many people are available to undertake this type of work. This high supply of labour relative to demand depresses wages. On the other hand, those with very specialist skills such as surgeons or with talents given to few (the few top sportsmen and women, such as Mike Atherton and Sally Gunnell) receive huge incomes because very few people are able to carry out these jobs.

Those jobs which require high skill levels (and hence long periods of training) tend to attract high pay because people want some return for long periods of training when they receive relatively low wages or salaries. Most teachers spend four years as a student in order to achieve the necessary qualifications. Students receive small grants from local authorities and are increasingly being forced to take out loans to see them through their period of training.

ACTIVITY

Look at the employment section in your local newspaper. Compile a list of the job titles and salaries advertised. Which occupations offer the highest wages? Can you explain why these posts should attract such high levels of pay?

THE UNDERGROUND ECONOMY

The underground or 'black' economy is that part of the UK's economic activity which is undisclosed. It covers economic activity that is not reported to the authorities such as the Inland Revenue, the Customs and Excise or the Benefits Agency. The reason that people choose not to report earnings from some of their activities is to avoid tax liability or reductions in social security benefits. It is notoriously difficult to assess the size of the underground economy, but estimates put it at between 5 per cent and 20 per cent of the total income of the UK. The Inland Revenue estimates that the actual figure lies at the bottom end of this range. Whatever the precise figure, it is a significant proportion of total economic activity. Earnings made in the underground economy do not appear in official statistics.

There are numerous examples of the underground economy. They include tradespeople who work for 'cash'. A local decorator may agree to paint a house for a lower figure if he or she is paid cash. The decorator may not declare this income on the tax return to avoid paying income tax on these earnings. An advantage to customers is that they should not be charged VAT in such circumstances.

People who sign on to receive unemployment benefit in spite of having paid employment are also part of the underground economy. Their earnings are obviously not declared to the tax and benefit authorities in these circumstances for fear of losing their entitlement to benefits and to avoid a possible prosecution for fraud.

Another significant part of the underground economy is crime. Earnings from crime, for example through the trade in illegal drugs, are estimated at many millions of pounds.

THE IMPACT OF THE CHANGING EMPLOYMENT TRENDS

The major trends in employment we have identified are:

- ❂ **increased numbers of women in employment;**
- ❂ **rising male unemployment;**
- ❂ **a substantial rise in the numbers of part-time workers;**
- ❂ **a move towards more flexible forms of working;**
- ❂ **increasing use of technology to replace unskilled workers.**

THE EFFECTS ON EMPLOYED INDIVIDUALS

Households have been substantially affected by the recent changes in employment patterns. It is much more common now for women to be working, though often on a part-time basis. Women are the major breadwinner for a significant number of households, with their partners either earning less or being unemployed. This shift in responsibilities is not always popular or welcome. Many men can find it difficult to adjust to this situation.

Probably the major effect on individuals is that the security of employment for most people has been eroded. People who were formerly on permanent contracts are now on temporary contracts; people who once were employed now run their own businesses; many people work part-time with less protection from employment legislation.

It has been argued that these patterns in employment are unlikely to lead to a healthy and productive workforce. As job security has been eroded, so the income levels for the poorest members of society have fallen in comparison to higher earners. The shift from direct to indirect taxation and the reforms of social security benefits have contributed to the hardship endured by the poorest groups in society over the last decade.

THE EFFECTS ON THE UNEMPLOYED

The level of unemployment in the UK is at a very high level. Strict comparisons over time are difficult because the way in which unemployemnt is recorded has been changed many times during the 1980s. However, unemployment is significantly higher than in the 1960s and 1970s. A high

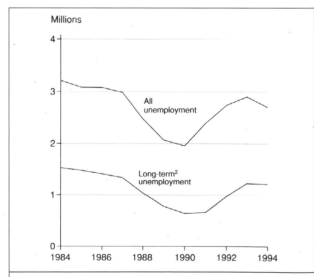

FIGURE 5.20: UK unemployment trends.
Source: *Social Trends 25*.

proportion of the UK's unemployed are **long-term unemployed** – that is, people who have been unemployed for at least a year.

The social and economic cost of unemployment is considerable. For the unemployed themselves, it means long periods on reduced incomes. They can also quickly become unfamiliar with current working practices which damages their prospects of re-employment. These factors can lead to a loss of confidence which makes it difficult for unemployed people to work again after prolonged periods of unemployment.

The lower incomes and the continuing stigma associated with unemployment can affect the health and social relationships of those who are without work.

THE EFFECTS ON COMMUNITIES

The changing patterns of employment have had significant social effects. The rise in the number of working women represents a real change; a generation ago, most women remained in the home as 'housewives'. For those households in which both partners work, the result in many cases has been higher incomes and enhanced living standards. As more women work, there has been a demand for new services like child-minding and nurseries.

One reason for the rise in unemployment has been the decline of a number of major manufacturing industries. The impact on those communities affected is a decline in prosperity, with other firms closing when the major industries shut down. For many smaller firms, the steel plants, textile mills and coal mines were major customers and some do not survive once the major industries close down. In these areas, all firms suffer as families cut spending in line with their incomes.

In areas with high levels of unemployment, communities suffer. They can become depressed, shabby and subject to increasing crime levels from those with little else to do. People will become part of the underground economy to protect their benefit entitlements. The health of these populations is often poor relative to more prosperous areas where people can afford better food and housing.

Ultimately the young, the skilled and the more enterprising move away from areas of high unemployment. They leave communities which are ageing and poor, in which people may have little sense of well-being.

THE EFFECTS ON GOVERNMENT REVENUE AND EXPENDITURE

The trend towards more people working part-time and the rise in unemployment hits the government twice in financial terms. First, income from taxation declines as the unemployed are not liable for income tax and those in part-time employment earn less and so pay less tax. At the same time, higher unemployment causes increased government expenditure on social security benefits. So the government faces higher expenditure as its income falls. This is one of the reasons which has led to the government reviewing its expenditure on social security.

Cutting benefits may not entirely solve the problem. It may encourage the underground economy. Low levels of benefits may push some unemployed people to supplement their benefits with some undeclared income – on which, of course, the government receives no tax revenue.

One bright point arising from the developing employment trend is that the government is enjoying a rising tax yield from women in employment and also from the self-employed. This will help offset the loss of tax income resulting from the decline of full-time employment.

PORTFOLIO ASSIGNMENT

This assignment requires you to write a report about the changing employment patterns in your area. As part of your investigation, you should focus in detail on particular industries. Choose at least one service industry and one manufacturing industry.

TASK 1

You first need to research your report. You need information on:

- ⊗ employment trends in local industries;

- ⊗ trends in full-time and part-time employment;

- ⊗ pay rates for a variety of occupations and industries.

You will need to draw on a number of sources. Approach your local council for information, possibly through its economic development office. Another useful source of information on the local labour market will be your Training and Enterprise Council.

You may need to find additional information on the national trends in specific industries. Follow up the sources of employment data listed in this unit (see page 297). You may also draw on the statistical information given in this element.

TASK 2

Write your report when you have obtained sufficient information, including detailed material on your chosen industries. It should be a formal report backed up by statistical data. Use statistical appendices as necessary. Your report should cover:

- ⊗ the changing pattern of local employment, including a focus on part-time and full-time employment and male and female employment;

- ⊗ pay rates and pay differentials between the various groups that make up the workforce;

- ⊗ a detailed investigation of the employment patterns in selected industries (including one service and one manufacturing industry);

- ⊗ an analysis of the implications of the changing employment patterns for employed and unemployed people;

- ⊗ a discussion of how the changes might affect local communities – for example, consider the possible consequences of greater female employment;

- ⊗ an assessment of the impact of changing employment patterns on the government, including the effect on tax revenue and the implications for the social security budget.

Examine the competitiveness of UK industry

THE PERFORMANCE OF THE UK ECONOMY

There are several ways of measuring the performance of the UK economy in relation to other developed economies. We will therefore use a variety of economic indicators to make this international comparison. Each of these indicators is in some way affected by the competitiveness of UK producers.

ECONOMIC GROWTH

Economic growth takes place when the value of the total output of the economy increases in real terms over a period of time. One measure of the output of the economy is **gross domestic product (GDP)**.

The performance of the UK economy in terms of its overall rate of economic growth can be a useful way of assessing the competitiveness of UK industry in relation to its major competitors. If a rise in the level of consumer spending leads to a similar rise in the total output of the UK economy, then this suggests that both consumers and those buying on behalf of firms see the output of UK firms

as representing value for money. An increase is likely to create more jobs and, therefore, produce a fall in unemployment. Economic growth raises the average level of household income and, therefore, improves living standards.

Rising income does not necessarily benefit the UK economy. There is a danger that much of it will be spent on imported goods and services reducing any beneficial impact on UK businesses. The UK economy suffered from rising imports during the prosperity enjoyed in the late 1980s. This may reflect a lack of competitiveness on the part of UK producers.

Even if UK producers can compete on price and quality, a large and sudden rise in consumer spending may lead to higher imports if producers do not have the capacity or skilled labour to meet this demand. This may be caused by a lack of investment in an earlier period. UK producers will, therefore, be less competitive on delivery dates; once customers are lost, it may be very difficult to regain them.

The UK's economic growth rate compared with other industrial economies is shown in *Fig. 5.21*. The negative figures, for example in 1990 and 1991, show that the UK's economy experienced a reduction in output. This is known as a **recession**.

ACTIVITY

Talk to your grandparents or other older relatives. Ask them about their lives half a century or so ago.

What were their luxuries?

What did they eat during the course of a normal day or week?

What forms of entertainment were available to them?

Reflect on the ways in which our standards of living have improved today. What reasons can you think of to explain this improvement?

Economic growth rates

Year	Industrial countries	France	Germany	Italy	Japan	UK	USA
1979	3.5	3.2	4.0	6.1	5.6	2.8	2.5
1980	0.9	1.6	1.0	4.1	3.5	−2.1	−0.5
1981	1.3	1.2	0.1	0.6	3.4	−1.3	1.8
1982	−0.1	2.5	−1.1	0.2	3.4	1.7	−2.2
1983	2.6	0.7	1.9	1.0	2.8	3.7	3.9
1984	4.5	1.3	3.1	2.7	4.3	2.3	6.2
1985	3.2	1.9	1.8	2.6	5.2	3.8	3.2
1986	2.7	2.5	2.2	2.9	2.6	4.3	2.9
1987	3.2	2.3	1.5	3.1	4.3	4.8	3.1
1988	4.4	4.5	3.7	4.1	6.2	5.0	3.9
1989	3.2	4.3	4.0	2.9	4.8	2.2	2.5
1990	2.0	2.5	4.9	2.1	4.8	0.4	0.8
1991	0.3	0.8	3.6	1.3	2.2	−2.2	−1.2
1992	1.9	1.2	0.8	0.9	1.3	−0.6	3.4
1993	1.8	−0.9	−2.1	–	−0.1	2.0	3.0

FIGURE 5.21: Growth of real GDP.
Source: *Economic Review - 1995 data supplement.*

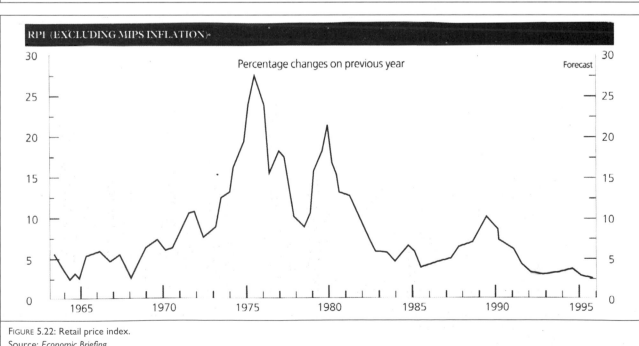

FIGURE 5.22: Retail price index.
Source: *Economic Briefing.*

INFLATION

Inflation describes the increase in the level of prices over time and the corresponding fall in the purchasing power of money. Since 1990, inflation has been much lower than the average for the previous 20 years (see *Fig. 5.22*).

High rates of inflation put businesses in the country concerned at a competitive disadvantage. Clearly, if a company's prices are rising more rapidly than those of its overseas rivals then it is likely to lose custom and, in all probability, profits.

ACTIVITY

Working in groups of two or three, make a list of the factors – other than price – that consumers may take into account when choosing a consumer durable. In what ways does the relative importance of price vary according to the product in question?

When seeking to measure what has happened to living standards it is important to take account of inflation. If, for example, the average level of household income has risen by 5 per cent when inflation is 3.5 per cent, then the rise in real income and spending power is only 1.5 per cent. All economies suffer from inflation but, as *Fig. 5.23* shows, their actual rates can differ considerably.

	UK	Germany	France	Italy	EU average	USA	Japan
1987	4.2	0.2	3.1	4.8	3.3	3.7	0.1
1988	4.9	1.3	2.6	5.0	3.6	4.1	0.7
1989	7.8	2.8	3.7	6.3	5.1	4.8	2.3
1990	9.4	2.7	3.4	6.5	5.7	5.4	3.1
1991	5.9	3.5	3.2	6.2	5.0	4.2	3.3
1992	3.8	4.0	2.3	5.2	4.2	3.1	1.7
1993	1.6	4.2	2.1	4.4	3.4	2.9	1.3
1994	2.5	3.0	1.8	4.0	3.1	2.6	0.7

FIGURE 5.23: Retail prices.
Source: *National Institute Economic Review.*

The UK government is concerned about the rate of inflation because a relatively high rate of inflation compared to other economies will damage the UK's international trading position. Retailers and wholesalers will find imported consumer goods more competitively priced; indeed UK producers themselves will increasingly turn to foreign suppliers of parts, components and equipment. At the same time, UK exports will become less competitive in overseas markets.

INVESTMENT

An important factor (and, perhaps, the most important factor) in making an economy competitive is the amount which firms are willing to invest in **plant**, **equipment**, **machinery** and **premises**. This kind of spending not only increases capacity, allowing firms to produce more, but can lead to significant improvements in both productivity and quality. By investing in the latest

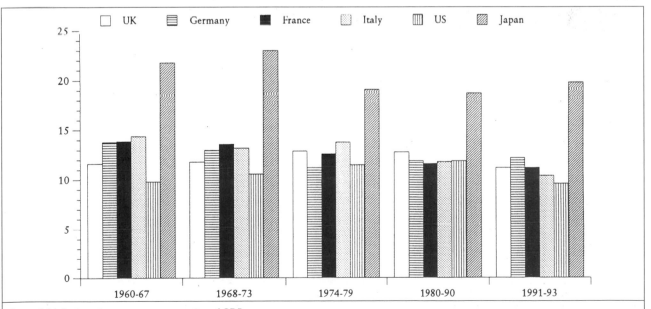

FIGURE 5.24: Business investment as a proportion of GDP.
Source: *National Institute Economic Review.*

technology, firms can produce higher quality goods more efficiently. *Fig. 5.24* shows that the UK's record on investment has improved relative to other major economies.

Investment in machinery and equipment by the manufacturing sector is seen as a particularly important factor in increasing productivity and stimulating economic growth. Businesses also increasingly recognise the importance of investing in staff training.

Many firms borrow money to finance their investment programmes. A rise in interest rates, which makes borrowed money more expensive, reduces the level of investment and damages the productivity of UK industry. During most of the post-war period, UK industry has experienced frequent changes in interest rates leading to fluctuations in the level of investment and variations in productivity improvements.

| | Interest rates | |
	Basic rate	Mortgage rate
1985	12.2	13.2
1986	10.9	11.8
1987	9.7	11.6
1988	10.1	10.9
1989	13.8	13.6
1990	14.8	15.1
1991	11.7	13.0
1992	9.6	10.8
1993	6.0	8.1
1994	5.5	7.8

FIGURE 5.25: Interest rates.
Source: *National Institute Economic Review.*

The UK has become an attractive location for many foreign companies. About 35 per cent of all Japanese investment in Europe comes to the UK. In 1993, foreign-owned companies employed nearly 20 per cent of the workforce and were responsible for about 40 per cent of the UK's exports of manufactures and one third of all capital investment in the manufacturing sector.

There has been significant inward investment in the car industry. Nissan, Toyota and Honda have all set up motor vehicle plants on greenfield sites and, as they have increased sales in both the UK and export markets, they have invested in extra capacity.

Foreign-owned companies and in particular those from Japan contribute to the competitiveness of UK firms through a number of spillover effects. In order to win contracts to supply these leading-edge companies, UK producers must meet such high quality standards that they also become much more competitive. They are in a better position to win business from overseas producers and gain market share elsewhere.

UK firms take on board new management styles. The Japanese approach to training and industrial relations has lessons for how to make more efficient use of the UK workforce. Foreign companies setting up new factories will use the opportunity to introduce the latest technology. Again, this carries lessons for UK firms and demonstrates the advantages of investment.

PRODUCTIVITY

We discussed the ways in which productivity can be measured at the beginning of this unit. If you are unsure about this concept, you should re-read the first section of element 1.

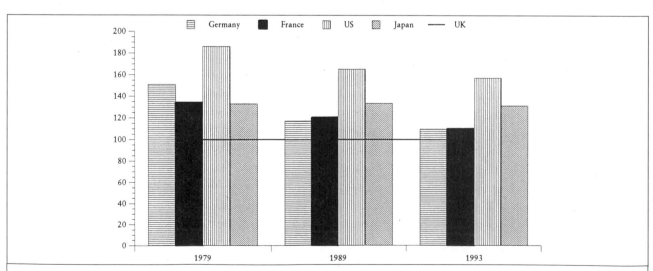

FIGURE 5.26: Manufacturing productivity.
Source: *National Institute Economic Review.*

Countries which regularly record improvements in the productivity of labour above the average for other economies will continue to strengthen their competitive positions. If, for example, a country has a manufacturing sector which records average annual improvements in productivity of 5 per cent, then unit costs and prices are likely to be relatively stable. This is because the average employer can meet pay increases of up to 5 per cent without suffering a rise in unit labour costs and needing to raise prices.

Countries with above average improvements in productivity also tend to have very low inflation. They are not likely to suffer from the very high wage demands which contribute to large price rises and a loss of competitiveness. This is because the overall rise in productivity not only makes more goods available but the extra production must mean a rise in income for those whose labour, capital and enterprise have been used in achieving the extra output.

Fig. 5.26 shows the extent to which productivity in the UK's manufacturing sector has been below that of other countries at various times since 1979. In 1979, for example, manufacturing productivity in France was about 35 per cent higher than that in the UK. This gap had closed to about 14 per cent in 1993.

ACTIVITY

1 **List the various factors which are likely to improve the productivity of labour in the manufacturing sector.**

2 **Imagine that you are a producer of manufactured goods in the UK. What benefits do you think that your business would enjoy if your productivity continually exceeded that of your competitors?**

EXPORTS

Exports provide perhaps the sternest test of the competitiveness of UK producers. When UK firms sell their products in overseas markets or provide services to foreigners, they have to compete against producers from all over the world. In recent years, the UK has faced increasing competition from the developing countries of the Far East such as South Korea, Malaysia and Hong Kong.

ACTIVITY

Using a library, research the share of world exports held by the UK in the period since the end of the Second World War. Identify the countries which have achieved a rising share of world trade over the same period.

Reflect upon what you have read earlier and comment upon the reasons for the changing share of world exports that you have researched.

THE EXCHANGE RATE

The exchange rate can be defined as the price of one currency expressed in terms of other currencies.

ACTIVITY

Use today's newspaper and find out the value of the pound in terms of the following currencies:

- ⊗ **French franc;**
- ⊗ **Spanish peseta;**
- ⊗ **US dollar;**
- ⊗ **German deutschmark;**
- ⊗ **Japanese yen.**

Research how the value of the pound against these currencies has altered over the past year.

The overall movement in the value of a country's currency over a period of years can also be used to assess the performance of an economy in relation to its major competitors. A high productivity, low inflation economy will be supplying goods and services which are very much in demand abroad. This will generate a high demand for its currency on foreign exchange markets as importers buy the currency to pay for its goods and services. Since a highly competitive economy will have a relatively low level of imported goods and services, the amount of its own currency being sold on foreign exchange markets to buy other currencies to pay for its imports will also be low. Thus, for a highly competitive economy, the amount of its own currency supplied to foreign exchange markets will be less than the amount demanded by the importers of its good and services. This will increase the 'price' of its currency as its currency will be relatively scarce.

The competitiveness of the German, US and Japanese economies therefore is a major reason why, in the long term, the pound has fallen in value against the deutschmark, dollar and yen. For example, the UK has generally imported more from Germany than it has exported; therefore, the supply of pounds onto foreign exchange

markets to buy deutschmarks is higher than the demand for pounds from Germans who wish to buy UK goods. As a consequence the value of the pound has fallen against the deutschmark. The overall movement in the value of the pound against major currencies is shown in *Fig. 5.27*.

BUSINESS STRATEGIES TO IMPROVE COMPETITIVENESS

In order to be as competitive as possible, firms should be continuously looking for ways of saving on costs or exploiting new market opportunities. In some cases, savings on costs and increased sales can be achieved without having to invest in the kinds of capital programmes that protect or improve competitiveness in the long term. Here are just some examples of how different departments or sections in a company can seek to improve competitiveness as part of their everyday work.

- **The purchasing department** should keep up to date with developments in markets for materials, parts, components and other inputs.

- **Workers may feel more motivated** to give the best of their ability if there is a mechanism for employee consultation; this might be the responsibility of the personnel or human resources department.

- **The market research department** should monitor trends in consumer tastes and preferences, the potential implications of social, demographic and economic changes, and the marketing strategies adopted by the company's competitors.

To achieve a more significant and longer-term improvement in competitiveness however, producers generally have to invest significant amounts of money. It usually takes some time before a return is achieved in the form of increased competitiveness and higher sales and profits. We will now concentrate on these longer-term strategies. They have attracted a great deal of attention in recent years. UK producers are likely to have to place a great deal of emphasis in the future on long-term strategies to improve their competitiveness.

IMPROVING QUALITY OF PRODUCTS AND SERVICES

As we saw in element 1, quality has become an increasingly important factor in the business world during the 1980s and 1990s. Japanese manufacturing companies have led the way in implementing new quality systems.

Year	US$/£	DM/£	Yen/£
1971	2.44	8.53	885.00
1972	2.50	7.98	752.00
1973	2.45	6.54	665.00
1974	2.34	6.05	683.00
1975	2.22	5.45	658.00
1976	1.80	4.55	535.00
1977	1.75	4.05	468.00
1978	1.92	3.85	403.00
1979	2.12	3.89	466.00
1980	2.33	4.23	526.00
1981	2.03	4.56	445.00
1982	1.75	4.24	435.00
1983	1.52	3.87	360.00
1984	1.34	3.79	317.00
1985	1.30	3.78	307.10
1986	1.47	3.18	246.80
1987	1.64	2.94	236.50
1988	1.78	3.12	227.98
1989	1.64	3.08	225.66
1990	1.79	2.88	257.38
1991	1.77	2.93	237.56
1992	1.77	2.75	224.00
1993	1.50	2.48	167.00
1994	1.53	2.48	156.40

Exchange rates (annual average)

FIGURE 5.27: The long-term fall in the value of the pound. Source: *Economic Review*.

Quality assurance tries to ensure that the customer is satisfied, with the aim of generating greater sales, value added and profits.

Total quality management attempts to create a culture of quality within an organisation. It aims to affect the behaviour of every employee within the organisation. Managers try to introduce a quality philosophy by getting each group or department within the business to think of those that they work for as customers as well as colleagues. As a result, they should aim to supply the best possible service to their colleagues. In this way, the overall quality of the business's product or service is improved.

Total quality management achieves change relatively slowly. It may involve the use of quality circles and discussion groups to help focus employees' thoughts upon achieving quality.

BS EN ISO 9000 is the new title for the main quality system standard. It replaces the old British Standard BS 5750. The new title reflects European (EN) and world-wide (ISO) recognition for this system, which was originally developed in the UK.

To obtain this certification, a supplier is required to establish, document and maintain an effective and economical quality system to ensure and demonstrate that the firm's materials, components and products conform to the specified requirements.

Critics consider that this system is a bureaucratic nightmare, but supporters believe it achieves reliable quality standards. Whatever the rights and wrongs, over 20,000 UK firms have achieved this certification.

TRAINING AND DEVELOPMENT

One of the factors which can prevent UK producers from taking full advantage of market opportunities both at home and abroad is a shortage of skilled workers. During the consumer spending boom of the late 1980s, for example, the skills shortages experienced by UK industry restricted the growth of output and forced more buyers to turn to imports. The skills shortages and the resulting bidding up of wages were also an important factor in the loss of price competitiveness.

During a period of depressed sales and falling profits, many firms may be tempted to make financial savings by cutting their training budgets. *Fig. 5.28* shows that when the recession took a hold in 1990 there was a decline in the number of employees receiving training. By cutting back on training, companies limit their ability to improve production techniques with consequent adverse implications for productivity and competitiveness.

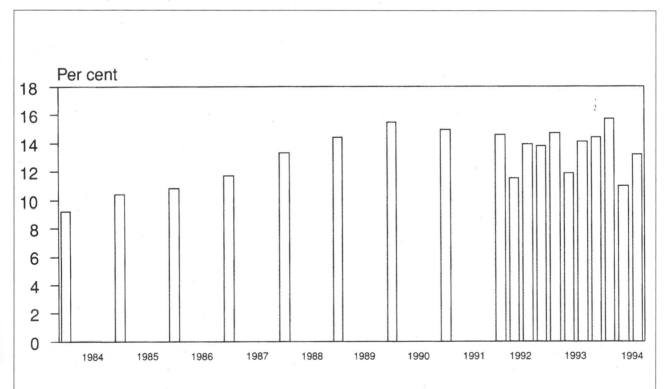

FIGURE 5.28: Percentage of employees receiving job-related training.
Source: *Skills and Enterprise Network*, Department for Education and Employment.

There are other important reasons why the training of employees and the development of management and supervisory skills improves competitiveness.

- **A lack of the necessary skills** as a firm seeks to expand may lead to a fall in productivity, a decline in quality, more output being scrapped or having to be made good, frequent breakdowns in machinery and more complaints from customers.

- **If the existing workforce can acquire a greater knowledge and range of skills,** then a firm has greater flexibility and can make more productive use of its workforce. This is particularly important when a producer has plans to introduce new working practices designed to trim the workforce in certain operations and cut labour costs.

- **Seeking a competitive advantage,** for example through a new design or improved performance, may involve changes to the final product or service. This may require new kinds of skills to match changes in the relevant processes or operations.

- **Training and development programmes** can help to increase job satisfaction and motivation. This not only helps to reduce labour turnover and absenteeism but also improves quality and productivity.

- **A skills development programme** is vital to ensure that a producer can make the most efficient use of capital investment projects which use the latest technology and which involve new production methods and skills.

NEW TECHNOLOGY AND RESEARCH AND DEVELOPMENT

Technological advance is so rapid that if a producer fails to research, develop or apply new technologies then its products or services will soon become outdated. Spending on **research and development (R&D)** must be maintained. Once the effort is relaxed and a rival establishes a competitive advantage, the rate of technological advance is such that it becomes very difficult to re-enter a particular field of R&D in an attempt to catch up.

In high-technology economies, spending on R&D is needed to produce new and improved products and materials. R&D is also needed to design new plant, machinery and equipment, and production processes which exploit the latest technology and raise the productivity of labour.

A growing part of world trade is in high-technology **capital goods**. These are goods such as lathes and production-line equipment used to produce other products. In 1994, for example, nearly 41 per cent of both the UK's exports and imports were capital goods. It is vital, therefore, that a firm involved in the design, development and manufacture of capital goods also invests in R&D in order to increase its share of the market for plant, machinery and equipment.

Only three UK companies appear in the world's top fifty companies, ranked in terms of spending on research and development. These are ICI, Glaxo and Shell Transport and Trading. Although spending on R&D per head of the

	% of GDP on R&D	% of private sector expenditure on R&D financed by government	Government expenditure on R&D as % of GDP
UK	2.22	13.8	0.87
Germany	2.50	9.8	1.00
France	2.40	18.3	1.27
Italy	1.31	9.9	0.79
USA	2.81	20.3	1.11
Japan	3.00	1.1	0.48*

*Excludes R&D in the social sciences and humanities

FIGURE 5.29: Government spending on research and development.
Source: Organisation for Economic Co-operation and Development (OECD).

population in the UK is only 20 per cent less than that of both Germany and France, it is about 40 per cent less than Japan and 45 per cent less than in the USA. Spending by the UK government to promote R&D is shown in *Fig. 5.29*. These figures include government spending on defence-related R&D. Defence-related expenditure accounts for about 45 per cent of UK government R&D spending compared with 33.5 per cent in France, 8.5 per cent in Germany and 6.1 per cent in Japan.

⊗ ACTIVITY

Select four products/services from the following list:

- ⊗ **air travel;**
- ⊗ **television programmes;**
- ⊗ **energy generation;**
- ⊗ **personal computers;**
- ⊗ **motor vehicles ;**
- ⊗ **telephones;**
- ⊗ **supermarkets;**
- ⊗ **music;**
- ⊗ **banking.**

Investigate how the products you have selected have been affected by new technology. Consider areas such as product innovation, production methods, materials and processes. Produce a report on your findings and, where possible, include photographs from magazines and brochures that feature your goods/services.

WAGES AND SALARY LEVELS

Because labour costs make up such a large part of a firm's total costs, any developments which moderate pay rises or help a firm to make more efficient use of its workforce will help to make the firm more competitive. A fall in unit labour costs can benefit a firm in several ways.

- ⊗ **If prices are kept at their existing levels,** then profit margins will widen. This means more funds available to finance future investment programmes.

- ⊗ **If the firm is operating in a market where sales are very sensitive to price changes,** then the

lower unit labour cost will allow a price cut without eating into the profit margin.

- ⊗ **The lower unit labour cost** may help to offset rises in other production costs.

It is for these reasons that employers are concerned about wage levels. They want to be free to manage their workforce in the most productive way. During the 1980s, employers supported the government's policy of reducing the power of trade unions. The trade unions were held mainly responsible for firms having to pay excessively high wage rates. These fed through into high prices and inflation. The government hoped that the reduction in trade union power would help the labour market to operate more like the markets for products and services. If, for example, there are more workers willing to supply their labour at current wage rates than employers want to hire – in other words, supply exceeds demand – then market forces should force wage rates down. Only when there are shortages of certain kinds of workers should the labour market produce a rise in wage rates.

	US	Japan	France	Germany	UK
1985	91.9	93.6	92.4	93.2	86.3
1986	95.3	97.2	96.4	96.7	93.3
1987	100.0	99.9	100.0	100.0	100.0
1988	105.7	104.0	104.4	103.2	108.2
1989	109.7	109.6	109.3	106.2	117.8
1990	115.9	116.7	115.3	111.4	129.0
1991	120.1	123.5	120.8	103.3	139.7
1992	126.1	126.8	126.2	112.7	147.7
1993	129.0	129.5	129.7	116.7	153.2
1994	133.0	132.4	132.3	119.7	157.6

FIGURE 5.30: Index of average earnings.

⊗ ACTIVITY

1 **Using the information in *Fig. 5.30* calculate the rate of increase of annual earnings for each economy.**

2 **Explain why you would need additional information in order to assess the effects of these increases in average earnings on the competitiveness of each economy.**

THE PROBLEM OF INDUSTRY-WIDE PAY INCREASES

Employers have argued that the collective bargaining power of trade unions and the threat of industrial action has led to excessive wage increases in sectors where trade unions have been strong. These increases were often regarded as excessive because they were seen as being above the level that could be justified by the profitability and productivity of the particular business sector. An industry-wide pay settlement also takes no account of the financial or competitive position of individual employers. This means, for example, that an employer might be faced with granting a pay increase which, given the competition from other local employers, was much higher than the level needed to retain or recruit certain kinds of labour. The wage rate would be above the rate that would be produced by the interaction of demand and supply in the local labour market.

Many UK employers regarded union power and the resulting increase in wage levels as a major reason why they found it difficult to compete on price with overseas producers. It was also argued that lower wage levels would encourage companies to take on more workers. Excessive pay rises were, therefore, partly to blame for the persistently high level of unemployment.

THE SHIFT TOWARDS LOCAL PAY SETTLEMENTS

By the early 1990s, prolonged unemployment and changes to the laws relating to trade unions had greatly reduced the bargaining power of unions. *Fig. 5.31* shows a sharp fall in the growth of unit labour costs.

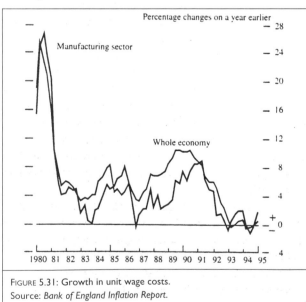

FIGURE 5.31: Growth in unit wage costs.
Source: *Bank of England Inflation Report.*

These developments have helped to produce a shift away from industry-wide negotiations on pay and conditions in favour of settlements on a local basis between employers and local trade union representatives. From the point of view of the employer, local pay agreements should bring advantages. Wage rates for particular kinds of workers will more closely reflect local labour market conditions. So a company in an area with relatively high unemployment for example would not expect to pay the same rate for the job as employers in areas where there are labour shortages.

Local agreements will be particularly important for companies which operate from several sites in different parts of the country. The larger pay increases needed to retain and recruit workers in those areas where certain skills are in short supply will not have to be paid to all employees.

PRODUCTIVITY AGREEMENTS

The decline in trade union power and the shift to local pay settlements has also increased the scope for **performance-related pay deals**. Companies might try to avoid rises in unit labour costs and so become more price competitive by linking pay increases to improvements in productivity. If, for example, there is an increase in productivity of 5 per cent and pay rates are increased by the same percentage, then the 5 per cent increase in total labour costs is spread over a 5 per cent increase in output. A pay rise of say 8 per cent however would increase unit labour costs by about 3 per cent.

PAY AND PROFITS

In a motor vehicle factory it is relatively easy to measure the physical productivity of various groups of workers and so link pay to performance. In the service sector it is more difficult to measure output and a different approach may have to be taken. A retail group, for example, may introduce pay increases related to the overall performance of the business rather than try to measure the extent to which individual employees have contributed to extra sales or cost-saving schemes. The company may therefore introduce a **profit-related pay scheme**. As with productivity agreements, profit-related pay is also a way of recognising that the overall improvement in a company's performance is very largely linked to the way in which its employees go about their work and deal with customers or clients.

POTENTIAL ADVANTAGES OF PERFORMANCE-RELATED PAY

Apart from the benefits already described in relation to unit labour costs and competitiveness, there are other points in favour of linking pay to performance. It gives employees a direct stake in the success of the business or the work of their department, section or team. They will recognise that at least part of their future income is directly linked to an improved performance by the company. Employers and employees will have a mutual interest in the future of the company and this will help to remove the 'them and us' attitude that has tended to produce conflict between management and workers. Some companies have also sought to involve the workforce by having employee representatives on their board in order to emphasise the stake which they have in the future competitiveness of the company.

Performance-related pay should improve motivation. Management will find that the workforce is much more willing to accept changes in working methods and practices. Previously, employees may have treated such changes with great suspicion and seen them largely as the means by which management could make some of them redundant. Performance-related pay, however, can produce a more positive view of such changes because the resulting improvement in productivity and quality will mean both higher pay and more secure jobs as the company strengthens its position in the market. Employees will also show greater enthusiasm for training and development programmes as well as becoming more involved in quality circles and suggestion schemes.

Trade unions have generally prevented pay from being cut during a period of slack demand and falling sales revenue. Since firms could not cut pay, they have only been able to reduce labour costs by making some workers redundant. With performance-related pay, however, it is claimed that employers will be under less pressure to lay people off and jobs will be more secure. If profits fall, companies may be able to freeze or reduce wage and salary levels. So, a loss of sales revenue may be partly compensated by a fall in total labour costs.

MINIMUM WAGES

As part of its policy of shaking up the labour market and making pay more responsive to market forces, the government finally abolished the remaining wages councils in 1993. These bodies had previously set minimum wage rates for a large number of industries. With their abolition, the UK differed from most European Union countries and the USA in having no legally enforceable minimum wage. These other countries either have a national minimum wage or agreements with unions which set the minimum level for different sectors.

The government is particularly concerned about the effects of a minimum wage on the competitiveness of UK producers in relation to producers overseas. However, there are a number of other arguments made to support the abolition of minimum wages. A key contention is that minimum wages **cost jobs**. If companies are forced to pay higher wages to comply with a legal minimum wage, it is argued that they will finance the increase by employing fewer people. Similarly, it is claimed that companies would employ more people if they could do so at a lower wage rate. Having to pay a minimum wage to young people, in particular, is said to be an important factor behind **youth unemployment**.

It is also argued that introducing a minimum wage will be **inflationary**. A minimum wage will reduce the gap between the lowest paid and the next group of workers in the wages ladder. Different groups of workers have traditionally sought to maintain pay differentials; a minimum wage could trigger off a knock-on effect as other workers demand a pay rise to restore wage differentials. This would mean a loss of price competitiveness in other sectors of the economy.

Finally, critics argue that a minimum wage is **unenforceable**. A minimum wage cannot necessarily be enforced where unions are weak or non-existent. Unscrupulous employers will simply give their employees the choice of either taking what is on offer or finding another job. There will also be employers who opt to operate in the black economy in order to avoid the wage regulations. The government will lose tax revenue through evasion. Businesses in the black economy will exist without the knowledge of those who inspect and enforce health and safety regulations; employees could be at risk in such an unregulated working environment.

There are alternative views on a minimum wage. Supporters of a minimum wage argue that low wages do not always benefit companies. They affect the morale and motivation of the workforce and, perhaps, encourage absenteeism. Productivity suffers and unit labour costs may actually rise.

It is also argued that it runs counter to the UK's long-term economic interests to encourage a low-wage economy. If companies in the manufacturing sector in particular can rely upon low wages to be competitive, there is less pressure to innovate and introduce the kind of technology which is important in promoting competitiveness in the long run. In any case, the UK cannot expect to compete on the basis of low wages with the growing number of cheap labour economies in the developing world such as China. An emphasis on low wages just diverts attention from the need to move into higher value added products.

Some dispute the arguments about job losses. If all the companies in a particular sector such as catering are faced with the same minimum wage, it is argued that they will all be under the same pressure to raise their prices. If the total market demand remains about the same, then there will be no job losses and the increased wage has simply been funded by consumers paying higher prices. The net effect, therefore, is a transfer of total purchasing power from customers to catering employees. Since total spending power in the economy as a whole is unchanged there should be no effect on total employment.

The potential effect of a minimum wage upon international competitiveness may not be a major factor because a large number of low-wage jobs are in the service sector. Here many businesses like shops, restaurants, hotels and cleaning companies do not compete with foreign companies in the UK market. A large number of low-paid jobs are also found in the public sector. Again, there is no direct international competition and pay rises can be funded by taxation.

Finally, the introduction of a minimum wage will not necessarily mean a loss of jobs to overseas producers if UK companies have to compete mainly with producers in countries where similar minimum wage levels exist such as the economies of the European Union.

ACTIVITY

Organise yourselves into two opposing groups to discuss the issue of a national minimum wage. Debate the following propositions:

(a) It is the responsibility of the government and not business to deal with poverty among the low paid.

(b) There is a moral argument for introducing minimum pay rates: nearly 17 per cent of women workers get paid less than £4 an hour compared with 8 per cent of men.

(c) If a minimum wage lifted the pay of a group of cleaners or bar staff from say £3.50 to £4.00 an hour, then some of them are bound to be made redundant.

(d) Companies that can only compete against cheap labour imports from the newly industrialising countries by paying their own workers very low wages will not survive for long anyway.

(e) Firms will hesitate to take on young workers if they are obliged to pay a national minimum wage.

A MORE FLEXIBLE WORKFORCE

We looked at labour market flexibility in element 2. We saw that achieving greater flexibility in the labour market allows firms to alter more easily the amount of labour which they employ in line with how busy they are.

Some employment legislation can make it difficult for businesses to use their labour force flexibly. It can be argued, for example, that employment protection legislation makes it difficult for a firm to lay off workers during periods of falling demand. Firms may also have problems in reducing unit labour costs, so making it difficult for them to offer the kinds of price cuts needed to compete for a falling number of customers. It can also be argued that employment protection rights discourage firms from taking on extra workers when demand is rising. Firms do not want to recruit staff, only to find it difficult to lay off workers if there is a fall off in sales.

Because employment protection rights are weaker for part-time employees, it is easier to lay-off such workers. This may be one of the factors behind the growth of part-time employment. It is also easier to alter the hours of part-time workers in response changes in demand. In recent years, for example, the Burton retail group shed 2,000 full-time jobs and replaced them with about 3,000 part-time positions.

Employers can achieve further flexibility in the employment of labour by offering jobs on fixed-term contracts. This gives them the option of not renewing contracts if they wish to cut labour costs sometime in future. The duration of a fixed-term contract can also be set so that the worker's period of continuous employment is too short to qualify for employment protection rights.

Companies may also seek to shed employees in favour of buying in the same kinds of skills from people who are self-employed. In 1994, just over 3 million people, one in eight workers, were self-employed. By using self-employed workers, companies can employ fewer people themselves and, instead, buy in services only for as long as they are needed.

ACTIVITY

Assume that you work for a retail organisation like Burton. It intends to replace many full-time jobs with part-time jobs.

1 As a senior member of the personnel department, produce a letter of no more than 350 words to be sent to employees

clearly listing the various reasons why the future of the company depends upon greater part-time employment. In your letter, explain why it is also in the interests of employees that they should accept the firm's decision.

2 You are asked for your views on the possible effects of this strategy upon labour turnover, staff morale, the quality of customer service, the calibre of new employees and the company's training programme. Respond in the form of a memorandum to the head of human resource management.

MERGERS AND TAKEOVERS

As *Fig. 5.32* shows, mergers and takeovers are a regular occurrence. They often involve a strategy where one or both of the companies concerned seeks to gain a competitive advantage. By increasing the scale of their operations, firms can improve their competitiveness, gain greater control over suppliers and gain access to new markets.

When expansion takes the form of companies joining together it is known as **integration**.

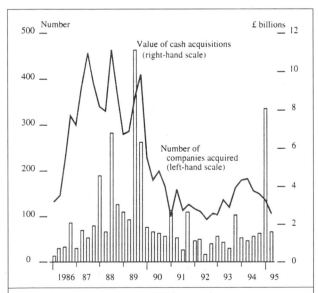

FIGURE 5.32: Aquisitions and mergers in the corporate sector.
Source: *Bank of England Inflation Report.*

HORIZONTAL INTEGRATION

Horizontal integration involves the joining of firms essentially in the same line of business into a single organisation. A number of examples of this type of merger have taken place in the financial sector; one example is the merger between the Halifax and Leeds building societies. Such a strategy is likely to provide opportunities to improve competitiveness through:

⊗ **rationalisation;**

⊗ **drawing on separate strengths;**

⊗ **economies of scale.**

Rationalisation programmes can be introduced to concentrate production in the most efficient factories or plant and high-cost units can be closed down. The remaining capacity should be better utilised as a result. Other areas where scope exists for rationalisation would be in transport and aspects of distribution and branch activity. For DIY chains and building societies, for example, mergers may lead to some outlets being closed to avoid the wasteful duplication of a service in the same area.

The rationalisation of other departments such as finance, marketing and personnel, for example, may also provide an ideal opportunity to introduce changes to the organisation's structure. This may involve setting up specialist divisions or the combining of operations, new management roles with a redistribution of responsibilities, new lines of communications and other changes aimed at trimming down management staff or the complete removal of certain layers of management.

Mergers may take place to draw on the **separate strengths** of individual firms. Two firms may recognise that each of them has a particular strength and that integration will produce a single but more competitive organisation. One firm, for example, may be strong on quality and product innovation while the other is widely recognised for its expertise in marketing and production management.

The larger output from a single organisation may lead to **economies of scale** which are not available to the separate producers. In particular, unit costs are likely to benefit from bulk buying and the introduction of plant and machinery with a purchase price and operating costs that do not increase in the same proportion as productive capacity.

VERTICAL INTEGRATION

Vertical integration involves mergers or takeovers between firms which have previously tended to concentrate on different stages in the production of a good or service. A building company, for example, may join with the manufacturers of building products and the suppliers of other building materials and then combine with a property company involved with the buying and development of land.

Vertical integration will benefit a producer in several ways. For example, if a motor vehicle manufacturer engages in **backward vertical integration** by merging with suppliers of materials and components, then its supplies will be more secure. Some industrial processes are more efficiently undertaken if carried out close to each other. Various stages in the production of metal, oil and chemical products, for example, need to be carried out at very high temperatures; energy, handling and transport costs can be saved if production is integrated and carried out on a single site.

Forward vertical integration involves mergers with a producer closer to the end product and the customers in the market. For example, a package tour operator may take over a string of travel agents in order to ensure that its own holidays are given as much exposure as possible. An airline that serves holiday destinations may acquire hotels in order to offer a wider service. In the manufacturing sector, a car maker may set up its own retail outlets or acquire existing businesses that can then be used to sell exclusively its own models. A television and video recorder manufacturer may set up its own video rental and direct selling business.

LATERAL INTEGRATION

Lateral integration is a strategy based on **diversification**. It is a strategy in which a firm widens the range of its output. For example, the Whitbread group has recently expanded its interests in the hotel and leisure industry by taking over the Happy Eater and Little Chef roadside restaurants.

A combination of factors may encourage the decision to compete in other markets. The same kinds of skills, parts and plant can be used for quite different products, so the motor-cycle producer Honda has diversified into petrol-driven lawn-mowers. The same retail outlets can be used; so DIY stores carry an increasing range of products with the 'Polycel' brand name ranging from paint stripper to secondary glazing systems.

Companies may diversify to exploit a high degree of brand loyalty and a logo that can be used to sell other products. Nike, the producer of sports trainers, has moved into clothing and accessories. Virgin has added air travel, condoms, a cola drink and an investment scheme to its

original interests that centred around the music business. Mars was the first of the confectionery producers to diversify into ice creams.

Diversification may also be motivated by a strategy designed to reduce the firm's reliance on a single product. Over the years, Walls has reduced its reliance on ice cream (which also tended to have a seasonal demand) and has added a range of both frozen and fresh food products to its range.

The experience gained in one market can be used to support diversification into other markets. So a company with a base in supplying and running pubs might move into other parts of the hospitality market such as restaurants, hotels and entertainment. Whitbread, for example, now has other interests such as TGI Friday, Travel Inns, Country Fayre, and less than 50 per cent of its profits now come from sales of beer.

ACTIVITY

Obtain copies of the annual report and accounts of a few large, well-known companies.

1 Find a company which is a good example of having expanded through a strategy based on integration. The names of subsidiary companies are usually listed in the back pages. The chairperson's report often refers to merger and takeover strategy and reports on the performance of subsidiaries.

2 Name some of the subsidiaries and describe how they might represent examples of various kinds of integration.

3 Explain what may have motivated some of the examples of integration.

4 Explain the reasons behind any integration involving an overseas operation.

GOVERNMENT STRATEGIES TO IMPROVE COMPETITIVENESS

The government has a number of methods through which it can improve the competitiveness of UK industry.

SUBSIDIES

One way for the government to make UK producers more competitive would be to give them large subsidies so that they could afford to charge lower prices than their overseas competitors. This, however, would be very expensive. It would mean higher taxes and it would tend to make UK producers very complacent if they were confident that the government would come to their rescue every time they experienced a rise in unit costs or needed capital to finance an improvement in competitiveness.

European Union policies are against state subsidies. The **single European market** seeks to ensure fair competition between member countries. As a founder member of the **World Trade Organisation**, the UK is committed to removing all distortions to trade. If the UK government did provide subsidies, it is likely to provoke other countries into a form of retaliation which could either restrict imports from the UK or involve subsidising their own producers.

Instead of using subsidies, governments have generally concentrated on measures which will neither reduce the incentive to be efficient nor upset our trading partners.

THE QUALITY OF THE WORKFORCE

TRAINING AND ENTERPRISE COUNCILS

In order to deal with the skills needs of particular industries and areas, the government set up the first Training and Enterprise Councils (TECs) in 1990. TECs are independent business-led companies funded by the government. Each TEC has a board of directors of around fifteen members; two-thirds must be from the private sector. They hope to attract directors with industrial and commercial expertise at a high level, such as chief executives or managing directors of local firms. Other directors may come from local government, education and the unions. TECs' staff are drawn from industrial, commercial and public sector backgrounds.

There are 81 TECs in England and Wales. (There are similar organisations in Scotland called Local Enterprise Companies.) They are responsible for analysing **local training needs** and **skills shortages**. They identify appropriate training schemes on offer from both public and private sector organisations. TECs, therefore, act as a kind of broker in that they bring together those that need training with those that supply it. They also encourage training networks which bring together employers' expertise and allow a sharing of training facilities. In order to assess the needs of the local labour market, TECs must consider skills shortages, likely areas of employment growth, the impact of new technology and the industries that are likely to be attracted to the area.

TECs are involved in the operation of government-backed schemes such as the **enterprise allowance** (for unemployed people setting up in business on their own), **youth training**, **youth credits** and **modern apprenticeships**. They also act very much on their own initiative. In 1994, for example, the Hertfordshire TEC offered more than twelve programmes covering many aspects of youth training and vocational education, over twenty-two programmes concerned with adult training, about twenty kinds of business services to help local enterprise as well as eight special projects such as promoting equal opportunities in local businesses and offering advice on setting up work-based nurseries to help returners to the workforce.

INVESTORS IN PEOPLE

TECs are also responsible for assessing firms that wish to be recognised publicly as 'Investors in People'. The idea behind the initiative is that investing in people is one of the most effective ways of improving business performance. To gain recognition as an Investor in People, companies must meet exacting training standards.

Regardless of its particular business objectives, a firm is likely to benefit in general from being an Investor in People. Improvements can be expected in areas such as quality, motivation and customer satisfaction. A firm should gain a reputation for being a well-organised and efficient company. This can enhance a business's standing and help it to recruit employees.

NATIONAL VOCATIONAL QUALIFICATIONS

National Vocational Qualifications (NVQs) are occupational qualifications based upon an employee's ability to achieve a certain level of skill or competence in carrying out various tasks connected with their particular occupation. The basis for awarding an NVQ is an assessment of an employee's level of competence and any necessary underpinning knowledge according to 'evidence' from his or her workplace.

NVQs form the basis of **education and training targets** endorsed by the government. One target is that by 1997 some 80 per cent of young people in the 16 to 24 age group should achieve NVQ level 2 (or its academic equivalent of four GCSEs grades A to C). Another key target is that by the year 2000 at least 50 per cent of young people should have achieved NVQ level 3 (or its academic equivalent of two A-levels).

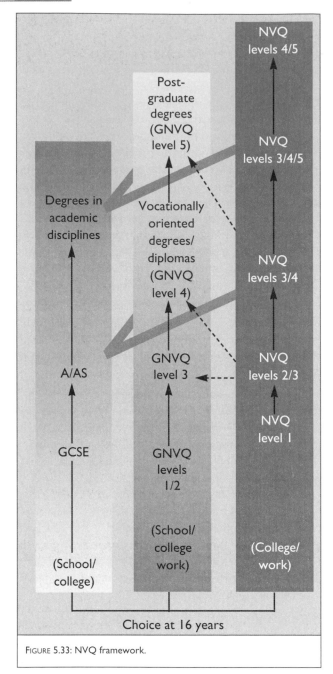

FIGURE 5.33: NVQ framework.

in Japan. *Fig. 5.35* shows that more young people now stay on in full-time education or training following their compulsory schooling. Despite these developments, however, more young people stay on in full-time education and training in the USA, Japan and most countries of the European Union than in the UK.

The growing number of students following full-time vocational courses such as the intermediate and advanced GNVQ will also play a vital part in raising the quality of the workforce. These courses will not only provide the essential knowledge aspects of a particular occupation but are competence-based and also develop the core skills which allow young people to play an effective role in other areas of employment.

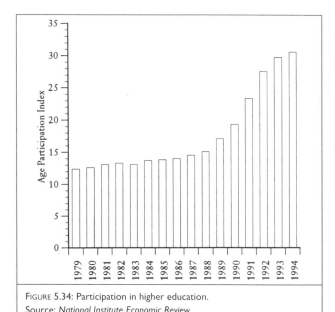

FIGURE 5.34: Participation in higher education.
Source: *National Institute Economic Review.*

Since NVQs take account of performance in the workplace rather than academic background, they should also motivate more mature employees to develop their skills and competence. NVQs have now been developed to meet the needs of all groups of employees from operative levels through to senior management.

EDUCATION

Education is as important as training in improving the quality of the workforce. There has been a substantial growth in the number of people in higher education in the UK (see *Fig. 5.34*). The percentage of young people graduating from university is now nearly as high as that

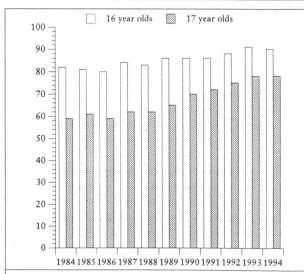

FIGURE 5.35: Proportion of 16 and 17 year-olds in full-time education and training.
Source: *National Institute Economic Review.*

PRIVATISATION AND DEREGULATION

The process of privatisation involves the conversion of nationalised industries or public sector corporations into public joint stock companies. From being state owned, they become owned by private shareholders. This aspect of government policy has received a great deal of media attention over recent years. Industries such as gas, electricity, the water companies and rail services have been returned to the private sector. The **policy of privatisation** began in the early 1980s. By 1995, most of the major industries previously owned by the state with the exception of the Post Office had been privatised.

The promoters of the privatisation programme claimed that when industries are owned by the state they are inefficient. It is argued that state-owned industries have less incentive to be efficient because they know that the government will eventually finance losses and provide the capital funds to finance their future investment. It is argued that previously state-owned companies like British Steel, British Airways, Jaguar, Rolls Royce and the coal industry should face very intensive foreign competition without the potential cushion of state aid; and, with private sector management, they will prosper.

The state-owned utilities such as telecommunications, gas, electricity and water were monopolies. It was hoped that privatisation would provide an opportunity to open up such industries to competition. This would prevent future price rises or even produce lower prices and would help the competitiveness of user industries through lower energy costs, for example.

The government announced its **deregulation initiative** at the beginning of 1994. This focuses on the scrapping, simplification or streamlining of any regulations and red tape which place too much of a burden on UK firms. The government has already identified 450 pieces of bureaucracy which it intends to tackle. It is particularly concerned about small businesses where 'unnecessary red tape leads to higher costs and missed opportunities' for manufacturing companies. The government is also considering amending other Acts of Parliament such as those governing health and safety laws and employment protection to remove or reduce further the burden on businesses. One measure advanced by the government is to give employers the right to make workers redundant regardless of accepted practice, putting the onus on the employee to claim unfair dismissal afterwards.

GOVERNMENT POLICY AND INFLATION

Governments have generally accepted responsibility for managing the economy as a whole. In this section, therefore, we concentrate on government policy designed to ease those pressures in the economy which lead to higher costs and higher prices and so cause a general loss of international competitiveness. For further discussion of how government policies affect markets see unit 1.

A sudden rise in consumer spending leading to an increase in demand for goods and services at a time when suppliers are unable to respond will lead to shortages of goods and services; it results in rising prices. Price rises can also be caused by rising costs, for example as a result of a pay settlement or a rise in the costs of imported raw materials. Inflation resulting from excessive levels of demand is termed **demand-pull inflation**; inflation caused by cost pressure is called **cost-push inflation**. The two can interact to create a **wage-price spiral** when rising costs and prices lead to workers making substantial wage claims thus fuelling inflationary pressure.

UK firms compete in world markets; they compete in terms of quality of goods and services, after-sales service, delivery dates, and so on. However, consumers find it easy to make price comparisons and a relatively high rate of inflation can set a country and its businesses at a significant competitive disadvantage.

POLICIES TO CONTROL INFLATION

Because inflation is often associated with an excessive level of total spending in the economy, the government's anti-inflationary polices are usually aimed at deflating total demand and helping to create a business environment where firms are under much more pressure to avoid cost and hence price increases. It is important to realise that sometimes the policies designed to cure inflation can inhibit the competitiveness of UK firms.

A RISE IN INTEREST RATES

If the government increases the cost of borrowing money, then a number of factors contribute to eventually slow down the rise in unit labour costs, and hence prices and the rate of inflation. When firms are faced with higher rates of interest, an immediate problem is to find the money to meet the higher charges on their existing bank loans and overdrafts. They are likely to pay more attention to the ways in which they use their labour in order to find ways of saving on labour costs. Changes in working practices to increase productivity and save on labour costs are likely to be given a greater priority by many firms. The burden of higher interest charges can only be met in the long term by making the kinds of savings which allow firms to make large reductions in the amounts they have borrowed. This exerts downward pressure on wage settlements; firms are likely to award low increases.

Higher interest rates will also increase the cost of consumer credit. They reduce the market demand for a wide range of goods and services; these cutbacks are likely to be most obvious in consumer durables such as washing machines and televisions. The fall in sales revenue will further increase the pressure on firms to resist wage demands.

The rise in mortgage interest payments will have a dramatic effects on the disposable income of many households; people will have to cut back in other areas to meet their mortgage repayments. The likely downturn in the housing market will further reduce the demand for consumer durables and home improvement products.

As the overall level of spending falls, it will increasingly becomes a buyer's market and producers will face greater price competition. Every effort must therefore be made to protect profit margins by avoiding cost increases. Greater competition between retailers with prolonged 'sales' and special offers means that they too will be looking for the best deals on prices from their suppliers.

HIGHER TAXES

In order to support a policy of higher interest rates, the government can also reduce total spending by increasing tax rates. A rise in income tax rates along with less generous tax allowances (that part of an individual's income not subject to income tax) will reduce average disposable income and thus lower spending power. Consumer spending will also fall if the government increases VAT and the excise duties paid on tobacco products, petrol and alcohol. The government can also extend VAT to items which are currently zero rated or introduce completely new taxes. Higher taxes on goods and services mean that people have to pay more for them and, because their income will not go as far as before, this will produce a fall in total demand.

CUTS IN GOVERNMENT SPENDING

Over 40 per cent of all spending in the economy is accounted for either directly or indirectly by the government. Cuts in government spending can therefore play an important role in an economic policy designed to curb total spending and reduce inflation. In 1995–6, for example, government spending was over £320bn. Cuts in capital projects such as bridges and other building programmes will affect the construction industry. Apart from those firms which receive fewer contracts from the

government, there will also be a knock-on effect on their suppliers. If people lose their jobs as a result, this will also mean less spending on a wide range of consumer goods and services.

ACTIVITY

In 1995, the government announced major cutbacks in its road-building plans. Working with other students, and using your local library, find out whether any plans to build roads in your region (such as a by-pass) have been delayed.

Write a short report which summarises the impact of the government's decision to cut its road building programme in your area, on the competitiveness of:

(a) local industries;

(b) UK industry, in general.

Government policies to tackle inflation and enhance industrial competitiveness have also sought to control sources of inflation by reducing the pressures on the costs of production. So, over the 1980s and early 1990s, governments passed legislation designed to limit the power of trade unions and reduce the inflationary impact of wage costs. At times, the government has also pursued a stable exchange rate policy with a view to avoiding rises in costs of imported raw materials.

SOME PROBLEMS WITH ANTI-INFLATION POLICIES

There is no doubt that if anti-inflationary policies are severe enough then the government will eventually succeed in reducing the rate of inflation. Unfortunately, the kinds of deflationary measures used are likely to produce a number of problems. For example, a large rise in interest rates will deter **investment** because:

⊙ **loan capital is more expensive;**

⊙ **the fall in profits cuts the level of capital funds generated internally;**

⊙ **business confidence will be depressed by the fall in market demand.**

The only long-term answer to a loss of competitiveness by UK producers is an actual increase in investment, but higher interest rates will actually cause firms to cut or postpone their capital investment programmes. Rather than an excessive reliance on interest rates as a way of dealing with inflation, it might be preferable to use higher income tax as a way of reducing the pressure of demand in the economy.

Higher interest rates will be very damaging for small firms, particularly those that have just borrowed money to finance an expansion in their operations. A rise in the cost of mortgages will depress the housing market and this will have a particularly severe effect on the house building industry. The collapse of the housing market may produce a fall in house prices and the problem of 'negative equity' in which home buyers have an outstanding mortgage which is greater than the value of their property. More generally, there may be a very serious decline in the level of consumer confidence because of higher mortgage interest payments, the threat of redundancy and a lack of job security.

Faced with these kinds of problems, households may save more of their income and also substantially reduce their take up of consumer credit. The result may then be a very much larger fall in total spending than the government expected and the economy could then slide into a deep recession. Consumer confidence, and willingness to spend, may be so severely damaged that the government may find it very difficult to stimulate the economy out of recession in the future.

Firms can lose their competitive edge at a time of falling sales. For example, they may lose the benefits of economies of scale if they have to reduce their output to match the fall in demand for their goods or services. Also, their unit costs can rise if they do not fully utilise their productive capacity. If, for example, they continue to pay the same rent and rates on their factory but produce only three-quarters of their previous output, then the amount of rent charged to each unit of output obviously rises.

THE EXCHANGE RATE AND INTERNATIONAL TRADE

As we discussed earlier, the exchange rate is simply the price of one currency in terms of another. In January 1996, one pound was worth 1.52 US dollars, 2.24 German deutschmarks or 160.25 Japanese yen. Movements in the exchange rate can have a major impact on the competitive position of UK producers when selling in overseas markets or competing against imports.

Sterling's value in other currencies	Prices of UK exports overseas	Prices of imported goods in UK
Appreciates (rises)	Increase	Fall
Depreciates (falls)	Fall	Increase

FIGURE 5.36: The effect of changes in exchange rates.

THE EFFECT OF A TRADE DEFICIT ON THE EXCHANGE RATE

If the rate of inflation in the UK is high relative to other economies then this makes UK exports less attractive to foreign buyers as well as causing more people in the UK to switch to imports. This may lead to a serious and persistent deficit in the UK's international trade. Because the UK economy as a whole is not earning enough foreign currency from exports to pay for its imports, the government may eventually be obliged to deal with the situation.

A trade deficit exerts a downward pressure on the pound in foreign exchange markets. The large rise in imports results in an increase in the quantity of pounds being sold on foreign exchange markets to obtain the foreign currencies needed to pay for imports. At the same time, a fall in the demand for UK exports means less demand for pounds from foreigners wishing to buy UK goods. Because the supply of pounds onto foreign exchange markets now exceeds the demand for pounds, the 'price' of the pound will fall. The government may decide to allow such a fall in the exchange rate in order to restore the competitive position of UK producers.

A FALL IN THE EXCHANGE RATE

Assume, for example, that at current exchange rates one pound is worth 2.50 deutschmarks (DM2.50). A German importer would have to pay DM2,500 to buy the pounds needed to purchase a UK product priced at £1,000. At this exchange rate, an importer in the UK would need £800 to buy the deutschmarks needed to purchase a product from a German supplier priced at DM2,000.

Now assume that the government is worried about the high rate of inflation in the UK. It allows the forces of demand and supply on foreign exchange markets to produce a fall in the exchange rate, so that a pound is only worth 2.25 deutschmarks. This depreciation in the pound means that the UK product priced at £1,000 will now only cost the German importer DM2,250 while the German product priced at DM2,000 will now cost a UK importer £888.88.

A fall in the exchange rate will therefore help to improve the competitive position of UK producers by lowering the prices of UK goods to foreigners in terms of their own currencies and raising the prices of imports in terms of pounds

SOME PROBLEMS WITH A FALL IN THE EXCHANGE RATE

Although a fall in the exchange rate seems to be a very easy and immediate way of helping UK producers to be more price competitive, there are several factors which may prevent the policy from having the desired effect. If producers are confident that the government will always allow a fall in the exchange rate to protect their competitive position against foreign producers, they may become complacent and have less incentive to become more efficient and keep their costs down.

The fall in the exchange rate will raise the production costs of those producers that rely on imported raw materials, parts and components as well as those involved in investment programmes using imported plant, machinery and equipment. Some of the advantage provided to exporters by the lower exchange rate may soon be wiped out by their higher import costs.

Imported consumer goods will also cost more and, along with the pressure of higher import costs on other prices, this will further increase the cost of living. Trade unions may then press for a pay rise which at least compensates for the rise in the cost of living. If pay increases, this will put yet more pressure on a firm's costs and hence its prices.

A fall in exchange rates will also fail to produce the expected benefits if UK firms lack the capacity to be able to take full advantage of the higher export demand or the switch away from imports. A lack of investment in an earlier period may mean that they do not have sufficient productive capacity to increase their output.

ACTIVITY

1 A UK company has unit costs of £2,000 and 20 per cent of these are due to imports of raw materials priced in US dollars and 10 per cent due to parts bought from Japan. On the foreign exchange markets the pound is currently worth $1.65 and 200 yen. Calculate the effects on the cost of a single unit of production of a 12 per cent fall in the value of the pound sterling against the US dollar and an 8 per cent fall against the yen.

2 Assume that a British car sells to a German distributor for £10,000, and the pound then falls from DM2.50 to DM2.25.

(a) What is the change in the deutschmark cost to the German distributor if the pound price is unchanged?

(b) What will be the extra annual sales revenue to the British manufacturer if the lower exchange rate produces an annual increase in sales of 8 per cent and the sales previously were 1,200 a month?

(c) What would be the effect of this same exchange rate movement on the price of a Volkswagen model selling to a UK distributor at DM30,500?

Instead of taking every step to exploit the price advantage provided by the fall in the exchange rate by investing in new capacity or by an aggressive marketing strategy, some UK firms may simply respond by raising their sterling prices. Firms will do this if they lack the confidence to plan for a possible long-term increase in the volume of their sales. This may be because they are uncertain about other future economic and financial developments in the UK economy as a whole.

Finally, allowing the exchange rate to fall does not deal with the actual cause of the loss of competitiveness. It is a short-term response to the loss of price competitiveness and simply gives UK producers a breathing space during which they should undertake the investment and training programmes needed to achieve a long-lasting improvement in competitiveness.

INTERNATIONAL COMPETITIVENESS AND A STRONG POUND

Rather than using a **lower exchange rate** to help make UK producers more competitive, the government may opt to maintain a **strong pound**; that is, to keep the exchange rate at a relatively high value. This is because a strong pound might actually help to tackle inflation.

If the government can convince firms that it will not allow a fall in the exchange rate to help offset the effects of price increases, then employers will be under greater pressure to resist pay rises that raise unit labour costs. UK producers will also need to pay more attention to other costs and to ways of increasing productivity.

A strong or rising exchange rate will also help to slow down inflation because of its effects on import costs. As long as the exchange rate does not fall, then at least the cost of a firm's imports will be unchanged at a time when other pressures are pushing up its domestic costs. Even a rise in the exchange rate may therefore be welcomed by the government because it will actually lower a firm's import costs and thus help to compensate for any rise in domestic costs.

Similarly, a strong pound will also help to moderate the rise in the cost of living and inflation because of its effect upon the prices of imported consumer goods. This will help firms to negotiate smaller pay rises.

COMPETITION AND EUROPEAN MARKET INTEGRATION

In the period leading up to the creation of the **single European market** in 1993, a great deal of discussion took place concerning the advantages to UK producers of operating in a **'home market'** of some 360 million. The removal of trade barriers such as import duties and quotas within the European Union would allow the free flow of goods and services and the resulting economic integration of the member states, it was argued, would create a single economy. Governments would also agree to eliminate subsidies which gave certain industries in their own countries an unfair advantage when competing in both home and foreign markets.

The European Union also seeks to **harmonise regulations** dealing with matters such as technical, safety and environmental standards. So a motor vehicle manufacturer, for example, would no longer have to change certain aspects of a car's specification in order to satisfy the different requirements in various member states. The process of harmonisation would also remove the possibility of a government using such regulations as a way of deliberately making it more difficult for imports to penetrate the home market.

Much of the support for the UK being part of a single European economy is based upon the advantages it would bring in terms of making UK producers more competitive.

ECONOMIES OF SCALE

The large European market and the eventual harmonisation of standards will offer much greater economies of scale and lower unit costs. This will help producers to be more price competitive not only within the European Union but also when competing in other parts of the world. Higher sales will generate extra profits and make funds available to pay for investment projects that will further strengthen competitiveness. The fall in unit costs may also help to offset the upward pressure upon prices caused by a rise in those costs over which businesses have no control such as higher interest charges or a rise in the world price of energy or raw materials.

THE RETURN ON CAPITAL PROJECTS

Capital-intensive industries with high fixed costs need the prospect of a large market, if they are to invest in new capacity and up-to-date technology. Similarly, firms that need to spend large amounts on research and development also require the potential of a large market if they are to undertake such projects. The abolition of import controls will create a market big enough to hold out the prospect of a good return on expensive investment. The general improvement in the level of business confidence will help to stimulate the capital spending that improves competitiveness and promotes economic growth.

PRODUCTION COSTS AND CHOICE OF SUPPLIERS

The abolition of import controls will allow producers a greater choice when purchasing materials, parts, components and capital goods. When balancing price and non-price factors, they will be able to select from a larger number of suppliers as imports will not be affected by import duties or quota restrictions. The competitive position of their own output will therefore benefit from this much wider choice.

STIMULATING GREATER EFFICIENCY AND INNOVATION

When producers are protected from imports, they face less competition and are under correspondingly less pressure to be keep their costs down and improve the quality of their output. If, however, the home economy is opened up to foreign competition, then home producers will have to respond to the threat of imports by paying greater attention to their costs, by offering more competitive prices and by introducing programmes aimed at making their product or service more attractive to potential customers. Those that fail to respond in this way will not survive for long in the much more competitive environment.

INCREASED TRADE AND ECONOMIC GROWTH

There is a very close connection between the rate of economic growth of an economy and the growth of its exports. Higher exports stimulate output and increase job opportunities, and the resulting rise in incomes will raise average living standards. In some cases, the opening up of home markets to imports can actually lead to lower prices and this will also help to raise the spending power of households. This extra spending power then leads to each country increasing its imports and so helps to sustain the growth in trade. A virtuous circle of events is therefore established: trade promotes economic growth and growth encourages trade.

INTERNATIONAL TRADE AGREEMENTS

Since 1945, the countries that have signed up to the **General Agreement on Tariffs and Trade (GATT)** have sought to dismantle barriers to trade and make export markets more competitive. As a member of GATT, the UK has played a part in the various rounds of trade talks. These can last many years before an agreement is reached to remove trade barriers.

The UK is more dependent upon international trade than most other industrialised countries as about one third of national output is exported. This is about the same as Germany but much higher than the US and Japan where only about 10 per cent of their national output is exported. The UK has always been a very 'open' economy and therefore has much more to gain than lose from international agreements that help to free world trade from protectionist measures such as tariffs and import quotas. The advantages arising out of an opening up of world trade are essentially the same as those which were used to support the UK becoming part of a single European market.

THE URUGUAY ROUND AND THE GATT AGREEMENT

At the end of 1993, and after a four-year preparation period followed by more than seven years of actual discussions, a round of GATT negotiations which started in Uruguay ended with 115 trade ministers agreeing to sign a package of reforms designed to further free world trade from protectionist measures.

ACTIVITY

1 Use the *Yellow Pages* to identify a group of manufacturing companies in your area. Note what goods they produce. You will need to get your teacher to co-ordinate this activity so that the same companies are not approached with similar requests for information.

2 Design a questionnaire that seeks to obtain information about the extent to which the companies do business with the European Union. Try to find out:

(a) exports to members of the EU as percentage of sales;

(b) imports from the EU and their advantages over UK suppliers;

(c) trends in exports and imports over the last five years;

(d) the roles of any employees who visit EU countries;

(e) any agents or businesses in the EU acting on their behalf.

3 Use the findings to produce a document that demonstrates the support which local industry gives to greater integration with Europe.

Gatt: who wins what

Total gains in Agriculture $73 billion; Textiles $85 billion; Services $29 billion; Other $23 billion: Total $209.4 billion

Total gain by regions $ bn

Region	$ bn
*Africa	-2.6
Asia Tigers	7.1
Asia	18.8
China	37.0
EU	61.3
E Europe	2.1
India	4.6
Japan	27.0
S America	8.0
US	36.4
Other	9.7

*Ex Egypt Lybia

Source: OECD GATT

1 US

Largest number of world's 500 biggest global companies, and biggest services exporter ($2 billion benefit). Aerospace, computer software, agriculture ($9.3 billion) and textile ($21.6 billion) sectors will also benefit. Total gain: $36 billion a year by 2002

2 Japan

Set to gain from liberalisation in high tech goods, Agriculture ($22 billion), manufacturing. Loses $0.5 billion through textile liberalisation. Total gain $27 billion a year by 2002

3 Asian Tigers

Gain $3.3 through farm liberalisation, $1.8 billion in textiles, $1.1 billion in services. $7.1 billion overall gain

4 EU

World's biggest exporting block. Agriculture to see income increase of $30 bln, textiles ($17.2 billion), services ($7 billion), manufacturing ($7.6 billion) all set to gain – but prospects differ in each country. Total gain: $61.3 billion a year by 2002

5 Eastern Europe

Textile, service sectors likely to benefit. Former Soviet Union set to gain by some $13 billion from liberalisation of services. Total Gain: $37 billion a year by 2002

6 Australia/New Zealand

Large gains from liberalisation of agriculture ($1.0 billion), textile ($1.1 billion). Total gain $2 billion a year by 2002

7 China

Set to gain $37 billion a year by 2002

8 India

Set to gain $4.6 billion a year by 2002

9 Africa (excluding Egypt and Libya)

The continent as a whole is set to lose $2.6 billion, with Nigeria alone down $1.0 billion. Morocco, Algeria and Tunisia together lose $0.6 billion, and South Africa loses $0.4 billion

10 South America

Set to gain $8.0 billion, with Brazil on its own up $3.4 billion.

The estimates also take no account of social costs arising from the structural adjustment of economies in the wake of trade liberalisation.

From the *Guardian*, December 15, 1993.

Lower prices will take time to work through

Shoppers would pay less for food, clothes and electronic gadgets after a GATT agreement, but not for at least two years, consumer groups claimed yesterday. But the Labour Party and the City said that dramatic high street price cuts were unlikely.

Mr Stephen Locke, of the Consumers Association, said lower prices would take time to filter through to the shops. 'The consumer has the right to expect lower prices in a few years, he said. 'But we cannot predict by how much.'

The GATT deal certainly includes important cuts in the huge subsidies paid to the European farmers under the Common Agricultural Policy, which costs every family in Britain at least £20 a week in dearer food and higher taxes. But although these should result in cheaper butter, beef and bread, for example, the benefits will be limited as France fought off bigger cuts in farm hand-outs. This means that inefficient farmers in countries like France, Germany and Italy will continue to be supported, although to a lesser extent, by both the consumer and the European taxpayer to the tune of tens of billions of pounds a year.

Meanwhile, supermarket groups played down the significance of lower farm costs for food prices in shops. 'Raw materials prices no longer have the same effect. Labour, marketing and packaging costs are more significant for food prices now,' said Elizabeth Hardwick of City bank SG Warburg.

Mr Locke said that imported clothing, such as socks, underpants, jeans and shirts, particularly in the budget ranges, would be at least five per cent cheaper because punitive import tariffs are to be scrapped. But shoppers may have to wait at least ten years to notice the difference because the European Community insisted on a long phasing-in period. Nevertheless, Sir James Goldsmith, the Anglo-French financier, has predicted that removing these tariffs will mean that Europe will be swamped by cheap goods from developing countries. It will be good for consumers but will have potentially disastrous consequences for jobs here.

Tariffs on many imported electronics goods, such as video recorders, televisions and compact disc players, are also to be abolished. But, once again, the consumer, who in Britain pays more than most for these goods, will have to wait for any lowering of prices.

Retailers remain cynical about the likely effect of the GATT deal on prices. 'We haven't even bothered to factor GATT in,' said one. 'Frankly, it's such a complicated deal, that it's impossible to say what it will mean.' But another claimed that it would offer the consumer more choice. Economists criticised the government and EC negotiators for making grandiose claims about the power of a GATT agreement to cut prices and create jobs and prosperity.

'The build-up to GATT has been an awful lot of hype, said Mr Dan Corry, of the Institute of Public Policy Research. 'While it is undoubtedly a good thing for the Western consumer, it is more because the alternative of damaging trade wars would have been so bad.'

Mr Nigel Griffiths MP, Labour spokesman on consumer affairs, said he was worried that retailers would fail to pass on the price cuts after the GATT agreement. He called on the government to take tougher action over retailers charging exceptionally high prices.

Daily Telegraph, 15 December 1994

ACTIVITY

Read the above article about the effects of the GATT deal.

1 Explain why the removal of financial support for farmers should mean both lower food prices and higher real disposable incomes for households.

2 Why might these developments lead to increased international trade and more jobs in non-food industries?

3 Assume that the raw material costs of a brand of butter are 20 per cent of its retail price which is 80p per 500 gm pack. If the GATT agreement reduces these costs by 25 per cent, what price could the producer afford to charge if all other costs remained unchanged?

4 You are the customer relations manager in a large company making frozen pizzas and your prices have continued to rise by an average of 2 per cent a year since the GATT agreement. Answer the accusation that the GATT agreement should have meant lower prices.

5 Select various kinds of food (such as biscuits, yoghurt, meat products, etc.) and describe the extent to which producers would bother to use any fall in the prices of their ingredients as a way of increasing sales.

The package of measures agreed during the Uruguay round covered ten times the value of trade dealt with by the previous seven GATT rounds put together. It is estimated that the resulting removal of various trade restrictions will stimulate demand and boost world trade by about $180bn a year by 2002. It is estimated that the GATT deal would mean an additional 416,000 jobs in Britain by 2005 because of the effect of falling tariffs, the greater competition upon prices and the resulting increases in real spending power. Service industries in particular are expected to benefit from being able to expand overseas.

OPENING UP TRADE IN AGRICULTURAL PRODUCTS

For many years, most governments in the developed economies had protected large parts of their agricultural sectors from low-cost food imports. The European Union, for example, has used a combination of guaranteed prices, subsidies and import controls that has encouraged over-production and the growth of food 'mountains' and 'lakes'. It has been estimated that the higher prices and tax revenues needed to support the **Common Agricultural Policy** mean that each European Union consumer is paying out about an extra £300 every year for food. A major achievement of the Uruguay Round therefore was an agreement that Europe would reduce farm subsidies and other kinds of financial support for farm products as well as lowering barriers to the import of farm products.

OPENING UP TRADE IN MANUFACTURES

One part of the Uruguay package that took effect immediately was a cut in tariffs on more than 20,000

products world-wide. The 116 GATT members had agreed to cut their average tariff rate by 36 per cent by the year 2000. Countries with high tariffs such as China and Brazil would have to make the largest cuts but since British tariffs were already very low this is unlikely to produce a sudden flood of cheaper imports into the UK.

The Uruguay agreement also sought to reduce government subsidies to industrial sectors, remove import quotas and deal with the problem of restricted tendering, a practice in which governments ensure that many major public sector contracts go to home producers. It also recognised the need to deal with non-tariff barriers designed to restrict imports such as differences in technical, safety and environmental regulations that made it difficult for a foreign supplier to compete against home producers.

Previous GATT rounds had made little progress in opening up world trade in textile products, and the developed countries had continued to protect their own markets through tariffs and the **Multi-Fibre Agreement (MFA)** which placed quotas on low-cost producers from the developing world. The Uruguay Round agreed to phase out the MFA over ten years.

OPENING UP TRADE IN SERVICES

The GATT deal has meant that for the first time services will also be subject to international trading rules. Although about 60 per cent of the European Union's total output is accounted for by services, very little progress had been made in removing the restrictions that prevented service sector companies from entering foreign markets. About 20 per cent of world trade is in services, and the figure continues to rise. Since Britain is already a very open market for services, it can expect to gain more from selling services abroad than it might lose from penetration of its home market.

The actual outcome of this particular round of GATT talks was, however, very limited in terms of opening up markets. Little real progress was made in areas such as shipping, air travel, financial services and film. There was some response to the growing concern for what is known as **'intellectual property rights'**. Steps will be taken to standardise regulations and conditions surrounding patent rights, copyrights and trademarks.

THE WORLD TRADE ORGANISATION
Until 1995, GATT had no real power to force members to comply with agreements or rulings on trade disputes.

However, the Uruguay deal set up the **World Trade Organisation (WTO)** to replace GATT with legally-enforceable powers to police world trade. There was also pressure for the WTO to play a part in the greater standardisation of competition laws in the same way that the European Commission has harmonised monopolies and mergers policy within Europe. It is hoped that this will stop home manufacturers acting as a cartel or having control over distribution systems that make it difficult for foreign producers to penetrate the home market. The WTO may also deal with the harmonisation of environmental regulations in an effort to stop countries from using either very strict or very weak environmental laws to give their own producers an advantage.

 ACTIVITY

The *Financial Times* regularly carries articles that cover developments in international trade that will affect UK companies either directly or indirectly. These reports are generally found on the European News, World Trade News and American News pages and, on some days, a 'World Trade News' section is also included.

Over a period of say two weeks, the class as a whole should share the responsibility for collecting articles that deal with either the opening up of international trade or with possible shifts towards protectionism.

The complete file of cuttings should then be made available to each student in order that they can analyse:

(a) the main countries or international organisations involved;

(b) the goods and services covered by the issue;

(c) the removal, reduction or imposition of certain kinds of trade barriers;

(d) the potential trading opportunities and problems raised in the articles;

(e) the possible effects of these opportunities and problems on particular UK companies.

PORTFOLIO ASSIGNMENT

1   Update the information in the charts and graphs in this element concerning the competitiveness of UK producers in relation to other developed economies. Research any additional information you think you require in order to assess the current competitive position of UK businesses.

2   Use an appropriate software package to display your results in such a way that rates of change in key economic data can be easily identified and compared.

3   Select a major manufacturing company in the UK which competes with foreign producers. Use its latest annual report and accounts and CD-ROM sources to identify aspects of its business strategy designed to strengthen its competitive position.

4   Where possible, identify ways in which 'your' company's performance may have been affected by actions of its competitors designed to improve their competitive position.

1 **Added value is:**

A the percentage rate at which VAT is levied

B the profit earned through production

C the difference between cost of materials and final selling price

D another term for contribution

2 **Quality assurance has become an important issue in the 1990s for all of the following reasons except:**

A European Union laws have made appropriate systems a legal requirement

B firms without such systems are at a competitive disadvantage

C some businesses insist on suppliers having a quality assurance system

D the costs of quality failure can be significant

3 **Which of the following is an advantage associated with just-in-time production:**

A stocks can be purchased more cheaply

B production and ordering systems can be simplified

C the risks of running out of raw materials are eliminated

D the costs of stock holding are reduced

4 **Which of the following is not an advantage of 'contracting out':**

A external suppliers often have specialist skills

B communication is easier with external suppliers

C external suppliers may benefit from economies of scale

D using external suppliers can result in new approaches to old problems

5 **Training the workforce can improve competitiveness for all of the reasons stated except:**

A it improves the motivation and performance of the workforce

B it reduces the level of costs faced by the firm

C it allows workers to develop new skills

D it helps businesses to recruit high class employees

6 **When a firm develops links with one supplier, at the expense of others, to reduce risk this is known as:**

A contracting out

B total quality management

C single sourcing

D lateral integration

7 **Labour productivity can be measured using which of the following formulae:**

A $\dfrac{\text{output per hour}}{\text{number of employees}}$

B $\dfrac{\text{number of employees}}{\text{output per hour}}$

C $\dfrac{\text{output per hour}}{\text{capital employed}}$

D $\dfrac{\text{output per hour}}{\text{wage per hour}}$

8 **A part-time worker is usually regarded as one who works less than:**

A twenty hours a week

B twenty-five hours a week

C fifteen hours a week

D sixteen hours a week

9 **Which of the following types of employment has become less common over recent years:**

A self-employment

B part-time employment

C male employment

D female employment

10 **Which of the following statements about part-time employees is untrue:**

A they are cheaper to employ

B they are a central element in a more flexible workforce

C they tend to be mainly young male employees

D part-time employees have fewer employment rights than full-time employees

11 **The 'underground' economy refers to:**

A any economic activity which is undeclared to the authorities

B any economic activity which is zero-rated for VAT purposes

C the mining and quarrying industries

D tertiary activities

12 **Pay differentials occur for all of the following reasons except:**

A regional differences

B differences in skill levels

C differences in demand for labour services

D differences in tax rates

13 **A rapid rate of economic growth is more likely in countries:**

A which are in recession and have a large pool of unemployed people

B with a high rate of inflation

C where a high proportion of total spending is accounted for by capital spending

D with high rates of interest

14 **An example of a rise in productivity would be:**

A total output in the economy rising faster than employment

B firms in general operating with spare capacity

C total output rising at the same rate as the population

D an increase in overtime working

15 A persistently healthy surplus on its international trade in manufactures is an indication of a country's competitiveness because:

A imports of raw materials must be low

B low levels of spending at home force firms to develop export markets

C both home and overseas buyers are attracted to its home products

D its currency will be in great supply on foreign exchange markets

16 If a company grants pay increases at its various plants which more closely reflect the conditions in local labour markets then:

A all of its workers will be paid the rate for the job

B the company will have no incentive to expand its operations in areas of high unemployment

C the pay rise granted to workers in one particular plant will always be the same as the average for other firms in that area

D the lower pay settlements in areas of high unemployment can be used to help finance the larger pay awards in areas of labour shortages

17 Which of the following is not a feature of capital investment:

A it can raise a firm's productive capacity

B it can raise output per worker

C it can contribute to improved quality

D it adds less to the country's growth than investment in works of art

18 Investment in training and development is:

A not necessary once labour is replaced by high technology machinery and equipment

B much less important in the service sector

C an important way of raising productivity

D only needed for manual and supervisory jobs

19 An example of backward vertical integration would be:

A a brewer merging with a producer of whisky

B a recording company taking over a chain of record shops

C a motor vehicle manufacturer acquiring a pressed steel works

D a bank buying up an estate agency business

20 Total quality management is:

A ensuring that defective products do not get through to customers

B inspecting all raw materials and components to ensure they are of the required quality

C managing in such a way that all processes and procedures are carried out right each and every time

D quality control based upon detection rather than prevention

✔ MULTIPLE CHOICE QUESTIONS

21 The word quality in the context of total quality management is best defined as:

A ensuring that the highest grade materials are used

B being able to sell at a higher price than competitors

C conformity to requirements

D a continuous improvement in reliability and more efficient after-sales services

22 If a pay rise is determined solely by an improvement in productivity then:

A employees will resist the introduction of new technology

B unit costs will not rise

C unit labour costs will remain unchanged

D employers will have to offer extra pay to encourage overtime working

23 Employing people on a flexible basis in terms of both total working hours and when they work:

A is only appropriate for those employing unskilled labour

B will be cost effective for employers in public transport services

C is a system which employers in the hotel and catering sector are likely to reject

D means that employers cannot introduce performance-related pay

24 A fall in the exchange rate for the pound against the US dollar will result in all of the following except:

A a rise in the dollar price of imports

B a fall in the dollar price of US imports from the UK

C a rise in the prices of dollar imports when priced in pounds

D visitors from the US getting more pounds for their dollars

25 A fall in consumer spending can be caused by all of the following except:

A a fall in disposable income

B a rise in the level of mortgage interest payments

C a rise in excise duties

D a fall in unemployment

26 If interest rates are high enough for long enough then inflation will eventually fall because:

A higher borrowing costs and falling sales will oblige firms to avoid a rise in unit labour costs

B higher interest rates will persuade all households to save much more and lower consumer spending will ease labour shortages

C the resulting fall in house prices will reduce the pressure for large pay rises

D the rise in the cost of consumer credit will reduce the demand for imported consumer durables

27 Capital investment programmes may be cut or postponed if:

A there is a fall in interest rates in other major economies

B a rise in consumer confidence leads to an increased take up of consumer credit

C the other major economies of the European Union achieve faster rates of economic growth

D the government is expected to respond to rising inflation by raising interest rates

28 UK membership of the European Union means that:

A the less efficient UK producers have a more secure future

B the potential economies of scale for efficient producers will increase export opportunities

C the UK will be able to restrict imports from Japan

D UK employers will pay the same wages as other employers in the European Union

29 Capital intensive industries in the UK will benefit from the opening up of international trade because:

A total fixed costs will fall

B borrowing costs will be lower

C the larger potential market will discourage takeovers by foreign firms

D the larger potential market offers the prospect of much lower average fixed costs

30 UK households benefit from the removal of import restrictions in the global economy because:

A producers offering the best value will have access to more markets

B there will be less emphasis on non-price competition

C imports will pay a lower rate of VAT

D excise duties on tobacco, wine and imported lagers will be lower

Financial Transactions, Costing and Pricing

CONTENTS

OUTLINE

In this unit, we consider some of the financial aspects of business, such as the procedures for buying and selling goods, how money moves through businesses, the documents required for recording financial details and security measures. We also discuss the different types of costs faced by a business and calculate the total costs of businesses. Finally, we consider how firms decide upon the prices they charge.

Money is the lifeblood of any business, circulating through it to keep it alive and allow it to grow and prosper. Money is required to set up and establish a business, to purchase equipment and supplies and to pay for the ongoing running costs of the business. It is vital, therefore, that businesses establish systems for controlling and recording the movement of money and operate these systems with accuracy and integrity. Equally, it is important for businesses to monitor their costs to ensure they are not losing money. They need to charge prices which will generate profits. Indeed, they want to charge the highest prices possible.

This unit introduces you to these financial concepts. There is further discussion of the financial aspects of business in unit 7.

This unit contains a single portfolio assignment covering topics discussed in all four elements and including all the evidence indicators that you need to demonstrate in completing this unit of your course. Work through the text and then tackle the portfolio assignment on page 402.

Explain added value, distribution of added value and money cycle

THE TRADING CYCLE

The aim of business is to trade with a view to making a profit, to receive more money from the sale of a product or service than it costs to supply it. A business is started by an individual or group of individuals who invest capital (money, vehicles, property and so on) plus time and effort. They do this in the hope that the business will make money for them – **a return on investment**. If the effort of running a business is to be worthwhile, the return on investment needs to be higher than that offered, for example, by a high-interest savings scheme. This is the key to all business activity and is achieved by giving **added value** to a product or service.

Most businesses are involved in the buying and selling of goods and/or services. **Goods** are tangible items which the business either extracts (through mining, for example), manufactures or buys for resale. **Services** range from washing-machine repair to banking and insurance. Recently the UK economy has exhibited a trend – common throughout the developed world – of the growth of tertiary or service industries and the relative decline of manufacturing industry.

Profit is generally viewed in two ways – **gross profit** and **net profit**. Gross profit is basically the difference in value between purchases and sales. For example, if a firm buys (or manufactures) goods worth £40,000 and sells them for £50,000, the gross profit is £10,000. Net profit is what remains after the expenses of running the business (selling and administration costs, rents, etc.) have been deducted from the gross profit. So, if the firm incurred running costs of £7,000 to generate a gross profit of £10,000, its net profit is £3,000.

Where does this profit come from? It comes from the added value that the firm has given to the product between purchasing and selling, during the **trading cycle**. Added value can be defined as the difference between the costs of materials and components and the price customers are prepared to pay for the finished product or service.

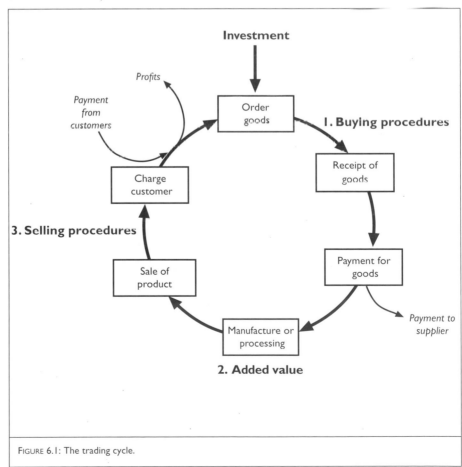

FIGURE 6.1: The trading cycle.

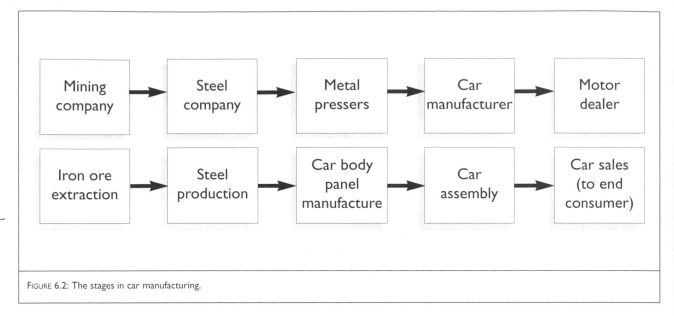

FIGURE 6.2: The stages in car manufacturing.

BUYING PROCEDURES

The first stage in the trading cycle involves buying goods and services. Buying goods is generally referred to as **purchasing**; obtaining services is known as **procurement**.

Let us consider what goods and services a business may require. Goods include the raw materials or components required to manufacture a product. These, in turn, may be used to produce a component for another manufacturer or to manufacture a finished product. Before Nissan decided to build a major new car production plant near Sunderland, the company would have considered where to purchase raw materials and components for its vehicles. *Fig. 6.2* shows how some of the material needed to produce a car moves through various businesses before reaching the consumer.

Extracted iron ore is the steel company's raw material. The company adds value by processing this raw material into sheet steel which, in turn, becomes the raw material for the metal pressers. It adds value by turning sheet steel into car body panels for firms such as Nissan. Each business in the chain is adding value through its knowledge, expertise, equipment and technical skills. Different companies purchase different raw materials, depending on the nature of their trade.

ACTIVITY

Using the example of steel car bodies as a model, identify the stages and types of business involved in the production of a wooden table. For each company in the chain, identify:

(i) **the raw material used;**

(ii) **the processes which add value;**

(iii) **the finished product sold.**

The services that a business may require include:

- **the supply of electricity, gas and water;**

- **transportation of finished goods to customers;**

- **external auditors to check the company's accounts;**

- **legal services;**

- **advertising agencies.**

This list is not exhaustive, there are numerous services which a business may require. Some will be directly involved in adding value to products, while others may be required for the overall running of the business. The ways in which these differences are dealt with, from a financial point of view, are dealt with later in this unit.

The aim of buying procedures is to ensure that:

- **the business receives the goods and services it needs to trade;**

- **the goods and services are supplied when they are needed;**

- **purchases are made at the right price;**

- **supplies are of the right quality;**

- **suppliers are reliable;**

- **no unauthorised purchases are made.**

When a business considers buying goods or services, the first step is to locate and assess potential suppliers. Locating suppliers may involve consulting trade journals and directories, or simply flicking through the *Yellow Pages*. The number of available suppliers varies, depending on the type of goods or services required. Potential suppliers are contacted and asked to send catalogues, price lists and specifications. Suppliers' representatives may visit customers to discuss their requirements or to demonstrate products. Sometimes a customer may have very detailed and specific requirements, which will involve lengthy consultation with potential suppliers.

There are a number of important factors to consider when selecting suppliers. These include cost, quality, reliability, versatility, location, capacity and delivery.

The most important consideration is usually how much the supplies will cost, although all other factors must be evaluated to avoid 'false economies'. The old adage 'you

get what you pay for' usually holds true. Improved transport and communications mean that companies can now look for potential suppliers throughout the world. UK electricity generating companies like PowerGen currently purchase supplies of coal from countries such as Poland in preference to domestic supplies. Given that coal is bulky and expensive to transport, the basic price differential must be very significant.

Quality is another key consideration. Purchasers need to know whether the supplies are going to be of the right quality. The delicate balance between quality and cost is sometimes difficult to achieve. Most companies are now accredited with the British Standards Institution standard BS 5750 (ISO 9000). This standard requires them to have a recognised and auditable quality assurance system. Most customers would expect their suppliers to be BS 5750 registered as a basic requirement. Quality is an important issue in the cost-conscious 1990s; a recent survey suggested that UK firms could save £6bn by eliminating the additional costs associated with producing poor quality goods and services.

In addition to checking cost and quality, a purchaser is likely to raise many other questions with potential suppliers. On reliability, a purchaser will want to know:

- **is the supplier always going to provide what is needed on time, every time?**

- **is the supply going to be of a consistent quality?**

- **is the supplier likely to go out of business (leaving us with no supplies)?**

On versatility:

- **can the supplier adjust to meet changing requirements and demand quickly?**

- **can one-off requirements be handled?**

- **can the supplier meet very specific and detailed specifications, if required?**

- **is the supplier prepared to invest in new facilities to meet the requirements?**

Location is another important factor. PowerGen, for example, would have to consider this issue very carefully before deciding to purchase Polish coal. In general, purchasers need to consider:

⊙ is the location of the supplier important?

⊙ will the location of the supplier affect purchasing costs (transport, labour costs, etc.)?

⊙ will the location of the supplier affect delivery times?

⊙ will location affect communication with the supplier?

On capacity, purchasers should ask:

⊙ does the supplier have the capacity to supply the required quantities?

⊙ how many other customers does the supplier have?

⊙ is the supplier planning to expand?

Finally, purchasers want to know about delivery:

⊙ how long does the supplier take to deliver?

⊙ can the supplier meet any special delivery requirements?

⊙ can a just-in-time (JIT) relationship (see below) be established with the supplier?

ACTIVITY

Using your school or college library, research the British Standard **BS EN ISO 9000**.

Write notes on what the standard requires and how companies can become **BS EN ISO 9000** accredited.

If services are required, the 'purchasing' process is known as procurement. Procuring services involves many of the same considerations. However, additional factors may be important, such as the expertise and qualifications of those offering to perform the service, whether they have the necessary resources and whether they can meet deadlines. Take training as an example. Many firms spend considerable sums training their employees. Before deciding upon a company offering training services, the purchaser may require evidence of the qualifications of the trainers, recommendations from other customers and, perhaps, samples of the service on offer.

Purchasers also need to check that suppliers meet any necessary legal requirements with respect to such things as auditing, legal services, and health and safety. Purchasers will also want to consider any discounts offered by suppliers, such as a cash discount (for prompt payment), trade discount or quantity discounts on large orders.

Selecting the right suppliers is the first key to successful purchasing and procurement. Having considered all the relevant factors, the purchaser will choose a supplier and negotiate the terms on which they will do business. Skilled negotiating is the second key to success. The aim is to obtain the best possible terms from the supplier. Successful negotiations result in a 'win-win' outcome, in which both parties feel that they have achieved an agreement that allows them to trade on a mutually profitable basis.

The most important factor in negotiations will be the price to be paid by the customer. The details need to be negotiated, including credit terms, such as the length of credit period, any discounts offered by the supplier, whether prices include delivery, and so on. Additionally, negotiations may involve establishing such things as the quantities required, default payments by suppliers if they fail to deliver goods or complete work on time, and the conditions applying to the supply and acceptance of goods. The details are likely to form part of a contract between purchaser and supplier.

Usually, the purchaser establishes a clear specification for the supplier to work to. This includes precise details of the products or services to be supplied including acceptable quality levels. Often, precise details regarding delivery are also specified. This is particularly true where the purchasing company is operating a **just-in-time (JIT)** system. Under a JIT system, a company holds as little stock of materials as possible by arranging for suppliers to deliver the materials and components it requires as, and when, they are needed. Obviously, communication between customer and supplier must be very reliable and efficient if this is to succeed (otherwise you could have a just-too-late situation). We consider JIT more fully in unit 5.

Having completed negotiations to the satisfaction of both parties, the customer places an order. A purchase order is a request for goods or services to be supplied. It is normally sent to the supplier on an order form (see *Fig. 6.7*, page 364). The customer itemises what is required and shows the prices quoted by the supplier. An order must be signed by an authorised person to ensure that only legitimate business purchases are made. Purchasing documents are described in detail later in this unit.

Once the goods have been received in good condition, or the service completed satisfactorily, the buyer pays the supplier. Payment procedures and documentation are detailed later.

ADDED VALUE

Having made purchases, the next stage in the trading cycle is adding value. We defined 'value added' as the difference between the total revenue of a firm (how much money it receives) and the cost of bought-in raw materials, services and components. Thus, it measures the value which the firm has 'added' to these bought-in materials and components by its production or handling processes. Value can be added in a number of ways. These include:

- **buying raw materials and manufacturing an entire product;**

- **buying raw materials and manufacturing components;**

- **buying components and assembling entire products;**

- **buying components and producing part-assembled products;**

- **buying entire products and distributing them;**

- **supplying a service.**

HOW IS VALUE ADDED?

An example of a company buying raw materials and manufacturing complete products is Pasta Foods. This

Great Yarmouth company purchases raw materials such as wheat and eggs and converts these into a variety of convenience foods. In this example, the value added is clear.

In contrast, QVC is an example of a company that adds value by buying products and distributing them. The satellite and cable television shopping channel sells and distributes a wide range of products including famous brands such as Black & Decker, Braun and Rowenta.

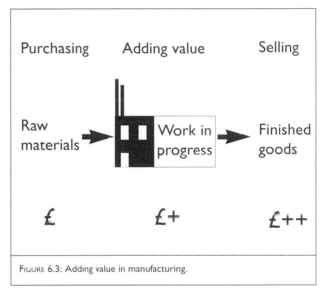

Purchasing   Adding value   Selling

Raw materials → Work in progress → Finished goods

£   £+   £++

FIGURE 6.3: Adding value in manufacturing.

Value is added in manufacturing when raw materials or components are processed to make a finished product. As *Fig. 6.3* shows, value is added as a result of the processes carried out in the factory. Raw materials arrive in the factory at cost price. Each process the material undergoes increases its value (accountants call these part-processed goods **'work in progress'**). Finally, the finished goods emerge from the factory. They are now worth considerably more than the raw materials that went in. Remember, one company's finished goods may be another company's raw material. Cost accounting determines how much each unit of production has actually cost to make; this is dealt with in more detail later. Accurate cost accounting is essential in order to price correctly the finished goods for resale (in other words, to decide how much to charge the customer).

A crucial factor in manufacturing is the amount of time spent in adding value. The money tied up in stocks of raw materials or in materials undergoing processing cannot be realised until the finished goods are sold. Therefore, any time wasted during processing, when value is not being added, is money wasted. For example, while a part-finished product is being stored, or is waiting for processing, it is not receiving added value. In fact, it is losing money for the business because it is tying up cash which could have been used to produce more products and make more money.

HELEN'S CASH CRISIS

Helen Godbolt owns a small business producing dried flower arrangements for shops and garden centres. There are no employees, Helen produces all the arrangements herself. She does not sell a large number of flower arrangements but she makes a considerable profit on each sale.

An arrangement can take many hours to complete. Helen knows that businesses order most flower arrangements in the period leading up to Christmas. So, Helen usually works on her arrangements steadily throughout the year and she likes to have a large variety of completed arrangements available to show to prospective customers.

Helen does not seem to be making much money from her business. No sooner has she received payment from her customers than it is swallowed up again buying materials for new arrangements. Helen complains that she never seems to have any cash in her pocket from the business.

ACTIVITY

1 Describe the value added by Helen's business.

2 Helen has turned to you for advice about her business. She wants to be able to take more cash out of the business. Advise her on what you think she ought to do.

Ideally, the time between buying raw materials and selling finished goods to customers (the 'added value' stage) should be as short as possible. Just-in-time (JIT) techniques, automated manufacturing, production improvement teams and project team management approaches are some of the strategies that have been adopted by companies to achieve this objective. The success of Japanese manufacturers is largely due to their ability to compress the manufacturing process by cutting out non-value adding activities. Many Japanese concepts and methods are being successfully adopted by manufacturers elsewhere.

It is easy to see how manufacturing processes add value – a complete rocking chair obviously has more value than the lengths of wood used to make it – but it is less easy to see the value added when goods are merely bought and re-sold or services are supplied.

The added value in the wholesale and retail trade normally has to do with scale. A corner shop may want to sell products manufactured by well-known producers such as Heinz. However, large producers like Heinz only sell in bulk. Obviously, the corner shop does not want to buy beans, for example, by the container lorry load. This is where wholesalers add value. They buy direct from the factory on a large scale and then distribute products (possibly via smaller wholesalers) to retailers, allowing them to buy smaller quantities. Wholesalers also distribute products geographically, transporting goods from factories throughout the world to a local supplier close to the corner shop.

Value is added in a huge variety of ways. Sometimes people add value by applying time and skill to a product. Often equipment and machinery is involved, particularly in manufacturing processes. Some businesses add value to products simply by repackaging them for their customers or by selling knowledge, expertise or facilities as a service. Sometimes a business will 'buy-in' goods or services from third parties in order to add value to their products.

One example of added value in services is investments and savings. When you invest in a bank savings or investment scheme, the bank adds value by increasing the money you deposit. It adds value to your initial investment, providing you with interest and the bank itself with a profit. The added value is supplied by the bank's expert knowledge of the investment market, enabling it to invest your money for the highest return. The bank's administrative service also adds value by allowing you to receive interest on your money without having to go to the trouble of deciding where, when and how to invest.

ACTIVITY

List three businesses that offer a service. Describe what added value they offer.

The fundamental point of the trading cycle is that a business adds value to produce new products or services. It is able to charge its customers for that added value and, thus, make a profit. The customers are prepared to pay more than the pure monetary value added because they do not have the expertise, equipment, facilities or time to undertake the processes themselves. Some companies, however, do process goods through several stages of the production process. For example, many oil companies extract crude oil, refine it and sell petrol, diesel and lubricants directly to the consumer. This helps to maximise the profit from the raw material and also assures the supply of raw material throughout the chain.

The level of profit that can be made, in addition to the added value, depends on what the customer is prepared to pay for the product or service. If the product or service is unique in some way, with few other companies supplying it, the potential for making a profit is high. Alternatively, if there is a great deal of competition, with many companies offering similar products and/or services, customers generally choose the least expensive option, and potential profits are lower.

SELLING PROCEDURES

The final stage in the trading cycle is selling. A sale is the provision of goods or services by a supplier to a customer in exchange for payment.

Sales can be made on either a cash or credit basis. The difference between the two is not (as you might think) the method of payment, but the time at which the payment is made. Cash transactions involve immediate payment; goods and services are paid for at the same time they are supplied. Generally, a **receipt** is given to the customer to confirm that payment has been received.

ACTIVITY

1 **Describe some types of business in which most sales are made via cash transactions.**

2 **Make a list of cash transactions you have been involved with during the last week. Record whether you were the supplier or the customer.**

3 **Compare your list with other members of the class.**

4 **List the advantages and disadvantages of cash-intensive businesses.**

Credit transactions involve payment for goods and services at some date after they have been supplied. The supplier sends the customer an **invoice**, which gives details of the items supplied and the amount owing. The time between the supply of the goods and services and the due date for payment is known as the **credit period** (usually 30 days). The credit period is part of the **credit terms** agreed between the customer and the supplier, which set out the basis on which they will trade.

Accountants have special terms for those involved in credit transactions. **Debtors** are those people (or companies) who owe money to a business for credit sales. **Creditors** are those people (or companies) to whom a business owes money for credit purchases.

When a business wishes to buy goods on a credit basis, the supplier must first establish the **credit worthiness** of the customer. This is usually done by asking the customer to complete a credit application form. The customer is asked for the following details:

- **name of business;**

- **registered address;**

- **registration and/or VAT numbers (if applicable);**

- **invoicing address;**

- **banking details and reference;**

- **trade credit references (other businesses with which the customer has credit facilities);**

- **auditor's/accountant's reference;**

- **amount of credit required;**

- **anticipated volume of purchases.**

These details are checked and, if the supplier is satisfied that the customer is likely to pay debts as they fall due, a credit account is opened. The terms of supply and payment will be established and the customer can begin to buy on credit.

When a sale is made on credit, the transaction needs to be recorded in such a way that the business can keep track of what is owed to them and by whom. This is done by entering the amount owing from the customer in an account in the **sales ledger**. This is part of the main accounting system and it contains an individual account for each customer (debtor) of the business. The sales ledger is sometimes referred to as the **debtors ledger**. All transactions (sales and payments received) are entered into the customer's account in the sales ledger.

The sales ledger is usually updated daily. It should be regularly monitored to ensure that customers pay invoices on time. This process of **credit control** ensures that customers do not exceed the agreed credit terms and that money is received regularly. When customers do not pay on time, reminders are sent out by the credit control department. If customers fail to respond to these reminders, legal action may be taken to recover the debt.

Sometimes customers either cannot or will not pay their debts. If it is not possible to recover the debt through legal action, it may have to be considered a **bad debt**. In the recession of the late 1980s and early 1990s, the high street banks (Lloyds, Barclays, etc.) suffered badly from bad debts. Many business customers ended up owing the banks money when their businesses failed. They were (at best) only able to pay back a proportion of the amount borrowed. For several years, the profits of the high street banks were badly affected by having to make allowance for very high levels of bad debts.

Bad debts are considered an expense of the business. They are included in the profit and loss account when the final accounts are prepared. They are a loss because the company has provided goods or services (at a cost) for no return. Final accounts are dealt with in detail in unit 7.

Another area of difficulty for businesses – and especially small businesses – is late payments. Many customers do settle their accounts eventually, but long after the firm has had to find the cash to purchase raw materials, components and services. This remains a major reason for the failure of small businesses. It does not mean that the business is fundamentally unprofitable, rather that it is not particularly well managed. Look again at the case study on page 356.

DISTRIBUTION OF ADDED VALUE

What happens to the added value generated by the trading cycle? The added value is represented financially by profits. We noted that the difference between gross and net profit is the amount spent on the running expenses of the business. These include such things as rents, stationery, telephone and postage, office expenses and so on. One major expense is the cost of employees; so much of the added value generated is distributed in the form of wages and salaries paid to the people who work for the firm. Likewise, interest payments to commercial lenders (bank loans, mortgages) are also treated as expenses. We examine the expenses of a business later in this unit.

Once the expenses of the business have been accounted for, the remaining net profit can be distributed. The distribution of profits is always detailed in the final accounts. Depending on the type of business structure, profits are variously distributed between four recipients:

- ✪ **government, through taxation;**

- ✪ **the owners of the business;**

- ✪ **financial backers;**

- ✪ **the business itself.**

The net profit (after tax) belongs to the owners of the business and must be distributed accordingly. In the case of sole traders, this is simply a matter of adding net

profit to the owner's capital. In partnerships, the profits are divided between the partners according to shares detailed in a partnership agreement. In companies, the profits are divided and distributed to the shareholders as **dividends**.

Sometimes part of the money needed to establish a business is raised by private loans, called **debentures**. Debenture holders are entitled to receive an agreed, fixed percentage of the amount of the loan on an annual basis.

Usually, some net profit is retained within the business itself. Undistributed profit retained is this way is called **reserves**. This allows a firm to pay for any major expenditure which may be necessary. For example, the firm's equipment may need replacing if it is old or obsolete. If the company plans to expand, money may be required for new premises, equipment or machinery.

A general reserve may also be retained, to even out profits from year to year. Profit held in reserve in a good year can be used to supplement low profit in a poor year to ensure that dividend payments to shareholders remain consistent. This is important because shareholders may lose confidence in the company if their dividend is very high one year and much lower the next.

THE MONEY CYCLE

The trading cycle could not operate without money. We now examine how money circulates in a business and what happens if the money cycle breaks down.

INITIAL CASH
The initial cash required for a business may come from a variety of sources. These include the owner (or owners) of the business, private loans, and finance from banks and other financial institutions. Usually the owners have to invest a substantial amount of their own money before other lenders are prepared to risk money on a new business venture. Much of this initial cash, known as **capital**, is used to purchase the <u>**fixed assets**</u> needed for the business to function. Fixed assets are items such as machinery, equipment, furniture and motor vehicles, which will be used in the business over a long period of time. The money used to purchase these long-term assets is known as **fixed capital**.

Additionally, if the business deals in goods of any kind, some cash is needed to buy the initial stock before the firm can begin trading. A manufacturing concern needs a stock of raw materials and components. **Stock** is the name given to the materials and goods which are for resale. The total stock includes raw materials and components, the work-in-progress materials and finished goods. The money circulating in the money cycle is known as **working capital**.

MONEY USED TO ADD VALUE
In addition to the money required to establish the business, there must be sufficient working capital available to allow the business to run on a day-to-day basis – to pay for expenses and wages. This is the money used in adding value to the product – an outflow of cash but an inflow of value.

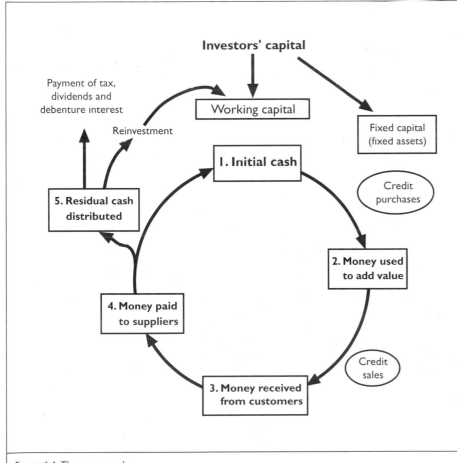

FIGURE 6.4: The money cycle.

MONEY RECEIVED FROM CUSTOMERS

Once products have been sold to customers, money flows back into the business as the customers pay their bills. The timing of payments can be critical; late payments can cause severe problems for firms. Businesses, and especially small businesses, must not tie up their money for too long in part-finished products or completed, but unsold, goods. The money cycle should move forward smoothly in line with the trading cycle to ensure funds are generated in time to purchase more raw materials.

MONEY PAID TO SUPPLIERS

Money flows out of the business in the form of payments to suppliers. It is in the interests of businesses to delay payment and so retain the cash within the business for as long as possible.

RESIDUAL CASH DISTRIBUTED

Provided the business is operating successfully, the amount of money flowing in (payments from customers) should be greater than the amount flowing out (paying suppliers and expenses). In this case, there is residual cash available for distribution – the company has made a profit. Ideally, every business should make a profit and be able to distribute its profits to its investors. However, if more money flows out than in, the business will make a loss. Obviously, this means no residual cash for distribution – investors will not receive any return, in fact they will lose some of their initial investment.

PROBLEMS WITH THE MONEY CYCLE

The major problem that occurs in the money cycle is a shortage of working capital. This usually results because a business buys too many fixed assets (machinery, vehicles, etc.), leaving insufficient circulating money to maintain the money cycle. A shortage of working capital might also be caused by poor credit control – allowing customers to take too long to pay.

Problems with working capital may leave insufficient money to pay creditors. This can cause delays in receiving supplies of raw materials. Delayed supplies will disrupt production and the distribution of products, thereby restricting sales to customers and generating an even lower level of working capital: the money cycle becomes a downward spiral.

ACTIVITY

Write down reasons why the credit terms given to customers might be important in maintaining the money cycle. Discuss your ideas with the rest of the class.

As you can see, the money cycle mirrors the trading cycle; the two cycles are interdependent. Without the money cycle, the trading cycle could not function. Without the trading cycle, the money cycle could not be maintained.

You should also now appreciate how important money is to a business. High sales are not necessarily a sign of success if the business is not earning enough to cover its costs and expenses.

Explain financial transactions and complete supporting documents

THE ACCOUNTING SYSTEM

Financial transactions involve a range of documents, each of which needs to be accurately completed and recorded. In this element, we examine these documents and why they are used. Firstly, however, we briefly look at the accounting system used to record these transactions and explain the importance of accounting records.

The accounting system consists of a series of steps (see Fig. 6.5). At each stage, financial transactions need to be recorded for a number of reasons, including:

⊗ **monitoring the performance of the business;**

⊗ **recording purchases and sales;**

⊗ **generating accounts;**

⊗ **meeting legal requirements.**

MONITORING THE PERFORMANCE OF A BUSINESS

Financial information is vital in planning and controlling the activities of a business. Managers need to know whether the business is making a profit or loss, how much money is available for buying equipment, whether they need to alter the way the organisation operates and so on. The owner(s), creditors and prospective investors need information about the performance and financial health of the organisation.

Some monitoring involves examining the historical financial records of the business to determine how it has performed over time and to assess the current situation. This information is contained in the **final accounts**, which are discussed in greater detail in unit 7.

Another form of monitoring involves comparing what is happening in the business with what was predicted to happen. This is known as **budgeting**. It requires managers to estimate sales and purchases over the coming months (or years) and, therefore, predict the performance of the organisation. This estimation is known as a **budget**. Actual sales and purchases are compared with the budget on an ongoing basis and actual performance is monitored against the budget forecasts. Because this method does not rely on historical data, it allows managers to adjust their planning and to exercise control quickly and effectively. We examine these methods further in unit 7.

RECORDING PURCHASES AND SALES

The majority of financial transactions involve either purchases or sales. These need to be recorded in order to calculate the organisation's profit (or loss) when the final accounts are drawn up.

Purchases and sales on credit need to be recorded in such a way that the organisation knows what money is owing – to its creditors and from its debtors. Without accurate records, payments to creditors may be overlooked or delayed, possibly resulting in supplies being stopped and legal action being taken to recover the debt. At the very least, it will damage relations with suppliers. Likewise, debtors may delay or not pay their invoices. These outstanding debts cannot be followed up if credit sales are not accurately recorded at the time they are made.

Purchases and sales of goods also need to be recorded so that stock can be controlled, and the correct goods sent to customers and received from suppliers.

GENERATING ACCOUNTS

It is essential that every transaction be recorded, accurately and completely, in order to generate complete and accurate accounts. Everything the business has bought or sold must be taken into account when calculating the profit (or loss) made. Likewise, everything the business owns or is owed by others (its **assets**) and everything it owes to others (its **liabilities**) must be shown on the **balance sheet**. In this way, the final accounts achieve their purpose and give a 'fair and true view' of the financial affairs of the business.

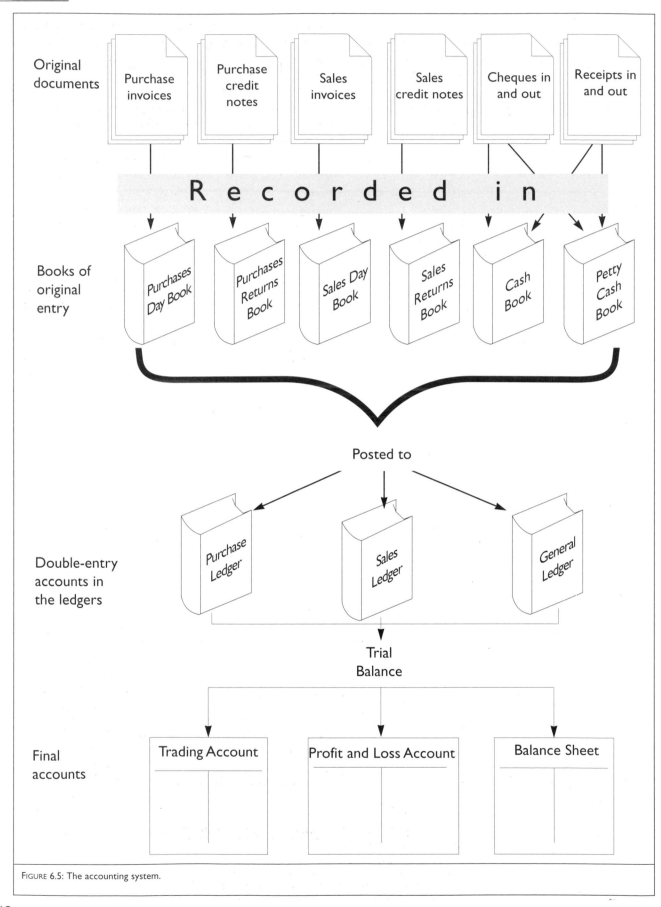

FIGURE 6.5: The accounting system.

MEETING LEGAL REQUIREMENTS

There is an enormous amount of legislation governing the way businesses conduct their affairs, including the way financial information is recorded and made available to interested parties.

All businesses are required to keep financial records in order that their liability for tax can be accurately determined. Information must be recorded and made available to the Inland Revenue and Customs and Excise. These bodies have legal rights to inspect the accounts and check that they are accurate and represent a 'fair and true' view of the business.

The Companies Acts 1985 and 1989 relate specifically to limited companies. These require companies to follow certain procedures in the preparation and presentation of accounts and the disclosure of financial and other information.

If a business pays employees, it must keep accurate **payroll records**, including any deductions made with respect to income tax (PAYE) and National Insurance. The Employment Protection (Consolidation) Act 1978 requires all employers to provide itemised, written pay slips to their employees in respect of their wages or salaries.

MUTUAL UNDERSTANDING

The use of written documents allows both buyer and seller to have a clear understanding of the trading arrangements. They confirm each stage of the transaction: the buyer's requirements; the prices to be paid to the seller; the delivery of the goods or services; the amount owed by the buyer; the time within which payment must be paid; and, finally, the amount paid. Documents constitute legally binding evidence in cases of dispute.

PURCHASES AND SALES

Now that we have an understanding of why financial transactions need to be recorded, we look at the documents used in the process. To start, we look at the flow of documents between a purchaser and a supplier in a typical transaction (see *Fig. 6.6*). Remember, the same documents will be purchase documents to the customer but sales documents as far as the supplier is concerned.

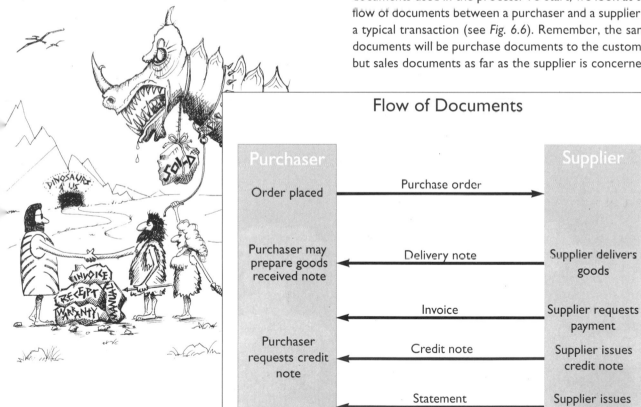

Flow of Documents

Purchaser		Supplier
Order placed	Purchase order →	
Purchaser may prepare goods received note	← Delivery note	Supplier delivers goods
	← Invoice	Supplier requests payment
Purchaser requests credit note	← Credit note	Supplier issues credit note
	← Statement	Supplier issues reminder
Purchaser makes payment	Payment with remittance advice →	

FIGURE 6.6: Flow of documents between a supplier and a purchaser.

ORDER FORM

The purchasing process begins when the customer sends an **order form** to the supplier, detailing what he or she wants to purchase. Each order form (sometimes referred to as a purchase order form) shows the following information:

- ☒ **name, address and telephone/fax details of customer;**

- ☒ **delivery address (if the goods are to be sent to a different address such as a warehouse);**

- ☒ **unique order number – used for reference on subsequent documents and for filing;**

- ☒ **date of order;**

- ☒ **a full description of the goods required (including any product code or catalogue numbers);**

- ☒ **the quantity required, including units where applicable (such as box of 20, pack of 2, ream);**

- ☒ **unit and total price(s) – as quoted by the supplier;**

- ☒ **authorised signature – the order must be signed and dated by someone authorised to place orders;**

- ☒ **required delivery date;**

- ☒ **whether quality/certification documentation is required.**

Fig. 6.7 shows an order placed by Morgan Publishers with one of its suppliers – Banville Business Supplies Limited. Look at the list of features of a purchase order form and locate them on this example.

▣ ACTIVITY

Working individually, list all the things which could be incorrectly completed on an order form and what the consequences would be in each case. Discuss your list with the rest of the class.

SECURITY

Orders are normally checked and approved by an authorised person, who has both the authority to approve purchases and the responsibility for justifying why they were made. The authorised person then signs the order, making it official. Authorised persons may be the managers of

Morgan *Publishers*

103-107 Dorien Park Road, Hammersmith, London W6 5TL
Telephone: 0181-643 5542
Fax: 0181-307 3556
Vat No: 267 7453 03

PURCHASE ORDER
Date: 21-12-95
Reference No: TRA/C136
Order No: 21/2455

Both the Order No. and Reference No. must be quoted on all correspondence.

To Banville Business
Supplies Limited
Manor Park Road
Weybridge
Surrey
KT11 4TM

Please supply:

Quantity:	Description	Cost centre	Price (exc. VAT)
		174.2	63.00
30 boxes	Punched Pockets A4 Clear (100 Pockets Per Box)	140.6	72.60
10 boxes	Nyrex Folders (Yellow) (25 Per box) – 022233	140.6	72.60
10 boxes	Nyrex Folders (Red) (25 Per box) – 022235	140.6	72.60
10 boxes	Nyrex Folders (Green) (25 Per box) – 022236	174.2	49.80
10 boxes	White self-seal Envelopes with windows – SE9112	174.2	63.00
10 boxes	Manilla, self-seal Envelopes – SE2103		

Deliver To Morgan Publishers
103-107 Dorien Park Road
Hammersmith
London
W6 5TL

Delivery Required A. S. A. P.

Authorised Signature *[signature]*

Invoice to Purchase Ledger Department
Morgan Publishers Ltd
North Hill Road
Glasgow G67 1RT

Registered as Morgan Publishers Ltd (Scotland 1948 No. 53987), North Hill Road, Bishopbriggs, Glasgow, G67 1RT

FIGURE 6.7: A purchase order.

different departments, or there may be a central purchasing department where all orders are issued and authorised.

Remember, a signed order form is a legal commitment to purchase what you have ordered, so errors could be very expensive. Additionally, receiving the wrong goods from a supplier may mean that you, in turn, are unable to supply your customers on time. That could prove even more expensive – especially if your customers find a new (and more reliable) supplier and stop buying from you.

DELIVERY NOTE

Having received an order, the supplier checks that the goods are available and arranges for them to be delivered, with an accompanying **delivery note**. This is issued by the supplier and lists the items that are being delivered.

When a delivery arrives, the customer checks the goods to ensure that what is listed on the delivery note has actually been delivered in good condition and then signs the delivery note to confirm receipt of the goods. If the goods are packaged in such a way that a full inspection is not possible at the time of delivery, the person receiving the goods should write 'unexamined' on the delivery note before signing it. In this way, the customer retains the right to notify the supplier if goods are found to be faulty or missing when the packaging is opened.

SECURITY

Once the goods have been signed for, there is a legal obligation to pay for them. It is important, therefore, that

FIGURE 6.8: A delivery note.

ACTIVITY

1 *Fig. 6.8* shows the delivery note for the order placed in *Fig. 6.7*. It arrives with the goods themselves. Can you think of ways in which this note helps both the supplier and the purchaser?

2 Working individually, list all the things which could be incorrectly completed on a delivery note and what the consequences would be in each case. Discuss your list with the rest of the class.

the number, specification and condition of the goods are checked against the original order and match the delivery note before the delivery is accepted. This responsibility usually rests with the warehouse supervisor or manager.

GOODS RECEIVED NOTE

Some organisations also prepare an internal document called a **goods received note**. This lists what has actually been received and is used by the accounts department to check that the purchase invoice, when it arrives, is correct. The goods received note illustrated in *Fig. 6.9* would have been drawn up by Morgan. Can you think of two groups of staff at Morgan who would need to know the information contained within this note?

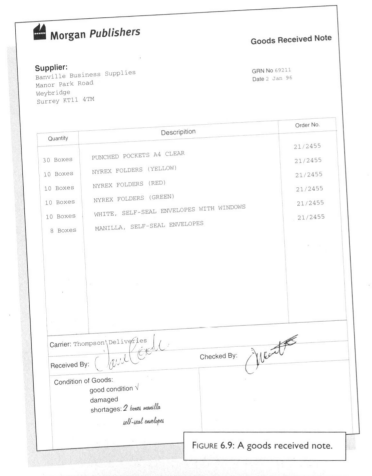

FIGURE 6.9: A goods received note.

INVOICE

Having confirmed receipt of the goods, the customer can now expect to receive an **invoice** from the supplier, stating how much money needs to be paid. These are normally sent by mail and usually arrive a few days after the goods are received.

As far as the supplier is concerned this document is a **sales invoice**. However, from the customer's viewpoint it is an incoming **purchase invoice**, detailing what has been bought and how much is due to the supplier.

The invoice shows details about the supplier, the customer, the date of sale, the details of goods or services supplied and the terms of trade. It has names and addresses:

- ☉ of the supplier;
- ☉ of the customer – to whom the invoice should be sent;
- ☉ to whom the goods were delivered (if different from the above).

The invoice date is the start of the credit period and is therefore important as it determines when payment is due. If VAT is included, it is also known as the **'tax point'** because it is the date at which the sale officially takes place and at which VAT is charged for tax purposes.

The invoice usually has several reference numbers. These include:

- ☉ **invoice number, an unique number – usually pre-printed;**
- ☉ **order number(s), enabling the customer to match the invoice to the original order form(s);**
- ☉ **delivery note number(s), enabling the invoice to be matched to the delivery note(s) and goods received note(s);**
- ☉ **customer's account number (for reference in the supplier's accounting system).**

It contains details of goods supplied:

- ☉ **code or catalogue numbers of the goods delivered – as shown on the original order(s) and delivery note(s);**
- ☉ **full description of each item of goods supplied;**
- ☉ **quantity of each item supplied – this should agree with the quantity ordered and delivered;**
- ☉ **unit (such as ream, box);**
- ☉ **unit price of each item;**
- ☉ **total price per item (unit price multiplied by quantity);**
- ☉ **discount – the percentage of trade discount allowed (usually given to regular customers in the same line of business);**
- ☉ **net amount due after the deduction of trade discount;**
- ☉ **goods total – the total of the net amount column;**

INVOICE

Banville

Manor Park Road
Weybridge
Surrey KT11 4TM

Tel: Sales 01831 657553
Fax: Sales 01831 558427

Tel: Accounts 01831 820244
Fax: Accounts 01831 857093

VAT REG. No. 121 6577321

YOUR ORDER No: 21/2455
OUR DELIVERY No: 1/DT 3573

INVOICE TO:

Morgan Publishers Ltd
Purchase Ledg Contract
(811)
North Hill Road
Glasgow
G67 1RT

DELIVERED TO:

Morgan Publishers
103-107 Dorien Park Road
Hammersmith
London
W6 5TL

CHEQUES PAYABLE TO:BANVILLE BUSINESS SUPPLIES LTD

INVOICE No. 1/I19601   PAGE 1   OF 1   Account   MORGAN   Date 20 Jan 96

PRODUCT	DESCRIPTION	QUANTITY	PRICE	PER	GROSS	DISCOUNT	NET VALUE
127529	PUNCHED POCKETS A4 CLEAR	3000	2.10	100	63.00		63.00
022233	NYREX FOLDER YELLOW	250	7.26	25	72.60		72.60
022235	NYREX FOLDER RED	250	7.26	25	72.60		72.60
022236	NYREX FOLDER GREEN	250	7.26	25	72.60		72.60
SE9112	WINDOW WHITE S/SEAL ENVELOPE	5000	4.98	500	49.50		49.50
SE2103	MANILLA ENV S/S	2500	6.30	250	63.00		63.00

CODE	GOODS VALUE	RATE	AMOUNT
A	393.60	17.50%	68.88

VAT ANALYSIS

Payment is due by 31 March 96

GOODS VALUE 393.60
VAT 68.88
AMOUNT PAYABLE 462.48

FIGURE 6.10: An invoice.

⊗ **cash discount** – a percentage of the goods total which may be deducted by customers if they pay within specified terms (see below);

⊗ **value added tax (VAT)** – an addition of a government-determined percentage (currently 17.5 per cent) to the total remaining after the deduction of any cash discount;

⊗ **invoice total** – the final amount due after all the above has been taken into account.

Finally, the invoice shows what terms for payment apply to the supply. For example:

⊗ **net 30 days** – means that the supplier expects the invoice to be paid in full (with no cash discount taken) within 30 days of the invoice date;

⊗ **10% 7 days** – means that the customer can deduct a 10 per cent cash discount (as shown on the invoice) if the invoice is paid within seven days of the invoice date;

⊗ **carriage paid** – means that the price of the goods includes the cost of delivering them;

⊗ **E & O E** – stands for 'errors and omissions excepted', this means that if there is a mistake on the invoice, or something has been left out, the supplier reserves the right to correct the mistake and demand the correct amount.

If the supplier is registered for VAT, the invoice must also show the supplier's VAT registration number.

ACTIVITY

1 *Fig. 6.10* shows the invoice sent by **Banville Business Supplies Limited** to **Morgan Publishers** in respect of the order and delivery that we have been following in this section. Can you identify three other elements that could be included on this invoice?

2 Working individually, list all the things which could be incorrectly completed on an invoice and what the consequences would be in each case. Discuss your list with the rest of the class.

CREDIT NOTE

Sometimes not all the goods that are ordered arrive in good condition. They may have been damaged or lost in transit, incorrect items or quantities may have been sent or they may be faulty. When this occurs, the supplier sends the customer a **credit note**. A credit note is very similar to an invoice but, instead of increasing the customer's debt to the supplier, a credit note reduces the debt. In other words, it is the opposite of an invoice for accounting purposes. Credit notes detail very similar information to invoices, usually with the addition of an explanation of why the credit is being issued. To avoid confusion, credit notes are often printed in red so that they are easily recognised by the customer's accounts department and not mistaken for invoices.

Credit notes are also issued if the customer has been overcharged on an invoice or if the customer has decided not to purchase some of the goods (provided the supplier is prepared to take them back). Occasionally deliveries are incomplete or damaged. Banville left two boxes of manilla envelopes off Morgan's order. *Fig. 6.11* represents a refund in recognition of this fact and means that Morgan does not have to pay for this part of the order.

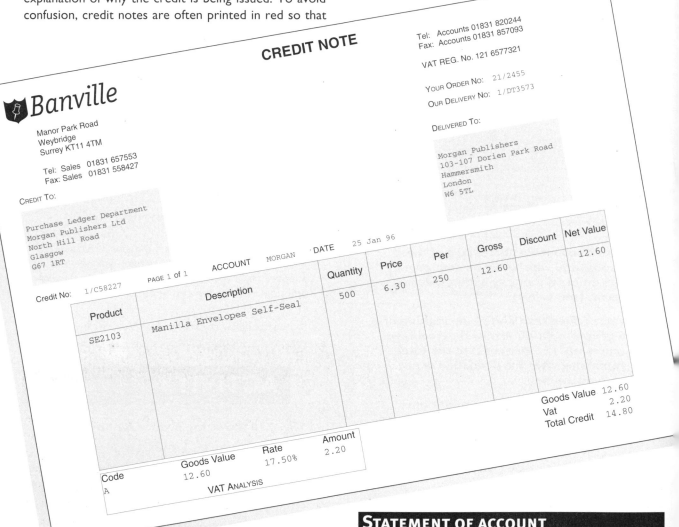

FIGURE 6.11: A credit note.

STATEMENT OF ACCOUNT

At the end of each month a supplier issues a **statement of account** to each of its customers. This lists all the invoices and credit notes that have been sent to the customer during the month, together with any payments that have been received from the customer. The total of the statement, therefore, is the outstanding amount currently due to be paid by the customer. In effect, the statement is a summary of all the transactions that have taken place between the two organisations during the

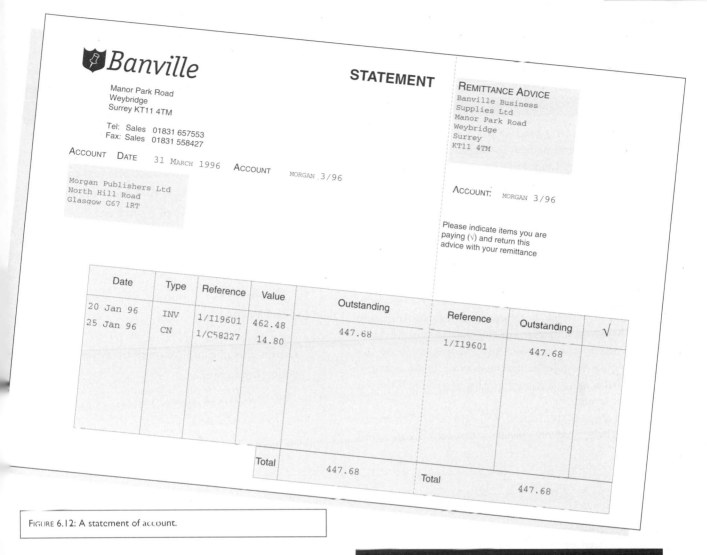

FIGURE 6.12: A statement of account.

MAKING PAYMENTS

month and a reminder to the customer of how much remains to be paid.

Fig. 6.12 shows the statement received by Morgan in respect of the order it placed with Banville Business Supplies Limited. Morgan may pay on receipt of a regular statement such as this rather than paying each invoice. In practice, it is likely that a statement received by Morgan would contain details of a number of invoices rather than a single one. You will also note that details of any credit notes are also recorded on this statement.

When the customer receives the statement, it is checked to ensure that it is correct. If the customer is satisfied that the statement of account is accurate and there are no items under dispute, a payment is sent to the supplier to settle the account. Sometimes the statement includes a tear-off section called a **remittance advice**, which is detached and returned by the customer with the cheque to confirm what is being paid. Some customers prepare their own remittance advices to be sent with their cheques.

Before any payments are made in response to an invoice or statement of account, checks are carried out to ensure that the goods were ordered by an authorised person and received in good condition. Usually, this is done by matching the invoices received from the supplier to the original purchase orders and delivery notes (and goods received notes if used). Any discrepancies or errors are notified to the supplier and the invoice held until the matter is resolved (usually upon receipt of a credit note or the outstanding goods). These security checks ensure that no supplier is paid in error.

Provided that everything is in order, the invoices will be approved for payment. A senior accountant or manager usually has responsibility for approving payments. Sometimes an 'authorisation box' is rubber-stamped on the front of the invoice, which is signed when it is approved for payment.

Ensuring that different people are responsible for the receipt of goods and the payment for goods reduces the opportunities for fraud. This is known as **segregation of duties**.

CHEQUE

A cheque instructs a bank to pay a specified amount of money to a named person (or organisation). The bank issues pre-printed cheques to its account-holders for use when they need to pay money to other people or organisations. Pre-printed on the cheque is the name, address and sort-code of the bank at which the account is held, together with the account-holder's name and account number.

The person writing out the cheque is known as the **drawer** and person to whom it is payable is known as the **payee**. Cheques must be written clearly, in ink, with the amount written in both words and figures. The name of the payee must appear and the cheque must be dated and signed by the drawer. Any changes made on the cheque must be initialled by the drawer. In this country, the life of a cheque is six months, after which time it becomes invalid.

Most cheques are marked 'A/C Payee only'. This means that the cheque can only be paid into a bank account held in the payee's name. This provides some measure of security against fraud and allows cheques to be sent safely through the mail.

ACTIVITY

1 Cheques are used a great deal in business for making payments. List one advantage and one disadvantage to a business of using cheques as a means of payment.

2 Look at the cheque in *Fig. 6.13*. Identify:

   (i) the drawer;
   (ii) the payee.

3 Could this cheque be used by anyone other than the payee?

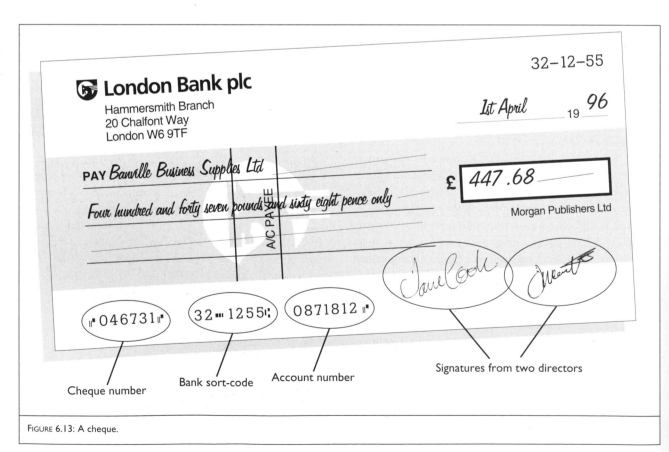

FIGURE 6.13: A cheque.

BANKERS AUTOMATED CLEARING SYSTEM (BACS)

Some businesses make use of a computer-based system known as BACS. This system has been established by the banks to facilitate inter-bank transfers of money via a computer network linking the banks and building societies. BACS dispenses with the need to use cheques. It is especially useful for paying regular suppliers and for making payroll payments.

BACS offers a number of payment methods. These include:

- ☉ **standing orders;**

- ☉ **autopay systems;**

- ☉ **direct debits.**

STANDING ORDERS

The account holder completes a written authorisation (a **standing order mandate**) instructing the bank to make regular payments. The mandate specifies how much to pay, to whom (the beneficiary) and when. These instructions are entered into the computerised BACS system and the money is automatically transferred to the correct account on the specified dates. Businesses use this service for making regular, fixed payments such as rentals or insurance premiums.

ACTIVITY

Fig. 6.14 shows a standing order mandate used by an organisation for teachers of business studies. List the ways in which you think that a direct debit mandate would differ from this standing order mandate.

AUTOPAY SYSTEMS

Where payments of variable amounts are made regularly to specified beneficiaries (such as staff payroll payments), the account holder can use a special type of standing order system known as **'autopay'**. Whenever payments need to be made, a schedule of amounts, dates and beneficiaries is sent to the bank. The information is entered into the BACS system and the money is automatically transferred to the beneficiaries' accounts.

DIRECT DEBITS

Direct debits differ from standing orders in that the amount to be paid, and/or the dates for payment, may be fixed or variable. Usually, an authorisation form (a **direct debit mandate**) is prepared by the beneficiary (such as a leasing company). The customer signs the mandate and returns it to the beneficiary. The mandate is then given to the beneficiary's bank, the computer instructions are set up and the original form sent to the payer's bank.

N A B S E

National Association for Business Studies Education

New Standing Order Mandate

To .... Bank

Branch ....

Address .... Sort Code ....../....../......

....

Please make payments

PLEASE COMPLETE THE FOLLOWING

Account to be debited * - your account name
                 - your account number

Beneficiary's name	Sorting code number	Account number
NABSE	05-09-40	48209734
Bank Yorkshire Bank	Branch title Sutton Coldfield	
Reference to be quoted NABMEM	Frequency of regular payment Annual	
Immediate payment required? YES	Amount of immediate payment *£95.00/£25.00	
Amount of regular payment *£95.00/£25.00	Amount of regular payment in words *Ninety five pounds only or twenty five pounds only	
Date of next regular payment 4/9/96		

* £95.00 inc VAT   Institutional Membership
* £25.00 inc VAT   Individual Membership

- please delete as necessary

PLEASE RETURN TO NABSE c/o CONFERENCE SUPPORT INTERNATIONAL LTD, 27-29 CHESTER ROAD, CASTLE BROMWICH, BIRMINGHAM, B36 9DA AND WE WILL FORWARD TO YOUR BANK

FIGURE 6.14: A standing order mandate.

Whichever BACS method of payment is used, a signed mandate detailing the following information is required by the bank:

- ⊗ **the name and bank account details (bank, branch, sort-code, account name and number) of the beneficiary (who is to receive the payments);**

- ⊗ **the name and bank account details of the account-holder (who is making the payments);**

- ⊗ **the amounts to be paid (unless this is variable – direct debits and autopay);**

- ⊗ **the dates on which sums are to be paid (unless this is variable – direct debits and autopay);**

- ⊗ **the signature of the account-holder authorising payment to be made;**

- ⊗ **the date on which the mandate is signed.**

ELECTRONIC DATA INTERCHANGE

Some organisations are linked to their suppliers via a computerised network system. This is known as **electronic data interchange (EDI)**. It allows the organisations to conduct financial transactions by sending electronic messages. This is an extension of **electronic mail (E-mail)** which is a method of sending messages from one computer to another. EDI dispenses with the need to send documents through the post. It can be used to transmit orders, invoices, credit notes and statements.

Organisations can extend their EDI system to include computer links with their banks. They can, therefore, instruct their banks directly, via the network, to make payments to suppliers. Usually, the computer network system is operated by a third party; this is known as a value added network (VAN). The VAN operates as an electronic post office, with each subscriber having their own electronic 'address'. Organisations transfer information to their suppliers and customers by E-mailing it to the appropriate 'address'.

The major advantage of EDI is that organisations can exchange information very quickly (electronic messages can be sent in seconds). This allows customers to order goods exactly when they are required, rather than holding large quantities in stock. Holding stock is expensive as it ties up money that could used elsewhere and also requires storage facilities. Similarly, payments are transferred faster via EDI.

Additional advantages include reduced costs in buying, handling and storing paper, reduced postage costs and greater accuracy. However, subscribing to the value added networks and the banking networks can be expensive, so many smaller businesses still use manual documentation systems.

PETTY CASH

Cheques and BACS methods are used for the majority of transactions. However, occasionally small purchases – such as postage stamps or a box of teabags for the tearoom – are made in cash by a member of staff. When this happens, the receipt is submitted to the person in charge of **petty cash**, who reimburses the person for the expense. Petty cash is normally held in a secure cash-box in the office, where it is readily available when needed. Each transaction is recorded on a **petty cash voucher**, which details the date, the amount spent and what was bought. The person in charge of petty cash signs the voucher to authorise payment; the person reimbursed signs the voucher to confirm receipt of the money. Petty cash transactions are recorded in the petty cash book, which forms part of the double-entry accounting system. Businesses would not expect to spend large sums through petty cash.

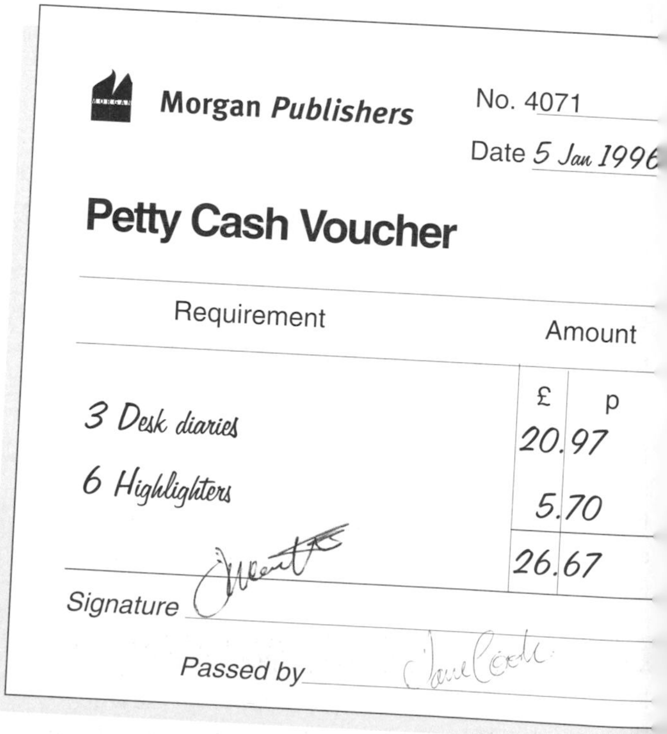

Morgan *Publishers*   No. 4071
Date 5 Jan 1996

Petty Cash Voucher

Requirement	Amount	
	£	p
3 Desk diaries	20	97
6 Highlighters	5	70
	26	67

Signature

Passed by

FIGURE 6.15: A petty cash voucher.

SECURITY

Payments can normally only be authorised by senior staff and only 'authorised signatories' can sign cheques or BACS documents. The authorised signatories give the bank specimens of their signatures. Banks will not make payments unless cheques or BACS documents are signed by one or more of the authorised signatories. Some organisations specify that two signatories must sign each document, reducing the risk of embezzlement and fraud (theft of money from the business).

Normally only one person has access to petty cash funds. He or she is responsible for ensuring that the contents of the petty cash box are correct at all times. Only small purchases can be paid through petty cash; usually firms set an upper financial limit. Larger items are referred to someone with greater purchasing authority.

SUPPORTING DOCUMENTS

Earlier in the unit, we discussed the difference between cash and credit transactions. Most credit transactions are paid for by cheque or BACS. These do not normally require further documentation because bank records confirm that payments have been made.

RECEIPTS

When a cash transaction is made, a **receipt** is normally issued to the customer as proof that the payment has been received. There is no need for further documentation or any record of the customer's details because there is no outstanding debt.

There are many different receipt formats, the most familiar being the till receipt issued by retail stores. Because many stores now use computerised tills, these often show exactly what items have been bought, in addition to the price and total. Alternatively, some retailers issue a hand-written receipt.

In either case, the receipt should show the name and (where applicable) the VAT registration number of the supplier, the date, the amount paid and the VAT amount. Not all till receipts show the amount of VAT charged, so an additional handwritten receipt, showing VAT, may be issued if required.

PAYING-IN SLIPS

Regardless of whether money comes into the business in the form of cash or cheques, it needs to be deposited in the business's bank account; a **paying-in slip** is used for this purpose. (BACS payments are received directly by the bank.)

```
        J SAINSBURY PLC
          ST NICHOLAS ROAD
           GREAT YARMOUTH
           NORFOLK NR30 1NN
      TELEPHONE NO. 01493 330313

                              £
       * SPKG APPL JUCE      0.79
         ONIONS 1KG          0.59
     GARLIC
           2 @   £0.18       0.36
     RED PEPPERS
     0.34 lb @   £0.79/lb    0.27
       * CIDER/GINGER        0.59
       * CORBIERES BLNC      2.49
       * JS CAB SYRAH        2.85
       * MEDTRNEAN CORD      1.49
       *JS VALPOLICELLA      3.09
       * CORBIERES           2.49
       * DRY CIDER X4        2.49
       * TWO DOGS CAN        0.89
       * FLEX COND PERM      1.85
       * A FRNCH FG FR       2.29
       * CWFT F/CON 1L       1.07
       * FLEX SHAMPOO        1.85
         JAFFA CAKE BARS     0.89
         CHKN B/TARRAGON     0.99
         LENTIL/BACN SOUP    0.59
         JS R/CAL SEAFOOD    0.65
       * WHKAS SEL CUT       0.46
         TAGLIATELLE 250G    0.59
       * WHISKAS MEAT        0.46
       * WHKAS SEL CUT       0.46
       * WHKAS SEL CUT       0.46
       * JS C/WL BALL        0.85
       * BIN LINERX20        2.15
       * N/LEANS BICARB      1.75
       * WHITE TISSUES       1.09
       * ANDREX SL/SIZE      1.25
         APPLE/B CRUMBLE     0.39
         APPLE/B CRUMBLE     0.39
     MULTIBUY
         BUY 2 SAVE 39P     -0.39
         CHOC MILKSHAKE      0.95
       * MESQUIK STRWBY      0.95
     MULTIBUY
         BUY 2 SAVE 48P     -0.48
         DORITOS X6          1.16
         JS FRENCH BRIE      0.90
         TURKEY STEAKS X4
         REDUCED PRICE       2.52
         CHICKN CASSEROLE    1.99
         CHICKN CASSEROLE    1.99
         GARLIC BREAD        0.59

       41 ITEMS PURCHASED
     BALANCE DUE            49.05

     EFT                    49.05
       4544 3266 0401 431
     CHANGE
                            0.00

     MULTIBUY SAVING        0.87
```

FIGURE 6.16: A till receipt.

ACTIVITY

The sample till receipt illustrated in *Fig. 6.16* contains most of the features one would expect.

1 Make a list of the details which Sainsbury's would include on each of its receipts.

2 Suggest ways in which Sainsbury's uses the information contained on receipt to help it manage the business.

Pre-printed books of blank paying-in slips are issued to account-holders by the banks. When a deposit is made, the account-holder completes the paying-in slip, listing the cash and cheques to be paid in to the bank.

Most businesses receive payments by cheque. *Fig. 6.17* relates to the account that Morgan used to pay Banville Business Supplies. You can see that Morgan is paying in three cheques and some cash.

FIGURE 6.17: A paying-in slip.

The following details must normally be completed on a paying-in slip:

- ☒ **the date of deposit;**

- ☒ **name, branch and sort-code of the bank where the account is held (normally pre-printed);**

- ☒ **account name and number into which the money is to be paid (normally pre-printed);**

- ☒ **the amount of cash being deposited (listed by denomination);**

- ☒ **the number of cheques being deposited;**

- ☒ **the total amount of the cheques being deposited (entered on the front of the slip);**

- ☒ **a list of cheques and their amounts (entered on the back of the slip);**

- ☒ **the total amount (cash plus cheques) being deposited;**

- ☒ **the counterfoil is completed (this is a record retained by the account-holder);**

- ☒ **the person making the deposit signs the slip.**

BANK STATEMENTS

On a regular basis (usually weekly or monthly), banks send each account-holder a **bank statement**. This is a statement of account which lists all the transactions that have taken place. The first entry shows the balance brought forward from the previous statement. All the deposits paid into the account are listed in the credit column, all payments from the account are listed in the debit column and the final column shows the balance (how much is left in the account). The balance is updated after each transaction – this is known as a **'running balance'**. Bank charges and interest also appear on the bank statement. Bank charges may include a monthly fee and a fee per transaction or they might be calculated on the amount of money passing through the account. Interest can be either paid (where the account is in credit) or charged (where it is overdrawn) by the bank.

Fig. 6.18 illustrates an extract from a bank statement received by Morgan Publishers for its account number 0871812. You will remember that it drew a cheque on this account to pay Banville Business Supplies Limited. The company also paid in some cheques and cash to the account. These details and other transactions are recorded on its bank statement.

The letter C beside the balance indicates that there is money in the account, while D indicates that the account is **overdrawn**. When an account becomes overdrawn, the account-holder is borrowing money from the bank and is charged interest. Overdrafts must be agreed with the bank in advance. This should only be a temporary measure because they are an expensive method of borrowing money as the interest charges are high.

When the business receives a bank statement, the entries are checked against the firm's records of receipts and payments. This record is kept in the cash book, an

London Bank plc

Hammersmith Branch
20 Chalfont Way
London W6 9TF

MORGAN PUBLISHERS LTD

Statement of Account

1996 sheet 612 Account No 0871812	DEBIT	CREDIT	BALANCE Credit=C Debit=D
JAN 1 OPENING BALANCE			31867.57C
JAN 1 Niller Printers 045441	14967.44		16900.13C
JAN 6 SUNDRIES		1322.00	18222.13C
JAN 8 Banville 045440	4217.94		14004.19C
JAN 8			
JAN 28 S Merrills 045592	500.00		23208.64C
JAN 29 SUNDRIES		1947.35	25155.35C
JAN 30 Parkinson Paper 045593	8472.87		16682.48C

FIGURE 6.18: A bank statement.

important component of the accounting system. This is known as preparing a bank reconciliation. It should be done regularly to ensure that both the bank and business records are correct.

COMPLETING DOCUMENTS

The financial documents we have examined in this element are the first step in the accounting process. It is essential, therefore, that they are prepared clearly, accurately and completely. Each document, whether written by hand, typed or prepared on computer, should be checked before being issued, to ensure that all details are correct and all necessary information has been entered. Particular care must be taken in preparing handwritten documents, to ensure that both text and figures are legible and unambiguous. Figures must be written neatly and clearly to avoid them being misread.

Failure to complete documents correctly results in inconvenience, expense and incorrect accounting records. Relationships with other businesses may be affected, especially if suppliers are not paid promptly or customers fail to receive deliveries. Incorrect accounting records result in incorrect final accounts. These will no longer reflect a 'fair and true' view of the business or its performance. Profits may be under- or overstated in the profit and loss accounts, while assets and liabilities may be incorrectly stated on the balance sheet.

At best, inaccurate documentation leads to inconvenience and wasted time. At worst, inaccurate accounting records may cause incorrect decision-making resulting in business failure or lead to charges of false accounting resulting in prosecution.

Calculate the cost of goods or services

DIRECT AND INDIRECT COSTS

We have emphasised how important finance and accurate documentation are to a business. It is equally important in managing a business that information should be available on the costs of production incurred by that business. This information can be used, as we describe later in this unit, in determining the **price** at which the product is sold. However, the relationship between costing and pricing is not always a close one. Businesses should charge the highest price which customers will pay for the product.

Costing aims to allocate costs between jobs and time periods. It provides the information to control costs effectively and to minimise the cost of production. A business normally aims to **reduce costs** and to improve its **productivity**. Profits are maximised by keeping prices high and costs low.

Dividing costs up into various categories is an important part of controlling costs. You may have already come across the terms **fixed costs** and **variable costs**, **direct costs** and **indirect costs**. These two sets of terms tend to be used interchangeably; however, they should not be. We shall consider fixed and variable costs later in this element.

Direct costs are those which can be directly attributed to the production of a particular product or service. Raw materials and sub-contracted labour are direct costs. Indirect costs are the opposite of direct costs – those costs which cannot be directly attributed to a particular product. Administration or rates are examples of indirect costs. Fixed costs are always indirect costs, but variable costs can be direct or indirect.

DIRECT COSTS OF PRODUCTION

Direct costs are those costs which can be linked to the production of a good or service or to some other **cost centre**. Examples of direct costs include expenditure on labour wages, materials and power. We briefly look at each of these in turn, below. Depreciation is sometimes considered a direct cost and sometimes an indirect cost, depending upon the nature of the asset which is being depreciated. We shall consider depreciation as an indirect cost.

LABOUR WAGES

Wages are payment in return for the services of labour. They are a significant part of the costs of most businesses, especially in service industries such as education and health. In many cases, the majority of a firm's costs are wage costs. Firms who are providing a service need to know how much to charge customers – plumbers, for example, charge on an hourly basis. To do this, it is necessary to know the wage costs involved in supplying the service.

Wage costs can be determined in a number of ways. Employees can be paid at an **hourly rate** throughout their working week. So, for example, an employee working a 40-hour week and paid at a rate of £5 per hour receives £200 (40 x £5) for a full week. Alternatively, some employees are paid on a **piece-rate** basis. This means they receive a payment for each unit of output they produce. People engaged as fruit pickers are frequently paid on the basis of the amount they pick, say, £1 for each kilo of strawberries.

ACTIVITY

Michael is employed as a bricklayer. In the past, he has been paid £64 for an eight-hour day. His employer has suggested a change in payment system: from next month Michael will be paid £10 for each 100 bricks he lays.

1 **Calculate how many bricks Michael will have to lay each day to earn the same amount as previously.**

2 **Suggest some benefits that Michael's employer might derive from introducing the piece-rate system.**

Employees often receive **overtime payments** if they work beyond their normal hours. The rate for this overtime work is normally in excess of the usual pay rates – perhaps one and a half times the standard rate. If an employer has to pay overtime, it can increase the cost of production of a good or service. However, it might still work out cheaper than the cost of hiring additional employees.

Employers face other employment costs beyond the wages they pay their employees. They have to pay a **national insurance** contribution related to the size of employees' wages. In addition, they may make a contribution towards employees' **pensions**.

MATERIALS

The cost of materials is the price that a business has to pay to acquire supplies of raw materials. A beer brewer, for example, requires supplies of malted barley and hops. For some manufacturing firms, such as car producers, materials can be a very substantial cost.

⚡ ACTIVITY

Imagine you are running a firm which builds houses.

1 **List all the raw materials you think are necessary to construct a building.**

2 **Suggest how a company could find out the cost of these raw materials.**

Firms operating in the primary and tertiary sectors are likely to have lower material costs. The **primary sector** includes firms involved in agriculture, forestry, fishing and the extractive industries such as coal mining. The **tertiary sector** covers all those industries supplying services, for example banking and insurance.

It is important that firms control the cost of materials as part of their cost control, if they are to achieve the highest possible profit. Because they are a direct cost, expenditure on materials varies with output. So, if a manufacturer of garden furniture decides to increase output in response to favourable market conditions, the material costs for the company will inevitably rise.

POWER

All businesses require power. You might immediately recognise that a major manufacturing business requires a great deal of power in the form of gas, electricity or coal. Jaguar, for example, requires power to operate its presses and drive its production lines. However, even service industries require power to heat and light offices and other work areas.

The cost of fuel, in whatever form, adds to the cost of each single unit of production. However, a certain proportion of power costs can be considered to be an indirect cost. For example, power is needed to heat and light the administration department of the business, and the costs of the administration department cannot be directly attributed to individual products – they are indirect costs.

INDIRECT COSTS

Indirect costs are those associated with the overall running of a business and cannot be easily apportioned to the production of a particular good or service. These costs can sometimes be difficult to control. Managers have to be aware of this and not allow indirect costs to become disproportionately high. Examples of indirect costs include some wage costs, depreciation, management, administration, marketing and some expenses such as rent, business rates and telephone charges.

OTHER WAGES

Some wage costs faced by businesses do not vary directly with the level of output produced by a firm. Perhaps the most obvious example of indirect wage costs is the salaries paid to the managers of a business. Managers may receive increased salaries if the business is successful. Indeed, many managers have a performance-related element in their salary package. But performance is usually measured in terms of profitability rather than the level of output or number of sales achieved by the business. This means that managers' salaries do not rise in direct proportion to increases in output, they are an indirect cost.

Some senior managers are also given shares in the business as part of their pay package. For example, in 1994 the chief executive of National Power sold his shares in the business realising over £600,000. Clearly share options cost the business money, but they are in no way a direct cost.

MARKETING

Many modern businesses describe themselves as **'market oriented'**. This means that they research the needs of their customers and they then produce the goods or services which meet those needs. The alternative approach is often described as **production orientation**; businesses produce goods or services and they then seek promotional strategies to persuade customers to buy these products.

Marketing covers a wide range of activities including market research, advertising and sales promotion. Once businesses have produced the goods or service which people want, it is important to inform potential customers through advertising and sales promotions to boost sales. The cost of these activities can be quite substantial; they should be included when calculating the production costs of a product.

ACTIVITY

Imagine that you are the marketing director for a company producing a range of confectionery. Your company wants to find out what potential customers think of a new chocolate bar that it intends to launch.

1 List two separate ways in which you could research the views of the public.

2 Describe the advantages and disadvantages of each of your chosen methods.

3 List the different groups of people that you would want to include in your research.

DEPRECIATION

You should be familiar with the idea that some items decline in value over time. A commonly quoted example is a car: each year, as it becomes older, its (second-hand) value declines until it is virtually worthless. The same decline in value is true of many fixed assets used by a firm. If a business purchases a fixed asset which has a working life of say four years, it will depreciate – or reduce – its value on the balance sheet over that period. In effect, it is saying the cost of this asset will be spread over the four years. That is why depreciation appears as a charge on the **profit and loss account.**

As an example, assume that a business purchases a piece of machinery for £12,000. It is expected to have a useful life of four years. At the end of its life, the machine will have no value – in other words, its residual value will

be zero. We can calculate the annual depreciation by using the formula:

$$\text{annual depreciation} = \frac{\text{original cost} - \text{residual value}}{\text{life of the asset in years}}$$

In this case, using the formula, we arrive at an annual depreciation figure of £3,000 (£12,000 divided by 4). This technique is known as the **straight line method of depreciation**. However, this is a notional charge because depreciation does not involve an annual movement of cash: it may be that the company paid in full for the asset at the beginning of the four-year period.

ACTIVITY

A company purchases a fixed asset with an expected life of four years. The asset costs £9,000. It is expected to have a residual (or selling) value of £1,000.

1 Assuming it is depreciated by the same amount over each of the four years of its life, calculate the annual depreciation figure entered into the profit and loss account.

2 Calculate the value of the asset that should be recorded each year on the balance sheet.

3 Discuss whether you think it is a reasonable policy to assume that an asset depreciates by the same amount each year of its life.

OTHER RUNNING EXPENSES

Running a business involves paying a lot of other expenses. A firm is likely to pay rent or, perhaps, a mortgage for the premises in which it operates. These payments can be quite substantial for a large business.

Additionally, it receives bills for services such as the telephone and water supply. Another significant cost is business rates; in areas of high unemployment, the government may subsidise rates in order to encourage job creation.

UNITS OF SERVICE

Many businesses base their prices on what is termed units of service. So, for example, an airline might calculate flight charges on the basis of passenger miles. Taking into account the number of people on a particular flight, the airline bases prices on the number of miles covered in the course of the flight. British Telecom adopts a similar approach (see *Fig. 6.20*). It provides firms with the standard cost of a three minute call made at different times of the day and over various distances. Similarly, garages charge for the services of a mechanic on an hourly basis.

ACTIVITY

Look at the invoice shown in *Fig. 6.19*. It is for the supply of gas to a domestic consumer.

1 **Compare this invoice to that shown in *Fig. 6.10*. What additional information is included in the invoice sent to Morgan Publishers? Why do you think this is the case?**

2 **Using the information contained in *Fig 6.19*:**

(a) **state the unit of production used by British Gas as a basis for the calculation of the charge to the domestic consumer;**

(b) **recalculate the invoice assuming that British Gas reduced its charge per unit by 0.1 pence per unit;**

(c) **suggest why British Gas includes a standing charge (based on a daily charge) as a part of its prices.**

FIGURE 6.19: Invoice for supply of gas to a household.

The cost of direct dial calls in the UK*	Time for 10p	Cost of 3 min call
Local calls		
cheap	105 secs	£0.20
standard	75 secs	£0.30
peak	52 secs	£0.40
National calls up to 56 kilometres		
cheap	75 secs	£0.30
standard	32.5 secs	£0.60
peak	24.5 secs	£0.80
weekend	76 secs	£0.30
National calls over 56 kilometres (low cost routes)		
cheap	47.5 secs	£0.40
standard	28.5 secs	£0.70
peak	21.5 secs	£0.90
weekend	76 secs	£0.30
National calls over 56 kilometres		
cheap	36 secs	£0.50
standard	23 secs	£0.80
peak	17 secs	£1.10
weekend	76 secs	£0.30
Calls to mobile phones		
cheap	12 secs	£1.50
standard	8 secs	£2.30
peak	8 secs	£2.30
Calls to BT premium rate service numbers		
cheap	7.6 secs	£2.40
standard	6.1 secs	£3.00
peak	6.1 secs	£3.00

Calls are rounded up to the nearest 10p.
*also applies to calls from Northern Ireland to the Republic of Ireland

FIGURE 6.20: British Telecom call charges.
Source: *A guide to call costs for BT Chargecard.*

ABSORPTION COSTING

To calculate the total cost of producing a single unit it is necessary to include all costs – both fixed and variable, direct and indirect. This process is known as **absorption costing** because all the costs of production for the whole business are absorbed into each cost unit. This process is complicated when a business produces more than one good or service.

Absorption costing 'absorbs' all costs involved in business operations, whether direct or indirect, and charges them to a particular **cost centre** associated with the good or service in question. Thus, if a business makes two products, absorption costing entails allocating (or 'absorbing') indirect costs as accurately as possible to the manufacture of the two products.

✪ **Costs such as rent, rates and fuel** could be allocated or apportioned according to relative floor spaces taken up by the production of the two products. So if product A takes up 60 per cent of the floorspace then 60 per cent of these indirect costs should be apportioned to product A.

✪ **Depreciation** could be apportioned according to the relative value of assets used in the production of the two products.

✪ **Indirect wage costs** associated with management and administrative staff could be allocated according to the number of people directly employed in the production of each product.

It may strike you that some of the bases used to decide upon the allocation of indirect costs are rather arbitrary and are unlikely to apportion costs in a meaningful manner.

ACTIVITY

Lichfield Engineering produces brass door furniture for the DIY market throughout Europe. The company sells its door furniture as sets. Each set comprises a door handle, a letter box and a door knocker. Its annual costs are:

	£
Direct labour costs	425,000
Raw materials	500,000
Fuel	65,000
Transport	125,000
Administration	240,000
Marketing	75,000
Rent and rates	250,000
Total	1,680,000

Lichfield Engineering produces only a single product, so its costs do not have to be apportioned to different products. In a year, the company produces and sells 84,000 units.

1 Calculate the total cost of producing a single set of door furniture when all costs – direct and indirect – are taken into account.

2 Identify which of the above costs are direct. We should expect these to increase as output rises. Calculate the total direct costs for the company for a year.

3 Assume that Lichfield Engineering increases its output by 10 per cent. Now recalculate the cost of producing a single set of door furniture. Remember direct costs will rise, but we would expect indirect costs to remain unchanged.

This is one of the arguments used against absorption costing. It is important that businesses are consistent in the way they allocate costs to cost centres.

Calculating the absorption cost for Lichfield Engineering is straightforward because the company only produces a single product. But, if the company produces, say, three products then the indirect costs would have to be divided up and allocated to each of the three product ranges. Can you think of ways in which you could do this?

We have assumed that only direct costs vary with the level of output of a company. In reality, businesses face constant change and most of their costs are variable. Extra factory space can be rented at short notice, extra managers can be hired and business rates may alter each year; normally in April, when the government sets the figure for the uniform business rate (UBR) for the financial year. In practice costs are, at best, only **semi-variable** and can alter fairly frequently.

For simplicity, we have worked with annual figures. Most businesses need to calculate costs and revenues over shorter time periods. Remember that monitoring and controlling costs is a crucial part of running a business successfully. Failing to monitor and control costs could result in the business running at a loss without the managers being aware of the true financial position. Hence, businesses need to have data available covering shorter time periods to allow informed decisions to be taken. Most businesses draw up monthly or quarterly budgets; they collect data to assess whether or not they are keeping their costs within the budgets they have allocated. This is why cost and revenue figures are provided regularly and frequently. In element 4, we look at revenue figures and link them to costs.

FIXED AND VARIABLE COSTS

Businesses have an alternative classification of their costs. As well as being classified direct or indirect, costs can be termed fixed or variable. This classification has its uses; for example, it is the basis of calculating breakeven which we look at later.

FIXED COSTS

Fixed costs are costs which do not vary with the level of output. They are linked to a time base rather than to a level of activity. Fixed costs exist even if a business is not producing any goods or services.

Thus, an example of a fixed cost is rent. This can be paid monthly or annually, but it does not vary according to whether that office or factory is used intensively to produce goods or services. If a manufacturer can double output and still use the same factory (but more intensively) the amount of rent does not alter – thus, it is a fixed cost. Similarly, the factory rent must be paid even during the period when the factory is closed for the annual summer holiday and there is no production.

You should be able to see that businesses benefit from using their facilities (and especially their premises) intensively. This is because their fixed costs do not alter as facilities are used more intensively but, because they are increasing their output of goods or services, they should be able to generate more revenue in higher sales.

Other examples of fixed costs include business rates, administration, management salaries, interest charges and depreciation. In the long term, fixed costs can alter. A manufacturer may decide to increase output significantly. This may not be achievable by using the existing facilities more intensively, instead it may require additional factory space and the negotiation of loans for additional capital equipment. Thus, rent will rise, as will interest payments. We can see that in the long term fixed costs may alter but, in the short term, they are – as their name suggests – fixed.

VARIABLE COSTS

Variable costs are those costs which vary directly with the level of output. They include payments made for the use of inputs such as labour, fuel and raw materials. If a manufacturer doubled output then these costs would rise significantly.

ACTIVITY

Assume a manufacturer doubles output. Suggest reasons why variable costs might not double along with output.

SEMI-VARIABLE COSTS

Our classification of costs into fixed and variable is simple and very convenient. In business, however, not all costs can be classified in this way. Take the case of an employee who is paid a salary which does not alter whatever the level of output of the business. We should argue that the employee's salary is a fixed cost. But if the business is particularly busy, and the employee is paid overtime to cope with the extra orders, an element of the labour cost becomes variable. In these circumstances, we should say that this labour cost is semi-variable, that is part fixed and part variable. Can you think of any more semi-variable costs?

When added together, fixed and variable costs (plus any semi-variable costs) give the total costs of a business. This figure is, of course, the same as the total direct and indirect costs of the same business. We have merely looked at different ways of dividing up the same total costs.

HELEN'S BUSINESS

In element.1, we looked at the business owned and operated by Helen Godbolt. She operates as a sole trader making flower arrangements for sale in the supermarkets and garden centres of her home town.

Helen runs her business from a workshop situated in a quiet part of the town. The business has annual fixed costs of £5,000, which covers rent, rates and interest charges. Helen's accountant calculates that the variable costs of each flower arrangement are approximately £5. This sum pays for the dried flowers, the oasis and the basket in which the arrangement is sold.

ACTIVITY

Read the case study about Helen's business.

1 If Helen did not produce any flower arrangements, but kept her workshop, what level of costs would she face?

2 Assume that Helen produces 1,000 arrangements during the year. Calculate her total costs. What proportion would be variable costs?

3 Now assume she increases production to 2,000 units per year. Calculate the proportion of Helen's total costs that are now fixed.

4 Describe the benefits that Helen gets from increasing her level of output.

5 Calculate Helen's profits if she produces 2,000 flower arrangements each year and sells them for an average price of £10 each.

MARGINAL COSTS

This is a simple concept, used more by economists than accountants. Marginal cost is simply the extra cost to an organisation of producing one extra unit of output. A brewery, for example, might find that the additional cost involved in producing an extra gallon of beer is only a few pence.

ACTIVITY

Look back at the case study above. If Helen produces an extra flower arrangement, then what is the extra or marginal cost?

Remember this is simply the cost of additional materials needed to produce the extra flower arrangement.

Explain basic pricing decisions and breakeven

The price of a good or service is the amount paid by a customer to the seller to purchase the item. Normally, this price would be sufficient to cover any costs of production and to provide for profit. When a firm takes a pricing decision, it will ensure that this decision is in line with the overall marketing of the business and that it helps to achieve the business's corporate objectives. However, it is important to emphasise that pricing is only one element of the marketing mix which we discussed fully in unit 3. Firms take pricing decisions alongside other marketing decisions, such as how much and where to advertise and which lines of distribution and retail outlets to use to sell their product.

EXTERNAL INFLUENCES ON PRICING

A large number of factors have to be taken into account by a business when deciding upon the price at which to sell its goods and services. Most businesses aim to set a price at which they will receive the highest level of profits. Profits for a business can be calculated by deducting costs from revenue; the surplus that remains, if any, is the profit.

As we shall see, this does not necessarily mean charging a very high price. In some circumstances, a lower price might be more profitable as the business might acquire customers from competitors who charge higher prices for a similar product. Some of the factors we shall discuss are external to the firm; for example, if the economy is going into recession then a firm may choose to reduce its price for fear of losing sales as consumers have less income to spend.

Other factors can be classified as internal: an obvious example is that if a business is going to make a profit on any one item it will have to charge a price which is higher than its cost of production. Later in this element we shall consider further internal influences upon pricing decisions and we shall explain the strategies firms might adopt in their pricing in the short and long term.

ACTIVITY

Make a list of five organisations which do not try to achieve the highest possible profit as their main commercial aim. In each case write down what you think their major aim might be.

THE NEED TO MAKE A PROFIT

Some organisations do not need – or even aim – to make a profit. However, the drive for profit is the overriding objective of the majority of businesses in the UK. This need for businesses to make a profit arises for a number of reasons. The owners of the business – shareholders, partners or perhaps the sole owner or trader – have put capital into the business in the expectation of earning a return on their investment at some stage. For this return to be made, the business has to earn a **surplus** of revenue over costs – it has to make a profit.

Other investors will be encouraged to put their money into a business if they see that it is making a profit. This is particularly important for public limited companies (plcs). Their share prices are quoted on the **Stock Exchange** and investment decisions usually depend upon the level of profitability of the company concerned.

The major source of funds for capital investment in new fixed assets such as factories and machinery is **retained profit**. Firms usually take a deliberate decision to hold on to some of their profits (called **undistributed profits**). The remainder of their profits are paid to the owners of the business. The undistributed profits are used to improve the efficiency of the business or, perhaps, to finance an expansion such as the building of a new factory.

Some firms engage in profit-maximising pricing. This entails researching the market to find the price which yields the largest profit. Note that the highest price is not necessarily the most profitable because a higher price usually results in fewer sales. Firms need to take account of the **price elasticity of demand** (as explained in unit 1) when seeking a profit-maximising price.

COMPETITION

A major factor that firms take into account when making pricing decisions is the extent, nature and possible reactions of competitors. Managers of businesses assess the market in which they are selling. They want to know:

- ✪ **how many firms are there in the market?**

- ✪ **how easy is it for new firms to enter the market?**

- ✪ **do competitors emphasise price in their marketing?**

- ✪ **are there close substitutes for the product being sold?**

Because all these factors interact, it is difficult to look at them in isolation. However, we shall use these questions as a structure for assessing the impact of competition on pricing decisions.

Economists classify markets according to the number of firms in that market. Some industries have only a single producer. This situation is termed a **monopoly**. (This is a pure monopoly; a legal monopolist, in the UK, is defined as a firm that controls 25 per cent or more of a market.) If a firm is a monopolist, then it has a degree of freedom in setting its prices because there are no rival firms to undercut them. Monopolists can abuse their market position particularly if no close substitute for their products exists.

A very common form of competition in UK markets is **oligopoly**. A market is deemed to be an oligopoly when there are few, relatively large suppliers within a market. The word oligopoly derives from the Greek *'oligoi'*, meaning a few. The markets for tobacco, daily newspapers and household detergents are oligopolistic; in each, the market is dominated by a small number of large producers.

In these circumstances, firms are very conscious of one another and their actions are influenced by what they believe will be the likely reactions of their competitors. Before an oligopolistic firm decides upon a price, it will consider very carefully the likely reaction of its rivals. Will competitors charge a similar price to avoid a **price war** or will they reduce their prices and, for example, advertise strongly the price differential? A judgement about the likely reaction will be an important factor shaping any final pricing decision.

Some oligopolistic markets are fiercely price competitive; in others, prices are so similar that there are accusations of collusion to maintain artificially high prices. Examples of highly price competitive oligopolistic markets are the overseas holiday market and, currently, the newspaper market. In contrast, the petrol retailing market is less price competitive and there have been allegations of collusion to maintain high prices and limit competition.

☀ ACTIVITY

Research the petrol retail market and the foreign holiday market.

1 **Find out the names of the major suppliers and what share of the market they have.**

2 **Collect some of their advertising materials and compare them. Consider to what extent firms in the two markets compete on price or on other factors such as promotions.**

3 **Write a short account of your findings.**

The oligopolistic market structure is an important influence on pricing decisions as it is becoming more common in developed economies. As products and services become more technical and complex to research, design and produce, they require larger businesses to produce them and to compete in the market-place. Oligopolistic markets can be highly price competitive which makes pricing decisions particularly critical; alternatively, prices can be relatively stable, with firms competing on quality and special promotions as well as other factors.

A final type of market structure recognised by economists exists where there are many small firms competing on an even basis because none has a competitive advantage. Economists sometimes refer to this type of market as being **perfectly competitive**. Consider the case of vegetable producers. Ignoring the market for organic produce, vegetables are pretty similar and at any time prices tend to 'bunch' around a given level. In such circumstances, the forces of demand and supply set the price, all producers set their prices closely around this market price. Such firms are sometimes referred to as **'price-takers'**.

In this type of 'perfect' market, the forces of demand and supply play a greater role than in markets with fewer and larger producers. Firms in competitive markets have little freedom in terms of pricing, particularly if their rivals produce virtually identical products.

However, not all competitive markets are ones in which identical products are sold. Some competitive markets do produce differentiated products. This type of market is called a **monopolistically competitive** market. Here firms differentiate their products through **branding**, when a product is given an identity of its own. This allows a firm greater freedom in price setting as the different nature of its product justifies price variation. It is more difficult for customers to compare prices with similar products. An example of this type of market is the market for legal services.

Markets can be especially price competitive if it is easy for new firms to enter and start trading. This is true of industries which require little capital investment and relatively few skills on the part of the workforce. Hairdressing and painting and decorating fall into this category. If firms tried to charge high prices, rivals would quickly enter a local market and, because of this, firms usually keep their prices low. This is another situation where the pricing decision is highly constrained.

In many markets, firms tend to compete in ways other than by price. They may advertise heavily, perhaps stressing

FIGURE 6.21: Competing on price.

the quality of their product, or they might use special promotions offering gifts or running competitions. They tend to follow the established price and try to avoid price changes. Companies fear that if they raise prices, their customers might purchase products from elsewhere, alternatively, if they lower prices, their rivals might lower their prices too. This might lead to a particularly damaging price war.

In general, if a business faces competition from a great number of similar products, it has less freedom in setting its prices. The price it charges is likely to be affected by the prices of others. When a business is able to make its product different from those of its competitors, or it has few rivals, then it has more freedom to establish its own price.

UNDER-USED CAPACITY

Capacity is the amount that a business can produce by fully utilising all its resources in the short run. It is the maximum amount that can be produced without acquiring additional fixed assets such as factories and machinery. It can be difficult to measure capacity accurately as it can be increased (using given resources) in a variety of ways. For example, better quality materials or a more highly motivated workforce can increase production without acquiring additional fixed assets. Businesses use a standard formula to calculate the extent to which the capacity of a firm's resources are being used.

$$\text{capacity utilisation} = \frac{\text{actual output per period}}{\text{full capacity output per period}} \times 100$$

It is important that a firm attempts to use its full capacity in order to minimise the impact of fixed overheads on the level of profits. Consider the following example: a business has fixed annual costs of £100,000 and produces 50,000 units of output each year. Thus, each unit bears £2 of the fixed overheads. If output falls to 25,000 units, this fixed overhead element in the cost of producing a single unit rises to £4. Thus, utilising the full capacity of a business is important in financial terms because it spreads fixed overheads over a larger number of units of output.

ACTIVITY

Developing this example further, assume that the firm has direct or variable costs of £5 per unit of production in addition to the fixed costs of £100,000. The product sells for £10.

1 Calculate the impact on total profits of reducing output from 50,000 units to 25,000 units annually.

2 What price should it now charge if the firm wants to maintain its original profit level?

If a business is not utilising all of its capacity, then it may well price any additional output at a level which covers all the variable (or marginal) costs such as wages, raw materials and fuel and makes some contribution towards fixed overheads. We consider this concept more fully later in this unit.

THE STATE OF THE ECONOMY

We considered how the government influences the markets in which businesses operate in unit 1. This highlighted the fact that the state of the economy is an important influence upon business behaviour. Similarly, the state of the economy has a significant impact on the pricing decisions taken by many firms.

Some firms might only be affected by the state of the local economy, if they price their goods or services to be sold in the immediate locality. Other firms might be affected by the state of the whole UK economy, because they sell products throughout the country. Finally, some particularly large or specialist firms sell throughout the world and so are dependent upon the state of the world economy.

ACTIVITY

Study the list of firms below. Classify those that would be affected by the state of the local economy, the national economy, and the international economy.

⊗ **Barclays Bank**

⊗ **BP**

⊗ **Paul's Motors**

⊗ **A corner grocery shop**

⊗ **Pressman Builders (UK) Ltd**

⊗ **British Gas**

⊗ **Norfolk Farms**

We need to establish how we would measure the state of the economy, whether it be local, national or international. There are a number of indicators that governments and the business community use to assess the state of the economy.

BANKRUPTCIES AND NEW BUSINESS STARTS

This is one way of assessing the general health of an economy. If the level of production in the economy is rising and the economy is broadly healthy, then the number of bankruptcies will be low because few businesses should be failing in such prosperous circumstances. These circumstances are sometimes termed an **economic boom**. When the economy is booming, a lot of people are tempted to go into business on their own and so the number of business start-ups rise. When the economy is healthy, firms have a degree of freedom to increase their prices as consumers may pay less attention to price and concentrate more on product quality, after-sales service and so on.

During an **economic recession**, the opposite is true. The number of bankruptcies increases and business start-ups decline in number. Firms tend to be cautious in their pricing strategies because consumers are likely to be very sensitive to price increases.

UNEMPLOYMENT

In many respects, unemployment is another way of measuring the general health of an economy, though unemployment can be confined to a particular industry or a particular locality rather than being widespread. When large numbers of people are without work, consumers have relatively little money to spend on the products and they cut back on non-essential products. Unemployment benefit is low, so many people are very price conscious when incomes are low.

INCOME LEVELS

In some areas, even those who are in employment receive low wages. In 1995, the average French income was 30 per cent higher than that of the UK. Similarly, people in London enjoyed incomes substantially in excess of the residents of Belfast. High incomes obviously mean that people have more money to spend. They may be willing to pay higher prices; indeed they may associate high prices with quality.

INFLATION

Inflation refers to the rate of change in prices, usually measured on an annual basis by the **retail price index (RPI)**. Firms are particularly aware of changes in the rate of inflation when taking pricing decisions. They have to take account of rising raw material and labour costs (their direct costs) and to adjust their prices accordingly to maintain profitability. If inflation is rising, then firms will not

want to lag behind their competitors in benefiting from rising sales revenue.

EXCHANGE RATE

Exchange rates are particularly important for the international economy, but they also have relevance to the national and local economies. The **exchange rate** can simply be defined as the price of one currency in terms of another. The pound is commonly expressed in terms of the US dollar, for example, £1 is worth $1.55 (November 1995). Increasingly, however, the pound is being valued in terms of the premier European currency; the German Deutschmark. The financial pages of newspapers print the previous day's exchange rate for the pound, usually expressed in terms of all the world's major currencies.

A fall in the value of the pound from, say, $1.55 to $1.45, has an impact both on firms in the UK and abroad. It means that UK exports become cheaper and that imported goods become more expensive.

ACTIVITY

A UK manufacturer sells coffee-making machines in France. These cost £10 to manufacture and export. So they could be sold in France for 100 frs. (French francs), assuming an exchange rate of 10 frs. to the pound. Similarly, a French firm's coffee-makers which cost 120 frs. to produce and export could be on sale in the UK for £12 (assuming the same exchange rate).

Now suppose the value of the pound falls, so that £1 is now worth 8 frs. Calculate the new selling prices of the two coffee-makers assuming no other changes take place. How much could the UK firm increase their prices (expressed in pounds) without forcing French customers to pay more in francs?

As the previous activity illustrates, a fall in the value of the pound gives firms the opportunity to raise their prices in overseas markets without actually increasing the cost to the consumer. This does not mean that they will necessarily choose to do so. They might prefer to increase their market share by holding prices down.

The effect on the home market of a fall in a currency is equally attractive for domestic businesses. Imports rise in price, giving home producers a price advantage over their foreign competitors. In these circumstances, domestic firms could raise their prices and enjoy larger profits or hold them down and hope for an increase in market share. However, firms which import raw materials or components will find their direct costs rising. This may force them to increase their prices.

A rise in the exchange rate of any currency has the opposite effect. You should be able to work through an example to illustrate that a rise in the exchange rate increases the price of exported goods and services and cuts the price of imports. This poses problems for domestic firms as their prices will become less competitive; in these circumstances, the advantage lies with foreign producers.

PRICING AND THE ENVIRONMENT

Many firms base their prices on the costs of producing the good or service in question. In recent years, businesses have incurred additional production costs meeting the demand for environmentally-friendly goods and services. Some of these costs are imposed by legislation designed to protect the environment. Other costs are related to market demands, the public wants to buy products which do not harm the environment (either in their production or use). Increased demand for recycled paper and aerosols without chlorofluorocarbons (CFCs) are examples of changing consumer tastes.

The prevention of pollution imposes significant additional costs for businesses. Imperial Chemical Industries (ICI), for example, has developed a substitute chemical for CFCs for use in refrigerators and freezers. The programme to develop this new material entailed investing in new factories at Runcorn in Cheshire and in Louisiana in the United States. However, ICI acknowledges that production costs for the substitute are 'at least five times as much … even after production economies of scale come into play'. This has obvious implications for the company's pricing policy.

Increased costs can also arise from introducing packaging which is not harmful to the environment. Companies are urged to use biodegradable packaging which will rot away over time. This type of packaging is more expensive than conventional materials. However, some firms can reduce their costs by reducing the amount of packaging they use. Robust products often have two or even three layers of packaging. Producers of household detergents such as Proctor and Gamble have recognised this, they now sell washing powder in more permanent storage containers which can be reused. Thus, the impact of environmentally friendly packaging on price varies according to the product in question.

Firms have to comply with an increasing amount of legislation designed to protect the environment. The main UK legislation in this area is the **Environmental Protection Act 1990**. It enshrines the principle that 'the polluter pays'. The Act sets high standards for industrial emissions, effluents, waste disposal and resource management and provides instruments for enforcement.

The **European Union** has passed more than 200 regulations and directives relating to environmental pollution. Directives cover the disposal of waste, control of air pollution and emissions from motor vehicles. As an example, under legislation introduced in March 1991, the production of all CFCs must be phased out by 1997. In May 1992, the **European Commission** proposed a carbon tax on fuels. This is intended to reduce demand for fuels which damage the environment. The proposed tax would put about a penny a litre on the price of petrol in the UK.

Meeting the new standards required by legislation inevitably imposes additional costs for businesses, particularly those in the so-called 'polluting sector' such as chemical manufacturing and oil refining. These additional costs are likely to be reflected in the pricing policies of the firms affected.

INTERNAL INFLUENCES ON PRICING

As we have seen, many of the factors which influence a business when setting prices are externally imposed. However, a range of other factors arise within the business itself.

THE OBJECTIVES OF THE BUSINESS

It is easy to assume that all businesses pursue maximum profits as their principal objective or aim. In practice, businesses may have other objectives.

GROWTH

Growth is the primary objective for a considerable number of firms, both small and large. Through growth businesses can become more secure as they accumulate larger reserves and produce a wider range of products. There is less risk if a particular product fails or if a certain market is lost because the firm has others on which to rely. If a firm can grow, it will probably increase its market share and may be able to raise its prices, thus increasing its long-term profitability.

A policy of growth means that a company has to price very competitively, particularly when it is entering a new market or acquiring new customers. This frequently results in multiple pricing, where firms charge different prices to different customers. Banks, for example, frequently offer genuinely free banking to students to encourage them to open accounts. However, at a later stage the normal account charges are imposed.

SOCIAL RESPONSIBILITY

Social responsibility concerns the extent to which individual firms serve social needs rather than the narrow financial interests of the owners and managers, even if this conflicts with the maximisation of profits. A business should be socially responsible to customers, shareholders, suppliers, employees, local residents as well as the environment. The Body Shop organisation run by Anita Roddick and her husband Gordon is well known for its sense of social responsibility. The Body Shop meets its social responsibilities in a number of ways. For example, it has organised the sending of relief supplies to eastern Europe, runs approximately 750 community projects and encourages recycling amongst its customers. *Fig. 6.22* is an advertisement designed to show the general public that British Gas is not an uncaring monopoly. It explains how British Gas has introduced a password system for its elderly and partially-sighted customers.

ELVIS LIVES,
CONFIRMS
METER READER,
BUT
WHEREABOUTS
REMAIN A SECRET.

Blind or partially sighted people may wish to take advantage of our special password scheme. It guarantees that when our representatives visit, customers can be sure we are who we say we are. All that remains is to choose the magic word. Believe it or not, Elvis lives just across the road from The Queen of Sheba.

British Gas

FIGURE 6.22: British Gas advertisement.

To some extent, the trend for firms to become more socially responsible has been a competitive one. If rival firms behave responsibly and publicise their activities then other firms will follow suit. Increasingly, governments and the European Union have passed legislation designed to protect consumers, employees and the environment.

Improving the image of a company will increase its costs which, in most cases, must be recovered through its pricing policy. It can be argued that such an objective may lead to firms raising their prices to ensure at least a minimum level of profits. They may do this in relatively hidden ways in order to protect their image. In 1995, British Telecom gave a lot of publicity to the price cuts it had introduced on overseas calls. At the same time, it increased the line rental charges paid by all of its customers.

Social responsibility does not always mean higher prices. In some circumstances, firms may offer reduced prices to vulnerable or less wealthy groups in society. Many businesses offer reduced rates for pensioners.

ACTIVITY

Research the local businesses in your area. To what extent do they publicise their socially responsible actions? Do they advertise lower prices for certain groups?

MAXIMISING SALES REVENUE

Some firms that are trying to establish themselves in a market seek to maximise sales revenue. This strategy is likely to be particularly favoured by employees who have salaries linked to sales figures. Salaries of a sales team might be linked, in part, to the volume of sales. Increasingly, however, companies link wages and salaries to profits rather than sales. Maximising sales revenue is likely to encourage companies to set relatively low prices. In this sense, it can be seen as a very different approach to profit maximisation which may involve fewer sales at a higher price.

OTHER OBJECTIVES

A number of business organisations pursue other objectives which have implications for their pricing policies. Examples are charities and voluntary organisations, such as Oxfam, one of the UK's better known charities.

Charities normally exist to dispense goods and services to those in need. Their prices are likely to be very low or they may even provide their goods or services without charge. Their pricing policy will be to provide the service at a minimal charge. They can afford to do this because they receive financial support from the general public and other organisations.

However, some organisations which have charitable status may pursue other pricing policies. Most public schools have charitable status and their services are provided at a substantial charge.

OTHER FACTORS

A number of other factors influence businesses when they are deciding upon their prices. Quite often, these are short term in their nature. A firm introducing a new product might aim to hold the price at a low level to allow the product to develop and to take a reasonable share of the market. Sky Television, for example, has offered some special deals in order to attract new customers to satellite television.

Alternatively, a business – having invested a considerable sum in the development of a new product – might want to charge a price which will be sufficient to repay its investment and provide some profit.

PRICING STRATEGIES

As we have described, a business is subject to a number of influences when determining its prices. If it is a large business, it may be able to have significant influence over the price at which its product is sold. Smaller businesses facing greater competition have less control and have to respond to, rather than shape, market price.

A business has to decide upon the pricing strategy that it wishes to pursue as well as the short-term tactical moves that it may use as a means of achieving its long-term strategy. In this section, we consider three pricing strategies:

- ⊗ **cost-plus pricing;**

- ⊗ **contribution pricing;**

- ⊗ **market-led pricing.**

In addition, we shall discuss the short-term pricing tactics that firms may employ.

COST-PLUS PRICING

Cost-plus pricing involves calculating the average cost of production of a particular good or service and then adding a certain percentage mark-up to generate a profit for the firm. The average cost of production is calculated by adding together fixed and variable costs for the product in question and then dividing by the quantity of the product that is produced. It is important that all costs are taken into account. In using cost-plus pricing, businesses need to use absorption costing techniques to apportion all costs (including indirect costs) to products.

This type of pricing strategy is most likely to be used when a business needs to make a profit. Adding an amount (the mark-up) to the cost of production guarantees a profit. However, this approach does not take into account what the consumer is prepared to pay, nor does it consider the actions of rival firms.

ACTIVITY

Consider a brand of soap with annual fixed costs of £100,000 and variable costs of 10p per bar. If the firm produces one million bars each year, calculate the average cost of producing a single bar.

Cost-plus pricing works like this: a firm calculates that the cost of producing a single product is £10. It may decide upon a mark-up of 20 per cent to provide its profit. So, it decides to sell its product for £12, earning £2 profit on each sale.

The simplicity of this approach is its major advantage. It is easy to do and firms can be confident that their earnings will be sufficient to cover their costs of production and create some profit.

The major drawback with this pricing strategy is that it ignores the market. Cost-plus pricing may determine a price which is acceptable to the firm and provides for a satisfactory profit, but it may be unacceptable to consumers. This may result in the firm achieving substantially less sales than it anticipated and profits may be low or even non-existent. Cost-plus pricing is usually inappropriate where a firm faces fierce competition.

CONTRIBUTION PRICING

Contribution pricing is based on the principle that if the price of a product exceeds the variable cost of production, then the product will be making a contribution towards the fixed costs of the business. This is a particularly appropriate strategy for a firm which produces a number of products. This approach is sometimes referred to as **marginal cost pricing**.

A firm calculates the **contribution** by subtracting the variable cost of production (the marginal cost) from the sales revenue. The key formula is:

contribution = sales revenue − marginal cost

Contribution can also be calculated for an individual unit of production by subtracting the marginal cost of producing a single unit of production from the price at which it sells.

We can illustrate this point with an example. South Norfolk Vineyards produce three wines which sell well throughout the UK and the European Union. The prices, variable costs and hence the contributions of the three varieties of wine are shown in *Fig. 6.23*. South Norfolk Vineyards has £147,000 available to pay its fixed costs and to provide for profit.

	Sales revenue £	Marginal cost £	Contribution £
Chateau Cromer	180,000	120,000	60,000
Weaver's Red	65,000	60,000	5,000
Norfolk Pride	284,000	202,000	82,000
		Total Contribution	147,000

FIGURE 6.23: Contribution pricing – South Norfolk Vineyards.

Under contribution pricing, each product is priced so that it makes some contribution towards paying fixed costs. The business will make an overall profit if enough units are produced and sold to ensure that the contribution earned exceeds total fixed costs. So, in our example, the vineyard would make a profit if its fixed costs are less than £147,000.

In the case of South Norfolk Vineyards, it could be argued that Weaver's Red is underpriced since it makes a very small contribution relative to its sales revenue, but this could be a new product that is steadily building up sales or simply a less successful product.

A benefit of contribution pricing is that separates out individual products and illustrates whether they can cover their own variable costs. If we calculate the total cost (the fixed plus variable costs) for each product, one or more products might show a loss. However, a product can be of value to a business if it makes a contribution towards fixed costs, which have to be paid even if the product is discontinued.

ACTIVITY

South Norfolk Vineyards has been told by its accountants that the total fixed costs of the business amount to £100,000. The accountants believe that 40 per cent of the fixed costs can be attributed to the production of Chateau Cromer, 10 per cent to Weaver's Red and the remaining 50 per cent to Norfolk Pride. Using this information, calculate the profits, if any, earned by each variety of wine. Do you think the company should stop producing Weaver's Red?

An important point arises from contribution pricing. If a business is already profitable, it can price any additional output at a level slightly in excess of the marginal cost of production. In these circumstances, because total fixed costs are already covered by the existing contribution, any further contribution is pure profit. This can be illustrated by the case of an airline. If sufficient seats have already been sold to cover the cost of a flight then any remaining seats only need to be priced at a level to cover the marginal cost of the extra passengers. The marginal costs include the cost of the extra fuel and the in-flight meals. These marginal costs are relatively small; so, airlines are able to offer very low prices to those able to fly at short notice.

MARKET-LED PRICING

Cost-plus and contribution pricing strategies are both based upon the costs of production of the product or products concerned. Although contribution pricing does allow some flexibility of price in response to market conditions, the main focus of this method is still cost. This is a very **product-oriented** view of pricing. It may have the advantage that it provides a profit for the company, but if competitors are selling products of equal quality more cheaply sales might be very low, generating tiny profits. Alternatively, consumers may actually be willing to pay more for the product. Cost-plus and contribution strategies can, therefore, lead to prices that are too low and the company loses an opportunity to make greater profits.

Many firms feel that their pricing strategies have to reflect the conditions that prevail in the market. We have discussed at some length how the competitive nature of a market might influence a firm's pricing of its products. Market-led pricing is a collective term for pricing methods that are based upon the conditions in the market. Market-led pricing methods can be carried out in a number of ways; many approaches or strategies are short term because once their objective has been achieved the business may change its approach. We now consider some short-term strategies.

MARKET SKIMMING

'Skimming the cream' takes the top of the milk. Market skimming takes the top of the market by selling at a very high price to the relatively few consumers who are willing to pay this price. It is only possible with an innovative product which has relatively little competition. This method of pricing is common in the pharmaceutical industry. A company may spend a lot of money researching and developing a new drug; it will deliberately set high prices until rivals bring out a competitive product. Companies producing technical products such as computers also employ this approach.

Some products are purchased because they are fashionable, and sometimes only the rich can afford them. Usually, firms in these markets hold prices high until increased competition forces them to drop prices. This can be a very profitable approach: companies can charge a high price early on and then drop their prices later, when competition intensifies, to attract the mass market.

However, high profits will attract competitors to enter the market, so the period of high profits may be relatively short term.

☀ ACTIVITY

Look through advertisements in magazines or newspapers to identify a product which has been priced at a level to 'skim the market'.

1 **What features in this product make it innovative?**

2 **What sort of people purchase it?**

3 **Watch the product over time to see if competitors appear and if the price begins to fall.**

MARKET PENETRATION

If a firm is looking to establish itself in a market, it may choose to price at a low level in order to build up **brand loyalty** and gain a share of the market. The firm may be producing a new product or introducing an established product into a new market. By developing brand loyalty, the company may be able to raise its prices at a later date and retain its customers. This approach can be particularly suitable for firms which anticipate high long-term sales. In the short-term, therefore, they are prepared to accept relatively small profits on each item sold.

This approach to pricing does have disadvantages. It can give the product a low-price image which can be associated with poor quality. Such an image can make it difficult for the company to raise its prices at a later date.

This pricing strategy was used by the publishers of the television listings magazine TV Quick. It initially had a cover price of 10p until it had established a reasonable level of sales. Then its price was raised to provide a profit for its publishers.

DESTROYER PRICING

This approach to pricing is also called **predatory pricing**. It entails setting a price sufficiently low to eliminate rival firms. Destroyer pricing is considered anti-competitive and firms suspected of employing it may be investigated by the **Office of Fair Trading (OFT)**.

Firms can use this method of pricing to knock out the opposition before raising their price again to generate larger profits. In the 1980s, Rentokil was told by the Office of Fair Trading to stop this practice. The OFT alleged that the company had used this pricing policy to knock out competitors throughout the UK before raising its prices and earning excessive profits. It has also been alleged that established airlines employed this tactic to force Laker Airlines out of business.

PRICE DISCRIMINATION

Price discrimination strategies involve offering the same product at different prices in different markets for reasons not associated with variations in costs. It is important that a supplier is able to keep parts of the market separate if this policy is to be a success.

One well-known price discriminator is British Telecom. It charges higher tariffs for calls made during the day than in the evenings or at the weekend. Utilities such as gas and electricity companies charge different prices to different groups of customers. Often, businesses are charged higher prices than domestic consumers.

CUSTOMER-VALUE PRICING

A customer-value approach involves charging the price that customers associate with the product and are prepared to pay. This is particularly used in pricing goods which have some status value. Chanel perfumes and Rolex watches have names which can command high prices. This is because customers perceive these goods to have high value.

UNDERCUTTING COMPETITORS

A pricing method employed by some companies is to choose a price that just undercuts the price charged by competitors. Some petrol retailers have followed this pricing method in an attempt to gain market share from their rivals.

Price wars commonly occur where there is over-supply within an industry, companies cut prices in an attempt to sell off their surplus stock. All companies tend to lose out in these circumstances as their price cuts tend to be matched by competitors leaving the businesses in the same relative position. The only winner from a price war is the consumer.

SPECIAL OFFERS

Special offers and promotions tend to be very short-term approaches to pricing. They may be used in combination with one of the other approaches outlined above.

A common type of special offer is the **loss leader**. A loss leader is sold at such a low price that a company makes a loss or a negligible profit on the sale. However, the company hopes that customers attracted by the cheap item will buy other standard-priced products to provide profit. So, loss leaders are used by businesses like

supermarkets which sell a range of products. Businesses usually advertise loss leaders extensively.

Companies also make **promotional offers** such as 'two for the price of one', run competitions or attach free gifts to products. This has to be done with care. In 1994, Hoover retained its standard prices but offered customers free airline tickets if they purchased certain products. The company was overwhelmed by the demand for its products and was unable in all cases to supply the free airline tickets desired by its customers. Amid a great deal of adverse publicity, Hoover was taken to court by disgruntled customers for failing to provide the tickets as promised.

BREAKEVEN ANALYSIS

It is important that a business knows how much its goods or services cost to produce. We looked in detail at costs earlier in this unit. Businesses also benefit from knowing how many products they have to produce and sell in order to cover all of their costs over a certain period of time. This level of output is known as the **breakeven point**. At this level of output, the revenue or income a firm receives from its sales are (just) sufficient to cover all its costs. In other words, at this level of output, the business concerned is neither making a profit nor a loss; it is breaking even.

You should note that to calculate the breakeven point you need information on both costs and, to forecast the firm's income, its prices too. As we see later, a change in costs or in the firm's pricing policy changes the level of output at which the firm breaks even.

Breakeven analysis is a fairly simple forecasting technique for businesses. It is also a valuable one, particularly in small businesses where the managers may not be able to employ more sophisticated techniques. Businesses can use breakeven analysis:

- ⊗ **to estimate the future level of output they will need to produce and sell;**

- ⊗ **to assess the impact of price changes upon profit and the level of output needed to break even;**

- ⊗ **to assess how changes in costs may affect profits and breakeven output.**

Breakeven output can be calculated and shown on a chart. First, we show how to forecast breakeven output through calculations before looking at breakeven charts.

ACTIVITY

Fig. 6.24 contains income and cost figures for Polly May. She runs a one-person business which produces pine chairs for sale in shops in Norwich.

1 Write down the number of chairs Polly has to produce and sell each week if her business is to break even.

2 Calculate how much profit she makes if she sells six chairs each week to shops in Norwich.

3 Work out the price that she receives for each of her chairs.

Output of chairs (weekly)	Sales income (£/weekly)	Total costs (£/weekly)
0	0	100
1	40	115
2	80	130
3	120	145
4	160	160
5	200	175
6	240	190

FIGURE 6.24: Polly May's income and costs.

CALCULATING BREAKEVEN

In order to calculate the breakeven point for a single product, we need to know the selling price of the product and its fixed and variable costs. As we described earlier in this unit, fixed costs are those expenses which do not alter in response to changes in demand or output. Fixed costs have to be paid whether or not the business is trading; examples include rent, business rates and interest charges. In contrast, variable costs do alter as demand and output change: a rise in output requires greater supplies of raw material and fuel, for example, and the cost of supplying these items will rise. A business does not incur variable costs if it is not trading.

We can calculate the breakeven point by using the total costs and total revenues of the firm. As an example, consider a pleasure boat which Jim Court uses to take tourists on sightseeing trips to the Isle of Lundy in the Bristol Channel. The boat makes one trip a day and Jim estimates that the cost of each trip is £200 in fuel, harbour dues, depreciation and wages for the crew. The trip includes a meal and wine for all the passengers and the landing fee charged by the owners of the island. These items cost an additional £5 for

each passenger on the boat. Jim is allowed to take a maximum of thirty passengers on each trip. Jim has priced the day trips at £15 per passenger. We can use the following equations to calculate the breakeven number of passengers for the day trips:

$$\text{total cost (TC)} = \text{fixed cost} + \text{variable cost}$$

$$\text{total revenue (TR)} = \text{price} \times \text{quantity sold (Q)}$$

For Jim's boat:

$$TC = 200 + 5Q$$

$$TR = 15Q$$

Here, Q is the number of passenger places sold. To break even, Jim needs a number of passengers such that he will not make a profit or a loss on each of his day trips. In other words, his total revenue should equal his total costs. At breakeven output:

$$TR = TC$$

$$\text{so } 15Q = 200 + 5Q$$

Now we need to find the value of Q (which is the number of passengers, remember) when total revenue equals total cost. This can be worked out by simple algebra:

$$15 Q - 5Q = 200$$

$$10 Q = 200$$

$$Q = \frac{200}{10} = 20$$

In other words, Jim needs 20 passengers on each of his day trips to break even.

ACTIVITY

Calculate how much profit Jim makes if he takes a day trip to the island with 25 passengers on the boat.

There is an alternative way to calculate break even. This is based on an understanding of the concept of **contribution**. Contribution is the amount of money left from sales revenue once the variable costs have been paid. So, we can calculate the contribution from each sale by subtracting the variable costs from the selling price. Now, if we divide this figure into our fixed costs, we will have calculated how many sales we need to pay all fixed and variable costs, that is to break even.

Now, let's calculate Jim's breakeven number of passengers using this method.

contribution per sale $=$ selling price $-$ variable cost

$$= £15 - £5 = £10$$

breakeven output $= \dfrac{\text{fixed costs}}{\text{contribution per sale}}$

$$= \frac{200}{10} = 20$$

Not surprisingly, and reassuringly, we arrive at the same answer using this contribution method of calculating breakeven.

ACTIVITY

Jim has asked for your help. He has decided to offer another day trip along the north Devon coast. This is a longer trip and the cost of running the boat in terms of wages, fuel, depreciation and harbour dues will be £250. He is planning to provide a tea on the boat and has arranged with a hotel further up the coast that his passengers should have lunch there. He estimates that the cost of food for each passenger will be £10. He is undecided whether to charge £20 or £22.50 per passenger. Remember, his boat holds a maximum of 30 passengers.

For the two prices separately, he needs to know how many passengers he would need in order to break even and how much profit he would make if the boat is full. Calculate the answers using either of the two methods outlined above.

BREAKEVEN CHARTS

Breakeven level of output can be calculated using the simple equations above, but more understanding of the sensitivity of the relationships between costs, sales and production is achieved through the use of **breakeven charts**.

A breakeven chart is constructed on a graph by first drawing the horizontal axis to represent the output of goods or services for the business in question. The vertical axis represents the values of costs and sales, usually in pounds sterling. On the horizontal axis, we mark output per time period – usually monthly or annual output.

We base our first breakeven chart on the following business scenario. Mark Cushion Limited manufactures confectionery. One of its most popular lines is Chewies – a fruit flavoured chew. These sweets sell for £1 a kilogram. The variable (or marginal) cost of production is 60p per kg. The fixed costs associated with this product are estimated at £50,000 a year. The company's maximum output of Chewies is 250,000 kg a year.

ACTIVITY

Using the contribution method, calculate the annual breakeven output in kilograms for Chewies.

To use breakeven charts, we should first put scales on our axes. The output scale needs to record up to the company's maximum annual output; this is 250,000 kg. The vertical axis records values of costs and revenues. Since revenue is usually the higher figure, we simply multiply the maximum output by the selling price and place values on the axis up to this figure. In this case, it needs to have a maximum value on the axis of £250,000 (£1 × 250,000).

Having drawn the axes, and placed scales upon them, the first line we enter is fixed costs. Since this value does not change with output, it is simply a horizontal line at the appropriate place on the chart. These costs cover rent and rates for the factory producing Chewies and also interest paid on loans taken out by Mark Cushion to set up production of Chewies.

Next, we add on variable costs to arrive at total costs. This is done by drawing a line to represent total costs. As shown in the middle graph in *Fig. 6.25*, the difference between total costs and fixed costs is variable costs. Now calculate the total cost when output is a convenient, and relatively high figure, say in the case of Chewies, 200,000 kg per year. The total cost is the fixed costs (£50,000) plus the variable costs of producing 200,000 kg (60p × 200,000 = £120,000); thus total cost at this level of output is £50,000 plus £120,000, that is £170,000. We now mark this point on our chart. If we draw a straight line from the extreme left of the fixed costs line through the point we have just marked, it will represent the total costs of production for Chewies. This is illustrated in the middle graph in *Fig. 6.25*.

Finally, we need to mark on the sales revenue earned by Chewies. We can draw this in a similar way to total costs. For the maximum level of output calculate the sales revenue and mark this on the chart. The maximum annual output of Chewies is 250,000 kg; we multiply this by the price per kilogram to work out the maximum income or revenue that the company can earn from Chewies, in this case £250,000 each year. We plot this on the graph, mark an income figure of £250,000 for an output level of 250,000 kg per year. Now if Mark Cushion does not produce and sell any Chewies, it will have zero income revenue: thus zero output means no income. We plot this too – this is the origin or the point where the two axes intersect. Join these two points with a straight line to represent the sales income of Chewies.

The breakeven chart brings together costs and revenues for a particular product. By drawing a line down from the point where lines representing total costs and sales revenue cross, we can find the annual level of output at which Chewies will break even. In this case, you can see that the breakeven output is 125,000 kg per year.

USING BREAKEVEN CHARTS

Reading off from breakeven charts is simple and informative. As well as showing the level of breakeven output, we can also see the level of profits earned, or losses incurred, by Chewies at various levels of output.

We can see that any level of output lower than 125,000 kilograms per year will mean the product makes a loss. The amount of the loss is shown by the vertical distance between the total cost and the total revenue line. For example, at an output level of 100,000 units per year Chewies would make a loss of £10,000 for Mark Cushion. At this level of output, sales are worth £100,000 but costs are £110,000 (£60,000 plus £50,000).

Any level of production in excess of 125,000 kg of Chewies per year earns the company a profit. If the company produces and sells 150,000 kg of Chewies yearly, it will earn a profit of £20,000. At this level of output, total revenue is £150,000 and total costs are £130,000. This is shown on the chart by the vertical distance between the total revenue line (which is now the higher) and the total cost line.

ACTIVITY

Read off the amount of profit or loss made by Chewies at the following operating points:

(i)   50,000 kg;

(ii)   120,000 kg;

(iii) 200,000 kg.

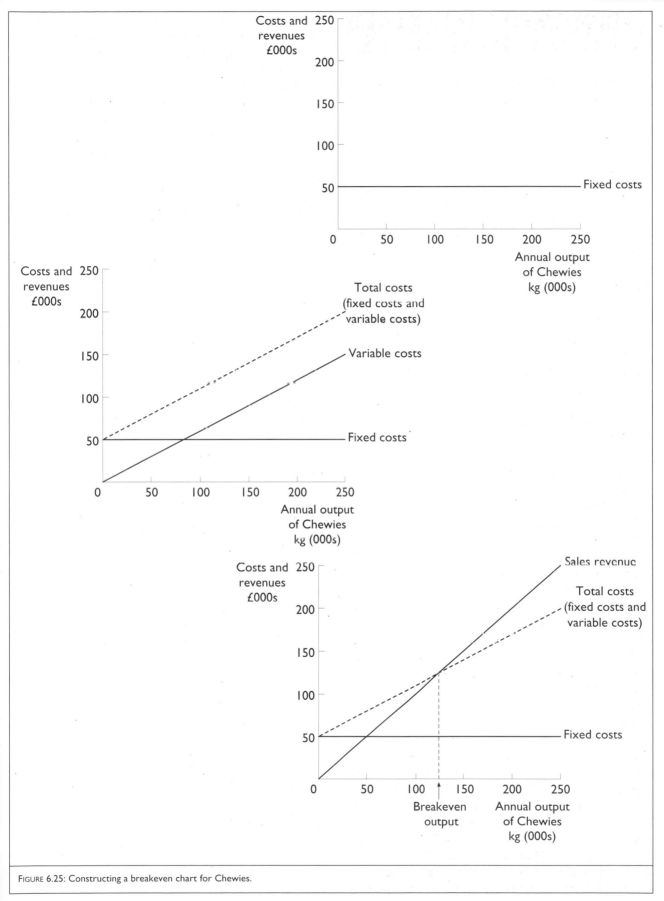

FIGURE 6.25: Constructing a breakeven chart for Chewies.

THE MARGIN OF SAFETY

One feature of breakeven analysis is the **margin of safety**. This can be defined as the amount by which current output exceeds the level of output necessary to break even.

The margin of safety can be calculated by subtracting the breakeven output from the current output and dividing the answer by the current level of output. So, if Mark Cushion is manufacturing and selling 150,000 kg of Chewies each year, with its breakeven output remaining at 125,000 kg, we can calculate:

$$\text{margin of safety} = \frac{\text{current output} - \text{breakeven output}}{\text{current output}}$$

$$= \frac{150,000 - 125,000}{150,000}$$

$$= 0.166 \text{ or } 16.67\%$$

Output could fall by 16.67 per cent before a loss-making situation developed.

ACTIVITY

Assume that Mark Cushion Limited faces new competition in the sweet market. As we noted earlier, an increase in supply can drive market prices down. As a consequence of this new competition, the company has to lower the price of Chewies to 90p per kg.

1   **Calculate the new breakeven figure for Chewies.**

2   **Illustrate your answer using a breakeven chart.**

3   **If current production is 180,000 kg per annum, calculate how much profit/loss is made on Chewies (at the new lower price) and what margin of safety, if any, exists.**

Your answer to this activity should highlight the importance of prices in determining breakeven points. If costs remain unchanged and prices fall, then this results in a higher breakeven level of production. Lower prices mean that more has to be produced and sold before a profit-making position can be reached. Conversely, a rise in price results in a lower breakeven level of production.

Costs have an equally important impact on breakeven levels. A rise in either fixed or variable (marginal) costs will result in a higher level of breakeven output. Similarly, a fall in costs reduces the amount which has to be produced and sold (each year, say) in order to break even.

If there is a rise in fixed costs, then the effect on the total costs line is to shift it upwards by the same amount at each level of output. In effect, the two total cost lines are parallel. This is because the rise in fixed costs is unaffected by the level of output at which the firm is producing. For example, a rise in rent for a factory has the same impact on total costs regardless of whether the firm is producing at half or full capacity. In contrast, a rise in variable or marginal costs increases the slope of the total costs line.

ACTIVITY

Mark Cushion has been advised that its variable or marginal costs are likely to rise by 10 per cent in the coming year. Redraw your breakeven chart showing the new breakeven level of output. Read off the new level of profit/loss for the following output levels of Chewies:

(i)   **50,000 kg;**

(ii)   **120,000 kg;**

(iii)   **200,000 kg.**

WHY DO BUSINESSES USE BREAKEVEN ANALYSIS?

As with most techniques of financial control, breakeven analysis has advantages and disadvantages. Breakeven analysis is simple to conduct and understand and it is cheap. It can show profit and loss at various levels of output, particularly when it is presented in the form of a chart. This may be of particular value when a business is first established. Indeed, financial institutions may require this sort of financial information before lending any money to an aspiring businessperson.

As we have seen, breakeven analysis can cope with changes in price: with a rise in price the total revenue line will pivot upwards causing breakeven at a lower quantity. Conversely, a fall in price will cause the line to pivot downwards increasing breakeven output. A change in costs can also be shown with rises in costs shifting the cost function upwards and falls in costs lowering it.

However, breakeven does have some drawbacks. It assumes that all of the output a firm produces is sold.

This may well not be true and, if so, would result in an inaccurate breakeven estimate. In times of recession, a firm may have difficulty in selling all that it produces. Although breakeven can cope with changes in prices and costs, in the real world such factors change regularly making it difficult to use as a forecasting technique. The model assumes that costs increase constantly and that firms do not benefit from economies of scale. Similarly, it assumes that a firm sells all its output at a single price. In reality, firms frequently offer discounts for bulk purchases. Finally, breakeven analysis is only as good as the data on which it is based: poor quality data can result in inaccurate conclusions being drawn.

Established in 1789, Armstrong's Ales is renowned throughout the UK for its high quality real ale. The firm's founder, Josiah Armstrong, built the first brewery at Aylsham, a few miles north of Norwich.

In spite of several take-over bids, Armstrong's remains one of the UK's few independent brewers. However, profits have declined in recent years and the company is considering ways in which operating costs can be reduced. The famous 'Cromer Bitter', which is made at a small brewery on the north Norfolk coast, is earning a low level of profit. The factory buildings are increasingly expensive to maintain. The council has given the factory listed building status, which has meant that Armstrong's has incurred additional costs.

Cromer Bitter: production costs 1995

	£
Wages – shop floor	48,500
Salaries – factory management	22,000
Raw materials (hops, yeast, etc.)	49,400
Power (electricity)	9,000
Factory rent and rates	11,000
Depreciation on machinery	1,500
Transport costs	16,000
Insurance	1,200
Factory maintenance and repair	16,400
Total annual production costs	**175,000**

Cromer Bitter: selling and administration expenses 1995

	£
Staff costs – administration	13,300
Office expenses	2,500
Depreciation on office equipment	1,200
Marketing costs	8,500
Telephone	2,000
Office rent and rates	9,000
Loan interest	1,000
Total annual administration costs	**37,500**

FIGURE 6.26: Production, selling and administration costs for Cromer Bitter.

TASK 1 – COSTING AND PRICING

The board of directors has asked for a breakdown of the production costs of Cromer Bitter. The annual production of Cromer Bitter is 25,000 gallons. The brewery receives on average £9 per gallon on sales. Using the information in *Fig. 6.26*, undertake the following financial analysis.

(a) Identify which of the costs in *Fig. 6.26* are indirect costs and which are direct costs. Some costs may be difficult to categorise in this way. Identify those which fall into this category and explain your choice(s).

(b) Calculate the annual direct costs of Cromer Bitter.

(c) Calculate the annual indirect costs of Cromer Bitter.

(d) Given that Armstrong's produces 25,000 gallons of Cromer Bitter each year, calculate the cost of producing one gallon.

(e) Now, classify the costs in *Fig. 6.26* as fixed or variable costs.

(f) Using your knowledge of the nature of costs, calculate the cost of producing an additional gallon of Cromer Bitter.

(g) Outline briefly the factors which Armstrong's may take into account when setting the price of a gallon of Cromer Bitter. Using your previous answers, suggest and explain an appropriate pricing policy for Cromer Bitter.

(h) Construct a breakeven chart for Cromer Bitter. Clearly mark the level of output needed for the brewery to break even. Write an explanation of your chart and explain why it might be helpful to the managers at Armstrong's Ales.

Task 2 – The trading and money cycles

Armstrong's Ales: annual trading figures	
	£
Initial working capital	10,000
Payments to creditors	49,400
Receipts from debtors	225,000
Production costs	125,600
Selling and adminstration costs	37,500

FIGURE 6.27: Summary financial information for Armstrong's Ales.

Fig. 6.27 contains annual trading figures for Armstrong's Ales.

(a) Using these figures, produce a diagram of the company's trading cycle to illustrate the flow of money and the residual cash available for distribution.

(b) Produce a spreadsheet illustrating the links between the trading cycle and the money cycle, starting and ending with cash.

(c) Include both your diagram and spreadsheet in a report which:

   (i) discusses and explains each stage of the trading cycle;
   (ii) explains the links between the trading and money cycles;
   (iii) suggests how the residual cash might be distributed.

Task 3 – Financial transactions

Imagine you work in the accounts office of Armstrong's Ales. Today's date is 30 September 1995. You have to work through the contents of your in-tray (see documents on pages 406–13). In completing this task, you should photocopy and complete as required the blank documents on pages 414–24.

(a) Armstrong's has received invoices from three suppliers: World Chemicals Inc., Heppleston Grains plc and NSS (Office Supplies) Ltd. Check the invoices against the purchase orders and delivery notes. If the invoices are correct, prepare a cheque ready for signature and a remittance advice. If there are any discrepancies, draft a letter to the supplier outlining the problem and asking for appropriate action to be taken.

(b) The next items in the in-tray are order forms from The Red Lion and The Court Hotel. For each of these orders, prepare a delivery note and an invoice. Note that the last delivery note issued was number 3247 and the last invoice issued was number 3974.

(c) While you are working through the in-tray, the receptionist asks you for £2.90 to pay for postage stamps she has bought for the office. You pay her from petty cash. Complete the petty cash voucher. Note, the last voucher number was 127.

(d) The next item in the in-tray is an invoice for Greenholme Golf Club. This needs to be included in the golf club's new statement of account. The previous statement of account showed that the club

owed Armstrong's a balance of £274.78. Since then, it has been sent one other invoice for £132.40 (invoice number 3956, dated 14 September 1995) and it paid £156.32 on 18 September 1995. Prepare a new statement of account for Greenholme Golf Club showing the position as of 30 September 1995.

(e) A deposit needs to be made at the bank. There are two cheques to pay in – one from The Buck Inn for £197.18, the other from Manor Hotels plc for £362.75 – and the following amounts of cash:

4	£20 notes
12	£10 notes
9	£5 notes
5	£1 coins
3	50p coins
9	20p coins
16	10p coins
23	5p coins
6	2p coins
31	1p coins

Prepare a paying-in slip for this deposit.

(f) The warehouse manager has requested some stationery items. Make out a purchase order to NSS (Office Supplies) Ltd. for two blue double-ring binders (reference SS391, net price £1.50 each) and one box of large paper clips (reference SS132, net price £1.30 for a box of 50). Note that the last purchase order was number 5734.

(g) A delivery of stationery arrives from NSS (Office Supplies) Ltd. Find the delivery note (number 70559) in your in-tray. All the items are in good condition. Complete a goods received note for this delivery. Note that the last goods received note was number 95/1224.

(h) A customer has returned a barrel of Cromer Bitter (net price £8.50). The valve on the barrel was faulty. Prepare a credit note for this item. The last credit note issued was number 474. The customer and transaction details are:

Customer:	The Boar Inn, Linkswood, Suffolk IP27 3BV
Order No:	3741
Delivery No:	4366
Invoice No:	3924

(i) One customer buys a barrel of Cromer Bitter direct from the brewery. The customer pays the net price £9.75 in cash. Make out a receipt for this transaction. Note that the last receipt issued was number 901.

(j) Finally, you come to the last item in the in-tray, a recent telephone bill. Photocopy the bill and complete the attached bank giro credit form for settling the account.

TASK 4 – ACCURACY AND SECURITY ISSUES

This task asks you to reflect on the purpose and function of the documents used in the previous task.

(a) Write a report explaining the purpose and function of each document used in task 3. Include an explanation of why it is important that all financial documents are completed fully, accurately and clearly. For each document, describe what problems could arise if the form is not completed correctly.

(b) Add a further section to your report
   outlining the security checks that should
   be undertaken when dealing with:

   (i) invoices for payment;
   (ii) delivery notes for goods being received;
   (iii) purchase orders from customers;
   (iv) cheques from customers.

(c) Finally, in your report explain what is
   meant by:

   (i)   authorisation of orders;
   (ii) authorised cheque signatories;
   (iii) segregation of duties.

The In-Tray

Heppleston Grains plc
Granstone Granary
Granstone
GR2 4XU

Tel: (02443) 123456
Fax: (02443) 123460

VAT Reg. No. 123 6543 76

Invoice

Customer:	Armstrong Ales		Invoice No:	HG/95/687
Address:	Norwich Road			
	Aylsham		Order Ref:	AA5532
	Norfolk			
	NR7 9AB		Invoice Date: (Tax Point)	25.08.95

Item	Description	Delivery Ref.	Qty	Unit	Unit Price	Net price
1	Grade A Hops	1001	3	tonne	275.00	825.00
2	Grade A Barley	1004	5	tonne	110.00	550.00
					Net Total	1375.00
					VAT	240.62
					Total due	£1615.62

This invoice is subject to VAT at 17.5%   Terms: 30 days nett

E & O E

Armstrong's Ales
Norwich Road
Aylsham
Norfolk
NR7 9AB

Tel: (01275) 675092
Fax: (01275) 674181

VAT Reg. No. 654 2080 61

Purchase Order

Supplier:	Heppleston Grains plc	Deliver to:	Armstrong's Ales	Order No:	AA5532
Address:	Granston Granary		Norwich Road		
	Granstone		Aylsham	Order Date:	08.08.95
	GR2 4XU		Norfolk		
			NR7 9AB	Contact:	P. Evans

Item	Code	Description	Unit	Qty
1	HG97644	Hops - Grade A	tonne	3
2	HG4372	Barley - Grade A	tonne	5

Ordered by:

| Name: | P Evans | Position: | Production Manager | Signature: | P Evans | Date: | 08/ 8 /95 |

World Chemicals Inc.

VAT Reg No: 642 9753 90

Invoice

Customer:	Armstrong Ales
Address:	Norwich Road
	Aylsham
	Norfolk
	NR7 9AB

Delivery Address (if different) _____

Invoice No: uk10034/09
Order Ref: AA5724
Tax Point: 03.09.95

Item	Code	Description	Qty	Unit	Unit Price	Net price
1	SCF2097	J30 Antigel	1	10 ltr	67.00	67.00
2	SCF2021	Y120 Inducer	3	10 ltr	43.00	129.00
3	SFF3003	Surfactant	10	10 ltr	24.50	245.00
4	BCF4587	J54 Anti-foam	5	10 ltr	103.00	515.00
5	ECA5263	E150 Colouring	5	1tr	38.00	1170.00
6	ECA5257	E129 Colouring	5	1tr	46.50	1147.50
7	ECA3244	E321 Antioxidant	15	1tr	28.75	2468.75

Net Total	5742.25
17.5% VAT	1004.89
Total	6747.14

E & O E

Terms: 30 days nett 15 days 5%

World Chemicals Inc. Harrow House, North Street, Flemingham, FM7 4AP Tel: (02542) 675519 Fax: (02542) 675682

Armstrong's Ales

Norwich Road
Aylsham
Norfolk
NR7 9AB

Tel: (01275) 675092
Fax: (01275) 674181

VAT Reg. No. 654 2080 61

Purchase Order

Supplier:	World Chemicals Inc
Address:	Harrow House
	North Street
	Flemingham
	FM7 4AP

Deliver to:	Armstrong's Ales
	Norwich Road
	Aylsham
	Norfolk
	NR7 9AB

Order No: AA5724
Order Date: 21.08.95
Contact: P. Evans

Item	Code	Description	Unit	Qty
1	SCF2097	J30 Anti-Gel		
2	SCF2021	Y120 Inducer	10 ltr	1
3	SFF3003	Surfactant	10 ltr	3
4	BCF4587	J54 Anti-foam	10 ltr	10
5	ECA5263	E150 Colour	10 ltr	5
6	ECA5257	E129 Colour	ltr	5
7	ECA3244	E321 Antioxidant	ltr	5
			ltr	15

Ordered by:

Name: P Evans   Position: Production Manager   Signature: P Evans   Date: 21/ 8 /95

NSS (OFFICE SUPPLIES) LTD.
Vat Reg: 986 3478 21

Invoice

Customer: Armstrong's Ales
Address: Norwich Road
Aylsham
Norfolk
NR7 9AB

Remit to: **NSS (Office Supplies) Ltd
Unit 6 Witham Lane
Norwich NR3 4XQ**
Tel: (01603) 113245 (5 lines)
Fax: (01603) 113278

Invoice No: 20135

Order Ref: AA5698

DN No: DN70518

Tax Point: 29.08.95

Item	P.Code	Description	Qty	Unit	Unit Price	Net price
1	PP506	Paper - White Bond	10	5 ream	11.00	110.00
2	SS107	Stapler	1	ea	4.50	4.50
3	SS409	Correction fluid	1	box 6	10.50	10.50
4	PP778	Envelopes - White Bond	1	box 100	9.00	9.00
5	SS096	Ballpoint pen - black	2	box 25	10.00	20.00
					Net Total	154.00
					17.5% VAT	26.95
					Total	180.95

E & O E

Terms: 30 days nett

NSS (Office Supplies) Ltd Unit 6 Witham Lane Norwich NR3 4XQ   Tel: (01603) 113245 (5 lines)   Fax: (01603) 113278

Armstrong's Ales
**Norwich Road
Aylsham
Norfolk
NR7 9AB**

Tel: (01275) 675092
Fax: (01275) 674181

VAT Reg. No. 654 2080 61

Purchase Order

Supplier: NSS (Office Supplies) Ltd
Address: Unit 6
Witham Lane
Norwich
NR3 4XQ

Deliver to: Armstrong's Ales
Norwich Road
Aylsham
Norfolk
NR7 9AB

Order No: AA5698

Order Date: 26.08.95

Contact: G. Owens

Item	Code	Description	Unit	Qty
1	PP506	Paper - White Bond	5 ream	10
2	SS107	Stapler	each	1
3	SS409	Correction Fluid	Box/6	1
4	PP778	Envelopes - White Bond	Box/100	1
5	SS096	Ballpoint pen - black	box/25	2

Ordered by:
Name: G Owens   Position: Admin. Manager   Signature: G Owens   Date: 26/ 8 /95

NSS (OFFICE SUPPLIES) LTD.
Vat Reg: 986 3478 21

Delivery Note

Customer: Armstrong's Ales
Address: Norwich Road
Aylsham
Norfolk
NR7 9AB

Delivery Address (if different): _____

Delivery Note No: DN70518
Delivery Date: 23.08.95
Order Ref: AA5698

Delivered by: own transport

Item	P.Code	Description	Qty	Unit
1	PP506	Paper - White Bond	10	5 ream
2	SS107	Stapler	1	ea
3	SS409	Correction fluid	1	box 6
4	PP778	Envelopes - White Bond	1	box 100
5	SS096	Ballpoint pen - black	2	box 25

Received by: _T Jones_ (Name) _T Jones_ (Signature) 23/8/95 (Date)

In good condition ☐ Incorrect/damaged/short delivered items ☒ Details: _both boxes of ballpoint pens returned - blue delivered, black required_

NSS (Office Supplies) Ltd Unit 6 Witham Lane Norwich NR3 4XQ Tel (01603) 113245 (5 lines) Fax (01603) 113278

Delivery Note

Heppleston Grains plc
Granstone Granary
Granstone
GR2 4XU

Tel: (02443) 123456
Fax: (02443) 123460
VAT Reg. No. 123 6543 76

Delivery: Armstrong Ales
Address: Norwich Road
Aylsham
NR7 9AB
NR7 9AB

Delivery: Armstrong Ales
Address: Norwich Road
Aylsham
Norfolk
NR7 9AB

Delivery No: 1001
Order Ref: AA5532
Delivery Date: 17.08.95

Item	Code	Description	Unit	Qty
			tonne	3
1	HG97644	Hops - Grade A		

Received by:
Name: _T Jones_ Position: _Warehouse manager_ Signature: _T Jones_ Date: 17/8/95

Delivery Note

Heppleston Grains plc
Granstone Granary
Granstone
GR2 4XU

Tel: (02443) 123456
Fax: (02443) 123460

VAT Reg. No. 123 6543 76

Delivery No:	1004

Delivery Address: Armstrong Ales, Norwich Road, Aylsham, NR7 9AB, NR7 9AB

Delivery Address: Armstrong Ales, Norwich Road, Aylsham, Norfolk, NR7 9AB

Order Ref: AA5532

Delivery Date: 19.08.95

Item	Code	Description	Unit	Qty
			tonne	5
1	HG4372	Barley - Grade A		

Received by:

Name: *T Jones*   Position: *Warehouse manager*   Signature: *T Jones*   Date: *19 / 8 / 95*

World Chemicals Inc.

VAT Reg No: 642 9753 90

Delivery Note

Customer: Armstrong's Ales
Address: Norwich Road
Aylsham
Norfolk
NR7 9AB

Delivery Address (if different): _____

Delivery Note No: uk10034/09/del
Delivery Date: 26.08.95
Order Ref: AA5724

Delivered by: Transpak

Item	Code	Description	Qty	Unit
1	SCF2097	J30 Antigel	1	10 ltr
2	SCF2021	Y120 Inducer	3	10 ltr
3	SFF3003	Surfactant	10	10 ltr
4	BCF4587	J54 Anti-foam	5	10 ltr
5	ECA5263	E150 Colouring	5	1tr
6	ECA5257	E129 Colouring	5	1tr
7	ECA3244	E321 Antioxidant	10	1tr

Notes: Only 10 of ECA3244 available for delivery. Remaining 5 will be despatched as soon as possible

Received by: *T Jones* (Name)   *T Jones* (Signature)   26.08.95 (Date)

World Chemicals Inc. Harrow House, North Street, Flemingham, FM7 4AP Tel: (02542) 675519 Fax: (02542) 675682

The Red Lion

The Street
Branwells
Norfolk
NR12 6DF

Tel:(01462) 870553
Fax:(01462) 871004
VAT Reg. No. 903 5381 72

Purchase Order

Supplier: Armstrong's Ales
Address: Norwich Road
Aylsham
NR7 9AB

Order No: 352

Order Date: 28.08.95

Item	Code	Description	Unit	Qty	Net Price
1	CB2	Cromer Bitter	bbl	3	9.25
2	SD5	*Armstrong's Ales' Ashtrays	each	2	1.35

Ordered by:

Name: K. Chivers   Signature: K. Chivers

The Court Hotel

Palace Court
Great Yarmouth
Norfolk
NR33 3HH
Tel: (01603) 972304
Fax: (01603) 972320
VAT Reg. No. 465 4217 22

Purchase Order

Supplier: Armstrong's Ales
Address: Norwich Road
Aylsham
NR7 9AB

Order No: 2975

Order Date: 27.08.95

Item	Code	Description	Unit	Qty	Net Price
1	CB2	Cromer Bitter	bbl	12	8.70

Ordered by:

Name: F Halland   Signature: F Halland   Date: 27/8/95

Armstrong's Ales
Norwich Road
Aylsham
Norfolk
NR7 9AB

Tel: (01275) 675092
Fax: (01275) 674181
VAT Reg. No. 654 2080 61

Invoice

Customer: <u>Greenholme Golf Club</u>
Address: <u>Greenholme</u>
<u>Norfolk</u>
<u>NR20 9LK</u>

Invoice No: <u>3974</u>

Order Ref: <u>GGC384</u>

Invoice Date: <u>30.09.85</u>
(Tax Point)

Item	Description	Ref.	Qty	Unit	Unit Price	Net price
1	Cromer Bitter	CB2	7	bbl	8.95	62.65
					Net Total	62.65
					VAT	10.96
					Total due	73.61

This invoice is subject to VAT at 17.5%

Terms: 30 days nett

E & O E

NSS (OFFICE SUPPLIES) LTD.
Vat Reg: 986 3478 21

Delivery Note

Customer: <u>Armstrong's Ales</u>
Address: <u>Norwich Road</u>
<u>Aylsham</u>
<u>Norfolk</u>
<u>NR7 9AB</u>

Delivery
Address
(if different)

Delivery Note No: <u>DN70559</u>
Delivery Date: <u>30.08.95</u>
Order Ref: <u>AA5717</u>

Delivered by: <u>own</u>

Item	P.Code	Description	Qty	Unit
1	PP525	Paper - White copier	5	5 ream
2	SS113	Two-hole punch	1	ea
3	SS409	Highlighter pen - yellow	1	box/6

Received by: _____ (Name) _____ (Signature) _____ (D

In good condition ☐   Incorrect/damaged/short delivered items ☐   Details: _____

NSS (Office Supplies) Ltd Unit 6 Withern Lane Norwich NR3 4XQ   Tel: (01603) 113245 (5 lines)   Fax: (01603) 113278

Phone bill for 0181-677 8903

Your bill is	£	124.32	**Call charges**
	£	40.275	for direct-dialled calls of £0.42 and under Details are in the Breakdown
	£	84.05	for direct-dialled calls (itemised) See Breakdown pages 2 - 5
plus	£	21.09	**Advance charges from 1 Aug 95 to 31 Oct 95**
	£	21.09	for the rental of your line
	£	145.41	Subtotal excluding VAT
plus	£	25.44	VAT at 17.5%
	£	**170.85**	**Total amount now due**

Please make sure that we receive payment by 7 September 1995 - thank you

0021125

British Telecommunications plc VAT Reg. No. 245 7193 48

BT *Payment slip*

Bank Giro Credit

Total amount due	£	**170.85**

Your Customer No.   LS 6806 6169 Q027 4G

Dear Customer
- Please fill in parts 1, 2, 3 and 4.
- Details of how to pay are shown overleaf.
- Please do not send cash by post.

Bank details

44-67-98

Midland Bank plc
Head Office Collection Acct.

		£	p
1 Signature			
2 Date			
3 Cash		£	p
or cheques		£	p
4 Total		£	p

Cashier's stamp and initials

No. cheques   Fee

Please do not fold, pin or staple this slip or write below this line.

03 LS 68066169 Q027   4G   170.85

<3LS68066169Q027< 446798+< 73   X

Armstrong's Ales
Norwich Road
Aylsham
Norfolk
NR7 9AB

Tel: (01275) 675092
Fax: (01275) 674181
VAT Reg. No. 654 2080 61

Remittance Advice

To: _____   Date: _____

Item	Description	Ref.	Dr	Cr	Balance
				Total Remitted	

Date _____

Payee _____

_____

_____

_____

£ [   ]

Royal Anglia Bank

Aylsham Branch
High Street
Aylsham A6N 2BA

12–04–77

_____ 19 ____

PAY _____

A/C PAYEE

£ [   ]

107655

ıı▪ 107655ıı▪   12 ▪▪04771:   0034702ıı▪

Date _____

Payee _____

_____

_____

_____

£ [   ]

Royal Anglia Bank

Aylsham Branch
High Street
Aylsham A6N 2BA

12–04–77

_____ 19 ____

PAY _____

A/C PAYEE

£ [   ]

107656

ıı▪ 107656ıı▪   12 ▪▪04771:   0034702ıı▪

Date _____

Payee _____

_____

_____

_____

£ [   ]

Royal Anglia Bank

Aylsham Branch
High Street
Aylsham A6N 2BA

12–04–77

_____ 19 ____

PAY _____

A/C PAYEE

£ [   ]

107657

ıı▪ 107657ıı▪   12 ▪▪04771:   0034702ıı▪

Armstrong's Ales

Norwich Road
Aylsham
Norfolk
NR7 9AB

Tel: (01275) 675092
Fax: (01275) 674181
VAT Reg. No. 654 2080 61

Invoice

Customer: _____

Address: _____

_____

_____

_____

Invoice No: _____

Order Ref: _____

Invoice Date: _____
(Tax Point)

Item	Description	Ref.	Qty	Unit	Unit Price	Net price
					Net Total	
					VAT	
					Total due	

This invoice is subject to VAT at 17.5%   Terms: 30 days nett   E & O E

Armstrong's Ales

Norwich Road
Aylsham
Norfolk
NR7 9AB

Tel: (01275) 675092
Fax: (01275) 674181
VAT Reg. No. 654 2080 61

Delivery Note

Customer: _____

Address: _____

_____

_____

Delivery No: _____

Order Ref: _____

Date: _____

Item	Description	Ref.	Unit	Qty

Received by: _____ (Name) _____ (Signature) _____ (Date)

n good condition ☐   Incorrect/damaged/short delivered items ☐ Details: _____

No. _____

Date _____

Petty Cash Voucher

Requirement	Amount	
	£	p

Signature _____

Passed by _____

No. _____

Date _____

Petty Cash Voucher

Requirement	Amount	
	£	p

Signature _____

Passed by _____

Armstrong's Ales

Norwich Road
Aylsham
Norfolk
NR7 9AB

Tel: (01275) 675092
Fax: (01275) 674181
VAT Reg. No. 654 2080 61

Statement

Customer: _____   Sheet No: _____
Address: _____
_____   A/C No: _____
_____
_____   Date: _____

Item	Description	Ref.	Dr	Cr	Balance
				Total due	

- -

Remittance Advice - Please attach this slip to your payment
Company Name: _____

Item	Description	Ref.	Dr	Cr	Balance
			Total	Remitted	

Date	Date	**bank giro credit**	Please detail cheques and cash overleaf

Date

Cashier's stamp

Date

Cashier's stamp

bank giro credit

Please detail cheques and cash overleaf

Notes £50
Notes £20
Notes £10
Notes £5
£1 coins
50p
Silver
Bronze

Royal Anglia Bank
Aylsham Branch

ACCOUNT   Armstrong Ale's

PAID IN BY

TOTAL CASH

Cheques/POs

Cash

Cheques
/POs

£

Number of
cheques

sorting code number	account number	tran.code
12–04–77	0034702	69

£

Please do not write below this line or fold this voucher

500074

⑄ 500074⑄   12 ⑄0477⑈   0034702⑄

Cheques etc.

	£			brought forward £		

| Carried forward | | | Carried over | | | |

Armstrong's Ales

Norwich Road
Aylsham
Norfolk
NR7 9AB

Tel: (01275) 675092
Fax: (01275) 674181

VAT Reg. No. 654 2080 61

Purchase Order

Order No: _____

Order Date: _____

Contact: _____

Supplier: _____
Address: _____

Deliver to:

Armstrong's Ales
Norwich Road
Aylsham
Norfolk
NR7 9AB

Item	Code	Description	Unit	Qty

Ordered by:

Name: _____   **Position:** _____   **Signature:** _____   **Date:** _____

Armstrong's Ales

Goods Received Note

Supplier: Heppleston Grains plc
1001

Delivery No:

GRN No: 95/1078

Order Ref: AA5532

Date: 17.08.95

Delivery Date: 17.08.95

Item	Code	Description	Unit	Qty
1	HG9764 4	Hops - Grade A	tonne	3

Received by:

Name: T Jones

Position: Warehouse Manager

Signature: T Jones

Date:

Armstrong's Ales

Norwich Road
Aylsham
Norfolk
NR7 9AB

Tel: (01275) 675092
Fax: (01275) 674181
VAT Reg. No. 654 2080 61

Credit Note

Customer: _____

Address: _____

_____

_____

_____

No: _____

Ref: _____

Date: _____
(Tax Point)

Item	Description	Ref.	Qty	Unit	Unit Price	Net price
					Net Total	
					VAT	
					Total	

E & O E

Armstrong's Ales

Norwich Road
Aylsham
Norfolk
NR7 9AB

Tel: (01275) 675092
Fax: (01275) 674181
VAT Reg. No. 654 2080 61

Receipt

Date: _____   Receipt No: _____

Received from: _____

Item	Description	Qty	Unit	Unit Price	Net price
				Net Total	
				VAT	
				Total paid	

1 **The difference between gross profit and net profit is best explained by:**

A the deduction of tax

B the deduction of the running expenses of the firm

C the deduction of added value

D the deduction of interest charges

2 **Debtors are:**

A people (or companies) to whom a business owes money

B companies who supply reports on credit worthiness

C people who draw up the sales ledger for a business

D people (or companies) who owe money to a business

3 **Which of the following is the purpose of a goods received note:**

A to inform the purchaser of the amount owed to the supplier

B to inform the supplier of the goods/services required

C to advise the supplier of the date delivery is required

D to allow the purchaser to check that the invoice is correct

4 **Which of the following is not usually included on a blank cheque:**

A the account number of the payee

B the account number of the drawer

C the bank's sort code number

D the account number on which the cheque is drawn

5 **What is the principal difference between a standing order and a direct debit:**

A with direct debits, the amounts paid can be varied

B standing orders are paid weekly and direct debits monthly

C only direct debits are part of the BACS system

D standing orders transfer money more quickly

6 **Which of the following is NOT a direct cost:**

A labour wages

B raw materials costs

C factory rent

D charges for fuel

7 **A business uses a machine which costs £11,000, lasts for five years and has a resale value of £1,000, what is the annual depreciation figure for this machine:**

A £2,000

B £2,500

C £10,000

D £1,000

8 **A firm which sells in competition with a few, large producers is called:**

A a monopoly

B a monopsony

C a nationalised industry

D an oligopoly

9 **A fall in the value of the pound will mean that:**

A exports become more expensive

B exports become cheaper

C imports become cheaper

D imports and exports do not change in price

10 The difference between sales revenue and marginal costs is known as:

A contribution

B variable cost

C fixed cost

D profit

11 The pricing policy which sells a new product at a high price to relatively few customers is called:

A penetration pricing

B destroyer pricing

C market skimming

D customer value pricing

12 The 'margin of safety' is:

A the amount by which current output exceeds breakeven output

B the level of profit earned at breakeven output

C the level of profit necessary to continue in business

D expenditure on health and safety

Financial Forecasting and Monitoring

CONTENTS

OUTLINE

This unit builds on the basic financial aspects of business developed in unit 6. In that unit, we considered business documentation, the types of costs faced by businesses and the pricing strategies available to them.

This unit extends that discussion to consider the sources from which a business might raise funds and the criteria which will help it to chose an appropriate source of finance. Financial forecasting is important to all businesses. It helps managers to decide whether a business is viable and gives a yardstick against which performance can be measured. We look at the compilation and structure of the major financial statements produced by businesses and we explain how these statements can be used to monitor the performance of a business.

The study of financial forecasting and monitoring will prove invaluable as an introduction to unit 8.

Explain sources of finance and financial requirements of business organisations

WHY BUSINESSES REQUIRE FINANCE

Businesses require finance for a number of reasons. A large public limited company such as Shell might want to raise many millions to purchase new oil exploration equipment. At the other end of the scale, a small corner shop might wish to carry a larger range of stock and may seek a loan of perhaps £1,000. The sources of loans are equally diverse: high street banks, merchant banks, investors, the government and its agencies. In this element, we look in some detail at the reasons why businesses need to raise finance and the sources from which they can raise such finance.

There are two principal reasons why businesses may seek to raise finance:

⊗ **to purchase more fixed assets such as premises and machinery;**

⊗ **to increase the working capital available to a business (to purchase items such as raw materials and stocks of components).**

⏣ ACTIVITY

Fig. 7.1 **is an advert placed in the business section of the** *Independent* **newspaper. Why do you think it was placed there? For what purposes would businesses borrow from Barclays Mercantile?**

PURCHASING ASSETS

Raising funds to purchase **fixed assets** such as vehicles and machinery usually requires medium to long-term finance; the amounts borrowed are normally large and repayments

Whatever equipment your business needs, come to Barclays and we'll deliver.

From heavy engineering to lighting rigs, Barclays Mercantile can help you find the best way for your business to acquire almost anything it needs. We'll assess your situation and, subject to status, recommend a method of payment that is tailored to your financial situation. All arrangements can be made locally, through a single point of contact. So you can save time as well. When you need to finance new assets, don't search the seven seas. Visit your local branch of Barclays.

 BARCLAYS

FIGURE 7.1: Barclays Bank's advertisement for financial services.

are likely to be spread over a reasonably long period. This form of finance is commonly referred to as **asset finance**.

Hutchison Telecom is a major company in the rapidly expanding mobile phone market. It is raising large sums of money to finance expansion (see newspaper cutting overleaf). Inevitably, a proportion of this finance will be asset finance.

The assets that might be purchased by Hutchison Telecom, or other companies raising asset finance are varied. In general, though, they are likely to be fixed assets,

Hutchison Telecom to raise £1bn

HUTCHISON Telecom, the mobile phone company that owns Orange, expects to improve its balance sheet with up to £1bn of bank debt within the next few months.

The Director of Finance for the company, Graham Howe, said, 'We are taking more and more market share. The business is capable of raising debt and we want to do so by the end of the year.'

The Times, 13 September 1995

that is those assets which are not bought for resale and remain in the business for more than one year.

We look more fully at the nature of assets in our discussion of balance sheets later in this unit. However, it is appropriate to consider fixed assets in more detail here. Fixed assets can be broken down into two categories: **tangible assets** and **intangible assets**.

TANGIBLE ASSETS

Tangible assets can be seen and have a physical existence. They include the following:

- ☉ **Land.** Businesses need somewhere for their premises. This land might be owned on a freehold basis. This gives the owner the right to use the land without having to pay any rent. Other land might be held on a leasehold basis, giving the user of the land the right to use it for a specified period of time in return for regular, usually annual, rent payments to the freeholder of the land.

- ☉ **Buildings.** These might be offices or factories or both, depending upon the nature of the business.

- ☉ **Equipment, plant and machinery.** The needs of individual businesses vary enormously, but this is an important requirement particularly for manufacturing businesses. For example, an engineering business requires lathes, drills and specialist machinery to allow it to function. These assets can be termed production assets.

ACTIVITY

List the plant, machinery and equipment that would be used by your local supermarket. Include the vehicles that they might possess in your list, even though vehicles are a separate category of fixed asset.

- ☉ **Vehicles.** Almost every business requires vehicles. You only need to look at the number of commercial vehicles that crowd the UK's roads to realise their importance. These fixed assets need replacing on a regular basis.

- ☉ **Office equipment.** This is an important category of fixed assets for service industries. The increased use of information technology has resulted in greater expenditure on office equipment.

- ☉ **Fixtures and fittings.** These include items such as shelving, display cases, furniture, lighting and counters. This can be a very significant item of expenditure for retailers.

ACTIVITY

Banks and other financial institutions have spent vast sums on information technology to improve their competitiveness. Can you think of any implications of banks increasing their use of information technology?

INTANGIBLE ASSETS

Intangible assets do not have a physical existence; unlike tangible assets, they cannot be seen and touched. A common example of an intangible asset is **goodwill** – the favour and prestige which a business enjoys. If significant, this usually generates a healthy number of customers and much repeat business. Other intangible assets are **patents** which give an inventor the exclusive right to make and sell an invention for a specified period and **copyrights** which grant protection to those who write books, write and record music and make films. Finally, **trademarks** assist in identifying a product and establishing consumer loyalty. A product such as Marmite has a widely known name and image and this contributes to healthy levels of sales.

WORKING CAPITAL

Working capital is the day-to-day finance needed to run a business. Once a business has all the fixed assets needed for operation, managers have to consider the requirements for working capital. Working capital is essential to begin the trading and money cycles which we considered in unit 6. *Fig.* 7.2 summarises the need for, and purposes of, working capital.

Working capital is necessary to establish and operate a business. Working capital is spent on:

- **Raw materials and components.** This can be a significant cost particularly for manufacturing businesses.

- **Work in progress.** Semi-completed goods will be on the production line of a manufacturing business at any time. The business has paid for the materials and components in work in progress but has not yet received an income from it. In industries with long production times, such as house building, work in progress can tie up large amounts of capital.

- **Labour costs.** These can be very high for service industries; for example, health care organisations employ large numbers of people but spend relatively small amounts on raw materials.

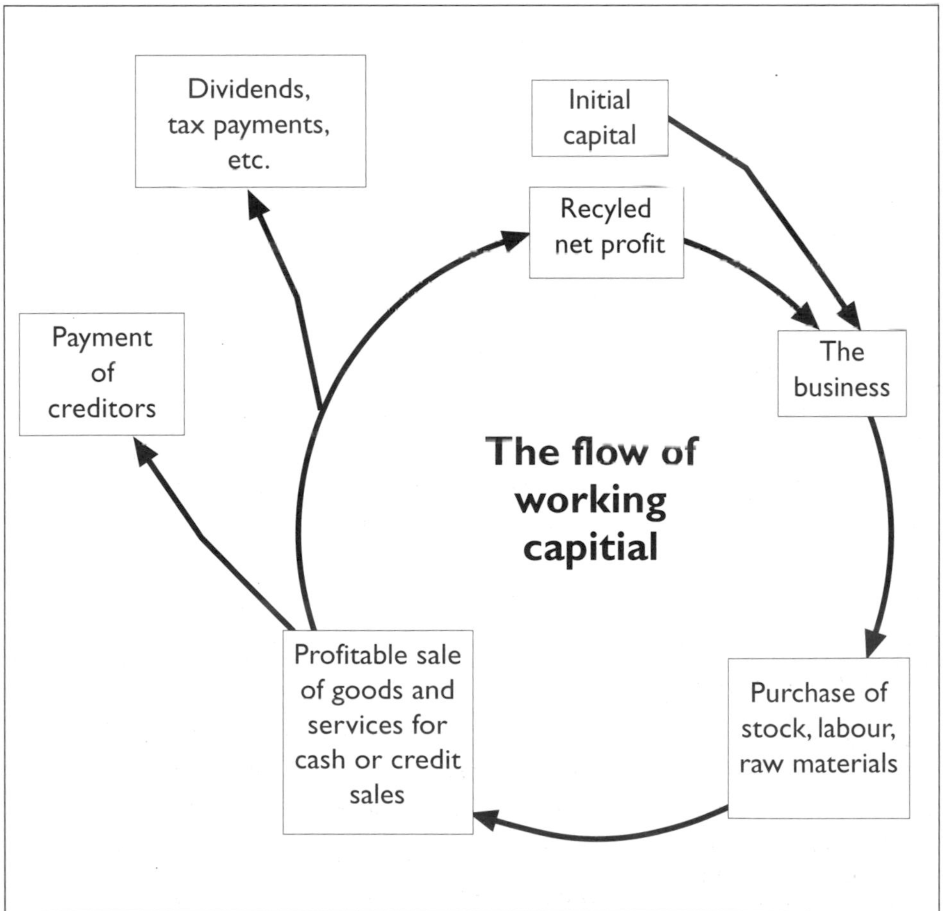

- **Stocks of finished goods.** As an example, retailers need to hold large quantities of stocks to offer sufficient choice to their customers.

- **Debtors.** To attract customers, many businesses have to offer credit, allowing their customers time to pay for goods and services. Businesses can often wait for up to three months for payment. Customers owing money become debtors to the business and represent another way in which money is tied up in the business.

- **Cash.** A business will require cash to meet day-to-day payments such as fuel for vehicles and stationery for the office.

FIGURE 7.2: The role of working capital.

Accountants define working capital as:

working capital = current assets − current liabilities

If a firm has too little working capital, it might be unable to finance increased production. It may not have the finance available to pay for the greater stocks of raw materials, more labour services and higher general running costs that an increase in production will require. In extreme cases, a shortage of working capital might mean that a business is unable to finance existing levels of production.

On the other hand, too much money tied up as working capital might mean that the business is short of asset finance.

METHODS OF FINANCING A BUSINESS

There are a number of ways in which business can raise the finance necessary to purchase assets and fund working capital. The method chosen by a business will depend upon:

- ⊗ **the amount of money required by the business;**

- ⊗ **the risk that the business represents to potential lenders;**

- ⊗ **the time period over which the loan is required.**

The time period over which the loan is required can be used as a means of classifying methods of finance into three categories:

- ⊗ **short-term finance;**

- ⊗ **medium-term finance;**

- ⊗ **long-term finance.**

SHORT-TERM FINANCE

A business may need short-term finance to fund its working capital. It may be that its customers are late in making payment for goods and services they have purchased or sales might be unexpectedly low. In either case, the firm is likely to be short of funds to purchase raw materials and to pay wages and salaries. Other unexpected problems such as sudden increases in the cost of raw materials can also create a need for short-term finance. Short-term finance is usually repayable within a one-year period.

There are three principal methods of short-term finance: **trade credit**, **overdrafts** and **debt factoring**.

TRADE CREDIT

Many suppliers grant their customers an interest-free period of grace in which to pay for the goods and services they have received. From the customer's point of view, this is a useful form of finance; it helps fund the customer's working capital at the expense of the seller's cash flow. The typical credit period offered to customers is 30 days. In practice, however, businesses take nearer 75 days to make their payments. In unit 6 we looked at the structure of invoices; one feature of these documents is that they include a statement concerning credit terms, for example 'Payment is due within 30 days'.

This form of credit is attractive to businesses because it is free, although some suppliers may offer a discount for prompt payment. In this case, where discount can be lost if trade credit is used, trade credit is not in effect interest-free. The use of trade credit is widespread. However, it is open to abuse; businesses can delay making payments for longer and longer periods. But, if customers exceed the trade credit period, suppliers may demand that payment is made in advance or may simply refuse to supply goods or services in the future.

OVERDRAFTS

Overdrafts are perhaps the best-known method of short-term finance. An overdraft is a facility offered by banks allowing businesses (and individuals) to borrow up to agreed limits without notification and for as long as they wish. Overdrafts are a very flexible form of finance as the amounts borrowed can vary so long as they are within the agreed overall limit. They are also simple to arrange – established business customers can often arrange, or increase the limit, without any form-filling.

Overdrafts are quite expensive. Interest is charged at between 2 per cent and 4 per cent over the bank's base lending rate. This is not usually a problem unless a business seeks to borrow on overdraft over a long period of time. In these circumstances, a business would be well advised to convert its overdraft to another longer-term method of finance.

It is unusual for an overdraft to be a secured loan. That is, banks and building societies do not normally require a business to lodge some form of security before agreeing to an overdraft. Secured loans are those where businesses have to offer collateral or security for the loan. Collateral frequently takes the form of property because these assets are less likely to fall in value over long time periods. Most other assets suffer routine depreciation. In the event of the loan not being repaid, the bank sells the collateral and uses the money raised to repay the original loan plus any outstanding interest.

ACTIVITY

Visit two high street banks such as Midland and Lloyds and ask for details of their overdraft rates for businesses. Find out what these banks charge for:

- agreed overdrafts;

- unauthorised overdrafts.

Compare the rates of the two banks. Do the banks provide similar services for their business customers?

DEBT FACTORING

Factoring is a service offered by financial institutions to help businesses recover debts and improve their cash flow. The financial institution provides up to 80 per cent of the value of an outstanding invoice as an immediate cash advance. It then organises the collection of the debt and makes a further payment to the business concerned. It is usual for the financial institution to retain about 5 per cent of the value of the invoice to cover its costs.

Many small firms consider that to lose 5 per cent of the value of their earnings makes factoring uneconomic. However, factoring does offer a number of benefits.

- **The factor (the bank or building society) takes the risk of bad debts, ensuring that the firm receives at least a proportion of the debt.**

- **The immediate cash provided by the factor means that the firm is likely to have lower overdraft requirements and will incur lower overdraft charges.**

- **The firm saves the administration costs of chasing late payments, for example, avoiding sending multiple invoices and telephoning customers who are slow to pay.**

- **Factoring brings forward the timing of cash flows and makes the earnings received by firms more predictable.**

ACTIVITY

Alan Williams owns and runs a garden centre. His local council is one of his major customers, purchasing a range of plants for its parks. Three months ago, Alan supplied the council with a large number of shrubs in addition to fulfilling their regular order. Alan sent an invoice for £3,000 to the council on his usual credit terms of 60 days.

Because Alan conducts much of his business on credit sales, he decided to factor this debt. He 'sold' the debt to his bank for an immediate payment of £2,400 (80 per cent of the total value) which enabled him to settle some of his own outstanding debts. Two months later the council paid the invoice and the bank sent him the balance of the invoice less a 5 per cent fee for the factoring service.

1 Calculate the value of the second cheque that Alan received from the bank assuming that the factoring fee had been deducted.

2 Read the rest of the section on short-term finance and then decide whether you think that Alan Williams was wise to use a factoring service in these circumstances. What else could he have done?

MEDIUM-TERM FINANCE

Medium-term finance is commonly used to replace some short-term finance, for example an overdraft which has been difficult to clear, or to provide start-up capital to establish a new business. Medium-term finance is usually repayable over a period of between two and eight years.

As with short-term finance, there are three principal methods of medium-term finance: **leasing**, **hire purchase** and **bank loans**.

LEASING

Leasing can be used to acquire assets other than property. With this method, a business simply leases (or rents) a fixed asset rather than buying it. Throughout the period of the lease, the ownership of the asset remains with the finance company and the amount of the rent is sufficient to provide the finance company with a level of profit. Examples of fixed assets which are leased include vehicles and office equipment such as photocopiers and computers.

Businesses often lease assets rather than purchasing them outright because this avoids the need for a large outlay of capital which can be used for other, more profitable, uses. Leasing also enables firms to update their equipment at relatively little extra charge. Some lease agreements allow the firm to purchase the leased asset for a relatively low price at the end of the lease period. It is common for a leasing agreement to include a maintenance contract to ensure that the asset is kept in good working order.

As with all methods of finance, leasing has disadvantages. Because the finance company providing the asset has to make a profit, it is inevitable that, over a period of time, leasing an asset will be more expensive than purchasing it outright. Furthermore, because the asset is never owned by the business, it does not appear as an asset on the balance sheet; this could make the business look less attractive to a potential investor.

HIRE PURCHASE

Hire purchase is a credit agreement enabling a business to purchase an asset by putting down a proportion of the asset's price as a deposit and paying the remainder in instalments over an agreed period of time. Individuals often use hire purchase to buy expensive items such as cars. In any hire purchase arrangement, the purchaser only owns the asset when the final instalment is paid.

The benefits of hire purchase are similar to those of leasing. Assets can be acquired without a large outflow of capital and this can improve the cash position of the business. In contrast to leasing agreements, the business's balance sheet position is improved because it owns the asset once the final payment is made. The principal disadvantage of this method of finance is that the cost of the asset will be considerably higher than if the business purchased it outright.

BANK LOANS

It is common for businesses to purchase assets by raising loans with banks or building societies. The financial institution advances the business a set figure and the business makes repayments over an agreed period of time. Bank loans are relatively straightforward to arrange if the business which is seeking the credit is solvent and has a satisfactory financial history. If the bank lending the capital considers that the loan is in any way risky, then it is likely to charge a higher rate of interest. Small businesses, in particular, suffer from this policy. Normally, banks charge about 2 per cent over their base rate of interest for these loans. In some cases, banks may also charge an arrangement fee for setting up a business loan.

Banks often require security for their loans. Borrowers usually secure loans against their property. Thus, if a business defaults on a loan, the bank can sell the property and recoup the money that it is owed. In this way, banks lower the degree of risk they incur in making loans to businesses.

The interest rates charged on bank loans can either be fixed or variable. Some businesses prefer fixed rates; because the interest payments and repayment schedule are fixed it is easier to plan and manage the business finances. Others are reluctant to take out fixed-rate loans; interest rates may fall after the loan is agreed, leaving those with fixed-rate loans paying higher charges than is necessary. Firms taking out variable-rate loans hope to benefit from lower interest rates.

When taking out loans firms have to be careful that they do not end up borrowing too much and leave themselves vulnerable to rises in interest rates. The balance between the amount of capital raised through loans and through selling shares is an important one for all businesses. This balance or ratio is known as gearing.

LONG-TERM FINANCE

All businesses need to raise long-term finance to purchase major capital assets such as land and buildings. They are also likely to seek long-term finance at times of expansion or when considering the takeover of another company. There are a number of ways in which businesses can raise long-term finance.

RE-INVESTING PROFITS

Profits are perhaps the major source of long-term finance, particularly for smaller businesses. A business can use or appropriate its profits in two ways: by **distributing**

profits to shareholders in the form of dividends or by **retaining profits** for investment and capital assets. By using profits for investment rather than taking out loans, a business avoids interest charges, but this may not be popular with shareholders who receive a lower dividend as a consequence. Furthermore, it is a method of finance only open to firms during profitable trading periods, and even then it may not provide sufficient funds to purchase the more expensive capital assets.

MORTGAGES

Mortgages are long-term loans granted by financial institutions for the purchase of land and buildings. The land or building is used as security for the loan. Typically, mortgages can be for up to approximately 85 per cent of the value of the property. These loans can be for long periods of time – often in excess of twenty years. They can have fixed or variable rates of interest. Mortgages are particularly suitable when a business wishes to raise a large sum of money.

Some businesses may choose to re-mortgage their premises to raise capital. A re-mortgage either increases the existing mortgage or establishes a mortgage where one did not exist before. This is a source of finance which is particularly used by small businesses.

SHARE OR EQUITY CAPITAL

Shares are a very common form of finance for both start-up capital and also for additional capital in a later stage of a business's life.

Firms raise capital by selling a share in their business to investors. The investors can gain in two possible ways from their purchase of shares. First, if the business is successful, the price of the shares might rise allowing them to be sold at a profit. Second, the company usually pays the shareholders a proportion of its profits, known as a dividend. This dividend is paid on every share, so the more shares an investor or shareholder has, the more he or she receives.

There are two main types of share.

- ☼ **Ordinary shares** give a variable dividend from year to year according to how well the company has done. They allow the shareholder a vote at the company's annual general meeting.

- ☼ **Preference shares,** as their name suggests, have priority over ordinary shares when it comes to paying dividends. If profits are small, it is the holders of ordinary shares who are likely to lose out. Preference shareholders usually receive a fixed dividend.

A share is simply a certificate giving the holder ownership of part (or a share) of a company. By selling large numbers of shares, companies can raise significant sums of capital. However, shareholders usually have the right to a say in the running of the company and, by selling too many shares, the owners can lose control of the company. Issuing shares is often administratively very expensive, which means it is only appropriate for raising very large sums of capital. Issuing shares is much more feasible for public limited companies which are quoted on the **London Stock Exchange**. Private limited companies (denoted by the letters Ltd after their names) are restricted in the ways in which they can sell their shares, which makes it more difficult to raise finance through increasing their share capital.

As members of the Stock Exchange, public limited companies have to meet very stringent regulations.

Preston reveals its new goal

PRESTON North End, one of the greatest names in football, is making an audacious bid to regain its former glory. In a scene straight out of *Roy of the Rovers*, the third division club is coming to the stock market in an attempt to cast off the legacy of two despairing decades.

Preston hopes to join the Alternative Investment Market (AIM) in a move expected to raise at least £4 million towards redevelopment. Fans were clamouring for the prospectus after the news broke on Preston radio yesterday.

Preston joins Manchester United, Millwall and Tottenham Hotspur on City dealing screens – even if its track record of late has been less than inspiring.

These can lead to higher administrative costs. In recent years, a parallel stock market – the **Alternative Investment Market** – has developed offering smaller companies many of the benefits of a full stock exchange quotation, most notably in terms of freer access to share capital.

There are a number of benefits from raising capital through the selling of shares or equity. In particular, a company is not committed to meeting fixed interest payments when raising finance in this way.

Although companies are expected to pay an annual return to shareholders, the level of this payment is not fixed and in an unprofitable year it may be possible for the company to avoid making any payment.

VENTURE CAPITAL

There are a number of organisations in the UK that specialise in providing venture capital to small and medium-sized businesses. These businesses are usually too small to be quoted on the London Stock Exchange and, therefore, cannot simply make a public issue of shares to raise capital. Venture capital is regarded as being a relatively high risk because the borrower is not a large firm and because it is usual for significant sums to be required. It is not unusual for sums in excess of £750,000 to be raised in this way.

Venture capitalists take a number of forms. **Merchant banks** (specialised commercial banks such as Rothschilds, Lazards and Hambros) commonly get involved in lending, or arranging, venture capital. There is also a specialist venture capital provider called **3i plc** (formerly Investors In Industry); this was originally a government-sponsored agency set up to promote economic growth by providing venture or risk capital to industry.

The charges associated with venture capital can be quite high, but are offset to some degree by the fact that most venture capitalists offer management support to those companies to whom they lend money.

GOVERNMENT AND EUROPEAN UNION GRANTS

Government grants to businesses can take a number of forms. Some financial assistance is only available in designated areas of the UK. These areas are shown in *Fig. 7.3*. There are two categories.

- **Development areas – which are those parts of the country which suffer the highest levels of unemployment and the lowest levels of prosperity.**

- **Intermediate areas – these suffer unemployment and poverty to a lesser degree than development areas but the problems are still acute.**

Companies in the designated areas can benefit from a number of schemes offered by the government or by agencies on its behalf.

- **Regional Selective Assistance.** Under this the government offers grants to firms who move to a designated area and create jobs.

- **Regional Enterprise Grants.** These are for firms with less than twenty-five employees who create jobs in development areas. The aid can help with investment up to a maximum of £25,000.

- **Consultancy Initiative.** Firms in all assisted areas, with fewer than 500 employees, can claim 66 per cent of the cost of hiring consultants.

- **Enterprise Zones.** Designed to revitalise inner cities these are areas of a few hundred acres. Firms can receive financial incentives to locate within them. Benefits include tax incentives and subsidised premises.

Venture cash set to pour into railways

BUSINESS analysts expect a flood of private capital to pour into Britain's under-invested railways after yesterday's successful £1.8 billion sale of three train fleet companies. The train fleet companies own 11,000 locomotives between them and lease them to the businesses which operate train services.

Venture capital organisations including Nomura, Charterhouse Development Capital and Babcock & Brown (each of whom were in groups investing at least £500 million) were amongst those putting up the money for the purchase of the three companies.

Adapted from *The Times*, 10 November 1995

FIGURE 7.3: Development and intermediate areas.
Source: Department of Trade and Industry.

Legend:
- Development Areas
- Intermediate Areas
- Government Office, Welsh Office Industry & Training Department and Scottish Office Industry Department boundaries

⊗ **Business Start-up Scheme.**
This scheme is run by Training and Enterprise Councils (TECs) to provide training and financial assistance to those who were previously unemployed and who wish to start businesses. These schemes vary from area to area, but applicants are normally expected to make a substantial capital investment into their business and, in return, receive a weekly wage and appropriate training from their local TEC.

Big sweetener draws Siemens to Britain

Sweeteners worth up to £200 million are thought to have persuaded Siemens, the German electronic group, to locate a £1.1 billion microchip plant in Tyneside.

Michael Heseltine, the Deputy Prime Minister, yesterday refused to put a figure on the incentive package attracting the company to the UK after it had considered sites in Ireland and Austria.

Mr Heseltine said it was not in the government's interests to publicise the figure for fear of setting high negotiating levels for other such arrangements. The Department of Trade and Industry was equally cagey. It referred to a regional selective assistance grant of £30 million with "the balance ... yet to be finalised".

Adapted from The Times, 5 August 1995

The government has offered substantial and undisclosed financial packages to a number of multinational companies in order to persuade them to locate in the UK. These grants and loans can be a significant source of finance for a company expanding within the UK.

The government also offers some financial support to businesses irrespective of their location within the UK.

⊗ **Loan Guarantee Scheme.** The government offers a guarantee for up to 85 per cent of a medium-term loan from a bank. This allows firms to borrow money for projects which would normally be considered too risky for banks to finance. This scheme has proved to be popular and successful.

The European Union also provides grants. There are three major sources of European support.

⊗ **European Regional Development Fund.** This provides financial and other help for businesses and for infrastructure projects such as roads and telecommunications.

⊗ **European Social Fund.** This provides money for training and other schemes designed to solve labour market problems.

⊗ **European Agricultural Guidance and Guarantee Fund.** This provides job opportunities in agricultural areas.

Finally, local authorities offer financial benefits to businesses, including:

⊗ **grants for business start-ups;**

⊗ **innovation grants;**

⊗ **job creation grants;**

⊗ **rent and rates free period;**

⊗ **guides to sources of finance;**

⊗ **loans to businesses.**

SOURCES OF FINANCE

Businesses can raise finance from a variety of sources. The actual source chosen is likely to depend upon the type and amount of finance that is required.

SUPPLIERS

If managed properly, suppliers can be a useful source of trade credit. It is important that firms pay before the due date to avoid the possibility of financial penalties and/or the withdrawal of this trade credit. Suppliers are unlikely to make trade credit available to new businesses or to those with a poor financial record.

ACTIVITY

For each of the following situations, state what you consider to be the most appropriate method of finance:

(a) a business wishes to finance a new fleet of cars for its salesforce;

(b) a company wants to build a major new factory costing £350m;

(c) a firm wishes to purchase more raw materials in order to increase its output;

(d) a small business needs to pay suppliers now but its customers are not expected to pay for a further two months;

(e) a services company is due to start up a branch, which will offer 100 jobs in an area of high unemployment;

(f) a large public limited company wishes to finance the development of a new range of products;

(g) a company wishes to install a new **IT** system but is conscious that the technology is changing rapidly;

(h) a firm that has little cash to spare, and which pays all its bills promptly, wishes to finance an increase in production;

(i) a business wishes to invest a substantial sum and anticipates steady profits over the next few years.

BANKS AND BUILDING SOCIETIES

The financial services offered by banks and, in particular, building societies have grown over recent years. Banks and building societies now provide similar services.

You will be familiar with the high street banks such as Lloyds and the National Westminster and building societies like the Halifax, but you may not have heard of merchant banks such as Rothschilds and Hambros. High street banks and building societies provide loans, overdrafts, leasing arrangements, factoring services and mortgages. Merchant banks are more likely to provide venture capital; they tend to accept higher risks than the high street banks in the hope of making higher profits.

Business Development Loan:

A straightforward LOAN with no Hidden costs

There may be times when you need to borrow money to develop your business. You may need to invest in new equipment to help you meet a particular order or contract, or to move to new premises or to expand your market. If so, a NatWest Business Development Loan could be the answer. With a Business Development Loan you can:

...benefit from a fixed interest rate, fixed term and fixed monthly payments;

...borrow any amount you can afford, from £2,000 to £250,000; and

...repay over a period from 1 to 20 years.

Source: NatWest Bank business finance leaflet.

HIRE PURCHASE AND LEASING COMPANIES

Some specialist companies provide leasing and hire purchase facilities. These companies are known as **finance houses**.

VENTURE CAPITAL INVESTORS

There are a number of specialist institutions covering the venture sector of the capital market, including the 3i plc and the venture capital arms of the high street and merchant banks. Venture capital investors originally concentrated most of their funding on small start-up businesses offering innovative products. Nowadays, they more frequently provide finance to allow management teams to buy out their companies (in so-called management buy-outs). The **British Venture Capital Association** represents firms and institutions operating in this area.

GOVERNMENT GRANTS

The government offers a substantial range of grants to businesses, as outlined earlier. In doing so, the government aims:

- **to promote jobs and the development of industry in less prosperous regions such as the north of England and Northern Ireland;**

- **to promote small firms through financial and managerial support in the hope that they will develop into larger firms;**

- **to support companies which export a significant volume of goods and services;**

- **to encourage industry to be more independent and self-reliant.**

OWNERS' FINANCE

Owners' finance is available to all types of businesses. A sole trader may put in a few thousand pounds of his or her savings. During the 1980s and early 1990s many sole traders financed their businesses with capital received as part of a redundancy package. Partnerships – of, for example, doctors, lawyers, accountants – can often use the same personal source of finance except that, because there are a number of partners, the sums available are likely to be larger. However, it is likely that the demand for capital will also be greater.

Over recent years, public limited companies have increasingly used **rights issues** as a means of raising finance. A rights issue allows shareholders in the company the chance to buy shares in proportion to their existing holdings (say, one new share for each ten already owned) at a reduced price. The company can afford to sell at a reduced price because the administrative costs of rights issues are relatively low. This, in effect, is just another means of raising more finance from the existing owners of the company.

SELLING SHARES

As an alternative to a rights issue, a company may make a **general shares issue** to attract additional investment. Public limited companies employ a merchant bank to advertise a share issue in the hope of attracting funds from both other companies and members of the public. A prospectus is published giving details of the company and its financial position (often in glowing terms). Adverts are usually placed in financial journals and newspapers. This is an expensive method of raising finance and it is only undertaken by a large company seeking to raise a substantial sum of capital.

INTERNAL SOURCES OF FINANCE

We have said that retained profits are a major source of finance for many businesses. There are also other ways in which companies can provide capital from within.

Companies may sell assets which are surplus to requirements to raise capital. Thus, the recently privatised water companies have sold off large parcels of land for which they have no use. The capital raised is available to finance investment in other aspects of their businesses.

Some companies use the technique of sale and leaseback. They sell major assets, often property, and then lease back the asset in question. In this way they continue to have the use of the asset whilst enjoying a large injection of capital at the same time.

Finally, some company directors may provide interest-free loans to the business from their personal resources. This tends to only happen in certain industries (for example, football clubs) and there are usually some strings attached. The company directors will expect something in return for an interest-free loan.

OTHER SOURCES OF FINANCE

There are a few other minor sources of finance which we have not yet covered. One major source of income for charities is fund-raising, although the introduction of the National Lottery in 1994 has resulted in a reduction of income for organisations such as Oxfam and Save The Children Fund. Charities hope that payments from the National Lottery fund will make up the shortfall.

Charities also receive finance through two other sources.

Deed of Covenant

NATIONAL **ASTHMA** CAMPAIGN
getting your breath back

If you pay income tax in your own right, we hope that you will agree to covenant your regular donations to us. *There would be no extra cost to you,* but we are able to reclaim the tax on your donations from the Inland Revenue. More than 1300 of our supporters already covenant their gifts to us.

The cheapest and most cost effective way for us to administer your covenanted donations is by Banker's Order. Please also complete the Banker's Order form if you are willing to make your donations by this method.

The completed Deed of Covenant and Banker's Order forms overleaf should be sent to us at the address below. *Please do not send them to your bank.*

National Asthma Campaign, Providence House, Providence Place, London N1 0NT
Tel: 071-226 2260   Fax: 071-704 0740

FIGURE 7.4: Covenants are an important source of income for charities.

○ **Covenants.** These are written agreements by a person to pay a specified sum of money to some other person or organisation for a given period of time. Covenants can be a beneficial form of income for charities as they provide a tax-efficient source of finance.

○ **Wills.** It is common for people to leave money to charitable organisations as a bequest in their wills.

Some clubs and associations have membership fees as a principal source of finance.

SOURCES AVAILABLE TO BUSINESS ORGANISATIONS

Different organisations have access to different sources of finance.

Fig. 7.5 summarises the major types of business organisation that exist within the UK and the main sources of funds that are available to each of those business organisations.

Type of Business Organisation	Examples	Sources of Finance
Sole Trader	Corner shop, window cleaner, painter and decorator.	Owner's savings, banks, suppliers, government grants and loans.
Partnership	Accountants, lawyers, dentists.	Partners' savings, banks, suppliers, government grants and loans, hire purchase and leasing companies.
Private Limited Company (Ltd)	These are generally small businesses operating in many areas of the economy that can also include larger nationally-known businesses, such as the Virgin Group.	Dependent upon the size of the private limited company, suppliers, banks, factoring, leasing and hire purchase companies, government grants and loans, venture capital institutions, private share issues.
Public Limited Company (plc)	Larger companies enjoying the benefits of selling shares on the Stock Exchange. Such companies include J Sainsbury plc and British Nuclear Fuels plc.	Suppliers, banks, factoring, leasing and hire purchase companies, government grants and loans, venture capital institutions, public share issues via the Stock Exchange.
Non-Profit-Making Organisation	Trade unions, for example UNISON, and charities such as Age Concern, companies limited by guarantee which are not established to make a profit, for example National Examination Boards.	Charitable donations.

FIGURE 7.5: Sources of business finance.

PORTFOLIO ASSIGNMENT

THE ANGLIA BANK PLC

You are employed by the Anglia Bank in its Norwich branch. You have recently been promoted to become the branch's business adviser.

One of your new duties at the bank will be to approve – or turn down – applications for loans from local businesses. Norwich has a mixture of businesses from large concerns such as Colmans and Norwich Union to a wide variety of small firms. The Anglia Bank is a major source of short and long-term finance for the businesses of Norwich. It has a reputation for offering advice as well as finance to businesses and, in particular, to small businesses.

As part of your training for your new post, you are given some mock cases (which are based on applications for loans received by the Norwich branch of the Anglia Bank). Your manager has asked you to write a formal report setting out both the options available to the borrowers and the type of finance you would provide in each case. She asks that, in each case, you set out the likely cost of the finance and whether any security should be demanded.

Your mock cases are printed opposite. They contain details of the customers and their financial needs. Read the case studies, and then write your formal reports.

(a) The Norwich Cannery Company Limited of Riverside Road, Thorpe St Andrew, is planning to build an extension to its factory following the success of its bid to can food for a major and prestigious high street retailer. The extension to the factory is expected to cost £250,000 with a further £100,000 necessary for fitting out the extension. The company has enjoyed a prosperous period recently. It is able to contribute £90,000 from its own reserves.

(b) Wilkinson and Humphries is a long-established firm of solicitors. The partnership has offices at Lime Tree Walk. The partners are seeking to introduce some sophisticated information technology into the partnership in order to improve both its image and the efficiency of the service which it provides. The expected cost of the equipment is £23,500.

(c) Paul Marsden runs his own printing business designing and producing stationery for businesses in Norfolk. In recent months, his business account has become heavily overdrawn. It currently has a deficit of £7,500. Paul's customers are increasingly delaying payment of their accounts with his business. He has provided evidence that he has £9,000 worth of outstanding invoices, but he has sought help because his creditors want him to settle his bills.

Produce and explain forecasts and a cash flow for a small business

CAPITAL BUDGETS AND TRADING FORECASTS

Forecasting is an important technique for all businesses and not least for small businesses. Estimating future outcomes, such as next year's sales figures or the likely expenditure on raw materials, is a central part of the successful management of a business. Forecasts can only be 'best guesses' as to what may happen in the future but there are techniques that firms can employ to help base their guesses on the most reliable information available.

⊗ **A business can base its forecasts on what has happened in the past by extending the trend into the future. This process is known as extrapolation.**

⊗ **Businesses can also undertake research into the area in which they have to produce a forecast. Thus, a forecast of next year's sales figures may be based on research into consumers' buying habits.**

In business, forecasts are generally referred to as budgets, though the term projection may also be used. Forecasts can relate to the income that the business expects to earn or to the expenditure – of whatever type – that the business is to undertake.

In this unit we shall use the term capital budget, but when discussing trading and cash flow we will refer to these as forecasts. This usage brings out the distinction between forecasts and budgets: a forecast is an estimate, a budget represents a target. *Fig. 7.6* illustrates that various forecasts and budgets are derived from a sales forecast.

In this element we shall concentrate on three areas in which businesses draw up forecasts:

⊗ **capital budgets;**

⊗ **trading forecasts;**

⊗ **cash flow forecasts.**

ACTIVITY

Distinguish clearly between a forecast and a budget. Which comes first in the process of business management?

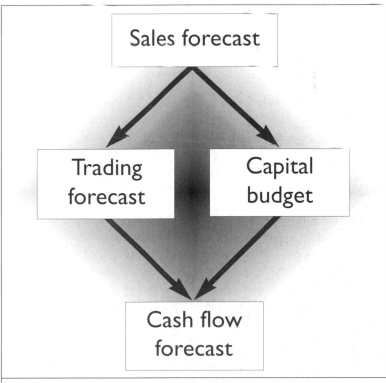

FIGURE 7.6: The development of budgets and forecasts.

THE PURPOSE OF FORECASTS

In the previous element, we reviewed the possible sources of finance available to a business. Many of these sources involve borrowing. Organisations (and individuals) that lend money to businesses will require some indication of what the owners of the business expect to happen in the coming months or years. Forecasts, and the budgets prepared from these forecasts, allow managers to set out how they think the business will develop and what they believe is likely to happen to it. It is one way of assessing the possible success of the business and it is an important step in persuading potential investors to lend money. Drawing up forecasts is an important part of preparing a business plan.

ACTIVITY

Talk to someone who runs a small business in your area. Ask them to predict what they think might happen to their business over the next year or so. Areas to discuss with them might include sales and income, costs, expenditure on capital items and competition. Ask them how they plan for such eventualities. Compare your results with those of other students following this course.

Banks and other financial institutions particularly expect information about the future of a business seeking finance before they are prepared to lend money. They require businesses to submit a business plan before they will advance a loan. The advice offered by Barclays Bank (see extract from its guide to financial planning, opposite) is typical.

A business plan should include details on the marketing strategy to be pursued by a business, its estimated costs of production and the overall financial implications of starting the business. The plan will help the entrepreneurs to think through their ideas and can help persuade others to put money into the business. The fact that a business plan is an integral part of starting – or expanding – a business is a powerful argument for the importance of forecasting in management. We consider business plans more fully in unit 8.

Managing a small business involves making decisions and choices. Forecasting can help businesses to decide

Thinking of starting a business?

Planning your way forward

BARCLAYS

What will the bank expect from you?

If you need to borrow money then your bank manager and your financial advisers need to understand how you see your business developing. They can then assess the viability of your plans and forecasts and give you advice.

Your bank manager will base the decision on whether or not to lend money to your business on his or her assessment of your business plan. Ultimately the decision has to be a financial one, but if you present your plan on the back of an envelope it is less likely to be successful. Such an approach may indicate that you have an unbusinesslike attitude which is unlikely to impress your potential customers.

Financial Planning for Your Business, Barclays Bank

between alternatives. Consider, for example, the choice faced by a restaurant owner who has to decide whether to open a new restaurant or to expand the existing one. Forecasts and budgets play a key role here. The owner will want to have some estimate of the likely sales in both cases and the potential costs in terms of wages and raw materials. It will also be useful to have some indication of possible expenditure on fixed assets in both circumstances. The process of forecasting and the creation of budgets from this data brings a quantifiable aspect to the process of deciding between alternative courses of action.

ACTIVITY

Imagine you have discovered that many of the people in your locality would be prepared to pay for a high-quality valeting and car cleaning service. You have to decide whether or not to give up your part-time job to pursue this business opportunity. Make a list of the information you would like to have to help you with this decision.

Most businesses set objectives and targets for a number of reasons. Managers might want to ensure that the business is managed coherently towards a common target, to provide motivation for employees by setting targets and also to have a figure against which to monitor performance. So, a salesperson might have a personal target of increasing sales by 5 per cent over the coming year. This will help the company to achieve its objective of growth and give the managers of the company something against which to measure the performance of the salesperson. However, all of this depends upon forecasts; the targets have to be reasonable and attainable. If they are not, then employees at all levels within the company can be demotivated. You can see that accurate forecasts are important in setting targets.

To summarise, forecasts have a number of purposes. They can help a business obtain finance, assist in choosing between alternative plans and projects, and can be used to provide targets and motivate staff. In addition, they also give managers a yardstick against which to measure the success of their enterprises.

CAPITAL BUDGETS

It is easy to think that business planning is restricted to a single year, and certainly one-year budgets are the most common. However, businesses will have long-term plans as well as short-term plans. Longer-terms plans are called **corporate plans**, and the corresponding short-term investment plans are called **capital budgets**, sometimes referred to as capital expenditure budgets.

A business has two short-term budgets: a **revenue budget** relating to planned sales and costs within the short-term – usually a year – and a **capital budget** associated with capital investments in the same period. In this element, we first consider capital budgets.

Expenditure on capital items, such as premises or machinery, is likely to be substantial. It is important that businesses remain within their budgets when undertaking such expenditure. However, it is equally important for businesses to appreciate the likely extent of capital expenditure.

ACTIVITY

You are considering opening a grocer's shop in a nearby town, specialising in high-quality foods and promising same-day delivery.

1 Make a list of the capital items you will be likely to need. Try and find out possible prices for these items.

2 Using the material in element 1, suggest how you might raise the finance for these purchases.

The capital expenditure budget outlines planned expenditure on fixed assets for the budget period, usually month by month. In a manufacturing organisation, it is normal to compare planned production levels and existing production facilities. If the facilities are inadequate, planned expenditure on fixed assets (for example, new premises and equipment) will have to take place over the budget period.

Fig. 7.7 shows a sample capital budget for Rusholme Engineering Ltd, a Suffolk-based business producing components for use in the motor vehicle industry. As is common with budgets and forecasts, a column for actual expenditure is included to allow managers to measure whether the business is performing to expectations. This allows planned and actual figures to be easily compared. For a medium-sized organisation such as Rusholme

	Planned	Actual
Premises	775,000	803,500
Vehicles	96,000	89,000
Equipment	135,750	129,000
Machinery	85,000	85,000
Total	1,091,750	1,106,500

FIGURE 7.7: Rusholme Engineering's capital budget.

Engineering, capital budgets may be drawn up after the departments or areas which comprise the business have made bids for capital.

Capital budgeting entails planning the total amount of capital spending over the next year or two on items such as premises, equipment, vehicles and machinery. Because the sums are large, the timing of capital expenditure is often critical to allow for the arrangement of suitable financing. Capital budgets are often updated quarterly, since both amounts and timing of payments can change quickly.

A number of financial techniques are available to help firms take decisions on whether to invest in capital items, or to help them choose between alternative capital investments. These techniques of investment appraisal compare expenditure on capital items with estimated earnings. Detailed knowledge of them is not part of the Advanced Business GNVQ syllabus.

TRADING FORECASTS

A trading forecast is a simple statement of intent, setting out planned production costs (for example, on raw materials and wages), overheads and sales. This type of forecast covers the other major area of expenditure faced by businesses besides capital expenditure. It also sets out anticipated revenue. In this sense, it is a forecast of the business's profit and loss account which we consider in detail later in this unit. Fig. 7.8 shows an example of a trading forecast (for a small business).

The exact make-up of a trading forecast depends on the type of business, but major items within the forecast will include:

- sales;
- raw materials;
- wages.

SALES

Forecast sales revenue is a key figure for any business. As we saw in Fig. 7.6, a sales forecast is the start of the budgetary process. Firms may undertake market research to assess consumer demand for their product at various prices. This information can then provide the basis for an estimate of sales revenue. Such figures are notoriously difficult to estimate as they are subject to many influences, including changes in tastes and fashions.

RAW MATERIALS

All manufacturing businesses require raw materials if they are to produce and sell goods. As we saw in unit 6, raw materials are a variable cost, that is they rise and fall in line with the level of production. This definition of raw materials can also extend to businesses such as retailing, where the raw materials are the products that the shops and supermarkets purchase to resell to customers. For example, in 1995 J Sainsbury plc sold £11.4bn of groceries and other items. Undoubtedly, Sainsbury's major cost would have been the purchase of the products which it sells to the public.

WAGES

Wages are an important cost faced by any business, particularly those in the tertiary sector. We saw in unit 1 that there is a trend within the UK and other advanced

Pittman's Pottery – Trading Forecast 1996–7

	£	£
Sales revenue		150,000
Expenditure		
Raw materials	46,000	
Wages	38,000	
Water rates	1,000	
Other running costs	52,000	
	137,000	
Annual profit		13,000

FIGURE 7.8: A trading forecast.

ACTIVITY

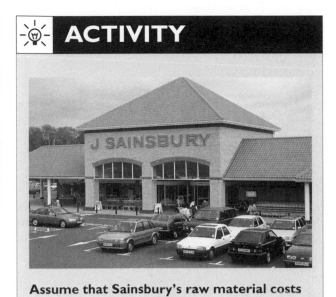

Assume that Sainsbury's raw material costs are 65 per cent of its sales value. How much would Sainsbury have paid for its raw materials in 1995?

economies for more people to be employed in tertiary or service industries. Because service industries, such as health and education, buy relatively few raw materials (by definition they do not produce goods but offer services) their major expenditure is on wages.

Like raw materials, wages are a variable cost. There is a close correlation between expenditure on wages and the level of sales achieved by a business. Forecasting wage costs can be complicated for a number of reasons. If employees suffer ill health and are unavailable for work but are still receiving sick pay, then wage costs increase as replacements have to be paid. Similarly, if workers are less productive than anticipated, or if unions are successful in obtaining higher than expected pay rises, then wage costs can exceed the forecast figure.

ACTIVITY

Give three reasons why actual expenditure on wages may be less than forecast expenditure.

Wages costs are subject to other influences. There is a trend for what is termed 'flexible' staffing in the UK at present. This involves greater use of part-time staff, employing more people on short-term contracts and more

use of self-employed personnel. This gives businesses greater flexibility to cope with short-term staffing needs caused, for example, by sudden changes in the level of demand for a firm's products. An additional advantage of flexible staffing arrangements is that the overheads incurred by the business are reduced.

OTHER COSTS
Firms face a variety of other costs. Some of these costs will be fixed and some will be variable. They include telephone expenses, postal charges, stationery costs and interest payments. All businesses have to pay overheads. These costs are usually fixed and include rent and business rates, water rates and the salaries of managers. These costs are not generated by the production process. The importance of these costs varies according to the nature of the business.

ACTIVITY

Consider the list of other costs above and identify which represent fixed costs and which are variable costs. Identify three other costs which a business might face.

CASH FLOW FORECASTS

A cash flow forecast is a detailed estimate of a firm's future cash inflows and outflows over a specified period. This is usually calculated on a monthly basis and by adding together the monthly figures the firm's cumulative cash position can be calculated. This is illustrated in *Fig. 7.9*.

Burrell Electronics			
(All figures in £000s)			
	Jan	Feb	Mar	Apr
Cash at start	100	90	70	95
Cash inflows	120	130	175	195
Cash outflows	130	150	150	145
Net cash flow	(10)	(20)	25	50
Cumulative cash	90	70	95	145

FIGURE 7.9: A cash flow summary.

Fig. 7.9 summarises a cash flow statement for Burrell Electronics for four months of the year. **Cash inflows** represent the earnings of the business, resulting from sales of its goods or services. These inflows could be the results of cash sales in the month in question, or the payment for credit sales which may have taken place in previous months.

Cash outflows represent the costs faced by businesses. These can be as a result of capital expenditure on fixed assets, or of current expenditure on, for example, rent and rates.

The net cash flow is simply the monthly balance between outflows and inflows. Thus for January the net cash flow is £120,000 minus £130,000, which is minus £10,000 or (£10,000). Remember that accounting convention places brackets around negative figures. The cumulative cash flow is simply calculated by adding the net cash flow for any month to the business's cash position at the beginning of that month. If we continue our example, we can see that the firm began January with a cash balance of £100,000, its net figure for the month was (£10,000) and so at the end of the month the firm had a cash balance of £90,000.

Both profit and cash flow are important to all businesses, but it is important to understand that they are not the same thing. A profitable company can experience cash shortages and, in extreme cases, these can result in bankruptcy. During the recession of the late 1980s and early 1990s many businesses, and especially small businesses, faced short-term cash difficulties due to a temporary decline in sales and an increase in interest charges. This put a strain on the financial position of firms, although fundamentally the businesses may have been profitable. Unfortunately, a large number of small businesses went bankrupt during this recession.

ACTIVITY

Assume that Burrell Electronics has a cash inflow of £150,000 in May and June and cash outflows of £170,000 in May and £140,000 in June. Calculate the net cash flows for the two months and the cumulative cash position at the end of this period.

The difference between profit and cash

Profit is a surplus earned in respect of a period of trading, after deducting all business expenses from sales turnover and any other income earned. **Cash** is a liquid asset owned by a business that enables it to purchase goods and services.

If a business sells its products for more than they cost, it has earned a profit. However, if its customers have not yet paid for these goods then it may have no cash available.

When a firm purchases fixed assets for which it may pay in cash, it does not deduct the whole cost of the assets from the profit made in the same period in which payment was made. Instead, the company's accounts usually charge only a proportion of the cost of the fixed assets as a depreciation expense in each period of the asset's life.

Thus, profit looks at the overall balance of income and expenditure, cash flow analysis (and of course cash flow forecasts) take into account the timing of payments and receipts.

THE PURPOSES OF A CASH FLOW FORECAST

Cash flow is an important part of financial planning for any business. Monitoring cash flows can ensure that the working capital for a business is sufficient and that funds are available to undertake day-to-day transactions. This planning and management ensures that cash is available to maintain any growth in the business. As an example, an expanding business may need to purchase additional stocks to allow higher production levels and to meet increased customer demand.

Cash flow forecasts can confirm that cash will be available to meet a variety of financial requirements. Expenditure may be necessary to meet the demands of capital budgets, ensuring that suitable fixed assets are available as and when the business requires them. Cash flow forecasts also indicate by how much a business may have to increase its sales or reduce its costs to meet the impending capital outlay. Alternatively, the cash flow forecast may highlight that some staging of the capital payments is essential: that is, payment for the fixed assets should be spread out over a longer time period. The business may also have to consider undertaking increased borrowing to meet its planned capital commitments.

Evidence of this kind of cash flow planning is likely to be helpful in attracting prospective investors or providers of finance. A positive cash flow position is likely to generate confidence in potential lenders. It will instil a belief that the business is well managed and has the ability to repay the debt.

Cash flow forecasts will also highlight the times at which funds are available to meet the current costs associated with trading. Thus, they identify when finance is available to pay major costs, such as rent and the purchase of raw materials. Equally, they make clear the timing of the receipts from the sale of goods or services.

Monitoring cash flows can also reduce the bank interest paid by the business. By monitoring and managing its cash flow, a business should have less need to use its overdraft facility or to require expensive short-term finance. This reduces the costs of the business and should improve its profitability. Control of such cash flows is a critical determinant in the success of a business.

Cash flow forecasts should also indicate the timing of cash surpluses. This can help firms to schedule projects in the anticipation that sufficient funds should be available for them. It is not in a firm's interests to have a very large surplus of cash; tying up resources in unproductive assets such as cash will not enhance profitability.

Each spending decision taken by a business should be dependent on the availability of cash: all business decisions should be considered from a cash flow perspective. Once a cash flow becomes negative, it can threaten the life of a business unless more cash is made available to the business.

THE STRUCTURE OF CASH FLOW FORECASTS

The precise format of cash flow forecasts can vary, although the basic principles remain the same. The format that is set out for Cumbers Trading Ltd (in *Fig. 7.10*) is one which is in common usage by businesses.

ACTIVITY

Visit a local branch of one of the high street banks and ask for information on starting your own business. Read carefully the section on constructing a cash flow forecast. Compare the format with that set out in *Fig. 7.10*.

	(All figures in £000s)			
	Jan	Feb	Mar	Apr
Cash inflows:				
Capital introduced	150	130	0	0
Receipts from loans	50	0	0	0
Receipts from sales	356	472	508	545
VAT recoveries	0	40	0	0
Total Inflow	**556**	**632**	**508**	**545**
Cash outflows:				
Payment for assets	275	0	0	0
Raw materials	60	65	60	65
Wages and salaries	115	125	125	125
Rent and rates	100	100	100	100
Water rates	0	0	0	23
Telephone	25	27	27	26
Office expenses	17	19	23	18
Interest payments	52	97	97	97
Loan repayments	20	34	34	34
VAT payments	0	0	198	0
Total outflow	**664**	**467**	**664**	**488**
Net cashflow	(108)	165	(156)	57
Opening balance	245	137	302	146
Closing balance	137	302	146	203

FIGURE 7.10: A cash flow forecast.

The cash flow forecast for Cumbers Trading is comprised of three sections. The top section records the **cash inflows** into the business and the middle section the **outflows** from the business. The final section shows the **net cash flow** from the business which is the balance between inflows and outflows over the month in question. This final section also records the cash position of Cumbers Trading at the beginning and end of each month. Frequently cash flow forecasts have two columns for each month – one to record the forecast and the second to give the actual figures for the month. This allows a business to see whether it is performing as well as expected. This is a format that we encountered when discussing capital budgets.

CASH INFLOWS

The cash inflows to a business can take a number of forms:

- **capital introduced;**
- **receipts from loans;**
- **sales receipts;**
- **VAT recoveries.**

Capital introduced is capital put into the business by the owners of the business. In the case of Cumbers Trading, this will be capital introduced to the business by the shareholders since it is a private limited company. This capital might have been raised by the company for a specific purpose, for example to finance the purchase of some machinery or new premises. When capital is introduced at the beginning of the life of a business, it is referred to as **start-up capital**. This might be required to alter and adapt premises before trading commences or for development and advertising costs to launch the new product. For a new business, this start-up capital could be the only inflow for some time until the business begins to earn revenue from selling its goods or services.

All businesses take out **loans** at some time or another. This is the alternative to raising funds from shareholders as mentioned above. The balance between capital raised through loans and through the sale of shares is a sensitive one. This balance is known as **capital gearing**. Cumbers Trading Ltd took out a loan in January and the business received £50,000 as a consequence. This is shown against 'receipts from loans' in its cash flow forecast. Loans are likely to be a very common feature on cash flow forecasts in the early stages of business trading

Sales receipts can fall into two categories: cash sales and credit sales. This is an important distinction when considering cash flow. **Cash sales** are sales for which payment is received in advance or at the time of purchase. These are likely to be sales to customers which the firm does not know well or who might have a bad track record in paying bills. This benefits the selling firm because it does not have to wait for payment when, of course, it has already had to pay many of the costs associated with production. **Credit sales** occur when the supplier allows the customer to purchase goods and services without making an immediate payment. For example, Cumbers Trading might allow reliable customers 30 days grace before payment has to be paid. In effect, Cumbers Trading is granting its customers an interest-free loan.

The income received from sales is recorded on the cash flow forecast at the time the money flows into the business. Thus, if Cumbers Trading makes a credit sale in February of £30,000 but does not receive payment until March, the £30,000 will be recorded as an inflow in March.

Our analysis of cash flow forecasts assumes that all the products manufactured by Cumbers Trading are sold. If this did not happen, then the sales income would be lower and the unsold output would be stored as stocks. This is a simplification: in real life, it is unlikely that a business will estimate market demand exactly and produce the correct quantity of goods and services.

Businesses will be charged **value added tax (VAT)** on most of the items that they purchase. Similarly, they will charge VAT on the products that they sell, unless they are zero-rated or exempt from VAT. Businesses have to pass on the VAT that they collect from their customers, but they are allowed to reclaim the VAT that they pay on their supplies. **VAT recoveries** are the repayments that a business receives from the **Customs and Excise** (which collects VAT on behalf of the government) and can appear in the cash flow forecast as shown in the case of Cumbers Trading Ltd. It is usual for businesses to pay VAT on a quarterly basis and also to receive VAT recoveries on the same basis. This explains why there is only a single entry for VAT recoveries during the four-month period covered by the cash flow forecast.

However, it is usual for businesses simply to pay the **net** amount of VAT that is due. That is, they pay the amount of tax they have charged on their sales **less** the amount they paid to suppliers. In this case, VAT recoveries would only appear as a separate item on a cash flow forecast if, for a particular VAT quarterly period, a business reclaimed more VAT from its suppliers than it collected from its customers.

ACTIVITY

Find three examples of goods which are exempt from VAT and three examples of goods which are zero-rated.

CASH OUTFLOWS

There are a number of forms of expenditure which can lead to a business incurring a cash outflow:

- **payments for assets;**
- **purchase of raw materials;**
- **wages;**
- **interest and loan payments;**
- **VAT payments;**
- **other running costs.**

Payments for assets refers to the purchase of fixed assets such as buildings, machines and vehicles. These appear in the capital budget; you may wonder why they should also appear in a cash flow forecast. The answer is that the capital budget is designed to tell managers that they have sufficient funds to purchase the assets, but the cash flow forecast looks at the timing of the expenditure in relation to expected receipts of funds. It is important for businesses to plan major items of expenditure to make sure that they occur at a time when the business has sufficient funds available.

Purchase of raw materials is often a particularly expensive item for manufacturing businesses. They can hold large stocks of raw materials, particularly if suppliers are unreliable. Manufacturers may also hold large stocks of raw materials as a hedge against inflation if they expect the price of raw materials to rise in the near future. However, part of the art of successful management is to order raw materials as they are required and to avoid tying up a large amount of cash in large stocks.

Recently Industry throughout Europe has been influenced by a number of Japanese management techniques. One, known as **just-in-time manufacturing**, involves minimising the level of stocks (including raw materials). Benetton, which is renowned for its controversial advertising campaigns, only produces knitwear once orders are received from stores. Benetton dyes its knitwear after the garments have been knitted to avoid holding large stocks of different coloured wool. This system relies upon a very efficient ordering system to ensure raw materials and components are available as required. We look more fully at just-in-time manufacturing in unit 5.

The purchase of raw materials can be treated in two ways in a cash flow forecast depending upon whether they have been purchased with cash or on credit. If purchased with cash, they should be recorded in the forecast immediately. If they are purchased on credit, they should be recorded when payment is made and the transaction is completed. This is likely to be two or three months later.

Wages are a major expense for many businesses. The timing of these payments are, to a great extent, beyond the control of a business. Delaying the payment of wages would do little to enhance industrial relations! Most cash flow forecasts will record an expenditure figure against wages in each month. It may be, in the early stages of a new business, that the owner of a business will draw the minimum amount possible to help his or her business establish itself.

Most businesses take out loans, particularly in their early stages. This, of course, means that a business will have to pay interest on the loans as well as repaying the loans themselves. **Interest payments** will be made each month and may be fixed. However, if a business takes out variable-rate loans, the amount of interest charged will rise or fall with variations in the general level of interest rates.

We discussed above that most businesses have to charge VAT on the products that they sell. They have to pass on the net **VAT payments** they have collected to the Customs and Excise on a quarterly basis. Most small businesses are registered for VAT on a cash payment basis. This means that they make VAT payments to the Customs and Excise each quarter based on the actual VAT paid and received during the quarter. So, if a business makes a credit sale, it does not include the VAT on the sale in its quarterly return to Customs and Excise until it has actually received payment from the customer.

Businesses face a range of other costs which will require expenditure at various times. In addition to the expenses listed above, most businesses also have to pay telephone charges, a mortgage and/or rent, business rates, charges for gas and electricity, stationery costs and marketing costs.

NET CASH FLOWS, OPENING AND CLOSING BALANCES

The remaining three rows of a cash flow forecast are usually the same. First, it is necessary to deduct the total cash outflow for the month from the total cash inflow for the same month. The resulting figure – which may be positive or negative – is termed the net cash flow figure. This, in turn, is added to the cash balance which the firm had at the beginning of the month or year – the opening balance. By adding the net cash flow to the opening balance, the closing balance for the firm is calculated. This is then carried forward to become the opening balance for the following month or year.

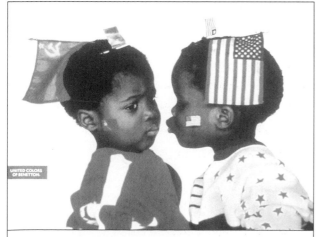

FIGURE 7.11: Benetton uses just-in-time techniques.

To illustrate this process, we have reproduced the final section of the cash flow forecast for Cumbers Trading (see *Fig. 7.12*). You can see that the net cash flow figure for January is (£108,000) – in other words, during this month £108,000 more cash flows out of the business than flows in. The cash available to the business at the start of the month is £245,000 – this is the opening balance. By adding together the net cash flow and the opening balance we arrive at the closing balance – in this case, it is (£108,000) plus £245,000, that is £137,000. This closing balance becomes the opening balance for the next month (February) and the process begins again.

	(All figures in £000s)			
	Jan	Feb	Mar	Apr
Net cash flow	(108)	165	(156)	57
Opening balance	245	137	302	146
Closing balance	137	302	146	203

FIGURE 7.12: Cumbers Trading – opening and closing balances.

ACTIVITY

Assume Cumbers Trading plans to take out a loan for £100,000 and the money is to be received by the business in May. It estimates that sales receipts will be £525,000 in both May and June. VAT recoveries in May are estimated at £50,000. The cash outflows in May and June are assumed to be identical to those in February and March respectively.

Draw up a cash flow forecast for Cumbers Trading for the months of May and June – following on from the one in *Fig. 7.12*.

THE TIMING OF RECEIPTS AND PAYMENTS

By now, you should be aware that the timing and receipts of payments are very important to a business. If you look at *Fig. 7.10*, which shows the four-month cash flow forecast

for Cumbers Trading Limited, you will see that, in addition to receipts from sales of £356,000, the business received £200,000 in January. This figure is made up of £150,000 capital introduced and £50,000 from an arranged loan. What would have happened had this money not been received until March? In particular, what would have been the closing balance for Cumbers Trading Limited at the end of January?

It is part of the task of management to manage the inflows and outflows of cash so that the business is not short of cash and, perhaps, unable to pay its creditors. Nor is a large surplus of cash desirable; this means the business has assets tied up in a form which is not earning any money. Management attempts to have sufficient, but not too much, cash available.

By negotiating purchases of items such as raw materials on credit terms, the business can improve its cash flow position. Credit terms often give between one and three months grace before payment is required. However, this benefit may be counter-balanced because many businesses have to offer similar credit terms to their customers. If they fail to do so, customers might take their business elsewhere.

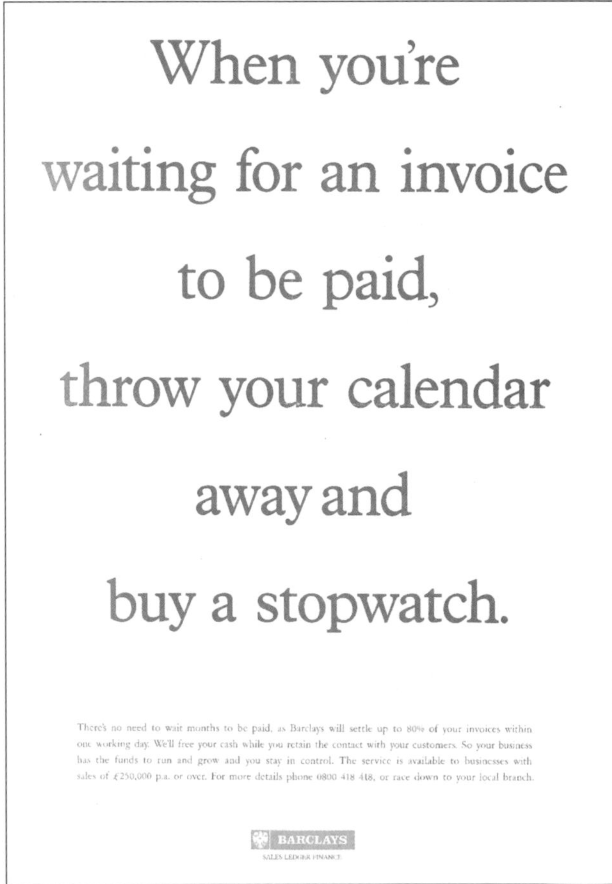

FIGURE 7.13: Banks can help businesses improve their cash flow. Source: Barclays Bank advert, *Independent*, 28 October 1995.

The fact that VAT is payable on a quarterly basis can help the cash position of a business. As we discussed earlier, a business will normally make a net payment to the Customs and Excise at the end of each quarter. This does, however, mean that the funds may be available to a company for a period of up to three months. Increasingly, financial institutions are offering services to help businesses improve their cash flows (see *Fig. 7.13*).

Remember, it is the timing of cash flows into and out of businesses which are critical, not the total amount of cash generated. Many experienced managers hold the view that companies do not go bust because they lose money, rather they fail because they run out of cash. Having sufficient cash is essential for commercial success.

THE CONSEQUENCES OF INCORRECT CASH FLOW FORECASTING

Incorrect cash flow forecasting can lead to a number of difficulties. The managers of a firm may receive a misleading impression that a business has more (or less) cash available than is actually the case. As a consequence, a business may arrange short-term loans or decide to invest in assets at times when these actions are not appropriate. Good decision-making by managers depends upon having good quality information on which to base decisions. Incorrect cash flow forecasting will not provide good quality information.

A potentially dangerous implication of incorrect cash flow forecasting is that a firm may have insufficient liquid assets for the day-to-day operation of the business. If this is the case, the business may not be able to pay its suppliers as their invoices arrive. This may result in suppliers being unwilling to continue to supply the business and they may take legal action to recover their debts. This lack of liquidity could lead to the business becoming insolvent and ceasing trading. A business is insolvent when it does not have sufficient liquid assets to meet its short-term liabilities; it is illegal to continue trading in these circumstances.

Managers can take a number of actions if they need to improve the cash flow of their business.

- ☻ **They can reduce the cash operating cycle by shortening the time between the purchase of raw materials and the sale of finished goods. This will mean that cash is not tied up for a long time in stocks and work-in-progress.**

- ☻ **They can delay payment to suppliers by retaining the cash within the company for longer.**

- ☻ **They can raise extra cash by arranging loans or selling fixed assets that are surplus to requirements.**

- ☻ **They can strictly control stocks, so avoiding tying up too much cash in the form of stock.**

- ☻ **By factoring their debts – that is, selling their debts to a factoring company for a high proportion of their total value – they can raise cash immediately.**

However, these actions can be avoided by the effective and efficient management of cash by the managers of a business.

PORTFOLIO ASSIGNMENT

THE BATH JEWELLERY

Gill Nolan and Peter Marsh are partners in a thriving jewellery business in Bath. Three years ago, the partners made the jewellery at home and sold it from a market stall. Since then, the partners have expanded their business. They now have a small shop in the centre of Bath, supplied from their workshop situated in a local small business centre.

As their business has grown the partners have had to adopt more sophisticated management techniques. Gill recently saw that a shop is for sale in nearby Bristol and has persuaded Peter that they should buy it to continue the expansion of the business. This expansion means that the partners need to arrange a sizeable loan with their local bank. The manager of the bank has no doubts about the viability of the existing parts of Gill and Peter's business. However, she wants to assess the likely financial future of the new venture in Bristol. She has asked for the following forecasts for the next trading year, before she will approve the loan for the Bath Jewellery:

⊗ a capital budget for the business focusing on the expansion in Bristol;

⊗ a trading forecast for the Bristol shop;

⊗ a cash flow forecast for the coming year for the Bristol shop.

Gill and Peter have turned to you for advice.

TASK 1

Using the information provided opposite, draw up the budget and forecasts for the coming year, starting in January. Use a spreadsheet package, so that Gill and Peter can add in the actual figures as the year progresses to effect a comparison.

TASK 2

Write an explanation of the figures and, in particular, highlight:

(a) any times at which the business might experience cash flow problems;

(b) additional finance that might be required to overcome these problems;

(c) how they might alter the timing of the income and expenditure to improve the financial position of the Bristol shop;

(d) other ways in which the business might overcome periods of financial difficulty;

(e) the consequences if these forecasts are incorrect.

Bath Jewellery

Financial forecasts
(January to December 1997)
The year will end on 31 December 1997.

Capital, trading and cash flow details

Sales amounting to £1,000 are expected for the first month rising to £1,600 per month for the next two months. The next four months will see a figure which is 25 per cent higher than in the second and third months. The period August to November sees sales running at a steady £2,500 per month and sales rise by 20 per cent from this figure for December. Gill and Peter expect to be paid in the month of supply for all their sales.

Purchases of raw materials are expected to be 40 per cent of sales throughout the year.

Expenditure on assets (in the form of start-up capital) will be £7,500 in January to fit out the new shop and (hopefully!) a loan amounting to £14,000 will be introduced in two stages, £7,000 in January and a further £7,000 in March.

A £3,000 lease on the property in Bristol will be payable in January. Solicitors' fees will amount to £400 for negotiating this lease.

Fuel costs are due to be paid quarterly starting with a payment in March. They are expected to be £300 each quarter. Gill and Peter believe they will have to spend £150 on advertising each quarter (from January) to start the business in Bristol. Wages and salaries are expected to be £500 each month – this will include employer's national insurance contributions.

Gill and Peter have set a budget of £75 per month to cover building repairs and maintenance. They plan to purchase a van in February at an anticipated cost of £4,000. Their loan payments will be £100 a month for January and February and £200 each month from then onwards.

The business will, of course, be liable to VAT. Gill and Peter's accountants have said that they should calculate a net figure by taking 17.5 per cent of sales value as their payment to the Customs and Excise, but assuming that they can claim 50 per cent of this figure back in the form of VAT that they have paid to suppliers. VAT will be payable quarterly, in arrears.

Stationery and administrative expenses are estimated at £50 per month. Business and water rates have been budgeted at £250 each quarter, with the first payment becoming due in February. Telephone charges are anticipated at £75 per quarter, with the first invoice due to arrive in March.

Finally, the anticipated motor expenses are expected to be £550 for tax and insurance when the van is purchased and £100 per month for running costs.

Produce and explain profit and loss statements and balance sheets

THE ACCOUNTING SYSTEM

In unit 6, we looked at the documents used in financial transactions and explained how and why they are used. In this element, we begin by examining the accounting system used to record financial information and to produce the **final accounts**, which summarise the financial affairs of the business. Then we shall examine the final accounts in more detail and discuss their importance.

The accounting system consists of a series of steps. These are illustrated in *Fig. 7.14*.

ORIGINAL DOCUMENTS

Also known as **prime documents**, original documents and their use are discussed in detail in unit 6. They are the documents used by firms to record and exchange financial information. The main original documents used in the accounting system are:

- ⊗ **sales invoice – for goods sold on credit;**

- ⊗ **sales credit note – for goods returned by customers;**

- ⊗ **purchases invoice – for goods bought on credit;**

- ⊗ **purchases credit note – for goods returned to suppliers;**

- ⊗ **cheques – sent to suppliers or received from customers;**

- ⊗ **other invoices – for fixed assets (such as machinery) or expense items (such as stationery) bought on credit;**

- ⊗ **receipts – for any items bought or sold on a cash basis.**

A word about cash and credit transactions

Sales (and purchases) can be made on either a cash or credit basis. The difference is not (as you might think) the method of payment, but the time at which the payment is made.

Cash transactions involve immediate payment; goods and/or services are supplied and paid for at the same time. Generally, a **receipt** is given to the customer to confirm that payment has been received. **Credit transactions** involve payment at a later date. The supplier sends the customer an **invoice**, which gives details of the items supplied and the amount owing. The time between the supply of the goods and/or services and the due date for payment is known as the credit period (usually 30 days). The **credit period** is part of the credit terms agreed between the customer and the supplier, which set out the basis on which they will trade.

Accountants have special terms for those involved in credit transactions. **Debtors** are those people (or companies) who owe money to a business for credit sales. **Creditors** are those people (or companies) to whom a business owes money for credit purchases.

If all transactions were made on a cash basis, the accounting system required to record the transactions could be very simple. No record would need to be kept of what is owed to whom and by whom. However, because credit transactions (mainly purchases and sales) make up the majority of transactions in modern businesses, a more complex system of accounting is required, in order to keep track of how much businesses owe their creditors and how much they are owed by their debtors.

Original Documents

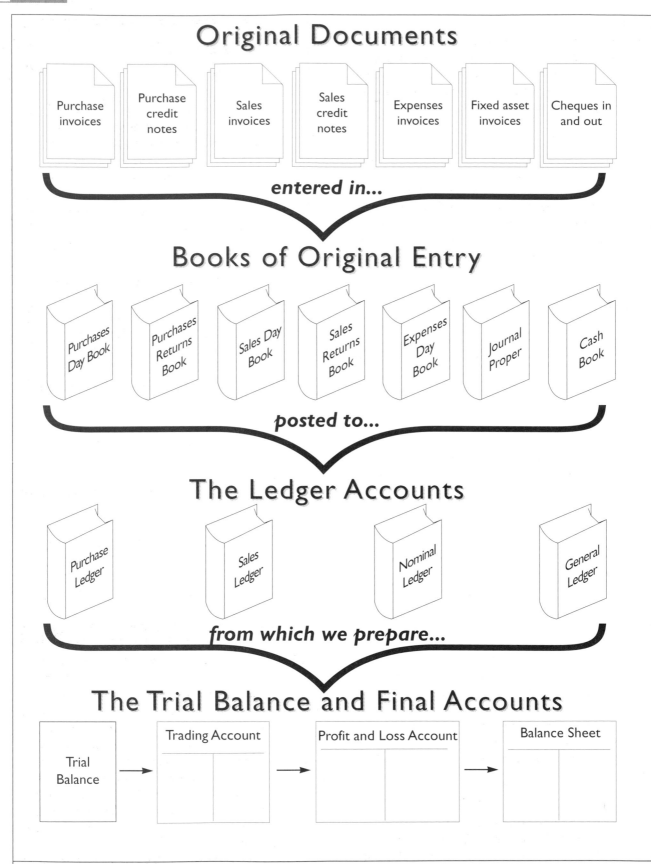

Purchase invoices

Purchase credit notes

Sales invoices

Sales credit notes

Expenses invoices

Fixed asset invoices

Cheques in and out

entered in...

Books of Original Entry

Purchases Day Book

Purchases Returns Book

Sales Day Book

Sales Returns Book

Expenses Day Book

Journal Proper

Cash Book

posted to...

The Ledger Accounts

Purchase Ledger

Sales Ledger

Nominal Ledger

General Ledger

from which we prepare...

The Trial Balance and Final Accounts

Trial Balance → Trading Account → Profit and Loss Account → Balance Sheet

FIGURE 7.14: The double-entry accounting system.

SALES INVOICE

Sales invoices are outgoing documents, sent to customers (a business's **debtors**) when sales have been made on credit. They detail what the customer owes for the goods or services supplied. Details of all sales invoices are recorded in a firm's **sales day book**.

SALES CREDIT NOTE

Sales credit notes are outgoing documents, also sent to customers. Credit notes are usually used for goods returned by the customer (because they are faulty, damaged or the wrong specification). In effect, credit notes are the opposite of invoices, in that they reduce the amount that the customer owes the business providing the goods or services. Sales credit notes are recorded in a firm's **sales returns book**.

PURCHASE INVOICE

Purchase invoices are incoming documents, received from suppliers (a business's **creditors**) for purchases that have been made on credit. They inform a firm about how much it owes its suppliers for goods or services it has received. Purchase invoices are recorded in a firm's **purchases day book**.

PURCHASE CREDIT NOTE

Purchase credit notes are also incoming documents. They are received from suppliers when a firm returns goods to them for some reason (because, for example, they are faulty or damaged). Purchase credit notes reduce the amount a firm owes to its suppliers. They are recorded in a firm's **purchases returns day book**.

Remember, the outgoing sales documents of one firm will be the incoming purchase documents of their customers.

CHEQUES

Firms need to record two types of cheques in their accounting systems – incoming and outgoing. Incoming cheques are received from a business's debtors when they pay for the goods or services that have been supplied to them (payment for sales). Outgoing cheques are sent to a business's creditors for the goods or services it has received (payment for purchases). Both incoming and outgoing cheques are recorded in the **cash book** (but on different sides!).

OTHER INVOICES

A business may receive other invoices apart from those for goods for resale. These may be for expense items or fixed assets bought on credit. They are handled differently in the accounting system from invoices for purchases. Expense items bought on credit are normally recorded

---

A word about sales and purchases

In accounting terminology, the words **sales** and **purchases** are reserved for **goods for resale** (that is, items of the stock for trade). Therefore, if a company's business is selling typewriters, sales of typewriters and purchases for resale would be considered **sales** and **purchases**. However, if a company selling table lamps bought typewriters for its office, these would not be considered part of its purchases but would be treated as **fixed assets**. Similarly, any items that are bought for use in the day-to-day running of a business (such as stationery) are also not included as purchases because they are not for resale. These items are treated as **expenses**. We discuss fixed assets and expenses in more detail later in the unit.

---

in an **expenses day book**, while credit purchases of fixed assets are recorded in the **journal proper**.

RECEIPTS

Receipts are used for cash transactions and are recorded in the **cash book**. They can be sales receipts (for things a business has sold on a cash basis) or purchases receipts (for things it has bought on a cash basis). Receipts may be for any type of expenditure (goods for resale, fixed assets or expense items) and will be accounted for accordingly in the main **books of account** (the ledgers).

THE BOOKS OF ORIGINAL ENTRY

Also known as the **books of prime entry**, the books of original entry are used to record all the details of original documents, including invoice or credit note numbers, cheque or receipt numbers, etc. This is important because in the main **books of account** (the ledgers) only the financial information is recorded. Therefore, the books of original entry form the link between the financial information in the ledgers and the original documents which supplied that information. Linking information is vital so that transactions can be traced through the accounts, to locate errors or to check for accuracy and authenticity (**auditing**).

All the information entered into the accounting system is linked via folio numbers. The folio number acts as a reference to where an entry came from or it went to.

For example, when an entry is made in the sales account, the folio reference quoted for that entry will be the sales day book page where the original entry was made. In the sales day book, the folio reference quoted will be the number allocated to the sales account.

This referencing system is vitally important when errors need to be traced and when the accounts are audited. Auditing is a process whereby the whole accounting system of a business is checked for accuracy and authenticity. The law requires that limited companies must produce audited accounts, but it is good practice for all businesses to audit their accounts. By using the folio numbers, it is possible to track each transaction through the system, from the original document to the entries in the ledger.

The main books of original entry are:

- **sales day book –** records the invoices a business sends to its customers for sales;

- **sales returns book –** records the credit notes a business sends to its customers for goods that have been returned;

- **purchases day book –** records the invoices a business receives from its suppliers for its purchases;

- **purchases returns book –** records the credit notes a business receives from its suppliers for goods returned to the suppliers;

- **expenses day book –** records the invoices a business receives from its suppliers for expense items bought on credit;

- **cash book –** records all incoming and outgoing payments (cheques), expense items bought on a cash (not credit) basis, cash sales and purchases and all bank transactions;

- **journal proper –** records purchases (and disposals) of all fixed assets (whether bought on a cash or credit basis); also used for other 'unusual' items, such as correction of errors, writing off bad debts, etc.

Once the details from the original documents have been recorded in the books of original entry, the next step is to transfer the financial information from the books of original entry to the ledger accounts. This is known as **posting** to the ledger. All postings to the ledger consist of 'balancing' entries, on either side of the ledger (but in different accounts). This is the fundamental principle of double-entry accounting. In this way, provided all the postings are completed correctly, the two sides of the ledger will balance. We shall examine these ideas of 'double-entry' and 'balancing' a little later in the unit.

THE LEDGER – THE MAIN BOOK OF ACCOUNT

Originally, the ledger was a single book containing all the accounts used by a business. However, as businesses have become larger and more complex, the ledger has been broken down into several separate books:

- **the sales ledger –** containing a separate account for each debtor (sometimes known as the debtors ledger);

- **purchases ledger –** containing a separate account for each creditor (sometimes known as the creditors ledger);

- **the nominal ledger –** containing a separate account for each expense of the business (for example, stationery account, telephone account, etc.);

- **the general ledger –** containing the remaining accounts of the business, such as fixed asset accounts (which may be divided into machinery account, vehicle account, etc.), and capital account;

- **the cash book –** although the cash book is a book of original entry, it is also part of the ledger because it contains the cash account and the bank account.

Note, in some businesses the subdivision between the nominal and general ledgers is not made, in which case the accounts described for each are combined in one ledger.

A word about the cash book

The cash and bank accounts are put into a bound book of their own for several reasons. First, they are very busy accounts, recording numerous transactions, so having them in a separate book allows one person to administer them. Second, they are vulnerable accounts, in that they are the most susceptible to fraud. Placing them in a bound book makes it difficult for pages to be removed and rewritten without detection. The cash book is usually administered by a senior bookkeeper or cashier, who is responsible for the cash and cheques passing through the business.

It is important to note that when accountants talk about 'the ledger' they are generally referring to all the ledger accounts, in total, regardless of the subdivisions we have just described.

THE LEDGER ACCOUNTS

There are three types of accounts in the ledger:

⊗ **personal accounts;**

⊗ **real accounts;**

⊗ **nominal accounts.**

Personal accounts are accounts for a business' debtors and creditors, the third parties with which it does business. They are located in the sales and purchases ledgers. Each account carries the name of the individual or organisation it concerns. For example, if a firm buys goods from Scotwells Ltd, there will be a page in its purchases ledger headed Scotwells Ltd. Similarly, if it sells goods to Peters & Sons, there will be an account in its sales ledger called Peters & Sons. Usually, accounts in the ledgers are arranged alphabetically to make them easy to use.

Real accounts are accounts for 'real things'; they include accounts for fixed assets (such as a machinery account) and current assets (for example, the cash account). They are located in the general ledger, with the exception of the cash account and the bank account, which are in the cash book.

Account Name							folio no.
Dr.							**Cr.**
Date	Details	F	Amount	Date	Details	F	Amount

FIGURE 7.15: Typical ledger account page.

Nominal accounts, found in the nominal ledger, record items 'in name only' and include all the expense accounts (such as the stationery account) and gain accounts (for example, the interest received account) of the business. They simply record why money was spent or received. For example, if a firm spends money on stationery, the real money is shown going out of the cash or bank account in the cash book, but the other half of the entry will be in the stationery account, recording where the money went.

At the end of the year, the stationery account will show how much the firm spent on stationery in the year.

THE DOUBLE-ENTRY SYSTEM

Having looked at the subdivisions of the ledger, and what types of accounts it contains, we now look at the double-entry system of accounting. The double-entry system has been in use for centuries and nobody has yet found a better way of recording financial information. There are many books dealing specifically with double-entry bookkeeping and you may be interested to examine the process in greater detail. However, we shall only discuss the basic principles here.

The fundamental principle of double-entry bookkeeping is that all postings to the ledger should consist of 'balancing' components. The ledger accounts are split into two 'sides' – the debit side (traditionally the left-hand side of the page) and the credit side (traditionally the right-hand side of the page). The debit side is usually abbreviated to Dr. and the credit side to Cr. *Fig. 7.15* shows the layout of a typical ledger account page.

We can think of the ledger as a set of scales. When we post to the ledger, each entry in a ledger account is like a 'weight' placed on one side of the scales.

FIGURE 7.16: 'Think of the ledger as a set of scales.'

Only if the total 'weight' of what is posted is equal on both sides will the scales be in balance. For example, if a firm sells goods worth £150 on credit to Johnson Ltd, the posting to the ledger would be:

⊗ **debit (on the left-hand side of the page) Johnson Ltd's account in the sales ledger by £150;**

⊗ **credit (on the right-hand side of the page) the sales account in the nominal ledger by £150.**

We can illustrate this posting in two ways. *Fig. 7.17* shows how our set of scales would look; *Fig. 7.18* shows the actual entries in the two accounts.

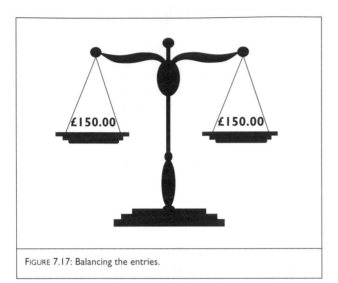

£150.00   £150.00

FIGURE 7.17: Balancing the entries.

Johnson Ltd   SL18

Dr.							Cr.
Date	Details	F	Amount	Date	Details	F	Amount
30/10	Sales	SD30	150.00				

Sales   GL44

Dr.							Cr.
Date	Details	F	Amount	Date	Details	F	Amount
				30/10	Johnson Ltd.	SD30	150.00

FIGURE 7.18: The two ledger accounts; Johnson Ltd and the sales account.

The same rule applies to every posting to the ledger. Regardless of how many entries are made or which accounts are involved, the two sides must always balance. Now consider a slightly more complicated example. Assume that VAT is charged on the goods sold to Johnson Ltd. *Fig. 7.19* shows how the entries in the accounts should be made.

Johnson Ltd   SL18

Dr.							Cr.
Date	Details	F	Amount	Date	Details	F	Amount
30/10	Sales	SD30	176.25				

Sales   GL44

Dr.							Cr.
Date	Details	F	Amount	Date	Details	F	Amount
				30/10	Johnson Ltd.	SD30	150.00

VAT   GL99

Dr.							Cr.
Date	Details	F	Amount	Date	Details	F	Amount
				30/10	Johnson Ltd.	SD30	26.25

FIGURE 7.19: The three ledger accounts; Johnson Ltd, sales account and VAT account.

In this case, one entry on one side of the ledger is balanced by two entries on the other side. If we forget to post the VAT amount, our set of scales would look like *Fig. 7.20* and the two sides of the ledger would not balance.

£150.00   £176.25

FIGURE 7.20: Unbalanced entries.

The basic principle of the double-entry system is that the two sides of the 'whole' ledger must always be equal. The main challenge of bookkeeping is learning which things go on which side!

ACTIVITY

Photocopy the blank ledger accounts on pages 487–8. Use these to post the following transactions:

(a) sales to Peter Bell of £673.20 (no VAT was chargeable);

(b) sales to Protac Ltd of £1,154.61, of which £171.11 was VAT;

(c) purchases from Lodenhall of £1,645.00, of which £245.00 was VAT.

Don't worry about folio numbers for your entries. Remember that both sides of the ledger must balance when all the entries have been made.

THE TRIAL BALANCE

On a regular basis (usually at least monthly), the accountant draws up what is known as the **trial balance**. This is a summary list detailing all the accounts in the ledger that have an account balance (accounts with a zero balance are ignored). If all postings to the accounts have been completed correctly, the total of the debit balances will equal the total of the credit balances.

THE ACCOUNT BALANCE

Each ledger account will, at any given time, have an account balance: either a debit balance, a credit balance or a zero balance. In the example shown in *Fig. 7.19* (assuming there are no other entries on these accounts), the accounts involved would have the following account balances at this point in time:

⊗ **Johnson Ltd – a debit balance of £176.25;**

⊗ **Sales – a credit balance of £150.00;**

⊗ **VAT – a credit balance of £26.75.**

Taking the three account balances above (and ignoring the fact that there would undoubtedly be other accounts in our ledgers), we could draw up a mini trial balance. This is illustrated in *Fig. 7.21*.

Company ABC Trial Balance as at 31 October 1995	Dr	Cr
Johnson Ltd	176.25	
Sales		150.00
VAT		26.25
	176.25	176.25

FIGURE 7.21: Trial balance (two-column format).

Note that we do not usually list every debtor and creditor individually. Instead, we bring a total balance for all debtors and a total balance for all creditors into the trial balance (otherwise the trial balance would be many pages long).

Fig. 7.21 shows a trial balance in the traditional format. An alternative style is to list all the accounts in a single column. In this format, debits and credits are distinguished in some way (sometimes by using + and − signs, sometimes by showing the credit balances in brackets). When this format is used, the total of the single column should equal zero, as shown in *Fig. 7.22*.

Company ABC Trial Balance as at 31 October 1995	
Johnson Ltd	176.25
Sales	(150.00)
VAT	(26.25)
	0

FIGURE 7.22: Trial balance (single-column format).

The main purpose of the trial balance is to carry out an arithmetic check of a firm's bookkeeping. However, it is important to note that some bookkeeping errors do not show up at the trial balance stage, because they do not result in the two sides of the ledger being unequal.

Additionally, the trial balance gives us a list of all the account balances from our ledger, in a useful format for preparing the final accounts.

ACTIVITY

Fig. 7.23 shows accounts for Elisabeth Ann's, a small business. Use these to draw up a trial balance as at 30 October 1995. Be sure to use the correct heading for your trial balance (as shown in earlier examples).

Account	Balance	Dr/Cr
Cash	343.58	Dr
Bank	4,784.17	Dr
Capital	9,600.23	Cr
Office equipment	3,250.00	Dr
Fixtures and fittings	2,100.00	Dr
Debtors	4,281.72	Dr
Creditors	2,294.81	Cr
Stock	6,341.50	Dr
Sales	28,692.80	Cr
Purchases	13,047.30	Dr
VAT	273.53	Cr
Stationery	412.67	Dr
Telephone	608.23	Dr
Light and heat	1,119.49	Dr
Office expenses	124.16	Dr
Rent	3,600.00	Dr
Rates	480.80	Dr
Postage	367.75	Dr

FIGURE 7.23: Account balances for Elisabeth Ann's as at 30 October 1995.

In order to see how figures are used in business, we will follow the financial information of a small business, Naomi's Novelties, as it evolves from trial balance to final accounts. Naomi Alexander is a sole trader and she started Naomi's Novelties three years ago. She has a small shop and the business buys and sells novelty and party items, gifts and cards. Most of her sales are cash, but she does have a few credit customers. Fig. 7.24 shows her trial balance for the financial year ended 31 December 1994. We will look again at Naomi's Novelties when we consider final accounts.

Naomi's Novelties
Trial Balance
as at 31 December 1994

	Dr	Cr
Cash	322.78	
Bank	8,869.91	
Shop fixtures	7,900.00	
Motor vehicles	6,600.00	
Office equipment	975.18	
Bank loan		5,000.00
Capital		24,748.73
Debtors	5,385.08	
Creditors		1,329.63
Drawings	8,750.00	
VAT		3,820.77
Stock	5,248.60	
Sales		64,513.46
Purchases	43,680.92	
Travel expenses	512.57	
Electricity	747.39	
Stationery	459.11	
Telephone	682.81	
Advertising	3,278.24	
Rent	6,000.00	
	99,412.59	99,412.59

FIGURE 7.24: Naomi's Novelties trial balance as at 31 December 1994.

WHY DOUBLE-ENTRY?

The elegance of the double-entry system lies in the way it records financial information in a format which allows us to see exactly what is going on in a business. It does this by recording the information in separate accounts, which can then be referred to individually or in combination (to produce the final accounts, which we will discuss later).

For example, the account balances shown in the trial balance in Fig. 7.22 tell us that:

☺ **Johnson Ltd owes £176.25;**

☺ **the business has made sales worth £150.00;**

☺ **it has collected £26.75 VAT on behalf of the Customs and Excise.**

Throughout the year, the accounts are constantly being updated by new postings. Some postings increase sales or purchases totals, some record debtors paying their accounts, some record expenses incurred by the business. At the end of the accounting period, the ledger accounts will contain information about every transaction that has taken place in the business, in a format which is easy to use in preparing the final accounts.

FINAL ACCOUNTS

Final accounts are prepared at the end of **accounting periods.** These might be quarterly (after every three months), half-yearly (after every six months) or annually (at the end of each year). Quarterly and/or half-yearly final accounts are drawn up by some businesses; annual accounts are prepared by all businesses. The **final accounts** summarise all the transactions that have taken place in the accounting period, and a **balance sheet** is drawn up which details the assets and liabilities of the business as at the date it is prepared.

One of the principles of accounting is that all income and expenditure of the business for a particular accounting period should be matched to the period under review. Sometimes this means that adjustments must be made to ensure that the correct amount is included in the appropriate accounting period. For example, if insurance cover for twelve months is taken out halfway through the current accounting year, only half the insurance premium (six months' worth) would belong in the current year's final accounts. The remaining six months' worth would need to be included in next year's final accounts (even though the money is actually paid in the current year). This is because half of the benefit from the expense (the insurance cover) would be received in the current accounting period, and half in the next.

These adjustments are important if the final accounts are to serve their purpose of presenting a 'perfectly accurate set of final accounts for the period under review, and a perfectly honest balance sheet as at the date it is prepared', which is one of the fundamental principles of accounting.

The term 'final accounts' is generally taken to include the **revenue accounts** (manufacturing account, trading account, profit and loss account and appropriation account) and the **balance sheet**. Strictly speaking, the final accounts of the business are the revenue accounts, which summarise the transactions which have taken place in the business during the accounting period and ultimately show the profit (or loss) made by the business. After these have been prepared, the remaining balances on the accounts will be displayed in the balance sheet, which details the assets and liabilities of the business as at a particular date.

We can think of the revenue accounts as being like a video, in that they show what has been happening throughout the accounting period. In contrast, the balance sheet is more like a photo – a snapshot of the state of the business on the date at which it is prepared.

Some businesses prepare manufacturing and/or trading accounts, depending on the type of business they are engaged in. In this unit, we shall only examine the **profit and loss account** and the **appropriation account**. The manufacturing and/or trading accounts reveal the **gross profit (or loss)** made by the business. The profit and loss account reveals the **net profit (or loss)** made and the appropriation account details how this net profit is distributed.

A word about gains and expenses

It is clearly important to distinguish between **business expenses** and **financial gains** to the business. An item like 'bank interest' could be a gain or an expense; it could be the interest a business **receives** on its cash deposits or it could be the interest a business **pays** on its loans and overdrafts.

Accountants use a convention to distinguish between gains and expenses. If an item could be read as either an expense or a gain, they use the term **'received'** to indicate that the item is a gain to the business. So, bank interest received is a financial gain but an accountant would assume that an item labelled simply 'bank interest' is an expense item.

A typical profit and loss account, in the traditional (horizontal) format is shown in *Fig. 7.25*. In recent times, the vertical format for presenting financial information has been more commonly adopted, as shown in *Fig. 7.26*. As you can see, the information is exactly the same, regardless of which format is used. Note that the profit and loss account is sometimes referred to as a profit and loss statement.

The **Companies Act 1985** specifies in great detail how companies must construct their published profit and loss accounts and balance sheets. Of course, if the accounts are drawn up for internal purposes only, they may be constructed in any way the company deems appropriate. The Act allows either horizontal or vertical formats to be used, although most companies use the vertical format – partly because it is easier to incorporate into the pages of a company's annual report! We deal specifically with company final accounts later in this element.

Company ABC
Profit and Loss Account
for the year ended 31 October 1995

			Gross profit			89,119.01
Electricity		896.25				
Stationery		765.32				
Insurance		1,374.73				
Salaries		27,372.50				
Rates		1,320.58				
Telephone		594.11				
Advertising		1,637.09				
Rent		26,987.00				
			60,947.58			
Net profit			28,171.43			
			89,119.01			89,119.01

FIGURE 7.25: Profit and loss account (horizontal format).

Company ABC
Profit and Loss Account
for the year ended 31 October 1995

Gross profit		89,119.01
Electricity	896.25	
Stationery	765.32	
Insurance	1,374.73	
Salaries	27,372.50	
Rates	1,320.58	
Telephone	594.11	
Advertising	1,637.09	
Rent	26,987.00	
Less expenses		60,947.58
Net profit		28,171.43

FIGURE 7.26: Profit and loss account (vertical format).

Now we return to Naomi's Novelties to see how final accounts look in practice. First, although we have not actually discussed them in any detail, we show a trading account to illustrate where the relevant items from the trial balance (see *Fig. 7.24*) would appear.

You can see that the figures for sales, purchases and stock have been taken from the trial balance (*Fig. 7.24*) and used in the trading account (*Fig. 7.27*). The figure for closing stock does not come from the trial balance; it is found by carrying out a physical stock take at the end of the accounting period. The trading account shows that Naomi's Novelties made a gross profit of £21,756.14 during the year.

Fig. 7.28 shows the balances that remain on the books after preparing the trading account. Some of these balances (the assets and liabilities) will appear on the balance sheet, which we look at later. But having determined the gross profit, the next step is to determine net profit. This is done by using some of the remaining balances to prepare the profit and loss account.

The profit and loss account (*Fig. 7.29*, see p.42) shows that in the accounting period 1 January to 31 December 1994 Naomi's Novelties made a net profit of £10,076.46. The remaining balances, which will appear on the balance sheet, are shown in *Fig. 7.30*.

Naomi's Novelties
Trading Account
for the year ended 31 December 1994

				Sales			64,513.46
Opening stock	5,248.60						
Add purchases	43,680.92						
Stock available		48,929.52					
Less closing stock		6,172.20					
Cost of sales			42,757.32				
Gross profit			21,756.14				
			64,513.46				64,513.46

FIGURE 7.27: Naomi's Novelties trading account.

Naomi's Novelties
Account balances remaining after the preparation of the Trading Account

	Dr	Cr
Cash	322.78	
Bank	8,869.91	
Shop fixtures	7,900.00	
Motor vehicles	6,600.00	
Office equipment	975.18	
Bank loan		5,000.00
Capital		24,748.73
Debtors	5,385.08	
Creditors		1,329.63
Drawings	8,750.00	
VAT		3,820.77
Travel expenses	512.57	
Electricity	747.39	
Stationery	459.11	
Telephone	682.81	
Advertising	3,278.24	
Rent	6,000.00	

FIGURE 7.28: Account balances remaining after preparing Naomi's Novelties trading account.

Naomi's Novelties
Account balances remaining after the preparation of the Trading and Profit and Loss Accounts

	Dr	Cr
Cash	322.78	
Bank	8,869.91	
Shop fixtures	7,900.00	
Motor vehicles	6,600.00	
Office equipment	975.18	
Bank loan		5,000.00
Capital		24,748.73
Debtors	5,385.08	
Creditors		1,329.63
Drawings	8,750.00	
VAT		3,820.77

FIGURE 7.30: Account balances remaining after preparing Naomi's Novelties profit and loss account.

Naomi's Novelties
Profit and Loss Account
for the year ended 31 December 1994

			Gross profit			21,756.14
Travel	512.57					
Electricity	747.39					
Stationery	459.11					
Telephone	682.81					
Advertising	3,278.24					
Rent	6,000.00					
		11,680.12				
Net profit		10,076.02				
		21,756.14				21,756.14

Figure 7.29: Naomi's Novelties profit and loss account.

A word about drawings and VAT

You should have noticed that neither drawings nor VAT appear in the revenue accounts. This is because neither of them are an expense of the business.

Drawings is the money that a sole trader or a partner in a partnership draws from the business for his or her personal use. As such, it can be viewed as a withdrawal of capital invested. This is how it is treated; it is shown as a deduction from capital on the balance sheet as we shall see later.

As we discussed in element 2, if a firm is registered for **VAT**, it must charge VAT on all sales invoices which involve VAT-chargeable goods. In doing so, the firm is collecting VAT on behalf of the Customs and Excise. At regular intervals, the firm makes a payment to Customs and Excise of the VAT it has collected after offsetting any VAT it has paid on its purchases. The important thing to remember is that VAT is not the firm's money and, therefore, it is not an expense of the business when it is paid. Usually, it is an amount owing to the VAT authorities at the end of an accounting period (a credit balance) and, therefore, a current liability on the balance sheet, which we shall discuss shortly.

Account	Balance	Dr/Cr
Cash	343.58	Dr
Bank	4,784.17	Dr
Capital	9,600.23	Cr
Office equipment	3,250.00	Dr
Fixtures and fittings	2,100.00	Dr
Debtors	4,281.72	Dr
Creditors	2,294.81	Cr
VAT	273.53	Cr
Stationery	412.67	Dr
Telephone	608.23	Dr
Light and heat	1,119.49	Dr
Office expenses	124.16	Dr
Rent	3,600.00	Dr
Rates	480.80	Dr
Postage	367.75	Dr
Gross profit (From Trading A/C)	10,359.20	Cr

FIGURE 7.31: Account balances for Elisabeth Ann's at 30 October 1995.

ACTIVITY

Look at the account balances in *Fig. 7.31*. You used these in an earlier activity to prepare a trial balance. Now select those that are relevant and prepare a profit and loss account for Elisabeth Ann's for the quarter ending 30 October 1995. Be sure to use the correct heading, as shown in earlier examples. (Note that this should be for the *quarter*, not the year.)

THE BALANCE SHEET

After the revenue accounts have been prepared, and the net profit figure has been determined, the remaining balances on the books need to be shown on the **balance sheet**. The balance sheet is an accounting statement of the firm's **assets** and **liabilities** on the last day of an accounting period. The balance sheet lists the assets which the firm owns and sets against these the balancing liabilities – the claims of those individuals or organisations who provided the funds to acquire the assets. Assets take the form of **fixed assets** and **current assets**; liabilities take the form of **capital**, **long-term liabilities** and **current liabilities**. The balance sheet can be seen as a snapshot of the firm's current state of affairs as at the date it is prepared.

FIXED ASSETS

Fixed assets are those assets, such as machinery, equipment and vehicles, that are bought for long-term use in the business rather than for resale. Long term is generally taken to be more than a year.

CURRENT ASSETS

Current assets (or circulating assets) are items such as stock, debtors, bank deposits and cash which are constantly undergoing short-term conversion within the current assets cycle (see *Fig. 7.32*).

CAPITAL

Capital is the funds invested in a business in order to acquire the assets the business needs to trade. It is also known as **owner's capital**, **equity capital** and **capital invested**. It is a liability because the business technically 'owes' it to the investors. In the case of a sole trader, the capital will have been invested by the sole owner of the business; in a partnership the partners normally each invest some capital, while the capital for a company is provided by the shareholders.

LONG-TERM LIABILITIES

Many businesses raise money by borrowing from external sources of medium and long-term finance, normally for a fixed period of time. These are long-term liabilities which have to be repaid over the 'long term' (a period longer than one year). Known also as loan capital, long-term liabilities include **mortgages, bank loans** and **debentures**.

CURRENT LIABILITIES

Current liabilities are debts of the business which have to be repaid in the short term (less than one year). The most common current liabilities are creditors and bank overdrafts.

So, the assets owned by a business are financed by its liabilities. If all the assets of the business are listed on one side of the balance sheet and all the liabilities of the business are listed on the other, the two totals should balance (we're back to the set of scales again). In a traditional balance sheet, this is exactly how the information is set out.

Fig. 7.33 shows two versions of a simple balance sheet for a sole trader. The first version shows a

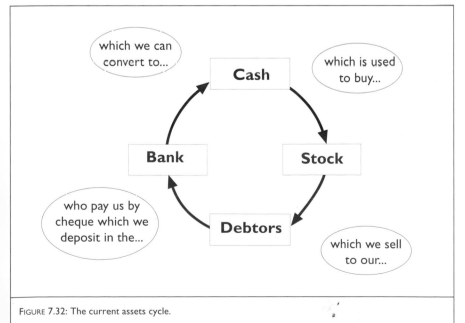

FIGURE 7.32: The current assets cycle.

which we can convert to...

which is used to buy...

Cash

Bank

Stock

who pay us by cheque which we deposit in the...

Debtors

which we sell to our...

R Fellows
Balance Sheet
as at 30 November 1995

Fixed assets				Capital (1.12.94)	23,500.00		
Machinery	9,500.00			Add net profit	9,565.50		
Computers	2,700.00					33,065.50	
Motor vehicles	6,900.00			Less drawings		7,300.00	
Current assets		19,100.00		Capital (30.11.95)			25,765.50
Stock	3,294.90						
Debtors	5,351.75			Long-term liabilities			
Bank	7,833.18			Bank loan			5,000.00
Cash	411.23			Current liabilities			
		16,891.06		Creditors		4,962.39	
				VAT		263.17	
							5,225.56
		35,991.06					35,991.06

R Fellows
Balance Sheet
as at 30 November 1995

Fixed assets				Capital (1.12.94)	23,500.00		
Machinery		9,500.00		Add net profit	9,565.50		
Computers		2,700.00				33,065.50	
Motor vehicles		6,900.00		Less drawings		7,300.00	
Current assets			19,100.00	Capital (30.11.95)			25,765.50
Stock	3,294.90						
Debtors	5,351.75			Long-term liabilities			
Bank	7,833.18			Bank loan			5,000.00
Cash	411.23						
		16,891.06					
Less current liabilities							
Creditors	4,962.39						
VAT	263.17						
		5,225.56					
Working capital			11,665.50				
			30,765.50				30,765.50

FIGURE 7.33: Balance sheets in traditional formats.

sole trader balance sheet in 'four-square', traditional format. The second version is a refinement of this layout, bringing the current liabilities across and deducting them from the current assets. Doing this allows the **working capital** figure to be displayed in the balance sheet. Working capital is the amount of money that is 'free' for use in the business and it has very important implications for cash flow. If, for example, too much money is tied up in stock or debtors are taking too long to pay, then the working capital would be reduced. This would result in a cash flow problem for the business, affecting its money cycle. (See unit 6 for a fuller discussion of the **money cycle**.)

Fig. 7.33 shows the balance sheet presented in the traditional, horizontal format. However, it is now common for firms, particularly companies, to use the vertical format shown in Fig. 7.34.

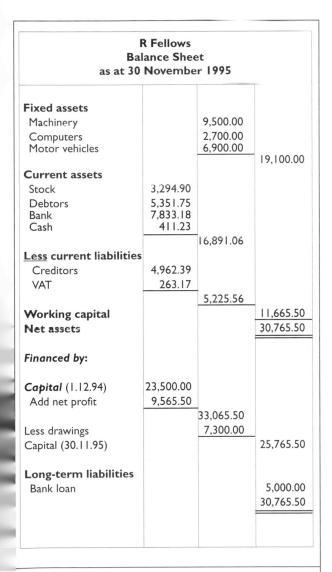

FIGURE 7.34: Sole trader balance sheet in vertical format.

ACTIVITY

Using the figures remaining after the profit and loss account has been prepared for Naomi's Novelties (see *Fig. 7.30*), draw up a balance sheet for the business, using the vertical format shown in *Fig. 7.34*.

FINAL ACCOUNTS OF COMPANIES

All the final accounts we have looked at so far have been those of sole traders. Company final accounts are set out slightly differently.

COMPANY PROFIT AND LOSS ACCOUNTS AND APPROPRIATION ACCOUNTS

Because all the net profit of a sole trader is added to the owner's capital, it is not necessary to include an appropriation account. However, other types of businesses have more than one owner. An **appropriation account** is used in partnership and company accounts to show how the net profit is to be distributed. It is prepared after the profit and loss account, and is sometimes included at the bottom of the profit and loss account. The appropriation account shows how much of the net profit has to be paid in **tax**, how much will be retained in the business in the form of **reserves**, and how much will be shared out as **dividends** to the **shareholders**.

SHAREHOLDERS

When a company is formed, capital can be raised by issuing shares in the company to investors. As we discussed in element 1, share capital is one source of long-term finance. In this way, a large group of people (the shareholders) each own a small part of the company. The capital of the company is referred to as the **shareholders' funds** (or **shareholders' equity**). In return for investing their money in the company, shareholders expect an annual return on their investment by receiving a share of the company's profits. These payments to shareholders are known as dividends.

AUTHORISED AND ISSUED SHARE CAPITAL

When a company is legally registered, it declares how many shares it intends to have (how many portions the company can be divided into) and what each share's face value is worth. This is known as the **authorised share capital**. However, most companies do not issue all their shares at once; instead, they issue shares in batches, only raising as much money as they need at any one time. The **issued shares capital**, therefore, represents the amount of money that has actually been invested in the company to date. The authorised share capital figure must, by law, appear on the balance sheet, but it is there for information purposes only.

RESERVES

Most companies retain some of the net profit within the business in the form of reserves. Some reserves are for specific items, such as the replacement of worn-out fixed assets, (held in specified holdings like the machinery reserve). The general reserve is unspecified and is often used to 'even out' dividends over the years, so that shareholders receive a consistent return on their investment, regardless of whether it has been a good or bad year for the company.

COMPANY BALANCE SHEETS

The layout of the balance sheet also changes for company accounts, to allow for a capital structure that involves shareholders' funds. Using another case study, Clark Ltd, we shall follow the preparation of a trading company's final accounts and its balance sheet, from the account balances remaining after completion of the trading account. Before we move on, we'll discuss some of the new terms that are used in this example.

DEBENTURES

Debentures are private, secured loans to the company (long-term liabilities), in return for which the lenders receive a specified rate of interest per annum. It is important to remember that debenture-holders are not shareholders and they do not receive a share of the company's profits in the form of dividends. They are merely paid their fixed rate of interest in the same way as the company would pay interest on money borrowed from the bank.

DEPRECIATION

Depreciation is the amount by which a fixed asset loses value over time. If you buy a new car, in two years' time it will not be worth what you paid for it. It will have lost value (depreciated). When companies buy fixed assets, they take into account what they paid for it, how long it is expected to be used in the business and estimate what it will be worth at the end of its useful life. From this, they calculate a 'depreciation per annum' figure, representing how much the asset devalues per year. There are many different methods of calculating depreciation, but the basic principle is the same.

Each year, the company will write off the annual depreciation amount as an expense (in the revenue accounts). The balance sheet shows the original value of the asset (**gross book value**, often abbreviated to **GBV**), the amount it has depreciated by so far (**accumulated depreciation**) and its 'true' current value (**net book value**, abbreviated to **NBV**). This information allows observers to see whether the asset is new, or worn out and in need of replacement soon.

A WORKED EXAMPLE

Now, we shall look at how company final accounts and balances sheets are prepared using Clark Ltd as an example. Clark Ltd is a trading company which buys and sells catering equipment. *Fig. 7.35* shows the account balances at the end of the financial year ending 31 January 1995, after calculating the cost of sales.

Clark Ltd
Account balances as at 31 January 1995

	Dr	Cr
Sales		626,000
Cost of sales	316,000	
295,000 £1 ordinary shares (issued)		295,000
General reserve		51,500
Profit and loss account balance 1.2.94		17,900
8% debentures		62,500
Bank	27,610	
Fixtures and fittings (at cost)	190,800	
Premises	285,000	
Stock	80,260	
Debtors	69,150	
Creditors		65,800
Salaries	52,000	
Commissions paid	5,000	
Administration expenses	50,834	
Selling expenses	72,846	
Depreciation of fixtures and fittings	30,800	

FIGURE 7.35: Account balances for Clark Ltd as at 31 January 1995.

To prepare the final accounts and balance sheet, we need some additional information. Clark Ltd has an authorised share capital of 400,000 £1 ordinary shares. The company policy is to depreciate fixtures and fittings by £20,000 each year. The directors of the company propose to pay an ordinary dividend of 9 per cent to the shareholders, to set aside a reserve for corporation tax of £11,150 and to add an additional £38,000 to the company's general reserve.

The first step is to prepare the profit and loss and appropriation accounts (see *Fig. 7.36*). You should notice that the year's depreciation on fixture and fittings has been charged as an expense in the profit and loss account.

Clark Ltd
Profit and Loss and Appropriation Account
for the year ended 31 January 1995

Turnover (net sales)	626,000	
Less cost of sales	316,000	
Gross profit		310,000
Expenses		
Salaries	52,000	
Commissions paid	5,000	
Administration expenses	50,834	
Selling expenses	72,846	
Depreciation of fixtures and fittings	20,000	
Total expenses		200,680
Net profit		109,320
Add profit and loss A/C balance 1.2.94		17,900
		127,220
Reserve for corporation tax	11,150	
General reserve	38,000	
Ordinary share dividend	26,550	
		75,700
Profit and loss A/C balance 31.1.95		51,520

FIGURE 7.36: Clark Ltd's profit and loss and appropriation account.

Having prepared the profit and loss account, the remaining balances (*Fig. 7.37*) appear on the balance sheet (*Fig. 7.38*). You should notice that the accumulated depreciation on fixtures and fittings that appears on the balance sheet is £50,800. This is the depreciation from previous years (amounting to £30,800) plus £20,000 for this year's depreciation. The proposed dividend of £26,550 (9 per cent of the £295,000 issued share capital) has not yet been paid out to shareholders and so it appears on the balance sheet as a current liability.

Clark Ltd
Account balances as remaining after the preparation of Revenue Accounts

	Dr	Cr
Profit and loss account balance		51,520
295,000 £1 ordinary shares (issued)		295,000
General reserve		51,500
8% debentures		62,500
Bank	27,610	
Fixtures and fittings (at cost)	190,800	
Premises	285,000	
Stock	80,260	
Debtors	69,150	
Creditors		65,800
Depreciation of fixtures and fittings	30,800	

FIGURE 7.37: Account balances remaining after preparing Clark Ltd's profit and loss and appropriation account.

Clark Ltd
Balance Sheet
as at 31 January 1995

	GBV	Acc. Dep	NBV
Fixed assets			
Premises	285,000	–	285,000
Fixtures and fittings	190,800	50,800	140,000
	475,800	50,800	425,000
Current assets			
Stock	80,260		
Debtors	69,150		
Bank	27,610		
		177,020	
Less current liabilities			
Creditors	65,800		
Proposed dividends	26,550		
		92,350	
Working capital			84,670
Net assets			**509,670**
Financed by:			
Capital and reserves	Authorised	Issued	
Share capital	400,000	295,000	
General reserve		89,500	
Profit and loss A/C bal.		51,520	
Shareholders' funds			436,020
Long-term liabilities			
6% debentures			62,500
Reserve for corp. tax			11,150
			509,670

FIGURE 7.38: Clark Ltd's balance sheet.

You will probably have noticed while working through the accounts of Clark Ltd that not all of the company's profit is distributed. This balance on the appropriation account is carried forward to the next financial period. It is added to the profit made in that period, when the next appropriation account is drawn up.

Although the format of company final accounts is different from that for sole traders, to allow for appropriation of profit and a more complicated capital structure, the basic principle is the same. The revenue accounts determine how much profit the company has made, while the balance sheet lists the assets of the firm and the liabilities that fund them.

THE PURPOSE OF ACCOUNTING STATEMENTS

Earlier in the unit, we said that the final accounts are a summary of all the financial transactions that have taken place in a business during a financial period. Financial transactions need to be recorded and summarised for a number of reasons, including:

- **helping managers monitor the performance of the business;**

- **informing the owners;**

- **securing and maintaining finance;**

- **meeting legal requirements.**

HELPING MANAGERS MONITOR THE PERFORMANCE OF THE BUSINESS

Financial information is vital in planning and controlling the activities of a business. Managers need to know whether the business is making a profit or loss, how much money is available for buying equipment, whether they need to alter the way the organisation operates, and so on. Only if up-to-date, accurate financial information is available can management make important decisions about the business or plan for the future.

INFORMING THE OWNERS

Whether the owners of businesses are sole traders, partners or shareholders, they will want to be kept informed about the performance and financial health of the business. They need to know whether the business is a worthwhile investment – whether it makes a healthy profit, and whether it has sufficient money to fund its cash flow. Obviously, financial considerations are not the only factors influencing investors' decisions (they will also be concerned with the firm's products, markets, etc.) but financial information is none the less very important.

SECURING AND MAINTAINING FINANCE

In much the same way as internal investors are influenced by and interested in the financial state of the business, so are external investors (banks, finance houses, etc.). Comprehensive and accurate financial information will be required by financiers whenever the company seeks to secure external finance. External investors will also want to monitor their investment as time goes by.

MEETING LEGAL REQUIREMENTS

There is an enormous amount of legislation governing the way businesses conduct their affairs, including the way financial information must be recorded and made available to interested parties. The Companies Acts 1985-9, which relate specifically to limited companies, require certain procedures to be followed in the preparation and presentation of accounts and the disclosure of financial and other information.

All businesses are required to produce accurate financial information in order that their liability for tax (income tax, corporation tax, value added tax) can be accurately determined. Information must be recorded and made available to the Inland Revenue and the Customs and Excise. These bodies have legal rights to inspect the accounts and check that they are accurate and represent a 'fair and true' view of the business.

Now work through element 4. At the end of element 4, you will be set a portfolio assignment that covers the material in elements 3 and 4.

Identify and explain data to monitor a business

Throughout this unit we have looked at the various types of financial data used in business. In this element, we bring together these concepts, discuss what the information is used for, by whom, and how it can assist in monitoring the performance of the business.

USERS OF ACCOUNTING INFORMATION

We identified some of the users of financial information earlier in the unit. These include owners, managers, providers of finance and the tax authorities. Additionally, the general public and the firm's employees may also have an interest in this information.

GENERAL PUBLIC

If the business is a company, the general public has a right to inspect its financial statements. Generally, existing or potential shareholders will be mainly interested in this information. However, companies' financial data are also used by researchers and other institutions which monitor general business activity.

EMPLOYEES

Employees obviously have a vested interest in the financial health of the business that employs them. This is particularly the case where the financial performance of the business affects them directly. This may be because they are involved in a profit-sharing scheme or because bonuses are based on financial performance. If employees have been set financial targets, they will want to know whether these have been achieved.

THE INFORMATION REQUIRED TO MONITOR A BUSINESS

In previous sections, we have looked at financial forecasting and the preparation of actual financial statements, both of which are used to monitor the performance of a business. Additionally, historical data from previous years offer a comparison between past and current performance. The key components include forecast, actual and historical **balance sheets**, **profit and loss accounts** and **cash flows**.

ACTIVITY

Contact a company in your area and ask for a copy of its annual report.

1 What general information does it offer?

2 What financial information does it contain?

3 Imagine you wanted to invest some money, would you invest in your chosen company? On what did you base your decision?

4 Compare your company with those chosen by other students on your course. What similarities and differences can you identify?

Other useful information includes data on **aged debtors** and **aged creditors** (actual and historical). These are analyses of how long debtors are taking to pay a business and how long it is taking to pay its creditors. This information is vital for **credit control purposes** (aged debtors) and in terms of maintaining **liquidity** (which we will examine shortly).

This financial information can be used in a variety of ways: to evaluate whether actual performance has matched the forecasts, to compare performance between different accounting periods and to make comparisons with other firms engaged in the same type of business activity. If a business finds a **variance** between what is forecast and what actually happens, or between different accounting periods, it needs to identify what caused the variance and what it can learn from it.

Accountants employ a range of ratios and percentage calculations which allow them to interpret the financial data provided by the final accounts. They use these to make the types of comparisons outlined above. We shall be examining some of these rational indicators in this element.

REASONS FOR MONITORING THE PERFORMANCE OF A BUSINESS

Monitoring business performance allows informed decisions to be made by owners and managers. Better decisions are made when people are well informed. Information is required both to understand all the possible outcomes that could arise and also to measure the value of these outcomes.

There are a number of important issues that the interpretation of financial information can identify or address. These include:

⊗ **solvency;**

⊗ **profitability;**

⊗ **taxation;**

⊗ **maintaining finance;**

⊗ **comparison with targets;**

⊗ **improving performance.**

We now take each of these issues in turn, examining what they represent, how they can be interpreted from the financial data and the significance of that interpretation to the performance of the business.

SOLVENCY

If a business is solvent, it has enough working capital to fund its cash flow requirements. A solvent business can pay its debts, as and when they fall due, in the short-term. If there is insufficient **liquidity** (that is, cash free to pay short-term debts) the business faces insolvency. As we discussed earlier, a profitable company can experience cash shortages which may, in extreme cases, lead to bankruptcy.

There are two main accounting ratios that can be used to measure a firm's solvency, the **current ratio** and the **acid test**.

CURRENT RATIO

The current ratio (also known as the **working capital ratio**) is the ratio of current assets to current liabilities. Both these figures are provided on the balance sheet.

The ratio is calculated by dividing current assets by current liabilities:

$$\text{current ratio} \quad = \quad \frac{\text{current assets}}{\text{current liabilities}}$$

For example, if a firm has current assets of £59,200 and current liabilities of £23,000 the current asset ratio would be:

$$\text{current ratio} \quad = \quad \frac{£52,900}{£23,000} \quad = \quad 2.3{:}1$$

This would be considered a satisfactory result. Generally speaking, a 'healthy' current ratio is at least 2:1. If the ratio falls below this, there would be concern about the firm's liquidity.

ACID TEST

Also known as the liquidity ratio, the acid test is a more precise measure of a firm's liquidity because it removes stock from the current assets figure. Stock takes time to convert to cash (you have to sell it and wait for payment) and, therefore, it cannot be considered a very liquid current asset. The acid test is calculated by dividing current assets less stock by current liabilities:

$$\text{acid test} \quad = \quad \frac{\text{current assets} - \text{stock}}{\text{current liabilities}}$$

Continuing the example we used above, if £18,400 of the firm's current assets are stock, the acid test result is:

$$\text{acid test} \quad = \quad \frac{£52,900 - £18,400}{£23,000} \quad = \quad \frac{£34,500}{£23,000} \quad = 1.5{:}1$$

Once again, this would be considered a satisfactory result. Generally speaking, a 'healthy' acid test result is at least 1:1. If the ratio falls below this, there would again be concern about the firm's liquidity.

ACTIVITY

The following figures are taken from the balance sheets of two different businesses. For each business, calculate the current ratio and the acid test. Which company gives the better result and why?

	Smith	Jones
Current assets (including stock)	£186,300	£182,500
Stock	£131,100	£94,900
Current liabilities	£69,000	£73,000

An important point to note is that even when a firm has a healthy current ratio, the acid test may indicate a liquidity problem which might threaten the firm's solvency. This results if a firm is holding too much stock, which cannot be readily converted into cash.

PROFITABILITY

Profitability is a measure of how much profit the business is making for its owners. It is usually measured in relation to the size of the business, by comparing the profit made with:

- ⊗ the value of the firm's assets;
- ⊗ the amount of capital originally invested;
- ⊗ the turnover; or,
- ⊗ the number of employees.

The most important interpretational tools for measuring profitability are the **gross profit percentage**, the **net profit percentage** and the **net assets percentage**.

GROSS PROFIT PERCENTAGE

The gross profit percentage calculates gross profit as a percentage of **turnover**. It is calculated as follows:

$$\text{gross profit percentage} = \frac{\text{gross profit}}{\text{turnover}} \times 100$$

For example, if a firm makes a gross profit of £58,800 from a turnover of £122,500, the gross profit percentage would be:

$$\text{gross profit percentage} = \frac{£58,800}{£122,500} \times 100$$
$$= 48\%$$

A word about absolute and relative change

An important point to note is the difference between absolute change and relative change. Comparing absolute figures does not always immediately give us an accurate picture of how a firm is doing. Relative changes, such as ratios and percentages, provide a much clearer indication. This difference is apparent when we look at figures for Dearing Ltd.

Dearing Ltd	Year 1	Year 2
Turnover	£200,000	£400,000
Gross profit	£50,000	£80,000

On the face of it, Dearing Ltd is a successfully expanding company. Gross profit has increased from £50,000 in year 1 to £80,000 in year 2. However, the change in absolute values can be misleading. If we apply the gross profit percentage, we can see whether things are really going so well. In year 1:

$$\text{gross profit percentage} = \frac{£50,000}{£200,000} \times 100 = 25\%$$

But in year 2

$$\text{gross profit percentage} = \frac{£80,000}{£400,000} \times 100 = 20\%$$

As the gross profit percentage shows, Dearing's profitability has fallen. So the relative change indicates that problems have arisen in year 2 which need to be investigated.

Generally speaking, the gross profit is relatively easy to control, given that a business should know how much it pays for the goods it purchases and how much it sells them for. However, should the gross profit percentage fall, the cause must be investigated. A number of factors can cause a fall in the gross profit percentage:

⊗ someone may be stealing the firm's cash takings;

⊗ someone may be stealing its stock;

⊗ stock may be being lost through breakages or deterioration;

⊗ poor purchasing decisions may result in the firm buying stock which it cannot sell;

⊗ the firm may have produced stock which it cannot sell;

⊗ the cost of purchasing goods may have risen and the firm may not have passed the increase on to its customers by raising prices.

Whichever reason is to blame, being aware that the gross profit percentage has fallen allows a business to take steps to remedy the situation.

ACTIVITY

Make a list of the problems that might have caused a drop in Dearing's gross profit percentage. What measures could the company take to remedy each type of problem?

NET PROFIT PERCENTAGE

The net profit percentage is calculated in a very similar way to the gross profit percentage. It expresses net profit as a percentage of turnover:

$$\text{net profit percentage} = \frac{\text{net profit}}{\text{turnover}} \times 100$$

For example, if a firm makes a net profit of £12,320 from a turnover of £112,000, the net profit percentage is:

$$\text{net profit percentage} = \frac{£12,320}{£112,000} \times 100 = 11\%$$

Unlike the gross profit percentage, the net profit percentage is subject to changes that are more difficult to control. This is because all the overhead expenses of the business affect the net profit. The major factors that need to be examined if the net profit percentage falls are:

⊗ has the gross profit percentage fallen?

⊗ have one or more expense items increased significantly?

⊗ have gains to the business (such as interest received) fallen significantly?

Again, whatever the cause, being aware that the net profit percentage has changed allows a business to take steps to remedy the situation.

NET ASSETS PERCENTAGE

The net assets percentage indicates the return on net assets. In other words, it shows how much profit has been made in relation to the net assets employed in generating that profit. The figures required for this calculation are found on the balance sheet (net assets) and the profit and loss account (net profit). The percentage is calculated as follows:

$$\text{net assets percentage} = \frac{\text{net profit}}{\text{net assets}} \times 100$$

For example, if a firm has net assets of £275,000 and it makes a net profit of £30,000 the net asset percentage would be:

$$\text{net profit percentage} = \frac{£30,000}{£275,000} \times 100 = 10.9\%$$

What represents a good return on assets depends on the type of business and the current economic climate. Therefore, this percentage is mostly used to compare performance between different accounting periods of the same firm or for comparisons between firms in the same type of business.

PERFORMANCE

A variety of ratios and percentages can be used to assess the overall performance of the business, as opposed to its solvency or profitability. These tell a business how much it costs to make its sales, how hard its assets are working for the business and how long accounts are taking to be paid.

SELLING

The **overheads percentage of turnover** expresses the overheads of the business as a percentage of the net sales:

$$\text{overheads percentage of turnover} = \frac{\text{overheads}}{\text{turnover}} \times 100$$

◦ ACTIVITY

1 Using the figures below, calculate the gross profit percentage, the net profit percentage and the net assets percentage for Balmar Ltd (accurate to one decimal place).

2 Compare your answers with the percentages for the previous year (as at 31 December 1993). What does this comparison tell you? Suggest reasons that may account for your findings.

Balmar Ltd

As at 31 December 1994

	£
Turnover (net sales)	628,870
Gross profit	315,530
Net profit	72,478
Net assets	750,000

Balmar Ltd

As at 31 December 1993

	%
Gross profit percentage	52.7
Net profit percentage	9.4
Net assets percentage	6.3

For example, if a firm has overheads of £63,000 and a turnover of £180,000 the percentage would be:

$$\text{overheads percentage of turnover} = \frac{£63,000}{£180,000} \times 100$$

$$= 35\%$$

This tells us that 35 per cent of the sales value is spent on the overheads required to run the business. Comparing this figure between different years tells a business whether it is costing more or less to achieve its sales.

ASSET TURNOVER

The **asset turnover ratio** shows how effective assets have been in generating sales, and how effectively a business's sales staff have used its assets to generate sales.

$$\text{asset turnover ratio} = \frac{\text{turnover}}{\text{net assets}}$$

For example, if a firm generates a turnover of £285,000 from net assets worth £322,000 the asset turnover would be:

$$\text{asset turnover ratio} = \frac{£285,000}{£322,000} = 0.89{:}1$$

STOCK TURNOVER

It is also useful to know how often the stock of a business turns over (how many times each year it sells its stock

holding). One way of estimating stock turnover is to divide sales by stock. This calculation can be used to give a quick answer for comparative purposes.

$$\text{stock turnover} = \frac{\text{annual sales}}{\text{stock}}$$

For example, if a firm generates a turnover of £285,000 and has a year-end stock of £57,000, the stock turnover would be:

$$\text{stock turnover} = \frac{£285,000}{£57,000} = 5 \text{ times per year}$$

Although this is a 'quick' method of examining stock turnover, it is not very accurate because the sales value is at selling price and the stock value is at cost price. A more accurate method is to use the rate of stock turn (ROST) calculation:

$$\text{rate of stock turn} = \frac{\text{cost of goods sold}}{\text{average stock}}$$

The cost of goods sold figure can be found in the revenue accounts. However, before we can use this equation we must find the value of the average stock. This is found by adding the opening stock value (at the start of the accounting period) to the closing stock value (at the end of the period) and dividing the result by two. This gives an average value for a business's stock holding over the period. The opening stock figure appears in the revenue accounts and the closing stock figure is shown

on the balance sheet.

$$average\ stock\ =\ \frac{opening\ stock\ +\ closing\ stock}{2}$$

This method uses more figures but, because all the values used are at cost price, the answer is more accurate.

ACTIVITY

Using the following figures, calculate Balmar's rate of stock turn during the year ended 31 December 1994 (accurate to one decimal place).

Balmar Ltd

	£
Cost of goods sold	313,340
Opening stock (1.1.94)	53,400
Closing stock (31.12.94)	42,910

DEBTORS AND CREDITORS

One way of keeping track of debtors and creditors is to prepare **aged analyses**. These show how much is owed (to a business or by a business) and how old those debts are. *Fig. 7.39* shows an example of an aged debtors analysis.

Aged debtors analysis

Debtor	Total	Current	30 days	60 days	60 days
L. Symonds	1,446.30	694.23	430.45	273.12	48.50
P. Halland	2,145.38	1,247.32	855.29	42.77	0
Jenson Ltd.	1,523.84	980.31	487.48	34.78	21.27
Totals	5,115.52	2,921.86	1,773.22	350.67	69.77

FIGURE 7.39: Aged debtors analysis.

DEBTOR DAYS

Another vitally important question for businesses is how long debtors are taking to settle their accounts, the **debtor collection period** or **debtors days**. Good credit control should ensure that customers pay their bills on time but should a firm's credit control slip, the length of time customers take to pay could start to slide beyond the credit period allowed them under the firm's terms of trade. We can calculate the average number of days that debtors are taking to pay using the following equation:

$$debtors\ days\ =\ \frac{debtors}{turnover\ (net\ sales)}\ \times\ 365$$

Should the debtors days start to creep up, a firm would need to improve its credit control methods.

CREDITOR DAYS

We can make a similar calculation to find the average number of days a firm is taking to pay its creditors. While a firm is obviously not so concerned with keeping this as low as possible, it also cannot afford to let its creditors days slide up too far or it will lose any trust that it has built with its suppliers. The average number of days that a firm is taking to pay its creditors can be calculated using the following equation:

$$creditors\ days\ =\ \frac{creditors}{net\ purchases}\ \times\ 365$$

ACTIVITY

Using the following figures, calculate Balmar's debtors days and creditors days as at 31 December 1994 (accurate to one decimal place).

Balmar Ltd

As at 31 December 1994

	£
Turnover (net sales)	628,870
Net purchases	298,970
Debtors	59,820
Creditors	36,210

The important point to note is that the time taken for accounts to be paid affects a firm's cash flow significantly. When debtors pay their bills there is an inflow of cash;

when a firm pays its creditors there is an outflow. If debtors days start to slide (that is debtors take longer to pay) there will be a delay in the inflow of cash. If, meanwhile, the firm is having to meet its outflow obligations (paying creditors, wages, etc.) then the cash cycle will begin to suffer (as discussed in unit 6). A firm may have to fund its cash requirements by taking out a loan or running a bank overdraft, costing money in interest payments. It is vital, therefore, that a firm maintains good credit control and ensures that its debtors pay what they owe promptly.

OTHER FACTORS

TAXATION

As we mentioned earlier, all business activity involves a tax liability. It is vitally important that a business establishes its tax liability accurately and, wherever possible, minimises that liability as it is legally entitled to do (by offsetting the legitimate expenses of the business against its profits). Obviously, this can only be achieved if the relevant financial data are available and accurate.

SECURING AND MAINTAINING FINANCE

Before any prospective source of external finance is prepared to lend money to a business, the potential investor needs to be satisfied that the loan will be repaid. The financial data provided by the business give the lender vital information to assess the risk involved in making the loan.

Having arranged the loan, lenders will want to monitor the performance of the business on an ongoing basis to ensure that the loan remains safe. Therefore, businesses need to provide regular financial data to lenders to maintain their external finance.

COMPARISON WITH TARGETS AND IMPROVING PERFORMANCE

The financial data used in business, together with the various interpretational tools we have discussed, allow owners and managers to compare the performance of their business with their targets and forecasts. Where there is variance between what was predicted or anticipated and what actually occurs, informed decisions can be made to improve the performance. Without accurate, well-interpreted financial data, it would be impossible to achieve any realistic levels of monitoring or improvement within a business.

In summary, then, financial data can provide vital information about the solvency, profitability and performance of a business. Accurate financial data and interpretation give owners and managers an opportunity to make informed decisions to avoid insolvency, maximise profits and improve performance. Interpretation of the data also allows comparisons to made between accounting periods of the same firm or to compare the performance of two separate firms in the same type of business. Accurate data are also essential to secure and maintain finance from external sources (lenders need to be sure that their money is safe) and to establish the firm's liability for tax.

PORTFOLIO ASSIGNMENT

RAPHAEL'S SANDWICH BUSINESS

TASK 1

Raphael's is a one-man business which sells sandwiches to firms on a local industrial estate. Most of Raphael's customers pay in cash but he has a few credit customers who settle their accounts monthly. He rents a small factory unit, where he prepares the sandwiches, and he then delivers by van. *Fig. 7.40* shows the account balances which remain after preparation of the trading account. Using these figures prepare:

(i)   a revised trial balance – for each item, indicate whether it would appear in the profit and loss account or on the balance sheet;

(ii) a profit and loss account for the quarter ending 31 August 1995;

(iii) a balance sheet as at 31 August 1995, which clearly shows the working capital figure.

The final accounts should be set out in the vertical format.

TASK 2

Write a brief report which explains the following:

(i)   a basic accounting system which could be used by a small business, including an explanation of how original documents are entered into the ledgers via the day books;

Account	Balance	Dr/Cr
Cash	110.00	Dr
Bank	333.00	Dr
Capital	13,800.00	Cr
Motor vehicle	6,500.00	Dr
Equipment	5,600.00	Dr
Debtors	1,050.00	Dr
Creditors	883.00	Cr
Drawings	350.00	Dr
Stationery	125.00	Dr
Telephone	130.00	Dr
Electricity	135.00	Dr
Delivery expenses	500.00	Dr
Rent	600.00	Dr
Gross profit (From Trading A/C)	2,250.00	Cr
Closing stock (31.8.95)	1,500.00	Dr

FIGURE 7.40: Account balances for Raphael's as at 31 August 1995.

(ii) what is meant by 'accounting periods';

(iii) what is meant by the following terms:

(a) overhead expenses;
(b) net profit;
(c) fixed assets;
(d) current assets;
(e) current liabilities;
(f) long-term liabilities;
(g) capital;
(h) drawings.

(iv) the purpose of the profit and loss account and the balance sheet.

TASK 3

Using the relevant data for Raphael's from task 1, plus the additional information given below, calculate the following:

⊗ **current ratio;**

⊗ **acid test;**

⊗ **gross profit percentage;**

⊗ **net profit percentage;**

⊗ **net assets percentage;**

⊗ **overheads to sales percentage;**

⊗ **asset turnover;**

⊗ **rate of stock turn.**

To complete task 3, you will need to use the following additional information:

Raphael's	£
As at 31 August 1995	
Turnover	4,600
Opening stock (1.6.95)	620
Cost of goods sold	2,350

TASK 4

Fig. 7.41 shows financial figures for Snax, another small business selling sandwiches to local firms. Interpret the data for Snax in the same way as you did for Raphael's in task 3.

	£
Turnover	5,650
Cost of goods sold	2,541
Gross profit	3,109
Net profit	509
Overheads	2,600
Current assets (including stock)	3,872
Current liabilities	1,712
Closing stock	2,500
Opening stock (1.6.95)	1,750
Net assets	16,872

FIGURE 7.41: Account balance for Snax as at 31 August 1995.

TASK 5

Prepare a report for Raphael, the owner of the first business, which outlines and compares the results of your interpretation of his financial data (from task 3) with that for Snax (from task 4). Explain the significance of your findings.

Include in your report a description of the key components of information used to monitor a business, explaining who might want to use the information and why. Clearly explain how the data you have provided can assist in comparisons and variance analyses and why these can be useful when monitoring the performance of a business.

✔ MULTIPLE CHOICE QUESTIONS

1 **Which of the following is a reason why businesses require finance for their working capital:**

A to purchase fixed assets

B to construct trading forecasts

C to purchase raw materials

D to allow factoring to take place

2 **Which of the following is an intangible asset:**

A vehicles

B goodwill

C fixtures and fittings

D buildings

3 **Which of the following is NOT an advantage of an overdraft as a form of short-term finance:**

A it is flexible

B increases in the overdraft (within an agreed limit) do not require notification

C they are simple to arrange

D interest is usually charged at between 2 per cent and 4 per cent above base rate

4 **Which of the following is NOT a form of medium-term finance:**

A leasing

B factoring

C hire purchase

D bank loans

5 **Covenants are a significant source of finance for:**

A sole traders

B partnerships

C non-profit making organisations

D public limited companies

6 **A rights issue is:**

A a method of selling shares

B a matter on which shareholders have the right to vote

C an issue of free shares

D a way in which plcs raise finance by selling assets

7 **The difference between a budget and a forecast is:**

A a forecast is long term

B a budget implies some sort of target

C only companies set budgets

D there is no difference

8 **Which of the following is NOT a purpose of a forecast:**

A to meet the legal obligations placed on companies

B to help a business obtain finance

C to assist in monitoring the performance of a business

D a means of motivating staff

9 **Value added tax is collected on behalf of the government by:**

A the Customs and Excise

B the Inland Revenue

C the Treasury

D the Department of Trade and Industry

10 **Which of the following will represent a cash outflow to a business:**

A capital introduced

B sales receipts

C VAT recoveries

D purchase of raw materials

11 **Which book of original entry records the invoices a business sends to its customers:**

A purchases day book

B expenses day book

C sales day book

D purchases returns book

12 **When the accountant for a business draws up a summary of all accounts contained in the ledger this is known as:**

A profit and loss account

B trial balance

C balance sheet

D the nominal ledger

13 **The difference between a business's gross profit and its net profit is:**

A current liabilities

B dividend payments

C additions to reserves

D the business's running expenses

14 **Which of the following is NOT a long-term liability to a business:**

A mortgages

B debentures

C overdraft

D bank loan

15 **Which of the following is a current asset:**

A debtors

B bank overdraft

C proposed dividends

D creditors

16 **Current assets minus current liabilities is also known as:**

A working capital

B authorised capital

C general reserve

D net assets employed

17 Which of the following is true:

A authorised and issued share capital are always equal

B issued share capital can exceed authorised share capital

C authorised and issued share capital can, on occasions, be equal

D authorised and issued share capital can never be equal

18 The acid test ratio is used to assess a company's

A solvency

B profitability

C credit control

D stock turnover

19 The net profit percentage compares net profit and:

A gross profit

B capital employed

C turnover

D net assets employed

20 Aged analyses are used to keep a track on:

A profit levels over a number of years

B the age profile of the workforce

C the length of period for which stock has been held

D debtors and creditors

Peter Bell

SL10

Dr.   **Cr.**

Date	Details	F	Amount	Date	Details	F	Amount

Protac Ltd

SL31

Dr.   **Cr.**

Date	Details	F	Amount	Date	Details	F	Amount

Lodenhall

PL22

Dr.   **Cr.**

Date	Details	F	Amount	Date	Details	F	Amount

Sales

<table>
<tr><td colspan="5"></td><td colspan="1" align="right">GL44</td></tr>
<tr><td colspan="6" align="center">**Sales**</td></tr>
<tr><td>**Dr.**</td><td></td><td></td><td></td><td></td><td align="right">**Cr.**</td></tr>
<tr><td>Date</td><td>Details</td><td>F</td><td>Amount</td><td></td><td></td></tr>
</table>

Date	Details	F	Amount	Date	Details	F	Amount

Purchases — Gl33

Date	Details	F	Amount	Date	Details	F	Amount

VAT — GL99

Date	Details	F	Amount	Date	Details	F	Amount

Business Planning

CONTENTS

OUTLINE

This unit clearly demonstrates how planning involves formulating a method by which something is to be done. It shows how planning can be applied to both personal and business situations. On a personal level, guidance is given on how to plan a career in the uncertain world of employment. In the context of business, the unit explains how to put forward business plans for new proposals and ideas. In the particular case of people who decide to work for themselves, these two forms of planning are interlinked to cover the setting up of a new business venture.

The unit offers an opportunity to bring together the knowledge and skills of all of the mandatory units. In particular, it focuses on the forces of demand and supply covered in unit 1. It also applies and extends the marketing concepts introduced in unit 3 into a market analysis and an outline sales and marketing plan. The planning process reflects the human resource issues discussed in unit 4 and the financial factors covered in units 6 and 7.

Students may wish to read through the third element on career planning before working through the first two elements on preparing and presenting a business plan.

Prepare work and collect data for a business plan

THE RANGE OF INFORMATION

Before developing a formal business plan, it is essential for any business organisation, or individual entrepreneur, to identify and collect the information necessary to assess the feasibility and viability of the business proposal. It is also important to determine how the proposal is to be implemented.

Information is generally collected in the following areas:

- the nature and form of the business idea and how it fits in with the organisation's objectives or purpose;

- the people skills and knowledge which are necessary to develop and exploit the business idea;

- the most suitable legal form for the business;

- the business environmental trends which may have led to, or influenced, the business idea, taking account of economic, social, legal, political and technological factors;

- the market, including potential customers, their needs and the possible competition; probable levels of sales and revenue, and the factors that might determine a suitable marketing strategy;

- where the business should be located and the type of premises it requires;

- the plant, machinery, equipment, fittings and vehicles required by the business and the financial implications of such expenditure;

- management and control systems;

- the legal constraints, requirements and supports for the business;

- the insurance needs of the business;

- a plan of action.

IDENTIFYING AND ENLISTING APPROPRIATE SUPPORT

It is a mistake to try and collect the information for a business proposal without consulting widely and getting considered advice. It is far more sensible to gain a wider perspective by enlisting appropriate support from within an organisation's existing management team and/or from an outside agency.

There are a number of agencies and organisations that can advise on new business proposals.

COMMERCIAL BANKS

Many banks have a team of business advisers who give help to both established and new businesses. In the case of a new business, the adviser may run through the various procedures associated with starting up the venture, raising finance and controlling the financial affairs of the business. As the business idea develops, further advice can be given on insurance, pensions, international trade services and money transmission.

PROFESSIONAL ADVICE

An accountant is able to help a new business with the preparation of the first cashflow forecasts, handling any business forms and dealing with income tax and value added tax (VAT). As the business becomes more established, the accountant can continue to give financial advice and can also audit the accounts.

A solicitor is able to advise on the completion of legal documents and other legal matters. The Law Society runs a scheme called Lawyers for Enterprise which directs people starting up in business to a suitable lawyer who will have a good knowledge of the local business environment and be able to give expert advice. The first half-hour's consultation is free.

TRAINING AND ENTERPRISE COUNCILS

The 81 Training and Enterprise Councils (TECs) throughout England and Wales provide training, advice and expertise to all types of businesses. In areas of high unemployment, and some inner city and urban communities, TECs are able to offer grants to those wishing to set up new businesses. They can also give general advice on grants from the European Union (EU), local authorities and other organisations. TECs administer a number of business start-up schemes which are aimed at people who want to set up their own business. These are generally in the form of consultancy advice and, where they are designed for unemployed people, they may include some sort of weekly allowance to compensate for any loss of benefits.

LOCAL ENTERPRISE AGENCIES

The 300 local enterprise agencies are run by managers recruited from industry and representatives of the local community. They generally offer free advice on starting up and running a business, provide relevant business training courses and give information on possible investors and sources of support.

DEPARTMENT OF TRADE AND INDUSTRY'S ENTERPRISE INITIATIVE

The Enterprise Initiative encourages business by promoting trade, both at home and abroad. The Department of Trade and Industry (DTI) aids the development of industry in general, and the small-firms sector and the regions in particular. As such, it provides grants, advice and consultancy services and acts as the channel through which European Union support is provided.

THE PRINCE'S YOUTH BUSINESS TRUST AND LIVEWIRE

These two initiatives are aimed at young people under 29 years of age who wish to set up in business. They provide training, counselling, advice, marketing support and, in certain cases, some finance.

THE BUSINESS IDEA AND THE ORGANISATION'S PURPOSE

For a business idea to be successful, it must link back directly to the organisation's aims and purpose. At a very early stage of the planning process, these aims should be clearly defined by the organisation. They are usually expressed in terms of the organisation's **mission statement** and objectives. These objectives will ultimately be translated into a series of tasks and action plans.

The mission statement covers what the organisation has been set up to achieve. It indicates the direction in which the organisation needs to move and the activities it should concentrate on. These activities need to be clearly defined in order to prevent the business from trying to do too many things at the same time. For example, the mission statement for Plumbright – a small plumbing business in the London area – reads:

'Work will be confined to domestic repairs and installations and, as well as doing a quality job well, will meet the customers' two needs: an accurate quotation and starting and completion dates which are met.'

This mission statement clearly shows the direction of the business, its market and how it is going to achieve a quality service. Larger organisations often have a broader and more general mission statement. For example, the Forte Company which owns hotels, restaurants, motorway and airport services, industrial catering operations and fast-food outlets, has a mission to become: 'host to the world – developing an international network of branded hotels and restaurants'. Similarly, Dupont, which is involved in petroleum, chemicals, polymers, fibres, agricultural products, medical products, electronic materials and publishing declares its mission to become: 'the most successful, customer-focused chemical and energy company in the world'.

Underlying the mission should be certain **organisational objectives**. These may be very general in nature such as making as much profit as possible, establishing commercial security or power, bringing about technological advancement or enhancing the reputation, status and prestige of the organisation. However, in order to meet the particular aims of the organisation's mission statement, there will also have to be some rather more specific objectives. For example, Plumbright's mission statement is supported by the following objectives:

- ✪ **to obtain 10 per cent of the local domestic repairs and installations market in the first year of trading;**

- ✪ **to achieve +/- 5 per cent accuracy in any quotation that is sent out;**

- ✪ **to start and complete all jobs within two days of the specified date.**

Having identified how the business idea links back to the organisation's aims and purpose, the next stage in the planning process is to break down the specific objectives into actual tasks. For example, the first objective for Plumbright – to win 10 per cent of the market – might generate the following tasks:

- ✪ **deliver leaflets to all houses in the area within three months;**

- ☺ **place an advertisement in the next edition of *Yellow Pages*;**

- ☺ **for the first two months of trading run a weekly advertisement in the local free newspaper.**

Each task then needs to be translated into an **action plan**. To deliver leaflets to all houses in the area, Plumbright needs to:

- ☺ **draft ideas to be included in the leaflet;**

- ☺ **send the draft to a promotions company to be designed and produced;**

- ☺ **arrange with a local newspaper group for leaflets to be delivered with a free newspaper.**

PEOPLE, SKILLS AND KNOWLEDGE

It is people who turn any business idea into a successful and profitable business venture. Therefore, it is essential to match any business proposal to the available people, skills and knowledge. Ultimately, it should be possible to demonstrate that the right people are available to run the business.

A new business start-up is likely to be more successful if the entrepreneur(s) display the sort of qualities shown in *Fig. 8.1*. For an established business considering a new business idea, people with entrepreneurial skills are just as important. However, such people generally need another dimension; they need political awareness if the idea is to be promoted successfully within the organisation and accepted by the major decision makers.

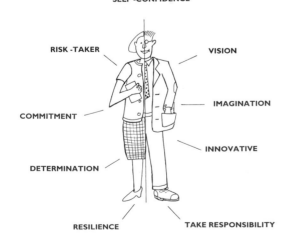

SELF-CONFIDENCE

RISK-TAKER

VISION

IMAGINATION

COMMITMENT

INNOVATIVE

DETERMINATION

RESILIENCE

TAKE RESPONSIBILITY

FIGURE 8.1: Entrepreneurial qualities.

When considering any business proposal, it is necessary to identify the type of knowledge and skills that the workforce require if they are to implement the proposal. This should involve all the major functional areas including production, marketing, finance, personnel and management information systems.

For both a new business start-up and the development of an established business, an **audit** needs to be undertaken to match the skills and knowledge of the people involved in the business to the key tasks that need to be performed. A new business start-up might have to supplement any skills shortages by employing people on a consultancy basis or through taking on part-time staff or people on short-term contracts. In an established business, after a complete review of existing skills, a decision would be taken on any training or recruitment that would be needed to deal with any skills shortage.

ACTIVITY

Imagine you are an aspiring entrepreneur who is considering the possibility of opening a fast-food outlet in your local area. You are planning on selling vegetarian burgers and health snacks. The business will provide both a take-away counter service as well as seating for 50 people to eat on the premises.

1 List the major tasks associated with managing and running such a venture.

2 Identify the particular knowledge and skills that people would require to complete the tasks.

3 Suggest how you might recruit the staff and what training might be necessary in order to overcome any possible skills shortage.

THE LEGAL FORM OF THE BUSINESS

When drafting a business proposal, it is important to decide upon the most suitable legal form for the business. For a new business start-up, this involves a choice between sole trader, partnership or private limited company. With an established business, it is unlikely that a new business proposal would cause a change in the legal status of the business, unless it involved such an expansion in the size of the business that it was forced to change from sole trader to limited company or from a private to a public limited company.

An accountant, bank manager or solicitor can provide advice about what is a suitable form for a business. Factors in making the decision include the ease of setting up, the costs, the proposed method of operation and legal responsibilities.

THE SOLE TRADER

The sole trader is the simplest, and by far the most common, form of business organisation in the UK. Basically, an individual person provides the capital, takes the decisions and assumes the risks of the business. It is a type of organisation particularly well suited to small retail outlets and local services such as hairdressing and window-cleaning, where customers value personal attention.

In general, there are no formal legal procedures to go through when setting up as a sole trader. However, if the business is being run under a name other than that of the owner, then the name and address of the proprietor must be shown on all business stationery and prominently displayed in the business premises. Also, if the business is to use a trade name, then it must ensure that it is not already being used by another business. For example, you could not open a fast-food outlet under the name 'Burger King'.

For some business activities it may be necessary for sole traders to obtain a licence, usually from the local authority, before they can lawfully trade. For example, licensing requirements apply to pet shops, betting shops, bingo halls, hairdressers, street traders, fruit machines, cinemas and theatres, pawnbrokers and riding stables. Sole traders may be required under certain circumstances to register with or notify various government agencies about their business.

Sole traders must submit annual accounts to the **Inland Revenue**. If their annual turnover exceeds the VAT threshold, they must register for VAT with **Customs and Excise**. Sole traders who employ staff need to contact the **Social Security** authorities for the purposes of National Insurance and sick pay. **The Factory Inspectorate** is interested in any business using industrial premises, and the local authority's **environmental health department** in all shops and offices (concerning the health and safety of staff) and in shops selling foods (concerning food hygiene).

Legally, sole traders have **unlimited liability**. This means that they are personally liable for all the debts of the business up to the limit of their personal estate. So, in the case of insolvency even the sole trader's house and car could be taken in order to settle business debts. In reality, it is possible to avoid some of these consequences by placing all major private assets in the name of a spouse, against whom creditors have no legal claim.

Sole traders act as their own bosses. They can implement policies when they see fit and they are answerable to no one apart from their customers. This means that the sole trader tends to survive against the competition of larger rivals by building up good personal relationships with customers and trying to ensure that service is of the highest standard.

Another method of survival has been sought by many sole traders competing with the large multiples in the retail trade. By grouping together, they have been able to enjoy some of the economies of scale associated with bulk purchasing. For example, the Spar (Society for the Protection of the Average Retailer) group of grocers' shops has formed its own purchasing and distribution system. Such associations are able to benefit from some of the other advantages of large-scale organisations, such as running advertising campaigns which might be beyond the means of an individual sole trader.

Economically, sole traders suffer from a lack of finance. This is because they are largely dependent upon borrowing from the commercial banking system and they are unable to command the same sort of credit as a larger organisation.

Sole traders cannot operate under the name of existing businesses.

ACTIVITY

You are considering the possibility of setting up as a sole trader and running a mobile snack bar. The intention is to target the lunch-time trade in the local industrial area.

1 List the government agencies you would need to contact before you can start trading.

2 Identify any legal requirements you would need to fulfil.

THE PARTNERSHIP

A partnership may legally consist of between two and twenty partners. However, the **Companies Act 1985** places no restriction on the number of partners making up a firm of solicitors, accountants or members of a recognised stock exchange. The partners provide the capital for the business and share the resulting profit or loss. This is an ideal form of organisation for a relatively small business requiring more capital than one person can provide. A partnership makes it possible to bring several sets of skills to the business. It is particularly suitable for groups of professionals such as doctors, dentists, accountants, architects and solicitors.

The legal regulations governing the ordinary or general partnership were established by the **Partnership Act 1890**. This states that in the absence of any statement to the contrary, all partners should share profits and losses equally and all partners have equal rights in the running of the firm. This has a number of serious implications. First, if one partner makes a costly business mistake, then all partners have to accept and pay for the consequences. Second, when it comes to liability for debts then under the law, all partners are 'jointly and severally responsible'. Ultimately, this means that the partnership's debtors can sue any partner for the entire sum; so if one partner runs off, then the other partner(s) are liable for that share of the debt.

An ordinary partnership is dissolved either compulsorily or voluntarily in the event of:

⊗ **the termination of the agreed period of its duration;**

⊗ **the completion of the venture for which the firm was founded;**

⊗ **the general agreement of the partners;**

⊗ **the death or bankruptcy of any partner;**

⊗ **the order of a court.**

In the majority of cases it is advisable for partners to have some form of partnership agreement. This allows for some variation from the provisions of the Partnership Act. An agreement would normally include:

- ☼ **the role of each partner;**

- ☼ **the apportioning of profits or losses;**

- ☼ **the arrangements for introducing new partners;**

- ☼ **the arrangements for existing partners who may wish to leave;**

- ☼ **the conditions under which the partnership may be terminated;**

- ☼ **the operation of the financial dealings of the partnership.**

Another variation from the ordinary partnership is the limited partnership. This was established by the **Limited Partnership Act 1907**. The advantage of this type of partnership is that it allows for the formation of a partnership between an **active partner** and one or more **'sleeping' partners**. Sleeping partners are not partners in the fullest sense as they take no part in the management of the firm. However, they enjoy the privilege of limited liability, which means that they are liable only for the debts of the business up to the extent of the capital they have put into the venture. Such partners are desired not for their expertise but rather for the capital they can put into the business.

Depending on the type of service provided or product sold, a partnership has to abide by the same licensing, registration and notification requirements as the sole trader. It is also subject to the same checks from local authorities and central government departments.

PRIVATE LIMITED COMPANY

A private company is a legal 'person' or entity quite separate from its members. For example, Multishade Limited manufactures sunglasses; its members (or shareholders) are John and Jenny Briggs, James Dean and Mike Kirby. As a private company, Multishade can sue and be sued in the courts and, if this resulted in the company being fined, then this fine would be taken out of company funds rather than the pockets of its shareholders.

A private company consists of an association of not less than two people who contribute towards a joint stock of capital through the ownership of shares for the purpose of carrying on business for profit. The term **'joint stock'** refers to the total assets of the company and it includes items such as plant, machinery, raw materials and stocks of finished goods. The ownership of these assets is vested in the **shareholders**; they have raised the finance with which the assets are acquired. In many private firms the majority of the shares may be held by the members of one family or by one or two key directors in the business.

There are two main types of shares, preference and ordinary. The difference between preference and ordinary shares lies in the degree of associated financial risk. The **ordinary share** is the most risky in that the financial return on the share depends entirely upon the fortunes of the company. Although there is always the prospect of a high dividend to compensate for the risk, there is also the danger of a nil return. As the fortunes of ordinary shareholders are so bound up with the fortunes of the company, they have the right to elect company directors.

The **preference share** is less risky. It carries a fixed dividend which is paid before the ordinary dividend is established. However, even these shareholders may receive nothing if the company has done very badly. Many preference shares are issued with **'cumulative' rights**. This means that unpaid dividends may be carried forward to future years when the company's fortunes might have improved. Due to the much smaller risk involved in cumulative preference shares, they very rarely entitle shareholders to any voting rights or say in the running of the company.

The private company is an ideal form of business enterprise for family concerns and for launching new ideas or ventures. It is often a natural development from the partnership or sole trader.

When forming a company it is necessary to satisfy certain legal requirements set out in the **Companies Act 1985**. A number of documents must be sent to the **Registrar of Companies**. The most important are:

- ☼ **the memorandum of association;**

- ☼ **the articles of association.**

The **memorandum of association** deals with the relationship of the company to the outside world. It covers:

- ☼ **the company's name and the address of its registered office;**

- ☼ **the objects of the company – these set out its purpose so, for example, Multishade is set up to manufacture sunglasses;**

- ☼ **the amount of authorised capital, that is the amount the company wants to have the power to raise.**

The memorandum also includes a statement that the liability of the shareholders is limited. This document must be signed by at least two people who must declare that they wish to be formed into a company and promise to pay for the shares they have agreed to take.

The **articles of association** deal with the internal control of the company. They cover such issues as the rights of shareholders, arrangements for meetings, powers of directors and transfer of shares.

If these two documents, together with a statement concerning the company's nominal capital and a declaration that the company has adhered to the Companies Acts, are approved by the Registrar of Companies, then the company will be issued with a **certificate of incorporation**. This makes the company a separate legal 'person'. It gives its members **limited liability** which means that each member's liability is limited to the value of the shares held. Thus, if the member holds 2,000 £1 shares, then that person can only be held liable for no more than £2,000.

Limited liability means that the degree of risk associated with any venture is clearly expressed. This means that individuals are more willing to invest in the enterprise, and larger amounts of capital become easier to raise. Because of the attractions of limited liability, many sole traders or partnerships are able, by forming themselves into private companies, to attract the type and amount of finance necessary to pursue new ventures, expand or modernise, which might otherwise have been impossible. However, a director may be asked to give a personal guarantee on certain loans and liabilities. Under these circumstances, if the company gets into difficulties, the director can be sued for the total amount of the personal guarantee that has been given.

The overall control of a private company is largely in the hands of its **directors** who have been elected by the shareholders. The extent of a shareholder's voting powers at a company meeting depends upon the number and type of shares he or she has bought. The interests of the company's shareholders, suppliers and customers are protected by legislation. The company's business affairs are kept very open. For example, it has to publish an annual set of accounts and hold an annual general meeting for the members.

PUBLIC LIMITED COMPANY

An established business may find it necessary to change its legal form, either as a result of taking up a new business proposal or in order to be large enough to enter into new areas of business. Such an expansion is often associated with some form of **horizontal**, **vertical** or **lateral integration**. For example, Multishade might merge with another manufacturer of sunglasses (horizontal integration), take over its suppliers of lenses (vertical integration), or diversify into the manufacture of suntan oil (lateral integration).

It is not unusual for a sole trader to become a limited company, or for a limited company that wants to attract more finance to become a public limited company. This allows the company to raise further capital by issuing shares to be sold to the general public, thus increasing its opportunity to attract more funds. It is always possible to identify when an organisation is a public limited company, because it must use the words 'public limited company' or plc in its name. So, for example, Multishade plc, Marks and Spencer plc and J Sainsbury plc are all public limited companies.

Most public limited companies started as private companies. Like private companies, they have to satisfy certain legal requirements and issue similar documents in order to qualify for a certificate of incorporation. They can then issue a **prospectus** in order to persuade members of the general public to invest in the company. The prospectus acts as a kind of advertisement for the company's shares. It must be drawn up according to guidelines set out in the Companies Act 1985. The prospectus gives details of the company's operations, history, financial position and directors. The actual sale of the shares will generally be handled by an issuing house.

The open sale of the shares means that anybody can become a shareholder in a public limited company. People are generally more willing to buy these shares, because they know that they can freely sell the shares if they so wish. Shares that are 'listed' or 'quoted' may be bought or sold on the Stock Exchange. Shares in public limited companies are increasingly being purchased by the financial institutions such as the insurance companies, private pension funds, unit trusts and investment trusts. These institutions tend not to become greatly involved in the affairs of the companies in which they are shareholders, unless the companies start getting into difficulties.

Wider share ownership means that there is an apparent divorce between ownership and management in the public limited companies. Although the shareholders own the company, they have little opportunity of directly influencing company policy, except possibly through annual general meetings or extraordinary meetings. Shareholder control is exercised through the elected board of directors. It is the directors who appoint the managers to run the business.

The public limited company is a form of organisation especially suitable for large-scale activities which require a great deal of capital investment. Public limited companies dominate in areas such as car production, the chemical and petrochemical industries, and the tobacco industry.

As a result of the ease with which the shares of public companies may be bought and sold, another form of business organisation – the **holding company** – has developed. Holding companies achieve financial control over other companies – known as **subsidiary companies** – through the acquisition of shares. In some cases, these subsidiary companies provide the holding company's only source of income. Financial control is achieved by the acquisition of 51 per cent of the ordinary shares of the subsidiary, though often a holding of less than 50 per cent can give effective control. Each subsidiary retains its original name and continues to function as a separate entity. However, the holding company may use its majority shareholding to direct the policy of the subsidiary. For example, the Walls Meat Company is a subsidiary of Unilever. In some cases, holding companies may own other companies abroad; these are known as **multinationals**. Unilever, for instance, operates through subsidiary companies in 75 different countries.

ACTIVITY

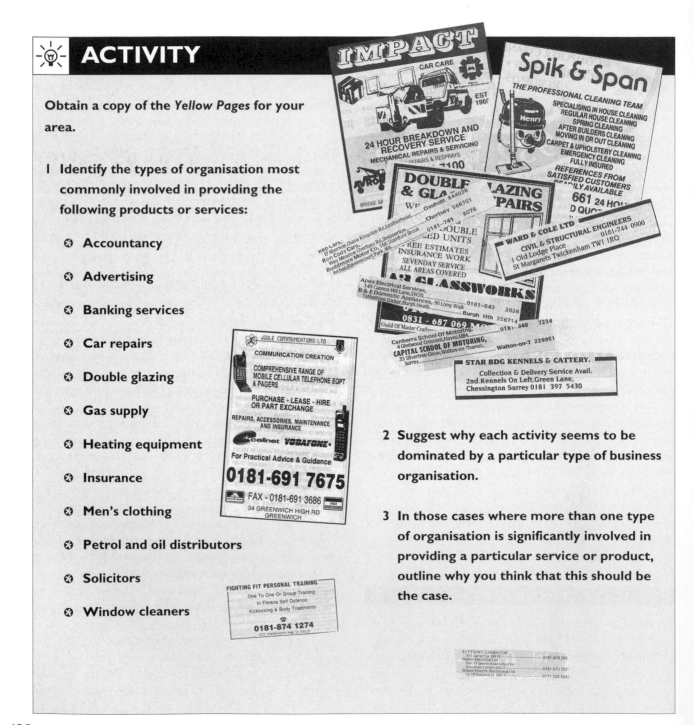

Obtain a copy of the *Yellow Pages* for your area.

1 Identify the types of organisation most commonly involved in providing the following products or services:

- ✪ **Accountancy**
- ✪ **Advertising**
- ✪ **Banking services**
- ✪ **Car repairs**
- ✪ **Double glazing**
- ✪ **Gas supply**
- ✪ **Heating equipment**
- ✪ **Insurance**
- ✪ **Men's clothing**
- ✪ **Petrol and oil distributors**
- ✪ **Solicitors**
- ✪ **Window cleaners**

2 Suggest why each activity seems to be dominated by a particular type of business organisation.

3 In those cases where more than one type of organisation is significantly involved in providing a particular service or product, outline why you think that this should be the case.

THE BUSINESS ENVIRONMENT

Business proposals must be developed within the context of the wider environment in which the organisation is operating. Trends and changes in the business environment have a dual effect. On the one hand, they generate **business opportunities**, on the other, they create **threats** and **pitfalls** for both new and existing businesses. The business environment must be constantly scanned for economic, legal, social, political and technological change, and this is as important for budding entrepreneurs as it is for established tycoons. The success of business people like Anita Roddick at the Body Shop or Bill Gates at the Microsoft Corporation has as much to do with their ability to identify change in the business world as it has with their ability to read a balance sheet. The ability to recognise a business opportunity and to exploit its market potential is the hallmark of a successful entrepreneur.

Business proposals may be affected by five main types of trends within the business environment:

- ⊗ **economic;**
- ⊗ **demographic and social;**
- ⊗ **legal;**
- ⊗ **political;**
- ⊗ **technological.**

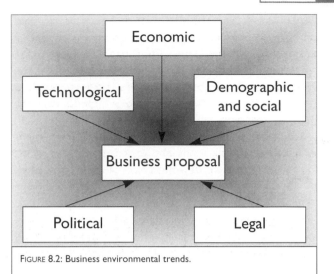

FIGURE 8.2: Business environmental trends.

ECONOMIC ENVIRONMENT

Businesses must monitor the level of economic activity in the economy. It is generally prudent to launch any new business proposal at the time of an upturn in the economy. Businesses need to consider movements in all of the major economic indicators (see *Fig. 8.3*).

Gross domestic product (GDP) is a useful indicator of the growth of output and hence the level of economic activity. **Consumer spending** refers to expenditure on goods and services by private households. It is a major determinant of the rate of increase of GDP. **Investment** includes expenditure on fixed assets such as buildings, plant and machinery. It is another major determinant of the rate of increase of GDP.

	GDP % ann.rise	Consumer spending % ann. rise	Investment % ann.rise	Exports % ann. rise	Imports % ann. rise	Retail prices % ann. rise	Unemployment Average (m) % of labour force	
1993	2.0	2.6	0.3	3.0	2.9	1.6	2.9	10.2
1994	3.4	2.7	7.0	8.7	7.3	2.6	2.6	9.1
1995	3.4	3.1	6.2	7.4	7.6	3.3	2.1	7.6
1993h1	1.6	2.2	-0.4	2.5	2.4	1.6	2.9	10.4
1993h2	2.4	2.9	1.1	3.8	3.3	1.6	2.8	10.1
1994h1	3.4	3.1	4.5	7.6	5.6	2.5	2.7	9.6
1994h2	3.4	2.4	8.9	9.7	9.0	2.7	2.4	8.7
1995h2	3.5	3.0	7.9	7.9	9.4	3.2	2.2	7.8
1995h2	2.2	3.2	4.5	7.0	5.8	3.5	2.1	7.5

FIGURE 8.3: Economic outlook.
Source: *Lloyds Bank Economic Bulletin*, Number 190, October 1994.

Trading activities abroad also have a significant effect on GDP. **Export expenditure** on goods and services is added to total expenditure, boosting GDP. Conversely, spending on imports is deducted from the total expenditure. This is because exports bring income into the economy, while imports remove income from the national economy.

Retail price indices show changes in the price of items which appear in the shops, and so represent a very good indicator of the **rate of inflation**. From a business point of view, inflation has implications for costs and relative competitiveness.

Unemployment generally falls as the economy expands, although the creation of new jobs may be limited by improvements in productivity or technology.

The economic indicators in *Fig. 8.3* relate to the national economy. Account should also be taken of regional economic trends which could have a direct impact on the rate of growth and, hence, business prospects in particular geographical segments of the market.

ACTIVITY

In small groups, study the trends shown in *Fig. 8.3*. Suggest whether the beginning of 1995 would have been an appropriate time to launch a new business manufacturing fitted kitchen units for home and overseas markets.

Businesses need to monitor changes in the government's economic policy, both in terms of its approach to managing the level of demand in the economy and its policies dealing with company taxation and investment. They need to take into account the extent and the nature of government intervention in the form of legislation dealing with consumer protection and other business activities.

Age and sex structure of the population

United Kingdom   **Percentage and millions**

	Under 16	16 – 39	40 – 64	65 – 79	80 and over	All ages (=100%) (millions)
Mid-year estimates						
1951	–	–	31.6	9.5	1.4	50.3
1961	24.8	31.4	32.0	9.8	1.9	52.8
1971	25.6	31.3	29.9	10.9	2.3	55.9
1981	22.2	34.9	27.8	12.2	2.8	56.4
1991	20.3	35.2	28.7	12.0	3.7	57.6
Males	21.4	36.5	29.1	10.7	2.3	28.1
Females	19.3	34.0	28.3	13.3	5.1	29.5
Mid-year projections						
2001	21.3	32.6	30.5	11.4	4.2	59.2
2011	20.1	30.0	33.7	11.7	4.5	60.0
2021	19.5	30.5	31.9	13.6	4.5	60.7
Males	20.2	31.6	32.1	12.7	3.4	30.0
Females	18.7	29.5	31.6	14.5	5.7	30.7

FIGURE 8.4: Age and sex structure of the population.
Source: *Social Trends* 23, 1993.

Businesses also need to note any changes in government economic policy which have a direct impact on the organisation's potential customers. For example, changes in personal taxation and benefits may have a direct impact on the distribution of income and wealth and, therefore, affect the levels of consumer spending in particular markets.

DEMOGRAPHIC AND SOCIAL TRENDS

Demographics concerns the total size, structure and distribution of the population. This is influenced by movements in the **birth rate**, **death rate** and **rate of migrations**. Demographic and social trends refer to changes in the composition of the population, including the size and type of household unit and its collective, material and employment needs. These changes reflect shifts in social attitudes, including views on the role of women, marriage and the family.

Demographic changes create opportunities and, in some cases, pose threats for organisations developing new business proposals. For example, if the population starts declining in size, then this would usually be accompanied by the population getting older. This older population, especially the relatively higher numbers of pensioners, would make greater demands on the welfare services. This would impose a larger tax burden on the already declining numbers making up the working population. This, in turn, would reduce consumer spending and, hence, business opportunities. However, the growing numbers of elderly people would create new patterns of demand; there would be new business opportunities to provide sheltered homes and to cater for retirement interests and special holidays.

LEGAL CHANGES

Any business organisation has to operate within a very broad legal framework. There are four fundamental ways in which the law may affect any organisation and, hence, the way in which it presents a business proposal.

- ✪ **It may influence the way in which the organisation conducts its business through legislation relating to contracts, consumer protection and international trade.**

- ✪ **It may determine how an organisation treats its employees through employment law and trade union law.**

- ✪ **It may affect how an organisation is structured and deals with its owners through the Companies Acts.**

- ✪ **It may influence how an organisation deals with the community as covered by criminal law.**

Changes in the law are normally fairly well publicised before legislation is enacted. A great deal of discussion may surround a bill as it passes through the various parliamentary stages to eventually become an Act of Parliament and the law of the land. This discussion may have been started at the outset by the publication of a white paper and, in some cases, a green paper. In the 1990s, businesses need to keep abreast of changes in the law which may be taking place in Europe as well as in the UK.

ACTIVITY

In small groups, identify the major trends revealed by _Fig. 8.4_.

Give five examples of business proposals that might be put forward in response to these trends.

ACTIVITY

With the aid of the research facilities in your library, obtain a copy of the speech made by the Queen at the last formal opening of Parliament.

From the speech, identify two items of future legislation that you feel would have a direct impact upon the activities of the business world and, hence, any future business proposals.

POLITICAL CHANGES

Political changes in the constitution and the make-up of the government and political parties can affect businesses. Governments stay in power by taking account of public opinion, pressure group activity and changing national and international circumstances. Their actions may create opportunities but they may equally pose threats.

When launching a new business proposal, it is necessary to take account of any political change. For example, considerable uncertainty exists in the run up to a British general election. This is because people fear that either the retention of the existing government may be accompanied by the continuation of a range of unpopular policies, or that a change of government might be accompanied by a change in policy which goes against the interests of the business.

TECHNOLOGICAL CHANGES

Technology involves the application of scientific and other organised knowledge to the advancement of techniques and systems for making and doing things. These techniques and systems generally involve people, organisations, living things and machines.

Changes in these techniques and systems may result in:

⊗ **new processes for producing a product or providing a service;**

⊗ **new ways of using labour;**

⊗ **the development of new or improved products.**

Ultimately, new technologies may help to lower production costs and create better quality goods and services. Since the Second World War, for example, new materials have been developed including plastics and glass fibre, which have been moulded into car and boat bodies. Some new materials have special properties; carbon fibre, for instance, is suitable for high-temperature turbine blades; certain types of material are resistant to high temperatures and are particularly suitable for heat shields on spacecraft. Lasers (light amplification by stimulated emission of radiation) have helped to provide a means of communicating over a very long distance. Pharmaceutical companies now attempt to design new drugs on the computer rather than in the laboratory. Information technology has allowed organisations to acquire, process, transmit and present information in all forms: audio, video, text and graphics.

Due to these rapid changes in technology, businesses have to be constantly researching and developing both their products and their methods of production if they are to remain competitive. It also means that new business proposals must reflect the latest developments in technology if they are to stand any chance of long-term success.

DEVELOPING A MARKETING STRATEGY

A sound understanding of the market is essential if a business proposal is ultimately to be turned into a successful and profitable business venture. Knowledge of the market should be used in an attempt to forecast sales and revenue and to plan an initial marketing strategy.

MARKET INFORMATION

Market information needs to be gathered through desk and field research to build up a picture of the potential customers, their needs and the possible competition.
This involves:

⊗ **finding out what potential consumers want in the context of changing tastes and preferences;**

⊗ **assessing the potential for new, improved or existing products or services;**

⊗ **determining the background of consumers in terms of sex, marital status, family size, socio-economic class and other elements that are important in product development and promotional activities;**

⊗ **conducting surveys relating to psychological factors such as image, social standing and personal values and how they influence consumer behaviour;**

⊗ **evaluating the various ways of approaching the market and distributing the product;**

⊗ **identifying the possible sources of existing or future competition and evaluating its strengths or weaknesses.**

Branson puts his fizz into Iceland

Michael Foster

RICHARD Branson has signed with cut-price food chain Iceland to supply Virgin Cola throughout its 700 stores. Iceland is a said to have found the price – and taste – of the new product so attractive that it has decided to stop selling Coca-Cola and Pepsi.

After a great deal of research into the popularity of Virgin's name, Iceland chief executive Malcolm Walker decided that its image was the best. But neither Iceland nor Virgin would comment on his decision to drop the leading brands.

The news will come as a hammer-blow to Coke and Pespi, following confirmation that Tesco will stock Virgin Cola. Never before in Britain have they faced the danger of seeing their brands forced off shelves.

Virgin Cola will be made by Cott Corporation of Canada, which already supplies cola to Sainsbury's. The supermarket chain says sales of Cott's product under its own name have grown to 60 per cent of cola sales since it was launched early this year.

Tesco believes that Virgin Cola, at 25p a can, could be its leading cola brand by Christmas. Virgin is hoping for a 75 per cent market share. Branson says: 'our agreement with Tesco is that Virgin Cola will not be sold through any other of the big five supermarket chains.' But he confirmed that he is talking to several independent suppliers.

Virgin has set up a 50-50 company with Cott, Virgin Cola, to produce soft drinks. 'It will be profitable from day one,' says Branson. He is interested in lending Virgin's name to other types of soft drink.

Virgin Cola could be a suitable candidate for a stock market float one day. Cott is already a quoted company. Its partnership with Wal-Mart of the US, the world's biggest retailer, has proved particularly successful.

The Observer, 16 October 1994

ACTIVITY

Read the article above about the launch of Virgin Cola.

1 **Identify the market information that would have encouraged Iceland to switch to Virgin and to drop Coca-Cola and Pepsi.**

2 **What type of market information would have made Virgin feel so confident about the prospects for its cola?**

FORECASTING SALES AND REVENUE

The techniques for measuring and forecasting sales are covered in detail in unit 3. Ultimately, the accuracy of such forecasts depends upon the quality of the data used in any desk research and the validity of any assumptions made in field research. In developing a business proposal, it is important to turn the sales forecasts into targets for the firm to achieve. Obviously, as the business gets underway, these targets should be regularly updated.

Achieving a sale is one thing, getting customers to part with their money and to pay for the product or service is quite another. Therefore, any forecast of revenue must include consideration of when bills will actually be paid. This often depends upon what are viewed as accepted practices within the industry. For example, in the building

Sales \ Month	1	2	3	4	5	6	7	8	9	10	11	12
Item A												
Units	100											
Price	£10											
Income	£1,000											
Item B												
Units					250							
Price					£20							
Income					£5,000							
Gross Income	£1,000				£5,000							
Receipts												
Cash Sales	£1,000											
Credit Sales											£5,000	
Total Sales Receipts	£1,000										£5,000	

FIGURE 8.5: Forecasting sales revenue.

Product

Design
Environmental features
Performance
Size
Accessories
Service
Guarantee

Place

Computer centres
Electrical shops
Electrical superstores
Department stores

Price

£399

List-price
Discount
Trade-ins
Payment period
Credit
Competition's prices

Promotion

Unique selling points
Sales promotion
Advertising
Personal selling
Publicity

FIGURE 8.6: Designing a marketing strategy for a new personal computer.

industry it is usual to use a system of staged payments: with an initial payment to cover materials, then so much at each stage of completion, and a final payment when the work has been completed and approved. Obviously, any projection of revenue would need to reflect this system. Similarly, if a business offers a discount for early payment, then any revenue forecast would need to reflect the probable effectiveness of the discount system and also its cost.

Fig. 8.5 provides a means of plotting the probable revenue from a business venture over a period of one year. Two examples have been given; one shows a cash sale in the first month of 100 units of item A at £10 per unit and the second a credit sale in the fifth month of 250 units of item B priced £20 per unit which is not paid for until six months have passed.

INITIAL PLANNING FOR A MARKETING STRATEGY

Even at the planning stage any business proposal must be supported by a well thought-out marketing strategy. This involves identifying what are considered to be the most important ingredients of the marketing operation and determining the best marketing mix of the four Ps – **product**, **price**, **place** and **promotion** – for the target market. In other words, it requires matching the product to consumer needs, determining the price, deciding upon how and where the product or service should be placed or distributed in the market and working out how best to promote it through publicity, advertising and sales techniques. These decisions should be based on the market information that has been gathered.

Fig. 8.6 illustrates the options available to a company which is proposing to launch a new personal computer onto the market. Ultimately, the chosen marketing strategy will reflect a mix of these factors.

PREMISES AND PHYSICAL RESOURCES

One of the major considerations of any business proposal involves where the business should locate and what type of premises it should use. Such decisions have serious financial and marketing implications. For example, expensive office premises may be necessary for a design consultancy wishing to attract wealthy clients; but, obviously, these premises would not be appropriate for a building firm wanting to store materials and equipment, and whose operations are carried out mainly on site, nor for a company whose dealings with clients are conducted in their homes or businesses.

In some cases, it may actually be appropriate to run a business from home. However, anybody considering running a business from home needs to review several factors.

- **The planning position** – is planning permission necessary to use a domestic dwelling for business purposes? This will depend upon the use that the premises are to be put to. For example, it might be acceptable to use office equipment, but quite unacceptable to create extra traffic through deliveries and customers, or to use machinery which creates noise, dirt or smell.

- **The tax position** – you may have to pay business rates or, when the home is sold, pay capital gains tax on any increase in the value of the property.

- **The legal position** – covenants in the deeds or lease of the house may forbid the carrying out of business activities on the premises.

- **Insurance** – house and contents insurance is unlikely to extend to business equipment and activity.

A compromise between working from home and renting expensive premises is to start in a small business unit. Many units are managed by local enterprise agencies. They often have the benefits of a pooled photocopier, answerphone and a receptionist/typist.

When considering a new business proposal, a more established business has to decide between either buying or leasing premises. Although buying is expensive, it has the advantage of providing useful collateral against which to borrow money and it guards against the possibility of sudden rent increases. However, leasing premises is the most usual method as it means that less capital has to be committed. It is important though to check carefully the obligations and conditions associated with the lease.

When deciding upon the geographical location of a business, consideration must be given to:

- **the costs and availability of sources of raw materials and the proximity of suppliers;**

- **the costs and availability of a suitable supply of labour;**

- **the proximity to the market;**

- **the communication links in terms of road, rail, air, waterways and sea;**

- **possible site requirements in terms of main services, storage, parking and the disposal of waste;**

- **potential external economies associated with working alongside other organisations already involved in similar activities, where savings might be made in terms of the availability of supplies of raw material and labour;**

- **possible government assistance in the form of grants, subsidies and training which is available in the assisted areas.**

ACTIVITY

In small groups, visit estate agents and enterprise agencies to find suitable premises in which to launch the following business ventures:

(a) an employment agency which employs six staff;

(b) a hairdresser's dealing exclusively with people between 15 and 25 years of age;

(c) a small building firm specialising in house extensions, which employs one office worker together with a bricklayer, a carpenter and a labourer.

In each case, provide details of the selected premises and justify the choice.

METHOD OF OPERATION OR PRODUCTION

At a fairly early stage of the development of a business proposal, a decision has to be made on how to actually conduct production or offer a service.

In the case of production, it is necessary to decide upon whether to make the product completely, to buy in components and assemble them or to purchase the product and sell it on. These three situations are illustrated below.

Case 1 – Abbey Pine designs and manufactures its own range of furniture, making use of cutting, turning and polishing tools and a finishing spray room. It purchases all its own wood and manufactures its products in batches of three or four.

Case 2 – Childcare Cottons designs and manufactures children's clothes. It designs the items, cuts them out and then sends the pieces to outworkers to make up. This provides considerable flexibility because the company only needs to employ a limited number of people to carry out the operation.

Case 3 – Officecoms Limited sells computer systems to small businesses. It designs and puts together the systems to meet the particular needs of the business. All the components are purchased as 'kit' parts.

Ultimately, the decision on how much of the production process should be undertaken by a business will depend upon the size of the organisation, the initial state of raw materials and components, the extent to which they must be worked upon, and the size of the production run which the firm can expect.

Similar decisions have to be made when deciding on how to run a service. A car-hire firm, an insurance company or a financial institution must organise themselves in such a way that their service is provided to clients as efficiently as possible. Whatever the nature of the undertaking, it is important to plan for the physical means by which the end product or service is to be achieved, where the activities should be located, the timetable for various stages of production and operation and the personnel to be involved at each stage.

The type of production or service to be undertaken will have a significant influence on the eventual choice and design of the premises. Mass production generally requires an extensive single-storey facility while other types of production may allow for a multi-storey building. The premises must be designed to meet production and operational requirements such as allowing for the most efficient use to be made of the technology available, siting certain activities in close proximity to each other, enabling easy movement of materials, components and personnel, and providing the conditions for a healthy and safe working environment.

THE PLANT, MACHINERY, EQUIPMENT, FITTINGS AND VEHICLES

Having identified the most appropriate premises for a business, it is then necessary to plan capital expenditure programmes. The premises may need extensive alterations, renovations and modernising; suitable fixtures and fittings have to be installed. For example, converting shop premises into a fast-food outlet would require extensive fittings for the bar and kitchen, suitable decorations for the customer service area and the installation of specialist cooking and other equipment.

Apart from fixtures and fittings, capital expenditure is often needed for:

- **plant,** equipment and machinery, such as that which might be used in a small engineering components business;

- **computer systems** and other high-tech equipment, which might be employed to control a production process to test the quality of a product or system, to store and access records and to administer a business;

- **motor vehicles** for transporting the work-force, sales force, supplies, components and finished product.

In an existing business, some capital items may already be owned by the company; in a new business start-up, they may have to be purchased for the first time. Whatever the circumstances, it is important for planning purposes to identify the exact capital items required. Fig. 8.7 shows a planning sheet that can be used to record capital requirements.

The entries on the planning sheet may be used to calculate the probable total capital requirements for the

Capital Item	Initial Cost	Date Purchased	Method of Payment	Useful Life
Example: Ford Transit	£14,500	1/1/95	Bank Loan	5 Years

FIGURE 8.7: Planning sheet for capital requirements.

business. These can then be incorporated into the financial plans and companies can begin to investigate appropriate sources of finance. Funds are generally obtained from one or a combination of the following sources:

- **money which belongs to the owners of the business – this is referred to as equity funding, and could include the original investment in the business or retained profits;**

- **loans in the form of mortgages, hire purchase, bank loans, bank overdrafts or credit from suppliers;**

- **other methods of securing capital assets such as leasing, hiring or renting.**

When planning to use these different sources, it is important to hit the right balance between lenders' money and owners' money. The ratio between the two is referred to as **gearing**. It is generally held that the **gearing ratio** should not exceed one, otherwise the business might be considered to be rather insecure.

Any decision to lend the business any money will be based on the lender's assessment of its prospects for success and whether it will be able to pay back the loan from profits. The degree of risk associated with the loan determines how much security is required by the lender. Business or personal assets may be used to cover a loan. Where these are insufficient, it may be possible for a bank to still provide finance by using the government's Small Firms Loan Guarantee Scheme.

MANAGEMENT AND CONTROL SYSTEMS

Even at the planning stage, it is very important to identify the information that will be necessary in order to manage and control the business. Businesses need systems for:

- marketing and sales;

- personnel management;

- finance.

MARKETING AND SALES

- **Plans** must be made to convert sales forecasts into realistic targets. This may be done by closely monitoring the early pattern of sales and making predictions based on these results.

- **A record system** should be designed to record all the orders placed, the goods and services delivered, invoices issued and payments received.

- **Arrangements** should be made to capture market information from the salesforce about who the customers are, what they buy, how often and in what quantities, what they like about the product/service and what related purchases they make.

PERSONNEL MANAGEMENT

- **A personnel record system should be designed.**

- **Job descriptions, person specifications and recruitment advertisements should be drafted.**

- **Plans should be made for suitable induction programmes and training courses.**

- **Consideration should be given to drafting suitable contracts of employment.**

- **Systems for PAYE and National Insurance should be established.**

FINANCE

To monitor the performance of any new business venture, it is important to plan for a suitable bookkeeping and accounting system. This should include the following items.

- **A cash book** to record the business's income and expenditure. This should include VAT and be matched against bank statements when they begin to arrive.

- **A sales day book** may be used to show who owes the business money. This may be devised on the basis of invoices sent out.

- **A purchase day book** may be used to show who the business owes money to. This may be devised on the basis of invoices coming in.

✪ **A petty cash account** may be used to record minor items of expenditure, such as coffee supplies, postage and small items of stationery. This will be supported by a cash float; drawings from the cash float should be covered by a receipt and when the float is replenished a record should be made in the cash book.

Obviously, many of these books can be kept on the computer. Many computerised financial systems allow business performance to be monitored by comparing actual figures against projections. Where significant differences occur, it will be necessary to investigate why this should be the case.

LEGAL CONSTRAINTS

The majority of new business proposals involve original ideas and documents which need protection; premises which need to be safely built and suitably located; workers who have employment rights and who need to be adequately protected in their working environments; and the provision of goods and services which are not faulty, conform to the necessary safety standards and are correctly described. There is legislation relating to all of these areas which needs to be acknowledged by any business about to embark on a new proposal.

LAW RELATING TO ORIGINAL IDEAS AND DOCUMENTS

The **Patents Act 1977** provides protection for any new invention with an industrial application. Essentially, by taking out a patent, it is possible to retain sole control over a particular product, process, mechanical device or type of material.

Applications to the **Patent Office** are normally made through an agent. A patent can be periodically renewed and lasts for a maximum of twenty years. It will be invalidated by idle talk which discloses the invention. It is possible to register designs and logos with the Patent Office.

The **Copyright, Designs and Patents Act 1988** protects owners' – often, but not always, the originators' or authors' – original written material, computer software, films, music and works of art. This protection should be formally acknowledged by the copyright sign (see *Fig. 8.8*). The sign warns people that the work is viewed as intellectual property.

FIGURE 8.8: The copyright symbol.

Consumer Credit Act 1974

1974 CHAPTER 39

An Act to establish for the protection of consumers a new system, administered by the Director General of Fair Trading, of licensing and other control of traders concerned with the provision of credit, or the supply of goods on hire or hire-purchase, and their transactions, in place of the present enactments regulating moneylenders, pawnbrokers and hire-purchase traders and their transactions; and for related matters.
[31st July 1974]

BE IT ENACTED by the Queen's most Excellent Majesty, by and with the advice and consent of the Lords Spiritual and Temporal, and Commons, in this present Parliament assembled, and by the authority of the same, as follows:—

PART I

DIRECTOR GENERAL OF FAIR TRADING

1.—(1) It is the duty of the Director General of Fair Trading ("the Director")— *General functions of Director.*

  (a) to administer the licensing system set up by this Act,

  (b) to exercise the adjudicating functions conferred on him by this Act in relation to the issue, renewal, variation, suspension and revocation of licences, and other matters,

  (c) generally to superintend the working and enforcement of this Act, and regulations made under it, and

  (d) where necessary or expedient, himself to take steps to enforce this Act, and regulations so made.

Consumer Protection Act 1987

1987 CHAPTER 43

An Act to make provision with respect to the liability of persons for damage caused by defective products; to consolidate with amendments the Consumer Safety Act 1978 and the Consumer Safety (Amendment) Act 1986; to make provision with respect to the giving of price indications; to amend Part I of the Health and Safety at Work etc. Act 1974 and sections 31 and 80 of the Explosives Act 1875; to repeal the Trade Descriptions Act 1972 and the Fabrics (Misdescription) Act 1913; and for connected purposes.
[15th May 1987]

BE IT ENACTED by the Queen's most Excellent Majesty, by and with the advice and consent of the Lords Spiritual and Temporal, and Commons, in this present Parliament assembled, and by the authority of the same, as follows:—

PART I

PRODUCT LIABILITY

1.—(1) This Part shall have effect for the purpose of making such provision as is necessary in order to comply with the product liability Directive and shall be construed accordingly. *Purpose and construction of Part I.*

(2) In this Part, except in so far as the context otherwise requires—

"agricultural produce" means any produce of the soil, of stock-farming or of fisheries;

"dependant" and "relative" have the same meaning as they have in, respectively, the Fatal Accidents Act 1976 and the Damages (Scotland) Act 1976; *1976 c. 30. 1976 c. 13.*

"producer", in relation to a product, means—

  (a) the person who manufactured it;

  (b) in the case of a substance which has not been manufactured but has been won or abstracted, the person who won or abstracted it;

Food Act 1984

1984 CHAPTER 30

...ct to consolidate the provisions of the Food and ...gs Acts 1955 to 1982, the Sugar Act 1956, the Food ... Drugs (Milk) Act 1970, section 7(3) and (4) of the ...opean Communities Act 1972, section 198 of the ...cal Government Act 1972 and Part IX of the Local ...vernment (Miscellaneous Provisions) Act 1982, and ...nnected provisions.
[26th June 1984]

BE IT ENACTED by the Queen's most Excellent Majesty, by and with the advice and consent of the Lords Spiritual and Temporal, and Commons, in this present Parliament ...mbled, and by the authority of the same, as follows:—

PART I

FOOD GENERALLY

Composition and labelling of food

...—(1) A person is guilty of an offence who— *Offences as to preparation and sale of injurious foods.*

  (a) adds any substance to food,

  (b) uses any substance as an ingredient in the preparation of food,

  (c) abstracts any constituent from food, or

  (d) subjects food to any other process or treatment,

LAW RELATING TO PREMISES

The **Town and Country Planning Act 1990** affects a business when it is choosing a suitable location and premises. The law requires that a business must apply to the local authority for planning permission before it starts any development. This includes the carrying out of building, engineering, mining or other operations in, on, over or under land, and the making of a material change in the use of any buildings or other lands. Essentially, the Act covers construction, demolition, major alterations and changes in the use of existing premises.

If the local planning authority turns down, or imposes unacceptable conditions on an application, then a business may appeal to the Secretary of State for the Environment. The appeal may be based on written evidence or, in some cases, it may go to a public inquiry.

Businesses that fail to apply for planning permission may be served with an **enforcement notice** by the local planning authority. This effectively requires the business to stop the offending activity. If the matter goes to appeal, then this may be supported by a **stop notice** which effectively stops the development from continuing.

Before acquiring premises, a business should seek professional help in ascertaining whether any restrictive covenants exist on the use of the land. A **deed of restrictive covenant** is an agreement between adjacent or adjoining land owners to limit the use that can be made of a particular piece of land. This agreement can affect the future owners of the land, which is why it is so important that a business organisation should ensure, through its professional advisers, that the right searches have been carried out into possible restrictions on the use to which the land may be put. For example, a restrictive covenant may be placed on land to limit its use to residential, educational or religious purposes.

The **Environmental Protection Act 1990** influences the way in which a business can use its premises or a particular area of land. In so doing, it can determine the suitability of a particular site for the location of that business. The Act sets out:

- ✪ **an integrated system of pollution control;**

- ✪ **tough regulations for the disposal of waste;**

- ✪ **a streamlined system for dealing with such statutory nuisances as air pollution;**

- ✪ **tough penalties for polluting controlled waters;**

- ✪ **public registration of land that may be contaminated.**

In small groups, discuss the implications of the Environmental Protection Act for each of the following business proposals:

(a) **a brewery;**

(b) **an arable farm;**

(c) **a paint manufacturer;**

(d) **a tannery;**

(e) **a pig farm.**

The **Landlord and Tenant Act 1954** determines the relationship between the tenant and landlord in any leasing arrangement. Leasing involves renting a property for a set period. It is particularly useful for businesses that are just starting out because they are unlikely to have sufficient funds to purchase premises outright.

It is very important for a business to seek professional advice from a solicitor before signing a lease. The obligations on the landlord and tenant need to be clearly established. An agreement should set out the responsibilities of the landlord and tenant relating to:

- ✪ **payment of rent;**

- ✪ **periods of review;**

- ✪ **sub-letting the premises;**

- ✪ **repair of the premises;**

- ✪ **insurance;**

- ✪ **the use to which the premises can be put.**

It is also important to establish the remedies that can be used for any breach in the tenant's obligations under the lease.

LAW RELATING TO EMPLOYMENT

FIGURE 8.9: Businesses must not discriminate on grounds of race, sex or religion.

The **Equal Pay Act 1970**, the **Sex Discrimination Act 1975** and the **Race Relations Act 1976** make it illegal for businesses to discriminate against any prospective or existing employee on grounds of race, sex or religion. Therefore, it is essential to check the employment aspects of any business proposal to ensure that it does not fall foul of the law.

Under the **Contracts of Employment Act 1972**, which was incorporated into the **Employment Protection (Consolidation) Act 1978**, a business must offer an employee written terms and conditions of employment within 13 weeks of employment. This statement is not the contract itself but the terms and conditions agreed in the contract. The statement must include:

⊗ **the names of the parties involved;**

⊗ **the date of issue of the statement;**

⊗ **the date of commencement of employment;**

⊗ **the job title;**

⊗ **the rate of remuneration and pay intervals;**

⊗ **the number of hours normally worked under the contract;**

⊗ **the employee's holiday entitlement including public holidays;**

⊗ **sick pay arrangements;**

⊗ **arrangements for pensions and pension schemes;**

⊗ **the employee's notice entitlement;**

⊗ **disciplinary rules that apply to the employee;**

⊗ **grievance procedures;**

⊗ **appeals procedures in matters of discipline and grievance.**

The **Health and Safety at Work Act 1974** is concerned with the health, safety and welfare of people in the work situation, and with the safety of the general public who come into contact with a work situation. The Act creates a framework for a healthy and safe working environment. It puts responsibility on both the employer and the employee to ensure that health and safety at work are both created and maintained. For any new business proposal, these issues have to be addressed.

Under the Act, the employer has a 'general duty' to ensure, as far as is reasonably practicable, the health, safety and welfare at work of all his or her employees. The employee has a 'general duty' to take reasonable care for the health and safety of himself or herself and of other people who may be affected by his or her acts or omissions at work. The employee also has a duty to co-operate with the employer as far as is necessary to meet or comply with any health and safety requirement. Employees must not interfere with or misuse anything provided in the interests of health, safety or welfare.

LAW RELATING TO THE SALE OF GOODS AND SERVICES

The **Trade Descriptions Acts 1968** and **1972** make it an offence for businesses to give inaccurate or false descriptions of the goods they are selling or the services they are offering. For example, it would be unlawful to describe a pair of ladies fashion boots as waterproof if they could not stand up to rain and snow.

The **Unsolicited Goods and Services Acts 1971** and **1975** are designed to control what is known as 'inertia selling', that is sending people goods through the post which they hadn't ordered and relying on their ignorance and/or apathy to extract payment. Fines can be imposed on businesses that demand payments for goods and services which are unsolicited.

The Acts provide that any unsolicited goods may be kept by the recipient without payment after a period of thirty days provided that the recipient gives notice to the sender asking that the goods be collected. Alternatively, the recipient can do nothing – that is, give no notice to the seller – and the goods become his or hers as an unconditional gift after six months.

The **Consumer Credit Act 1974** regulates the way in which a business may offer credit facilities to its credit consumers (or debtors). The Act places a number of obligations on businesses that would have to be allowed for in any business proposal.

- ☻ **Every credit agency must obtain a licence from the Director-General of Fair Trading.**

- ☻ **There is control over advertisements for credit which may be misinterpreted or may be misleading.**

- ☻ **The credit agreement must be properly drawn up and contain terms laid down in regulations. For example, the agreement should state the debtor's principal rights and duties.**

- ☻ **The credit arrangement must show the APR (the annual percentage rate of interest) which will allow consumers to make an accurate comparison between different offers.**

- ☻ **The debtor is entitled to a copy of the agreement at the time of the contract, and to a second copy within seven days if the agreement is accepted at a later date.**

The **Sale of Goods Acts 1979** and **1994** and the **Supply of Goods and Services Act 1982** clearly indicate the responsibility of any business in selling goods and services. A legal contract exists between the buyers and sellers of goods or services. Once the offer to buy goods has been accepted, then the seller and not the manufacturer has to deal with any complaint.

The Acts lay down three basic conditions regarding the quality of goods and services that a business may sell. These concern **quality**, **product description** and **fitness for purpose**.

- ☻ **Merchantable quality:** goods must be as fit for the purpose or purposes for which goods of that kind are commonly bought as it is reasonable to expect having regard to the description applied to them. For example, a 'new' car should not have a damaged and dented door panel.

- ☻ **Correspondence with description:** nearly every sale will involve some kind of description; if the buyer makes a purchase relying upon description, then the goods must be as described. If, however, the goods do not correspond with description then there is a breach of implied condition, and the goods can be rejected by the buyer. For example, a belt described as leather must be made out of leather and not plastic.

- ☻ **Fitness for purpose:** this right covers any sales where the buyer clearly informs the seller of the particular purpose for which he or she requires the goods. If the seller is not confident that the goods will meet the buyer's requirements, he or she must make it clear that the buyer cannot rely upon the seller's skill or judgement. For example, if the sole comes off a pair of shoes then this suggests that they are not fit for the purpose of being footwear.

A business cannot attempt to remove any of these rights by getting customers to sign a guarantee which offers less protection than is already available under the law.

The **Food Act 1984** and the **Food Safety Act 1990** lay down regulations governing the production, distribution and sale of food. Local authority environmental health officers enforce these regulations. Criminal prosecution may result if, for example, food or drink is being sold which is felt to be unfit for human consumption, or if the content of any food has been wrongly described or claims have been made about the nutritional value of food which are misleading.

The **Weights and Measures Act 1985** provides detailed rules regarding the weighing and measurement of goods. For example, in the case of prepacked meat or cheese, the weight must be accurately marked on the packet. Breaches of rules can result in prosecution.

The **Consumer Protection Act 1987** makes it a criminal offence to supply any consumer goods which do not meet with general safety requirements. Businesses have a general duty to trade safely. Products like furniture (with regard to fire hazards) electrical appliances, toys and babies' dummies must be manufactured to specified standards.

ACTIVITY

Consider the following business scenarios. Identify the major piece(s) of legislation that a business would need to take into account in each case.

(a) **A car manufacturer bringing out a revolutionary, lightweight, electrical car.**

(b) **Plans to turn redundant college buildings into a supermarket with an adjoining petrol station.**

(c) **Insuring rented premises against fire.**

(d) **Advertising for a hotel receptionist.**

(e) **Installing a new computerised machine in a clothing factory.**

(f) **Advertising second-hand cars on a garage forecourt with special finance arrangements attached to them.**

(g) **Operating a mobile sandwich bar.**

INSURANCE

Business planning is about trying to anticipate and forecast the future; however, it is not always possible to cover every eventuality, such as fire or accident causing injury to a customer or employee in the work place. Therefore, it is necessary to protect the business by taking out adequate insurance.

It is sensible for any new or existing business, at the stage of putting a new business proposal together, to contact a number of insurance brokers to ask for their impartial advice. Their services are normally free and the broker carries professional indemnity insurance which means that the business can sue if it suffers as a result of the broker's negligence.

At its simplest, any business would require insurance cover for the following eventualities.

✪ **To protect premises** which the business owns against fire, lightning, explosion, storm, tempest and flood. In the case of leasehold premises, it is usual for the landlord to insure them.

✪ **To cover plant,** machinery, computer systems and stock against fire, lightning, explosion, storm, tempest, flood, theft and accidental damage.

✪ **Protection against loss of profits** following an interruption to business, usually for interruptions caused by the risks covered in the premises insurance as well as those resulting from a supplier who has caused a breakdown in business.

○ **To cover the use of motor vehicles** for business purposes. This type of insurance is also compulsory.

○ **To cover specialist risks** such as protection against loss of licence, computer breakdown, embezzlement and fraud, and professional negligence.

○ **To cover the business against its public liability** to third parties for causing death, personal injury or damage to their property. This includes risks associated with the ownership, occupation or management of premises, such as causing pollution and causing injury to, or damage to the property of, visitors. Public liability insurance also covers risks arising from the activities of employees and agents which may cause death, bodily injury or damage to property. In this case, the employer is said to have a 'vicarious liability' for their actions.

○ **To cover the business against loss**, damage or bodily injury arising **from selling a defective product**. This product liability insurance covers the business for the obligations it has under the Consumer Protection Act 1987, Sale of Goods Acts 1979 and 1994 or under the common rules of negligence.

○ **To cover the business against its liability towards its employees** for any bodily injury or disease that they might sustain arising out of their employment. Employer's liability insurance is compulsory, but the employee has to prove that the injury was due to negligence by the employer, or breach of the Health and Safety at Work Act, or personal negligence of a fellow employee.

ACTIVITY

You are considering setting up as a general builder carrying out renovation work, alterations and small extensions. You are to operate from a small builder's yard where you can store equipment and materials and house one part-time office worker. You will have three other employees with bricklaying, carpentry and labouring skills.

1 Identify the different risks you will need to insure against.

2 Contact a number of insurance companies and identify suitable policies and the approximate cost.

A PLAN OF ACTION

An important part of the planning process involves drawing up a plan of action to cover the major decisions associated with the business proposal. Estimates should be made of the time needed for the implementation of each decision. These should then be ordered in a logical sequence. For example, a business must advertise for, select, interview, appoint, induct and train its staff before it can commence trading.

By adopting this logical analytical approach, decisions should be taken at the right time and in the right order. To help with this process information may be presented on a simple **critical path analysis chart** (see *Fig. 8.10*).

The vertical key decision lines reflect the activities which can all be started at the same time. The amount of time needed for the completion of each activity is shown as a horizontal line. Obviously, the activity with the longest horizontal line determines when it is possible to move on to the next key decision vertical line. By combining these longest horizontal lines, it is possible to identify the critical path, that is the total length of time that it will take to complete in a logical fashion the implementation of the business proposal. By planning in this way, it is possible to draw up a timetable for action and in so doing to improve decision-making by concentrating the energies of the business on the most important areas.

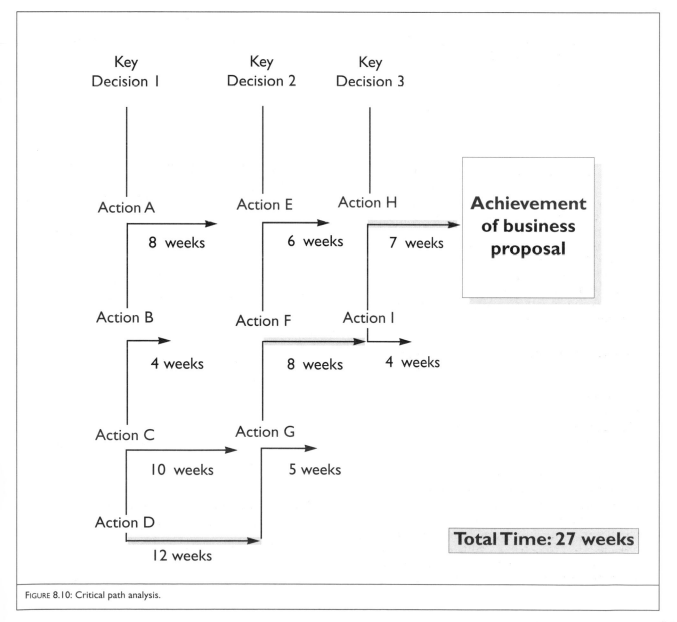

FIGURE 8.10: Critical path analysis.

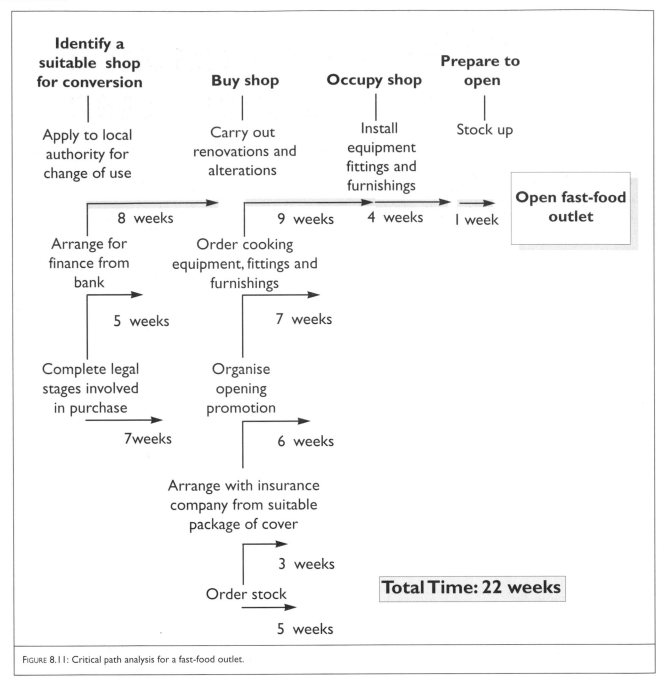

Identify a suitable shop for conversion

Apply to local authority for change of use

8 weeks

Arrange for finance from bank

5 weeks

Complete legal stages involved in purchase

7 weeks

Buy shop

Carry out renovations and alterations

9 weeks

Order cooking equipment, fittings and furnishings

7 weeks

Organise opening promotion

6 weeks

Arrange with insurance company from suitable package of cover

3 weeks

Order stock

5 weeks

Occupy shop

Install equipment fittings and furnishings

4 weeks

Prepare to open

Stock up

1 week

Open fast-food outlet

Total Time: 22 weeks

FIGURE 8.11: Critical path analysis for a fast-food outlet.

Fig. 8.11 shows the critical path of activities associated with the opening of a fast-food outlet. It can be seen that there are four key decisions; none can be made until the previous one has been completed. For example, the shop cannot be purchased until finance has been applied for, the legal points resolved and the change of use determined. Similarly, the shop cannot be occupied until the renovations and alterations have been completed. The horizontal lines represent a series of paths of time towards the ultimate goal of opening the fast-food outlet. The total time needed to implement the plan and the critical path is determined by the longest line in each case. Data can be taken from the chart to draw up a timetable for action with target dates.

Now go on to element 2. At the end of element 2, you will be set a portfolio assignment that covers material in elements 1 and 2 and incorporates all the evidence indicators needed for these two elements.

Produce and present a business plan

THE VALUE AND PURPOSE OF BUSINESS PLANNING

Business planning involves assembling, evaluating, analysing and presenting relevant information in order to improve decision making and the future performance of new and existing businesses.

During the 1980s, an average of half a million businesses started up each year. They ranged from builders to florists, software specialists to garden centres, recording studios to haulage firms. Generally, 40 per cent failed within the first three years of operation. In many cases, the reason for failure was poor initial planning. It is equally important to plan very carefully when expanding or changing the direction of an established business.

A well-researched business plan acts as a kind of map, which obviously improves the chances of the business reaching its desired destination.

A well-written business plan has particular value for the decision making of three groups. The investors in the business, together with the people and organisations who lend money to the business, are particularly interested in looking at issues of profitability and cash flow. The people who run and manage the business on a day-to-day basis need to be assured of its financial viability. They will want to monitor its overall performance in terms of sales, costs, turnover and profits.

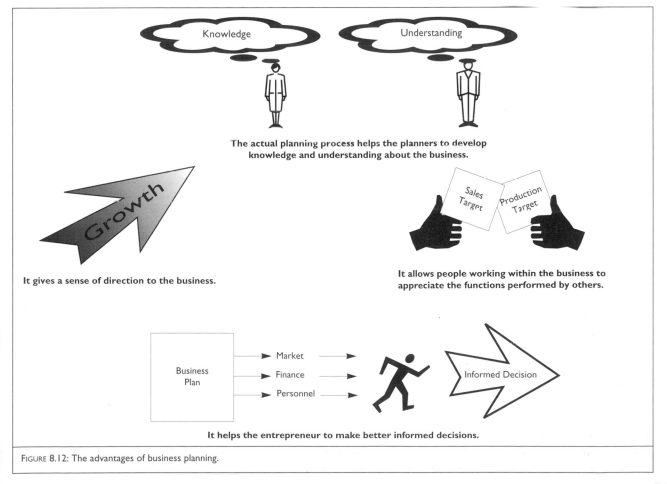

FIGURE 8.12: The advantages of business planning.

THE STRUCTURE OF A BUSINESS PLAN

Having assembled and evaluated the information needed to assess the feasibility and viability of a business proposal, it is necessary to present it as a **formal business plan**. This could be presented to a bank or other source of finance describing what the business intends to do and explaining what its costs will be, what it expects to earn, how it will repay money and how soon it will make a profit.

There is no set format and structure for a business plan; it varies according to the type of business. However, each of the major commercial banks suggest a structure for a business plan in their information packs for small businesses, and these tend to have a standard format. All have the following in common:

⊗ **a description of the business and its objectives;**

⊗ **an outline marketing plan;**

⊗ **a production plan;**

⊗ **an outline of the resources needed;**

⊗ **the finances of the business.**

These five parts need to be presented and communicated in a very professional and persuasive manner as the objective of the plan is ultimately to sell the business idea. In the financial section, banks expect to see a start-up balance sheet, projected profit and loss, a cash-flow forecast and a projected balance sheet. Generally, a number of copies of the plan are required, which are often sent out in advance of an interview for finance.

In this element, we concentrate on the five parts of the plan. We use as reference material the standard formats put forward by Barclays Bank and the National Westminster Bank.

Business plan form

Use this form to help you structure your own business plan. The various headings may well be relevant to your business, but don't worry if they're not. Use the form to suit your business rather than planning your business to suit the form.

Details of the Business

Name of business _____

Business address _____

_____

Format (limited company, sole trader etc.) _____

Type of business _____

Telephone _____

Date business began (if you have already started trading) _____

Business activities _____

_____

FIGURE 8.13: Business plan form.
Source: Barclays Bank.

Key Staff

Name, age and qualifications	Position	Date joined	Salary

Please also attach full details on separate sheets of your staff's past experience, job responsibilities and general health

Number of employees (including directors or partners) _____

FIGURE 8.14: Details of key staff.
Source: NatWest Bank.

A DESCRIPTION OF THE BUSINESS AND ITS OBJECTIVES

INTRODUCTION

The opening pages of the business plan are crucial. They must attract and hold the attention of the reader (who could be providing the finance) and make the rest of the plan very accessible. This can be achieved by using clear and simple language, highlighting the opportunities associated with the business proposal and providing a clear route through the plan. Consequently it is good practice to include:

- **the name and address of the business;**

- **an executive summary which clearly and briefly describes the business proposal;**

- **a clear list of the contents showing the five parts of the plan, appropriate subheadings and any supporting appendices.**

The executive summary should highlight the type of venture, outline the features of the product or service, indicate the business environmental trends which have helped to create the market opportunity, stress the uniqueness of the venture, describe the process involved in producing the product and getting it to the market, introduce the people involved in the venture and list their management expertise and experience, state the amount of money invested in the business to date and how much additional funding is required, and forecast the probable returns and prospects for the business.

DETAILS OF THE BUSINESS

This section provides the background information necessary for the records of the bank or any other potential source of finance. Typically, it would cover the details shown in *Fig. 8.13*.

When completing the section on business activities it is very important to use simple terms which are intelligible to an outside reader who may not be familiar with the business, or its associated jargon and technical terms. It is also important to cover any applications or uses of the product and/or service which are not apparent to the reader.

BUSINESS OBJECTIVES

The organisation's mission statement should be supported by a declaration of both its general and more specific objectives and an indication of the major tasks on which it needs to concentrate. In all cases, it is appropriate to include a statement of short-term objectives (up to twelve months); and then, where a business can look more to the future, it may include medium term (one to three years) or long-term (up to five years) objectives. For very small businesses, especially sole traders, it is often appropriate to include both personal and organisational objectives.

The objectives need to be written in positive and confident terms and should convey a sense of direction for the business. They need to be clearly and concisely expressed and should reflect what is realistic and achievable.

KEY STAFF

Details should be given of the background and experience of the main people responsible for helping the organisation to achieve its objectives. This can either be done on a standard form (see *Fig. 8.14*) or, if more details are required, then full CVs (curriculum vitae) may be included in the appendices.

AN OUTLINE MARKETING PLAN

This part of the business plan is very important as it helps to demonstrate to a bank or other source of finance that the organisation has a good understanding of the market, that it is possible to penetrate it and that there is a demand for the product or service. It shows that the organisation is in control of the crucial success factors that will enable it to enter the market, obtain a niche, maintain a market share and reach its sales goals and financial targets.

The evidence from the analysis of the business environmental trends and from the desk and field market research should provide sufficient market information to draft an outline plan. This should cover:

- **the features of the product or service, the proposed price and unique selling points;**

- **the features, size and potential of the market, where it is located, who the customers are, and whether it is growing, static or in decline;**

- **the competitors and their prices, strengths and weaknesses;**

- **the proposed marketing mix of product, place, promotion and price and how it will provide a strategic marketing advantage;**

- **brief details of the size of the marketing budget;**

- **a sales forecast and estimate of revenue for the first year (see *Fig. 8.5*);**

- **an indication of the level of sales necessary for the business to break even.**

To add credence to the outline marketing plan, reference should be made to the research methods that have been employed to gather the market information.

PRODUCTION PLAN

Potential financial backers will be most interested in this section as it is where most business plans tend to fall short and, ultimately, it accounts for most business failures.

It is important to demonstrate that the organisation has a very sound understanding of the manufacturing or service process and operation. In particular, the plan should show that adequate consideration has been given to legal and insurance issues relating to the organisation's operations, and to responsibilities towards its workforce and consumers.

The plan should be presented under the following subheadings:

- **premises and location;**

- **plant, machinery, equipment and vehicles;**

- **manufacturing or service process and operation;**

- **labour requirements.**

PREMISES AND LOCATION

This should cover:

- **a description of the location** or proposed location including a review of the other businesses in the area, communication links, proximity to markets, availability of raw materials, suitability of local labour, special site requirements, local environmental requirements and relevant local licenses;

- **details of the premises** selected showing costs, valuation, proposed renovations or alterations, insurance arrangements, and whether the premises are freehold or leasehold.

Suitable maps, photographs and details from the estate agents may be used for illustration and/or included in the appendices.

PLANT, MACHINERY, EQUIPMENT AND VEHICLES

This should cover:

- **all capital items (see *Fig. 8.7*) with details of costs, method of payment and useful life;**

- **the insurance, maintenance and replacement requirements of the capital items;**

- **an indication of any advantages of the capital items over those used by similar businesses;**

- **the long-term plans for capital items in the future.**

MANUFACTURING/SERVICE PROCESS AND OPERATION

This should cover:

✪ **a description of the methods and processes** involved, including an indication of what will be done internally, what will be subcontracted and how quality will be monitored and controlled;

✪ **a description of the raw materials** and/or components required, who will supply them and on what terms and conditions;

✪ **a sketch of the layout** of the manufacturing or service unit, showing the overall size of the facility needed, the positioning of equipment, and the path of materials and finished goods.

LABOUR REQUIREMENTS

This should cover:

✪ **a description of the major tasks that need to be carried out;**

✪ **summary job descriptions for key positions;**

✪ **details of the basis on which people are to be employed, that is, full-time, part-time, consultancy or casual;**

✪ **a statement of the terms and conditions of employment to show that the Employment Protection (Consolidation) Act 1978 has been complied with;**

✪ **a description of how recruitment, selection, induction and training are to be carried out;**

✪ **an indication as to how wages and salaries compare with other companies;**

✪ **a brief description of the arrangements for PAYE, National Insurance and pensions;**

✪ **a statement on health and safety issues and insurance.**

AN OUTLINE OF THE RESOURCES NEEDED

The information relating to resource needs will have been collected and analysed on planning sheets like *Fig. 8.7* (on page 507). This has to be presented in the business plan so that it is clear to the prospective financial backer how much finance is required, what proportion is to be invested by the owner and what assets are available for security. The following headings may be used:

✪ **resource needs** – shown as a list of capital items, individually and totally costed;

✪ **finance required** – shown as a list of those capital items which have been financed from various sources and the amounts involved in each case;

✪ **own financial resources** – shown as the difference between the resource needs and the finance required;

✪ **collateral** – shown as a list of the assets available for security and their value.

Fig. 8.15 shows an example of how this information is presented in a business plan for Build-it Limited, which is a small building firm specialising in renovations, alterations and extensions.

THE FINANCES OF THE BUSINESS

This part of the business plan will be very carefully looked at by potential investors. (In some cases, they may actually decide to undertake an independent financial analysis of the venture.) Therefore, it must be thorough and convincing and any projections should be very realistic. Where it is necessary to make any assumptions, they should be explained and accompanied by a statement indicating why they are felt to be valid and what alternatives may be followed if they are not achieved.

Many of the techniques which are needed for the presentation and analysis of the financial data are covered in units 6 and 7.

Four sets of financial data and forecasts should be produced. First, a **start-up balance sheet**, which provides a picture of the business when it first starts trading. Second, a **profit and loss forecast** which may be presented on the standard form (see *Fig. 8.16*). This may also be used for calculating the breakeven level of sales by using the formula:

$$\frac{\text{total overhead}}{\text{gross profit margin}} \times 100 = \text{breakeven sales level}$$

Third, a **cash-flow forecast** is needed. Again, this can be presented as a standard form (see *Fig. 8.17*). This is particularly important because managing cash badly is one of the main reasons for business failure. By monitoring cash flow properly a business is able to identify when there may be a shortage, recognise when extra cash may be made and used, and ensure that there is sufficient cash to cover any necessary capital expense.

BUILD-IT LIMITED – BUSINESS PLAN

An outline of the resources needed

a) Resource Needs

Capital Item	Cost (£)
Builder's yard and mobile building	£75,000
Plant and equipment	£60,000
Office computer and other equipment	£15,000
Vehicles (lorry plus van)	£25,000
Materials and working capital	£20,000
Total	**£195,000**

b) Finance Required

Capital Item	Source of Finance and Amount	
Yard and building (freehold)	Bank mortgage	£40,000
Plant and equipment	Bank loan	£30,000
Materials and working capital	Bank overdraft	£20,000
	Total	**£90,000**

c) Own Financial Resources

£105,000

d) Collateral

Assets	Value (£)
Yard and building (freehold)	£80,000 (value at 1/1/90)
Other fixed items	£100,000 (at cost)
Total	**£180,000**

FIGURE 8.15: Build-it Limited – business plan.

The flow of cash will obviously be influenced by the period of credit the organisation gives its customers or takes from its suppliers. In both cases, these need to be set at a realistic level. As VAT is a cash settlement, it needs to be shown in the cash flow forecast, but not in the profit and loss because it is not treated as a charge against either.

Fourth, a **projected balance sheet** for the end of twelve months is needed. This will indicate the anticipated growth and development of the business.

These four sets of financial calculations and presentations will make it possible to monitor and, ultimately, to control business performance. By continually comparing the actual figures against the budgeted figures, it should be possible to spot difficulties early on and to put them right.

APPENDICES

We have already mentioned some material which might usefully go in appendices. In addition, it would also be advisable to include a detailed 'plan of action'. This should cover the major stages of the implementation of the business plan. It will allow the reader to see at a glance the logical order in which tasks are to be carried out and the amount of time involved in each case.

Profit & Loss Forecast

Year beginning _____

BARCLAYS

	Month		Month		Month		Month		Month		Month		Sub totals	
	Budget	Actual	Budget	Actual	Budget	Actual	Budget	Actual	Budget	Actual	Budget	Actual	Budget	Actual
Sales (a)														
Less: Direct Costs														
Cost of Materials														
Wages														
Gross Profit (b)														
Gross Profit Margin (% x 100%)														
Overheads														
Salaries														
Rent/Rates/Water														
Insurance														
Repairs/Renewals														
Heat/Light/Power														
Postages														
Printing/Stationery														
Transport														
Telephone														
Professional Fees														
Interest Charges														
Other														
Other														
Total Overheads (c)														
Trading Profit (b) – (c)														
Less: Depreciation														
Net Profit Before Tax														

*These headings may vary according to the needs of your business. You may therefore need to amend any that are not applicable.

PTO

FIGURE 8.16: Profit and loss forecast.
Source: Barclays Bank.

Cashflow Forecast

Year beginning _____

*	Month		Month		Month		Month		Month		Month		Sub totals	
	Budget	Actual	Budget	Actual	Budget	Actual	Budget	Actual	Budget	Actual	Budget	Actual	Budget	Actual
Receipts														
Cash Sales														
Cash from Debtors														
Capital Introduced														
Total Receipts (a)														
Payments														
Payments to Creditors														
Salaries/Wages														
Rent/Rates/Water														
Insurance														
Repairs/Renewals														
Heat/Light/Power														
Postages														
Printing/Stationery														
Transport														
Telephone														
Professional Fees														
Capital Payments														
Interest Charges														
Other														
VAT payable (refund)														
Total Payments (b)														
Net Cashflow (a-b)														
Opening Bank Balance														
Closing Bank Balance														

*These headings may vary according to the needs of your business. You may therefore need to amend any that are not applicable.

PTO

FIGURE 8.17: Cash-flow forecast.
Source: Barclays Bank.

PORTFOLIO ASSIGNMENT

AN ENTERPRISING START

Imagine you have completed your Advanced Business GNVQ and you have recently inherited £40,000. You view this as an opportunity to launch your own business venture, either individually or with one other person. Select a business idea from this list:

- a fast-food outlet;
- home catering;
- a market stall;
- a small shop;
- business services;
- building services;
- garden services;
- cleaning services;
- manufacture of craft/engineering products;
- a disco;
- a band.

1 Carry out preparatory work on your idea, recording your activities in a diary. Prepare detailed notes on:

- the organisation's mission and objectives;
- the choice of legal form;
- the business environmental trends which support your business venture;
- the findings from desk and field research regarding the target market, possible competition, potential sales and revenue;
- a suitable marketing strategy;
- the reasons for choice of premises and where they are located;

- a planning sheet for the major capital items;
- sources of finance;
- management and control systems for marketing, personnel and finance;
- legal issues regarding the protection of ideas, premises, employing people and the consumer;
- insurance issues;
- a plan of action.

2 Discuss your ideas with a bank manager, or accountant, or solicitor, or representative from the TEC, a local enterprise agency, the Prince's Trust or Livewire. (This should be arranged or simulated by your school/college.) In the light of the discussion, make any necessary amendments or, where it has been suggested, conduct further research.

3 Write a full business plan which is to be sent to a bank in advance of an interview for finance. Prepare the plan on a computer. Your plan should have five sections:

- a description of the business and its objectives;
- an outline marketing plan;
- a production plan;
- an outline of the resources needed;
- the finances of the business.

4 Attend an interview with a bank manager to support your request for finance. You will be required to explain your business idea, answer questions about the plan and justify your request for finance. (The interview should be arranged or simulated by your school/college.)

5 Assume that your business has been trading for a year and has proved to be a great success. In order to inspire other budding young entrepreneurs, you are invited to give a talk to the local chamber of commerce to explain the reasons for your success and, in particular, to stress the advantages of detailed planning. Prepare a set of briefing notes for your talk and make the presentation in front of your business studies group.

Plan for employment or self-employment

THE NEED TO WORK

The majority of adult members of society need to work. At a very basic level people need the opportunity to find employment, so that they can produce sufficient to meet their own material needs and to support those who are dependent upon them, such as their families, the elderly and the sick.

These two reasons effectively cover what can be called a person's physiological and safety needs. In *Motivation and Personality*, Abraham Maslow categorised people's different needs. Maslow felt that people's needs may be ordered in a hierarchy (see *Fig. 8.18*).

FIGURE 8.18: Maslow's hierarchy of needs.
Source: *Motivation and Personality*, Abraham Maslow.

Most people have to achieve their physiological and safety needs before they can consider anything else from a job. Social needs and self-esteem stem from those things which people feel they need to do in terms of their job. For example, they may feel that they need to work with others, receive friendship, have contact with other people

and be recognised for what they do through receiving promotion and some sort of status. Having satisfied all of these needs, it may then be possible for a person to strive for self-actualisation, that is to be the kind of person they want within the job. This could include being independent, taking risks, accepting a challenge, helping society or being creative.

FACTORS INFLUENCING THE AVAILABILITY OF WORK

Unfortunately, in the modern world it is not always possible for people to find work; and, even where it is available, it may not allow people to satisfy the higher order needs identified by Maslow. The availability of work depends upon the level of activity in the economy. The type of work available depends upon the stage of technological development.

In recent years, a number of factors have had, and will continue to have, a direct impact upon the number of jobs that are available.

DEINDUSTRIALISATION

During the past three decades, the UK economy has experienced a period of deindustrialisation. This has involved a decline in the relative importance of the manufacturing sector in terms of both output and employment opportunities. Much of the decline in manufacturing has been due to the lack of competitiveness of UK goods in relation to foreign goods, both at home and abroad. Reasons for this decline include relatively high interest and exchange rates, poor quality products, a failure to invest in research and development and new productive ideas, and 'footloose' multinationals moving their production out of the UK and taking advantage of the lower labour costs in newly industrialising countries.

This decline in manufacturing has been accompanied by a corresponding growth in the service sector, especially in the banking, finance, insurance, catering, travel, leisure, tourism and retailing sectors.

FIGURE 8.19: New markets in Eastern Europe.

THE EXPANSION OF MARKETS ABROAD

In the new era of **glasnost** (openness) and **perestroika** (reconstruction), trade between Eastern and Western Europe has taken on a new significance and direction. Western companies wanting to sell products or technology to Eastern Europe as it rapidly embraces capitalism, have never felt the climate to be so favourable; the potential market is vast. Companies taking advantage of these changes will be creating more job opportunities.

A similar growth in opportunities is associated with the opening up of the single market in Europe and the increase of European membership to fifteen countries. This will provide more opportunities for British firms to trade abroad with a resultant improvement in job prospects.

TECHNOLOGICAL DEVELOPMENTS

Since the Second World War, jobs have been changed by developments in technologies. There is greater automation, computerisation and use of robotics. The rate of technological change has been accelerated in recent years by the application and development of information technology. As a result, workers are increasingly involved in handling information about operations rather than having to carry out the operations themselves.

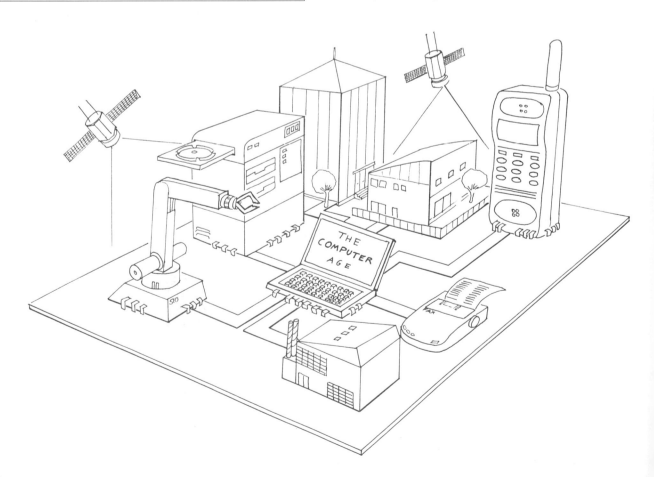

The new technologies associated with new products or developments such as colour televisions, space travel, antibodies, communication satellites, video recorders and computer disks have all created new job opportunities. For example, the development of colour television has created jobs in research, production, retailing, servicing and the making of programmes.

In the modern labour market, people need to try and predict the areas where technological developments will create jobs in the future.

ACTIVITY

Identify where employment might have been created as a result of the development of the new technologies associated with:

(a) mobile phones;

(b) CD-i (interactive CD–ROM).

TRENDS IN THE LABOUR MARKET

The three factors identified above – deindustrialisation, expansion abroad and new technology – have obviously influenced the recent trends in the labour market. By looking at these trends, it is possible to build up a picture of what is likely to happen in the future and where jobs will be available.

Due to the recession, the number of people with jobs in Great Britain fell by some two million between June 1990 and March 1993 to 24.2 million. However, it is projected that the number of people with jobs will grow to over 26 million by the turn of the century.

	per cent
Corporate Managers and Administrators	+17
Managers/Proprietors in Agriculture and Services	+11
Science and Engineering Professionals	+18
Health Professionals	+16
Teaching Professionals	+4
Other Professional Occupations	+42
Science and Engineering Associated Professionals	+10
Health Associate Professionals	+2
Other Associate Professionals	+25
Clerical Occupations	−3
Secretarial Occupations	−2
Skilled Construction Trades	+11
Skilled Engineering Trades	−14
Other Skilled Trades	1
Protective Service Occupations	+7
Personal Services Occupations	+28
Buyers, Brokers and Sales Representatives	+4
Other Sales Occupations	+7
Industrial Plant and Machine Operatives	0
Drivers and Mobile Machine Operators	0
Other Occupations in Agriculture	−13
Other Elementary Occupations	−10
All Occupations	**+7**

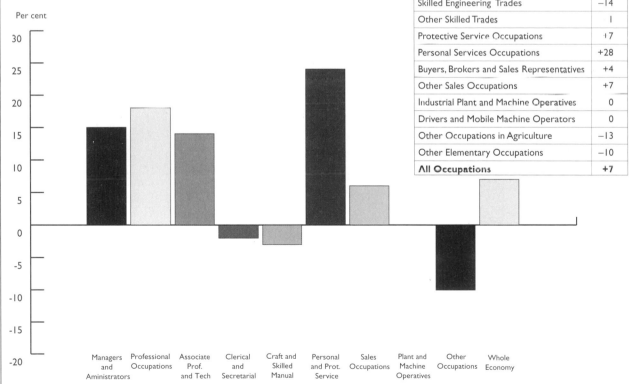

FIGURE 8.20: Change in employment by occupation.
Source: Institute for Employment Research, University of Warwick.

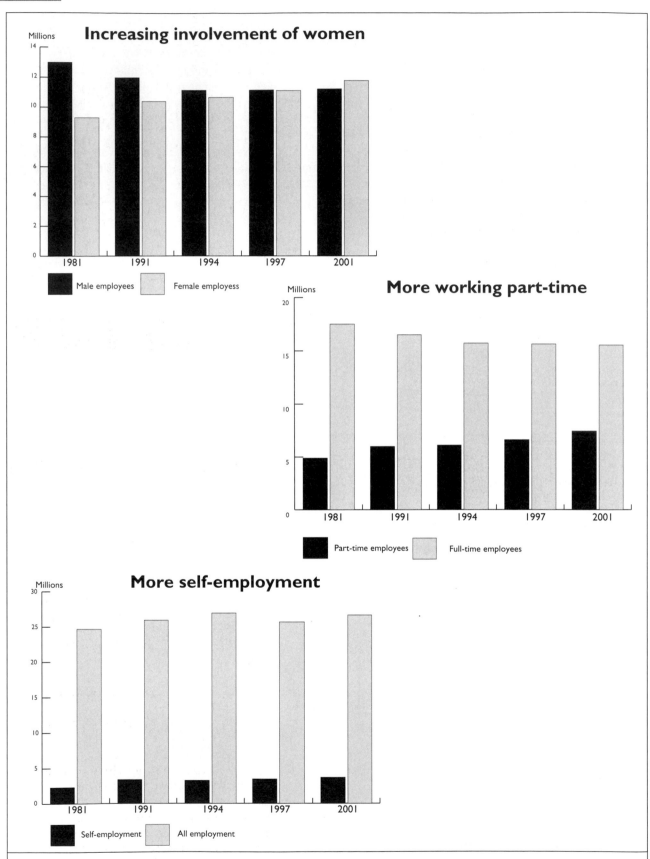

FIGURE 8.21: Labour market trends.
Source: Institute for Employment Research, University of Warwick.

Fig. 8.20 shows that most of the growth in employment will be in higher level jobs with extra managerial and professional opportunities. There will also be a decline in basic secretarial and clerical work. It is forecast that jobs will increase in the service sector and there will be more jobs in sales. There will be more skilled jobs in construction, but fewer in engineering. The number of operative jobs in manufacturing will remain stable, but there will be a decline in jobs in the primary industries.

Fig. 8.21 demonstrates how, since 1981, there has been a significant increase in the involvement of women in the workforce, more part-time employment opportunities and a larger number of people working for themselves. All these increases are projected to continue to the year 2001.

During the past decade, these changes have been accompanied by a shift towards various forms of flexible working. In the early 1990s, some 10 per cent of employers were using home-based workers and 5 per cent were employing teleworkers. It is likely that these proportions will increase during the decade.

These trends demonstrate that employment opportunities are constantly shifting. It is, therefore, necessary for people within the workforce to try and anticipate the next movement.

ACTIVITY

Study the list of jobs below. Which, in your judgement, are likely to be required in the future? Rank the jobs in order, from the most needed to unlikely to be needed. Comment on your ranking.

- **Social worker**
- **Secretary**
- **Retail manager**
- **Machine operator**
- **Garage mechanic**
- **Lorry driver**
- **Computer programmer**

- **Leisure centre manager**
- **Hotel receptionist**
- **TV aerial installer**
- **Nurse**
- **Insurance clerk**
- **Bank manager**

TYPES OF EMPLOYMENT

This section considers the different types of employment. As *Fig. 8.22* shows, employment can be viewed in a variety of categories and contexts.

PAID WORK FOR OTHERS

There are many advantages of working for someone else. A full-time employee is actually entitled to many benefits.

- **Within thirteen weeks of starting employment, an employee receives a written statement of the terms and conditions of employment, including details of pay, sick pay, hours, holiday entitlement, pension arrangements, period of notice, disciplinary rules, grievance procedures and appeals procedure.**

- **Employees receive an itemised pay slip showing gross wages and any deductions for tax, National Insurance, pension and final net pay.**

- **Employees should have a healthy and safe working environment.**

- **Where a woman has worked for an employer for more than two years, she is entitled to maternity leave and the right to return to the job three months after giving birth.**

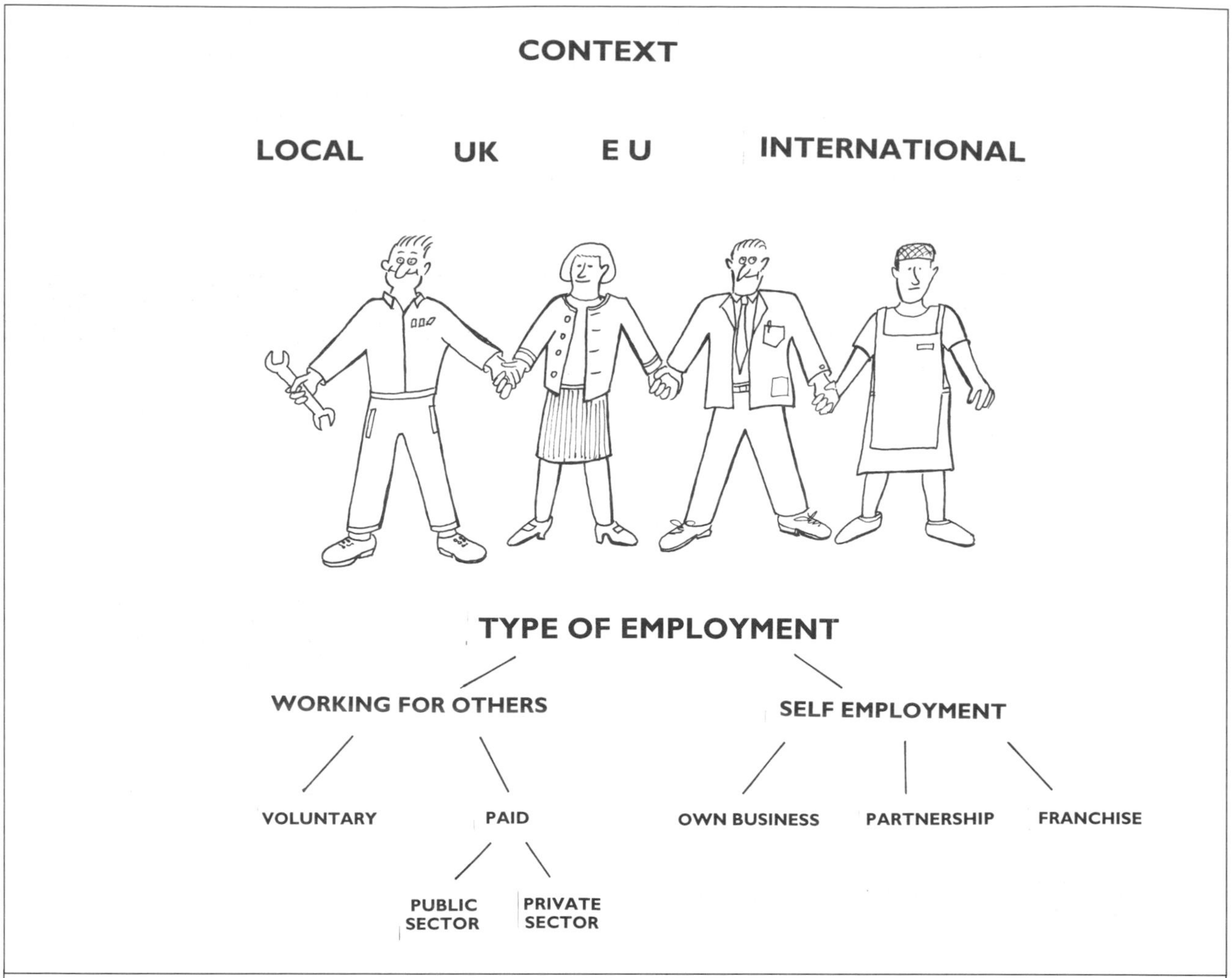

FIGURE 8.22: Types of employment.

The diagram shows:

CONTEXT

LOCAL   UK   E U   INTERNATIONAL

TYPE OF EMPLOYMENT

WORKING FOR OTHERS → VOLUNTARY, PAID (PUBLIC SECTOR, PRIVATE SECTOR)

SELF EMPLOYMENT → OWN BUSINESS, PARTNERSHIP, FRANCHISE

- ❂ **Where an employee has worked for the same employer for more than two years, he or she is entitled to a redundancy payment.**

- ❂ **Where employees have worked for the same employer for more than two years, he or she is entitled to compensation for unfair dismissal providing the claim is proven.**

- ❂ **Depending upon the length of time an employee has been with an employer, he or she is entitled to a period of notice.**

- ❂ **Employees should have the right to join a trade union.**

- ❂ **Employees receive equal pay regardless of sex or race.**

There are certain differences between the type of paid work in the two main sectors of the economy, the public sector and the private sector.

In the **public sector**, which is that part of the economic system controlled by the government, job opportunities may arise in both business and administrative organisations.

The nationalised industries, such as British Rail and the Post Office, were taken under public control for economic, organisational, strategic and social reasons. However, working for the nationalised industries is now not dissimilar to working for any other business organisation. Their objectives have largely been brought into line with the private sector in preparation for privatisation.

People who are employed in the central government services are called **civil servants**. They are responsible for administering government activities such as defence, overseas aid, support for agriculture, fisheries, food and forestry policy, support for trade and industry, the employment services, the system of law and order, the health policy, the social security system, and the Scottish, Welsh and Northern Ireland offices.

In **local government**, employees run and administer services such as housing, education, planning, transport, recreation, the arts, personal social services, environmental services, the police and the fire brigade.

In general, the major motivation for people working in the public sector is to **maximise social welfare** by providing an efficient service within a fixed budget.

In the **private sector**, that part of the economic system which is largely privately owned and independent of government control, job opportunities arise in large, medium and small-scale business organisations in the primary, secondary and tertiary sectors.

Private sector business organisations employ people in jobs which make use of mechanical, practical, artistic, literary, verbal, computational, administrative, managerial, advisory, entrepreneurial and scientific skills. The private sector covers areas as diverse as finance, commerce, the media, retailing, leisure, hotels and catering, mining, engineering, manufacturing, construction, transport, travel, science, the law, personal services and domestic services.

In general, the major motivation for people working in the private sector is to **maximise profits** for the business employer.

VOLUNTARY WORK

Over 40 per cent of adults in the UK undertake some form of voluntary work. They are generally employed by a voluntary agency. The National Council for Voluntary Organisations defines a voluntary agency as 'a self-governing body of people who have joined together voluntarily to take action for the betterment of the community'. Examples include the National Society for the Prevention of Cruelty to Children (NSPCC), Shelter and the Royal National Institute for the Blind (RNIB).

Voluntary organisations are not run for commercial gain. They are funded from voluntary contributions and, in some cases, they may receive some sort of grant from the government; although, even when this is the case, they still retain their independence.

Voluntary work is usually carried out on a part-time basis. It can involve a wide range of activities including helping to provide care for the disadvantaged or disabled, carrying out routine, office, clerical or administrative support, and trying to promote greater awareness of the voluntary organisation and its causes. In many cases, the efforts of the voluntary workers are co-ordinated by a team of paid permanent staff who act as professional administrators and fund raisers and who deal with public relations.

People who become involved in voluntary work are generally motivated by a desire to help others. However, in some cases voluntary work may be viewed by some people as an opportunity to develop their own ability to work effectively with others and to take responsibility, thus enhancing skills which may be useful when trying to secure paid employment in the future.

ACTIVITY

Split into groups of four. Using library sources, identify a voluntary organisation in which you are all particularly interested.

1 Contact the organisation and ask for information about its activities. Obtain leaflets and posters which promote its causes.

2 Draw up a plan of action for an awareness-raising day, including a collection for the voluntary organisation within your school or college.

3 As a class, evaluate each group's plans and decide which are the best.

4 The tutor should then formally contact the voluntary group which is the subject of the best plan, giving details of the plans for the awareness-raising day and the collection. The whole class should work as a team to run the awareness-raising day and conduct the collection.

OWN BUSINESS

During the last two decades, there has been a 60 per cent increase in the proportion of the workforce which is self-employed. This represents a larger increase than in any other European country. This growth reflects:

- ☺ changes in the pattern of employment with many large employers in all sectors deciding to reduce their permanent staff and to buy in services from outside;

- ☺ people viewing self-employment as an alternative to unemployment;

- ☺ more people making a positive decision to work for themselves rather than someone else, because job security no longer exists in the rapidly changing business world;

- ☺ governments giving a great deal of encouragement to the self-employed through local enterprise agencies and Training and Enterprise Councils.

Self-employment is strongest in the service sector. In particular, the major growth has been in financial, business and personal services such as catering and cleaning. There are also a large number of self-employed people working in trades relating to building, home improvements and maintenance. Opportunities in the future appear to be for creating a business around a one-off service which can deal with a sudden emergency or breakdown in a piece of industrial, commercial or home equipment.

To make a success of self-employment, people need the following qualities:

- ☺ initiative and drive;

- ☺ capacity to organise time efficiently;

- ☺ good health;

- ☺ an ability to cope with stress;

- ☺ clear personal objectives and a realistic sense of their own strengths and weaknesses;

- ☺ overwhelming optimism tempered with common sense;

- ☺ an ability to cope with failure and an acceptance that things will go wrong;

- ☺ a sense of perspective;

- ☺ an ability to read the market and respond rapidly to changes and developments.

Self-employment is not a soft option. It generally involves working long hours and provides a fluctuating rather than steady income. You have to take calculated risks, acting as a 'jack of all trades' with financial, administrative, technical and marketing skills. You have to accept pressures from financial backers and be prepared for both successes and failures.

Looking at the above list of qualities, you might ask why people decide to work for themselves. The answer lies in a basic need to be independent, a desire to be free to make their own decisions, a wish to create a business in their own image and to be rewarded directly for their own efforts.

There are a variety of different ways for people to enter business on their own behalf. The choice is normally determined by the extent to which a person is prepared to take a risk and the level of independence that is sought.

BUSINESS START-UP

Starting a business from scratch involves identifying a gap in the market, and having the drive, determination and organisational ability to exploit it. This involves:

- ☺ conducting extensive market and business environmental research;

- ☺ clearly identifying the objectives of the business;

- ☺ recognising the people skills and knowledge which are necessary to develop and exploit the idea;

- ☺ deciding upon a suitable legal form;

- ☺ identifying the resources necessary to run the business;

- ☺ identifying the possible sources of finance;

- ☺ testing the commercial and financial viability of the business idea.

A large proportion of new businesses start as sole traders. This means that a single person provides the capital, takes the decisions and assumes the risks of the business. The attraction of operating and working as a sole trader is that it is relatively easy to set up, and it provides considerable scope for the development of the owner's ideas and initiatives. However, this can often be at the cost of having to work very long hours, accepting heavy responsibilities, taking considerable business risks and experiencing financial problems.

GOVERNMENT ENTERPRISE SCHEME

Some people view self-employment as a way out of unemployment. In an attempt to regenerate business activity, especially in depressed areas of the country, the government has tried to encourage this attitude. The 81 Training and Enterprise Councils located throughout England and Wales administer a number of business start-up schemes. Some of these are aimed at unemployed people who wish to set up their own business but who do not wish initially to be made worse off by sacrificing their benefits. Generally, these schemes provide consultancy advice on business planning, together with some sort of weekly allowance which makes up or compensates for the loss of benefits.

The provision of schemes varies across the country. *Fig. 8.23* provides details of the scheme that operates in Hertfordshire. This is one of the most generous in the country providing extensive training, consultancy advice and some financial assistance. It is offered through Business Link which is a collaborative arrangement between the Hertfordshire TEC, the Hertfordshire Chamber of Commerce and Industry, the Hertfordshire County Council and the University of Hertfordshire. Its business start-up scheme has a very impressive success rate; after 12 months 84 per cent of people on the scheme remain in business, after 18 months 83 per cent are still in business (the national average is 60 per cent).

arting a business

comprehensive and flexible programme is for anyone wanting to start iness successfully in Hertfordshire. It offers support at every stage of ng a business including information, advice, training, and counselling.

ho is it for? Anyone based in ertfordshire who wants to start in business. If your business has arted, but is new (ie in the first 12 onths of trading), you will still be le to take advantage of some rts of the programme.

hat are the benefits? ailored training and support at very stage of development through ur first 18 months. The ogramme takes you step-by-step rough starting and running a isiness successfully. You will be le to test the viability of your isiness idea and define the amount f further advice, support and nance that will be needed.

How does it work?

Step One - Introduction: a half-ay introduction to planning and arting a new business. This xplains in straightforward terms hat is involved and how the rogramme works and helps you xamine the viability of your ideas.

Step Two - Developing the business idea: Helps you prepare a sound business plan. Your plan ill support the successful resentation of your idea to banks, financiers, support agencies and other organisations who can help turn it into reality. An intensive one-day seminar shows you the vital elements of a viable business plan - how to research markets, establish pricing, determine and test profitability and project cash flow. You are then set the assignment of developing your own business plan for an initial assessment to determine your individual needs.

Step Three - The action plan: a half-day assessment workshop which gives you the opportunity to assess the viability of your business plan. The workshop leader works with you to develop your own action plan of further support from a flexible programme covering business information, advice, training and counselling. Training options within the programme include workshops on the fundamentals of starting a business (eg marketing, selling, book-keeping and accounts). Further specific workshops on topics such as taxation, VAT, telephone techniques, computing and information technology, letter writing, promotion and raising finance are also offered.

Step Four - Continuous advice and support: regular one-to-one counselling/monitoring meetings with an expert small business counsellor to help keep development of your business on track and recommend solutions to problems as they arise.

♦ **What does it cost?** The commercial value of the programme, ie all four steps, is over £2,000. Sponsorship for your action plan from Hertfordshire TEC makes it available *completely free of charge to successful applicants starting a business in Hertfordshire.*

♦ **Financial support for special circumstances:** If you want to start up in business and fulfil the criteria below* you may be eligible for one of two schemes to assist your finances during your critical start-up period.

- *A cash grant* worth a total of £390.00 - paid at £30.00 per week for eight weeks with a bonus of £150.00 after six months from commencement of your action plan. Under this scheme you are free to develop your business independently, but to receive the grant you must sign off the unemployment register and be accepted onto the programme by demonstrating the quality and viability of your business plan

- or -

- *Enterprise Rehearsal* which allows you to try out your business without affecting any of your benefit claims. During your 'business rehearsal' period of 3 months you will receive an additional training allowance of £10.00 per week and be able to develop your business under weekly supervision from an experienced business counsellor. At the end of the period, you can assess the on-going viability of your business with your counsellor and then decide the most appropriate plan of action for the future from a basis of sound business experience.

♦ **Next step:** Contact the information line on 0727 813 813.

* To be eligible for financial support you must be registered unemployed for at least 6 months, registered disabled, a victim of a large scale redundancy, returning to work after a break of at least 2 years or be an ex-forces regular

FIGURE 8.23: Support for new business start ups.
Source: Hertfordshire Business Link.

☀ ACTIVITY

1 Contact your local TEC and obtain details of its business start-up scheme.

2 Compare and contrast the package that is available with that which is on offer in Hertfordshire (see *Fig. 8.23*).

3 In groups of four, discuss whether you would be persuaded to become involved in a business start-up on the basis of what is on offer from your local TEC.

PARTNERSHIP

When planning and developing a new business, it is often easier to work with a partner. It allows for the sharing of responsibilities, the pooling of financial resources, the opportunity to discuss and bounce ideas off each other, and the bringing together of complementary business and technical skills. Partners provide additional capital for the business, sharing the resulting profit or loss.

As much care should be taken in selecting a suitable business partner as in deciding upon a marriage partner because, ultimately, if the partners fall out the business will go under. Personalities must match, skills should complement each other, and relative strengths and weaknesses need to balance out.

FAMILY BUSINESS

The growth in small family businesses has provided a very useful training ground for budding entrepreneurs. Typically, such businesses are in retailing, personal services or small engineering activities.

Finding employment in a family business can have several advantages.

- ☺ **There is scope to tailor the job to meet the precise needs, strengths and interests of the person concerned, thus providing better training and more satisfying work.**

- ☺ **From the owners' point of view, a family member should be more committed, more flexible, less inclined to defraud and easier to induct into the working ways of the business.**

- ☺ **In the long-term, it provides for the future survival of the business as it can be handed on to the next generation.**

However, there can be a number of difficulties in working for a parent or close relative.

- ☺ **Family relationships do not necessarily transfer easily into business relationships. In some cases, resentments may develop – some people may find it difficult to work for an older brother or sister or a parent. Conversely, an older relative's judgement may be clouded by their emotional relationship with the younger new recruit, for example they may be too easy going or hypercritical.**

- ☺ **Businesses need a constant injection of new ideas to flourish and grow. The danger is that a family member may be less inclined to criticise and more accepting of the traditional family way of doing things.**

- ☺ **Other employees, who are not relatives, may resent the position, and what may be viewed as the preferment, of the family member.**

- ☺ **Under some circumstances, family members may be paid less than the going rate for the job. This may be justified on the grounds that they will be compensated in the future when they inherit the business.**

FRANCHISE

To reduce the danger of business failure, it is often worthwhile buying into a franchise. This involves a contractual licence granted by the franchiser to the franchisee. The licence is normally purchased for an initial franchise fee (usually exclusive of future royalty payments). The franchisee then receives a complete business package from the franchiser, including expertise and market research, financial planning, training, and the use of the corporate name and its promotion through advertising. This allows the franchisee to operate the business to the same standard and format as all the other units in the franchised chain. Essentially, this means that someone can run their own business according to a format which already has a proven track record.

Franchises often have a well-established name backed in many cases by national and international advertising. Under these circumstances, there is a far higher probability

FIGURE 8.24:
Some UK
franchises.

of the business being successful. Franchised operations can be found in a wide range of activities including retailing, catering, fast food, print shops, parcel delivery, home maintenance, cleaning, drain cleaning and plumbing. *Fig. 8.24* shows some of the major franchises in operation in the UK.

If a person wishes to work in their own franchised business, they need to carry out a very careful evaluation of the franchise contract and arrangement. They should consider:

- **the exact terms, conditions and responsibilities under the contract;**

- **whether the market for the franchised product or service is growing, static or declining;**

- **how competitive the franchised product or service is in relation to local competition;**

- **how close is the nearest operator of the same franchise located;**

- **the history, track record and performance of the franchiser;**

- **the true cost of the franchise in terms of initial fee and royalty on turnover;**

- **whether advertising is dedicated to the franchise as a whole or for promoting an individual outlet;**

- **who pays for training and what it provides;**

- **how often the operating manual is changed and updated;**

- **whether the franchiser is a member of the British Franchise Association.**

Some people may not enjoy running their own business as part of a franchise. This is because it may be viewed as limiting the opportunity to express personal initiative in terms of product, service or design. Also, where the franchiser's product or service receives bad publicity, this will obviously have an effect on the franchisee. Finally, failure of a franchiser may leave a franchisee with a business which is not viable on its own.

WORKING ABROAD

Many people are motivated to look for either short-term or in some cases permanent jobs abroad. Reasons include:

- **a desire to travel the world;**

- **a wish to improve language skills;**

- **an interest in other cultures;**

- **a wish to enjoy a better climate;**

- **a desire to help those living in less fortunate circumstances.**

The actual availability of job opportunities abroad is affected by political, economic and social factors. For example, if a country has high unemployment it will often legislate to give priority in the jobs market to its own nationals. This is why countries such as New Zealand, Australia, the United States and Canada have become

FIGURE 8.25: The European Union.

increasingly selective in their choice of immigrants and have restricted work opportunities for visitors to agreed schemes.

British subjects can freely seek employment within a European Union country. Technically, British people are entitled to the same treatment as the citizens of the European country in which they are seeking employment. They should receive equality in terms of pay, working conditions, social security, vocational training, income tax and trade union rights. However, the reality is that to get a job in a European Union country, especially during a period of high unemployment, it is necessary to have well-developed language skills and vocational skills which are in high demand. There is, for example, a free market for footballers, but continental clubs only want British players with the skills of a Gary Lineker or a Paul Gascoigne.

The **Overseas Placing Unit** helps people who are looking for jobs in Europe. It is part of the Department for Education and Employment and provides advice and guidance to people who are looking for vacancies. It has the facility to access all overseas vacancies held on the **National Vacancy System** and the **Oracle Jobfinder Service**. For example, Belgium, which is very cosmopolitan, often has vacancies for English speakers to work in technical and administrative jobs. In France, businesses are often looking for people with secretarial

skills. In Germany, opportunities often arise for skilled trades people.

Job opportunities in Austria, Norway and Sweden may come up on the **International Clearing of Vacancies Scheme** under which the UK Employment Service exchanges applications for employment in these countries. Anyone finding a job under this scheme would require a work permit.

Finding a permanent job overseas is very difficult and it is generally achieved by working for a multinational company. Jobs in the oil and construction industries often involve the opportunity of a posting abroad.

People with teaching or library skills or who have a scientific background may be able to find a posting abroad with the **British Council**. Working for the British Council involves promoting an understanding of Britain in other countries, through cultural, educational and technical co-operative activities. Some job opportunities may also arise in international organisations such as the World Bank, the United Nations and the European Commission.

People who are looking for work abroad very often do so out of a desire to travel the world while earning money to help pay for their trip. Some of the more popular ways of doing this are to work in an international work camp, find a place in an Israeli kibbutz, or secure suitable seasonal tourist-based work.

Many voluntary societies also recruit people to work abroad. Generally they are looking for independent recruits who have relevant specialist skills. **Voluntary Service Overseas (VSO)**, for example, sends people to Africa, Asia, the Caribbean, Papua New Guinea and the Pacific, and Eastern Europe. VSO is looking for people with skills relating to education, health, technical trades, crafts and engineering, agriculture, and social, community and business development.

STATUTORY REQUIREMENTS

Once people start work, they have to pay income tax if they are earning above a certain level and make National Insurance contributions.

Income tax is a form of direct taxation levied on all people receiving an income above a minimum threshold. The threshold varies, it is largely determined by allowances relating to taxpayers' marital status or age. Certain deductions are also allowed for some employment expenses, retirement annuities, loans, maintenance payments, and personal pension payments. The balance is taxed on a sliding scale, currently (in 1994-5) rising from 20 per cent to 25 per cent and, finally, to 40 per cent.

A full record of **national insurance** payments entitles a person to state benefits if his or her personal circumstances permit. These include:

- **sickness benefit;**
- **invalidity benefit;**
- **retirement pension;**
- **widows' benefit;**
- **unemployment benefit.**

The Department of Social Security administers the National Insurance system. The fund out of which the benefits are paid is created partly by the exchequer out of taxation and partly through contributions from both the employer and employee. The latter are only made if the employee's earnings are over a certain minimum level.

All contributions are earnings related. Where employers can demonstrate that they can provide a pension scheme equal to or better than the state provision they may contract out of the state scheme. Under these circumstances, National Insurance contributions by both the employer and employee will be lower as they are not paying for the pension element.

The employer is responsible for deducting both income tax and National Insurance. Income tax is deducted under the **Pay-As-You-Earn (PAYE)** scheme. It is paid by the employer to the Collector of Taxes at the Inland Revenue. The employer also deducts contributions for Class 1 National Insurance. This is sent with their own contributions to the Inland Revenue. Below a certain limit, currently £57 per week for National Insurance and £67.78 per week for income tax, the employer does not have to make any deductions.

STATUTORY REQUIREMENTS FOR THE SELF-EMPLOYED

When they are starting out in business, far too many people get themselves into difficulties because they fail to take account of the need to make arrangements for income tax, National Insurance and value added tax (VAT).

INCOME TAX
As soon as someone starts a business they should inform the Inland Revenue. This can be done by completing form 41G and sending it to the local tax office. The form gathers information about the owners of the business, the business itself, and the personal circumstances of the person who is filling out the form.

If the owner(s) have given up previous employment to start the business then they should give their local tax office the form P45 which was handed to them when they left their last employment.

The owner of a business must keep full and accurate records and proper accounts from the moment the business starts trading. These accounts will be used by the Inland Revenue to assess the owner's tax liability. In April 1997, the Inland Revenue will issue new-style tax returns under a new self-assessment system. These returns must contain full details of income, capital gains, allowances, reliefs and deductions. Taxpayers will be able to choose either to calculate their own tax liability or to leave it to the Inland Revenue to calculate their tax bill.

The owners of the business can decide the accounting year on which their tax assessments are based. For example, the 'accounting date' – the date on which the accounting year ends – may be on the anniversary of the date the business started trading. Or it may be to the end of the calendar year ending on 31 December, or to the end of the tax year on 5 April. Where a business has a seasonal pattern of activity, it may be an advantage to work to an accounting date when trade is slower and stocks are down. Whatever date is chosen, a self-employed person should receive a tax return each April and is expected to make two annual tax payments (in January and July) on the basis of assessed taxable profit.

It is sensible for anybody in business to get advice and help from an accountant. An accountant can draw up the accounts, agree the amount of taxable profit with the tax office, and help claim any reliefs that may be due. The assistance of a qualified accountant will become even more important when self-assessment is introduced in April 1997.

Self Assessment

A guide for
the self-employed

SA/BK2

Inland Revenue

NATIONAL INSURANCE

On commencing business, it is important to inform the local Social Security office, which administers national insurance contributions.

Flat rate class 2 contributions are payable every week by all self-employed individuals of working age unless they have applied for and been granted small earnings exception or are over retirement age. Payment may be made by a monthly direct debit or by settlement of a quarterly invoice from the Department of Social Security. The class 2 contribution secures the self-employed person's entitlement to normal pension and sickness benefits.

When profits exceed a certain level, class 4 contributions are levied. These are collected by the Inland Revenue, normally at the same time as income tax on the business profits. Half of these class 4 contributions are allowable against tax. These contributions do not secure any further state benefits. For the 1994-5 financial year,

these contributions were charged at 7.3 per cent of the profits between £6,490 and £22,300, with a maximum payment of £1,158.51.

VALUE ADDED TAX (VAT)

The owner of a business is legally required to register within 30 days with the Customs and Excise VAT office if they feel that taxable turnover for the previous 12 months is about to exceed the annual limit. In 1994-5, the annual limit was £45,000.

VAT is levied at each stage of the production of goods or services. It is payable on the added value as raw materials are used to produce components, as the components are assembled into a product and as the product is distributed through the wholesaler and retailer to the consumer. Each party in this process must account to Customs and Excise for the tax on their output but they may deduct from this figure the amount of tax already paid by the party supplying them.

Obviously for this system to work efficiently, it is very important to keep accurate records of both purchases and sales, indicating where VAT has been paid or charged. These records will be regularly inspected by Customs and Excise.

PORTFOLIO ASSIGNMENT

CAREER PLANNING

This element has provided you with a sound overview of the different types of employment available locally, nationally and abroad. It has also investigated the factors which determine the availability of employment and self-employment opportunities. In the case of each type of job opportunity, there has been an indication of the particular specialist vocational skills it draws upon and the personal and organisational skills and qualities that are required to undertake it. It is this final aspect which needs further elaboration and investigation in order to help you plan for your future career.

This assignment is designed to help you identify and analyse your strengths and weaknesses in relation to the skills and qualities that are required in particular areas of employment. It will also help you to develop a clear picture of yourself so that you can draw up a curriculum vitae (CV). This is a summary of your personal details, including educational record, qualifications, interests, hobbies and achievements, and work experience. Your CV can be used as a focus for your research with the various careers guidance services, and should ultimately allow you to develop a suitable short-term and long-term personal career plan.

TASK 1 – SKILLS AND QUALITIES AUDIT

An audit enables you to identify the skills and qualities that you already have. These may have been developed and demonstrated through your GNVQ course, through your hobbies and interests, through work experience or any positions of responsibility you may have held within your school or college.

The skills and qualities are classified under three main headings:

- ⊗ core skills;

- ⊗ personal skills and qualities;

- ⊗ organisational skills.

Core skills relate to communication, application of number and information technology. These skills are transferable between different vocational areas and underpin all jobs. Personal skills and qualities which are essentially individual to you and cover how you relate to other people, how they view you and how you conduct yourself in general. Organisational skills relate to how effective you are at organising yourself and other people and running events.

To undertake your audit:

(a) Photocopy and then complete the skills and qualities audit sheets (see pages 544–9).

(b) Ask a friend or member of your family to comment on your ratings and the validity of your evidence. In the light of their comments make any necessary amendments.

(c) Highlight the skills and qualities that you have rated as being 'well developed' and the context (evidence) in which they have been demonstrated.

(d) Write a series of statements which summarise your findings such as 'I have well developed oral communication skills which were recognised in the local "Youth

Speaks" public speaking competition, which I helped my school/college to win last year.'

These statements may be used for job/higher education applications, for your CV, or as a basis for discussion with your careers guidance officer. In certain cases, you may find it helpful to turn the statement round to read: 'I was a member of my school's/college's public speaking team, which won the local "Youth Speaks" competition. This experience has helped to develop my oral communication skills.'

(e) Highlight the skills and qualities you have rated as 'partly developed' and suggest where appropriate the actions you might take to improve upon them.

TASK 2 – WORKING FOR OTHERS OR SELF-EMPLOYMENT

To decide whether you want to be self-employed or work for someone else, photocopy and complete the form '*Thinking of Starting a Business*' (see page 546). This form has been taken from Barclays Bank's publication for aspiring business persons. Ask a friend or member of your family to verify your results.

TASK 3 – PRODUCE A CV

Photocopy and then complete the blank curriculum vitae (CV) forms (see pages 547–8). Your summary statement from task 1 should be helpful when completing sections 4 and 6.

Your CV may be placed at the front of your record of achievement (if you have one). It will provide a useful focus for any discussions with a careers guidance counsellor, prospective employer, or higher education establishment.

TASK 4 – REVIEWING THE OPTIONS

(a) Study the literature available in your school's/college's careers room or library, and also at the local careers office. Identify at least three types of employment that interest you. Conduct detailed research into one of them, listing opportunities in the UK, European Union or other international location with relevant sources of information and statutory requirements.

(b) Arrange an interview with the following people:
   (i) school/college careers or guidance counsellor;
   (ii) advisers at the local careers office.

(c) Attend any careers conventions held in your local area. These provide an opportunity to meet with local and national employers.

(d) If you are interested in higher education attend open days at universities and colleges.

(e) If you are thinking of setting up your own business, arrange an interview with the following people:
   (i) business adviser at the bank;
   (ii) an adviser/consultant at the local Training and Enterprise Council or local enterprise agency.

(f) At each stage of the review process keep records of your findings and any conclusions you might have reached. Record the date you undertake each activity, describe what trips you make and the findings and conclusions you draw from each visit or interview.

TASK 5 – PERSONAL CAREER PLAN

To prepare a personal career plan:

(a) Photocopy the personal career plan form (see page 549).

(b) Fill in your name and your current academic programme: 'Advanced Business GNVQ'.

(c) Your long-term career aim should be expressed in terms of qualifications and job, such as 'to qualify as a certified accountant and to work in retailing'.

(d) Your academic career plan should reflect your next stage, such as:
- ⊗ BTEC HND/C;
- ⊗ degree in accountancy;
- ⊗ accounting technicians' exams.

(e) The actions you need to take should include research, consultations, interviews, visits, and qualifications needed.

(f) Identify the relevant statutory requirements.

(g) The long-term academic/career plan needs to indicate the stages during the next five years which are necessary to achieve your aim, such as:
- ⊗ GNVQ with distinction;
- ⊗ three-year degree in accountancy;
- ⊗ trainee accountancy position in retailing;
- ⊗ pass certified accountancy exams.

(h) The actions you need to take should include research, consultations, interviews, applications, visits and qualifications needed.

Core Skills	Well developed	Developing	Not yet developed	Evidence
Oral communication				
Written communication				
IT – information handling				
IT – applications				
Collecting and processing numerical data				
Tackling numerical problems				
Communicating through number				

Organisational Skills and Qualities	Well developed	Developing	Not yet developed	Evidence
Know how to identify and collect information relevant to a particular problem or issue				
Recognise the possible solutions to a problem and determine the most appropriate one				
Make a decision but be willing to modify it in the light of experience				

Personal Skills and Qualities	Well developed	Developing	Not yet developed	Evidence
Work effectively as a member of a team				
Head a small team				
Head a large team				
Carry out instructions from superiors				
Accept criticism and use it to improve own performance				
Identify and try to overcome personal weaknesses				
Accept responsibility for looking after other people				
Accept responsibility for completing a project on time				
Get on well with people from different backgrounds				
Deal effectively with the general public				
Ability to sell people things or ideas				

Thinking of starting a business

Ask yourself these questions to help you assess whether or not you have what it takes to set up and run a business.

1. I often feel I'm the victim of outside forces I cannot control.   YES ☐   NO ☐

2. It's not unusual for me to work later than planned.   YES ☐   NO ☐

3. Some days seem to go by without me having achieved a thing.   YES ☐   NO ☐

4. Given a bad situation, I'll always get something out of it.   YES ☐   NO ☐

5. I think a well ordered pattern of life with regular hours suits me best.   YES ☐   NO ☐

6. I'm much happier not having to rely on other people.   YES ☐   NO ☐

7. I've never been one to follow the crowd.   YES ☐   NO ☐

8. There's no point starting something unless you're going to see it through.   YES ☐   NO ☐

9. People often tell me how good I am at seeing things from their point of view.   YES ☐   NO ☐

10. I tend not to be too ambitious to avoid being disappointed.   YES ☐   NO ☐

11. It's very important to me that people recognise my success.   YES ☐   NO ☐

12. When I find myself talking to a telephone answer machine, I usually hang up without leaving a message.   YES ☐   NO ☐

13. I'm prepared to take risks only when I've carefully thought through all possible consequences.   YES ☐   NO ☐

14. All that matters is how much I earn regardless of how hard I work to get it.   YES ☐   NO ☐

How to score
For questions 2,4,7,8,9,11 and 13, score 2 points for every yes response and zero points for every no.
For questions 1,3,5,6,10,12 and 14, score 2 points for every no response and zero points for every yes.
The maximum score is 28 points. The higher your score, the better equipped you should be for your venture.

CURRICULUM VITAE

I. PERSONAL DETAILS

FULL NAME

_____

_____

ADDRESS

_____

_____

TELEPHONE

_____

2. EDUCATION

Dates	Establishment
_____	_____
_____	_____
_____	_____
_____	_____
_____	_____
_____	_____
_____	_____
_____	_____
_____	_____
_____	_____

3. EDUCATIONAL QUALIFICATIONS

SCHOOL/COLLEGE	DATES	QUALIFICATIONS
_____	_____	_____
_____	_____	_____
_____	_____	_____
_____	_____	_____
_____	_____	_____
_____	_____	_____
_____	_____	_____
_____	_____	_____
_____	_____	_____
_____	_____	_____
_____	_____	_____
_____	_____	_____

4. WORK EXPERIENCE (FULL AND PART-TIME)

COMPANY/ORGANISATION

DATES EMPLOYED

JOB TITLE

MAIN DUTIES INVOLVED

PERSONAL ACHIEVEMENT
FROM JOB

5. HOBBIES AND INTERESTS

6. PERSONAL QUALITIES
AND CHARACTERISTICS

7. REFERENCES

Educational

Personal

SIGNED

DATE

Personal Career Plan

Name:

Current academic programme:

Long-term career aim:

Academic/career plans for the end of **GNVQ** year:

Action to be taken

Action	By when	Date achieved

Relevant statutory requirements

Academic/career plans for the next five years:

Action to be taken

Action	By when	Date achieved

I **All of the following are advantages of business planning, except:**

A it helps the business to clearly identify its goals

B it helps the entrepreneur to make better informed decisions

C it allows people working within a particular functional area to plan independently from each other

D it allows for mistakes to be made on paper and not in the actual marketplace

2 **Which of the following statements is false:**

A local enterprise agencies offer free advice on starting-up and running a business

B the Department of Trade and Industry concentrates on encouraging new businesses to trade abroad

C the commercial banks offer advice on raising finance and controlling the financial affairs of business

D the Law Society helps new businesses through its scheme called 'Lawyers for Enterprise'

3 **Which of the following business activities would a sole trader be least likely to undertake:**

A a hairdressing business

B an accountancy business

C the production of colour television sets

D a building business

4 **Which of the following would not appear in a company's memorandum of association:**

A the company's name

B the address of the company's registered office

C the company's objectives

D details as to the way in which shareholders' meetings are to be conducted

5 **The ordinary partnership would generally be dissolved either compulsorily or voluntarily in the event of all of the following except:**

A the death or bankruptcy of any partner

B a disagreement over the hiring of a temporary shorthand-typist

C the completion of the venture for which the firm was founded

D a court order

6 **Which of the following statements is (or are) true:**

⊗ **it is generally prudent to launch any new business proposal at the time of an upturn in the economy**

⊗ **a reduction in the rate of growth of the economy is normally associated with an increase in GDP**

⊗ **rising prices make companies more competitive**

⊗ **a new business is less likely to be launched during the run up to a general election**

⊗ **rapid changes in technology mean that businesses have to be constantly developing their products if they are to remain competitive**

A the second and fourth statements

B the first, fourth and fifth

C the first and the last

D the last three statements

7 Which of the following issues should be considered before a business is run from the owner's home:

○ **whether any special covenants relate to the home**

○ **the coverage of the house and contents insurance**

○ **local planning regulations**

○ **parking for clients and suppliers making deliveries**

A the first and the last statements

B the last two statements

C all of them

D the second statement only

8 Which of the following statements is false:

A plant, machinery, equipment, fittings and vehicles are all items of capital expenditure

B equity funding relates to bank loans and overdrafts

C gearing relates to the ratio between lenders' money and owners' money

D mortgages, hire purchase and credit from suppliers all represent forms of loans

9 Under the Consumer Protection Act 1987 which of the following does not apply:

A it is a criminal offence to supply any consumer goods which do not meet with general safety requirements

B businesses have a general duty to trade safely

C businesses must reach certain standards regarding furniture and fire hazards

D businesses must ensure that all consumers read operating instructions and safety rules

10 Which of the following statements is false:

A an insurance broker must have professional indemnity insurance

B public liability insurance covers a business against causing death, personal injury or damage to the property of a third party

C product liability insurance covers a business against loss, damage or bodily injury arising from selling a defective product

D vicarious liability means that an employee or agent of a business accepts responsibility for any action which may cause death, bodily injury or damage to property

Answers to multiple choice questions

UNIT 1
1 B
2 D
3 B
4 A
5 B
6 D
7 D
8 B
9 C
10 C
11 C
12 B
13 A
14 B
15 A
16 A
17 B
18 D
19 B
20 B
21 C
22 D
23 A
24 A
25 B
26 C
27 B
28 C
29 D
30 C
31 C
32 C
33 C

UNIT 3
1 B
2 C
3 B
4 D
5 B
6 D
7 B
8 B

9 A
10 D
11 B
12 D
13 C
14 D
15 D
16 D
17 D
18 B
19 D
20 C

UNIT 4
1 B & C
2 A & C
3 A, C & D
4 None of these
5 B, C & D
6 A & D
7 A & D
8 C & D
9 A, B, C & D
10 A & C
11 B
12 C & D
13 C
14 A & D
15 A & C
16 A & D

UNIT 5
1 C
2 A
3 D
4 B
5 B
6 C
7 A
8 D
9 C
10 C
11 A

12 D
13 C
14 A
15 C
16 D
17 D
18 C
19 C
20 C
21 C
22 C
23 B
24 A
25 D
26 A
27 D
28 B
29 D
30 A

UNIT 6
1 B
2 D
3 D
4 A
5 A
6 C
7 A
8 D
9 B
10 A
11 C
12 A

UNIT 7
1 C
2 B
3 D
4 B
5 C
6 A
7 B
8 A

9 A
10 D
11 C
12 B
13 D
14 C
15 A
16 A
17 C
18 A
19 C
20 D

UNIT 8
1 C
2 B
3 C
4 D
5 B
6 B
7 C
8 B
9 D
10 D

Index

minimum wages 327–8
mining and quarrying 28–9
MIS *see* management information systems
MMC *see* Monopolies and Mergers Commission
money cycle 359–60, 471
monopolies 42, 51–7, 386–7
  natural 57
  privatisation 59
Monopolies and Mergers Commission (MMC) 52
mortgages 8, 435
multi-purpose systems 133
multi-tasking systems 133
mutuality sector 84, 89

National Health Service 61, 83
national insurance 378, 539–40
National Lottery 90, 440
National Vocational Qualifications 331–2
nationalised industries 57–8
negative equity 8
net asset percentage 478
net profit percentage 478
networks 108, 139–40
non-contract employment 304

objectives 81–4
Office of Fair Trading (OFT) 51–4, 394
  regulatory agencies 59
Office of Population Censuses and Surveys (OPCS) 168
Offices, Shops and Railways Premises Act 106
Official Listed Market 85
Official Secrets Act 105
oligopolies 39–42, 386–7
order forms 364–5
ordinary shares 88, 435, 496
organisational structures 92–5
  centralisation 94
  committee 93–4
  decentralisation 95
  functional 93
  line 93
  matrix 94
original documents 457–9
overdrafts 89, 375, 432–3
overheads 98
Overseas Placing Unit 538
  see also international employment
ownership types 84–92

packaging 147
Partnership Act 86, 495
partnerships 86–7, 495–6, 536
part-time employment 300–2, 309
party plan selling 184
Patents Act 509
pay
  see also wages
  differentials 312–13
  Equal Pay Act 312, 511
  increase problems 326
  levels 325–8
  local settlements 326
  minimum wages 327–8
  performance-related 326–7
  productivity agreements 326
  profit-related 326
paying-in slips 373–4

payments 369–74
  timing of 452–3
payroll records 363
pensions 299, 378
permanent employment 302
personality tests 258
personnel management 508
personnel officers 235, 245
personnel profile 248–9
PEST factors 81, 159–63
petty cash 372
pollution 44–5
predatory pricing 24, 394
preference shares 88, 435, 496
premises 507, 510
  insurance 513–14
press releases 182
price
  see also pricing
  cartels 40
  complementary products 5
  demand changes 3–4, 23
  discrimination 394
  elasticity of demand 10–12
  marketing 149–51
  products 3–4
  profits 20–4
  restraints 58
  substitutes 4–5
  wars 386, 395
Prices Act 194
pricing
  see also price
  basic decisions 385–405
  breakeven 395–401
  business objectives 390–2
  capacity 388
  competition 386–8
  contribution 392–3
  cost-plus 150, 392–3
  economic considerations 388–90
  environmental influences 385–90
  external influences 385–90
  internal influences 390–2
  marketing mix influences 149–51
  market-led 393–5
  objectives 149
  social responsibilities 391
  strategies 392–5
  units of service 380
Prince's Youth Trust 492
private costs 42
private limited companies 84, 496–7
private sector businesses 84–8, 533
privatisation 58–61, 90–1
  monopolies 59
procurement *see* buying procedures
product(s)
  complementary 5
  demand 3–4
  development 157–74
  differentiation 37
  knowledge 192
  life cycle 148
  marketing 146–9
  promotion 152–4
  research 157–8